WORLD POLITICS
Trend and Transformation

2011–2012 Update Edition

Charles William Kegley
Carnegie Council for Ethics in International Affairs
and
Shannon Lindsey Blanton
The University of Memphis

WADSWORTH
CENGAGE Learning·

Australia · Brazil · Japan · Korea · Mexico · Singapore · Spain · United Kingdom · United States

WADSWORTH
CENGAGE Learning

World Politics: Trend and Transformation
Charles William Kegley, Shannon Lindsey Blanton

Publisher: Suzanne Jeans

Executive Editor: Carolyn Merrill

Development Editor: Rebecca Green

Associate Development Editor: Katie Hayes

Assistant Editor: Laura Ross

Editorial Assistant: Angela Hodge

Media Editor: Laura Hildebrand

Marketing Manager: Lydia LeStar

Marketing Coordinator: Josh Hendrick

Senior Marketing Communications Manager: Heather Baxley

Art Director: Linda Helcher

Print Buyer: Fola Orekoya

Senior Rights Acquisitions Manager, Images: Jennifer Meyer Dare

Senior Rights Acquisitions Manager, Text: Katie Huha

Production Service: Christian Holdener, S4Carlisle Publishing Services

Cover Designer: Pier Design

Cover Image: nico_blue/iStockphoto

For product information and technology assistance, contact us at
Cengage Learning Customer & Sales Support, 1-800-354-9706
For permission to use material from this text or product,
submit all requests online at **www.cengage.com/permissions.**
Further permissions questions can be emailed to
permissionrequest@cengage.com.

Library of Congress Control Number: 2010943353

Student Edition:
ISBN-13: 978-0-495-90655-1
ISBN-10: 0-495-90655-7

Wadsworth
20 Channel Center Street
Boston, MA 02210
USA

Cengage Learning is a leading provider of customized learning solutions with office locations around the globe, including Singapore, the United Kingdom, Australia, Mexico, Brazil and Japan. Locate your local office at **international.cengage.com/region**

Cengage Learning products are represented in Canada by Nelson Education, Ltd.

For your course and learning solutions, visit **www.cengage.com.**

Purchase any of our products at your local college store or at our preferred online store **www.CengageBrain.com.**

Printed in Canada
1 2 3 4 5 6 7   14 13 12 11

DEDICATION

To my loving wife Debbie

and

the Carnegie Council for Ethics in International Affairs,
in appreciation for its invaluable contribution to building through
education a more just and secure world
– Charles William Kegley

To my husband Rob

and

our sons Austin and Cullen,
in appreciation of their love, support, and patience
– Shannon Lindsey Blanton

brief contents

Preface xvii
Acknowledgments xxvii
Meet Your Authors xxxi

Part 1   Trend and Transformation in World Politics   2
Chapter 1   Interpreting World Politics   4
Chapter 2   Theories of World Politics   29

Part 2   The Globe's Actors and Their Relations   62
Chapter 3   Great Power Rivalries and Relations   64
Chapter 4   The Global South in a World of Powers   101
Chapter 5   Nonstate Actors and the Quest for Global Community   136
Chapter 6   International Decision Making   188

Part 3   Confronting Armed Aggression   228
Chapter 7   The Threat of Armed Aggression to the World   230
Chapter 8   The Military Pursuit of Power through Arms and Military Strategy   273
Chapter 9   Alliances and the Balance of Power   314
Chapter 10   Negotiated Conflict Resolution and International Law   342
Chapter 11   Institutional and Normative Approaches to Collective Security   374

Part 4   Human Security, Prosperity, and Responsibility   412
Chapter 12   The Globalization of International Finance   414
Chapter 13   International Trade in the Global Marketplace   446
Chapter 14   The Demographic and Cultural Dimensions of Globalization   483
Chapter 15   The Promotion of Human Development and Human Rights   516
Chapter 16   Global Responsibility for the Preservation of the Environment   553

Part 5   Thinking about the Future of World Politics   594
   Chapter 17   Looking Ahead at Global Trends
                  and Transformations   596

   Glossary   616
   References   627
   Name Index   659
   Subject Index   662

contents

Part 1 Trend and Transformation in World Politics   2

CHAPTER 1

INTERPRETING WORLD POLITICS   4

The Challenge of Investigating World Affairs   6

How Perceptions Influence Images of International Reality   7

The Nature and Sources of Images   8

CONTROVERSY *Should We Believe What We See?*   9

The Impact of Perceptions on World Politics   12

Keys to Understanding World Politics   14

Introducing Terminology   15

Distinguishing the Primary Transnational Actors   15

Distinguishing Levels of Analysis   18

Distinguishing Change, Cycles, and Continuities   20

Preparing for your Journey into World Politics   24

The Book's Approach   24

The Book's Organization   25

CHAPTER 2

THEORIES OF WORLD POLITICS   29

Theories and Change in World Politics   30

Realist Theory   31

The Realist Worldview   32

The Evolution of Realist Thought   33

The Limitations of Realism   36

Liberal Theory   37

The Liberal Worldview   37

The Evolution of Liberal Thought   40

The Limitations of Liberalism   42

CONTROVERSY *Can International Relations Theory Address a Zombie Outbreak?*   43

Constructivist Theory   46

The Constructivist Worldview   46

The Evolution of Constructivist Thought   48

The Limitations of Constructivism   49

What's Missing in Theories of World Politics?   51

The Radical Critique   51

The Feminist Critique   53

Theorizing about Theory   56

International Theory and the Global Future   57

CONTROVERSY *Can Behavioral Science Advance the Study of International Relations?   58*

Part 2   The Globe's Actors and Their Relations   62

CHAPTER 3

GREAT POWER RIVALRIES AND RELATIONS   64

The Quest for World Leadership   66

The First World War   67

The Causes of World War I   68

The Consequences of World War I   71

The Second World War   73

The Causes of World War II   74

The Consequences of World War II   78

The Cold War   80

The Causes and Evolutionary Course of the Cold War   80

CONTROVERSY *Was Ideology the Primary Source of East–West Conflict?   82*

The Consequences of the Cold War   88

The Post–Cold War Era   88

CONTROVERSY *Why did the Cold War End Peacefully?   89*

America's Unipolar Moment   91

The Rise of the Rest? From Unipolarity to Multipolarity   93

Looking Ahead: The Future of Great Power Relations   95

CHAPTER 4

THE GLOBAL SOUTH IN A WORLD OF POWERS   101

The Colonial Origins of the Global South's Current Circumstances   103

The First Wave of European Imperialism   105

The Second Wave of European Imperialism   107

Self-Determination and Decolonization in the Twentieth Century   109

North and South Today: Worlds Apart   111

Theoretical Explanations of Underdevelopment   115

Internal Factors: Classical Economic Development Theory's Interpretation   115

International Factors: Dependency Theory's Interpretation   116

Closing the Gap? The Global South's Prospects in a World of Great Powers   117

CONTROVERSY *Theories of Development: A Return to Modernization?   118*

Fueling Growth through Oil and Technology   119

The Global East   120

Military Security   121

Reform of the Economic Order   122

Regional Trade Regimes   123

Foreign Aid and Remittances   124

Trade and Foreign Direct Investment   127

Debt Management   130

CONTROVERSY *Multinational Corporations in the Global South: Do They Help or Hurt?   131*

The Global South's Future   133

CHAPTER 5

NONSTATE ACTORS AND THE QUEST FOR GLOBAL COMMUNITY   136

Nonstate Actors in World Politics   138

Intergovernmental Organizations (IGOs)   138

Nongovernmental Organizations (NGOs)   140

Prominent Intergovernmental Organizations   141

The United Nations   141

Other Prominent Global IGOs   149

Regional Intergovernmental Organizations   153

The European Union   154

Other Regional IGOs   159

Prominent types of Nongovernmental Organizations   162

CONTROVERSY *Will Global IGOs Replace States as the Primary Actors in World Politics?   163*

Nonstate Nations: Ethnic Groups and Indigenous Peoples   164

Transnational Religious Movements   168

CONTROVERSY *Are Religious Movements Causes of War or Sources of Transnational Harmony?   171*

Transnational Terrorist Groups   173

Multinational Corporations   176

Issue-Advocacy Groups   181

Nonstate Actors and the Future of World Politics   184

CHAPTER 6

INTERNATIONAL DECISION MAKING   188

Foreign Policy Making in International Affairs   189

Transnational Actors and Decision Processes   190

Influences on the Making of Foreign Policy Decisions   190

Decision Making by Transnational Actors: Three Profiles   195

Decision Making as Rational Choice   196

The Bureaucratic Politics of Foreign Policy Decision Making   202

The Leverage and Impact of Leaders   208

CONTROVERSY *Do Leaders Make a Difference?   213*

The Global and Domestic Determinants of States' International Decisions   214

International Influences on Foreign Policy Choice   215

The Domestic Sources of Foreign Policy Decisions   218

CONTROVERSY *Are Democracies Deficient in Foreign Affairs?   223*

Part 3   Confronting Armed Aggression   228

CHAPTER 7

THE THREAT OF ARMED AGGRESSION TO THE WORLD   230

Changes in Interstate War and Armed Aggression   232

Armed Aggression within States   235

Intrastate Conflict   237

The International Dimensions of Internal Conflict   240

Terrorism   243

The New Global Terrorism   246

Counterterrorism   248

CONTROVERSY *Can the War Against Global Terrorism Be Won?   251*

What Causes Armed Aggression?   252

The First Level of Analysis: Individuals' Human Nature   252

The Second Level of Analysis: States' Internal Characteristics   255

The Third Level of Analysis: The Global System   265

Armed Aggression and its Future   270

CHAPTER 8

THE MILITARY PURSUIT OF POWER THROUGH ARMS AND MILITARY STRATEGY   273

Realist Approaches to War and Peace   274

Power in World Politics   275

The Elements of State Power   277

Trends in Military Spending   281

The Changing Character of Power   283

CONTROVERSY *Does High Military Spending Lower Human Security?   284*

Changes in Military Capabilities   286

Trends in the Weapons Trade   287

Trends in Weapons Technology   293

Military Strategies   301

Coercive Diplomacy Through Military Intervention   308

Rival Realist Roads to Security   311

CHAPTER 9

ALLIANCES AND THE BALANCE OF POWER   314

Realist Interpretations of Alliances in World Politics   317

CONTROVERSY *Do the Advantages of Alliances Outweigh the Disadvantages?   319*

Realism and the Balancing of Power   320

Rules for Rivals in the Balancing Process   322

Difficulties With the Maintenance of a Balance of Power   324

Balancing Power in the Contemporary Global System   327

Models of the Balance of Power—Past and Present   327

What Lies Ahead?   334

CONTROVERSY *Is a Unipolar, Bipolar, or Multipolar System the Most Stable?   337*

CHAPTER 10

NEGOTIATED CONFLICT RESOLUTION AND INTERNATIONAL LAW   342

Liberal and Constructivist Routes to International Peace   344

International Crises and the Negotiated Settlement of Disputes   345

CONTROVERSY *Can Women Improve Global Negotiations and the Prospects For World Peace?   349*

Law at the International Level   351

The Characteristics of International Law   352

Core Principles of International Law Today   353

Limitations of the International Legal System   354

The Abiding Relevance of International Law   357

The Legal Control of Armed Aggression   359

Just War Doctrine: The Changing Ethics Regarding the Use of Armed Force   360

CONTROVERSY *Was the War in Iraq a Just War?   363*

New Rules for Military Intervention   365

The Judicial Framework of International Law   367

Law's Contribution to Peace and Justice   370

CHAPTER 11

INSTITUTIONAL AND NORMATIVE APPROACHES TO COLLECTIVE SECURITY   374

Beating Swords into Plowshares   376

Disarmament versus Arms Control as Routes to Peace   378

Bilateral Arms Control and Disarmament   379

Multilateral Arms Control and Disarmament   380

The Problematic Future of Arms Control and Disarmament   383

CONTROVERSY *Arms Races and the Prisoner's Dilemma   385*

Maintaining Collective Security Through International Organizations   389

The League of Nations and Collective Security   390

The United Nations and Peacekeeping   392

Regional Security Organizations and Collective Defense   396

Uniting One World in a Common Culture of Shared Moral Values   400

Trade Ties of Common Interest   401

A Democratic Peace Pact   403

CONTROVERSY *Is Taiwan "Living Proof" of the Liberal Path to Peace and Prosperity?   406*

Institutions, Norms, and World Order   408

Part 4   Human Security, Prosperity, and Responsibility   412

CHAPTER 12

THE GLOBALIZATION OF INTERNATIONAL FINANCE   414

Interpreting Contemporary Economic Change   416

International Political Economy   416

What Is Globalization?   417

Money Matters: the Transnational Exchange of Money   419

The Globalization of Finance   419

Monetary Policy: Key Concepts and Issues   423

The Bretton Woods System   428

Financial and Monetary Aspects of the Bretton Woods System   430

The End of Bretton Woods   432

Floating Exchange Rates and Financial Crises   433

CONTROVERSY *The IMF, World Bank, and Structural Adjustment Policies: Is the "Cure" Worse than the "Disease"?   435*

The Crisis of 2008   436

Reforming the International Financial Architecture?   441

CHAPTER 13

INTERNATIONAL TRADE IN THE GLOBAL MARKETPLACE   446

Globalization and Trade   447

Trade, Multinational Corporations, and the Globalization of Production   449

The Globalization of Labor   452

Contending Trade Strategies for an Interdependent World   455

The Shadow of the Great Depression   455

The Clash between Liberal and Mercantilist Values   457

Trade and Global Politics   461

The Fate of Free Trade   466

Trade Tricks   467

The Uneasy Coexistence of Liberalism and Mercantilism   469

Triumph or Trouble for the Global Economy?   471

The Development of the WTO   471

CONTROVERSY *Globalization's Growing Pains: Is the World Trade Organization a Friend or Foe?   474*

An Emerging Regional Tug-of-War in Trade?   476

World Trade and the Financial Crisis   478

CHAPTER 14

THE DEMOGRAPHIC AND CULTURAL DIMENSIONS OF GLOBALIZATION   483

Population Change as a Global Challenge   485

World Population Growth Rates   485

Global Migration Trends   493

New Plagues? The Global Impact of Disease   499

The Global Information Age   503

The Evolution of Global Communications   504

The Politics and Business of Global Communication   507

Globalization and the Global Future   510

CONTROVERSY *Is Globalization Helpful or Harmful?   513*

CHAPTER 15

THE PROMOTION OF HUMAN DEVELOPMENT AND HUMAN RIGHTS   516

Putting People into the Picture   517

How does Humanity Fare? The Human Condition Today   519

Measuring Human Development and Human Security   523

Globalization, Democratization, and Economic Prosperity   525

Human Rights and the Protection of People   528

Internationally Recognized Human Rights   529

The Precarious Life of Indigenous Peoples   530

CONTROVERSY *What is Security?* 533

Gender Inequality and Its Consequences 534

Slavery and Human Trafficking 539

Children and Human Rights 541

Responding to Human Rights Abuses 544

The Human Rights Legal Framework 545

The Challenge of Enforcement 546

CONTROVERSY *Should Tyranny and Human Rights Violations Justify Humanitarian Intervention?* 547

CHAPTER 16

GLOBAL RESPONSIBILITY FOR THE PRESERVATION OF THE ENVIRONMENT 553

The Globalization of Environmental Dangers 554

Framing the Ecological Debate 555

CONTROVERSY *Why is there a Global Food Crisis?* 557

The Ecopolitics of the Atmosphere 560

The Ecopolitics of Biodiversity, Deforestation, and Water Shortages 567

Toward Sustainability and Human Security 575

The Tragedy of the Global Commons 576

Global Solutions 580

National and Local Solutions 588

Part 5   Thinking About the Future of World Politics   594

CHAPTER 17

LOOKING AHEAD AT GLOBAL TRENDS AND TRANSFORMATIONS 596

Global Trends and Forecasts 597

How to Think about How People Think about the World 598

The Global Predicament: Key Questions about a Turbulent World 600

Is Globalization a Cure or a Curse? 601

Will Technological Innovation Solve Pressing Global Problems? 604

What Types of Armed Aggression Will Become the Major Fault Line in the Geostrategic Landscape? 605

Will the Great Powers Intervene to Protect Human Rights? 606

Is the World Preparing for the Wrong War? 608

Is This the "End of History" or the End of Happy Endings? 609

A New World Order or New World Disorder? 610

Glossary 616

References 627

Name Index 659

Subject Index 662

maps

Mercator Projection 10

Peter's Projection 10

Orthographic Projection 11

"Upside Down" Projection 11

Territorial Changes in Europe Following World War I 72

World War II Redraws the Map of Europe 75

Emerging Regions of Power in the Twenty-First-Century Global Hierarchy 95

The Global North, Global South (and Global East) 102

A Legacy of Mistrust 105

Global Imperialism 1914 108

Sending Money Back Home 127

Pirates on the Open Sea 142

The UN's Headquarters and Global Network 144

From Few to Many: The Expansion of the European Union, 1951–2010 156

Ethnolinguistic Divisions 166

The World's Major Civilizations: Will Their Clash Create Global Disorder? 167

Major Religions of the World 169

Geographic Influences on Foreign Policy 217

How Free Is Your Country? 222

The Threat of Failed States 236

The Persistent Threat of Global Terrorism 244

Demographic Stress and the Likelihood of Civil War 260

Two Measures of Power Potential: State Wealth and Size of National Armies 280

Military Expenditures as a Percentage of GDP 284

Which World Court? 371

Trick or Treaty? Can Arms-Control Treaties Arrest the Proliferation of Weapons? 388

UN Peace Missions since 1948 394

The Enlarged NATO in the New Geostrategic Balance of Power 398

Countries Dependent on Trade 403

Globalization around the World 418

The Global Supply Chain 450

Economic Freedom in the World 465

The World Trade Organization Goes Global 472

Trade Flows within and between Major Regions 477

The Geographic Population Divide 489

A World That Is "Spiky," Not Flat   494

From Whence Do They Flee?   497

Pandemic (H1N1) 2009 . . . and Counting   503

The Digital Divide in Information and Communication Technologies   508

Where Poverty Prevails in the World: The Share of People Living on Less Than $1.25 a Day   522

The Map of Human Development   527

Gender Politics   537

Locating Biodiversity Bastions and Endangered Biodiversity Hot Spots   569

Loss of Forest and Ground to Deserts   572

preface

Understanding twenty-first-century world politics requires accurate and up-to-date information, intellectual analysis, and interpretation. In a globe undergoing constant and rapid change, it is imperative to accurately describe, explain, and predict the key events and issues unfolding in international affairs. These intellectual tasks must be performed well so that world citizens and policy makers can harness this knowledge and ground their decisions on the most pragmatic approaches to global problems available. Only informed interpretations of world conditions and trend trajectories and cogent explanations of why they exist and how they are unfolding can provide the tools necessary for understanding the world and making it better. By presenting the leading ideas and the latest information available, *World Politics: Trend and Transformation* provides the tools necessary for understanding world affairs in our present period of history, for anticipating probable developments, and for thinking critically about the potential long-term impact of those developments on countries and individuals across the globe.

World Politics: Trend and Transformation aims to put both changes and continuities into perspective. It provides a picture of the evolving relations among all transnational actors, the historical developments that affect those actors' relationships, and the salient contemporary global trends that those interactions produce. The major theories scholars use to explain the dynamics underlying international relations—realism, liberalism, and constructivism, as well as feminist and radical interpretations—frame the investigation. That said, this book resists the temptation to oversimplify world politics with a superficial treatment that would mask complexities and distort realities. Moreover, the text refuses to substitute mere subjective opinion for information based on evidence and purposefully presents clashing and contending views so that students have a chance to critically evaluate the opposed positions and construct their own judgments about key issues. It fosters critical thinking by repeatedly asking students to assess the possibilities for the global future and its potential impact on their own lives.

OVERVIEW OF THE BOOK

To facilitate student learning and provide the tools and information for analyzing the complexities of world politics, this book is organized into five parts. Part 1 introduces the central concepts essential to understanding world politics, global trends, and their meaning. It introduces the leading theories used to interpret international relations. Part 2 examines the globe's transnational actors—the great powers, the less developed countries of the "Global South," intergovernmental organizations (IGOs), and nongovernmental organizations (NGOs). It looks at relations and interactions between them, and now considers the processes and procedures by which transnational actors make decisions. Part 3 examines armed threats to world security, and places emphasis on contending ideas and theoretical perspectives about how to best confront armed aggression. Part 4 explores the ways in which human security and prosperity are truly global issues, and looks at the economic, demographic, and environmental dimensions of the global human condition. The book concludes with Part 5, which considers scenarios about the likely future of world politics and poses six questions raised by prevailing trends in order to stimulate further thinking about the global future.

CHANGES IN THE 2011–2012 UPDATE EDITION

In order to keep you and your students abreast of the latest developments, World Politics has always changed in response to unfolding events around our world. Since the publication of the 2010–2011 edition in February 2010, numerous changes have taken place in international relations. While retaining the major structural and pedagogical changes added in the thirteenth major revision of this textbook, this 2011–2012 update edition incorporates the latest global events and scholarly research to provide students the most current information.

Updates to Content by Chapter

This text continues to take pride in identifying and reporting the most recent developments in international affairs and in providing the latest data on the most significant related trends. The 2011–2012 update edition includes current coverage on the most important issues on the global agenda, from the spread of nuclear capabilities to the continued oppression of people around the globe; from instability and the outbreak of armed conflict to the volatility of global finance and worldwide poverty; from risks posed by global warming to the implications of technological innovation.

As always, this leading text incorporates many thematic shifts in emphasis that capture the latest changes in the understanding of key issues and problems in our world. This update edition includes 11 new maps, figures, and tables—in addition to revisions of most existing ones—to incorporate the latest data available. There are 21 brand new pictures as well as accompanying background information. An all-new Controversy box is also included to facilitate learning about international relations theory.

The following descriptions pinpoint the most important changes to each chapter in the 2011–2012 update edition:

- Chapter 1, "Interpreting World Politics," clearly presents the book's approach and organization, with key concepts—such as world politics, foreign policy, power, and ethnic groups—now introduced early in the chapter. A new introduction also incorporates recently available information on current events. The coverage of levels of analysis has been revised, and discussion about the impact of perceptions on world politics has been updated and takes into account developments in U.S. involvement in Iraq.

- Chapter 2, "Theories of World Politics," now places greater emphasis on constructivism and, for the first time, includes scholarship on cultural theory. The revised discussion on realism now distinguishes between classical and neoclassical realism. Insights from President Obama's administration are also included. Additionally, the chapter features a brand-new Controversy box that evaluates various international relations theories through the pop-culture prism of a zombie outbreak.

- Chapter 3, "Great Power Rivalries and Relations," consolidates prior coverage of national security strategies. The treatment of the causes and course of the Cold War has been revised in both the text and the Controversy box. The new emphasis on uni-multipolarity, with increased attention to the implications of the "rise of the rest," is enhanced with a revised discussion of the U.S. unipolar moment and new definitions for unipolarity and polarization in the margins. There is revised discussion of multipolar powers, with new coverage of China as a growing economic player.

- Chapter 4, "The Global South in a World of Powers," is revised to reflect changes in the challenges facing Global South countries and the possibilities for narrowing the divide between wealthy and poor countries. There is new discussion of "outsourcing" and the legacy of mistrust between the developed and developing worlds. Focusing on relations between the Global South and Global North today, there is enhanced coverage of the global financial crisis, capital flows, and military spending. New discussion of the G-20 meeting is also included, as well as updates to include the most recent data on an array of issues such as foreign aid, remittances, trade and global debt.

- Chapter 5, "Nonstate Actors and the Quest for Global Community," consolidates material on intergovernmental organizations and nongovernmental organizations that was spread across two chapters in prior editions of *World Politics*. The discussion of the United Nations has been updated, as has coverage on the World Bank, APEC, Amnesty International, and the Lisbon Treaty. New discussion of the far-reaching consequences of the global economic crisis is included, as well as enhanced coverage of terrorism, indigenous groups, ethnic minorities, and multinational corporations.

- Chapter 6, "International Decision Making," brings Part 2 to a close so that a survey of decision making follows the introduction of the globe's actors. Discussion of decision making as rational choice, the influence of domestic divisions, and the reticence of leaders to acknowledge and address failures has been revised, as has coverage of the role of bureaucratic politics. Discussion on polarity, polarization, and the rise of Global East powers has also been enhanced; a new map depicts the number of electoral democracies in the world as of 2010. There is also new discussion of the potential for threat inflation, as well as a brand new definition to further explain the concept.

- Part 3 on "Confronting Armed Aggression" positions discussion of military threats, and global responses to them, earlier in the book than in prior editions. Chapter 7, "The Threat of Armed Aggression to the World," begins the section with updated discussion and data on armed conflicts and failed states. There is enhanced discussion of aggression within states, coup d'états, cyclical theories of warfare, and terrorism. A brand new map depicts the persistent threat of terrorism across the globe, and figures on the tools of terrorist warfare and statistics on terrorist incidents have been revised. There is also coverage of conflicts and civil unrest in Afghanistan, Sudan, Iran, and elsewhere.

- Chapter 8, "The Military Pursuit of Power through Arms and Military Strategy," introduces the core premises and policy prescriptions underlying realist approaches to war and peace. The latest international trends in military preparation are captured in updated data and coverage on military expenditures, robotic military technology, and the proliferation of nuclear and chemical weapons. There is an expanded discussion on trends in the weapons trade, with a brand new table that identifies the top twenty arms-producing companies. The chapter also includes updated discussion of missile defense and the expanding missile gap.

- Chapter 9, "Alliances and the Balance of Power," emphasizes realist interpretations of the influence of arms control in stabilizing the balance of power. There is an updated discussion of NATO, which includes the prospects for incorporating Russia in NATO expansion. Revised discussion of the United States as a global hegemon considers the possibilities of a power transition and the importance of alliances in U.S. national security strategy. There is updated data on economic competition, with coverage of balancing by "emerging markets" that emphasizes the enhanced geopolitical importance of Eurasia and the BRIC countries.

■ Chapter 10, "Negotiated Conflict Resolution and International Law," was extensively reorganized with the thirteenth major revision. The emphasis on the liberal theoretical tradition was supplemented with greater attention to constructivist theory throughout the chapter. In this updated edition, coverage of legality and legitimacy in international law has been enhanced, as has discussion of positivist legal theory. There is updated coverage on issues such as the Guantanamo detention site, international crime, the International Court of Justice, and the International Criminal Court. Discussion on the preventive and preemptive use of force has also been revised.

■ Chapter 11, "Institutional and Normative Approaches to Collective Security," retains the emphasis on international security approaches most strongly advocated by liberals. The chapter also includes the expanded discussion on constructivist and feminist perspectives introduced in the thirteenth major revision of *World Politics*. This updated edition includes a major retreatment of multilateral arms control and disarmament. There is also new discussion on the global response to nuclear developments in Iran, North Korea, China, and elsewhere. Expanded coverage focuses on current issues facing the United Nations and its future prospects. There is also updated information on global trade ties and the democratic peace.

■ Part 4, "Human Security, Prosperity, and Responsibility," assesses the global condition and how the erosion of national borders is transforming world politics and affecting human welfare. Chapter 12, "The Globalization of International Finance," expands discussion of globalization and its implications for international finance, in particular the geopolitical ramifications of the global economic crisis. China's rising economic power and the debate surrounding dollar-yuan exchange rates are discussed. There is also enhanced coverage of the global financial institutional framework, with updates on the G-20 summit, WTO, global inflation, exchange rates, and balance of trade.

■ Chapter 13, "International Trade in the Global Marketplace," continues coverage of the international political economy. There is expanded discussion of the globalization of production, with a new emphasis on outsourcing. The chapter proceeds with a revised discussion on foreign direct investment, including new data and figures on FDI inflows and destinations. There is a new look at the concept of comparative advantage and updated data on an array of measures from tariffs to corruption to agricultural subsidies. Consideration of regional trade agreements is enhanced, and a revised discussion of the linkage between trade, the financial crisis, and its aftermath is included.

■ Chapter 14, "The Demographic and Cultural Dimensions of Globalization," examines trends in global population changes and the challenges they pose. There is revised discussion of the demographic divide between the Global North and Global South, with an emphasis on the implications of differences in replacement-level fertility. This chapter discusses issues such as youth bulges in some countries and aging populations in others. The text now also reviews the distinction between chronological and biological aging. The chapter also includes updated discussion on urbanization, refugees, and the spread of global diseases. A new discussion on the growth of cross-border communications emphasizes the increasing significance of social networks.

■ Chapter 15, "The Promotion of Human Development and Human Rights," enhances the treatment of human development and human rights. There is revised discussion of the divide in human development between the Global North and Global South, with updated data on poverty, income inequality, adult literacy, and life expectancy. Coverage of the status of women includes new information on gender inequalities, women and economic growth, and the role of women in public office. The section on human trafficking introduced with the thirteenth major revision is significantly revised, and there is new discussion of gendercide and how gender discrimination is tied to human rights violations. The section on children and human rights has been updated, with revised data on slavery, child mortality, and child soldiers.

■ Chapter 16, "Global Responsibility for the Preservation of the Environment," puts into perspective an entire range of global ecological issues, including revised discussions of climate change and global warming, ozone depletion, desertification, and animal and plant extinction. There is enhanced discussion of ecopolitics addressing the challenges of energy supply and demand, water and food shortage, and the struggle for advantages in access to oil. The chapter provides extensive updates to data on greenhouse gas emissions, deforestation, energy consumption, nuclear power, and environmental performance—as well as coverage of recent natural and man-made disasters around the globe, including the oil spill in the Gulf of Mexico. The chapter concludes with consideration of the possibilities for sustainability.

■ Part 5, "Thinking about the Future of World Politics," closes with Chapter 17, "Looking Ahead at Global Trends and Transformations." The chapter continues to inventory insights from philosophers and policy makers about the interpretation of the global condition. It also introduces six leading debates about the global future. In this updated edition, there is revised discussion of globalization and the nature of human security. The chapter concludes with a challenge to students to formulate their own ideas about the possibilities for humanity's common future.

Changes to Structure, Presentation, and Pedagogical Aids

In addition to the content updates identified above, this 2011–2012 update edition continues to reflect structural and pedagogical modifications introduced with the thirteenth major revision of *World Politics*.

■ **A significant reorganization of the material that consolidates coverage of previously dispersed topics, alters the thematic order of the chapters, and more fully integrates theoretical perspectives throughout the book.** As a result, there are five parts and seventeen chapters, with chapters focusing on armed aggression and the military preceding those on economics, human security, demographics, and the environment in order to enhance the flow of the book as a whole. Discussions of the theoretical contributions of constructivism and feminism are enhanced and highlighted across the book's chapters. Although the organization has been consolidated, *World Politics*' depth of coverage remains unchanged.

■ **A design that makes the book more attractive and easier to use.** The 2011–2012 edition retains the streamlined chapter-openers with traditional chapter outlines so students can preview and review the material presented. It continues to incorporate thought-provoking quotations in each chapter to broaden awareness of competing ideas and to stimulate interest with insightful opinions. The featured quotations are limited and strategically placed in order to enhance the material's relevance while minimizing breaks to the flow of the primary text.

■ **Revised and new Controversy boxes that feature critical thinking questions.** Long a mainstay of the book, each Controversy box examines opposing positions in major debates in international relations. Addressing both classic dilemmas in international affairs and the most heated current debates, Controversy boxes offer excellent starting points for class discussions or research papers. With the thirteenth major revision, for the very first time, *World Politics* features "What Do You Think?" questions to further develop critical thinking skills and facilitate student assessment of opposing viewpoints, development of their own opinions, and application of the main ideas to other global affairs dilemmas. A completely new Controversy box has been added in the 2011–2012 update edition, and others have been revised to reflect recent developments and data.

■ **Revised, up-to-date map and illustration program.** One of the most popular pedagogical features of the text, the illustration program, has been revised to broaden the book's coverage, provoke interest, and enable students to visualize the central developments and most recently available data. Students today are often woefully uninformed about world geography, and the extensive map program helps remedy this problem. Building upon the extensive revisions of the 2010–2011 edition, this updated edition includes more than two dozen new photographs, maps, tables, and figures selected to introduce the timeliest topics and include detailed captions explaining their relevance to the larger issues discussed in the text.

■ **Revised treatment of key terms.** Key terms continue to be highlighted with bold-faced text and glossed definitions in the margins when the terms are first introduced. Each term is glossed the first time it is introduced, and a single definition is used to familiarize students with the term's broadest and most common meaning. If a term is used again in subsequent chapters, the term is identified in *italics* the first time it appears within a given chapter as a reminder that the definition can be found in the glossary.

■ **A revised glossary of key term definitions.** This reference tool appears at the end of the text, so students can easily access terms they may not remember from previous chapters. New terms have been added to keep students up-to-date with key concepts in the study of world politics.

■ **New margin icons for online exercises.** With the thirteenth edition, margin icons were introduced at key points throughout each chapter to alert students to relevant online activities they can access through the book's CourseMate site.

■ **New end-of-chapter coverage.** "Key Terms" have been removed from the end of the chapter and are now listed in the margins of the text and in the end-of-book glossary. In the 2011–2012 update edition, revised listings of "Suggested Readings" are included at the end of each chapter to bring attention to the most recent and authoritative scholarship on discussed topics. There is also a prompt at the conclusion of each chapter encouraging students to take an online quiz to assess their knowledge and understanding of the presented material.

SUPPLEMENTS

The publisher proudly offers the following state-of-the-art supplements prepared specifically for *World Politics: Trend and Transformation.*

FOR THE INSTRUCTOR

PowerLecture DVD with JoinIn and ExamView

ISBN-10: 1439082049 | ISBN-13: 9781439082041

- Interactive **PowerPoint Lectures set,** a one-stop lecture and class preparation tool, makes it easy for you to assemble, edit, publish, and present custom lectures for your course. You will have access to a set of PowerPoints with outlines specific to each chapter of *World Politics* as well as photos, figures, and tables found in the book. You can also add your own materials—culminating in a powerful, personalized, media-enhanced presentation.

- A **Test Bank** in Microsoft Word and ExamView computerized testing offers a large array of well-crafted multiple-choice and essay questions, along with their answers and page references.

- An **Instructor's Manual** includes learning objectives, chapter outlines, discussion questions, suggestions for stimulating class activities and projects, tips on integrating media into your class (including step-by-step instructions on how to create your own podcasts), suggested readings and Web resources, and a section specially designed to help teaching assistants and adjunct instructors.

- **JoinIn** on Turning Point offers book-specific "clicker" questions that test and track student comprehension of key concepts. Political Polling questions simulate voting, engage students, foster dialogue on group behaviors and values, and add personal relevance; the results can be compared to national data, leading to lively discussions. Visual Literacy questions are tied to images from the book and add useful pedagogical tools and high-interest feedback during your lecture. Save the data from students' responses all semester—track their progress and show them how political science works by incorporating this exciting new tool into your classroom. It is available for college and university adopters only.

- The **Resource Integration Guide** outlines the rich collection of resources available to instructors and students within the chapter-by-chapter framework of the book, suggesting how and when each supplement can be used to optimize learning.

WebTutor

WebTutor on WebCT IAC

ISBN-10: 1439082359 | ISBN-13: 9781439082355

WebTutor on Blackboard IAC

ISBN-10: 1439082375 | ISBN-13: 9781439082379

WebTutor on Angel IAC

Rich with content for your international relations course, this Web-based teaching and learning tool includes course management, study/mastery, and communication tools. Use WebTutor to provide virtual office hours, post your syllabus, and track student progress with WebTutor's quizzing material.

For students, WebTutor offers real-time access to interactive online tutorials and simulations, practice quizzes, and Web links—all correlated to *World Politics*.

FOR THE STUDENT

CourseMate Instant Access Code

ISBN-10: 1439082022 | ISBN-13: 9781439082027

CourseMate for *World Politics: Trend and Transformation* offers a variety of rich learning resources designed to enhance the student experience. These resources include an interactive eBook, podcasts by the text's authors; simulations that can be assigned as homework; animated learning modules; case studies, which consist of Internet exercises and activities that correspond to instructor goals and challenges for the course; key term flashcards; and videos, all corresponding with concepts taught in each chapter. CourseMate also offers interactive timelines and maps and NewsNow.

Bring the news right into your classroom! Available in both student and instructor versions, NewsNow is a combination of Associated Press news stories, videos, and images that bring current events to life. For students, a collection of news stories and accompanying videos is served up each week via the Premium Website that accompanies their international relations text. For instructors, an additional set of multimedia-rich Power-Point slides is posted each week to the password-protected area of the text's companion. Instructors may use these slides to take a class poll or trigger a lively debate about the events shaping the world right now. And because this all-in-one presentation tool includes the text of the original newsfeed, along with videos, photos, and discussion questions, no Internet connection is required!

Interactive eBook

ISBN-10: 0538733594 | ISBN-13: 9780538733595

We provide separate options for the delivery of an interactive, multimedia eBook that contains links to simulations, flashcards, and other interactive activities.

CengageBrain and Companion Website

www.cengagebrain.com/shop/ISBN/0495802204

On CengageBrain.com students will be able to save up to 60% on their course materials through our full spectrum of options. Students will have the option to rent their textbooks, purchase print textbooks, e-textbooks, or individual e-chapters and audio books all for substantial savings over average retail prices. You'll also find Cengage Learning's broad range of homework and study tools, including the Companion Website for *World Politics*: learning objectives, tutorial quizzes, chapter glossaries, flashcards, and crossword puzzles—all correlated by chapter. Instructors also have access to the Instructor's Manual and PowerPoints.

International Politics Atlas

ISBN-10: 0618837132 | ISBN-13: 9780618837137

Free when bundled with a Wadsworth textbook, this atlas offers maps of the world showing political organization, population statistics, and economic development; maps highlighting energy production and consumption, major world conflicts, migration, and more; and extensive regional coverage. Students will find it useful for understanding world events and to supplement their studies in international politics.

ACKNOWLEDGMENTS

Many people—in fact, too many to identify and thank individually—have contributed to the development of this leading textbook in international relations (including especially Eugene R. Wittkopf, who served as coauthor of the first six editions of *World Politics* and to whom the eleventh edition was dedicated following his tragically premature death). Those who made the greatest contributions to making this, the 2011–2012 update edition, better include the following, whose assistance is most appreciatively acknowledged.

In the first category are the constructive comments and suggestions offered by reviewers. In particular, gratitude is hereby expressed to the professional scholars who provided blind reviews, including:

Bossman Asare, Graceland University

Cristian A. Harris, North Georgia College and State University

Todd Myers, Grossmont College

Christopher Sprecher, Texas A&M University

John Tuman, University of Nevada, Las Vegas

In a second category are scholars who provided advice and data. These include:

Ruchi Anand at the American Graduate School of International Relations and Diplomacy in Paris;

Osmo Apunen at the University of Tampere;

Chad Atkinson at the University of Illinois;

Andrew J. Bacevich at Boston University;

Yan Bai at Grand Rapids Community College;

George Belzer at Johnson County Community College;

John Boehrer at the University of Washington;

Robert Blanton at The University of Memphis;

Linda P. Brady at the University of North Carolina-Greensboro;

Leann Brown at the University of Florida;

Dan Caldwell at Pepperdine University;

John H. Calhoun at Palm Beach Atlantic University;

John Candido at La Trobe University;

Roger A. Coate at Georgia College & State University;

Jonathan E. Colby at the Carlyle Group in Washington, D.C.;

Phyllis D. Collins at Keswick Management Inc. in New York City;

Reverend George Crow at Northeast Presbyterian Church;

Jonathan Davidson at the European Commission;

Philippe Dennery of the J-Net Ecology Communication Company in Paris;

Gregory Domin at Mercer University;

Thomas Donaldson at the Wharton School of the University of Pennsylvania;

Ayman I. El-Dessouki and Kemel El-Menoufi of Cairo University;

Robert Fatton at the University of Virginia;

Matthias Finger at Columbia University;

Eytan Gilboa at Bar-Ilan University in Israel;

Giovanna Gismondi at the University of Oklahoma;

Srajan Gligorijevic at the Defense and Security Studies Centre of the G-17 Plus Institute in Belgrade Serbia;

Richard F. Grimmett at the Congressional Research Office;

Ted Robert Gurr at the University of Maryland;

Russell Hardin at New York University;

James E. Harf at Maryville University in St. Louis;

Charles Hermann at Texas A&M University;

Margaret G. Hermann at Syracuse University;

Stephen D. Hibbard at Shearman & Sterling LLP;

Steven W. Hook at Kent State University;

Jack Hurd at the Nature Conservatory;

Lisa Huffstetler at The University of Memphis;

Patrick James at the University of Southern California;

Loch Johnson at the University of Georgia;

Christopher M. Jones at Northern Illinois University;

Christopher Joyner at Georgetown University;

Michael D. Kanner at the University of Colorado;

Mahmoud Karem of the Egyptian Foreign Service;

Deborah J. Kegley at Kegley International, Inc.;

Mary V. Kegley at Kegley Books in Wytheville, Virginia;

Susan Kegley at the University of California-Berkeley;

Lidija Kos-Stanišić at the University of Zagreb in Croatia;

Matthias Kranke at the University of Tier;

Barbara Kyker at The University of Memphis;

Imtiaz T. Ladak of Projects International in Washington D.C.;

Jack Levy at Rutgers University;

Carol Li at the Taipei Economic and Cultural Office, New York;

Urs Luterbacher of the Graduate Institute of International and Development Studies in Geneva;

Gen. Jeffrey D. McCausland at the U.S. Army War College in Carlisle, Pennsylvania;

James McCormick at Iowa University;

Kelly A. McCready at Maria College, Albany, New York;

Mahmood Monshipouri at San Francisco State University;

Robert Morin at Western Nevada Community College;

Ahmad Noor at Youth Parliament Pakistan;

Anthony Perry at Henry Ford Community College;

Jeffrey Pickering at Kansas State University;

Karen Ann Mingst at the University of Kentucky;

James A. Mitchell at California State University;

Donald Munton at the University of Northern British Columbia;

Desley Sant Parker at the United States Information Agency;

Albert C. Pierce at the U.S. Naval Academy;

Alex Platt at the Carnegie Council for Ethics in International Affairs;

Ignacio de la Rasilla at the Université de Genève;

James Ray at Vanderbilt University;

Gregory A. Raymond at Boise State University;

Neil R. Richardson at the University of Wisconsin;

Peter Riddick at Berkhamsted Collegiate;

James N. Rosenau at George Washington University;

Joel Rosenthal at the Carnegie Council for Ethics in International Affairs;

Tapani Ruokanen at Suomen Kuvalehti, Finland;

Alpo M. Rusi, Finnish Ambassador to Switzerland;

Jan Aart Scholte at University of Warwick, UK;

Rebecca R. Sharitz at International Association for Ecology;

Shalendra D. Sharma at the University of San Francisco;

Richard H. Shultz at the Fletcher School of Law and Diplomacy, Tufts University;

Dragan R. Simić at the Centre for the Studies of the USA in Belgrade, Serbia;

Michael J. Siler at the University of California;

Bengt Sundelius at the National Defense College in Stockholm;

David Sylvan of the Graduate Institute of International and Development Studies in Geneva;

William R. Thompson of Indiana University;

Rodney Tomlinson at the U.S. Naval Academy;

Deborah Tompsett-Makin at Riverside Community College, Norco Campus;
Denise Vaughan at Bellevue Community College;

Rob Verhofstad at Radmoud University in Nijmegen the Netherlands;
William C. Vocke, Jr. at the Carnegie Council for Ethics in International Affairs;

Jonathan Wilkenfeld at the University of Maryland; and Samuel A. Worthington at InterAction.

Also helpful in a third category was the input provided by graduate students Maggie Sommer, Katharine Nelson, and Drew Dickson at The University of Memphis, who provided invaluable research assistance. Thanks are also given for the insights and advice of professorial colleagues in the Fulbright American Studies Institute, which Kegley co-directed with Don Puchala in 2003, 2004, and 2005.

The always helpful and accommodating project manager Madhavi Prakashkumar with S4Carlisle Publishing Services and Photo Researcher Jaime Jankowski with Pre-Press PMG made valuable contributions to this book. In addition, also deserving of special gratitude are our highly skilled, dedicated, and helpful editors at Wadsworth: Executive Editor Carolyn Merrill and Development Editor Rebecca Green, who exercised extraordinary professionalism in guiding the process that brought this edition into print, assisted by the project management of Josh Allen and Permissions Editors Jennifer Meyer Dare and Katie Huha. Gratitude is also expressed to the always instructive advice of Lydia LeStar, Wadsworth's skilled Political Science Marketing Manager.

Charles William Kegley

Shannon Lindsey Blanton

meet your authors

CHARLES WILLIAM KEGLEY is currently the Vice Chair of the Board of Trustees of the Carnegie Council for Ethics in International Affairs. The Distinguished Pearce Professor of International Relations, Emeritus at the University of South Carolina, Kegley is also a past President of the International Studies Association (1993-1994). A graduate of American University (B.A.) and Syracuse University (Ph.D.) and a Pew Faculty Fellow at Harvard University, Kegley has held faculty appointments at Georgetown University, the University of Texas, Rutgers University, the People's University of China, and the Institut Universitaire de Hautes Études Internationales Et du Développement in Geneva, Switzerland. A founding partner of Kegley International, Inc., a publishing, research, and consulting foundation, Kegley is a recipient of the Distinguished Scholar Award in Foreign Policy of the International Studies Association, and he has widely published his primary research in the leading scholarly journals. Among his more than fifty books, Kegley has recently published *The New Global Terrorism* (2003); *Controversies in International Relations Theory* (1995); and, with Gregory A. Raymond, *The Multipolar Challenge* (2008), *After Iraq: The Imperiled American Imperium* (2007); *The Global Future* (third edition, 2010); *From War to Peace* (2002); *Exorcising the Ghost of Westphalia* (2002); *How Nations Make Peace* (1999); *A Multipolar Peace? Great-Power Politics in the Twenty-First Century* (1994); and *When Trust Breaks Down: Alliance Norms and World Politics* (1990). Kegley has also coauthored and edited with Eugene R. Wittkopf a number of leading texts, including *American Foreign Policy: Pattern and Process* (seventh edition, 2007, with Christopher Jones); *The Global Agenda* (sixth edition, 2001); *The Future of American Foreign Policy* (1992); *The Nuclear Reader* (second edition, 1989); and *The Domestic Sources of American Foreign Policy* (1988). Kegley has also published widely in leading scholarly journals, including *Armed Forces and Society, Asian Forum, Brown Journal of International Affairs, Comparative Political Studies, Conflict Management and Peace Science, Cooperation and Conflict, Ethics and International Affairs, Fletcher Forum of World Affairs, Futures Research Quarterly, Harvard International Review, International Interactions, International Organization, International Politics, International Studies Quarterly, Jerusalem Journal of International Relations, Journal of Conflict Resolution, Journal of Peace Research, Journal of Politics, Korean Journal of International Studies, Orbis,* and the *Western Political Quarterly.*

SHANNON LINDSEY BLANTON is Professor of Political Science at The University of Memphis, where she is also the Vice Provost for Undergraduate Programs. She oversees all undergraduate programs and provides leadership in curriculum planning, general education, the Center for International Programs and Services, the Honors Program, and the Learning Communities. She is a past department chair and undergraduate coordinator, and has served nationally as a facilitator for leadership development in higher education. A graduate of Georgia College (B.A.), the University of Georgia (M.A.), and the University of South Carolina (Ph.D.), she has received numerous research awards and was named in 2007 as the recipient of The University of Memphis' prestigious *Alumni Association Distinguished Research in the Social Sciences and Business Award*. She specializes in the areas of international relations and foreign policy, with an emphasis on human rights, democracy, international political economy, and the arms trade. She has served on a number of editorial boards, including those for three of the discipline's foremost journals, *International Studies Quarterly*, *Foreign Policy Analysis* and *International Studies Perspectives*. Her work has been published extensively in leading scholarly journals, including the *American Journal of Political Science*, *Journal of Politics*, *International Studies Quarterly*, *Journal of Peace Research*, *International Interactions*, *Social Science Journal*, *Journal of Third World Studies*, *Journal of Political and Military Sociology*, *Business and Society*, *Conflict Quarterly*, and *Leadership*.

Together Kegley and Blanton have coauthored publications appearing in *The Brown Journal of World Affairs*, *Futures Research Quarterly*, *Mediterranean Quarterly*, *Rethinking the Cold War*, and *World Politics* (twelfth edition update and 2010–2011 edition).

WORLD POLITICS
Trend and Transformation

2011–2012 Update Edition

Part 1
TREND AND TRANSFORMATION IN WORLD POLITICS

"There is no scientific antidote [to the atomic bomb], only education. You've got to change the way people think. I am not interested in disarmament talks between nations. . . . What I want to do is to disarm the mind. After that, everything else will automatically follow. The ultimate weapon for such mental disarmament is international education."

—Albert Einstein, Nobel Peace Prize physicist

Rajesh Kumar Singh/AP Photo

WHAT FUTURE FOR HUMANKIND? Many global trends are sweeping across a transforming planet. Among those that pose a serious threat are the heatwaves and droughts that have spread across the globe, such as that pictured here in Allahabud, India. Arresting global warming is one of the many global challenges that face humanity.

THESE ARE TURBULENT TIMES, INSPIRING BOTH ANXIETY AND HOPE. What lies ahead for the world? What are we to think about the global future? Part 1 of this book introduces you to the study of world politics in a period of rapid change. It opens a window on the many trends that are unfolding, some of them in contrary directions. The combined force of these trends may transform many aspects of international relations, even though they may persist.

There are obstacles that prevent us from understanding world politics accurately. Chapter 1 explains how our perceptions of global realities can lead to distortions, and suggests how to get beyond these barriers by providing four keys to understanding world politics as well as an outline of the book's thematic approach and organization. Chapter 2 introduces the major rival theories (realism, liberalism, and constructivism) that scholars have developed to help policy makers and citizens better describe, explain, and predict the evolving nature of international relations. It also illuminates two powerful critiques of these mainstream theories: radicalism and feminism. Such theories are important tools that can help you construct more accurate images of the complexity of world politics and better interpret emerging trends and transformations.

CHAPTER 1
INTERPRETING WORLD POLITICS

CHAPTER OUTLINE

THE CHALLENGE OF
INVESTIGATING WORLD AFFAIRS

HOW PERCEPTIONS INFLUENCE
IMAGES OF INTERNATIONAL
REALITY

The Nature and Sources
of Images

CONTROVERSY: Should We
Believe What We See?

The Impact of Perceptions on
World Politics

KEYS TO UNDERSTANDING
WORLD POLITICS

Introducing Terminology

Distinguishing the Primary
Transnational Actors

Distinguishing Levels
of Analysis

Distinguishing Change, Cycles,
and Continuities

PREPARING FOR YOUR JOURNEY
INTO WORLD POLITICS

The Book's Approach

The Book's Organization

The world is at a critical juncture, and so are you . . . Go ahead and make your plans . . . and don't stop learning. But be open to the detours that lead to new discoveries.

—Kofi Annan, former UN Secretary General

NASA

A WORLD OF POSSIBILITIES As viewed from outer space, planet Earth looks as if it has continents without borders separating states and people. Reflecting on his Space Shuttle experience, astronaut Sultan bin Salman Al-Saud remarked that "the first day or so we all pointed to our countries. The third or fourth day we were pointing to our continents. By the fifth day, we were aware of only one Earth." As viewed from newspaper headlines, however, world politics looks much different.

Imagine yourself returning home from a two-week vacation on a tropical island where you had no access to the news. The trip gave you a well-deserved break before starting a new school term. But now you are curious about what has happened when you were away. As you glance at a newspaper, the headlines catch your eye. They indicate that there is a downsizing of resources and troops in Iraq, though tensions and unrest persist. Instead, the focus is on the battle against Al Qaeda and the Taliban in Afghanistan and parts of Pakistan, where the United States-led coalition forces face not only violent resistance from militants but also rampant corruption and lack of economic opportunity that threaten to undermine the prospects for success. As you ride home from the airport, you hear a radio broadcast that describes protests and strikes in Greece and Spain that are waged in response to austerity measures being taken to address rampant debt and poor public finance. In China, the government has decided to unpeg its currency from the U.S. dollar and allow it to fluctuate and potentially rise in value. You wonder if this will have any effect on the price of the new laptop that you want to buy. Shortly after arriving home, you connect to the Internet and find that the consequences of the oil spill in the Gulf of Mexico is more dire than initially thought—killing untold numbers of wildlife and dramatically affecting the livelihood of those in the coastal region—with some estimating more than 2.6 million gallons of oil a day surging from the damaged oil well into the ocean waters. Finally, while listening to CNN later that evening, you hear several other reports: There are concerns over efforts by Iran and North Korea to develop their nuclear capabilities, and the leaders of both countries are belligerent in the face of international censure. There are signs that the economic decline in the United States is leveling off, and you hope that conditions improve before you graduate and go on the job market. In addition, there is coverage of the violence by drug cartels in Mexico, and you worry about whether this will affect your plans for a study abroad tour over the winter break.

The scenario just described is not hypothetical. The events identified record what actually occurred during the month of June 2010.

Undoubtedly, many individuals experienced fear and confusion during this turbulent period. But it is, uncomfortably, not so different from other eras. Putting this information about unfolding events together, you cannot help but be reminded that the world matters and that those changes in it affect your circumstances and future powerfully. The "news" you received is not really new, because it echoes many old stories from the past about the growing sea of turmoil sweeping contemporary world circumstances. Nevertheless, the temptation to wish that this depressing kind of chaotic world would just go away is overwhelming. If only the unstable world would stand still long enough for a sense of predictability and order to prevail. Alas, that does not appear likely. You cannot escape the world or control its turbulence, and you cannot single-handedly alter its character.

We are all a part of this world, and this world is an integral part of each of us. Hence, if we are to live adaptively amid the fierce winds of global change, we must face the challenge of discovering the dynamic properties of *world politics.*

world politics
the study of how global actors' activities entail the exercise of influence to achieve and defend their goals and ideals, and how it affects the world at large.

Because every person is influenced increasingly by world events, all can benefit by investigating how the global system works and how changes are remaking our political and economic world. Only through learning how our own decisions and behavior contribute to the global condition, as well as those of powerful state governments and nonstate transnational actors, and how all people and groups in turn are heavily conditioned by changes in world politics, can we address what former U.S. President Bill Clinton defined as "the question of our time—whether we can make change our friend and not our enemy."

Great things are achieved by guessing the direction of one's century.

—Giuseppe Mazzini, Italian political leader

THE CHALLENGE OF INVESTIGATING WORLD AFFAIRS

American poet Walt Whitman wrote in 1888, "I say we had best look at our times and lands searchingly, like some physician diagnosing some deep disease." His advice is as timely today as it was then. We must perceive our times accurately in order to best understand the political convulsions that confront the globe's 6.8 billion people.

Interpreting the world in which we now live and anticipating what lies ahead for the globe's future—and yours—presents formidable challenges. We are constantly bombarded with a bewildering amount of new information and new developments. Forging a meaningful understanding of the messages about world affairs we receive every day could be the most difficult task you will ever face. Why? Partly because the study of international relations requires taking into account every factor that influences human behavior. This is a task that, as the seminal scientist Albert Einstein believed, is extremely challenging. He once hinted at how big the challenge of explaining world politics was when he was asked, "Why is it that when the mind of man has stretched so far as to discover the structure of the atom we have been unable to devise the political means to keep the atom from destroying us?" He replied, "This is simple, my friend; it is because politics is more difficult than physics."

Another part of the challenge stems from the tendency of people to resist unfamiliar information and ideas that undermine their habitual ways of viewing and thinking about world affairs. We know from repeated studies that people do not want to accept ideas that do not conform to their prior beliefs.

A purpose of this book is to help you to cultivate a questioning attitude about your preexisting beliefs about world affairs and about the many actors on the world stage. To that end, we will ask you to evaluate rival perspectives on global issues, even if they differ from your current images. Indeed, we will expose you to schools of thought prevailing today that you may find unconvincing, and possibly repugnant. Why are they included? Because many other people make these views the bedrock of their interpretations, and these viewpoints accordingly enjoy a popular following.

For this reason, this text will describe some visions of world politics with which even your authors may not agree, so that you may weigh the wisdom or foolishness of contending perspectives. The interpretive challenge, then, is to try to observe unfolding global realities objectively, in order to describe and explain them accurately.

To appreciate how our images of reality shape our expectations, we begin with a brief introduction to the role that subjective images of reality play in understanding world politics. This will be followed by a set of analytic tools that this book will use to help you overcome perceptual obstacles to understanding world politics, and to empower you to more capably interpret the forces of change and continuity that affect our world.

> *It is the tragedy of the world that no one knows what he doesn't know and the less a man knows, the more sure he is that he knows everything.*
>
> —Joyce Carey, English author

HOW PERCEPTIONS INFLUENCE IMAGES OF INTERNATIONAL REALITY

We already hold mental images of world politics, although we may not have attempted to explicitly define our perceptions about the world in our subconscious. But whatever our levels of self-awareness, our images perform the same function: They simplify "reality" by exaggerating some features of the real world while ignoring others. Thus, we live in a world defined by our images.

These mental pictures, or perceptions, are inevitably distortions, as they cannot fully capture the complexity and configurations of even physical objects, such as the globe itself (see Controversy: Should We Believe What We See?).

Many of our images of the world's political realities may be built on illusions and misconceptions. Even images that are now accurate can easily become outdated if we fail to recognize changes in the world. Indeed, the world's future will be determined not only by changes in the "objective" facts of world politics but also by the meaning that people ascribe to those facts, the assumptions on which they base their interpretations, and the actions that flow from these assumptions and interpretations—however accurate or inaccurate they might be.

The Nature and Sources of Images

The effort to simplify one's view of the world is inevitable and even necessary. Just as cartographers' projections simplify complex geophysical space so that we can better understand the world, each of us inevitably creates a "mental map"—a habitual way of organizing information—to make sense of a confusing abundance of information. Although mental maps are neither inherently right nor wrong, they are important because we tend to react according to the way the world appears to us rather than the way it is. How we view the world (not what it is really like) determines our attitudes, our beliefs, and our behavior. Political leaders, too, are captives of this tendency (Kirkpatrick 2007). As Richard Ned Lebow (1981, p. 277) warns, "Policymakers are prone to distort reality in accord with their needs even in situations that appear . . . relatively unambiguous."

Most of us—policy makers included—look for information that reinforces our preexisting beliefs about the world, assimilate new data into familiar images, mistakenly equate what we believe with what we know, and deny information that contradicts our expectations. We also rely on our intuitions without thinking and emotionally make snap judgments (Gladwell 2005; Weston 2007).

schematic reasoning
the process of reasoning by which new information is interpreted according to a memory structure, a schema, which contains a network of generic scripts, metaphors, and simplified characterizations of observed objects and phenomena.

In addition, we rely on learned habits for viewing new information and for making judgments, because these "schema" guide our perceptions and organize information for us. Research in cognitive psychology shows that human beings are "categorizers" who match what they see with images in their memories of prototypical events and people when attempting to understand the world by *schematic reasoning*. The absentminded professor, the shady lawyer, and the kindly grandmother are examples of "stock" images that many of us have of certain types of people. Although the professors, lawyers,

CONTROVERSY:

SHOULD WE BELIEVE WHAT WE SEE?

Many people assume that seeing is believing without questioning whether the ways they have organized their perceptions are accurate. But is there more to seeing than meets the eye? Students of perceptual psychology think so. They maintain that seeing is not a strictly passive act: what we observe is partially influenced by our preexisting values and expectations (and by the visual habits reinforced by the constructions society has inculcated in us about how to view objects). Students of perception argue that what you see is what you get, and that two observers looking at the same object might easily see different realities. To illustrate this, perceptual psychologists are fond of displaying the following drawing, which, depending on how the viewer looks at it, can be seen as either a goblet or two faces opposing each other. Both images are possible.

This principle has great importance for investigation of international relations, where, depending on one's perspective, people can vary greatly on how they will view international events, actors, and issues. Intense disagreements often arise from competing images.

To appreciate the controversies that can result when different people (with different perspectives) see different realities even though they are looking at the same thing, consider something as basic as objectively viewing the location and size of the world's continents. There exists a long-standing controversy among cartographers about the "right" way to map the globe, that is, how to make an accurate projection. The accuracy of their rival maps matters politically because they shape how people view what is important. All maps of the globe are distorted because it is impossible to perfectly represent the three-dimensional globe on a two-dimensional piece of paper. The difficulty cartographers face can be appreciated by trying to flatten an orange peel. You can only flatten it by separating pieces of the peel that were joined when it was spherical. Cartographers who try to flatten the globe on paper, without ripping it into

separate pieces, face the same problem. Although there are a variety of ways to represent the three-dimensional object on paper, all of them involve some kind of distortion. Thus cartographers must choose among the imperfect ways of representing the globe by selecting those aspects of the world's geography they consider most important to describe accurately, while making adjustments to other parts.

Cartographers' ideas of what is most important in world geography have varied according to their own global perspectives. These four maps (Maps 1.1, 1.2, 1.3, and 1.4) depict the distribution of the Earth's land surfaces and territory, but each portrays a different image. Each is a model of reality, an abstraction that highlights some features of the globe while ignoring others.

(*continued*)

SHOULD WE BELIEVE WHAT WE SEE? (Continued)

MAP 1.1

MERCATOR PROJECTION This Mercator projection, named for the Flemish cartographer Gerard Mercator, was popular in sixteenth-century Europe and presents a classic Eurocentric view of the world. It mapped the Earth without distorting direction, making it useful for navigators. However, distances were deceptive, placing Europe at the center of the world and exaggerating the continent's importance relative to other landmasses. Europe appears larger than South America, which is twice Europe's size, and two-thirds of the map is used to represent the northern half of the world and only one-third the southern half.

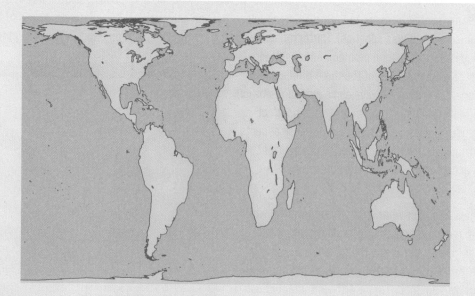

MAP 1.2

PETER'S PROJECTION In the Peter's projection, each landmass appears in correct proportion in relation to all others, but it distorts the shape and position of the Earth's landmasses. In contrast with most geographic representations, it draws attention to the less developed countries of the Global South, where more than three-quarters of the world's population lives today.

MAP 1.3

ORTHOGRAPHIC PROJECTION The orthographic projection, centering on the mid-Atlantic, conveys some sense of the curvature of the Earth by using rounded edges. The sizes and shapes of continents toward the outer edges of the circle are distorted to give a sense of spherical perspective.

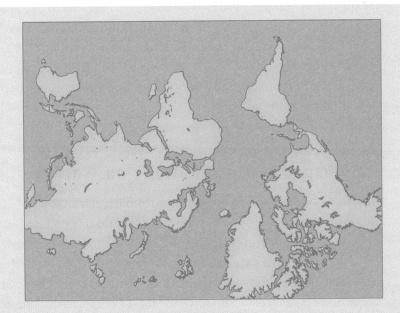

MAP 1.4

"UPSIDE DOWN" PROJECTION This projection gives a different perspective on the world by depicting it upside down, with the Global South positioned above the Global North. The map challenges the modern "Eurocentric" conceptualization of the positions of the globe's countries and peoples by putting the Global South "on top."

(*continued*)

SHOULD WE BELIEVE WHAT WE SEE? (Continued)

WHAT DO YOU THINK?

- What are some of the policy implications associated with the image of the world as depicted in each of the respective images of the world?

- How does history play a role in the features of a map that are distorted? Can you think of any ways modern cartographers might modify any of these world projections?

- In thinking about images and the important role they play in foreign policy, should a consensus be made as to the world projection that is "least" distorted? Why or why not?

and grandmothers that we meet may bear only a superficial resemblance to these stereotypical images, when we know little about someone, our expectations will be shaped by presumed similarities to these characters.

Many factors shape our images, including how we were socialized as children, traumatic events we may have experienced growing up that shape our personalities and psychological needs, exposure to the ideas of people whose expertise we respect, and the opinions about world affairs expressed by our frequent associates such as close friends and coworkers. Once we have acquired an image, it seems self-evident. Accordingly, we try to keep that image consistent without other beliefs and, through a psychological process known as *cognitive dissonance* (Festingner 1957), reject information that contradicts how it portrays the world. In short, our minds select, screen, and filter information; consequently, our perceptions depend not only on what happens in daily life but also on how we interpret and internalize those events.

cognitive dissonance
the general psychological tendency to deny discrepancies between one's preexisting beliefs (cognitions) and new information.

The Impact of Perceptions on World Politics

We must be careful not to assume automatically that what applies to individuals applies to entire countries, and we should not equate the beliefs of leaders, such as heads of states, with the beliefs of the people under their authority. Still, leaders have extraordinary influence, and leaders' images of historical circumstances often predispose them to behave in particular ways toward others, regardless of "objective" facts. For instance, the loss of twenty-six million Soviet lives in the "Great Patriotic War" (as the Russians refer to World War II) reinforced a long-standing fear of foreign invasion, which caused a generation of Soviet policy makers to perceive U.S. defensive moves with suspicion and often alarm. Similarly, the founders of the United States viewed eighteenth-century European power politics and its repetitive wars as corrupt, contributing to two seemingly contradictory tendencies later evident in U.S. foreign policy: (1) America's impulse to isolate itself (its disposition to withdraw from world affairs), and (2) its determination to reform the world in its own image whenever global circumstances become highly threatening. The former led the country to reject membership in the League of Nations after World War I; the latter gave rise to the U.S. globalist foreign policy since World War II, which committed the country to active involvement nearly everywhere on nearly every issue. Most Americans, thinking of their country as virtuous, have difficulty understanding why others sometimes regard such far-reaching international activism as arrogant or threatening; instead, they see only good intentions in active U.S. interventionism. As former President Jimmy Carter once lamented, "The hardest thing for Americans to understand is that they are not better than other people."

Because leaders and citizens are prone to ignore or reinterpret information that runs counter to their beliefs and values, mutual misperceptions often fuel discord in world politics, especially when relations between countries are hostile. Distrust and suspicion arise as conflicting parties view each other in the same negative light—that is, as *mirror images* develop.

mirror images
the tendency of states and people in competitive interaction to perceive each other similarly—to see others the same hostile way others see them.

This occurred in Moscow and Washington during the Cold War. Each side saw its own actions as constructive but its adversary's responses as hostile, and both sides erroneously assumed that their counterparts would misinterpret the intentions of their own policy initiatives. When psychologist Urie Bronfenbrenner (1961) traveled to Moscow, for example, he was amazed to hear Russians describing the United States in terms that were strikingly similar to the way Americans described the Soviet Union: Each side saw itself as virtuous and peace-loving, whereas the other was seen as untrustworthy, aggressive, and ruled by a corrupt government.

Mirror-imaging is a property of nearly all *enduring rivalries*—long-lasting contests between opposing groups. For example, in rivalries such as Christianity against Islam during the Crusades in the Middle Ages, Israel and Palestine since the birth of the sovereign state of Israel in 1948, and the United States and Al Qaeda today, both sides demonize the image of their adversary while perceiving themselves as virtuous. Self-righteousness often leads one party to view its own actions as constructive but its adversary's responses as negative and hostile. When this occurs, conflict resolution is extraordinarily difficult. Not only do the opposing sides have different preferences for certain outcomes over others, but they do not see the underlying issues in the same

enduring rivalries
prolonged competition fueled by deep-seated mutual hatred that leads opposed actors to feud and fight over a long period of time without resolution of their conflict.

light. Further complicating matters, the mirror images held by rivals tend to be self-confirming. When one side expects the other to be hostile, it may treat its opponent in a manner that leads the opponent to take counteractions that confirm the original expectation, therein creating a vicious circle of deepening hostilities that reduce the prospects for peace (Deutsch 1986; Sen 2006). Clearing up mutual misperceptions can facilitate negotiations between the parties, but fostering peace is not simply a matter of expanding trade and other forms of transnational contact, or even of bringing political leaders together in international summits. Rather, it is a matter of changing deeply entrenched beliefs.

Although our constructed images of world politics are resistant to change, change is possible. Overcoming old thinking habits sometimes occurs when we experience punishment or discomfort as a result of clinging to false assumptions. As Benjamin Franklin once observed, "The things that hurt, instruct." Dramatic events in particular can alter international images, sometimes drastically. The Vietnam War caused many Americans to reject their previous images about using military force in world politics. The defeat of the Third Reich and revelations of Nazi atrocities committed before and during World War II caused the German people to confront their past as they prepared for a democratic future imposed by the victorious Allies. More recently, the human and financial costs of the prolonged U.S. war in Iraq led many policy makers and political commentators to reexamine their assumptions about the meaning of "victory" and its implications as U.S. engagement moved beyond initial combat to address issues of governance and stability. Often, such jolting experiences encourage us to construct new mental maps, perceptual filters, and criteria through which we may interpret later events and define situations.

Video: Determining
Foreign Policy

As we shape and reshape our images of world politics and its future, we need to think critically about the foundations on which our perceptions rest. Are they accurate? Are they informed? Should they be modified to gain greater understanding of others? Questioning our images is one of the major challenges we all face in confronting contemporary world politics.

KEYS TO UNDERSTANDING WORLD POLITICS

If we exaggerate the accuracy of our perceptions and seek information that confirms what we believe, how can we escape the biases created by our preconceptions? How can we avoid overlooking or dismissing evidence that runs counter to our intuition?

There are no sure-fire solutions to ensure accurate observations, no ways to guarantee that we have constructed an impartial view of international relations. However, there are a number of tools available that can improve our ability to interpret world politics. As you undertake an intellectual journey of discovery, a set of intellectual roadmaps will provide guidance for your interpretation and understanding of past, present, and future world politics. To arm you for your quest, *World Politics: Trend and Transformation* advances four keys to aid you in your inquiry.

Introducing Terminology

A primary goal of this text is to introduce you to the vocabulary used by scholars, policy makers, and the "attentive public" who routinely look at international developments. You will need to be literate and informed about the shared meaning of common words used worldwide to discuss and debate world politics and foreign policy. Some of this language has been in use since antiquity, and some of it has only recently become part of the terminology employed in diplomatic circles, scholarly research, and the media—television, newspapers, and the Internet. These words are the kind of vocabulary you are likely to encounter long after your formal collegiate education (and the course in which you are reading *World Politics*) has ended. It is also the terminology your future employers and educated neighbors will expect you to know. Some of these words are already likely to be part of your working vocabulary, but others may look new, esoteric, pedantic, and overly sophisticated. Nonetheless, you need to know their meaning—immediately and forever. Your use of them will facilitate your ability to analyze and discuss world affairs and mark you hereafter as a knowledgeable, educated person. So take advantage of this "high definition" feature of *World Politics*. Learn these words and use them for the rest of your life—not to impress others, but to understand and communicate intelligently.

To guide you in identifying these terms, as you may already have noticed, certain words are printed in **boldface** in the text, and a broad definition is provided in the margins. In cases when a word is used again in a different chapter, it will be highlighted at least once in *italics,* although the marginal definition will not be repeated. In all cases, the primary definition will appear in the Glossary at the end of book.

Distinguishing the Primary Transnational Actors

The globe is a stage, and the players in the drama are many. It is important to identify and classify the major categories of actors (sometimes called agents) who take part in international activities. The actions of each transnational

actor
an individual, group, state, or organization that plays a major role in world politics.

actor, individually and collectively at various degrees of influence, shape the trends that are transforming world politics. But how do scholars conventionally break the types of actors into categories and structure thinking about the classes of players?

World Politics follows accepted legal conventions about distinctions. The essential building-block units, of course, are individual people—all 6.8 billion of us. Every day, whether each of us choose to litter, light a cigarette, or parent a child affects in small measure how trends in the world will unfold. Humans, however, join in various groups. All of these combine people and their choices in various collectivities and thereby aggregate the *power* of each expanding group. Such groups often compete with one another because frequently they have divergent interests and goals.

power
the factors that enable one actor to manipulate another actor's behavior against its preferences.

For most periods of world history, the prime actors were individual groupings of religions, tribes whose members shared ethnic origins, and empires or expansionist centers of power. When they came into contact, they sometimes collaborated with each other for mutual benefit; more often they competed and fought over valued resources.

The Emergence of the Nation-State System   The more than eight thousand years of recorded international relations between and among these groups provided the precedent for the formation of today's system of interactions. As a network of relationships among independent territorial units, the modern state system was not born until the Peace of Westphalia in 1648, which ended the Thirty Years' War (1618–1648) in Europe. Thereafter, rulers refused to recognize the secular authority of the Roman Catholic Church, replacing the system of papal governance in the Middle Ages with geographically and politically separate states that recognized no superior authority. The newly independent states all gave to rulers the same legal rights: territory under their sole control, unrestricted control of their domestic affairs, and the freedom to conduct foreign relations and negotiate treaties with other states. The concept of *state sovereignty*—that no other actor is above the state— still captures these legal rights and identifies the state as the primary actor today.

state sovereignty
a state's supreme authority to manage internal affairs and foreign relations.

state
an independent legal entity with a government exercising exclusive control over the territory and population it governs.

The Westphalian system continues to color every dimension of world politics and provides the terminology used to describe the primary units in international affairs. Although the term nation-state is often used interchangeably with "state" and "nation," technically the three are different. A *state* is a legal entity that enjoys a permanent population, a well-defined territory, and a government capable of exercising sovereignty. A *nation* is a collection of people who, on the basis of ethnic, linguistic, or cultural commonality, so construct their reality as to primarily perceive themselves to be members of the same group, which defines their identity. Thus, the term nation-state implies a convergence between territorial states and the psychological identification of people within them. However, in employing this familiar terminology, we should exercise caution because this condition is relatively rare; there are few independent states comprising a single nationality. Most states today are populated by many nations, and some nations are not states. These "nonstate nations" are *ethnic groups*—such as Native Americans in the United States, Sikhs in India, Basques in Spain, or Kurds in Iraq, Turkey, Iran, and Syria—composed of people without sovereign power over the territory in which they live.

nation
a collectivity whose people see themselves as members of the same group because they share the same ethnicity, culture, or language.

ethnic groups
people whose identity is primarily defined by their sense of sharing a common ancestral nationality, language, cultural heritage, and kinship.

The Rise of Nonstate Actors   The history of world politics ever since 1648 has largely been a chronicle of interactions among states that remain the dominant political organizations in the world. States' interests, capabilities, and goals are the most potent shaping forces of world politics.

However, the supremacy of the state has been severely challenged in recent years. Increasingly, world affairs are also influenced by the new, big players in international affairs: "intergovernmental organizations" (IGOs) that transcend national boundaries, such as global international organizations whose members are states like the United Nations (UN) and regional organizations such as the European Union (EU). Such international organizations carry out independent foreign policies and therefore can be considered global actors in their own right. In addition, as noted, individual people band together to form coalitions of private citizens in order to participate in international affairs. Multinational corporations are an example of "nongovernmental organizations" (NGOs). Diverse in scope and purpose, these nonstate actors also push their own agendas and increasingly exert global influence.

In thinking about world politics and its future, we shall probe all these "units" or categories of actors. The emphasis and coverage will vary, depending on the topics under examination in each chapter. But you should keep in mind that all actors (individuals, states, and nonstate organizations) are simultaneously active today, and their importance and power depend on the trend or issue under consideration. So continuously ask yourself the question, now and in the future: Which actors are most active, most influential, on which issues, and under what conditions? That probing should cast doubt on outdated images of international relations.

Distinguishing Levels of Analysis

When we describe international phenomena, we answer a "what" question. What is happening? What is changing? When we move from description to explanation, we face the more difficult task of answering a "why" question. Why did event X happen? Why is global warming occurring? Why is the gap between rich and poor widening?

One useful key for addressing such puzzles is to visualize an event or trend as part of the end result of some unknown process. This encourages us to think about the causes that might have produced the phenomenon we are trying to explain. Most events and developments in world politics and its future are undoubtedly influenced simultaneously by many determinants, each connected to the rest in a complex web of causal linkages.

World Politics provides an analytic set of categories to help make interpretive sense of the multiple causes that explain why international events and circumstances occur. This analytic distinction conforms to a widespread scholarly consensus that international events or developments can best be analyzed and understood by first separating the multiple pieces of the puzzle into different categories, or levels. Most conventionally, investigators focus on one (or more) of three levels. Known as *levels of analysis*, as shown in Figure 1.1, this classification distinguishes individual influences, state or internal influences, and global influences for the system as a whole.

levels of analysis
the different aspects of and agents in international affairs that may be stressed in interpreting and explaining global phenomena, depending on whether the analyst chooses to focus on "wholes" (the complete global system and large collectivities) or on "parts" (individual states or people).

To predict which forces will dominate the future, we also must recognize that many forces are operating at the same time. No trend or trouble stands alone; all interact simultaneously. The future is influenced by many determinants, each connected to the rest in a complex web of linkages. Collectively, these may produce stability by limiting the impact of any single disruptive force. If interacting forces converge, however, their combined effects can accelerate the pace of change in world politics, moving it in directions not possible otherwise.

individual level of analysis
an analytical approach that emphasizes the psychological and perceptual variables motivating people, such as those who make foreign policy decisions on behalf of states and other global actors.

The *individual level of analysis* refers to the personal characteristics of humans, including those responsible for making important decisions on behalf of state and nonstate actors, as well as ordinary citizens whose behavior has important political consequences. Here, for example, we may properly locate the impact of individuals' perceptions on their political attitudes, beliefs, and behavior. We may also explore the questions of why each person is a crucial part of the global drama and why the study of world politics is relevant to our lives and future.

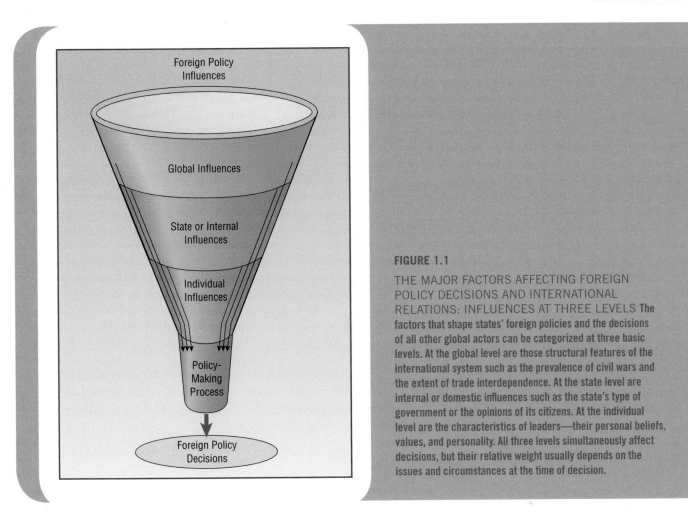

FIGURE 1.1

THE MAJOR FACTORS AFFECTING FOREIGN POLICY DECISIONS AND INTERNATIONAL RELATIONS: INFLUENCES AT THREE LEVELS **The factors that shape states' foreign policies and the decisions of all other global actors can be categorized at three basic levels. At the global level are those structural features of the international system such as the prevalence of civil wars and the extent of trade interdependence. At the state level are internal or domestic influences such as the state's type of government or the opinions of its citizens. At the individual level are the characteristics of leaders—their personal beliefs, values, and personality. All three levels simultaneously affect decisions, but their relative weight usually depends on the issues and circumstances at the time of decision.**

The *state level of analysis* consists of the authoritative decision-making units that govern states' foreign policy processes and the internal attributes of those states (e.g., their type of government, level of economic and military power, and number of nationality groups), which both shape and constrain leaders' foreign policy choices. The processes by which states make decisions regarding war and peace and their capabilities for carrying out those decisions, for instance, fall within the state level of analysis.

state level of analysis
an analytical approach that emphasizes how the internal attributes of states influence their foreign policy behaviors.

The *global level of analysis* refers to the interactions of states and nonstate actors on the global stage whose behaviors ultimately shape the international political system and the levels of conflict and cooperation that characterize world politics. The capacity of rich states to dictate the choices of poor states falls properly within the global level of analysis. So does the capacity (or incapacity) of the UN to maintain peace.

global level of analysis
an analytical approach that emphasizes the impact of worldwide conditions on foreign policy behavior and human welfare.

Examples abound of the diverse ways in which global trends and issues are the product of influences at each level of analysis. Protectionist trade policies by an importing country increase the costs to consumers of clothing and cars and reduce the standard of living of citizens in the manufacturing states. Such policies are initiated by a state government (national level), but they diminish the quality of life of people living both within the protectionist country and those living abroad (individual level) and reduce the level of global trade while threatening to precipitate retaliatory trade wars (global level). Of course, for some developments and issues, factors and forces emanating primarily from one or two particular levels provide more analytical leverage than do those from the other level(s). Accordingly, as we confront specific global issues in subsequent chapters, we emphasize those levels of analysis that provide the most informative lens for viewing them.

Distinguishing Change, Cycles, and Continuities

Once we have identified factors from different levels of analysis that may combine to produce some outcome, it is useful to place them in a chronological sequence. Anyone who owns a combination lock knows that the correct numbers must be entered in their proper order to open the lock. Similarly, to explain why something happened in world politics, we must determine how various individual-, state-, and global system–level factors fit together in a configuration that unfolds over time.

One key to anticipating probable human destiny is to look beyond the confines of our immediate time. It is important to appreciate the impact of previous ideas and events on current realities. As philosopher George Santayana cautioned, "Those who cannot remember the past are condemned to repeat it." Similarly, former British Prime Minister Winston Churchill advised, "The farther backward you look, the farther forward you are likely to see." Thus, to understand the dramatic changes in world politics today and to predict how they will shape the future, it is important to view them in the context of a long-term perspective that examines how transnational patterns of interaction among actors have changed and how some of their fundamental characteristics have resisted change. What do evolving diplomatic practices suggest about the current state of world politics? Are the episodic shock waves throughout the world clearing the way for a truly new twenty-first–century world order? Or will many of today's dramatic disruptions ultimately prove temporary, mere spikes on the seismograph of history?

We invite you to explore these questions with us. To begin our search, we discuss how the differences between continuities, changes, and cycles in world history can help you orient your interpretation.

Every historical period is marked to some extent by change. Now, however, the pace of change seems more rapid and its consequences more profound than ever. To many observers, the cascade of events today implies a revolutionary restructuring of world politics. Numerous integrative trends point to that possibility. The countries of the world are drawing closer together in communications and trade, producing a globalized market. Yet at the same time, disintegrative trends paint a less promising picture. Weapons proliferation, global environmental deterioration, and the resurgence of ethnic conflict all portend a restructuring fraught with disorder.

To predict which forces will dominate the future, we must recognize that no trend stands alone, and that divergent trends may produce stability by limiting the impact of any single disruptive force. It is also possible for converging trends to accelerate the pace of change, moving world politics in directions not possible otherwise.

It appears that the world is now going through a transition period in world politics. The opposing forces of integration and disintegration point toward the probable advent on the horizon of a *transformation*, but distinguishing true historical watersheds from temporary change is difficult. The moment of transformation from one system to another is not immediately obvious. Nevertheless, another useful key for students of world history is to recognize that certain times are especially likely candidates. In the past, major turning points in world politics usually have occurred at the conclusion of wars with many participants, which typically disrupt or destroy preexisting international arrangements. In the twentieth century, World Wars I and II and the Cold War caused fundamental breaks with the past and set in motion major transformations, providing countries with incentives to rethink the premises underlying their interests, purposes, and priorities. Similarly, many people concluded that the terrorist attacks on September 11, 2001 (9/11), produced a fundamental transformation in world affairs. Indeed, 9/11 seemed to change everything: In former U.S. President George W. Bush's words, "Night fell on a different world."

To analyze change in world politics, it is equally important to look also for the possibility of *continuity* amidst apparent transformation. Consider how, despite all that may appear radically different since the 9/11 terrorist attacks, much also may remain the same. As William Dobson (2006) wrote on the eve of the fifth anniversary of 9/11, "what is remarkable is how little the world has changed." "The massive forces of international trade and globalization were largely unaffected by the attacks," notes historian Juan Cole (2006, p. 26) in a similar vein. "China's emergence as an economic giant continues with all its economic, diplomatic, and military implications." Decades-old

transformation
a change in the characteristic pattern of interaction among the most active participants in world politics of such magnitude that it appears that one "global system" has replaced another.

Case Studies: The End of History or the Clash of Civilizations and Terrorism?

flash points remain, including the conflicts between India and Pakistan, North Korea and the United States, and Israel and militants in southern Lebanon and the Palestinian territories. "For all their visibility and drama," concludes Cole (2006, p. 26), "the 9/11 attacks left untouched many of the underlying forces and persistent tensions that shape international politics."

We often expect the future to bring changes automatically, and later are surprised to discover that certain patterns from the past have reappeared. Headlines are not trendlines. Given the rapid changes that are occurring alongside enduring continuities, it is dangerous to assume that a major transformation in world politics is under way.

What criteria can help determine when an existing pattern of relationships gives way to a completely new global system? Follow Stanley Hoffmann (1961), who argues that we can identify a new global system when we have a new answer to one of three questions: (1) What are the system's basic units? (e.g., states or supranational institutions for global governance); (2) What are the predominant foreign policy goals that these units seek with respect to one another? (e.g., territorial conquest or material gain through trade); and (3) What can these units do to one another with their military and economic capabilities?

These criteria might lead us to conclude that a new system has now emerged.

Carmen Taylor/AP Photo

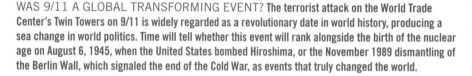

WAS 9/11 A GLOBAL TRANSFORMING EVENT? The terrorist attack on the World Trade Center's Twin Towers on 9/11 is widely regarded as a revolutionary date in world history, producing a sea change in world politics. Time will tell whether this event will rank alongside the birth of the nuclear age on August 6, 1945, when the United States bombed Hiroshima, or the November 1989 dismantling of the Berlin Wall, which signaled the end of the Cold War, as events that truly changed the world.

First, new trade partnerships have been forged in Europe, the cone of South America, North America, and the Pacific Rim, and these trading blocs may behave as unitary, or independent, nonstate actors as they compete with one another. Moreover, international organizations such as the EU now flex their political muscles in contests with individual states, and transnational religious movements such as Islamic extremist groups challenge the *global system* itself. International law still defines this system as being composed primarily of each state consisting of various nationality groups who perceive themselves as unified by a common language, culture, or ethnic identity. At the same time, some states have disintegrated into smaller units.

global system
the predominant patterns of behaviors and beliefs that prevail internationally to define the major worldwide conditions that heavily influence human and national activities.

Second, territorial conquest is no longer states' predominant foreign policy goal. Instead, their emphasis has shifted from traditionally military methods of exercising influence to economic means. Meanwhile, the ideological contest between democratic capitalism and the Marxist-Leninist communism of the Cold War era no longer comprises the primary cleavage in international politics, and a major new axis has yet to become clear.

Third, the proliferation of weapons technology has profoundly altered the damages that enemies can inflict on one another. Great powers alone no longer control the world's most lethal weapons. Increasingly, however, the great powers' prosperity depends on economic circumstances throughout the globe, reducing their ability to engineer growth.

The profound changes in recent years of the types of actors (units), goals, and capabilities have dramatically altered the hierarchical power ranking of states, but the hierarchies themselves endure. The economic hierarchy that divides the rich from the poor, the political hierarchy that separates the rulers from the ruled, the resource hierarchy that makes some suppliers and others dependents, and the military asymmetries that pit the strong against the weak—all still shape the relations among states, as they have in the past. Similarly, the perpetuation of international *anarchy*, in the absence of institutions to govern the globe, and continuing national insecurity still encourage preparations for war and the use of force without international mandate. Thus, change and continuity coexist, with both forces simultaneously shaping contemporary world politics.

anarchy
a condition in which the units in the global system are subjected to few if any overarching institutions to regulate their conduct.

The interaction of constancy and change will determine future relations among global actors. This perhaps explains why *cycles,* as periodic sequences of events that resemble patterns in earlier periods, so often appear to characterize world politics: Because the emergent global system shares many characteristics with earlier periods, historically minded observers may experience

cycles
the periodic reemergence of conditions similar to those that existed previously.

déjà vu—the illusion of having already experienced something actually being experienced for the first time.

PREPARING FOR YOUR JOURNEY INTO WORLD POLITICS

World Politics warns about the obstacles to accurate perceptions of international relations and then provides some guideposts to help you travel on your journey to discovery. This introduction concludes with a brief outline of the book's thematic approach and organizational roadmap.

> *The ability to learn how to learn will be the only security you have.*
>
> —Thomas L. Friedman, *political journalist*

The Book's Approach

Because world politics is complex and our images of it are often dissimilar, scholars differ in their approaches to understanding world politics. Some view the world through a macropolitical lens, meaning they look at world politics from a "bird's eye view" and explain the behavior of world actors based on their relative position within the global system. Other scholars adopt a micropolitical perspective that looks at world politics from the "ground-up," meaning the individual is the unit of analysis from which aggregate behavior is extrapolated. Both approaches make important contributions to understanding world politics: the former reveals how the global environment sets limits on political choice; the latter draws attention to how every transnational actor's preferences, capabilities, and strategic calculations influence global conditions. By looking at world politics from a macropolitical perspective, we can see why actors that are similarly situated within the system may behave alike, despite their internal differences. By taking a micropolitical perspective, we can appreciate why some actors are very different or behave differently, despite their similar placement within the global system (see Waltz 2000).

From this analytic point of departure, *World Politics* will accordingly inspect (1) the major macro trends in world politics that set the boundaries for action, (2) the values, interests, and capabilities of the individual actors affected by these global trends, and (3) the ways these actors interact in their individual and collective efforts to modify existing global circumstances and how these interactions shape the ultimate trajectories of global trends.

This analytic approach looks at the dynamic interplay of actors and their environment as well as how the actors respond and seek to influence each others' behavior.

The approach outlined here can open a window for you not only to understand contemporary world politics but also to predict the likely global future. The approach has the advantage of taking into account the interplay of proximate and remote explanatory factors at the individual, state, and global levels of analysis while avoiding dwelling on particular countries, individuals, or transitory events whose long-term significance is likely to decrease. Instead, *World Politics* attempts to identify behaviors that cohere into general patterns that measurably affect global living conditions. Thus, you will explore the nature of world politics from a perspective that places historical and contemporary events into a larger, lasting theoretical context, to provide you with the conceptual tools that will enable you to interpret subsequent developments later in your lifetime.

The Book's Organization

Part 1 of this book, "Trend and Transformation in World Politics," introduces the world of politics and its rapidly changing nature and sets the stage for the constantly changing aspects of international relations. Chapter 1 explains how our perceptions of global events and realities lead to distorted views, and suggests how to move beyond the limited scope of those views by providing four keys to understanding world politics. The chapter also provides an outline of the book's organization and thematic approach. Your journey continues in Chapter 2 with an overview of the realist, liberal, and constructivist theoretical traditions that scholars and policy makers use most often to interpret world politics. It also considers the radical and feminist critiques of these mainstream traditions. The comparison of these contending theories provides the intellectual roadmap for the description and explanation of the issues and developments treated in the remaining chapters.

Part 2, "The Globe's Actors and Their Relations," turns attention to each of the various types of transnational actors and examines how their characteristics, capabilities, and decision-making processes affect their interests and influence in the world. Chapter 3 covers the ***great powers*** (those wealthy countries with the largest militaries) and their current national security strategies and relationships. Chapter 4 incorporates into the picture the place of the weaker states, that is, the less developed countries of the Global South, and explains how the fate of this group of states is shaped by their relations

great powers
the most powerful countries, militarily and economically, in the global system.

with great powers, the rising "Global East" emerging economic powerhouses, as well as the most powerful nonstate actors and international institutions active in world politics. Chapter 5 expands the account to cover IGOs such as the United Nations and the European Union. It also captures the impact on world politics of such transnational NGOs as ethnic groups and indigenous peoples, transnational religious movements and terrorist groups, multinational corporations, and issue-advocacy groups. This coverage describes how IGO and NGO actors interact with states and increasingly challenge the supremacy of all states, including even the great powers, by either transcending or subverting states' sovereign control over their destinies. Your understanding of world politics is further strengthened in Chapter 6, which introduces three ways of looking at international decision-making processes by all transnational actors. It concludes by focusing on the global and domestic determinants of states' international behavior, because states remain the principal actors in world politics.

Part 3, "Confronting Armed Aggression," examines some clear and present dangers to global security, and looks at contending ideas and theoretical perspectives about how to best confront violent conflict. Chapter 7 considers changes in violence involving wars between states, civil wars within states, and global terrorism, and considers causes of these three forms of armed aggression at three levels of analysis: human nature, the internal characteristics of countries, and changes in global circumstances. Chapter 8 reviews realist theoretical accounts of power in world politics, trends in military spending and capabilities, military strategies, and coercive diplomacy through military intervention abroad. The picture is completed in Chapter 9, which explores the role of alliances in world politics, with an emphasis on the realist perspective. Through liberal and constructivist lenses, Chapter 10 looks at both the negotiated settlement of disputes through diplomacy and the legal control of armed aggression. Chapter 11 focuses on arms control and disarmament, the maintenance of collective security through international organizations, and the creation of a shared international moral consensus through the expansion of free trade and democratic institutions.

Part 4, "Human Security, Prosperity, and Responsibility," shifts to the economic, demographic, human, and environmental dimensions of globalization. Chapter 12 explores the international financial system and issues surrounding the worldwide flow of capital. Chapter 13 follows with a discussion of trends in the globalization of international trade, and the various strategies pursued in the quest for wealth and power. Coverage is continued in Chapter 14 by inspecting population change, migration patterns, the global health crisis, and the global information age as agents of global transformation. Chapter 15 examines relative levels of human rights and security and the expanding global commitment, as well as the inherent difficulties, to protecting and improving the human condition. Chapter 16 probes the multiple environmental challenges facing our world today, and the consequences that they pose for our continued survival and well-being.

In Part 5, "Thinking about the Future of World Politics," the major changes and issues surveyed throughout the book are revisited. Drawing on the ideas and information presented in earlier chapters, Chapter 17 considers contending perspectives about the probable shape of the global future by focusing on some of the most hotly debated questions on the global agenda. These dilemmas are likely to dominate discussion of world politics during the next decade.

Courtesy of Carla Martinez

IT'S A SMALL WORLD **As you begin your journey of discovery to extend your knowledge of world politics, it is important to be aware of the images that you hold and be open to new experiences and interpretations of the world around you. Take full advantage of all of your opportunities to study and learn about the global community. Shown here are U.S. students from The University of Memphis enjoying their study abroad program in San Jose, Costa Rica.**

Take an Online Practice Quiz

www.cengagebrain.com/shop/ISBN/0495802204

| *Suggested Readings* |

Cetron, Marvin J. and Owen Davies. (2005) *53 Trends Now Shaping the Future*. Bethesda, MD: World Future Society.

Ellis, David C. (2009) "On the Possibility of "International Community'," *The International Studies Review* 11 (March):1–26.

Friedman, Thomas L. (2005) *The World Is Flat: A Brief History of the Twenty-first Century*. New York: Farrar, Straus and Giroux.

Holsti, K. J. (2004) *Taming the Sovereigns: International Change in International Politics*. New York: Cambridge University Press.

Jervis, Robert. (2008) "Unipolarity: A Structural Perspective," *World Politics* 61:188–213.

Shapiro, Robert J. (2008) *Futurecast: How Superpowers, Populations, and Globalization Will Change the Way You Live and Work*. New York: St. Martin's Press.

CHAPTER 2
THEORIES OF WORLD POLITICS

There is an inescapable link between the abstract world of theory and the real world of policy. We need theories to make sense of the blizzard of information that bombards us daily. Even policy makers who are contemptuous of "theory" must rely on their own (often unstated) ideas about how the world works in order to decide what to do. . . . Everyone uses theories—whether he or she knows it or not.

—Stephen M. Walt, political scientist

CHAPTER OUTLINE

THEORIES AND CHANGE IN WORLD POLITICS

REALIST THEORY

The Realist Worldview

The Evolution of Realist Thought

The Limitations of Realism

LIBERAL THEORY

The Liberal Worldview

The Evolution of Liberal Thought

CONTROVERSY: Can International Relations Theory Address a Zombie Outbreak?

The Limitations of Liberalism

CONSTRUCTIVIST THEORY

The Constructivist Worldview

The Evolution of Constructivist Thought

The Limitations of Constructivism

WHAT'S MISSING IN THEORIES OF WORLD POLITICS?

The Radical Critique

The Feminist Critique

THEORIZING ABOUT THEORY

CONTROVERSY: Can Behavioral Science Advance the Study of International Relations?

INTERNATIONAL THEORY AND THE GLOBAL FUTURE

Herbert SA House - Lank/Superstock/PhotoLibrary

THEORETICAL CHALLENGES We live in a world of ever-changing international conditions. Many trends are unfolding, some in contrary directions, and obstacles exist to understanding world politics accurately. As you begin your study of trends and transformations in world politics, your challenge is to interpret theoretically the meaning of a changing world.

Imagine yourself the newly elected president of the United States. You are scheduled to deliver the State of the Union address on your views of the current global situation and your foreign policy to deal with it. You face the task of both defining those aspects of international affairs most worthy of attention and explaining the reasons for their priority. To convince citizens that these issues are important, you must present them as part of a larger picture of the world. Therefore, based on your perceptions of world politics, you must think theoretically. At the same time, you must be careful, because your interpretations will necessarily depend on your assumptions about international realities that your citizens might find questionable. The effort to explain the world, predict new global problems, and sell others on a policy to deal with them is bound to result in controversy because even reasonable people often see realities differently.

When leaders face these kinds of intellectual challenges, they fortunately benefit from various theories of world politics from which they can draw guidance. A *theory* is a set of conclusions derived from assumptions (axioms) and/or evidence about some phenomenon, including its character, causes, and probable consequences, and their ethical implications. Theories provide a map, or frame of reference, that makes the complex, puzzling world around us intelligible.

theory
a set of hypotheses postulating the relationship between variables or conditions advanced to describe, explain, or predict phenomena and make prescriptions about how positive changes ought to be engineered to realize particular goals and ethical principles.

THEORIES AND CHANGE IN WORLD POLITICS

Choosing which theory to heed is an important decision, because each rests on different assumptions about the nature of international politics, each advances different claims about causes, and each offers a different set of foreign policy recommendations. Indeed, the menu of theoretical choice is large. Rival theories of world politics abound, and there is no agreement about which one is the most useful. The reason is primarily because the world is constantly undergoing changes, and no single theory has proven capable of making international events understandable for every global circumstance. So there are fads and fashions in the popularity of international theories; they rise and fall over time in popularity and perceived usefulness, depending on the global conditions that prevail in any historical period.

The history of the world is the history of changes in the theoretical interpretation of international relations. In any given era, a *paradigm*, or dominant way of looking at a particular subject such as international relations, has arisen to influence judgments regarding which characteristics of the subject are most important, what puzzles need to be solved, and what analytic

paradigm
derived from the Greek *paradeigma*, meaning an example, a model, or an essential pattern; a paradigm structures thought about an area of inquiry.

criteria should govern investigations. These paradigms, or "fundamental assumptions scholars make about the world they are studying" (Vasquez 1997), tend eventually to be revised in order to explain new developments. Cycles are embedded in history, and theory is forever evolving in an effort to stay in sync with history's pendulum.

Throughout history, paradigms have been revised or abandoned when their assertions have failed to mirror the prevailing patterns of international behavior. Major wars have been especially potent in bringing about significant changes in the theoretical interpretation of world affairs. "Every war . . . has been followed in due course by skeptical reassessments of supposedly sacred assumptions" (Schlesinger 1986, p. 165) and has influenced "what ideas and values will predominate" (Gilpin 1981). Three such system-transforming wars dominated the twentieth century: World War I, World War II, and the Cold War; and likewise, the 9/11 terrorist attacks in 2001 shattered the preexisting international order. Each shaped policy makers' perceptions of world politics, and each provided lessons critical to developing policies to best preserve world order. Thus, the theories that guide the thinking of policy makers and scholars in different historical circumstances tell us much about world politics itself.

The purpose of this chapter is to compare the assumptions, causal claims, and policy prescriptions of realism, liberalism, and constructivism—the most common theoretical perspectives policy makers and scholars use to interpret international relations. Moreover, the chapter broadens coverage of the range of contemporary international theorizing by introducing you also to the radical and feminist critiques of these three dominant schools of thought.

He who loves practice without theory is like the sailor who boards ship without a rudder and compass and never knows where he may cast.

—*Leonardo da Vinci, artist*

REALIST THEORY

Realism is the oldest of these three contending schools of thought, and has a long and distinguished history that dates back to Thucydides' writings about the Peloponnesian War in ancient Greece. Other influential figures that contributed to realist thought include sixteenth-century Italian philosopher Niccolò Machiavelli and seventeenth-century English philosopher Thomas Hobbes. Realism deserves careful examination because its worldview continues to guide much thought about international politics.

realism
a paradigm based on the premise that world politics is essentially and unchangeably a struggle among self-interested states for power and position under anarchy, with each competing state pursuing its own national interests.

The Realist Worldview

Realism, as applied to contemporary international politics, views the state as the most important actor on the world stage because it answers to no higher political authority. States are sovereign: they have supreme *power* over their territory and populace, and no other actor stands above them wielding the legitimacy and coercive capability to govern the global system. Given the absence of a higher authority to which states can turn for protection and to resolve disputes, realists depict world politics as a ceaseless, repetitive struggle for power where the strong dominate the weak and there is inherently a constant possibility of war. Because each state is ultimately responsible for its own survival and feels uncertain about its neighbors' intentions, realism claims that prudent political leaders seek arms and allies to enhance national security. In other words, international anarchy leads even well-intentioned leaders to practice *self-help*, increase their own military strength, and opportunistically align with others to deter potential threats. Realist theory does not preclude the possibility that rival powers will cooperate on arms control or on other security issues of common interest. Rather, it asserts that cooperation will be rare because states worry about the unequal distribution of *relative gains* that can result from cooperation to the disadvantage of one of the parties and the possibility that the other side will cheat on agreements. Leaders should never entrust the task of self-protection to international security organizations or international law, and should resist efforts to regulate international behavior through global governance.

At the risk of oversimplification, realism's message can be summarized by the following assumptions and related propositions:

self-help
the principle that because in international anarchy all global actors are independent, they must rely on themselves to provide for their security and well-being.

relative gains
conditions in which some participants in cooperative interactions benefit more than others.

- People are by nature selfish and are driven to compete with others for domination and self-advantage. Machiavelli captures the realist view of human nature in his work *The Prince*, arguing that people in general "are ungrateful, fickle, and deceitful, eager to avoid dangers, and avid for gain, and while you are useful to them they are all with you, offering you their blood, their property, and their sons so long as danger is remote, but when it approaches they turn on you."

- By extension, the primary obligation of every state—the goal to which all other national objectives should be subordinated—is to promote its *national interest* and to acquire power for this purpose. "Might makes right," and a state's philosophical or ethical preferences are neither good nor bad. What matters is whether they serve its self-interest. As Thucydides put it, "The standard of justice depends on the equality of power to compel . . . the strong do what they have the power to do and the weak accept what they have to accept."

national interest
the goals that states pursue to maximize what they perceive to be selfishly best for their country.

- World politics is a struggle for *power*—in the words of Thomas Hobbes, "a war of all against all"—and the possibility of eradicating the instinct for power is a hopeless utopian aspiration. In the pursuit of power, states must acquire sufficient military capabilities to deter attack by potential enemies and to exercise influence over others; hence states "prepare for war to keep peace." Economic growth is important primarily as a means of acquiring and expanding state power and prestige and is less relevant to national security than is military might.

- International anarchy and a lack of trust perpetuate the principle of self-help and can give rise to the *security dilemma*. As a state builds up its power to protect itself, others inevitably become threatened and are likely to respond in kind. An arms race is commonly seen as a manifestation of the security dilemma, for even if a state is truly arming only for defensive purposes, it is rational in a self-help system for opponents to assume the worst and keep pace in any arms buildup.

security dilemma
the tendency of states to view the defensive arming of adversaries as threatening, causing them to arm in response so that all states' security declines.

- If all states seek to maximize power, stability will result by maintaining a *balance of power*, facilitated by shifts in the formation and decay of opposing alliances that counter each other's expansionist motives. Thus allies might be sought to increase a state's ability to defend itself, but their loyalty and reliability should not be assumed, and commitments to allies should be repudiated if it is no longer in a state's national interests to honor them (see Chapter 9 for further discussion).

balance of power
the theory that peace and stability are most likely to be maintained when military power is distributed to prevent a single superpower hegemon or bloc from controlling the world.

With their emphasis on the ruthless nature of international life, realists often question letting ethical considerations enter foreign policy deliberations. As they see it, some policies are driven by strategic imperatives that may require national leaders to disregard moral norms. Embedded in this "philosophy of necessity" is a distinction between private morality, which guides the behavior of ordinary people in their daily lives, and reason of state (raison d'état), which governs the conduct of leaders responsible for the security and survival of the state. Actions that are dictated by national interest must be carried out no matter how repugnant they might seem in the light of private morality. Reflecting upon his decision to send additional U.S. troops to Afghanistan in 2010, in his acceptance speech of the Nobel Peace Prize, President Obama noted that "I face the world as it is, and cannot stand idle in the face of threats to the American people."

The Evolution of Realist Thought

We have seen how the intellectual roots of realism reach back to ancient Greece. They also extend beyond the Western world to India and China. Discussions of "power politics" abound in the *Arthashastra*, an Indian treatise

REALIST PIONEERS OF POWER POLITICS In *The Prince* (1532) and *The Leviathan* (1651), Niccolò Machiavelli (left) and Thomas Hobbes (right), respectively, argued for basing international decisions on self-interest, prudence, power, and expediency above all other considerations. This formed the foundation of what became a growing body of modern realist thinking that accepts the drive for power over others as necessary and wise statecraft.

on statecraft written during the fourth century BCE by Kautilya, as well as in works written by Han Fei and Shang Yang in ancient China.

Modern realism emerged on the eve of World War II, when the prevailing belief in a natural harmony of interests among states came under attack. Just a decade earlier, this belief had led numerous countries to sign the 1928 ***Kellogg-Briand Pact***, which renounced war as an instrument of national policy. Now, with Nazi Germany, fascist Italy, and Imperial Japan all violating the treaty, British historian and diplomat E. H. Carr (1939) complained that the assumption of a universal interest in peace had allowed too many people to "evade the unpalatable fact of a fundamental divergence of interest between nations desirous of maintaining the status quo and nations desirous of changing it."

In an effort to counter what they saw as a utopian, legalistic approach to foreign affairs, Reinhold Niebuhr (1947), Hans J. Morgenthau (1948), and other realists painted a pessimistic view of human nature. Echoing seventeenth-century philosopher Baruch Spinoza, many of them pointed to an innate conflict between passion and reason; furthermore, in the tradition of St. Augustine, they stressed that material appetites enabled passion to overwhelm reason. For them, the human condition was such that the forces of light and darkness would perpetually combat for control.

The realists' picture of international life appeared particularly persuasive after World War II. The onset of rivalry between the United States and the Soviet Union, the expansion of the Cold War into a wider struggle between

Kellogg-Briand Pact
a multilateral treaty negotiated in 1928 that outlawed war as a method for settling interstate conflicts.

East and West, and the periodic crises that threatened to erupt into global violence all supported the realists' emphasis on the inevitability of conflict, the poor prospects for cooperation, and the divergence of national interests among incorrigibly selfish, power-seeking states.

Whereas these so-called classical realists sought to explain state behavior by examining assumptions about peoples' motives at the individual level of analysis, the next wave of realist theorizing emphasized the global level of analysis. Kenneth Waltz (1979), the leading proponent of *neorealism* (sometimes called "structural realism"), proposed that international anarchy—not some allegedly evil side of human nature—explained why states were locked in fierce competition with one another. The absence of a central arbiter was the defining structural feature of international politics. Vulnerable and insecure states behaved defensively by forming alliances against looming threats. According to Waltz, balances of power form automatically in anarchic environments. Even when they are disrupted, they are soon restored (see Controversy: Can International Relations Theory Address a Zombie Outbreak?).

There are several members of the realist family as shown in Table 2.1. Classical realism focuses primarily on "the sources and uses of national power . . . and the problems that leaders encounter in conducting foreign policy" (Taliaferro et al. 2009, p. 16). Structural realism as envisioned by Kenneth Waltz is often referred to as defensive realism to distinguish it from the more recent variant, offensive realism. Although both are structural realist theories, defensive realism sees states as focused on maintaining security by balancing others and essentially preserving the status quo, while offensive realism sees states as seeking to ensure security by aggressively maximizing their power. Neoclassical realism draws on both classical realism and structural realism

neorealism
a theoretical account of states' behavior that explains it as determined by differences in their relative power within the global hierarchy, defined primarily by the distribution of military power, instead of by other factors such as their values, types of government, or domestic circumstances.

Table 2.1 Comparing Variants of Contemporary Realism

Variant	Primary State Objective	View of International System	Systemic Pressure	Rational State Preference
Classical Realism	Varies (e.g., security, power, or glory)	Somewhat important	Defensive or Offensive	Status quo or revisionist
Defensive Realism	Survival	Very important	Defensive	Status quo
Offensive Realism	Survival	Very important	Offensive	Revisionist (hegemons excepted)
Neoclassical Realism	Varies (e.g., security, power, or glory)	Important	Defensive or Offensive	Status quo or revisionist

Source: Based on Taliaferro et al. 2009; Rynning and Ringsmose 2008.

as it emphasizes "how systemic-level variables are 'translated through unit-level intervening variables such as decision-makers' perceptions and domestic state structure'" (Rynning and Ringsmose 2008, 27).

The Limitations of Realism

However persuasive the realists' image of the essential properties of international politics, their policy recommendations suffered from a lack of precision in the way they used such key terms as *power* and *national interest*. Thus, once analysis moved beyond the assertion that national leaders should acquire power to serve the national interest, important questions remained: What were the key elements of national power? What uses of power best served the national interest? Did arms furnish protection or provoke costly arms races? Did alliances enhance one's defenses or encourage threatening counteralliances? From the perspective of realism's critics, seeking security by amassing power was self-defeating. The quest for absolute security by one state would be perceived as creating absolute insecurity for other members of the system, with the result that everyone would become locked in an upward spiral of countermeasures that jeopardized the security of all (Vasquez 1998).

Because much of realist theorizing was vague, it began to be questioned. Realism offered no criteria for determining what historical data were significant in evaluating its claims and what epistemological rules to follow when interpreting relevant information (Vasquez and Elman 2003). Even the policy recommendations that purportedly flowed from its logic were often divergent. Realists themselves, for example, were sharply divided as to whether U.S. intervention in Vietnam served American national interests and whether nuclear weapons contributed to international security. Similarly, whereas some observers used realism to explain the rationale for the 2003 U.S. invasion of Iraq (Gvosdev 2005), others drew on realist arguments to criticize the invasion (Mansfield and Snyder 2005a; Mearsheimer and Walt 2003).

A growing number of critics also pointed out that realism did not account for significant new developments in world politics. For instance, it could not explain the creation of new commercial and political institutions in Western Europe in the 1950s and 1960s, where the cooperative pursuit of mutual advantage led Europeans away from the unbridled power politics that brought them incessant warfare since the birth of the nation-state some three centuries earlier. Other critics began to worry about realism's tendency to disregard ethical principles and about the material and social costs that some of its policy prescriptions seemed to impose, such as hindered economic growth resulting from unrestrained military expenditures.

Despite realism's shortcomings, many people continue to think about world politics in the language constructed by realists, especially in times of global tension. A recent example can be found in the comments by former Bush administration adviser Michael Gerson (2006) about how the United States should deal with Iran's nuclear ambitions. Arguing from the realist assumption that "peace is not a natural state," he called for a robust American response based on a steely-eyed focus on preventing the proliferation of weapons of mass destruction in the Middle East. "There must be someone in the world capable of drawing a line— someone who says, 'This much and no further.'" Peace, he concluded, cannot be achieved by "a timid foreign policy that allows terrible threats to emerge." Unless those who threaten others pay a price, "aggression will be universal."

Case Study: *Realism*

LIBERAL THEORY

Liberalism has been called the "strongest contemporary challenge to realism" (Caporaso 1993, p. 465). Like realism, it has a distinguished pedigree, with philosophical roots extending back to the political thought of John Locke, Immanuel Kant, and Adam Smith. Liberalism warrants our attention because it speaks to issues realism disregards, including the impact of domestic politics on state behavior, the implications of economic interdependence, and the role of global norms and institutions in promoting international cooperation.

The Liberal Worldview

There are several distinct schools of thought within the liberal tradition. Drawing broad conclusions from such a diverse body of theory runs the risk of misrepresenting the position of any given author. Nevertheless, there are sufficient commonalities to abstract some general themes.

Liberals differ from realists in several important ways. At the core of liberalism is a belief in reason and the possibility of progress. Liberals view the individual as the seat of moral value and assert that human beings should be treated as ends rather than means. Whereas realists counsel decision makers to seek the lesser evil rather than the absolute good, liberals emphasize ethical principle over the pursuit of power, and institutions over military capabilities (see Doyle 1997; Zacher and Matthew 1995). Politics at the global level is more of a struggle for consensus and mutual gain than a struggle for power and prestige.

Several corollary ideas give definition to liberal theory. These include (1) the need to substitute attitudes that stress the unity of humankind for those who stressed parochial national loyalties to independent sovereign states; (2) the importance of individuals—their essential dignity and fundamental equality

liberalism
a paradigm predicated on the hope that the application of reason and universal ethics to international relations can lead to a more orderly, just, and cooperative world; liberalism assumes that anarchy and war can be policed by institutional reforms that empower international organization and law.

throughout the course of history, and the analogous need to place the protection and promotion of human rights and freedom ahead of national interests and state autonomy; and (3) the use of the power of ideas through education to arouse world public opinion against warfare.

Instead of blaming international conflict on an inherent lust for power, liberals fault the conditions under which people live. Reforming those conditions, they argue, will enhance the prospects for peace. The first element common to various strands of liberal thought is an emphasis on undertaking political reforms to establish stable democracies. Woodrow Wilson, for example, proclaimed that "democratic government will make wars less likely." Franklin Roosevelt later agreed, asserting "the continued maintenance and improvement of democracy constitute the most important guarantee of international peace." Based on tolerance, compromise, and civil liberties, democratic political cultures are said to shun lethal force as a means of settling disagreements. In place of force, *diplomacy* provides a means for achieving mutually acceptable solutions to a common problem, and enables leaders to negotiate and compromise with each other in a peaceful manner. Politics is not seen as a *zero-sum* game, as the use of persuasion rather than coercion, and a reliance on judicial methods to settle rival claims is the primary means of dealing with conflict.

diplomacy
communication and negotiation between global actors that is not dependent upon the use of force and seeks a cooperative solution.

zero-sum
an exchange in a purely conflictual relationship in which what is gained by one competitor is lost by the other.

According to liberal theory, conflict-resolution practices used at home can also be used when dealing with international disputes. Leaders socialized within democratic cultures share a common outlook. Viewing international politics as an extension of domestic politics, they generalize about the applicability of norms to regulate international competition. Disputes between democratic governments rarely escalate to war because each side accepts the other's legitimacy and expects it to rely on peaceful means of conflict resolution. These expectations are reinforced by the transparent nature of democracies. The inner workings of open polities can be scrutinized by anyone; hence, it is difficult to demonize democratically ruled states as scheming adversaries.

The second thrust common to liberal theorizing is an emphasis on free trade. The idea that commerce can reduce conflict has roots in the work of Immanuel Kant, Charles de Secondat Montesquieu, Adam Smith, Jean-Jacque Rosseau, and various Enlightenment thinkers. "Nothing is more favourable to the rise of politeness and learning," noted liberal philosopher David Hume (1817), "than a number of neighboring and independent states, connected by commerce." This view was later embraced by the Manchester School of political economy and formed the basis for Norman Angell's (1910) famous rebuttal of the assertion that military conquest produces economic prosperity.

The doctrine that unfettered trade helps prevent disputes from escalating to wars rests on several propositions. First, commercial intercourse creates a material incentive to resolve disputes peacefully: War reduces profits by interrupting vital economic exchanges. Second, cosmopolitan business elites who benefit most from these exchanges comprise a powerful transnational interest group with a stake in promoting amicable solutions to festering disagreements. Finally, the web of trade between countries increases communication, erodes national selfishness, and encourages both sides to avoid ruinous clashes. In the words of Richard Cobden, an opponent of the protectionist Corn Laws that once regulated British international grain trade: "Free Trade! What is it? Why, breaking down the barriers that separate nations; those barriers, behind which nestle the feelings of pride, revenge, hatred, and jealousy, which every now and then burst their bounds, and deluge whole countries with blood."

Finally, the third commonality in liberal theorizing is an advocacy of global institutions. Liberals recommend replacing cutthroat, balance-of-power

The Granger Collection Christie's Images/CORBIS

PIONEERS IN THE LIBERAL QUEST FOR WORLD ORDER A product of the Enlightenment, Scottish philosopher David Hume (left) tried to temper his realist concern that reason is a "slave of the passions" by embracing the liberal faith in wealth-generating free markets and free trade that could cohesively bind people together to create a peaceful civil society. Influenced by David Hume and Jean-Jacques Rousseau, Immanuel Kant (right) in *Perpetual Peace* (1795) helped to redefine modern liberal theory by advocating global (not state) citizenship, free trade, and a federation of democracies as a means to peace.

politics with organizations based on the principle that a threat to peace anywhere is a common threat to everyone. They see foreign policy as unfolding in a nascent global society populated by actors who recognize the cost of conflict, share significant interests, and can realize those interests by using institutions to mediate disputes whenever misconceptions, wounded sensibilities, or aroused national passions threaten peaceful relations.

The Evolution of Liberal Thought

Contemporary liberal theory rose to prominence in the wake of World War I. Not only had the war involved more participants over a wider geographic area than any previous war, but modern science and technology made it a war of machinery: Old weapons were improved and produced in great quantities; new and far more deadly weapons were rapidly developed and deployed. By the time the carnage was over, nearly twenty million people were dead.

For liberals such as U.S. President Woodrow Wilson, World War I was "the war to end all wars." Convinced that another horrific war would erupt if states resumed practicing power politics, liberals set out to reform the global system. These "idealists," as they were called by hard-boiled realists, generally fell into one of three groups (Herz 1951). The first group advocated creating global institutions to contain the raw struggle for power between self-serving, mutually suspicious states. The League of Nations was the embodiment of this strain of liberal thought. Its founders hoped to prevent future wars by organizing a system of *collective security* that would mobilize the entire international community against would-be aggressors. The League's founders declared that peace was indivisible: an attack on one member of the League would be considered an attack on all. Because no state was more powerful than the combination of all other states, aggressors would be deterred and war averted.

collective security
a security regime agreed to by the great powers that sets rules for keeping peace, guided by the principle that an act of aggression by any state will be met by a collective response from the rest.

A second group called for the use of legal procedures to adjudicate disputes before they escalated to armed conflict. Adjudication is a judicial procedure for resolving conflicts by referring them to a standing court for a binding decision. Immediately after the war, several governments drafted a statute to establish a Permanent Court of International Justice (PCIJ). Hailed by Bernard C. J. Loder, the court's first president, as the harbinger of a new era of civilization, the PCIJ held its inaugural public meeting in early 1922 and rendered its first judgment on a contentious case the following year. Liberal champions of the court insisted that the PCIJ would replace military retaliation with a judicial body capable of bringing the facts of a dispute to light and issuing a just verdict.

A third group of liberal thinkers followed the biblical injunction that states should beat their swords into plowshares and sought disarmament as a means of avoiding war. Their efforts were illustrated between 1921 and 1922 by the Washington Naval Conference, which tried to curtail maritime competition among the United States, Great Britain, Japan, France, and Italy by placing limits on battleships. The ultimate goal of this group was to reduce international tensions by promoting general disarmament, which led them to convene the 1932 Geneva Disarmament Conference.

Although a tone of idealism dominated policy rhetoric and academic discussions during the interwar period, little of the liberal reform program was ever seriously attempted, and even less of it was achieved. The League of Nations failed to prevent the Japanese invasion of Manchuria (1931) or the Italian invasion of Ethiopia (1935); major disputes were rarely submitted to the PCIJ; and the 1932 Geneva Disarmament Conference ended in failure. When the threat of war began gathering over Europe and Asia in the late 1930s, enthusiasm for liberal idealism receded.

The next surge in liberal theorizing arose decades later in response to realism's neglect of *transnational relations* (see Keohane and Nye 1971). Although realists continued to focus on the state, the events surrounding the 1973 oil crisis revealed that nonstate actors could affect the course of international events and occasionally compete with states. This insight led to the realization that *complex interdependence* (Keohane and Nye 1977) sometimes offered a better description of world politics than realism, especially on international economic and environmental matters. Rather than contacts between countries being limited to high-level governmental officials, multiple communication channels connect societies. Instead of security dominating foreign policy considerations, issues on national agendas do not always have a fixed priority; and although military force often serves as the primary instrument of statecraft, other means frequently are more effective when bargaining occurs between economically interconnected countries. In short, the realist preoccupation with government-to-government relations ignored the complex network of public and private exchanges crisscrossing state boundaries. States were becoming increasingly interdependent, that is, mutually dependent on, sensitive about, and vulnerable to one another in ways that were not captured by realist theory.

Although interdependence was not new, its growth during the last quarter of the twentieth century led many liberal theorists to challenge the realist conception of anarchy. Although they agreed that the global system was anarchic, they also argued that it was more properly conceptualized as an "ordered" anarchy because most states followed commonly acknowledged normative

transnational relations interactions across state boundaries that involve at least one actor that is not the agent of a government or intergovernmental organization.

complex interdependence a model of world politics based on the assumptions that states are not the only important actors, security is not the dominant national goal, and military force is not the only significant instrument of foreign policy; this theory stresses crosscutting ways in which the growing ties among transnational actors make them vulnerable to each other's actions and sensitive to each other's needs.

standards, even in the absence of hierarchical enforcement. When a body of norms fosters shared expectations that guide a regularized pattern of cooperation on a specific issue, we call it an ***international regime*** (see Hansenclever, Mayer, and Rittberger 1996). Various types of regimes have been devised to govern behavior in trade and monetary affairs, as well as to manage access to common resources such as fisheries and river water. By the turn of the century, as pressing economic and environmental issues crowded national agendas, a large body of liberal "institutionalist" scholarship explored how regimes developed and what led states to comply with their injunctions.

international regime
embodies the norms, principles, rules, and institutions around which global expectations unite regarding a specific international problem.

Fueled by the recent history that suggested that international relations can change and that increased interdependence can lead to higher levels of cooperation, *neoliberalism* emerged in the last decade of the twentieth century to challenge realism and neorealism. This new departure goes by several labels, including "neoliberal institutionalism" (Grieco 1995), "neoidealism" (Kegley 1993), and "neo-Wilsonian idealism" (Fukuyama 1992a).

neoliberalism
the "new" liberal theoretical perspective that accounts for the way international institutions promote global change, cooperation, peace, and prosperity through collective programs for reforms.

Like realism and neorealism, neoliberalism does not represent a consistent intellectual movement or school of thought. Whatever the differences that divide them, however, all neoliberals share an interest in probing the conditions under which the convergent and overlapping interests among otherwise independent transnational actors may result in cooperation (see Controversy: Can International Relations Theory Address a Zombie Outbreak?). Neoliberalism departs from neorealism on many assumptions. In particular, neoliberalism focuses on the ways in which influences such as democratic governance, public opinion, mass education, free trade, liberal commercial enterprise, international law and organization, arms control and disarmament, collective security, multilateral diplomacy, and ethically inspired statecraft can improve life on our planet. Because they perceive change in global conditions as progressing over time, haltingly but still in the same trajectory through cooperative efforts, neoliberal theorists maintain that the ideas and ideals of the liberal legacy could describe, explain, predict, and prescribe international conduct in ways that they could not during the conflict-ridden Cold War.

Case Study: *Liberal Idealism*

The Limitations of Liberalism

Liberal theorists share an interest in probing the conditions under which similar interests among actors may lead to cooperation. Taking heart in the international prohibition, through community consensus, of such previously entrenched practices as slavery, piracy, dueling, and colonialism, they emphasize the prospects for progress through institutional reform. Studies of European integration during the 1950s and 1960s paved the way for the liberal

CONTROVERSY:

CAN INTERNATIONAL RELATIONS THEORY ADDRESS A ZOMBIE OUTBREAK?

A number of humorous and insightful efforts have been made of late that use a lens of pop culture to elucidate the different actors and concepts of international relations theories (see Table 2.2) and to evaluate their relative merit. Drawing on a constructivist perspective, the concept of sovereignty and the foundations of modern rule have been critically evaluated by assessing UFOs (Unidentified Flying Objects) (Wendt and Duvall 2008). Similarly, the movie *The Godfather* is used to explore theories of American foreign policy statecraft as represented by Don Vito Corleone and his sons (Hulsman and Mitchell 2009, 2008). Here, we draw on assessments of the sociopolitical ramifications of a potential zombie outbreak to provoke critical review of various international relations theories.

Zombies are a "popular figure in pop culture/entertainment and they are usually portrayed as being brought about through an outbreak or epidemic," as noted by researchers at Carleton University and the University of Ottawa (Munz et al, 2009, p. 133) who mathematically modeled the spread of the lethal infection. Zombies also have been used as an allegory for various threats such as the spread of Communism, the outbreak of AIDS, and the destruction of human civilization through our own folly or excesses. Viewing a zombie outbreak as a strategic threat, and assessing the relative usefulness and applicability of different international relations theories, offers a fun way to learn about theories by applying them to clearly hypothetical (we hope) situations. But there are real insights to be gained through such an exercise, for "given the present changes in the world's power structure," such efforts can provide "a startlingly useful metaphor for the strategic problems of our times" (Hulsman and Mitchell 2008).

Along these lines, consider these questions: In a world suffering from a zombie outbreak, what effects would different systemic international relations theories predict? Would the outcomes be of little consequence, or would they result in the demise of human society as we know it?

- Structural Realism. Due to an uneven distribution of capabilities, structural realism would anticipate that some countries would be better able than others to ward off zombies. Despite differences in the individual characteristics or domestic institutions of humans and zombies, the basic structure of world politics would persist as both actors would be subject to the constraints of a global system that is anarchical. Balance of power politics could ensue, with human states aligning with other human states to counter the global spread of zombieism. Or, as political analyst Daniel Drezner (2010, p.37) suggests, "states could also exploit the threat from the living dead to acquire new territory, squelch irredentist movements, settle old scores, or subdue enduring rivals."

- Liberal Institutionalism. As a strand of liberalism, liberal institutionalism would see a zombie outbreak as a problem that transcends national borders and threatens the global community writ large. Therefore, prudent states would seek to cooperate with one another and coordinate efforts to contain and squash the zombie threat. Both global and regional regimes and institutions could serve as important means for facilitating communication and directing the human response. For example, a World Zombie Organization (WZO) could be

(*continued*)

CAN INTERNATIONAL RELATIONS THEORY ADDRESS A ZOMBIE OUTBREAK? (Continued)

helpful in codifying international rules and procedures for responding to the zombie outbreak, while the United States could lead the way in creating a North American Fight Zombies Agreement (NAFZA) (see Drezner 2009).

• Social Constructivism. With its emphasis on the development of norms and ideas, social constructivism would envision a number of different scenarios. On one hand, relations between humans and zombies could best be reflected by the Hobbesian "kill or be killed" norm. Alternatively, a Kantian pluralistic anti-Zombie community could emerge "that bands together and breaks down nationalist divides in an effort to establish a world state" (Drezner 2009). Hostilities between humans and zombies could also strengthen group identity, where humans who have not been infected identify with one another as opposed to zombies, who seem to recognize each other as fellow "brain-eaters."

WHAT DO YOU THINK?

• If you were the leader of your country, which theoretical orientation do you think would best help you address a zombie outbreak? Why?

• Reflect upon the "real" global challenges facing us today, from the threat of terrorism to global warming to the worldwide economic downturn. Which concerns have the greatest impact upon our security, and how do realism, liberalism, and constructivism deal with these threats?

• Should a country work toward international cooperation or international dominance? Draw on realism, liberalism, or constructivism to frame your response.

institutionalist theories that emerged in the 1990s. The expansion of trade, communication, information, technology, and migrant labor led Europeans to sacrifice portions of their sovereign independence to create a new political and economic union out of previously separate units. These developments were outside of realism's worldview, creating conditions that made the call for a theory grounded in the liberal tradition convincing to many who had previously questioned realism. In the words of former U.S. President Bill Clinton, "In a world where freedom, not tyranny, is on the march, the cynical calculus of pure power politics simply does not compute. It is ill-suited to the new era."

Yet, as compelling as contemporary liberal institutionalism may seem at the onset of the twenty-first century, many realists complain that it has not transcended its idealist heritage. They charge that just like the League of Nations and the PCIJ, institutions today exert minimal influence on state behavior. International organizations cannot stop states from behaving according to balance-of-power logic, calculating how each move they make affects their relative position in a world of relentless competition.

Critics of liberalism further contend that most studies supportive of international institutions appear in the arena of commercial, financial, and environmental affairs, not in the arena of national defense. Although it may be difficult to draw a clear line between economic and security issues, some scholars note that "different institutional arrangements" exist in each realm, with the prospects for cooperation among self-interested states greater in the former than the latter (Lipson 1984). National survival hinges on the effective management of security issues, insist realists. Collective security organizations naïvely assume that all members perceive threats in the same way, and are willing to run the risks and pay the costs of countering those threats.

Because power-lusting states are unlikely to see their vital interests in this light, global institutions cannot provide timely, muscular responses to aggression. On security issues, conclude realists, states will trust in their own power, not in the promises of supranational institutions.

A final realist complaint lodged against liberalism is an alleged tendency to turn foreign policy into a moral crusade. Whereas realists claim that heads of state are driven by strategic necessities, many liberals believe moral imperatives can guide and constrain leaders. Consider the 1999 war in Kosovo, which pitted the North Atlantic Treaty Organization (NATO) against the Federal Republic of Yugoslavia. Pointing to Yugoslav leader Slobodan Milosevic's repression of ethnic Albanians living in the province of Kosovo, NATO Secretary General Javier Solana, British Prime Minister Tony Blair, and U.S. President Bill Clinton all argued that humanitarian intervention was a moral necessity. Although nonintervention into the internal affairs of other states had long been a cardinal principle of international law, they saw military action against Yugoslavia as a duty because human rights were an international entitlement and governments that violated them forfeited the protection of international law. Sovereignty, according to many liberal thinkers, is not sacrosanct. The international community has an obligation to use armed force to stop flagrant violations of human rights.

To sum up, realists remain skeptical about liberal claims of moral necessity. On the one hand, they deny the universal applicability of any single moral standard in a culturally pluralistic world. On the other hand, they worry that adopting such a standard will breed a self-righteous, messianic foreign policy. Realists embrace *consequentialism*. If there are no universal standards covering the many situations in which moral choice must occur, then policy

consequentialism
an approach to evaluating moral choices on the basis of the results of the action taken.

decisions can be judged only in terms of their consequences in particular circumstances. Prudent leaders recognize that competing moral values may be at stake in any given situation, and they must weigh the trade-offs among these values, as well as how pursuing them might impinge on national security and other important interests. As former U.S. diplomat and celebrated realist scholar George Kennan (1985) once put it, the primary obligation of government "is to the interests of the national society it represents, not to the moral impulses that individual elements of that society may experience."

> *It's important that we take a hard clear look . . . not at some simple world, either of universal goodwill or of universal hostility, but the complex, changing, and sometimes dangerous world that really exists.*
>
> —Jimmy Carter, U.S. President

CONSTRUCTIVIST THEORY

Since the end of the Cold War, many students of international relations have turned to constructivism in order to understand world politics. With intellectual roots in the twentieth-century Frankfurt School of critical social theory, contemporary scholars who have influenced the theoretical development of this perspective include Alexander Wendt, Friedrich Kratochwil, and Nicholas Onuf, among others. *Constructivism* merits careful consideration because awareness of how our understandings of the world are individually and socially constructed, and of how prevailing ideas mold our beliefs about what is unchangeable and what can be reformed, allows us to see world politics in a new and critical light.

The Constructivist Worldview

Sometimes described as more of a philosophically informed perspective than a fully fledged general theory (Ruggie 1998), constructivism includes diverse scholars who agree that the international institutions most people take for granted as the natural and inevitable result of world politics need not exist (Hacking 1999). Like the institutions of slavery and even war, these practices are mere ideational constructs that depend on human agreement for their existence. They are therefore changeable.

Although constructivism is "a loose paradigm of related interpretations [that] share certain assumptions with realists and liberals" (Steele 2007, p. 25), it departs from realism and liberalism in important ways. In contrast to

constructivism
a paradigm based on the premise that world politics is a function of the ways that states construct and then accept images of reality and later respond to the meanings given to power politics; as consensual definitions change, it is possible for either conflictual or cooperative practices to evolve.

realism and liberalism, which emphasize how material factors such as military power and economic wealth affect relations among states, constructivism emphasizes how ideas define identities, which in turn impart meaning to the material capabilities and behavior of actors. As discussed in the previous chapter, international reality is defined by our images of the world. Constructivists stress the intersubjective quality of these images—how perceptions are shaped by prevailing attitudes.

As shown in Table 2.2, constructivists differ from realists and liberals most fundamentally by insisting that world politics is individually and socially constructed. That is to say, material conditions acquire meaning for human action only through the shared knowledge that circulating ideas ascribe to them. Socially popular visions of realities provide transnational actors with certain identities and interests, as well as material capabilities with certain meanings (see Onuf 1989; Hopf 1998; Smith and Owens 2005). Hence, the meaning of a concept such as "anarchy" depends on underlying shared knowledge. An anarchy among allies, for example, holds a different meaning for the states in question than an anarchy composed of bitter rivals. Thus, British nuclear weapons are less threatening to the United States than the same weapons in North Korean hands, because shared Anglo-American

Table 2.2 A Comparison of Realist, Liberal, and Constructivist Theories

Feature	Realism	Liberalism	Constructivism
Core concern	War and security How vulnerable, self-interested states survive in an environment where they are uncertain about the intentions and capabilities of others	Institutionalized peace How self-serving actors learn to see benefits to coordinating behavior through rules and organizations in order to achieve collective gains	Social groups' shared meanings and images How ideas, images and identities develop, change, and shape world politics
Key actors	States	States, international institutions, global corporations	Individuals, nongovernmental organizations, transnational networks
Central concepts	Anarchy, self-help, national interest, relative gains, balance of power	Collective security, reciprocity, international regimes, complex interdependence, transnational relations	Ideas, images, shared knowledge, identities, discourses, and persuasion leading to new understandings and normative change
Approach to peace	Protect sovereign autonomy and deter rivals through military preparedness and alliances	Institutional reform through democratization, open markets, and international law and organization	Activists who promote progressive ideas and encourage states to adhere to norms for appropriate behavior
Global outlook	Pessimistic: great powers locked in relentless security competition	Optimistic: cooperative view of human nature and a belief in progress	Agnostic: global prospect hinges on the content of prevailing ideas and values

expectations about one another differ from those between Washington and Pyongyang. The nature of international life within an anarchy, in other words, is not a given. Anarchy, as well as other socially constructed concepts such as "sovereignty" and "power," are simply what states make of them (Wendt 1995).

The Evolution of Constructivist Thought

The unraveling of the Warsaw Pact and subsequent disintegration of the Soviet Union stimulated scholarly interest during the 1990s in constructivist interpretations of world politics. Neither realism nor liberalism foresaw the peaceful end to the Cold War, and both theories had difficulty explaining why it occurred when it did (see Chapter 4 Controversy: Why Did the Cold War End Peacefully?). Constructivists attributed this to the material and individualist orientation of realism and liberalism, and argued that an explanation that addressed the role of changing ideas and identities provided for superior explanation of this systemic change.

social constructivism
a variant of constructivism that emphasizes the role of social discourse in the development of ideas and identities.

There are several strands of thought within the constructivist perspective. One of the most prominent is *social constructivism*, which emphasizes collective identity formation. Alexander Wendt, who is widely credited with the contemporary application of social constructivism to world politics, challenges the material and individualist foundations of realism and liberalism. He posits that "structures of human association are determined primarily by shared ideas rather than material forces" (Wendt 1999, p. 1). Likewise, interests and identities stem from shared ideas and are not reducible to individuals. So, for example, social constructivists see the structure of the international system in terms of the distribution of ideas, whereas neorealists view systemic structure within the context of the distribution of material capabilities and neoliberals see it as the distribution of capabilities within an institutional superstructure. According to social constructivism, all of us are influenced by collective conceptions of world politics that are reinforced by social pressures from the reference groups to which we belong.

According to Cynthia Weber (2005, p. 76), constructivism as exemplified in the work of Alexander Wendt reifies states by picturing these collectives like individuals whose decisions become the authors or producers of international life; that is, it treats them as objects that already exist and says little about the "practices that produce states as producers." Thus, there is concern that social constructivism overemphasizes the role of social structures at the expense of the purposeful agents whose practices help create and change these structures (Checkel 1998). A second strand of constructivism, *agent-oriented constructivism*, takes a different approach by emphasizing individualist influences on identities. Independent actors in world politics may differ in terms of their internal ideas or identities, and agent-oriented constructivists contend that the domestic identities of actors "are crucial for their perceptions of one another in the international arena" (Risse-Kappen 1996, p. 367). An actor can hold both an internal and external identity, which is shaped by respective dialogue at home and within the international community. Social constructivists attribute the shaping of ideas and identities to repetitive social practices and view most identity as shared or collective. Agent-oriented constructivists allow for individual or autonomous identity and credit the development of ideas in part to individual actors with the capacity for independent and critical thinking. It is possible to construct new ideas and change existing social structures. Accordingly, agent-oriented constructivists pointed to the challenge that Mikhail Gorbechev's "new thinking" posed to traditional ideas about national security. New thinking, they suggested, led to the rise of new *norms* governing the relations between Moscow and Washington.

For constructivists, the game of international power revolves around actors' abilities, through debate about values, to persuade others to accept their ideas. People and groups become powerful when their efforts to proselytize succeed in winning converts to those ideas and norms they advocate, and a culture of shared understandings emerges. Building upon such ideas of society, culture, and identity formation, Richard Ned Lebow (2009) emphasizes the role of self-esteem as a universal human need that has a profound influence upon political behavior.

The capacity of some activist transnational nongovernmental organizations, such as Human Rights Watch or Greenpeace, to promote global change by convincing many people to accept their ideas about political liberties and environmental protection are examples of how shared conceptions of moral and legal norms can change the world. Consensual understandings of interests, self-identities, and images of the world—how people think of themselves, who they are, and what others in the world are like—demonstrably can alter the world when these constructions of international realities change (Adler 2002; Barnet 2005; Onuf 2002).

The Limitations of Constructivism

The most common criticism of constructivism concerns its explanation of change. If changes in ideas through discussions and discourses lead to behavioral changes within the global system, what accounts for the rise and fall of

agent-oriented constructivism
a variant of constructivism that sees ideas and identities as influenced in part by independent actors.

norms
generalized standards of behavior that, once accepted, shape collective expectations about appropriate conduct.

INTERFOTO Pressebildagentur/Alamy Limited dpa/Landov Media

Arne Dedert/dpa/Landov

PIONEERING INFLUENCES ON CONSTRUCTIVIST THOUGHT **Many constructivists have been influenced by critical theory, especially as it was developed by Max Horkheimer (1947), left, and Jurgen Habermas (1984), right. Rather than viewing the world as a set of neutral, objective "facts" that could be perceived apart from the situation in which observation occurred, critical theorists saw all phenomena as being embedded within a specific socio-historical context ascribing normative meaning to information (Price and Reus-Smit 1998).**

different ideas and discourses over time? How, when, and why do changes in shared knowledge emerge? "Constructivists are good at describing change," writes Jack Snyder (2004, p. 61), "but they are weak on the material and institutional circumstances necessary to support the emergence of consensus about new values and ideas." Moreover, critics charge that constructivists remain unclear about what factors cause particular ideas to become dominant whereas others fall by the wayside. "What is crucial," asserts Robert Jervis (2005, p. 18), "is not people's thinking, but the factors that drive it." Constructivists, he continues, have excessive faith in the ability of ideas that seem self-evident today to replicate and sustain themselves; however, future generations who live under different circumstances and who may think differently could easily reject these ideas. For constructivists, socially accepted ideas, norms, and values are linked to collective identities—stable, role-specific understandings and expectations about the self (Wendt 1994). Although constructivists recognize that shared identities are not predetermined and can change over time, critics submit that constructivists cannot explain why and when they dissolve. Critics also charge that constructivism does not adequately deal with the issue of uncertainty, and that the assumption that "states typically know a lot about the other's motives is an unsupported empirical statement" (Copeland 2006, p. 11).

And though the constructivist approach is increasingly viewed as a vital perspective for understanding world politics, it is still criticized for its limited attention to methodological issues. According to Amir Lupovici (2009, p. 197), "scholars have tended to neglect the methodological dimension, providing little guidance on how to conduct a constructivist study." In an effort to address this deficiency, scholars have begun to call for a more systematic and unified framework that combines a number of existing methods so as to enable us to "examine the mutual influences of constitutive effects upon causal effects and vice versa" (Lupovici 2009, p. 200; Pouliot 2007). In other words, such a pluralistic methodology would help us to consider both the material and ideational factors that shape world politics.

Despite these criticisms, constructivism is a very popular theoretical approach in world politics. By highlighting the influence that socially constructed images of the world have on your interpretations of international events, and by making you aware of their inherent subjectivity, constructivism can remind you of the contingent nature of all knowledge and the inability of any theory of world politics to fully capture global complexities.

WHAT'S MISSING IN THEORIES OF WORLD POLITICS?

Although realism, liberalism, and constructivism dominate thinking about international relations in today's academic and policy communities, these schools of thought have been challenged. Two of the most significant critiques have come from radicalism and feminism.

The very idea that there is another idea is something gained.

—Richard Jeffries, English author

The Radical Critique

For much of the twentieth century, socialism was the primary radical alternative to mainstream international relations theorizing. Although there are many strands of socialist thought, most have been influenced by Karl Marx's argument that explaining events in world affairs requires understanding capitalism as a global phenomenon. Whereas realists emphasize state security, liberals accentuate individual freedom, and constructivists highlight ideas and identities, socialists focus on class conflict and the material interests of each class (Doyle 1997).

"The history of all hitherto existing society," proclaimed Marx and his coauthor, Friedrich Engels (1820–1895), in the Communist Manifesto, "is the history of class struggles." Capitalism, they argued, has given rise to two antagonistic classes: a ruling class (bourgeoisie) that owns the means of production and a subordinate class (proletariat) that sells its labor but receives little compensation. According to Marx and Engels, "The need of a constantly expanding market for its products chases the bourgeoisie over the whole surface of the globe." By expanding worldwide, the bourgeoisie gives "a cosmopolitan character to production and consumption in every country."

imperialism
the policy of expanding state power through the conquest and/or military domination of foreign territory.

Vladimir Ilyich Lenin (1870–1924) in the Soviet Union extended Marx's analysis to the study of *imperialism*, which he interpreted as a stage in the development of capitalism when monopolies overtake free-market competition. Drawing from the work of British economist John Hobson (1858–1940), Lenin maintained that advanced capitalist states eventually face the twin problems of overproduction and underconsumption. They respond by seeking foreign markets and investments for their surplus goods and capital, and by waging wars to divide the world into spheres of influence that they can exploit. Though his assertions have been heavily criticized on conceptual and empirical grounds (see Dougherty and Pfaltzgraff 2001), the attention given to social classes and uneven development stimulated several new waves of theorizing about capitalism as a global phenomenon.

INTERFOTO Pressebildagentur/Alamy Limited

KARL MARX CHALLENGES INTERNATIONAL THEORETICAL ORTHODOXY **Pictured here is the German philosopher Karl Marx (1818–1883). His revolutionary theory of the economic determinants of world history inspired the spread of communism to overcome the class struggles so pronounced in most countries. The target of his critique was the compulsion of the wealthy great powers to subjugate foreign people by military force and to create colonies for purposes of financial exploitation. Imperial conquest of colonial peoples could only be prevented, Marx warned, by humanity's shift from a capitalist to a socialist economy and society.**

One prominent example is *dependency theory*. As expressed in the writings of André Gunder Frank (1969), Amir Samin (1976), and others (Dos Santos 1970; see Chapter 4), dependency theorists claimed that much of the poverty in Asia, Africa, and Latin America stemmed from the exploitative capitalist world economy.

As they saw it, the economies of less developed countries had become dependent on exporting inexpensive raw materials and agricultural commodities to advanced industrial states, while simultaneously importing expensive manufactured goods from them. Theotonio Dos Santos (1971, p. 158), a prominent dependency scholar, described dependency as a "historical condition which shapes a certain structure of the world economy such that it favors some countries to the detriment of others." Dependency theory was criticized for recommending withdrawal from the world economy (Shannon 1989), and eventually theoretical efforts arose to trace the economic ascent and decline of individual countries as part of long-run, system-wide change (Clark 2008).

dependency theory
a theory hypothesizing that less developed countries are exploited because global capitalism makes them dependent on the rich countries that create exploitative rules for trade and production.

World-system theory, which was influenced by both Marxist and dependency theorists, represents the most recent effort to interpret world politics in terms of an integrated capitalist division of labor (see Anderson 2005; Chase-Dunn and Wallerstein 2005 and 1988). The capitalist world economy, which emerged in sixteenth-century Europe and ultimately expanded to encompass the entire globe, is viewed as containing three structural positions: a core (strong, well-integrated states whose economic activities are diversified and centered on possession and use of capital), a periphery (areas lacking strong state machinery and engaged in producing relatively few unfinished goods by unskilled, low-wage labor), and a semiperiphery (states embodying elements of both core and peripheral production). Within the core, a state may gain economic primacy by achieving productive, commercial, and financial superiority over its rivals. Primacy is difficult to sustain, however. The diffusion of technological innovations and the flow of capital to competitors, plus the massive costs of maintaining global order, all erode the dominant state's economic advantage. Thus, in addition to underscoring the exploitation of the periphery by the core, world-system theory calls attention to the cyclical rise and fall of hegemonic superpowers at the top of the core hierarchy.

world-system theory
a body of theory that treats the capitalistic world economy originating in the sixteenth century as an interconnected unit of analysis encompassing the entire globe, with an international division of labor and multiple political centers and cultures whose rules constrain and share the behavior of all transnational actors.

Whereas the various radical challenges to mainstream theorizing enhance our understanding of world politics by highlighting the roles played by corporations, transnational religious movements, and other nonstate actors, they overemphasize economic interpretations of international events and consequently omit other potentially important explanatory factors. According to feminist theorists, one such factor is gender.

The Feminist Critique

Beginning in the late 1980s, feminism began challenging conventional international relations theory. Cast as a "critical theory," contemporary feminist scholars called for a "shift from mechanistic causal explanations to a greater interest in historically contingent interpretive theories" (Tickner 2010, p. 37). In particular, feminist theory was concerned with the gender bias inherent in both mainstream theory and the practice of international affairs, and sought to demonstrate how a gendered perspective is relevant to understanding and explaining world politics. As *feminist theory* evolved over time, it moved away from focusing on a history of discrimination and began to explore how gender identity shapes foreign policy decision making and how gendered hierarchies reinforce practices that perpetuate inequalities between men and women (see Ackerly and True 2008; Bolzendahl 2009; Enloe 2004; Peterson and Runyan 2009; Tickner 2005).

feminist theory
body of scholarship that emphasizes gender in the study of world politics.

According to the feminist critique, the mainstream literature on world politics dismisses the plight and contributions of women and treats differences in men's and women's status, beliefs, and behaviors as unimportant. Feminism challenges the fundamentals of traditional international relations theory in four primary ways:

- **The scientific study of world politics:** As we have previously discussed, traditional international relations theory—particularly neorealism—has influenced the scientific study of world politics, which attempts to explain the behavior of states in the international system by universal, objective laws. Yet feminism questions the true objectivity of these approaches. Spike Petersen, a prominent feminist theorist, notes that there was an explicit masculine bias in the scientific revolution of the seventeenth century, with science and reasoning attributed as a "male" trait and emotion and rationality as a "female" one. Somewhat similar to *social constructivism*, the feminist critique emphasizes the role of identity in the construction of knowledge, and contends that the study of international relations draws heavily on male experiences to explain international affairs, largely dismissing the feminine dimension.

- **Fundamental gender bias:** Feminism notes that the basic assumptions of the mainstream theoretical literature, as well as the practice of foreign policy, are heavily colored by a masculinist tradition of thought. For example, although "Hobbes' description of human behavior in the state of nature refers explicitly to that of adult males, contemporary realism has taken this behavior as constitutive of human nature as a whole" (Tickner 2010, p. 39). This can be seen in Morgenthau's classical realist depiction of states in an anarchical environment engaged in a persistent pursuit of power to further their own self-interest (Hutchings 2008). Yet feminism challenges the heavy reliance on such assumptions, and posits that characteristics dismissed due to their "feminine" quality play an important role as well. Indeed, for life to have persisted in the state of nature, cooperative activities such as child rearing must have occurred.

- **Reformulation of core concepts:** Feminists call for a closer examination of key concepts in world politics—such as state, power, interest, and security—and ask whether a "masculine" conceptualization of these ideas shapes the conduct of foreign policy. Realism, for instance, attributes to the state masculine characteristics of sovereignty that emphasize a hierarchical leader, the capacity to wage war, desirability of wealth and reputation, and the conduct of international affairs as separate from the domestic concerns of its populace. Feminist scholars such as Cynthia Enloe (2007), however, argue that power relations are influenced by gender in ways that shape practices of war and diplomacy, and that alternative formulations of key concepts allow for the relevance of a wide range of other issues and structures, including social and economic ones, in world politics.

- **Incorporation of the female perspective:** Historically, the role of women has been marginalized in most societies. In order to understand how unequal gender relations have excluded women from foreign policy, perpetuated injustice and oppression, and shaped state interests and behavior, it is critical to purposively examine the female experience. Christine Sylvester's (2002) examination of women's cooperatives in Zimbabwe and women's peace activism at Greenham Common reflects a feminist commitment to a more flexible understanding of security that expands upon the traditional state-centric conceptualization as protection from external aggressors to include threats to economic and family concerns as well. The "idea that theorizing is 'objective'" is rejected by feminism in favor "of a perspectival approach, which links the possibility of insight to specific standpoints and political agendas" (Hutchings 2008, p. 100).

Although all feminists stress the importance of gender in studying international relations, there are several contending schools of thought within feminist scholarship. Some feminists assert that on average there are no significant differences in the capabilities of men and women; others claim differences exist, with each gender being more capable than the other in certain endeavors; still others insist that the meaning ascribed to a person's gender is an arbitrary cultural construct that varies from one time or place to another (Goldstein 2002). Regardless of the position taken on the issue of gender differences, feminist scholars demonstrate that many women have proven to be very capable leaders who have left deep footprints on international affairs. More than simply acknowledging the impact of female leaders such as Britain's Margaret Thatcher, Indonesia's Megawati Sukarnoputri, Israel's Golda Meir, the Philippines' Corazón Aquino, Pakistan's Benazir Bhutto, Germany's Angela Merkel, Argentina's Christina Fernandez de Kirchner, or

Chile's Michelle Bachelet, they urge us to examine events from the personal perspectives of the countless women who have been involved in international affairs as caregivers, grassroots activists, and participants in the informal labor force. The feminist critique continues to expand across a range of issues, from foreign policy to humanitarian intervention to terrorism, and a variety of actors, from states to nongovernmental organizations. "Women have never been absent in world politics," writes Franke Wilmer (2000). They have, for the most part, remained "invisible within the discourse conducted by men." As prominent feminist scholar J. Ann Tickner (2010, p. 38) urges, "We must search deeper to find ways in which gender hierarchies serve to reinforce these socially constructed boundaries which perpetuate inequalities between women and men."

Case Study: *Liberal Idealism*

THEORIZING ABOUT THEORY

To understand our changing world and to make reasonable prognoses about the future, we must begin by arming ourselves with an array of information and conceptual tools, entertain rival interpretations of world politics in the global marketplace of ideas, and question the assumptions on which these contending worldviews rest. Because there are a great (and growing) number of alternative, and sometimes incompatible, ways of organizing theoretical inquiry about world politics, the challenge of capturing the world's political problems cannot be reduced to any one simple yet compelling account (Chernoff 2008). Each paradigmatic effort to do so in the past has ultimately lost advocates as developments in world affairs eroded its continuing relevance.

Although grand theories fade with the passage of time, they often regain their attractiveness when global transformations make them useful once again. In fact, world politics is so resistant to clear, comprehensive,

David Caulkin/AP Photo

PROTESTING FOR PEACE **Between 1981 and 2000, tens of thousands of British women mobilized to protest against nuclear proliferation and the stationing of U.S. nuclear air missiles at the Greenham Common Airbase in Berkshire, England. They saw peace as a feminist issue, and asserted their power by holding hands and creating a fourteen-mile chain around the airbase with their bodies. Not only did they see nuclear weapons as a direct threat to themselves and their children, they protested that trillions were being spent on weapons of mass destruction while so many around the world suffered from a lack of food and water, inadequate healthcare, and underfunded schools. Their nearly two-decade demonstration attracted worldwide media attention and generated the support of millions throughout the world.**

and convincing analysis that some advocates of so-called *deconstructivism* contend that international change and complexity defy description, explanation, and prediction. Deconstructionists share the philosophical view that all peoples' conceptions of global realities are relative to their understandings. Thus, biased interpretation is inevitable and "objectivity" a myth, so that the validity of all conceptions is dependent on one's own personal point of view (any interpretation is as valid as any other), and there is no point in attempting to develop a shared conception of the world. At the extreme, the nihilistic advocates of deconstructivism maintain that theories of international relations grounded in behavioral science that attempt to understand or discover objective truths about the world are meaningless creations of the methods on which they are built (see Controversy: Can Behavioral Science Advance the Study of International Relations?). "Perspectivism," or the claim that any account of international reality can be only given from personal perspectives, rejects the application of reason to interpret evidence because no "facts" can be taken as really true (Behe 2005).

deconstructivism
the postmodern theory that the complexity of the world system renders precise description impossible and that the purpose of scholarship is to understand actors' hidden motives by deconstructing their textual statements.

The vast majority of scholars rejects this defeatist deconstructivist posture to understanding and continues to struggle in the pursuit of theory and knowledge about international affairs. However, because no single general-purpose theory exists that is able to account for all questions regarding international relations, a number of scholars have returned to reconsider the basic questions of *epistemology* that are fundamental to evaluating the relative value and validity of rival theoretical frameworks (see Agnew 2007). How do we know what to believe? What principles of analysis can lead us to recognize the strengths and weaknesses of various theories? How do we separate fact from fiction and sense from nonsense? What is the relative descriptive accuracy and explanatory power of different theories, and how much confidence should be placed in their explanations of world politics? As you review various theoretical interpretations of global circumstances, it is important to evaluate the premises on which each contending account is based.

epistemology
the philosophical examination of the ways in which knowledge is acquired and the analytic principles governing the study of phenomena.

INTERNATIONAL THEORY AND THE GLOBAL FUTURE

As you seek to understand changing global conditions, it is important to be humble in recognizing the limitations of our understandings of world politics and at the same time inquisitive about its character. The task of

CONTROVERSY:

CAN BEHAVIORAL SCIENCE ADVANCE THE STUDY OF INTERNATIONAL RELATIONS?

How should scholars construct theories to interpret international behavior? The answer to that question has never been satisfactorily resolved, and the long-standing debate about how best to construct theories of international relations continues today. Some scholars, known as advocates of "postmodern deconstructivism," challenge the ability of intellectuals to provide a satisfactory theoretical account of why states and people act as they do in international relations. These scholars devote their efforts to criticizing and "deconstructing" the theories of world politics to expose their inherent limitations. Most scholars, however, remain motivated by the theoretical quest to interpret and comprehend the complexities of international relations, and they challenge the pessimistic view that world politics defies meaningful understanding, despite the obstacles and limits to knowledge.

This evolving epistemological controversy took an important step in the 1960s when a movement known as **behavioralism** arose to challenge interpretations of international relations that were based more on speculative assessment than on systematic observable evidence. Behavioralism was not a new theory of international relations so much as a new method of studying it, based largely on the application of scientific methods to the study of global affairs (Knorr and Rosenau 1969; Knorr and Verba 1961). Behavioralism advances principles and procedures for formulating and stringently testing **hypotheses** inferred from theories to reach generalizations or statements about international regularities that hold true across time and place. Science, the behavioralists claim, is primarily a generalizing activity. From this perspective, a theory of international relations should state the relationship between two or more variables that specifies the conditions under which a relationship holds and explain why the relationship should hold. To uncover such theories, behavioralists lean toward using comparative cross-national analyses rather than case studies of particular countries at particular times. Behavioralists also stress the need for data about the characteristics of transnational actors and how they behave toward one another. Hence, the behavioral movement encourages the comparative and quantitative study of international relations (see, for example, Rosenau 1980; Singer 1968).

What makes behavioralism innovative is its attitude toward the purposes of inquiry: replacing subjective beliefs with verifiable knowledge, supplanting impressions with testable evidence, and substituting data and reproducible information for mere opinion or the assertions of politicians claiming to be authorities. Behavioralism is predicated on the belief that the pursuit of knowledge about the world through systematic analytic methodologies is possible and productive. The behavioral research agenda is based on the conviction that although laws of international behavior cannot be proven outside the approach used to uncover them, Albert Einstein was correct in arguing that there exists a world independent of our minds, and that this world is rationally organized and open to human understanding (Holt 2005). In this sense, behavioralists embrace liberalism's "high regard for modern science" and its "attacks against superstition and authority" (J. Hall 2001). In place of the self-proclaimed and often mistaken opinions of "experts" (Tetlock 2006), behavioral scientists seek to acquire knowledge cumulatively by suspending judgments about truths or values until they have sufficient evidence to support them. They attempt to overcome the tendency of traditional inquiry to select facts and cases to fit preexisting hunches. Instead, all available data, those that contradict as well as those that support existing theoretical hypotheses, are to be examined. Knowledge, they argue, would advance best by theorists assuming a cautious, skeptical attitude toward any empirical statement. The slogans "Let the data, not the armchair theorist, speak," and "Seek evidence, but distrust it" represent the behavioral posture toward the acquisition of knowledge.

WHAT DO YOU THINK?

- Is the scientific analysis of patterns of international relations a reasonable undertaking? Or, as deconstructionists argue, are explanations of international relations impossible?

- While behavioralism is merited for its capacity for predictive power, it is criticized for its lack of explanatory power. When determining the strength of a theory on international relations, is prediction or explanation more important? Why?

- Another critique of theories explaining international relations is the incorporation, or lack thereof, of change over time. Are they correct in assuming that aspects of human behavior remain invariant over time? What are the implications for exclusion of the element of time for the theories derived from behavioralist methodologies?

interpretation is complicated because the world is itself complex. Donald Puchala theoretically framed the challenge in 2008 by observing:

> Conceptually speaking, world affairs today can be likened to a disassembled jigsaw puzzle scattered on a table before us. Each piece shows a fragment of a broad picture that as yet remains indiscernible. Some pieces depict resurgent nationalism; others show spreading democracy; some picture genocide; others portray prosperity through trade and investment; some picture nuclear disarmament; others picture nuclear proliferation; some indicate a reinvigorated United Nations; others show the UN still enfeebled and ineffective; some describe cultural globalization; others predict clashing civilizations.
>
> How do these pieces fit together, and what picture do they exhibit when they are appropriately fitted?

All theories are maps of possible futures. Theories can guide us in fitting the pieces together to form an accurate picture. However, in evaluating the usefulness of any theory to interpret global conditions, the historical overview in this chapter suggests that it would be wrong to oversimplify or to assume that a particular theory will remain useful in the future. Nonetheless, as American

behavioralism
the methodological research movement to incorporate rigorous scientific analysis into the study of world politics so that conclusions about patterns are based on measurement, data, and evidence rather than on speculation and subjective belief.

hypotheses
speculative statements about the probable relationship between independent variables (the presumed causes) and a dependent variable (the effect).

poet Robert Frost observed, any belief we cling to long enough is likely to be true again someday because "most of the change we think we see in life is due to truths being in and out of favor." So in our theoretical exploration of world politics, we must critically assess the accuracy of our impressions, avoiding the temptation to embrace one worldview and abandon another without any assurance that their relative worth is permanently fixed.

Although realism, liberalism, and constructivism are the dominant ways of thinking about world politics today, none of these theories is completely satisfactory. Recall that realism is frequently criticized for relying on ambiguous concepts, liberalism is often derided for making naïve policy recommendations based on idealistic assumptions, and constructivism is charged with an inability to explain change. Moreover, as the challenges mounted by radicalism and feminism suggest, these three mainstream theories overlook seemingly important aspects of world politics, which limits their explanatory power. Despite these drawbacks, each has strengths for interpreting certain kinds of international events and foreign policy behaviors.

Because we lack a single overarching theory able to account for all facets of world politics, we will draw on realist, liberal, and constructivist thought in subsequent chapters. Moreover, we will supplement them with insights from radicalism and feminism, where these theoretical traditions can best help to interpret the topic covered.

> *When I was working in Washington and helping formulate American foreign policies, I found myself borrowing from all three types of thinking: realism, liberalism, and constructivism. I found them all helpful, though in different ways and in different circumstances.*
>
> —Joseph S. Nye, international relations scholar and U.S. policy maker

Take an Online Practice Quiz

www.cengagebrain.com/shop/ISBN/0495802204

Suggested Readings

Drezner, Daniel W. (2010) *Theories of International Politics and Zombies*. Princeton, NJ: Princeton University Press.

Keohane, Robert O. and Joseph S. Nye. (2000) *Power and Interdependence*. 3rd ed. Upper Saddle River, N.J.: Pearson.

Lebow, Richard Ned. (2009) *A Cultural Theory of International Relations*. New York: Cambridge University Press.

Lobell, Steven E., Norrin M. Ripsman, and Jeffrey W. Taliaferro. (2009). *Neoclassical Realism, The State, and Foreign Policy*. New York: Cambridge University Press.

Peterson, V. Spike and Anne Sisson Runyan (2009) *Global Gender Issues in the New Millennium*. 3rd ed. New York: Westview Press.

Puchala, Donald J. (2003) *Theory and History in International Relations*. New York: Routledge.

Part 2
THE GLOBE'S ACTORS AND THEIR RELATIONS

"Everybody has accepted by now that change is unavoidable. But that still implies that change is like death and taxes—it should be postponed as long as possible and no change would be vastly preferable. But in a period of upheaval, such as the one we are living in, change is the norm."

—Peter Drucker, American futurologist

Narong Sangnak/EPA/Landov

MARCHING FOR CHANGE   People, like states and international organizations, are transnational actors. Mobilized publics often use protest demonstrations to express their dissent and to draw global attention to their cause. Show here in Bangkok, Thailand on September 19, 2010 are protesters, known as the Red Shirts, who oppose the government and are calling for greater democracy and popular participation. Many believe the conflict reflects deep divisions between the elite and poor, while others see it as a battle between two distinct groups of elites. As Thai newscaster Karuna Buakamsri says, "Even after this is over, the conflicts in Thai society will remain for many years to come."

SHAKESPEARE WROTE THAT "ALL THE WORLD'S A STAGE AND ALL THE MEN AND WOMEN MERELY PLAYERS." When it comes to world politics, not just people but also organizations, groups, and countries have a variety of roles to play on the global stage. Part 2 identifies the major actors in world politics today and describes the roles they perform, the policies they pursue, and the predicaments they face.

The first three chapters in Part 2 each focus on a prominent type of global actor. Chapter 3 opens by giving you a view of the great powers—the actors with the greatest military and economic capabilities. Chapter 4 compares the great powers with the weaker, economically less developed countries now known as the Global South, whose fates are powerfully shaped by others. The rise of the Global East to its new status as rival to the traditional great powers is also covered. Chapter 5 examines the role of intergovernmental organizations, such as the United Nations and the European Union, and non-governmental organizations, such as Greenpeace and Amnesty International, whose members actively work for global change. A window is opened for you to also explore the activities of other nonstate global actors, including multinational corporations, ethnic groups, and religious movements. Finally, Chapter 6 explains how states and all other transnational actors go about the task of making foreign policy decisions. It also identifies the intellectual and political barriers that often reduce the ability of transnational actors to make rational choices about their interests, policy goals, and workable paths for promoting them.

CHAPTER 3
GREAT POWER RIVALRIES AND RELATIONS

CHAPTER OUTLINE

THE QUEST FOR WORLD LEADERSHIP

THE FIRST WORLD WAR

The Causes of World War I

The Consequences of World War I

THE SECOND WORLD WAR

The Causes of World War II

The Consequences of World War II

THE COLD WAR

The Causes and Evolutionary Course of the Cold War

CONTROVERSY: Was Ideology the Primary Source of East-West Conflict?

CONTROVERSY: Why Did the Cold War End Peacefully?

The Consequences of the Cold War

THE POST–COLD WAR ERA

America's Unipolar Moment

The Rise of the Rest? From Unipolarity to Multipolarity

Looking Ahead: The Future of Great Power Relations

Great powers fear each other. They regard each other with suspicion, and they worry that war may be in the offing. They anticipate danger. There is little room for trust. . . . From the perspective of any one great power, all other great powers are potential enemies. . . . The basis of this fear is that in a world where great powers have the capability to attack each other and might have the motive to do so, any state bent on survival must be at least suspicious of other states and reluctant to trust them.

—John Mearsheimer, realist political theorist

FDR Library

ALLIES OR NEW RIVALS? The "Big Three" (Winston Churchill, Franklin Roosevelt, and Joseph Stalin) meet at Yalta as victorious great power allies to establish rules for all states to follow in the post–World War II global order, but that cooperation would soon be replaced by bitter competition.

Who's number one? Who's gaining on the leader? What does it mean for the future if the strongest is seriously challenged for the predominant position?

These are the kinds of questions sports fans often ask when the rankings of the top teams are adjusted after the preceding week's competition. World leaders also adopt what former U.S. Secretary of State Dean Rusk called a "football stadium approach to diplomacy." And many people throughout the world habitually make comparisons of countries, asking which states are the biggest, strongest, wealthiest, and most militarily powerful and evaluating which states are rising and which are falling relative to one another.

When making such rankings, both groups are looking at world politics through the lens of realism. They see a globe of competitors, with winners and losers in an ancient contest for supremacy. And they look most closely at the shifting rankings at the very top of the international hierarchy of power—at the rivalry and struggle among the "great powers." Moreover, they picture this conflict as perpetual. As Arnold J. Toynbee's (1954) famous cyclical theory of history explains: "The most emphatic punctuation in a uniform series of events recurring in one repetitive cycle after another is the outbreak of a great war in which one power that has forged ahead of all its rivals makes so formidable a bid for world domination that it evokes an opposing coalition of all the other powers."

Toynbee's conclusion lies at the center of realism. The starting point for understanding world politics, elaborates Hans J. Morgenthau (1985), a leading post–World War II realist theorist, is to recognize that "all history shows that nations active in international politics are continuously preparing for, actively involved in, or recovering from organized violence in the form of war." Cycles of war and peace colored twentieth-century world politics, with three global wars breaking out. World Wars I and II were fought with fire and blood; the Cold War was fought without the same magnitude of destruction but with equal intensity. Each of these wars triggered major transformations in world politics.

This chapter explores the causes and consequences of great power rivalries. By understanding the origins and impact of these three struggles over world leadership, you will be better positioned to anticipate whether the great powers will be able to avoid yet another global war in the twenty-first century.

The price of greatness is responsibility.

—Winston Churchill, British prime minister

THE QUEST FOR WORLD LEADERSHIP

Rivalry between great powers has long characterized world politics, and there is a strong probability that this historical pattern is cyclical and unfolds through a series of distinct phases. According to *long-cycle theory*, over the past five centuries, periods of global war have been followed by periods of international rule-making and institution building. Shifts in the cycle have occurred alongside changes in the major states' relative power, changing their relations with one another (see Chase-Dunn and Anderson 2005). Each past global war led to the emergence of a *hegemon*. With its unrivaled power, the hegemon has reshaped the rules and institutions of the global system to preserve its preeminent position.

Hegemony always imposes an extraordinary burden on the world leader. A hegemon must bear the costs of maintaining political and economic order while protecting its position and upholding its dominion. Over time, as the weight of global engagement takes its toll, every previous hegemon has overextended itself. As challengers have arisen, the security agreements so carefully crafted after the last global war have come under attack. Historically, this struggle for power has set the stage for another global war, the demise of one hegemon and the ascent of another. Table 3.1 summarizes five hundred years of the cyclical rise and fall of great powers, their global wars, and their subsequent efforts to restore order.

Critics note that long-cycle theorists disagree on whether economic, military, or domestic factors produce these cycles. They also express frustration with the deterministic tone of the theory, which to them implies that global destiny is beyond policy makers' control. Must great powers rise and fall as if by the law of gravity—what goes up must come down? Still, long-cycle theory suggests you should consider how shifts in the relative strength of great powers affect world politics. It rivets attention on hegemonic transitions, the rise and fall of leading states in the global system, and in so doing provokes questions about whether this long cycle can be broken in your future. Long-cycle theory also forces you to evaluate *hegemonic stability theory* and that theory's predictions. Is the theory correct that a future stable world order will require a sustained global leader dominant enough to punish aggressors who challenge the global status quo in their pursuit of hegemony?

To underscore the importance of struggles over world leadership and their impact on trends and transformations in world politics, this chapter accordingly asks you to inspect the three great power wars of the twentieth century, as well as the lessons these clashes suggest for the twenty-first century.

long-cycle theory
a theory that focuses on the rise and fall of the leading global power as the central political process of the modern world system.

hegemon
a preponderant state capable of dominating the conduct of international political and economic relations.

hegemonic stability theory
a body of theory that maintains that the establishment of hegemony for global dominance by a single great power is a necessary condition for global order in commercial transactions and international military security.

Table 3.1   The Evolution of Great Power Rivalry for World Leadership, 1495–2025

Dates	Preponderant State(s) Seeking Hegemony	Other Powers Resisting Domination	Global War	New Order after Global War
1495–1540	Portugal	Spain, Valois, France, Burgundy, England	War of Italy and the Indian Ocean, 1494–1517	Treaty of Tordesillas, 1517
1560–1609	Spain	The Netherlands, France, England	Spanish-Dutch Wars, 1580–1608	Truce of 1608; Evangelical Union and the Catholic League formed
1610–1648	Holy Roman Empire (Hapsburg dynasty in Spain and Austria-Hungary)	Shifting ad hoc coalitions of mostly Protestant states (Sweden, Holland) and German principalities as well as Catholic France against remnants of papal rule	Thirty Years' War, 1618–1648	Peace of Westphalia, 1648
1650–1713	France (Louis XIV)	The United Provinces, England, the Hapsburg Empire, Spain, major German states, Russia	War of the Grand Alliance, 1688–1713	Treaty of Utrecht, 1713
1792–1815	France (Napoleon)	Great Britain, Prussia, Austria, Russia	Napoleonic Wars, 1792–1815	Congress of Vienna and Concert of Europe, 1815
1871–1914	Germany, Turkey, Austria-Hungary	Great Britain, France, Russia, United States	World War I, 1914–1918	Treaty of Versailles creating the League of Nations, 1919
1933–1945	Germany, Japan, Italy	Great Britain, France, Soviet Union, United States	World War II, 1939–1945	Bretton Woods, 1944; United Nations, Potsdam, 1945
1945–1991	United States, Soviet Union	Great Britain, France, China, Japan	Cold War, 1945–1991	NATO/Partnerships for Peace, 1995; World Trade Organization, 1995
1991–2025?	United States	China, European Union, Japan, Russia, India	A cold peace or hegemonic war, 2010–2025?	A new security regime to preserve world order?

THE FIRST WORLD WAR

World War I rumbled onto the global stage when a Serbian nationalist seeking to free his ethnic group from Austrian rule assassinated Archduke Ferdinand, heir to the Hapsburg throne of the Austrian-Hungarian Empire, at Sarajevo in June 1914. This assassination sparked a series of great power actions and reactions in the five weeks that followed, shattering world peace.

By the time the first major European war in the previous century had ended, nearly ten million people had died, three empires had crumbled, new states

Karim Kadim/AP Photo

MIGHT MAKES FRIGHT Shown here is one example of resistance to U.S. global preeminence: In September 2008, protesters in Sadr City in Baghdad held "Go Out USA" signs. Home to two million Shia and the anti-American cleric Muqtada al-Sadr, Sadr City had been one of the most dangerous areas of Iraq and was the site of intense fighting between the United States and insurgents earlier in the year. Following American construction of a wall across the district, a tenuous calm emerged that was nonetheless regularly interrupted by protests and bombings.

had been born, seven decades of communist rule in Russia had begun, and the world geopolitical map had been redrawn in ways that paved the way for the rise of Adolf Hitler in Nazi Germany.

The Causes of World War I

How can such a catastrophic war be explained? Multiple answers are possible. Most popular are structural neorealist explanations, which hold that World War I was inadvertent, not the result of anyone's master plan. Neorealists believe that it was a war bred by circumstances beyond the control of those involved, one that people neither wanted nor expected. Revisionist historians, however, have argued that the war was the result of deliberate choices—"a tragic and unnecessary conflict . . . because the train of events that led to its outbreak might have been broken at any point during the five weeks of crisis that preceded the first clash of arms, had prudence or common goodwill found a voice" (Keegan 1999, p. 3).

structuralism the neorealist proposition that states' behavior is shaped primarily by changes in the properties of the global system, such as shifts in the balance of power, instead of by individual heads of states or by changes in states' internal characteristics.

Structuralism　Framed at the *global level of analysis*, *structuralism* postulates that the changing distribution of power within the anarchical global system is the primary factor determining states' behavior. Looking at the circumstances on the eve of World War I, many historians hypothesize that the way in which the great powers were aligned against one another created an environment conducive to an armed conflict. The great powers' prior rearmament efforts, as well as their alliances and counteralliances, created a momentum that, along with the pressures created by the mobilization of armies and arms races, dragged European statesmen toward war (Tuchman 1962).

This structural explanation concentrates attention on the nineteenth century, when Britain dominated world politics. Britain was an island country isolated from continental affairs by temperament, tradition, and geography. Britain's sea power gave it command of the world's shipping lanes and control over a vast empire stretching from the Mediterranean to Southeast Asia. This dominance helped to deter aggression. However, Germany would mount a challenge to British power.

After becoming a unified country in 1871, Germany prospered and used its growing wealth to create a formidable army and navy. With this strength came ambition and resentment of British preeminence. As the predominant military and industrial power on the European continent, Germany sought to compete for international position and status. As Kaiser Wilhelm II proclaimed in 1898, Germany had "great tasks outside the narrow boundaries of old Europe." With Germany ascendant, Germany's rising power and global aspirations altered the European geopolitical landscape.

Germany was not the only newly emergent power at the turn of the century, however. Russia was also expanding and becoming a threat to Germany. The decline in power of the Austrian-Hungarian Empire, Germany's only ally, heightened Germany's fear of Russia, which was reflected in Germany's strong reaction to the assassination of Archduke Ferdinand. Fearing that a long war might result in an unfavorable shift in the *balance of power*, Germany sought a short localized war with a more favorable outcome. Germany thus supported Austria-Hungary's unrestrained assault on Serbia.

While the logic behind Germany's calculation was clear—a victorious war would bolster Austria-Hungary and hamper Russian influence—it turned out to be a serious miscalculation. France and Russia joined forces to defend Serbia, and were soon joined by Britain in an effort to oppose Germany and defend Belgian neutrality. In April 1917, the war became truly global in scope when the United States, reacting to German submarine warfare, entered the conflict.

Here we observe, again at the global level of analysis, the dynamics of shifts in the *balance of power* as a causal factor: the historic tendency for opposed conditions to form so that the distribution of military power is "balanced" to prevent any single power or bloc from seriously threatening others. And that is what *did* happen in the decade prior to Archduke Ferdinand's assassination. European military alignments had become polarized, pitting the Triple Alliance of Germany, Austria-Hungary, and the Ottoman Empire against the Triple Entente of Britain, France, and Russia. According to this structural interpretation, after Russia mobilized its armies in response to Austria's attack on Serbia, cross-cutting alliance commitments pulled one European great power after another into the war.

Nationalism   As an alternative interpretation of the origins of World War I at the *state level of analysis*, many historians view the growth of *nationalism*, especially in southeastern Europe, as having created a climate of opinion that made war likely. Groups that glorified the distinctiveness of their national heritage began championing their own country above all others (Woodwell 2008). Long-suppressed ethnic prejudices soon emerged, even among leaders. Russian foreign minister Sergei Sazonov, for example, claimed to "despise" Austria, and Kaiser Wilhelm II of Germany proclaimed "I hate the Slavs" (Tuchman 1962).

nationalism a mind-set glorifying a particular state and the nationality group living in it, which sees the state's interest as a supreme value.

Domestic unrest inflamed these passions, making it hard to see things from another point of view. Believing that they were upholding their national honor, the Austrians could not comprehend why Russians labeled them the aggressors. German insensitivity to others' feelings prevented them from understanding "the strength of the Russians' pride, their fear of humiliation if they allowed the Germans and Austrians to destroy their little protégé, Serbia, and the intensity of Russian anger." (White 1990). With each side belittling the national character and ethnic attributes of the other, diplomatic alternatives to war evaporated.

Rational Choice   At the *individual level of analysis*, *rational choice theory* offers a third interpretation of the causes of World War I. From this perspective—which emphasizes that leaders make decisions based upon careful evaluation of the relative usefulness of alternative options for realizing the best interests of themselves and their states (see Chapter 6)—the war's outbreak was a result of German elites' preference for a war with France and Russia in order to consolidate Germany's position on the continent, confirm its status as a world power, and divert domestic attention from its internal troubles (Kaiser 1990). The people gathered at the Imperial Palace in Berlin are seen as having pushed Europe over the brink.

The rational choice model of decision making suggests that World War I is best seen as a consequence of the purposive goal of rival great powers to compete against one another for global power. This is a drive that realists believe is an "iron law of history." It resulted from "an attempt by Germany to secure its position before an increasingly powerful Russia had achieved a position of equality with Germany (which the latter expected to happen by 1917)" (Levy 1998b).

As these rival interpretations suggest, the causes of World War I remain in dispute. Structural explanations emphasize the global distribution of power, domestic interpretations look at causal factors *within* states, and rational choice explanations direct attention to the calculations and goals of particular leaders. All partially help us to understand the sequences that produced the world's first truly global war.

The Consequences of World War I

World War I destroyed both life and property and changed the face of Europe (see Map 3.1). In its wake, three multi-ethnic empires—the Austrian-Hungarian, Russian, and Ottoman (Turkish)—collapsed, and in their place the independent states of Poland, Czechoslovakia, and Yugoslavia emerged. In addition, the countries of Finland, Estonia, Latvia, and Lithuania were born. The war also contributed to the independence of the Republic of Ireland from Britain in 1920 and the overthrow of the Russian czar in 1917 by the Bolsheviks. The emergence of communism under the leadership of Vladimir Lenin produced a change in government and ideology that would have geopolitical consequences for another seventy years.

Despite its costs, the coalition consisting of Britain, France, Russia, and (later) the United States and Italy defeated the threat of domination posed by the Central powers (Germany, Austria-Hungary, Turkey, and their allies). Moreover, the war set the stage for a determined effort to build a new global system that could prevent another war.

> For most Europeans, the Great War had been a source of disillusionment. When it was all over, few remained to be convinced that such a war must never happen again. Among vast populations there was a strong conviction that this time the parties had to plan a peace that could not just terminate a war, but a peace that could change attitudes and build a new type of international order. . . .
>
> For the first time in history, broad publics and the peacemakers shared a conviction that war was a central problem in international relations. Previously, hegemony, the aggressive activities of a particular state, or revolution had been the problem. In 1648, 1713, and 1815, the peacemakers had tried to resolve issues of the past and to construct orders that would preclude their reappearance. But in 1919 expectations ran higher. The sources of war were less important than the war itself. There was a necessity to look more to the future than to the past. The problem was not just to build a peace, but to construct a peaceful international order that would successfully manage all international conflicts of the future (K. Holsti 1991, pp. 175–176, 208–209).

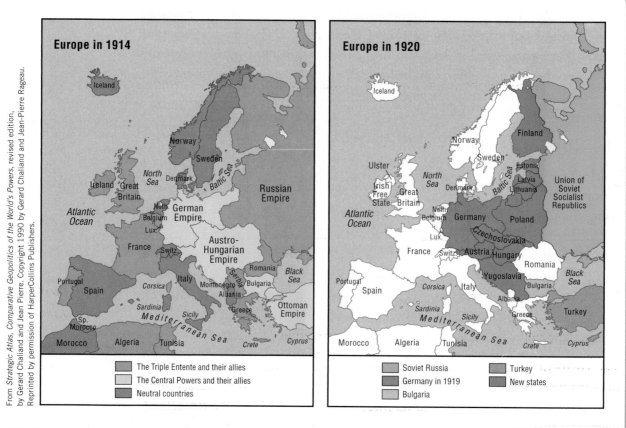

From *Strategic Atlas, Comparative Geopolitics of the World's Powers*, revised edition, by Gerard Chaliand and Jean Pierre. Copyright 1990 by Gerard Chaliand and Jean-Pierre Rageau. Reprinted by permission of HarperCollins Publishers.

MAP 3.1

TERRITORIAL CHANGES IN EUROPE FOLLOWING WORLD WAR I | The map on the left shows state boundaries on the eve of war in 1914, as well as the members of the two major opposing coalitions that formed. The map on the right shows the new borders in 1920, with the nine new states that emerged from the war.

World War I evoked revulsion for war and theories of *realism* that justified great power competition, armaments, secret alliances, and *balance-of-power* politics. The staggering human and material costs of the previous four years led many of the delegates to the 1919 peace conference convened at Versailles, outside Paris, to reevaluate their convictions about statecraft. The time was ripe for a new approach to building world order. Disillusioned with realism, many turned to *liberalism* for guidance on how to manage the global future.

The decade following World War I was the high point of liberal idealism. Woodrow Wilson's ideas about world order, as expressed in his January 1917 "Fourteen Points" speech, were anchored in a belief that by reordering the global system according to liberal principles, the "Great War" (as World War I was then called) would be "the war to end all wars." Wilson's chief proposal was to construct a League of Nations that allegedly would guarantee the independence and territorial integrity of all states. His other recommendations included strengthening international law, settling territorial claims on the basis of self-determination, and promoting democracy, disarmament, and free trade.

However, once the peace conference began, the knives of parochial national interest began whittling away at the liberal philosophy underpinning Wilson's proposals. Many European leaders had been offended by the pontificating American president. "God was content with Ten Commandments," growled Georges Clemenceau, the cynical realist French prime minister. "Wilson must have fourteen."

As negotiations at the conference proceeded, hard-boiled power politics prevailed. Ultimately, the delegates were only willing to support those elements in the Fourteen Points that served their national interests. After considerable wrangling, Wilson's League of Nations was written into the peace treaty with Germany as the first of 440 articles. The rest of the treaty was punitive, aimed at stripping the country of its great power status. Similar treaties were later forced on Austria-Hungary and Germany's other wartime allies.

Case Study:
Liberal Idealism

The Treaty of Versailles grew out of a desire for retribution. In brief, Germany's military was drastically cut; it was forbidden to possess heavy artillery, military aircraft, or submarines, and its forces were banned from the Rhineland. Germany also lost territory in the west to France and Belgium, in the south to the new state of Czechoslovakia, and in the east to the new states of Poland and Lithuania. Overseas, Germany lost all its colonies. Finally, in the most humiliating clause of the treaty, Germany was assigned responsibility for the war and charged with paying heavy financial reparations for the damages. On learning of the treaty's harsh provisions, the exiled German Kaiser is said to have declared that "the war to end wars has resulted in a peace to end peace."

THE SECOND WORLD WAR

Germany's defeat in World War I and its humiliation under the Treaty of Versailles did not extinguish its hegemonic aspirations. On the contrary, they intensified them. Thus conditions were ripe for the second great power war of the twentieth century, which pitted the Axis trio of Germany, Japan, and Italy against an unlikely "grand alliance" of four great powers who united despite their incompatible ideologies—communism in the case of the Soviet Union and democratic capitalism in the case of Britain, France, and the United States.

The world's fate hinged on the outcome of this massive effort to defeat the Axis threat. The Allied powers achieved success, but at a terrible cost: twenty-three thousand lives were lost each day, and at least fifty-three million people died during six years of fighting. To understand the origins of this devastating conflict, we will once again examine causal factors operating at different *levels of analysis.*

The Causes of World War II

Following Germany's capitulation in 1918, a democratic constitution was drafted by a constituent assembly meeting in the city of Weimar. Many Germans had little enthusiasm for the Weimar Republic. Not only was the new government linked in their minds to the humiliating Versailles Treaty, but it also suffered from the 1923 French occupation of the industrial Ruhr district, various political rebellions, and the ruinous economic collapse of 1929. By the parliamentary elections of 1932, over half of the electorate supported extremist parties that disdained democratic governance. The largest of these was the Nazi, or National Socialist German Workers, party. This was to be the start of a tragic path.

Proximate Causes on the Road to War   On January 30, 1933, the Nazi leader, Adolf Hitler, was appointed chancellor of Germany. Less than a month later, the Reichstag (Parliament) building burned down under mysterious circumstances. Hitler used the fire to justify an emergency edict allowing him to suspend civil liberties and move against communists and other political adversaries. Once all meaningful parliamentary opposition had been eliminated, Nazi legislators passed an enabling act that suspended the constitution and granted Hitler dictatorial power.

In his 1924 book *Mein Kampf* ("My Struggle"), Hitler urged Germany to recover territories taken by the Treaty of Versailles, absorb Germans living in neighboring lands, and colonize Eastern Europe. During his first year in power, however, he cultivated a pacifist image, signing a nonaggression pact with Poland in 1934. The following year, the goals originally outlined in *Mein Kampf* climbed to the top of Hitler's foreign policy agenda as he ignored the *Kellogg-Briand Pact* (prohibiting the use of force). In 1935, he repudiated the military clauses of the Versailles Treaty; in 1936, he ordered troops into the demilitarized Rhineland; in March 1938, he annexed Austria; and in September 1938, he demanded control over the Sudetenland, a region of Czechoslovakia containing ethnic Germans. To address the Sudeten German question, a conference was convened in Munich, attended by Hitler, British prime minister Neville Chamberlain, and leaders of France and Italy (ironically, Czechoslovakia was not invited). Convinced that *appeasement* would halt further German expansionism, Chamberlain and the others agreed to Hitler's demands.

appeasement
a strategy of making concessions to another state in the hope that, satisfied, it will not make additional claims.

Rather than satisfying Germany, appeasement whetted its appetite and that of the newly formed fascist coalition of Germany, Italy, and Japan, which aimed to overthrow the international status quo. Japan, disillusioned with Western liberalism and the Paris settlements, and suffering economically from the effects of the Great Depression of the 1930s, embraced militarism. In the might-makes-right climate that Germany's imperialistic quest for national aggrandizement helped to create, Japanese nationalists led their country on the path to imperialism and *colonialism.* Japan's invasions of Manchuria in 1931 and China proper in 1937 were followed by Italy's absorption of Abyssinia in 1935 and Albania in 1939, and both Germany and Italy intervened in the 1936–1939 Spanish civil war on the side of the fascists, headed by General Francisco Franco, whereas the Soviet Union supported antifascist forces.

colonialism
the rule of a region by an external sovereign power.

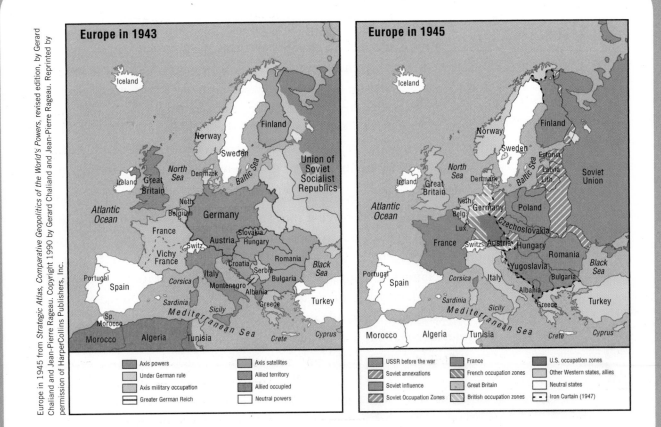

Europe in 1945 from *Strategic Atlas, Comparative Geopolitics of the World's Powers,* revised edition, by Gerard Chaliand and Jean-Pierre Rageau. Copyright 1990 by Gerard Chaliand and Jean-Pierre Rageau. Reprinted by permission of HarperCollins Publishers, Inc.

MAP 3.2

WORLD WAR II REDRAWS THE MAP OF EUROPE The map on the left shows the height of German expansion in 1943, when it occupied Europe from the Atlantic Ocean and the Baltic Sea to the gates of Moscow in the Soviet Union. The map on the right shows the new configuration of Europe after the "Grand Coalition" of Allied forces—Great Britain, the United States, and the Soviet Union—defeated the Axis's bid for supremacy.

After Germany occupied the rest of Czechoslovakia in March 1939, Britain and France formed an alliance to protect the next likely victim, Poland. They also opened negotiations with Moscow in hopes of enticing the Soviet Union to join the alliance, but the negotiations failed. Then, on August 23, 1939, Hitler, a fascist, and the Soviet dictator, Joseph Stalin, a communist, stunned the world with the news that they had signed a nonaggression pact, promising not to attack one another. Now confident that Britain and France would not intervene, Hitler invaded Poland. However, Britain and France honored their pledge to defend Poland, and two days later declared war on Germany. World War II began.

The war expanded rapidly. Hitler next turned his forces to the Balkans, North Africa, and westward, as the mechanized German troops invaded Norway and marched through Denmark, Belgium, Luxembourg, and the Netherlands. The German army swept around the Maginot line, the defensive barrier on the eastern frontier that France boasted could not be breached. Within six weeks France surrendered, even though Germany's forces were measurably inferior to those of France and its allies. The alarming and nearly bloodless German victory forced the British to evacuate a nearly 340,000-strong expeditionary force from the French beaches at Dunkirk. Paris itself fell in June 1940. Meanwhile, to deter the United States from participating in the looming war, in September 1940 Japan forged the Tripartite Pact with Germany and Italy that pledged the three Axis powers to come to one another's aid if attacked by another nonbelligerent great power, such as the United States.

In the months that followed, the German air force, the Luftwaffe, pounded Britain in an attempt to force it into submission as well. Instead of invading Britain, however, the Nazi troops launched a surprise attack on the Soviet Union, Hitler's former ally, in June 1941. On December 7th of that same year, Japan launched a surprise assault on the United States at Pearl Harbor. Almost immediately, Germany also declared war on the United States. The unprovoked Japanese assault and the German challenge ended U.S. aloofness and *isolationism*, enabling President Franklin Roosevelt to forge a coalition with Britain and the Soviet Union to oppose the fascists.

isolationism
a policy of withdrawing from active participation with other actors in world affairs and instead concentrating state efforts on managing internal affairs.

multipolarity
the distribution of global power into three or more great power centers, with most other states allied with one of the rivals.

Underlying Causes at Three Analytic Levels   At the global level of analysis, many historians regard the reemergence of *multipolarity* in the global power distribution as a key factor in the onset and expansion of World War II. The post–World War I global system was precarious because the number of sovereign states increased at the same time the number of great powers declined. In 1914, Europe had only twenty-two key states, but by 1921 the number had nearly doubled. When combined with resentment over the Versailles treaty, the Russian Revolution, and the rise of fascism, the increased number of states and the resurgence of nationalistic revolts and crises made "the inter-war years the most violent period in international relations since the Thirty Years' War and the wars of the French Revolution and Napoleon" (K. Holsti 1991, p. 216).

The 1930s collapse of the global economic system also contributed to the war. Great Britain found itself unequal to the leadership and regulatory roles it had performed in the world *political economy* before World War I. Although the United States was the logical successor, its refusal to exercise leadership hastened the war. The 1929–1931 Depression was followed in 1933 "by a world Monetary and Economic Conference whose failures—engineered by the United States—deepened the gloom, accelerated protectionist barriers to foreign trade such as tariffs and quotas, and spawned revolution" (Calvocoressi, Wint, and Pritchard 1989, p. 6). In this depressed global environment, heightened by deteriorating economic circumstances at home, Germany and Japan sought solutions through *imperialism* abroad.

At the state level of analysis, collective psychological forces also led to World War II. These included "the domination of civilian discourse by military propaganda that primed the world for war," the "great wave of hypernationalism [that] swept over Europe [as] each state taught itself a mythical history while denigrating that of others," and the demise of democratic governance (Van Evera 1990–1991, pp. 18, 23).

For example, domestically, German nationalism inflamed latent *irredentism* and rationalized the expansion of German borders both to regain provinces previously lost in wars to others and to absorb Germans living in Austria, Czechoslovakia, and Poland. The rise of *fascism*—the Nazi regime's *ideology* championing anti-Semitic racism against the Jews, flag, fatherland, nationalism, and imperialism—animated this renewed imperialistic push and preached the most extreme version of realism, *matchpolitik* (power politics), to justify the forceful expansion of the German state and other Axis powers that were aligned with Germany. "Everything for the state, nothing outside the state, nothing above the state" was the way Italy's dictator, Benito Mussolini, constructed his understanding of the fascist political philosophy, in a definition that embraced the extreme realist proposition that the state was entitled to rule every dimension of human life by force.

The importance of leaders at the individual level of analysis stands out. The war would not have been possible without Adolf Hitler and his plans to conquer the world by force. World War II arose primarily from German aggression. Professing the superiority of Germans as a "master race" along with

political economy
a field of study that focuses on the intersection of politics and economics in international relations.

irredentism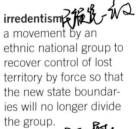
a movement by an ethnic national group to recover control of lost territory by force so that the new state boundaries will no longer divide the group.

fascism
a far-right ideology that promotes extreme nationalism and the establishment of an authoritarian society built around a single party with dictatorial leadership.

ideology
a set of core philosophical principles that leaders and citizens collectively construct about politics, the interests of political actors, and the ways people ought to behave.

matchpolitik
the German realist philosophy in statecraft that sees the expansion of state power and territory by use of armed force as a legitimate goal.

Art Media/PhotoLibrary

THE RISE OF HITLER AND GERMAN NATIONALISM Consistent with the realist view that states have an inherent right to expand, Adolf Hitler persuaded the German people of the need to persecute the Jews and expand German borders through armament and aggression. He constructed and cultivated a wide spread perception in Germany that, in his words, "an evil exists that threatens every man, woman and child of this great nation. We must take steps to ensure our domestic security and protect our homeland." Pictured here on April 20, 1941, Hitler (far right) confers with senior Nazis leaders.

virulent anti-Semitism and anticommunism, Hitler chose to wage war to create an empire that he believed could resolve once and for all the historic competition and precarious coexistence of the great powers in Europe by eliminating Germany's rivals.

The broad vision of the Thousand-Year Reich was . . . of a vastly expanded—and continually expanding—German core, extending deep into Russia, with a number of vassal states and regions, including France, the Low Countries, Scandinavia, central Europe, and the Balkans, that would provide resources and labor for the core. There was to be no civilizing mission in German imperialism. On the contrary, the lesser peoples were to be taught only to do menial labor or, as Hitler once joked, educated sufficiently to read the road signs so they wouldn't get run over by German automobile traffic. The lowest of the low, the Poles and Jews, were to be exterminated. . . . To Hitler . . . the purpose of policy was to destroy the system and to reconstitute it on racial lines, with a vastly expanded Germany running a distinctly hierarchical and exploitative order. Vestiges of sovereignty might remain, but they would be fig leaves covering a monolithic order. German occupation policies during the war, whereby conquered nations were reduced to satellites, satrapies, and reservoirs of slave labor, were the practical application of Hitler's conception of the new world order. They were not improvised or planned for reasons of military necessity (Holsti 1991, pp. 224–225).

The Consequences of World War II

Having faced ruinous losses in Russia and a massive Allied bombing campaign at home, Germany's Thousand-Year Reich lay in ruins by May 1945. By August, the U.S. atomic bombing of Hiroshima and Nagasaki forced

Japan to end its war of conquest as well as well as brace itself, after its shattering defeat followed by six years of U.S. military occupation, to meet the challenge of socially constructing acceptance of new values.

The Allied victory over the Axis redistributed power and reordered borders, resulting in a new geopolitical terrain. The Soviet Union absorbed nearly 600,000 square kilometers of territory from the Baltic states of Estonia, Latvia, and Lithuania, and from Finland, Czechoslovakia, Poland, and Romania—recovering what Russia had lost in the 1918 Treaty of Brest-Litovsk after World War I. Poland, a victim of Soviet expansionism, was compensated with land taken from Germany. Germany itself was divided into occupation zones that eventually provided the basis for its partition into East and West Germany. Finally, pro-Soviet regimes assumed power throughout Eastern Europe (see Map 3.2). In the Far East, the Soviet Union took from Japan the four Kurile Islands—or the "Northern Territories," as Japan calls them—and Korea was divided into Soviet and U.S. occupation zones at the Thirty-Eighth Parallel.

With the defeat of the Axis, one global system ended, but the defining characteristics of the new system had not yet become clear. Although the United Nations was created to replace the old, discredited League of Nations, the management of world affairs still rested in the hands of the victors. Yet victory only magnified their distrust of one another.

The "Big Three" leaders—Winston Churchill, Franklin Roosevelt, and Joseph Stalin—met at the *Yalta Conference* in February 1945 to design a new world order. But the vague compromises they reached concealed the differences percolating below the surface. Following Germany's unconditional surrender in May, the Big Three (with the United States now represented by Harry Truman) met again in July 1945 at Potsdam. The meeting ended without agreement, and the facade of Allied unity began to disintegrate.

Yalta Conference the 1945 summit meeting of the Allied victors to resolve postwar territorial issues and voting procedures in the United Nations to collectively manage world order.

In the aftermath of the war, the United States and the Soviet Union were the only two great powers that were still strong and had the capacity to impose their will. The other major-power victors, especially Great Britain, had exhausted themselves and slipped from the apex of the world-power hierarchy. The vanquished, Germany and Japan, also fell from the ranks of the great powers. Thus, as Alexis de Tocqueville had foreseen in 1835, the Americans and Russians now held in their hands the destinies of half of humankind. In comparison, all other states were dwarfs.

In this atmosphere, ideological debate arose about whether the twentieth century would become "the American century" or "the Russian century." Thus, perhaps the most important product of World War II was the *transformation*

bipolarity
a condition in which power is concentrated in two competing centers so that the rest of the states define their allegiances in terms of their relationships with both rival great power superstates, or "poles."

it caused, after a short interlude, in the distribution of global power from *multipolarity* to *bipolarity*. In what in 1949 became known as the Cold War, Washington and Moscow used the fledgling United Nations not to keep the peace but to pursue their competition with each other. As the third and last hegemonic struggle of the twentieth century, the Cold War and its lessons still cast shadows over today's geostrategic landscape.

> *The United States should take the lead in running the world in the way that the world ought to be run.*
>
> —Harry S Truman, U.S. President

THE COLD WAR

The second great war of the twentieth century, without parallel in the number of participants and destruction, brought about a global system dominated by two superstates whose nuclear weapons radically changed the role that threats of warfare would play in world politics. Out of these circumstances grew the competition between the United States and the Soviet Union for hegemonic leadership.

The Causes and Evolutionary Course of the Cold War

Cold War
the forty-two-year (1949–1991) rivalry between the United States and the Soviet Union, as well as their competing coalitions, which sought to contain each other's expansion and win worldwide predominance.

power transition
a narrowing of the ratio of military capabilities between great power rivals that is thought to increase the probability of war between them.

sphere of influence
a region of the globe dominated by a great power.

The origins of the twentieth century's third hegemonic battle for domination are debated because the historical evidence lends itself to different interpretations (see Leffler and Westad 2009). Several postulated causes stand out. At the global level of analysis, the first is advanced by realism: the *Cold War* resulted from the *power transition* that propelled the United States and the Soviet Union to the top of the international hierarchy and made their rivalry inescapable. "As both sides searched beyond their core alliances for strategic advantage, the Cold War began to affect the trajectories of states and political movements across the globe" (Freedman 2010. p.137). Circumstances gave each superpower reasons to fear and to struggle against the other's potential global leadership and encouraged each superpower competitor to carve out and establish dominant influence in its own *sphere of influence*, or specified area of the globe.

A second interpretation, at the state level of analysis, holds that the Cold War was simply an extension of the superpowers' mutual disdain for each other's professed beliefs about politics and economics. U.S. animosity toward the Soviet Union was stimulated by the 1917 Bolshevik Revolution, which brought to power a government that embraced the radical Marxist critique of capitalistic imperialism (see Chapter 2). American fears of Marxism stimulated the emergence of anticommunism as an opposing ideology. Accordingly, the United States embarked on a missionary crusade of its own to contain and ultimately remove the atheistic communist menace from the face of the Earth.

Similarly, Soviet policy was fueled by the belief that capitalism could not coexist with communism. The purpose of Soviet policy, therefore, was to push the pace of the historical process in which communism eventually would prevail. However, Soviet planners did not believe that this historical outcome was guaranteed. They felt that the capitalist states, led by the United States, sought to encircle the Soviet Union and smother communism in its cradle, and that resistance by the Soviets was obligatory. As a result, ideological incompatibility may have ruled out compromise as an option (see Controversy: Was Ideology the Primary Source of East–West Conflict?).

A third explanation, rooted in decision making at the individual level of analysis, sees the Cold War as being fueled by the superpowers' misperceptions of each other's motives. From this constructivist perspective, conflicting interests were secondary to misunderstandings and ideologies. Mistrustful actors are prone to see only virtue in their own actions and only malice in those of their adversaries. This tendency to see one's opponent as the complete opposite, or *mirror image*, of oneself makes hostility virtually inevitable. Moreover, when perceptions of an adversary's evil intentions are socially constructed and become accepted as truth, a self-fulfilling prophecy can develop and the future can be affected by the way it is anticipated. Thus, viewing each other suspiciously, each rival giant acted in hostile ways that encouraged the very behavior that was suspected.

Additional factors, beyond those rooted in divergent interests, ideologies, and images, undoubtedly combined to produce this explosive Soviet–American hegemonic rivalry. To sort out the relative causal influence of the various factors, evaluate how, once it erupted after the 1945–1948 gestation period, the Cold War changed over its forty-four-year duration. The character of

Bettmann/CORBIS

LOST OPPORTUNITIES? The U.S. thermonuclear standoff that became the Cold War might not have occurred had the two rivals made other choices: "The Cold War was not predetermined," argues Melvyn Leffler (2007). "These leaders made choices." Shown here are Harry Truman (left) and Joseph Stalin (right).

CONTROVERSY:

WAS IDEOLOGY THE PRIMARY SOURCE OF EAST—WEST CONFLICT?

Cold War America was gripped by a "great fear" not simply of the Soviet Union but of communism. Senator Joseph McCarthy led the most infamous hunt for communist sympathizers in government, Hollywood production companies blacklisted supposed communist sympathizers, and average American citizens were often required to take loyalty oaths at their offices. Everywhere, communism became synonymous with treasonous, un-American activity. As the nuclear arms race escalated and the U.S. government took military action to contain the Soviet Union, its justification was almost always expressed in terms of ideology. The threat, as the population learned to perceive it, was that of an atheistic, communistic system that challenged the fundamental American principles of democratic capitalism. Also, according to the **domino theory**, which states that communism was driven to knock over one country after another, Soviet communism was inherently expansionistic. The other side also couched its Cold War rhetoric in terms of ideology, objecting to the imperialistic, capitalist system that the Soviets said America planned to impose on the whole world.

Some would argue that fear of the other side's world dominance may have been more important in the Cold War than pure ideology. Both the American and the Soviet governments may have entered the Cold War to secure their relative power in the world order as much as to protect pure principles. After all, the United States and the Soviet Union had managed to transcend differing ideologies when they acted as allies in World War II. After World War II, however, a power vacuum created by the demise of Europe's traditional great powers drew them into conflict with each other, and as they competed, ideological justifications surfaced.

Liberalism, communism, socialism, and capitalism are examples of ideologies of international politics. Ideologies help us to interpret life and its meaning and are for that reason indispensable for organizing thought and values. As social constructivism suggests, ideology provides meaning within a social context and enables a society to use its domestic values and norms to frame its interests and convictions. But commitment to an ideology may at times cause hatred and hostility. Institutional proponents of particular ideologies are prone to perceive other ideologies competitively—as challenges to the truth of their own ideology's core beliefs. However, ideology can also become an excuse for armed violence. Communist theoretician Vladimir Lenin described the predicament that he perceived to underlie the Cold War—prophetically, it turned out—when he predicted: "As long as capitalism and socialism exist, we cannot live in peace; in the end, either one or the other will triumph—a funeral dirge will be sung either over the Soviet Republic or over world capitalism." Although scholars are still debating the causes of the Cold War, we need to ask whether it was, in fact, an ideological contest over ideas, or a more general contest for power.

WHAT DO YOU THINK?

- Was the Cold War really an ideological contest between international communism and the free-market capitalism espoused by the liberal democracies, or were there other, deeper conflicts of interest involved?

- Did the end of the Cold War signify the triumph of Western values over communist ones? What is the potential for ideological differences to reemerge and fuel conflict between the two countries?

- Can you think of other examples in more recent years where ideological differences have appeared to play a role in shaping conflict between countries?

the Cold War shifted in three phases over its long history (see Figure 3.1), and several distinct patterns emerged that not only provide insights into the impetus behind the Cold War but also illustrate the properties of other great power rivalries.

domino theory
a metaphor popular during the Cold War that predicted that if one state fell to communism, its neighbors would also fall in a chain reaction, like a row of falling dominoes.

Confrontation, 1947–1962 Though a brief period of wary Soviet–American cordiality prevailed in the immediate aftermath of World War II, this goodwill rapidly vanished as the two giants' vital interests collided. At this critical juncture, George F. Kennan, then a diplomat in the American embassy in Moscow, sent to Washington his famous "long telegram" assessing the sources of Soviet conduct. Published in 1947 by the influential journal *Foreign Affairs*, and signed as "X" to conceal his identity, Kennan argued that Soviet leaders would forever feel insecure about their political ability to maintain power against forces both within Soviet society and in the outside world. Their insecurity would lead to an activist—and perhaps aggressive—Soviet foreign policy. However, the United States had the power to increase the strains under which the Soviet leadership would have to operate, which could lead to a gradual mellowing or final end of Soviet power. Kennan concluded: "In these circumstances it is clear that the main element of any United States policy toward the Soviet Union must be that of a long-term, patient but firm and vigilant containment of Russian expansive tendencies" (Kennan 1947).

Soon thereafter, President Harry S Truman made Kennan's assessment the cornerstone of American postwar foreign policy. Provoked in part by violence in Turkey and Greece, which Truman and others believed to be communist inspired, Truman declared that he believed "it must be the policy of the United States to support free peoples who are resisting attempted subjugation by armed minorities or by outside pressures." Eventually known as the *Truman Doctrine*, this statement defined the strategy that the United States would

Truman Doctrine
the declaration by President Harry S Truman that U.S. foreign policy would use intervention to support peoples who allied with the United States against communist external subjugation.

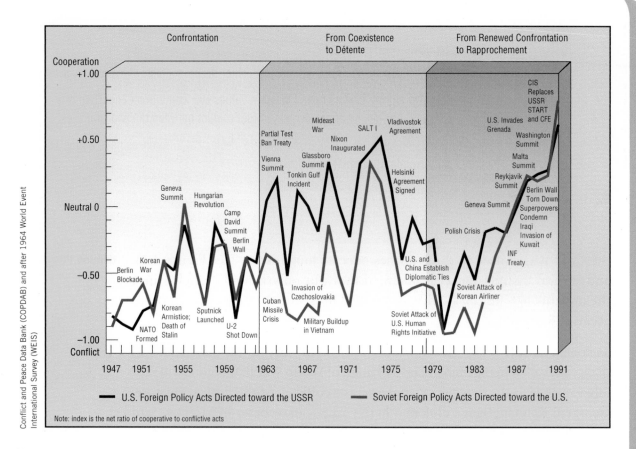

FIGURE 3.1

KEY EVENTS IN THE EVOLUTION OF THE U.S.–SOVIET RELATIONSHIP DURING THE COLD WAR, 1947–1991
The evolution of U.S.–Soviet relations during the Cold War displays a series of shifts between periods of conflict and cooperation. As this figure shows, each superpower's behavior toward the other tended to be reciprocal, and, for most periods before 1983, confrontation prevailed over cooperation.

containment
a strategy to prevent a great power rival from using force to alter the balance of power and increase its sphere of influence.

Case Study:
The Cold War

pursue for the next forty years, over Kennan's objections. This strategy, called *containment*, sought to prevent the expansion of Soviet influence by encircling the Soviet Union and intimidating it with the threat of a military attack.

A seemingly endless series of new Cold War crises soon followed. They included the communist coup d' état in Czechoslovakia in 1948; the Soviet blockade of West Berlin in June of that year; the communist acquisition of power on the Chinese mainland in 1949; the outbreak of the Korean War in 1950; the Chinese invasion of Tibet in 1950; and the on-again, off-again Taiwan Straits crises. The Soviets finally broke the U.S. atomic monopoly in 1949. Thereafter, the risks of massive destruction necessitated restraint and changed the terms of the great powers' rivalry.

Because the Soviet Union remained strategically inferior to the United States, Nikita Khrushchev (who succeeded Stalin upon his death in 1953) pursued a policy of *peaceful coexistence* with capitalism. Even so, the Soviet Union at times cautiously sought to increase its power in places where opportunities appeared to exist. As a result, the period following Stalin's death saw many Cold War confrontations, with Hungary, Cuba, Egypt, and Berlin becoming the flash points.

In 1962, the surreptitious placement of Soviet missiles in Cuba set the stage for the greatest test of the superpowers' capacity to manage their disputes—the Cuban Missile Crisis. The superpowers stood eyeball to eyeball. Fortunately, one (the Soviet Union) blinked, and the crisis ended. This painful learning experience both reduced enthusiasm for waging the Cold War by military means and expanded awareness of the suicidal consequences of a nuclear war.

From Coexistence to Détente, 1963–1978   The growing threat of mutual destruction, in conjunction with the approaching parity of American and Soviet military capabilities, made coexistence or nonexistence appear to be the only alternatives. At the American University commencement exercises in 1963, U.S. President John F. Kennedy warned that

> . . . should total war ever break out again—no matter how—our two countries would become the primary targets. It is an ironical but accurate fact that the two strongest powers are the two in the most danger of devastation. . . . We are both caught up in a vicious and dangerous cycle in which suspicion on one side breeds suspicion on the other and new weapons beget counter-weapons. In short, both the United States and its allies, and the Soviet Union and its allies, have a mutually deep interest in a just and genuine peace and in halting the arms race. . . .
>
> So let us not be blind to our differences, but let us also direct attention to our common interests and to the means by which those differences can be resolved. And if we cannot end now our differences, at least we can help make the world safe for diversity.

Kennedy signaled a shift in how the United States hoped thereafter to bargain with its adversary, and the Soviet Union reciprocally expressed its interest in more cooperative relations. That movement took another step forward following Richard Nixon's election in 1968. Coached by his national security adviser, Henry A. Kissinger, President Nixon initiated a new approach to Soviet relations that in 1969 he officially labeled *détente*. The Soviets also adopted this term to describe their policies toward the United States, and relations between the Soviets and Americans "normalized." Arms control stood at the center of the dialogue surrounding détente. The *Strategic Arms Limitation Talks (SALT)*, initiated in 1969, sought to restrain the threatening,

peaceful coexistence
Soviet leader Nikita Krushchev's 1956 doctrine that war between capitalist and communist states is not inevitable and that inter-bloc competition could be peaceful.

détente
in general, a strategy of seeking to relax tensions between adversaries to reduce the possibility of war.

Strategic Arms Limitation Talks (SALT)
two sets of agreements reached during the 1970s between the United States and the Soviet Union that established limits on strategic nuclear delivery systems.

expensive, and spiraling arms race by limiting the deployment of antiballistic missiles. As Figure 3.1 shows, cooperative interaction became more commonplace than hostile relations. Visits, cultural exchanges, trade agreements, and joint technological ventures replaced threats, warnings, and confrontations.

From Renewed Confrontation to Rapprochement, 1979–1991   Despite the careful nurturing of détente, its spirit did not endure. When the Soviet invasion of Afghanistan in 1979 led to détente's demise, President Jimmy Carter defined the situation as "the most serious strategic challenge since the Cold War began." In retaliation, he declared America's willingness to use military force to protect its access to oil supplies from the Persian Gulf, suspended U.S. grain exports to the Soviet Union, and attempted to organize a worldwide boycott of the 1980 Moscow Olympics.

Relations deteriorated dramatically thereafter. President Ronald Reagan and his Soviet counterparts (first Yuri Andropov and then Konstantin Chernenko) exchanged a barrage of confrontational rhetoric. Reagan asserted that the Soviet Union "underlies all the unrest that is going on" and described the Soviet Union as "the focus of evil in the modern world." The atmosphere was punctuated by Reagan policy adviser Richard Pipes's bold challenge in 1981 that the Soviets would have to choose between "peacefully changing their communist system . . . or going to war." Soviet rhetoric was equally unrestrained and alarmist.

As talk of war increased, preparations for it escalated. The arms race resumed feverishly, at the expense of addressing domestic economic problems. The superpowers also extended the confrontation to new territory, such as Central America, and renewed their public diplomacy (propaganda) efforts to extol the virtues of their respective systems throughout the world. Reagan pledged U.S. support for anticommunist insurgents who sought to overthrow Soviet-supported governments in Afghanistan, Angola, and Nicaragua. In addition, American leaders spoke loosely about the "winability" of a nuclear war through a "prevailing" military strategy that included the threat of a "first use" of nuclear weapons in the event of conventional war. Relations deteriorated as these moves and countermoves took their toll. The new Soviet leader, Mikhail Gorbachev, in 1985 summarized the alarming state of superpower relations by fretting that "The situation is very complex, very tense. I would even go so far as to say it is explosive."

rapprochement
in diplomacy, a policy seeking to reestablish normal cordial relations between enemies.

However, the situation did not explode. Instead, prospects for a more constructive phase improved greatly following Gorbachev's advocacy of "new thinking" in order to achieve a *rapprochement*, or reconciliation, of the rival

Biber/SIPA Press

EASING TENSIONS: U.S.–SOVIET DÉTENTE **Pictured here, President Richard Nixon, one of the architects of the U.S.** *"linkage" strategy* **along with Secretary of State Henry Kissinger, toasts Soviet Premier Leonid Brezhnev and fellow dignitaries at their meeting to discuss approaches to relaxing tensions between the superpowers.**

"linkage" strategy
a set of assertions claiming that leaders should take into account another country's overall behavior when deciding whether to reach agreement on any one specific issue so as to link cooperation to rewards.

states' interests. He sought to settle the Soviet Union's differences with the capitalist West in order to halt the deterioration of his country's economy and international position. Shortly thereafter, Gorbachev embarked on domestic reforms to promote democratization and the transition to a market economy, and proclaimed his desire to end the Cold War contest. "We realize that we are divided by profound historical, ideological, socioeconomic, and cultural differences," he noted during his first visit in 1987 to the United States. "But the wisdom of politics today lies in not using those differences as a pretext for confrontation, enmity, and the arms race." Soviet spokesperson Georgi Arbatov elaborated, informing the United States that "we are going to do a terrible thing to you—we are going to deprive you of an enemy."

Surprisingly, to many adherents of *realism* who see great power contests for supremacy as inevitable and strategic surrender or acceptance of defeat as impossibile, the Soviets did what they promised: they began to act like an ally instead of an enemy. The Soviet Union agreed to end its aid to and support for Cuba, withdrew from Afghanistan, and announced unilateral reductions in military spending. Gorbachev also agreed to two new disarmament agreements: the START (Strategic Arms Reduction Treaty) treaty for deep cuts in strategic arsenals and the Conventional Forces in Europe (CFE) treaty to reduce the Soviet presence in Europe.

In 1989, the Berlin Wall came down, and by 1991 the Cold War had truly ended when the Soviet Union dissolved, accepted capitalist free-market principles, and initiated democratic reforms. To nearly everyone's astonishment, the Soviet Union acquiesced in the defeat of communism, the reunification of Germany, and the disintegration of its east European bloc of allies, the Warsaw Pact (see Controversy: Why Did the Cold War End Peacefully?). The conclusion of the enduring rivalry between East and West, and with it the end of the seventy-year ideological dispute as well, was a history-transforming event. "Liberalism seemed to have triumphed—not merely capitalism but democracy and the rule of law, as represented in the West, and particularly in the United States" (Keohane and Nye 2001a).

The collapse of the Cold War suggested something quite different from the lesson of the twentieth century's two world wars, which had implied that great power rivalries are necessarily doomed to end in armed conflict. The Cold War was different; it came to an end peacefully, as a combination of factors contributed at various stages in the Cold War's evolution to transform a global rivalry into a stable, even cooperative, relationship. This suggests that it is sometimes possible for great power rivals to reconcile their competitive differences without warfare.

The Consequences of the Cold War

Although they were locked in a geostrategic rivalry made worse by antagonistic ideologies and mutual misperceptions, the United States and the Soviet Union avoided a fatal showdown. In accepting the devolution of their empire, Russian leaders made the most dramatic peaceful retreat from power in history. The end of the Cold War altered the face of world affairs in profound and diverse ways. With the dissolution of the Soviet Union in 1991, no immediate great power challenger confronted American hegemonic leadership. However, a host of new security threats emerged, ranging from aspiring nuclear powers such as North Korea and Iran to terrorist networks such as Al Qaeda. As the turbulent twentieth century wound down, the simple Cold War world of clearly defined adversaries gave way to a shadowy world of elusive foes.

THE POST–COLD WAR ERA

Rapid, unanticipated changes in world politics create uncertainty about the global future. To optimists, the swift transformations following the collapse of communism "ushered in a generation of relative political stability" (Zakaria

CONTROVERSY:

WHY DID THE COLD WAR END PEACEFULLY?

How history is remembered is important because those memories shape future decisions about the management of great power rivalries. Why did the Cold War end without the use of armed force? That question remains a puzzle that still provokes much controversy, in part because the Cold War's abrupt end came as such a surprise to most observers. Also, the unanticipated outcome undermined confidence in the adequacy of conventional realist theories—which argued that no great power would ever accept the loss of position to another hegemonic rival without a fight. In considering your view on this issue, consider the diversity of opinions, at three *levels of analysis,* reflective of realist, liberal, and constructivist theorizing:

Contending Interpretations of the Causes of the Cold War's End

Level of Analysis	Theoretical Perspective		
	Realism	Liberalism	Constructivism
Individual	Hardball Power Politics	Leaders as Movers of History	External Influences on Leadership
	"The people who argued for nuclear deterrence and serious military capabilities contributed mightily to the position of strength that eventually led the Soviet leadership to choose a less bellicose, less menacing approach to international politics."—Richard Perle, U.S. presidential adviser	"[The end of the Cold War was possible] primarily because of one man— Mikhail Gorbachev. The transformations . . . would not have begun were it not for him."—James A. Baker III, U.S. Secretary of State	"Reagan's 'tough' policy and intensified arms race [did not persuade] communists to 'give up.' [This is] sheer nonsense. Quite the contrary, this policy made the life for reformers, for all who yearned for democratic changes in their life, much more difficult. . . The [communist hard-line] conservatives and reactionaries were given predominant influence . . . . Reagan made it practically impossible to start reforms after Brezhev's death (Andropov had such plans) and made things more difficult for Gorbachev to cut military expenditures."—Georgi Arbatov, Director of the USSR's Institute for the USA and Canada Studies

(continued)

WHY DID THE COLD WAR END PEACEFULLY? (Continued)

State	Economic Mismanagement	Grassroots Movements	Ideas and Ideals
	"Soviet militarism, in harness with communism, destroyed the Soviet economy and thus hastened the self-destruction of the Soviet empire."—Fred Charles Iklé, U.S. Deputy Secretary of Defense	"It was man who ended the Cold War in case you didn't notice. It wasn't weaponry, or technology, or armies or campaigns. It was just man. Not even Western man either, as it happened, but our sworn enemy in the East, who went into the streets, faced the bullets and the batons and said: we've had enough."—John Le Carré, author	"The root of the conflict was a clash of social systems and of ideological preferences for ordering the world. Mutual security in those circumstances was largely unachieveable. A true end to the Cold War was impossible until fundamental changes occurred in Soviet foreign policy."—Robert Jervis, political scientist

Global	Containment	International Public Opinion	Cross-Border Contagion Effects
	"The strategy of containment that won the Cold War was the brainchild of realists . . . Containment focused first and foremost on preventing Moscow from seizing the key centers of industrial power that lay near its borders, while eschewing attempts to "roll back" Communism with military force."—Stephan Walt, political scientist	"The changes wrought by thousands of people serving in the trenches [throughout the world] were at least partially responsible [for ending the Cold War]."—David Cortright, political scientist	"The acute phase of the fall of communism started outside of the Soviet Union and spread to the Soviet Union itself. By 1987, Gorbachev made it clear that he would not interfere with internal experiments in Soviet bloc countries. . . . Once communism fell in Eastern Europe, the alternative in the Soviet Union became civil war or dissolution."—Daniel Klenbort, political journalist

Evaluate the validity of these contending hypotheses about the causes of the Cold War's peaceful end. They can't all be correct. So act like a detective looking for clues about causation. And keep in mind the epistemological warning about approaches to analysis voiced by the fictional master detective Sherlock Holmes: "It is a capital mistake to theorize before one has data. Insensibly one begins to twist facts to suit theories, instead of theories to suit facts" (Borer and Bowen 2007).

WHAT DO YOU THINK?

- What was the cause of the Cold War's collapse? Do explanations at one level of analysis better explain the end of the Cold War than others?

- Which theoretical perspective is best? Is a particular theory more useful than others depending upon on which level of analysis you focus?

- As constructivism warns, the lessons drawn from the Cold War drama remain important because they affect how leaders are likely to manage new great power rivalries throughout the twenty-first century. How has this been seen in the handling of conflicts since the end of the Cold War?

2009) and signaled "the universalization of Western liberal democracy as the final form of government" (Fukuyama 1989). To pessimists, these sea changes suggested not history's end but the resumption of contests for hegemonic domination and opposition over contested ideas and ideologies. Both groups recognized that, in the years immediately following the end of the Cold War, bipolarity was superseded by *unipolarity*—a hegemonic configuration of power with only one predominant superstate. As time passed, however, other great powers began to vie for increased influence and visibility in world politics, and there is ongoing debate as to whether *multipolarity* better describes the emerging distribution of power today. Of interest is what this might mean for relations among the great powers in meeting the new and difficult challenges in world politics in the post—Cold War era.

unipolarity
a condition in which the global system has a single dominant power or hegemon capable of prevailing over all other states.

America's Unipolar Moment

Unipolarity refers to the concentration of power in a single preponderant state. With the end of the Cold War, in a historical "moment" in world history (Krauthammer 2003), the United States stood alone at the summit of the international hierarchy. It remains the only country with the military, economic, and cultural assets to be a decisive player in any part of the world it chooses. Its military is not just stronger than anybody else's; it is stronger than everybody else's, with defense expenditures in 2011 larger than nearly all other countries combined. Complementing America's military might is its awesome economic strength. With less than 5 percent of the global population, the United States accounts for a fifth of global income and two-fifths of the entire world's combined spending on research and development. Further, America continues to wield enormous *soft power* because it is the hub of

soft power
the capacity to co-opt through such intangible factors as the popularity of a state's values and institutions, as opposed to the "hard power" to coerce through military might.

global communications and popular culture, through which its values spread all over the world (Galeota 2006; Nye 2008). In the words of former French Foreign Minister Hubart Vedrine, the United States is not simply a super-power; it is a "hyperpower."

This rare confluence of military, economic, and cultural power gives the United States what might appear to be an extraordinary ability to shape the global future to its will. This is why America's unique superpower position atop the global pyramid of power seemingly allows it to act independently without worries about resistance from weaker powers. Rather than working in concert with others, a strong and dominant hegemon can address inter-national problems without reliance on global organizations and can "go it alone," even in the face of strident foreign criticism.

unilateralism
an approach that relies on self-help, inde-pendent strategies in foreign policy.

Such *unilateralism* derives from the desire for control over the flexible con-duct of a great power's foreign relations, independent of control by or pres-sure from other great powers. Unilateralism can involve isolationism; an attempt to exert hegemonic leadership; a strategy of *selective engagement* that concentrates external involvements on vital national interests; or an effort to play the role of a "balancer" that skillfully backs one side or another in a great power dispute (but only when necessary to maintain a military equilibrium between the other great power disputants).

selective engagement
a great power grand strategy using eco-nomic and military power to influence only important particular situations, countries, or global issues by striking a balance between a highly interventionist "global policeman" and an uninvolved isolationist.

Unilateralism has its costs, however. Acting alone may appear expedient, but it erodes international support on issues such as combating terrorism, on which the United States is in strong need of cooperation from others. At the extreme, unilateralism can lead the global leader to play the role of international bully, seeking to run the world. And overwhelming power, observes Henry Kissinger, "evokes nearly automatically a quest by other societies to achieve a greater voice . . . and to reduce the relative position of the strongest."

The status of being a superpower, the single "pole" or center of power, without a real challenger, has fated the United States with heavy and grave responsibilities. Although the United States may hold an unrivaled posi-tion in the world today, in the long run, *unipolarity* is very unlikely to endure. Indeed, every previous leading great power has been vulnerable to *imperial overstretch*, the gap between internal resources and external com-mitments (Kennedy 1987). Throughout history, *hegemons* repeatedly have defined their security interests more broadly than other states, only to slip from the pinnacle of power by reaching beyond their grasp. Excessive costs to preserve America's empire by military means could prove to burst "the bubble of American supremacy" (Sanger 2005; Soros 2003).

imperial overstretch
the historic tendency for hegemons to sap their own strength through costly imperial pursuits and military spending that weaken their economies in rela-tion to the economies of their rivals.

Since the terrorist attacks on the United States on September 11, 2001, the U.S. Congress has approved $944 billion for military operations, base security, reconstruction, foreign aid, embassy costs, and veterans' healthcare for the wars in Afghanistan and Iraq, and other programs related to the battle against terrorism. While defense expenditures declined due to a withdrawal of troops from Iraq, these decreases were largely offset by the expense of sending additional troops to Afghanistan. For fiscal year 2010, Defense Secretary Robert Gates estimated that an additional $139 billion was needed, which would bring total war-related funding to $1.08 trillion (CRS 2009). In May 2010 Gates proposed to cut $10 billion from the current defense budget by terminating what he saw as unnecessary high-priced weapons systems and shift existing resources to more fully fund military personnel and more relevant weapons programs. Nonetheless, defense spending by the United States has more than doubled since the terrorist attacks and, when adjusted for inflation, remains at the highest level since World War II.

Simulation:
Explaining U.S. Intervention in Iraq

The trade-offs posed by allocating enormous national resources to military preparedness are reflected in former U.S. President Dwight Eisenhower's warning that "the problem in defense spending is to figure out how far you should go without destroying from within what you are trying to defend from without." Expressing a similar sentiment, Gates called for a review of the U.S. force structure and expressed concerns that it is likely out of scale to existing threats. "Does the number of warships we have and are building really put America at risk when the U.S. battle fleet is larger than the next thirteen navies combined, eleven of which belong to allies and partners? Is it a dire threat that by 2020 the United States will have only twenty times more advanced stealth fighters than China?"

The Rise of the Rest? From Unipolarity to Multipolarity

Yet it is not only the financial cost of expansive military commitments that has some worried about America's ability to sustain its predominant position in the international system; there are political costs to U.S. assertiveness as well. Washington's neglect of the politics of compromise and consensus building over most of the past decade has "reduced America's standing in the world and made the United States less, not more, secure" (Freedland 2007; see also Johnson 2007). As Richard Haass, president of the Council on Foreign Relations (a premier nonpartisan think tank), warns: "America remains the world's preeminent actor, but it is also stretched militarily, in debt financially, divided domestically, and unpopular internationally."

The United States' predominance in the world has been further eroded by the financial crisis of 2008, which originated in the United States and spread throughout the global financial system. Foreseeing a world characterized by the "rise of the rest," realist political journalist Fareed Zakaria attributes transformative significance to the economic growth experienced by countries throughout the globe during the post—Cold War period, and the subsequent economic challenges posed by what many perceive as the worst downturn since the Great Depression:

> The rise of the rest is at heart an economic phenomenon, but the transition we are witnessing is not just a matter of dollars and cents. It has political, military, and cultural consequences. As countries become stronger and richer, and as the United States struggles to earn back the world's faith, we're likely to see more challenges and greater assertiveness from rising nations (Zakaria 2009, p. xxiii).

uni-multipolar
a global system where there is a single dominant power, but the settlement of key international issues always requires action by the dominant power in combination with that of other great powers.

There is growing recognition that the distribution of power in the international system is shifting to what political scientist Samuel Huntington (2005) has described as *uni-multipolar*. According to this perspective, while the United States continues to be the only superpower, other states are not easily dominated. U.S. involvement remains critical in addressing key international issues, but resolution of transnational problems also requires action by some combination of other major states. Yet the potential for great power rivalry is increased, as the great powers in Europe and Asia have begun to resist American hegemony, and there is a growing gap between the U.S. view of its own power and how other countries see that power (Brooks 2006).

As diplomatic historian Paul Kennedy (2006) notes, there are growing limits on American domination: "The United States possesses the world's single largest national economy but faces huge trade and budget deficits and economic rivalries from an equally large European Union and a fast-growing China. Its armed forces look colossal, but its obligations look even larger." If some combination of U.S. imperial overstretch alongside rising economic and political influence by America's chief challengers transforms the current distribution of global power, many scholars and policy makers predict that a *multipolar* global system with more than two dominant centers of power will emerge.

Because multipolar systems include several comparatively equal great powers, they are complex. The interplay of

RIA-Novosti, Mikhail Klimentyev, Presidential Press Service/AP Photo

A RESURGENT RUSSIA "Following years of post-Cold War irrelevance and decline, Russia has more recently gone to great lengths to prove to the rest of the world that it matters internationally . . . whether supporting separatist groups in neighboring states, cutting off gas to Belarus and Ukraine, or standing up for Iran at the UN Security Council" (Mankoff 2009, p. 6). Shown here, Russian President Medvedev and Prime Minister Vladimir Putin enjoy the Victory Day military parade through Moscow's Red Square to celebrate Russia's victory over Nazi Germany during World War II.

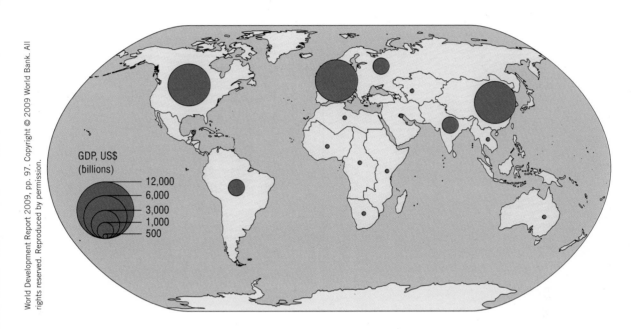

MAP 3.3

EMERGING REGIONS OF POWER IN THE TWENTY-FIRST CENTURY GLOBAL HIERARCHY **To estimate which countries are the most powerful and which are relatively weak, analysts frequently rely on the size of states' economies because that measure predicts the *power potential* of each state (that is, their relative capacity to project power and exercise global influence). This map pictures the proportionate economic clout of the leading great powers (measured by gross domestic product), showing the United States, Europe, and China as today's leading economic powerhouses.**

military and economic factors, with great powers competing as equals, is fraught with uncertainty. Differentiating friend from foe becomes especially difficult when allies in military security may be rivals in trade relationships. As Map 3.3 and Figure 3.2 show, the long-term economic trajectories based on differential national growth rates point to a world in which China is likely to overtake the United States. "Over the past decade, China's own internal market has grown; its exports to non-Western countries are now significant; it has vast capital surpluses of its own" (Zakaria 2010, p. 35). Moreover, a united Europe and perhaps other great powers, such as India or a resurgent Russia, may eventually also challenge American financial preeminence.

Looking Ahead: The Future of Great Power Relations

There is a deepening sense that shifts in the global distribution of power are underfoot. Of current debate is the extent to which the United States will continue to hold its position as the principal global leader. Leslie Gelb, a renowned foreign policy expert, rejects the idea that we are moving into a period where the United States will be no more significant than the other

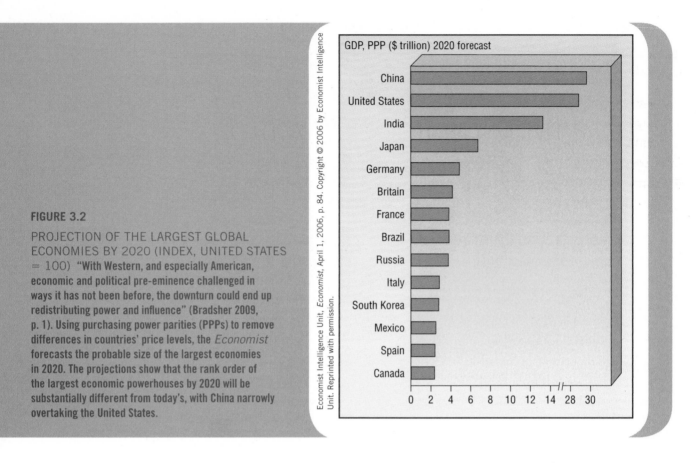

FIGURE 3.2

PROJECTION OF THE LARGEST GLOBAL ECONOMIES BY 2020 (INDEX, UNITED STATES = 100) "With Western, and especially American, economic and political pre-eminence challenged in ways it has not been before, the downturn could end up redistributing power and influence" (Bradsher 2009, p. 1). Using purchasing power parities (PPPs) to remove differences in countries' price levels, the *Economist* forecasts the probable size of the largest economies in 2020. The projections show that the rank order of the largest economic powerhouses by 2020 will be substantially different from today's, with China narrowly overtaking the United States.

great powers. He shares the view that the United States will remain an indispensable leader for years to come:

> The shape of global power is decidedly pyramidal—with the United States alone at the top, a second tier of major countries (China, Japan, India, Russia, the United Kingdom, France, Germany, and Brazil), and several tiers descending below. Even the smallest countries now occupy a piece of the international pyramid and have, particularly, enough power to resist the strong. But among all nations, only the United States is a true global power with global reach (Gelb 2009, p. xv).

Others see the world from a somewhat different perspective, perceiving a great transformation marked by the ascendance of other great powers in what has been coined a "post-American" world where many other state and nonstate actors help to define and direct how we respond to global challenges. "At the politico-military level, we remain in a single-superpower world. But in every other dimension—industrial, financial, educational, social, cultural—the distribution of power is shifting, moving away from American dominance" (Zakaria 2009, p. 4).

Predicting what cleavages and partnerships will develop among the great powers in the future twenty-first-century system will be difficult because it will be hard to foresee what will become the next major axis of conflict. Competition could emerge from any pair of great powers, but it may be restricted to one sphere of interaction. For example, the United States, Japan, China, and India are highly competitive in their commercial relations; nevertheless, they also display continuing efforts to manage their security relations collaboratively, as shown by their cooperation in fighting terrorism (Mead 2006). After years of decline following the end of the Cold War, Russia seeks to restore what it sees as its rightful place as a global leader among the great powers, though it is not particularly interested in directly challenging the West (Mankoff 2009).

China's status as an economic powerhouse has led to predictions that global power is shifting from the United States to China. By some estimates, the Chinese economy will reach $123 trillion by 2040, which will be nearly triple the size of the economic output of the entire world in 2000. Per capita income in China will reach $85,000, twice the predicted income for people living in the European Union and even more than that for those living in India and Japan. While it will not surpass the United States in per capita wealth, China's 40 percent share of global GDP will eclipse that of the United States (14 percent) and the European Union (5 percent), leading to speculation that

Frederic J. Brown/AFP/Getty Images

A NEW GLOBAL HEGEMON? According to Chris Patten, a former British governor of Hong Kong, China was the world's leading economic power for eighteen of the past twenty centuries. From the Chinese perspective, the idea of an ascendant China is not novel but rather a return to the status quo. "To the West, the notion of a world in which the center of global economic gravity lies in Asia may seem unimaginable. But," economist Robert Fogel (2010, p. 75) reminds us, "it wouldn't be the first time." Shown here, President Barack Obama and President Hu Jintao review the honor guard during a welcoming ceremony in Beijing.

we are entering the "Asian Century " (Fogel 2010). However, while Asia is indeed increasing its economic footprint in the world, "it still lags far behind the United States in military might, political and diplomatic influence, and even most measures of economic stability." Notes Joshua Kurlantzick (2010), a Senior Fellow at the Council of Foreign Relations, "Asia's growth, the source of its current strength, also has significant limits - rising inequality, disastrous demographics, and growing unrest that could scupper development."

Pervasive hostilities could emerge between any pair of great powers, such as between the globe's two major contenders for supremacy, the United States and China, if their competition escalates and they practice containment to prevent their rival's quest for hegemony. However, this kind of armed rivalry need not develop; cooperation could increase instead. Quite different and inconsistent political types of great power relations could emerge in the economic and military spheres. There is the probability of economic rivalry growing as global trade expands the integration of states' economies in an ever-tightening web of interdependence. However, the likelihood of security cooperation for many of these same relationships is also high. Under these circumstances, the danger of ***polarization*** could be managed if the great powers develop international rules and institutions to manage their fluid, mixed-motive relationships. Table 3.2

polarization
the formation of competing coalitions or blocs composed of allies that align with one of the major competing poles, or centers, of power.

Table 3.2   The New Great Power Chessboard: Simultaneously Unfolding Military and Economic Rivalries

Economic Rivalry				
	United States	European Union	Russia	China
United States	—			
European Union	H	—		
Russia	L	M	—	
China	H	M	M	—
Military Rivalry				
	United States	European Union	Russia	China
United States	—			
European Union	L	—		
Russia	H	H	—	
China	H	H	M	—

Note: The symbols H=high, M=medium, and L=low predict the probability of increasing future rivalries in various bilateral relationships.

presents a projection of the kind of cross-cutting bilateral relationships that could develop among the great powers throughout the twenty-first century. It estimates the probability of military cooperation and economic conflict between any pair of the five major powers.

Today the paradox prevails that many pairs of great powers that are the most active trade partners are also the greatest military rivals, but the key question is whether economic cooperation will help to reduce the potential for military competition in the future. The opportunities and challenges that we face in the world today call for a multilateral approach, with all of the great powers working cooperatively to achieve global solutions.

One possibility along these lines is the development of a *concert*, or a cooperative agreement, among the great powers to manage the global system jointly and to prevent international disputes from escalating to war. The Concert of Europe, at its apex between 1815 and 1822, is the epitome of previous great power efforts to pursue this path to peace. The effort to build a great power coalition to wage a war against global terrorism following 9/11 is a more recent example of *multilateralism* to construct a concert through collective approaches. Some policy makers also recommend that today's great powers unite with the lesser powers in constructing a true system of *collective security*. The formation of the League of Nations in 1919 is the best example of this multilateral approach to peace under conditions of *multipolarity,* and despite Russia's invasion of neighboring Georgia in 2008, some believe Russia's pledge to cooperate with NATO is representative of a collective security quest to maintain peace through an alliance of powerful countries.

concert
a cooperative agreement in design and plan among great powers to manage jointly the global system.

multilateralism
cooperative approaches to managing shared problems through collective and coordinated action.

> *Challenge and opportunity always come together—under certain conditions one could be transformed into the other.*
>
> —Hu Jintao, Chinese President

Of course, we have no way of knowing what the future holds. Patterns and practices can change, and it is possible for policy makers to learn from previous mistakes and avoid repeating them. What is crucial is how the great powers react to the eventual emergence of a new global system where power and responsibility are more widely distributed. It is clear that the choices the great powers make about war and peace will determine the fate of the world. In Chapter 4, we turn your attention from the rich, powerful, and commercially active great powers at the center of the world system to the poorer, weaker, and economically dependent states in the Global South and the rising powers in the Global East.

Take an Online Practice Quiz

www.cengagebrain.com/shop/ISBN/0495802204

Suggested Readings

Gelb, Leslie H. (2009) *Power Rules: How Common Sense Can Rescue American Foreign Policy.* New York: HarperCollins.

Ikenberry, G. John. (2008) "The Rise of China and the Future of the West," *Foreign Affairs* 87: 23–37.

Kegley, Charles W., Jr. and Gregory Raymond. (2007) *After Iraq: The Imperiled American Imperium.* New York: Oxford University Press.

Mankoff, Jeffrey. (2009) *Russian Foreign Policy: The Return of Great Power Politics.* New York: Rowman and Littlefield.

Mearsheimer, John J. (2001) *The Tragedy of Great Power Politics.* New York: W.W. Norton.

Zakaria, Fareed. (2009) *The Post-American World.* New York: W.W. Norton.

CHAPTER 4
THE GLOBAL SOUTH
IN A WORLD OF POWERS

*A global human society based on poverty for many and prosperity
for a few, characterized by islands of wealth surrounded by a sea
of poverty, is unsustainable.*
—Thabo Mbeki, former president of South Africa

CHAPTER OUTLINE

THE COLONIAL ORIGINS OF THE
GLOBAL SOUTH'S CURRENT
CIRCUMSTANCES

The First Wave of European
Imperialism

The Second Wave of European
Imperialism

Self-Determination and
Decolonization in the Twentieth
Century

NORTH AND SOUTH TODAY:
WORLDS APART

THEORETICAL EXPLANATIONS
OF UNDERDEVELOPMENT

Internal Factors: Classical
Economic Development Theory's
Interpretation

International Factors: Dependency
Theory's Interpretation

CONTROVERSY: THEORIES OF
DEVELOPMENT: A RETURN TO
MODERNIZATION?

CLOSING THE GAP? THE GLOBAL
SOUTH'S PROSPECTS IN A
WORLD OF GREAT POWERS

Fueling Growth through Oil
and Technology

The Global East

Military Security

Reform of the Economic Order

Regional Trade Regimes

Foreign Aid and Remittances

Trade and Foreign Direct
Investment

Debt Management

CONTROVERSY: MULTINATIONAL
CORPORATIONS IN THE GLOBAL
SOUTH: DO THEY HELP OR HURT?

THE GLOBAL SOUTH'S FUTURE

SUPRI/Reuters/Landov

MAKING NEW FRIENDS Increasingly, the small powers of the Global South are having the opportunity to participate and wield influence in world politics. Pictured here with schoolchildren in Indonesia, recognition of this is reflected in Hillary Clinton's decision to make Asia the destination of her first trip as Secretary of State—something that had not been done since Dean Rusk's 1961 visit. Not only does Southeast Asia want American engagement as a counterbalance to China's expanding military might, but the United States sees its future shaped by Asia as well.

Earth is divided into two hemispheres, north and south, at the equator. This artificial line of demarcation is, of course, meaningless except for use by cartographers to chart distance and location on maps. However, this divide also represents a popular way of describing the inequalities that separate rich and poor states. By and large, these two groups are located on either side of the equator (see Map 4.1).

Life for most people in the Northern Hemisphere is very different from that in the Southern Hemisphere. The disparities are profound, and in many places appear to be growing. The division in power and wealth characterizing the *Global North* and *Global South* poses both moral and security problems. As the philosopher Plato in fifth-century BCE Greece counseled, "There should exist neither extreme poverty nor excessive wealth, for both are productive of great evil." While poverty and inequality have existed throughout recorded history, today the levels have reached extremes. The poor countries find themselves marginalized, in a subordinate position in the global hierarchy. What

Global North
a term used to refer to the world's wealthy, industrialized countries located primarily in the Northern Hemisphere.

Global South
a term now often used instead of "Third World" to designate the less developed countries located primarily in the Southern Hemisphere.

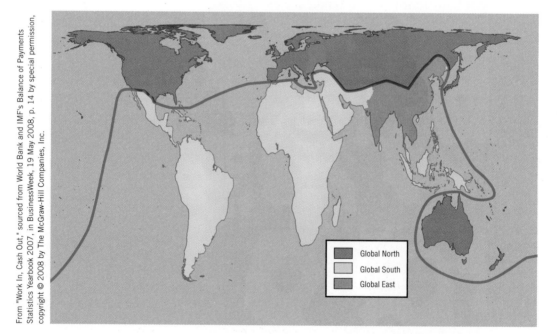

From "Work In, Cash Out," sourced from World Bank and IMF's Balance of Payments Statistics Yearbook 2007, in BusinessWeek, 19 May 2008, p. 14 by special permission, copyright © 2008 by The McGraw-Hill Companies, Inc.

Legend:
- Global North
- Global South
- Global East

MAP 4.1

THE GLOBAL NORTH, GLOBAL SOUTH (AND GLOBAL EAST) Global North countries are wealthy and democratic. In contrast, according to the World Bank, the Global South countries are home to 84 percent of the world's population, but the impoverished people living there possess only 27 percent of the world's gross national income (WDI 2010, p. 34). As shall be seen, into this picture should now be placed "the Global East," countries that have arisen from the former Global South and are now positioned to rival the levels of prosperity that the Global North has enjoyed in the last two decades.

are the causes and consequences of the pronounced inequalities between the great powers and the disadvantaged countries trapped in poverty? That is the central question that you will consider in this chapter.

THE COLONIAL ORIGINS OF THE GLOBAL SOUTH'S CURRENT CIRCUMSTANCES

Many analysts trace the roots of today's inequalities among states at the *global level of analysis* because they believe that the global system has properties built into it that account for the inability of most poor countries to close the gap with the wealthy countries. Taking their hypothesis that prevailing worldwide conditions are part of a much longer historical pattern, they note that the rules governing international politics today were constructed in the 1648 Peace of Westphalia following Europe's Thirty Years' War. These rules were crafted by the most powerful actors on the world stage—the great powers at the time—to serve their parochial self-interests in preserving their predominant positions at the top of the global pyramid of power by preventing less-powerful states from joining them (see Kegley and Raymond 2002).

The origins and persistence of the inequalities of states stem in part from the fact that today's modern global system was initially, and remains, a socially constructed reality by, of, and for the most powerful states. The powerful did not design a global system for equals; the great powers followed the prescription of realist thought to always seek self-advantage. Accordingly, they did not build the global system with an eye to preventing the victimization of the weak and the disadvantaged.

So, a good starting place is to begin your inquiry by taking into consideration the legacy of this seedbed for today's global system. Many analysts see the history of *colonialism*, the European conquest of *indigenous peoples* and the seizure of their territory for exclusively European gain, as the root source of the problem. They note that almost all of the independent sovereign states in the Southern Hemisphere were at one time colonies. These analysts argue that today's inequalities are a product of this past colonization.

During the Cold War, the term ***Third World*** was used to distinguish the growing number of newly independent but economically less developed states that, for the most part, shared a colonial past with those states aligned with either the communist East or the capitalistic West. However,

indigenous peoples
the native ethnic and cultural inhabitant populations within countries, referred to as the "Fourth World."

Third World
a Cold War term to describe the less developed countries of Africa, Asia, the Caribbean, and Latin America.

the "Third World" soon was used to refer to those countries that had failed to grow economically in a way that was comparable to countries of the *First World* industrialized great powers such as Europe, North America, and Japan. The so-called *Second World*, consisting of the Soviet Union and its allies in other communist countries, was distinguished by a communist ideological commitment to planned economic policies rather than reliance on free-market forces. The terms Second World and Third World carry obsolete Cold War baggage. Today the term Global North, which refers to what was previously known as the First World, and Global South, which refers to the less developed countries in the Southern Hemisphere, are now commonplace. These contemporary terms largely correspond to the distinction between *great powers* and *small powers* as well (see Chapter 5, also Kassimeris 2009).

The placement of particular states within these categories is not easy. Although journalists, policy makers, and scholars frequently generalize about the Global South, considerable diversity exists within this grouping of states. For example, it includes low-income countries such as Ghana and Haiti, where a majority of the population tries to survive through subsistence agriculture; middle-income countries such as Brazil and Malaysia, which produce manufactured goods; and some countries such as Kuwait and Qatar, whose petroleum exports have generated incomes rivaling those of Global North countries.

Global South countries are different in other ways as well. Included among their ranks is Indonesia, an archipelago of more than seventeen thousand islands scattered throughout an oceanic expanse larger than the United States, and Burundi, a landlocked state slightly smaller than Maryland. Also included is Nigeria, with 148 million inhabitants, and Uruguay, with just three million people. In addition to these geographic and demographic differences, Global South countries also vary politically and culturally, ranging from democratic Costa Rica to autocratic Myanmar.

The emergence of the Global South as an identifiable group of states is a distinctly contemporary phenomenon. Although most Latin American countries were independent before World War II, not until then did other countries of the Global South gain that status. In 1947, Great Britain granted independence to India and Pakistan, after which *decolonization*—the freeing of colonial peoples from their dependent status—gathered speed. Since then, a profusion of new sovereign states has joined the global community, nearly all carved from the British, Spanish, Portuguese, Dutch, and French empires built under colonialism four hundred years ago.

First World
the relatively wealthy industrialized countries that share a commitment to varying forms of democratic political institutions and developed market economies, including the United States, Japan, the European Union, Canada, Australia, and New Zealand.

Second World
during the Cold War, the group of countries, including the Soviet Union, its (then) Eastern European allies, and China, that embraced communism and central planning to propel economic growth.

small powers
countries with limited political, military, or economic capabilities and influence.

decolonization
the achievement of sovereign independence by countries that were once colonies of the great powers.

Today, few colonies exist and the decolonization process is almost complete. However, the effects persist. Most of the ethnic national conflicts that are now so prevalent have colonial roots, as the imperial powers drew borders within and between their domains with little regard for the national identities of the indigenous peoples. Similarly, the disparity in wealth between the rich Global North and the poor Global South is attributed in part to unequal and exploitative relations during the colonial period, as is a legacy of mistrust and insecurity that persists not only across this global divide but also within the former colonial countries themselves (see Map 4.2).

The First Wave of European Imperialism

The first wave of European empire building began in the late fifteenth century, as the Dutch, English, French, Portuguese, and Spanish used their naval power to militarily conquer territories for commercial gain. Scientific innovations made the European explorers' adventures possible, and merchants followed in their wake, "quickly seizing upon opportunities to increase their

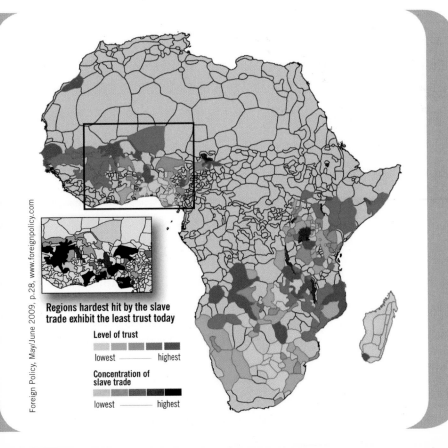

MAP 4.2

A LEGACY OF MISTRUST Spurred by the quest for labor in the New World (Africans proved much more resistant than the indigenous peoples to the diseases brought over by Europeans), the expanding colonial powers eagerly participated in a transatlantic slave trade from the mid-1500s through the late 1700s. Harvard economist Nathan Nunn attributes the stalled economic development of much of Africa to the trauma of this colonial legacy, arguing that major shocks can "change people's behavior in ways that seem pretty permanent." Indeed, in "regions of Africa where the slave trade was most concentrated, people today extend less trust to other individuals: not only to foreigners, but also to relatives and neighbors" (Keating 2009, p. 28).

Foreign Policy, May/June 2009, p.28, www.foreignpolicy.com

Regions hardest hit by the slave trade exhibit the least trust today

Level of trust
lowest ——— highest

Concentration of slave trade
lowest ——— highest

business and profits. In turn, Europe's governments perceived the possibilities for increasing their own power and wealth. Commercial companies were chartered and financed, with military and naval expeditions frequently sent out after them to ensure political control of overseas territories" (Cohen 1973, p. 20).

The economic strategy underlying the relationship between colonies and colonizers during this era of "classical imperialism" is known as *mercantilism*—an economic philosophy advocating government regulation of economic life to increase state power. European rulers believed that power flowed from the possession of national wealth measured in terms of gold and silver, and that cultivating mining and industry to attain a favorable balance of trade (exporting more than they imported) was the best way to become rich. "Colonies were desirable in this respect because they afforded an opportunity to shut out commercial competition; they guaranteed exclusive access to untapped markets and sources of cheap materials (as well as, in some instances, direct sources of the precious metals themselves). Each state was determined to monopolize as many of these overseas mercantile opportunities as possible" (Cohen 1973, p. 21). States wedded to realist justifications of the competitive drive for global power saw the imperial conquest of foreign territory by war as a natural by product of active government management of the economy.

mercantilism
a government trade strategy for accumulating state wealth and power by encouraging exports and discouraging imports.

By the end of the eighteenth century, the European powers had spread themselves, although thinly, throughout virtually the entire world. But the colonial empires they had built began to crumble. Britain's thirteen North American colonies declared their independence in 1776, and most of Spain's possessions in South America won their freedom in the early nineteenth century. Nearly one hundred colonial relationships worldwide were terminated in the half-century ending in 1825 (Bergesen and Schoenberg 1980).

classical liberal economic theory
a body of thought based on Adam Smith's ideas about the forces of supply and demand in the marketplace, emphasizing the benefits of minimal government regulation of the economy and trade.

As Europe's colonial empires dissolved, belief in the mercantilist philosophy also waned. As liberal political economist Adam Smith argued in his 1776 treatise, *The Wealth of Nations*, national wealth grew not through the accumulation of precious metals but rather from the capital and goods they could buy. Smith's ideas about the benefits of the "invisible hand" of the unregulated marketplace laid much of the intellectual foundation for *classical liberal economic theory*. Following Smith and other liberal free-trade theorists, faith in the precepts of *laissez-faire economics* (minimal government interference in the market) gained widespread acceptance (see also Chapter 12). Henceforth, European powers continued to seek colonies, but the rationale for their imperial policies began to change.

laissez-faire economics
the philosophical principle of free markets and free trade to give people free choices with little government regulation.

*All history is only one long story to this effect: Men have struggled
for power over their fellow men in order that they might win the
joys of Earth at the expense of others, and might shift the burdens of
life from their own shoulders upon those of others.*

—William Graham Summer, American realist economic-sociologist

The Second Wave of European Imperialism

From the 1870s until the outbreak of World War I, a second wave of imperialism washed over the world as Europe, joined later by the United States
and Japan, aggressively colonized new territories. The portion of the globe
that Europeans controlled was one-third in 1800, two-thirds by 1878,
and four-fifths by 1914 (Fieldhouse 1973). As illustrated in Map 4.3, in
the last twenty years of the nineteenth century Africa fell under the control of seven European powers (Belgium, Britain, France, Germany, Italy,
Portugal, and Spain), and in all of the Far East and the Pacific, only China,
Japan, and Siam (Thailand) were not conquered. However, the foreign great
powers carved China into separate zones of commerce, which they each individually controlled and exploited for profit. Japan itself also imperialistically occupied Korea and Formosa (Taiwan). Elsewhere, the United States
expanded across its continent, acquired Puerto Rico and the Philippines in
the 1898 Spanish-American War, extended its colonial reach westward to
Hawaii, leased the Panama Canal Zone "in perpetuity" from the new state
of Panama (an American creation), and exercised considerable control over
several Caribbean islands, notably Cuba. The preeminent imperial power,
Great Britain, in a single generation expanded its empire to cover one-fifth
of the earth's land area and comprised perhaps one-fourth of its population
(Cohen 1973). As British imperialists were proud to proclaim, it was an
empire on which the sun never set.

So why did most of the great powers—and those that aspired to great power
status—engage in this expensive and often vicious competition to control
other peoples and territories? What explains the new imperialism?

One answer lies in the nature of the global economy. With the Industrial
Revolution, capitalism grew—emphasizing the free market, private ownership of the means of production, and the accumulation of wealth. Radical
theorists following Karl Marx and Vladimir Lenin, who called themselves
adherents of *communism*, saw imperialism's aggressive competition as
caused by capitalists' need for profitable overseas outlets for their surplus
("finance") capital. Sharing a critical perspective of the capitalist world

communism
the radical ideology
maintaining that if soci-
ety is organized so that
every person produces
according to his or her
ability and consumes
according to his or her
needs, a community
without class distinc-
tions will emerge,
sovereign states will
no longer be needed,
and imperial wars of
colonial conquest will
vanish from history.

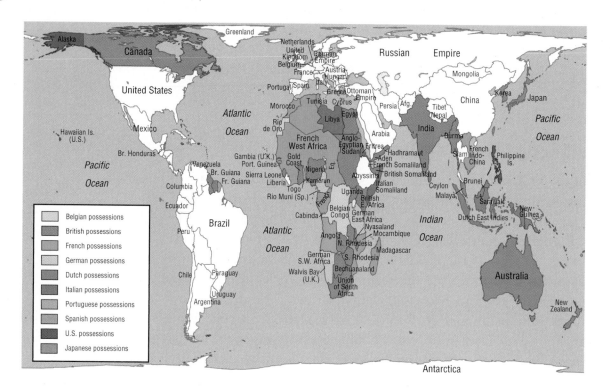

MAP 4.3

GLOBAL IMPERIALISM 1914 The ten major imperial powers competed for colonies throughout the globe in the present-day Global South, and on the eve of World War I, their combined territories covered much of the world.

economy, *world-system theory* saw a world division of labor where the (industrial) "core" areas exploit the (nonindustrial) "periphery," and colonization provided a means for imperial control over foreign lands. Liberal economists, by contrast, regarded the new imperialism not as a product of capitalism but, rather, as a response to certain maladjustments that, given the proper will, could be corrected. What the three perspectives shared was the belief that economics explained the new imperialism: It was rooted in the material needs of advanced capitalist societies for cheap raw materials, additional markets to consume growing production, and places for the investment of new capital (see Chapter 2).

Another explanation emphasizes purely political factors as the source of the second wave of imperialism. As liberal British economist J. A. Hobson argued in his seminal 1902 book, *Imperialism,* jockeying for power and prestige between competitive empires had always characterized the great powers' behavior in the European balance-of-power system. Hobson believed that imperialism through overseas expansion was simply a global extension of this inter-European competition for dominance inspired by the *realpolitik*

realpolitik
the theoretical outlook prescribing that countries should increase their power and wealth in order to compete with and dominate other countries.

theoretical premise that all states have an unquenchable thirst for more and more power.

By the 1800s, Britain emerged from Europe's perpetual conflict as the world's leading power. By 1870, however, British hegemony began to decline. Germany emerged as a powerful industrial state, as did the United States. Understandably, Britain tried to protect its privileged global position in the face of growing competition from the newly emerging core states. Its efforts to maintain the status quo help to explain the second wave of imperial expansion, especially in Africa, where partition served the imperial powers at the expense of local populations.

Self-Determination and Decolonization in the Twentieth Century

The climate of opinion turned decidedly against imperialism when the 1919 Versailles peace settlement that ended World War I embraced *liberalism*—the body of theoretical thought that stresses the importance of ideas, ideals, and institutions to generate progress, prosperity, and peace. Part of that reform program was the principle of national *self-determination* championed by U.S. President Woodrow Wilson. Self-determination advocated that indigenous nationalities should have the moral right to decide which authority would rule them. Wilson and other *liberal theorists* (see Chapter 2) reasoned that freedom would lead to the creation of states and governments that were content with their territorial boundaries and therefore less inclined to make war. In practice, however, the attempt to redraw states' borders to separate nationality groups was applied almost exclusively to war-torn Europe, where six new states were created from the territory of the former Austrian-Hungarian Empire (Austria, Czechoslovakia, Hungary, Poland, Romania, and the ethnically divided Yugoslavia). Other territorial adjustments also were made in Europe, but the proposition that self-determination should be extended to Europe's overseas empires did not receive serious support.

Still, the colonial territories of the powers defeated in World War I were not simply parceled out among the victorious allies, as had typically happened in the past. Instead, the territories controlled by Germany and the Ottoman Empire were transferred under League of Nations auspices to countries that would govern them as "mandates" until their eventual self-rule. Many of these territorial decisions gave rise to subsequent conflicts such as in the Middle East and Africa. For example, the League of

JOSE GOITIA /The New York Times/Redux Pictures

A NEW FACE OF GLOBAL SOUTH SOCIALISM **Having replaced his elder brother, long-time communist ruler Fidel Castro, in 2008 as president of Cuba, Raul Castro pledged to "improve people's spiritual and material lives." However, disappointingly little has been done thus far to alleviate poverty and repression, and despite a purge of eleven government ministers, it is expected that under Raul's leadership the radical perspective of Marxist-Leninism will persist and there will be "continued one-party rule and a state-run economy that will be tweaked, rather than radically reformed" (Economist, April 18, 2009, p. 40).**

self-determination
the liberal doctrine that people should be able to determine the government that will rule them.

Nations called for the eventual creation of a Jewish national homeland in Palestine and arranged for the transfer of control over Southwest Africa (called Namibia) to what would become the white minority regime of South Africa.

The principle implicit in the League of Nations mandate system gave birth to the idea that "colonies were a trust rather than simply a property to be exploited and treated as if its peoples had no rights of their own" (Easton 1964, p. 124). This set an important precedent after World War II, when the defeated powers' territories placed under the United Nations (UN) trusteeship system were not absorbed by others but were promised eventual self-rule. Thus, support for self-determination gained momentum.

The decolonization process accelerated in 1947, when the British consented to the independence of India and Pakistan. War eventually erupted between these newly independent states as each sought to gain control over disputed territory in Kashmir in 1965, in 1971, and again as the nuclear-armed states clashed in 2002. Violence also broke out in Vietnam and Algeria in the 1950s and early 1960s when the French sought to regain control over their pre–World War II colonial territories. Similarly, bloodshed followed closely on the heels of independence in the Congo when the Belgians granted their African colony independence in 1960, and it dogged the unsuccessful efforts of Portugal to battle the winds of decolonization that swept over Africa as the 1960s wore on.

Rene Burri/Magnum Photos New York

NEW STATES After the decolonization process runs its complete course, more new countries can be expected because many existing states are fragmenting. When World War I broke out, only sixty-two independent countries existed; now there are more than two hundred. Many new sovereign states are very small. Pictured here is the "micro" state of Nauru, which has a president, a supreme court, and the full apparatus of government to rule its tiny population. Half the globe's countries have populations less than that of the U.S. state of Massachusetts.

Despite these political convulsions, decolonization for the most part was not only extraordinarily rapid but also remarkably peaceful. This may be explained by the fact that World War II sapped the economic and military vitality of many of the colonial powers. World-system analysts contend that a growing appreciation of the costs of empire also eroded support for colonial empires (Strang 1990, 1991). Whatever the underlying cause, colonialism became less acceptable. In a world increasingly dominated by rivalry between East and West, Cold War competition for political allies gave both the superpower rivals incentives to lobby for the liberation of overseas empires. Decolonization "triumphed," as Inis Claude (1967, p. 55) explains, in part "because the West [gave] priority to the containment of communism over the perpetuation of colonialism."

Many Global South countries feared, however, that they would become entrapped in the Cold War and that their right to self-determination would be compromised, so they adopted foreign policies based on *nonalignment*. The strategy energized both the United States and the Soviet Union to renew their efforts to attract the uncommitted Global South countries to their own network of allies, often offering economic and military aid as an inducement. Some states aligned themselves with either the United States or the Soviet Union; others avoided taking sides in the Cold War. The latter approach gathered momentum in 1955, when twenty-nine *nonaligned states* from Asia and Africa met in Bandung, Indonesia, to construct a strategy to combat colonialism. Six years later, leaders from twenty-five countries met in Belgrade, Yugoslavia, and created the *Nonaligned Movement (NAM)*. The membership of this coalition would later grow to more than one hundred countries.

The Cold War's end eroded the bargaining leverage nonalignment had provided the Global South. As a strategy, nonalignment "died" with the Cold War. But the passion of Global South leaders to eradicate global inequities lives on, as can be seen in the 2003 *Non-Aligned Kuala Lumpur Summit Declaration*, which raised questions about the inability of many Global South countries to advance. Thus, the Global South worries that in the future, even newer forms of great power imperialism might continue to destroy any Global South hopes for progress.

As the old order crumbled—and as the leaders in the newly emancipated territories discovered that freedom did not translate automatically into autonomy, economic independence, or domestic prosperity—the conflict between the rich Global North and the emerging states of the Global South began.

nonalignment
a foreign policy posture that rejects participating in military alliances with rival blocs for fear that formal alignment will entangle the state in an unnecessary involvement in war.

nonaligned states
countries that do not form alliances with opposed great powers and practice neutrality on issues that divide great powers.

Nonaligned Movement (NAM)
a group of more than one hundred newly independent, mostly less developed, states that joined together as a group of neutrals to avoid entanglement with the superpowers' competing alliances in the Cold War and to advance the Global South's primary interests in economic cooperation and growth.

NORTH AND SOUTH TODAY: WORLDS APART

The Global South is sometimes described today as a "zone of turmoil" or an "axis of upheaval," in large measure because, in contrast with the peaceful and democratic Global North, most of the people in the Global South face chronic poverty amidst war, tyranny, and anarchy. In the poorest countries of the Global South where preexisting conditions of dictatorships and dismal financial prospects persist, the odds increase that these countries will experience civil wars and armed conflicts with each other (Collier 2005; Ferguson 2009). Indeed, more than 90 percent of the inter- and intrastate conflicts and 90 percent of the casualties in the past sixty years occurred within the Global South (see Chapter 7).

Democracy has spread rapidly and widely since the 1980s, becoming the preferred mode of governance throughout much of the Global South as a means of promoting both economic development and peace. Because the Global North's history suggests that "economic and technological development bring a coherent set of social, cultural, and political changes . . . and they also bring growing mass demands for democratic institutions and for more responsive behavior on the part of elites" (Inglehart and Welzel 2009, p. 39), the continuing expansion of Global South market economies under capitalism appears likely to hasten democratization.

Even so, the continued enlargement of the liberal democratic community is not guaranteed, with some seeing democracy as failing even while elections become more commonplace. In many places, democratization is only "skin deep." As Oxford economist Paul Collier (2009, p. 149) points out

> In the average election held among the bottom billion poorest of the world's population, despite the fact that voters usually have many grounds for complaint, the incumbent "wins" a healthy 74 percent of the vote. In elections with particularly weak restraints, it is an even healthier 88 percent. Somehow or other, incumbents in these societies are very good at winning elections.

developing countries
a category used by the World Bank to identify low-income Global South countries with an annual GNI per capita below $975 and middle-income countries with an annual GNI per capita of more than $975 but less than $11,905 (WDI 2010).

gross national income (GNI)
a measure of the production of goods and services within a given time period, which is used to delimit the geographic scope of production. GNI measures production by a state's citizens or companies, regardless of where the production occurs.

Furthermore, many Global South countries lack well-developed domestic market economies based on entrepreneurship and private enterprise. Indeed, the global financial crisis has exacerbated the disappointment of some in the Global South with "the failure of free-market policies to bring significant economic growth and reduce the region's yawning inequality" (Schmidt and Malkin 2009, p. 5), and has generated a renewed interest in the radical ideas of Karl Marx, who would likely have seen the crisis as the natural by-product of "the 'contradictions' inherent in a world comprised of competitive markets, commodity production and financial speculation" (Panitch 2009, p. 140).

The fact that 84 percent of the world's population is poor is both a reflection and cause of these unequally distributed resources. To measure the disparities, the World Bank differentiates the "low-income" and "low- and middle-income," economies in *developing countries*, whose *gross national income (GNI)* is an average of $15,649 billion for each state, from the "high-income" developed countries, which average $42,415 billion for each state (WDI 2010). Among the *developed countries*, wide variations in economic performance (growth and inflation rates, debt burdens, and export prices, for example) and international circumstances (such as the availability of oil and other fuels) are evident.

Numbers paint pictures and construct images, and the data on the division between the Global North and Global South point to brutal disparities and inequalities. When we compare the differences on some key indicators differentiating low- and middle-income countries from high-income countries (at the peak of development), we discover huge gaps (see Table 4.1).

developed countries
a category used by the World Bank to identify Global North countries with an annual GNI per capita of $11,906 or more (WDI 2010).

Table 4.1   Two Worlds of Development: An International Class Divide

Characteristic	Developing Global South	Developed Global North
Number of countries/economies	135	66
Population (millions)	5,629	1,069
Average annual population growth rate, 2005–2015	1.2%	0.5%
Population density (people for each sq km)	59	32
Women in parliaments	18%	22%
Land area (thousands of km²)	98,797	35,299
Gross national income for each person	$2,780	$39,678
Average annual % growth of GDP per person, 2006–2007	4.5%	-0.2%
Net foreign direct investment inflows (% of GDP)	3.6%	2.8%
Exports- Goods and Services ($ billions)	$5,938	$13,709
Imports- Goods and Services ($ billions)	$5,503	$13,741
Workers' remittances received (in millions)	$335,789	$107,603
Refugees by country of origin (thousands)	10,059	109.4
Access to improved sanitation (% of population)	55%	100%
Prevalence of undernourishment (% of population)	16%	5%
Health expenditure (% of GDP)	5.4%	11.2%
Daily newspapers for each 1,000 people	59	261
Internet users for each 100 people	15.3	69.1
Life expectancy at birth	67	80
Population living in cities (%)	45%	78%
Number of motor vehicles for each 1,000 people	70	621

(continued)

Table 4.1 Two Worlds of Development: An International Class Divide (Continued)

Characteristic	Developing Global South	Developed Global North
Personal computers for each 100 people	5.2	67.8
Electric Power consumption per person (kWh)	1,478	9,753
Armed forces (thousands)	21,745	5,724

Where people live on Earth influences how they live. As this information shows, the situation is much more favorable—and the quality of life is relatively advantageous—in the developed countries of the Global North than it is in the Southern Hemisphere, where nearly all the Global South countries are located.

Source: World Bank, 2010 World Development Indicators.

least developed of the less developed countries (LLDCs) the most impoverished countries in the Global South.

This picture darkens even more when the focus shifts to the plight of the poorest in the low-income developing countries. More than 976 million people (15 percent of humanity) live in one of the forty-three countries at the bottom of the global hierarchy, the ***least developed of the less developed countries (LLDCs)***, where barter of one agricultural good for another (rather than money) typically is used for economic exchanges (WDI 2010). Sometimes described as the "Third World's Third World," these countries are the very poorest, with little economic growth and rapid population growth that is increasingly straining their overtaxed society and environment. These countries are not emerging or reemerging to break the chains of their destitution; they are falling behind the other Global South countries.

A daunting scale of misery and marginalization is thus evident across the Global South, from which only a fraction of its countries have begun to escape. For most Global South countries, the future is bleak, and the opportunities and choices most basic to freedom from fear and poverty are unavailable. The aggregate pattern underlying global trends in the last twenty years shows that more than sixty countries today are worse off than they were and are falling ever further behind the levels achieved by the countries in the Global North. When we consider that nearly all the population growth in the twenty-first century will occur in the Global South, the poorest countries cut off from circulation in the globalized marketplace, it is hard to imagine how the gap can close and how the soil of poverty can be prevented from producing terrorism and civil war.

This tragic portrayal of unspeakable despair for so many Global South states raises the basic theoretical question: Why does the Global South, at this historical juncture, suffer from such dismal destitution?

THEORETICAL EXPLANATIONS OF UNDERDEVELOPMENT

Why has the Global South lagged far behind the Global North in its comparative level of well-being and *development*? And why have the development experiences even within the Global South differed so widely?

The diversity evident in the Global South invites the conclusion that underdevelopment is explained by a combination of factors. Some theorists explain the underdevelopment of most developing economies by looking primarily at *internal* causes within states. Other theorists focus on *international* causes such as the position of developing countries in the global political economy. We will take a brief look at each of these schools of thought.

development
the processes, economic and political, through which a country develops to increase its capacity to meet its citizens' basic human needs and raise their standard of living.

Internal Factors: Classical Economic Development Theory's Interpretation

Liberal economic development theories of *modernization* first emerged in the early post–World War II era. They argued that major barriers to development were posed by the Global South countries' own internal characteristics. To overcome these barriers, most classical theorists recommended that the wealthy countries supply various "missing components" of development, such as investment capital through foreign aid or private foreign direct investment.

Once sufficient capital was accumulated to promote economic growth, these liberal theorists predicted that its benefits would eventually "trickle down" to broad segments of society. Everyone, not just a privileged few, would begin to enjoy rising affluence. Walt W. Rostow, an economic historian and U.S. policy maker, formalized this theory in *The Stages of Economic Growth* (1960). He predicted that traditional societies beginning the path to development would inevitably pass through various stages by means of the free market and would eventually "take off" to become similar to the mass-consumption societies of the capitalist Global North. Even though the rich are likely to get richer, it was argued, as incomes in the world as a whole grow, the odds increase that a preindustrialized economy will grow faster and eventually reduce the gap between it and richer countries.

modernization
a view of development popular in the Global North's liberal democracies that wealth is created through efficient production, free enterprise, and free trade, and that countries' relative wealth depends on technological innovation and education more than on natural endowments such as climate and resources.

The Global South rejected that prognosis and the premises on which it was based. Leaders there did not accept the classical liberal argument that the Global North became prosperous because they concentrated on hard work, innovative inventions of new products, and investments in schooling.

Furthermore, by the mid 1970s, it was apparent that assistance from the rich countries of the Global North had not brought about significant progress toward prosperity or democracy in the Global South as expected. The Global South was instead persuaded by the rival theory that attributed their lack of development to the international links between developing countries and the Global North's leadership in the global political economy.

International Factors: Dependency Theory's Interpretation

Whereas classical theory attributes the causes of most developing countries' underdevelopment to internal conditions within states, *dependency theory* emphasizes international factors in general and the Global South's dependence on the dominant great powers in particular. As noted in Chapter 2, dependency theory builds on Vladimir Lenin's radical critique of imperialism, but it goes beyond it to account for changes that have occurred in recent decades. Its central proposition is that the structure of the capitalist world economy is based on a division of labor between a dominant core and a subordinate periphery. As a result of colonialism, the Global South countries that make up the periphery have been forced into an economic role whereby they export raw materials and import finished goods. Whereas classical liberal theorists submit that specialization in production according to comparative advantage will increase income in an unfettered market and therein help close the gap between the world's haves and have-nots, dependency theorists maintain that global inequalities cannot be reduced so long as developing countries continue to specialize in producing primary products for which there are often numerous competing suppliers and limited demand.

import-substitution industrialization
a strategy for economic development that centers on providing investors at home incentives to produce goods so that previously imported products from abroad will decline.

export-led industrialization
a growth strategy that concentrates on developing domestic export industries capable of competing in overseas markets.

Breaking out of their dependent status and pursuing their own industrial development remains the greatest foreign policy priority for countries in the Global South. To this end, some countries (particularly those in Latin America) have pursued development through an *import-substitution industrialization* strategy designed to encourage domestic entrepreneurs to manufacture products traditionally imported from abroad. Governments (often dictatorships) became heavily involved in managing their economies and, in some cases, became the owners and operators of industry.

Import-substitution industrialization eventually fell from favor, in part because manufacturers often found that they still had to rely on Global North technology to produce goods for their domestic markets. The preference now is for *export-led industrialization*, based on the realization that "what had enriched the rich was not their insulation from imports (rich countries do, in fact, import all sorts of goods) but their success in manufactured exports, where higher prices could be commanded than for [Global South] raw materials" (Sklair 1991).

Dependency theorists also argue that countries in the Global South are vulnerable to cultural penetration by multinational corporations (MNCs) and other outside forces, which saturate them with values alien to their societies. Once such penetration has occurred, the inherently unequal exchanges that bind the exploiters and the exploited are sustained by elites within the penetrated societies, who sacrifice their country's welfare for personal gain. The argument that a privileged few benefit from dependency at the expense of their societies underscores the dual nature of many developing countries.

Dualism refers to the existence of two separate economic and social sectors operating side by side. Dual societies typically have a rural, impoverished, and neglected sector operating alongside an urban, developing, or advanced sector—but with little interaction between the two. *Multinational corporations (MNCs)* contribute to dualism by favoring a minority of well-compensated employees over the rest that increases gaps in pay and by widening differences between rural and urban economic opportunities.

Although dependency theory has great appeal within the Global South, it cannot easily explain the rapid economic development of what many people refer to as the *newly industrialized countries (NICs)* in the *Global East*. Neither does it do a good job of explaining the lack of sustained development of countries such as Cuba, Myanmar, and North Korea that focused their economic growth efforts inwardly and have had little involvement in global trade. Recently, however, there has been a reincarnation of modernization theory that once again looks at how internal characteristics, such as social and cultural conditions, may shape political and economic development (see Controversy: Theories of Development: A Return to Modernization?).

dualism
the separation of a country into two sectors, the first modern and prosperous centered in major cities, and the second at the margin, neglected and poor.

multinational corporations (MNCs)
business enterprises headquartered in one state that invest and operate extensively in many other states.

newly industrialized countries (NICs)
the most prosperous members of the Global South, which have become important exporters of manufactured goods as well as important markets for the major industrialized countries that export capital goods.

Global East
the rapidly growing economies of East and South Asia that have made those countries competitors with the traditionally dominant countries of the Global North.

CLOSING THE GAP? THE GLOBAL SOUTH'S PROSPECTS IN A WORLD OF GREAT POWERS

The vast political, economic, and social differences separating the Global North and the Global South suggest that the remaining countries in the Global South are increasingly vulnerable, insecure, and defenseless, and that these conditions are products of both internal and international factors. Given the multiple problems standing in the way of Global South security and prosperity, ask yourself how you, were you to become a head of state

CONTROVERSY:

THEORIES OF DEVELOPMENT: A RETURN TO MODERNIZATION?

Over time, the perceived effectiveness and credibility of theories have waxed and waned depending in part upon their ability to explain and predict current world events. Such has been the case with theoretical explanations of modernization. During its heyday in the 1960s, classical theory prescribed countries to emulate the path of industrial democracies in order to develop. However, it was apparent by the 1970s that such efforts had not resulted in widespread prosperity or democracy. For example, many countries in Latin America, such as Chile, Argentina, and Brazil, suffered from authoritarian rule and abject poverty. Dependency theory grew in popularity at this time, with its focus on the global capitalist system—rather than the internal problems of the Global South countries—as the reason for persistent underdevelopment. Yet the relevance of this theoretical explanation came to be questioned as well, particularly in light of the success of the Global East countries that experienced meaningful growth by participating in the global market and pursuing export-oriented strategies.

As both perspectives fell out of vogue, critics suggested that modernization theory was dead. However, since the end of the Cold War, a nuanced version of modernization theory has emerged and is gaining credibility. Responding to changes in the world such as the demise of communism and the economic success of East Asian countries, its core premise is that producing for the world market enables economic growth; investing the returns in human capital and upgrading the work force to produce high-tech goods brings higher returns and enlarges the educated middle class; once the middle class becomes large and articulate enough, it presses for liberal democracy—the most effective political system for advanced industrial societies (Inglehart and Welzel 2009, p. 36).

Like earlier incarnations of modernization theory, this more recent version similarly sees economic development as eliciting important and predictable changes in politics, culture, and society. Yet it provides a more complex understanding in a number of ways (Inglehart and Welzel 2009):

- History Matters. As constructivists would argue, a society's beliefs, values, and traditions shape its larger worldview and its engagement with the forces of modernization.

- Modernization Is Not Westernization. The success of industrialization in the Global East, and the role of countries other than the United States as models for development, challenges earlier ethnocentric assumptions of modernization theory.

- Modernization Is Not Democratization. While economic development tends to produce certain societal changes linked to modernization, increases in per capita GDP do not automatically result in democracy, as seen in the case of Kuwait and the United Arab Emirates.

- Modernization Is Not Linear. There are multiple inflection points, as individual phases of modernization tend to be associated with particular changes in society; industrialization tends to be linked to bureaucratization, hierarchy, and secularization while post-industrialization tends to emphasize individual autonomy and self-expression values.

This debate over the sources of modernization provides us ideas about why some countries develop to a greater extent than others. It also illustrates a feedback loop between real-world events and trends and the construction and testing of theory.

WHAT DO YOU THINK?

- How are liberalism, constructivism, and radical perspectives (such as Marxism) reflected in the various versions of modernization theory?

- What are the implications of the new modernization theory for the rise of gender equality? For democratization? For the role of international organizations as instruments of development?

- New modernization theory suggests that the rise of the middle class is an important component in a country's development into a democracy. How might this be an important policy perspective for decision makers, both domestically and internationally? What might some policy outputs look like, taking new modernization theory into account?

of a Global South country, would approach these awesome challenges. Your choices would undoubtedly benefit by considering the different approaches Global South countries have taken to pursue their objectives, particularly in their relationships with the Global North.

Fueling Growth Through Oil and Technology

Consider one category of Global South states whose relative wealth contrasts sharply with the LLDCs' poverty: those Global South states that have fossil fuels to consume and export. The sixteen developing-country exporters of oil and other fuels, and especially the twelve members of the Organization of Petroleum Exporting Countries (OPEC), have escaped the LLDCs' grim fate. Notably, OPEC members Kuwait, Qatar, and the United Arab Emirates have risen to the high-income group's standards of living and now rival or exceed that of some countries in the Global North.

Simulation: OPEC

The Global North and the Global South differ in terms of their technological capabilities. Typically, Global South countries have been unable to develop an indigenous technology appropriate to their own resources and have been dependent on powerful Global North multinational corporations (see Chapter 5) to transfer technical know-how. This means that research and development expenditures are devoted to solving the Global North's problems, with technological advances seldom meeting the needs of the Global South. And in the information age, technology has not been distributed equally geographically: the lowest density of computer connections to the Internet is in the Global South. Nonetheless, emerging multinationals in the Global South have made advances,

Face to Face/UPPA/Photoshot, Inc.

EMERGING MARKET GIANTS Launched in March 2009, the Tata Nano is the world's cheapest car and is the innovation of an emerging multinational in Mumbai, India. With low-cost production models based on inexpensive local labor and growing domestic markets, companies in the Global South are competing with the rich-country multinationals in the Global North.

and are "spooking the rich world's established multinationals with innovative products and bold acquisitions" (*The Economist*, March 28, 2009, p. 20).

The Global East

Another group of countries that inspires hope and awe is the "middle-income" and rapidly rising *newly industrialized countries* in East and Southern Asia. This new contingent of countries, called the Global East, has arisen from the former Global South and is now positioned to rival the levels of prosperity that the Global North has enjoyed in the last two decades (Mahbubani 2009). A loose definition of the Global East would include not only Japan and the four *Asian Tigers* (South Korea, Singapore, Taiwan, and Hong Kong), but also China, India, Malaysia, and Thailand (see Map 4.1).

Asian Tigers
the four Asian NICs that experienced far greater rates of economic growth during the 1980s than the more advanced industrial societies of the Global North.

purchasing power parity (PPP)
an index that calculates the true rate of exchange among currencies when parity—when what can be purchased is the same—is achieved; the index determines what can be bought with a unit of each currency.

Together, these nine Asian economies account for roughly one-fourth of the total world gross national income, adjusted for *purchasing power parity (PPP)* (WDI 2010, pp. 32–34). They are experiencing even greater success than the oil-exporting countries. Their achievement lies in moving beyond the export of simple unfinished goods such as crude oil to the export of manufactured goods and to providing service and expertise in the digital revolution of the information age. Today, the NICs are among the largest exporters of manufactured goods and are leaders in the information processing industry. They have climbed from the periphery into the *semiperiphery* and beyond to rival the Global North.

Their growth has been energized by the *outsourcing* of jobs from the labor-costly Global North to skilled Asian workers capable of performing the same labor at less expense. Outsourcing and corporate restructuring are promoted as critical to facilitating business without borders, enhancing corporate growth and profitability, and better using skilled staff in both the Global North and the Global South. However, there is widespread controversy regarding the threat that the offshore transfer of labor poses to workers in the Global North as "even highly educated tech and service professionals . . . compete against legions of hungry college grads in India, China, and the Philippines willing to work twice as hard for one-fifth the pay" (Engardio, Arndt, and Foust 2006). The recent global recession that

Jon Arnold Images/Alamy

Ashraf Shazly/AFP/Getty Images

FROM RAGS TO RICHES A number of formerly poor Global South countries have catapulted to affluence, either through free markets and aggressive trade or by capitalizing on abundant natural resources. Dubai, shown here (left), is a prime example of the latter. Rising oil prices have created a boom that is transforming this Arab kingdom into a zone of prosperity, as exemplified by the construction of the world's largest shopping mall with the world's largest aquarium and a five-story underwater hotel. Not to be outdone, Saudi and Kuwaiti investors have developed a huge financial center in war-torn but oil-rich Sudan, Africa's largest country. Pictured (right) are Sudanese crossing the bridge to witness the inauguration ceremony for the financial center.

began in 2007 has accelerated this structural shift in the economy. Former U.S. Secretary of Labor Robert Reich (2010) recently noted that

> Companies have used the downturn to aggressively trim payrolls, making cuts they've been reluctant to make before. Outsourcing abroad has increased dramatically. Companies have discovered that new software and computer technologies have made many workers in Asia and Latin America almost as productive as Americans and that the Internet allows far more work to be efficiently moved to another country without loss of control.

The success of the NICs in elevating themselves above the rest of the Global South has inspired faith in the neoclassical theorists' export-led strategies and now encourages other Global South countries to copy them by removing still other obstacles standing in the way of economic growth, such as speeding up transitions toward fuller economic liberalization and democratic governance.

Military Security

Global South countries must face the fateful question of whether they dare to call for help from the great powers and dominating international organizations when violence, terrorism, and anarchy prevail. The cry for assistance poses risks, because where there is outside involvement, there tends to be outside influence, some of which may be unwelcome. There is a fine line between external involvement and interference. On top of this concern is another: the threat of great power indifference or inability to agree about when, where, why, and how they should collectively become involved within Global South borders where violence, ethnic cleansing, and terrorism occur.

semiperiphery
to world-system theorists, countries midway between the rich "core," or center, and the poor "periphery" in the global hierarchy, at which foreign investments are targeted when labor wages and production costs become too high in the prosperous core regions.

outsourcing
the transfer of jobs by a corporation usually headquartered in a Global North country to a Global South country able to supply trained workers at lower wages.

Faced with seemingly endless conflict at home or abroad, and a desire to address military insecurity on their own terms, it is not surprising that the Global South countries have joined the rest of the world's quest to acquire modern weapons of war—including nuclear weapons, as in the cases of China, India, North Korea, and Pakistan. As a result, the burden of military spending (measured by the ratio of military expenditures to GNP) is highest among those least able to bear it (SIPRI 2010). In the Global South, military spending typically exceeds expenditures on health and education; impoverished states facing ethnic, religious, or tribal strife at home are quite prepared to sacrifice expenditures for economic development in order to acquire weapons.

Few Global South states produce their own weapons. Weak Global South governments, paralyzed by fears of separatist revolts, have invested increased proportions of their country's modest national budgets in arms rather than reallocate those scarce revenues to reduce poverty and enhance social and economic development. Most Global South countries have increased their military spending to purchase arms produced in the Global North at higher rates than do their Global North counterparts (SIPRI 2010). Thus, in responding to a world of powers, the Global South appears to be increasing its dependence for arms purchases on the very same rich states whose military and economic domination they historically have most feared and resented.

Reform of the Economic Order

Although some Global South countries benefit from global economic integration and prosper, others remain immune to the alleged benefits of globalization and are especially vulnerable to recessions in the global economy. How to cope with dominance and dependence thus remains a key Global South concern. The emerging Global South countries were born into a political-economic order with rules they had no voice in creating. In order to gain control over their economic futures, they began coordinating their efforts within the United Nations, where their growing numbers and voting power gave them greater influence than they could otherwise command.

Group of 77 (G-77)
the coalition of Third World countries that sponsored the 1963 *Joint Declaration of Developing Countries* calling for reform to allow greater equality in North–South trade.

In the 1960s, they formed a coalition of the world's poor, the *Group of 77 (G-77)*, and used their voting power to convene the UN Conference on Trade and Development (UNCTAD). UNCTAD later became a permanent UN organization through which the Global South would express its interests concerning development issues. A decade later, the G-77 (then numbering more than 120 countries) again used its UN numerical majority to push for a *New International Economic Order (NIEO)* to replace the international economic regime championed by the United States and the other capitalist powers since World War II. Motivated by the oil-exporting countries' rising bargaining power, the Global South sought to compel the Global North to abandon practices perceived as perpetuating their dependence.

Not surprisingly, the Global North rebuffed many of the South's proposals, although some of the issues that were raised (such as debt relief) remain on the global agenda. At the 2003 World Trade Organization meeting in Cancún, Mexico, for example, the poor countries united to demand major concessions from the wealthy countries, especially with regard to foreign subsidies. In 2008 another step was taken when "Banco del Sur" (Bank of the South) was launched by founding members Brazil and Argentina to compete directly with the World Bank and thereby fund big infrastructure projects through the region's new oil wealth to go around Global North interference.

New International Economic Order (NIEO)
the 1974 UN policy resolution that called for a North–South dialogue to open the way for the less developed countries of the Global South to participate more fully in the making of international economic policy.

Regional Trade Regimes

With the failure of reform envisioned by the NIEO, the integration of Global South countries into the globalization process will occur according to the rules dictated by the Global North. Are there alternatives? Can regional arrangements enable Global South states to take advantage of growing economic interdependence to achieve their development goals?

To promote growth through regional economic agreements, in the 1990s the global economy began to subdivide into three "trade blocs"—one in Europe, with the European Union (EU) as its hub; a second in the Americas, with the United States at the center; and a third in the Global East, with Japan and China dominant. Consider some recent developments:

■ In the Americas: The Central America-Dominican Republic Free Trade Agreement (CAFTA-DR) aims to emulate NAFTA and create a free-trade zone that includes the United States, Dominican Republic, Guatemala, El Salvador, Nicaragua, Honduras, and Costa Rica. Intent on liberalizing U.S. and Central American markets, the agreement is the first major "sub-regional" agreement between very unequal trading partners—excluding the United States, the combined GDP of CAFTA members is less than 1 percent of U.S. GDP (WDI 2010). Mercosur, commonly referred to as the "Common Market of the South," is the largest trading bloc in South America and aims for full economic integration of the region. Full members include Argentina, Brazil, Paraguay, Uruguay, and Venezuela, with Bolivia, Colombia, Ecuador, Peru, with Chile holding associate membership status.

- In Asia: The association of Asia-Pacific Economic Cooperation (APEC), an informal forum created in 1989, has committed itself to creating a free-trade zone during the next twenty-five years. In addition, the members of the Association of Southeast Asian Nations (ASEAN), first established in 1967 by Brunei, Indonesia, Malaysia, the Philippines, Singapore, and Thailand and now including Vietnam, agreed to set up a free-trade area.

- In Sub-Saharan Africa: The Southern African Development Community (SADC) is the largest of twelve regional free-trade areas in the region.

Will the lofty expectations of these regional politico-economic groups be realized? In the past, political will and shared visions have proven to be indispensable elements in successful regional trade regimes that set rules for members' collaboration. Economic complementarity is another essential component, as the goal is to stimulate greater trade among the members of the free-trade area, not simply between it and other regions.

Foreign Aid and Remittances

One approach for closing the gap between the Global South and the Global North is through the distribution of foreign assistance. Urging the wealthy countries to help the poorest, Chinese president Hu Jintao declared in February 2009 that "developed countries should assume their responsibilities and obligations, continue to deliver their aid, [keep their] debt relief commitments, maintain and increase assistance to developing countries and effectively help them maintain financial stability and economic growth."

foreign aid
economic assistance in the form of loans and grants provided by a donor country to a recipient country for a variety of purposes.

bilateral
interactions between two transnational actors.

official development assistance (ODA)
grants or loans to countries from donor countries, now usually channeled through multilateral aid institutions such as the World Bank for the primary purpose of promoting economic development and welfare.

Some *foreign aid* consists of outright grants of money, some of loans at concessional rates, and some of shared technical expertise. Although most foreign aid is *bilateral* and is termed *official development assistance (ODA)*—meaning the money flows directly from one country to another—an increasing portion is now channeled through global intergovernmental institutions such as the World Bank, and hence is known as "multilateral aid" (see Chapter 5). Moreover, the purposes of aid are as varied as its forms. Commonly stated foreign aid goals include not only the reduction of poverty through economic development but also human development, environmental protection, reduced military spending, enhanced economic management, the development of private enterprise, increased power for women, the promotion of democratic governance and human rights, and humanitarian disaster relief and assistance to refugees (Dimiral-Pegg and Moskowitz 2009, Woods 2008, Barrett 2007). However, security objectives traditionally have figured prominently as motives of donors' allocations of both economic aid and military assistance, and still do. For example, the United States continues to target Israel and Egypt as major recipients to symbolize friendship, maintain a balance of power, and tilt the scales toward peace in the Middle East. Also, security was the primary motive behind the doubling of the U.S. foreign assistance budget following 9/11 to provide funds for allies' use in the global war on terrorism.

The assumption that development will support other goals, such as fostering solidarity among allies and promoting commercial advantage, free markets, or democratization, still underpins most donors' assistance programs. With the Millennium Challenge Account (MCA), the United States committed to provide from 2006 onward at least $5 billion each year in aid to seventeen eligible countries that "govern justly, invest in their people, and encourage economic freedom." This represented the largest increase in U.S. development assistance since the Marshall Plan in 1948. The general global trend for the past fifteen years in foreign aid allocations has been toward slowly rising increases, with contributions expected to reflect an 11 percent increase between 2008 and 2010 due in part to greater expenditures by a number of multilateral agencies (OECD 2010). However, due to the global economic downturn, many donor countries will not meet their targeted ODA levels.

Video: *Embarrassing the Rich to Help the Poor*

Many aid donors have become frustrated with the slow growth rates of many of the Global South recipients and have grown impatient and doubtful of the effectiveness of their aid programs, despite strong evidence that foreign aid has made a positive difference (Easterbrook 2002). Critics particularly resent what they perceive to be an entrenched state of mind in many Global South cultures that stands in the way of development, which—while bemoaning poverty—at the same time condemns the profit motive, competition, and consumerism that lie at the heart of capitalism. Donors are especially resentful that the countries seeking aid do not value the core Western values of hard work, economic competition, and entrepreneurial creativity believed to be crucial for progress and prosperity.

In response to this viewpoint, donors have grown increasingly insistent on "conditionality," or demands that aid recipients must meet to receive assistance. Donors also persist in their habit of making development assistance "tied" to the donors for their benefit, such as requiring purchases from the donors, even though the World Bank estimates this practice reduces the value of aid by 15 to 30 percent, decreases its efficiency, and violates the same free-market principles that the Global North promotes.

On top of this, Global South countries complain that the Global North donors have been promising for the past forty years to allocate 0.7 percent of their gross national product (GNP) to foreign aid, but only a few have kept the promise or even come close (see Figure 4.1). This is true despite the evidence that more assistance does indeed contribute to development when it is designed properly and is delivered in a sustained way to countries with records of improving democratic governance (Sachs 2005). Recently, however, many Global South leaders have joined Global North critics of foreign aid, interpreting it as an instrument of neocolonialism and neoimperialism and resenting the conditionality criteria for receiving aid imposed by the International Monetary Fund (IMF) and other multilateral institutions. As Rwandan President Paul Kagame explained in May 2009, "We appreciate support from the outside, but it should be support for what we intend to achieve ourselves."

Much more money—more than double the global total in foreign aid—is primarily funneled into Global South economies through the ***remittances*** that

remittances
the money earned by immigrants working in rich countries (which almost always exceeds the income they could earn working in their home country) that they send to their families in their home country.

FIGURE 4.1

BROKEN PROMISES
With UN Resolution 2626, the wealthy countries of the Global North agreed in 1970 to allocate 7 percent of their GNP as aid for the long-term development of the poorer countries of the Global South. Though the Global North has given $2.98 trillion in aid since that time, the amount falls far short of the promised assistance, which would now come to $4.01 trillion (Shah 2010).

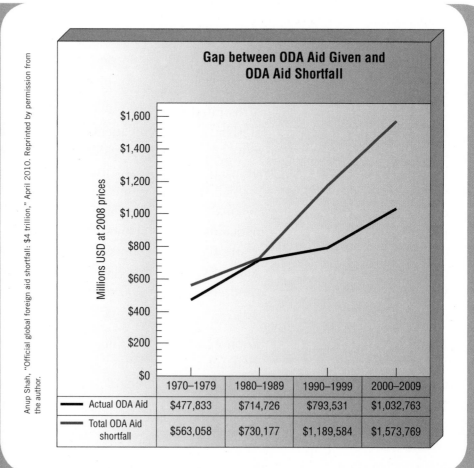

Anup Shah, "Official global foreign aid shortfall: $4 trillion," April 2010. Reprinted by permission from the author.

Gap between ODA Aid Given and ODA Aid Shortfall

Millions USD at 2008 prices

	1970–1979	1980–1989	1990–1999	2000–2009
Actual ODA Aid	$477,833	$714,726	$793,531	$1,032,763
Total ODA Aid shortfall	$563,058	$730,177	$1,189,584	$1,573,769

migrant laborers working in the Global North earn each paycheck and faithfully send home to their families. For some countries, such as Jamaica, Lebanon, and Tajikistan, remittances in some years comprise more than a fifth of their GDP. Global remittances rose steadily each year since the 1970s and reached $420 billion in 2009 from only $170 billion in 2002. Though the World Bank expected remittances to decline in 2009, remittances are not as sensitive to economic downturns as private-capital flows. The World Bank estimates that $317 billion of the $420 billion in remittances "went to developing countries, involving some 192 million migrants or 3 percent of the world population. The money received is an important source of family (and national) income in many developing economies, representing in some cases a very relevant percentage of the GDP of the receiving countries" (World Bank 2010).

Trade and Foreign Direct Investment

The developing countries have long pleaded for "trade, not aid" to improve their global position, turning to the NIC's and the Global East experience to support the view that access to the Global North's markets is critical to Global South economic growth. And those requests for

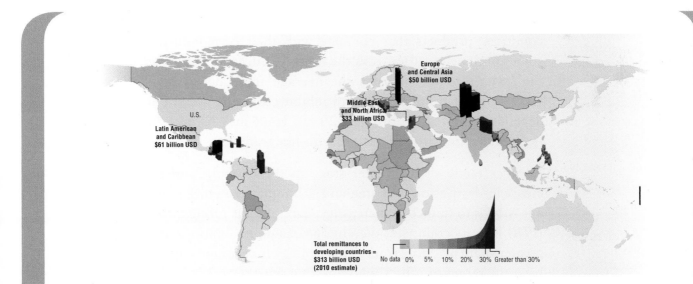

MAP 4.4

SENDING MONEY BACK HOME The billions of dollars that migrant workers send home each year is vital to developing countries. For example, in Tajikistan, remittances amount to almost 36 percent of the gross domestic product. As the global economy continues to experience ups and downs at the start of 2011, the stream of revenue may slow. This concerns governments such as Mexico's, where fewer Latin American immigrants in the United States are sending money back home.

greater trade through reduced barriers have met with success: the number of free-trade agreements between Global South and Global North countries increased to 186 (WTO 2010), from only 23 in 1990 (Bigelow 2005). Indeed, many countries of the Global South have benefited from a "virtuous cycle" (Blanton and Blanton 2008), wherein trade leads to improved domestic conditions that in turn facilitate trade. In an effort to shore up the global economy, global leaders pledged to finance trade, resist protectionist measures, and assist the Global South. These efforts met with success, as seen in the recovery of global trade volumes by the start of 2010 following their sharp decline in 2008 (Gregory et al. 2010). However, as evidenced by the shift at the G-20 summit meeting in Toronto in 2010 from an emphasis on spending programs to debt reduction as a response to the global economic crisis, there is a potential for the developed and emerging market economy countries to reduce spending, enact protectionist measures, and focus on their own economic problems—an approach that could disrupt the fragile recovery of the worldwide economy and disadvantage the Global South.

The "North-South gap has not narrowed so far during the most recent globalization era" (Reuveny and Thompson 2008, p. 8). Many Global South countries have not improved their lot: market access remains difficult because domestic pressure groups in these low-growth Global South countries have lobbied their governments to reduce the imports of other countries' products that compete with their own industries. Moreover, some continue to suffer from the negative effects of trade deficits—among the lower-income countries the average trade deficit is 13 percent of GDP—and such imbalances can inhibit economic growth and encourage dependency in the South (WDI 2010). Trade may be preferred to aid, but political barriers often interfere with free trade.

foreign direct investment (FDI)
a cross-border investment through which a person or corporation based in one country purchases or constructs an asset such as a factory or bank in another country so that a long-term relationship and control of an enterprise by nonresidents results.

externalities
the unintended side effects of choices that reduce the true value of the original decision, such as trade protectionism against foreign imports increasing the costs of goods to consumers and stimulating inflation.

Another tactic sitting center stage in the Global South's strategies for escaping destitution and stagnant economic growth has been to encourage MNCs to funnel an increasing share of their *foreign direct investment (FDI)* into its countries, thereby increasing its export earnings to gain a greater share of global trade. This strategy for economic growth has always been the target of critics who question whether the investment of capital by MNCs (and, to a lesser extent, private investors) into local or domestic business ventures is really a financial remedy. The strategy has always been controversial, because there are many hidden costs, or *externalities*, associated with permitting corporations controlled from abroad to set up business within the host state for the purpose of making a profit. Who is to be the ultimate beneficiary, the foreign investor or the states in which the investments are made? Considerable risks are entailed, as are a number of trade-offs among competing values (see Controversy: Multinational Corporations in the Global South: Do They Help or Hurt?).

The primary danger with this strategy is the potential for foreign investments to lead to foreign control and the erosion of sovereign governments' capacities to regulate the economy within their borders. An additional danger is the probability that the multinational foreign investors will not invest their profits locally but channel them abroad for new investments or disburse them as dividends for their wealthy Global North shareholders. However, despite the risks, many developing countries have relaxed restrictions in order to attract foreign investors, with less emphasis placed on liberalizing investment restrictions and encouraging open domestic economic competition than on offering tax and cash enticements and opportunities for joint ventures. This has stimulated a recent surge in the flow of capital investments to the Global South (see Figure 4.2).

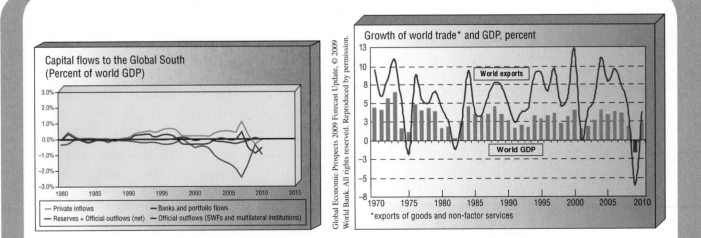

FIGURE 4.2

THE RISE AND FALL OF THE GLOBAL ECONOMY Over the past decade, fixed investment has been a primary source for growth in the Global South. Developing countries in East and Central Asia, as well as Europe, saw an investment contribution to overall growth of roughly 4 percentage points. However, the recent global economic downturn has challenged future growth. Both private and official capital flows to the Global South experienced great volatility between 2007 and 2009, before becoming more stable by 2011 (see left). According to the World Bank, the contraction of world trade and GDP in 2009 was unparalleled and had a negative interaction with investment, as "firms around the world had to scale-back production and postpone capital spending plans" (shown right).

The impact of this new infusion of foreign investments in developing countries has been substantial, given the Global South's relatively small economies. It has paved the way for emerging markets to expand their rates of economic development—despite the resistance of local industries that are threatened by the competition and the critics who complain about the income inequalities that the investments are causing. Such fears and consequences notwithstanding, developing countries are intensifying their competition for foreign investment capital in order to liberate themselves from dependence and destitution (Blanton and Blanton 2009). And foreign direct investment is the leading cause of the shift from farm work to service jobs in Global South urban areas (now 61.5 percent of the developing countries' labor force) that is lifting millions of people out of poverty while at the same time outsourcing skilled jobs from the Global North (WDI 2010, p. 72).

Debt Management

The prospects for either foreign aid, trade, or foreign direct investments to contribute to the future development of, and relief of poverty in, the Global South will depend on a number of other factors. Foremost is the extent to which the staggering level of debt facing many Global South countries can be managed. The World Bank estimates that Global South debt in 2008 exceeded $3,718 billion and that the debt-service payments of these countries were equivalent to over 22 percent of their gross national income (WDI 2010). This is unsustainable and threatens their economic health and future growth.

heavily indebted poor countries (HIPCs)
the subset of countries identified by the World Bank's Debtor Reporting System whose ratios of debt to gross national product are so substantial they cannot meet their payment obligations without experiencing political instability and economic collapse.

Worse off are the forty *heavily indebted poor countries (HIPCs)*. In an effort to provide debt relief within a framework of poverty reduction, the joint IMF-World Bank "Initiative for Heavily Indebted Poor Countries" (HIPC Initiative) coordinated efforts through multilateral organizations and governments to reduce the severe external debt of HIPCs to a level that they could sustain. To provide even further debt relief, a group of Global North great powers proposed the "Multilateral Debt Relief Initiative" (MDRI) in 2005. Under this program, four multilateral lending institutions—the International Development Association (IDA), International Monetary Fund (IMF), African Development Fund (AfDF), and Inter-American Development Bank (IDB)—provide 100 percent debt relief on eligible debts owed to them by HIPCs once thoses countries have completed key structural reforms as required by the "HIPC Initiative" process and have already received the initial HIPC Initiative assistance. This was partly done out of compassion but also was a result of the economic self-interest of the Global North, which sees in debt relief a pragmatic method for preventing an economic collapse that could threaten the entire world economy in the age of interdependent globalization.

CONTROVERSY:

MULTINATIONAL CORPORATIONS IN THE GLOBAL SOUTH: DO THEY HELP OR HURT?

Within the Global South, widespread concern has existed about the impact of multinational corporations' (MNCs) activities on the local economy and its growth rate. Part of the concern stems from the historic tendency for MNCs to look to Global South countries as production sites so they can take advantage of cheap labor for production and avoid labor-union pressure that for years was virtually nonexistent. MNCs can either promote or inhibit development, depending on how they channel investments and, when they do, how they operate in the host country. Despite these concerns about MNCs as powerful, potentially neocolonial, nonstate actors that may compromise national sovereignty and undermine local prosperity, many Global South countries have overcome their fears and now welcome global companies to stimulate rapid growth despite the many potential risks and costs that MNC penetrations often incur.

MNCs continue to be alternately praised and condemned, depending on how their performance is viewed. The record is mixed and can be evaluated on different criteria. The following "balance sheet" summarizes the major arguments for and against MNCs. Using this summary of contending interpretations, you can easily see why the role and impact of MNCs is so controversial.

Positive	Negative
• Increase the volume of trade	• Give rise to huge merged conglomerations that reduce competition and free enterprise
• Assist the aggregation of investment capital that can fund development	• Raise capital in host countries (thereby depriving local industries of investment capital) but export profits to home countries
• Finance loans and service international debt	
• Lobby for free trade and the removal of barriers to trade, such as tariffs	• Limit the availability of commodities by monopolizing their production and controlling their distribution in the world marketplace
• Underwrite research and development initiatives that allow technological innovation	• Create "sanctuary markets" that restrict and channel other investments to give MNCs an unfair advantage
• Introduce and dispense advanced technology to less developed countries	• Export technology ill-suited to underdeveloped economies
• Reduce the costs of goods by encouraging their production according to the principle of *comparative advantage*	• Inhibit the growth of infant industries and local technological expertise in less developed countries while making Global South countries dependent on Global North technology

(continued)

DO THEY HELP OR HURT? (Continued)

Positive	Negative
• Produce new goods and expand opportunities for their purchase through the internationalization of production	• Limit workers' wages
• Disseminate marketing expertise and mass advertising methods	• Limit the supply of raw materials available in international markets
• Provide investment income to facilitate less developed countries' modernization	• Erode traditional cultures and national differences, leaving in their place a homogenized world culture dominated by consumer-oriented values
• Generate income and wealth	• Widen the gap between rich and poor countries
• Advocate peaceful relations between and among states to preserve an orderly environment conducive to trade and profits	• Increase the wealth of local elites at the expense of the poor
• Generate employment	• Support and rationalize repressive regimes in the name of stability and order
• Encourage the training of workers	• Challenge national sovereignty and jeopardize the autonomy of states
	• Create monopolies that contribute to inflation

WHAT DO YOU THINK?

- Some may argue that, in light of the Global South being so far behind, *any* positive results from MNCs are a good thing, even if they come with negatives consequences as well. Are the negative effects worth it as a cost of developing, or is there a better way to raise the Global South's level of development?

- Does regime type matter when evaluating the potential for an exploitative or constructive relationship between MNCs and countries in the Global South? Why or why not?

- Thinking ahead, what potential role could intergovernmental organizations such as the UN or the IMF play in regulating MNCs?

Yet these reforms may not be as successful as their advocates claim. On the one hand, China and Singapore have enjoyed rapid economic growth without undertaking significant political liberalization. On the other hand, many Global South countries that have implemented economic liberalizing reforms have not experienced growth (Collier 2007). Some have even experienced increased hardship, civil conflict, and human rights repression (Abouharb and Cingranelli 2007). Indeed, Joseph Stiglitz, a Nobel Laureate in economics and former chief economist of the World Bank, complains that the policies produce disappointing results because they are anchored in a free-market dogma that ignores the unique sociocultural contexts of the countries where they are applied. Given the diversity of the Global South, development strategies for the future should avoid grandiose claims of universality and one-size-fits-all policies. What works in one country may be impractical or undesirable in another.

> *The twenty-first century is going to be about*
> *more than great power politics.*
>
> —Bill Clinton, U.S. President

THE GLOBAL SOUTH'S FUTURE

It is useful to remember the historical trends underlying the emergence of the Global South as an actor on the global stage. Those states that came to regard themselves as its members share important characteristics. Most were colonized by people of another race, experienced varying degrees of poverty and hunger, and felt powerless in a world system dominated by the affluent countries that once controlled them and perhaps still do. Considerable change occurred among the newly emergent states as post–World War II *decolonization* took place, but much also remained the same.

The relationships between the world's great and small powers will no doubt continue to change—exactly how remains uncertain. However, the future of Global South development is certain to depend in the near term on the activities of the Global North. A turn inward toward isolationist foreign policies in the Global North could lead to a posture of "benign neglect" of the Global South. Conversely, a new era of North-South-East cooperation could commence, dedicated to finding solutions to common problems ranging from commercial to environmental and security concerns. Elements of both approaches are already evident.

Animated Learning Module: *International Organizations and Transnational Actors*

Relations between the Global South and the Global North remain dominated by the great powers. That domination is funneled in part through the powerful international organizations, such as the United Nations and the World Bank, that the great powers have created. At the same time, intergovernmental organizations (IGOs) provide an opportunity for the small powers of the Global South to exert influence on world politics. To understand world politics and the roots of changes in international affairs, it is important to inspect the impact of these influential IGOs as actors in the global arena. To complete the picture, you also need to inspect the thousands of nongovernmental organizations (NGOs), whose presence and pressure as nonstate actors are also transforming international politics, for both the Global North and the Global South. We turn to both of these transnational actors in Chapter 5.

Take an Online Practice Quiz

www.cengagebrain.com/shop/ISBN/0495802204

Suggested Readings

Chant, Sylvia and Cathy McIlwaine. (2009) *Geographies of Development in the 21st Century: An Introduction to the Global South.* New York, NY: Edward Elgar Publishing.

Mahbubani, Kishore. (2009) *The New Asian Hemisphere: The Irresistible Shift of Global Power to the East.* New York, NY: Basic Civitas Books.

Reuveny, Rafael and William R. Thompson, eds. (2008) *North and South in the World Political Economy.* Malden, MA: Blackwell.

Williams, Glyn, Paula Meth, and Katie Willis (2009) *New Geographies of the Global South: Developing Areas in a Changing World.* New York, NY: Taylor & Francis.

Woodward, Susan L. (2009) "Shifts in Global Security Policies: Why They Matter for the South," *IDS Bulletin* 40:121–128.

World Bank. (2009) *Atlas of Global Development,* 2nd edition. Washington, D.C.: World Bank.

CHAPTER 5
NONSTATE ACTORS AND THE
QUEST FOR GLOBAL COMMUNITY

CHAPTER OUTLINE

NONSTATE ACTORS IN WORLD POLITICS

Intergovernmental Organizations (IGOs)

Nongovernmental Organizations (NGOs)

PROMINENT INTERGOVERNMENTAL ORGANIZATIONS

The United Nations

Other Prominent Global IGOs

REGIONAL INTERGOVERNMENTAL ORGANIZATIONS

The European Union

Other Regional IGOs

CONTROVERSY: Will Global IGOs Replace States as the Primary Actors in World Politics?

PROMINENT TYPES OF NONGOVERNMENTAL ORGANIZATIONS

Nonstate Nations: Ethnic Groups and Indigenous Peoples

Transnational Religious Movements

CONTROVERSY: Are Religious Movements Causes of War or Sources of Transnational Harmony?

Transnational Terrorist Groups

Multinational Corporations

Issue-Advocacy Groups

NONSTATE ACTORS AND THE FUTURE OF WORLD POLITICS

A novel redistribution of power among states, markets, and civil society is underway, ending the steady accumulation of power in the hands of states that began with the Peace of Westphalia in 1648.
—Jessica T. Mathews, international relations scholar

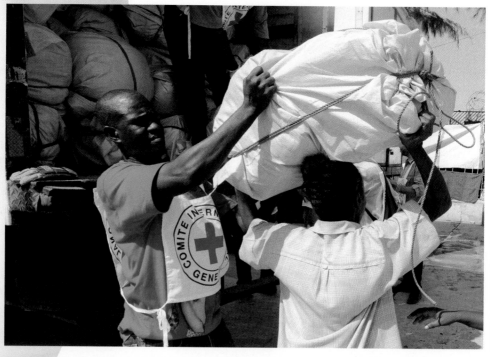

Thony Belizaire/AFP/Getty Images

PEOPLE POWER Shown here are members of the Red Cross, an international humanitarian movement, working in a spirit of global community to provide relief to the people of Haiti, who faced an array of devastating challenges in 2010. The Red Cross provided supplies in the wake of a series of destructive earthquakes that began in January, and in November provided health care to Haitians suffering from a severe cholera outbreak and helped respond to the damage and hardship caused by flooding brought on by Hurricane Tomas.

Y ou are a member of the human race, and your future will be determined to a large degree by the capacity of humanity to work together as a global society to manage the many common problems that confront the entire world. How is the world responding to this challenge?

The answer for centuries has been reliance primarily on sovereign territorial states. As *realism* posits, countries remain the most influential actors on the world stage. It is *states'* foreign policy decisions and interactions that, more than any other factor, give rise to trends and transformations in world politics. Today, however, as liberal theory observes, the extraordinary power of states over global destiny is eroding as our world becomes increasingly complex and interdependent, and nonstate actors continue to multiply and seek greater influence in the global community. Moreover, a new construction of the concept of *responsible sovereignty* is gaining traction among global leaders—one that "entails obligations and duties to one's own citizens and other states" and provides for a greater role by IGOs and NGOs as it "differs from the traditional interpretation of sovereignty (sometimes called *Westphalian sovereignty*) as nonintereference in the internal affairs of states" (Jones et al. 2009, p. 9).

responsible sovereignty a principle that requires states to protect not only their own people but to cooperate across borders to protect global resources and address transnational threats.

A critical question to consider, then, is if the predicted decline of states' sovereign authority and independence will ultimately prove to be a cure for global problems or a curse, by reducing states' ability to rely on *self-help* measures to address problems unilaterally as each state seeks solutions that best serve its own self-interests.

This chapter provides information and insight that can help you evaluate this question. More specifically, it will enable you to confront and assess the theoretical hypothesis advanced by world leader Jean-Francois Rischard, a former World Bank Vice President for Europe, who argues, "One thing is sure: global complexity [is creating a] global governance crisis that will have to be solved through new ways of working together globally, and bold departures from old, trusted concepts."

Global problems, without a doubt, often require global solutions. There have arisen impressive numbers of nonstate actors on the world stage that are increasingly flexing their political muscle in efforts to engineer adaptive global changes. This chapter will explore two broad types of nonstate actors—international organizations that carry out independent foreign policies as transnational actors and NGOs made up of individual people who band together in coalitions of private citizens to exercise international influence. To introduce this, we begin with a look at the general characteristics of both types of nonstate actors.

The quest for international security involves the unconditional surrender by every nation, in a certain measure, of its liberty of action, its sovereignty that is to say, and it is clear beyond all doubt that no other road can lead to such security.

—Albert Einstein, leading scientist of the twentieth century

NONSTATE ACTORS IN WORLD POLITICS

intergovernmental organizations (IGOs)
institutions created and joined by states' governments, which give them authority to make collective decisions to manage particular problems on the global agenda.

nongovernmental organizations (NGOs)
transnational organizations of private citizens maintaining consultative status with the UN; they include professional associations, foundations, multinational corporations, or simply internationally active groups in different states joined together to work toward common interests.

What distinguishes the two principal types of nonstate actors is that *intergovernmental organizations (IGOs)* are international organizations whose members are states, whereas *nongovernmental organizations (NGOs)* are associations comprised of members who are private individuals and groups. Both types experienced a sharp increase in their numbers during the twentieth century: In 1909 there were 37 IGOs and 176 NGOs, by 1960 this number had risen to 154 IGOs and 1,255 NGOs, and at the start of 2010 the number had escalated to 247 conventional IGOs and 8,003 conventional NGOs (see Figure 5.1). This does not include the 742 unconventional IGOs and 4,443 unconventional NGOs (organizations such as international funds and foundations) that are recorded by the Yearbook of International Organizations (2009/2010, p. 33).

Intergovernmental Organizations (IGOs)

IGOs are purposely created by states to solve shared problems. This gives IGOs whatever authority they possess for the purposes states assign them, and IGOs are generally regarded as more important than NGOs. In part, this is because IGOs are defined by the fact that their members are the governments of states and also by the permanence of their institutions. IGOs meet at regular intervals, and they have established rules for making decisions and a permanent secretariat or headquarters staff.

IGOs vary widely in size and purpose. Only thirty-three IGOs qualify as "intercontinental organizations" and only thirty-four are, like the UN, "universal membership" IGOs. The rest, accounting for more than 72 percent of the total, are limited in their scope and confined to particular regions. Table 5.1 illustrates these differences. The variation among the organizations in each subcategory is great, particularly with single-purpose, limited-membership IGOs. The North Atlantic Treaty Organization (NATO), for example, is primarily a military alliance, whereas others, such as the Organization of American States (OAS), promote both economic development and democratic reforms. Still, most IGOs concentrate their activities on specific economic or social issues of special concern to them, such as the management of trade or transportation.

States and Conventional IGOs

Conventional NGOs

Source: Figures for states are based on the Correlates of War (COW) (2010); IGOs and NGOs are from the Yearbook of International Organizations 2009–2010, p. 33); and moving averages are from prior volumes.

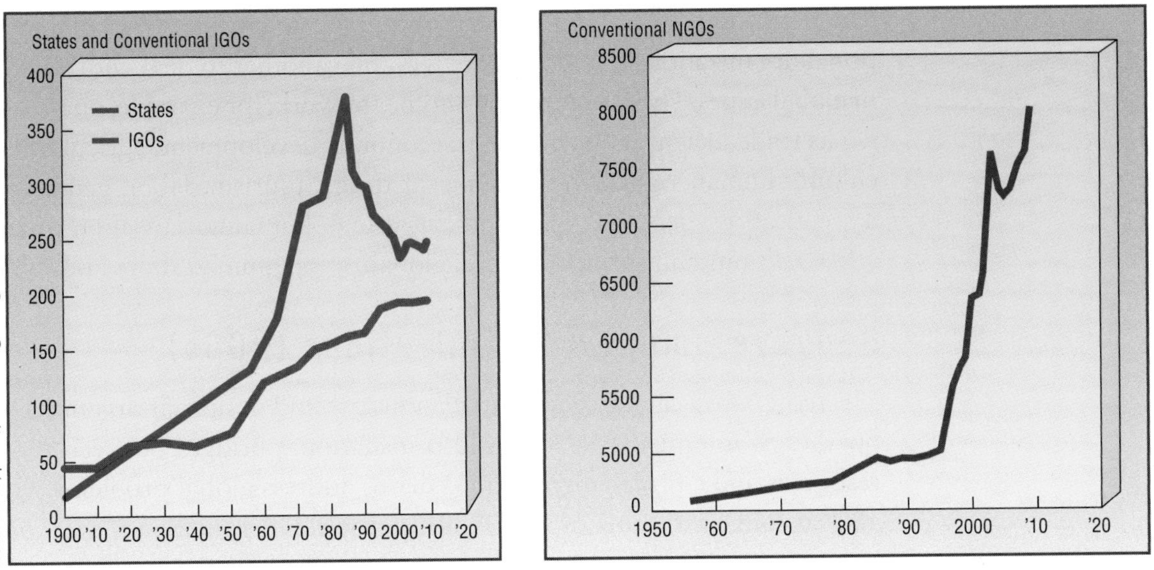

FIGURE 5.1

TRENDS IN THE NUMBER OF IGOs, NGOs, AND STATES SINCE 1900 Since 1900 the number of independent states has increased dramatically, and that growth accelerated especially after World War II when the decolonization movement began. But note that the number of NGOs has grown even more rapidly in this period, declining only since the late 1980s when a number of formerly independent IGOs began to merge with one another. The number of NGOs has grown even more rapidly, with more than 8,000 NGOs in existence worldwide.

Table 5.1 A Simple Classification of Intergovernmental Organizations (IGOs)

Geographic Scope of Membership	Range of Stated Purpose	
	Multiple Purposes	Single Purpose
Global	United Nations, World Trade Organization, UNESCO, Organization of the Islamic Conference	World Health Organization, International Labor Organization, International Monetary Fund, Universal Postal Union
Interregional, regional, subregional	European Union, Organization for Security and Cooperation in Europe, Organization of American States, Organization of African Unity, League of Arab States, Association of Southeast Asian Nations	European Space Agency, Nordic Council, North Atlantic Treaty Organization, International Olive Oil Council, International North Pacific Coffee Organization, African Groundnut Council

The expansion of IGOs has created a complex network of overlapping international organizations that cooperate with one another to deal with a wide range of global issues. They support one another to work, for example, on issues as varied as trade, defense, disarmament, economic development, agriculture, health, culture, human rights, the arts, illegal drugs, tourism, labor, gender inequality, education, debt, the environment, crime, humanitarian aid, civilian crisis relief, telecommunications, science, globalization, immigration, and refugees.

Nongovernmental Organizations (NGOs)

The term *NGO* can be applied to *all* nonstate and nonprofit organizations that operate as intermediaries to build transnational bridges between those with resources and a targeted group in order to address global problems. Thus, it is also customary to think of NGOs as intersocietal organizations that contribute to negotiations between and among states in the hope of reaching agreements for global governance on nearly every issue of international public policy. NGOs link the global society by forming "transnational advocacy networks" working for policy changes (Keck and Sikkink 2008). According to a constructivist perspective, they are inspired to action by their interests and values.

Like IGOs, NGOs differ widely in their characteristics. For example, some are small with membership in the hundreds; others are huge, with the biggest being Amnesty International, which in 2010 included 2.8 million members spread across one hundred fifty countries and regions. At the beginning of 2010, the Union of International Associations categorized the major "conventional" NGOs as split, with over 5 percent as "universal," almost 14 percent as "intercontinental," and the vast majority, almost 80 percent, as "regionally oriented." Functionally, NGOs span virtually every facet of political, social, and economic activity in an increasingly borderless globalized world, ranging from earth sciences to ethnic unity, health care, language, history, culture, education, theology, law, ethics, security, and defense.

> Nongovernmental organizations are not a homogeneous group. The long list of acronyms that has accumulated around NGOs can be used to illustrate this. People speak of NGOs, INGOs (International NGOs), BINGOs (Business International NGOs), RINGOs (Religious International NGOs), ENGOs (Environmental NGOs), QUANGOs (Quasi-Non-Governmental Organizations—i.e., those that are at least partially created or supported by states), and many others. Indeed, all these types of NGOs and more are among those having consultative status at the UN. Among the NGOs . . . are the Academic Council on the UN System, the All India Women's Conference, the Canadian Chemical Producers Association, CARE International, the World Young Women's Christian Association, the World Wide Fund for

Nature International, the Union of Arab Banks, the Women's International League for Peace and Freedom, the World Energy Council, the World Federation of Trade Unions, and the World Veterans Association. Thus, it is difficult to generalize about NGOs at the UN (Stephenson 2000, p. 271).

In general, the socially constructed image of NGOs widely accepted throughout the world is very positive—most pursue objectives that are highly respected and therefore do not provoke much opposition. This perspective is reflected in the World Bank's definition of NGOs as "private organizations that pursue activities to relieve suffering, promote the interests of the poor, protect the environment, provide basic social services, or undertake community development" (World Bank, June 7, 2010). For example, NGOs such as Amnesty International, the International Chamber of Commerce, the International Red Cross, Save the Children, and the World Wildlife Federation enjoy widespread popular support. Others, however, are more controversial because they unite people for collective action in ways that can harm others, as in the case of terrorist groups, international drug rings, or transnational pirates!

Many NGOs interact formally with IGOs. For instance, more than three thousand NGOs actively consult with various agencies of the extensive UN system, maintain offices in hundreds of cities, and hold parallel conferences with IGO meetings to which states send representatives. Such partnerships between NGOs and IGOs enable both types to work (and lobby) together in pursuit of common policies and programs. As IGOs and NGOs rise in numbers and influence, a key question to contemplate is whether a "global society" will materialize to override the traditional global system centered on sovereign states, and, if so, whether this structural transformation will democratize or disrupt global governance.

PROMINENT INTERGOVERNMENTAL ORGANIZATIONS

Let us continue our analysis of nonstate actors in world affairs by examining the most prominent and representative IGOs: the United Nations, the European Union, and various other regional organizations. As we do so, ask yourself whether IGOs' activities are adequate for dealing with the pressing threats to human welfare, whether these IGOs are undermining states' continuing autonomy, and, if so, whether an erosion of state power will prove helpful or harmful.

The United Nations

The United Nations (UN) is the best-known global organization. What distinguishes it from most other IGOs is its nearly universal membership, today

Ships captured
by pirates in 2010
Source: IMB

MAP 5.1

PIRATES ON THE OPEN SEA According to the International Maritime Bureau, during the first half of 2010, more than fifty percent of the 196 pirate attacks worldwide were carried out by Somali pirates. Seventy vessels were boarded, with 597 crew members taken hostage. Attacks by Somali pirates continue to widen, spreading from the Gulf of Aden and the southern part of the Red Sea to the coasts off Tanzania, Kenya, the Seychelles, and even Madagascar in the Indian Ocean and Oman in the Arabian Sea. Protecting more than 23,000 merchant vessels that sail near the Horn of Africa each year from this new kind of actor is a challenging task—the pirates appear to be motivated by monetary gain rather than ideology. Pictured left are suspected pirates in the Gulf of Aden as they are being seized by the U.S. Navy. Pictured right are pirate attacks in 2010.

including 192 independent member states from across the Global North, Global South, and Global East. The UN's nearly fourfold growth from the fifty-one states that joined it at the UN's birth in 1945 has been spectacular, but the admission process has from the start been governed by political conflicts that show the extent to which the organization reflects the relationships of the five great powers that created it and govern it through veto authority in the Security Council. In principle, any sovereign state that accepts the UN's goals and regulations can join, but the great powers have often let *realpolitik*—the belief that countries should put their own national interest above concern for the global community—guide their decision making about which new countries should be admitted. This was especially true during the Cold War, when both the United States and the Soviet Union prevented countries aligned with their adversary from joining.

The UN's Agenda Peace and security figured prominently in the thinking of the great powers responsible for creating the UN and its predecessor, the League of Nations. Following each twentieth-century global war, world leaders created new institutions to keep peace. These institutional reforms were inspired by the liberal conviction that both war and the management of other global problems can best be controlled by removing global *anarchy*—the absence of supranational authority to regulate relations between states—from the international scene. The League of Nations sought to prevent a recurrence of the catastrophic World War I by replacing the balance-of-power system with one based on the construction of a *collective security* regime made up of rules for keeping peace, guided by the principle that an act of aggression by any state would be met by a collective retaliatory response from the rest. When the League failed to restrain expansionistic aggression by Germany, Japan, and Italy during the 1930s, it collapsed. At the start of World War II, the U.S., British, and Russian allies began planning for a new international organization, the United Nations, to preserve the postwar peace because it was believed that peace could not be maintained unilaterally by any one great power acting alone. Article 1 of the UN Charter defines the UN's objectives as centered on:

- Maintaining international peace and security

- Developing friendly relations among states based on respect for the principle of equal rights and the self-determination of peoples

- Achieving international cooperation in solving international problems of an economic, social, cultural, or humanitarian character and in promoting and encouraging respect for human rights and for fundamental freedoms for all

- Functioning as a center for harmonizing the actions of countries to attain these common ends

The history of the UN reflects the fact that countries from both the Global North and the Global South have successfully used the organization to promote their own foreign policy goals, and this record has led to the ratification of more than three hundred treaties and conventions consistent with the UN's "six fundamental values": international freedom, equality, solidarity, tolerance, respect for nature, and a sense of shared responsibility. Though faith in the UN's ability eroded when it soon became paralyzed by the unforeseen Cold War conflict between the United States and the Soviet Union, in the post–Cold War era it was freed from paralysis and returned to its original mission. The UN now manages an expanding agenda of urgent military and nonmilitary problems, and in response to these global demands has evolved over time into a vast administrative machinery (see Map 5.2). To assess the capacity of the United Nations to fulfill its growing responsibilities, let us consider how it is organized.

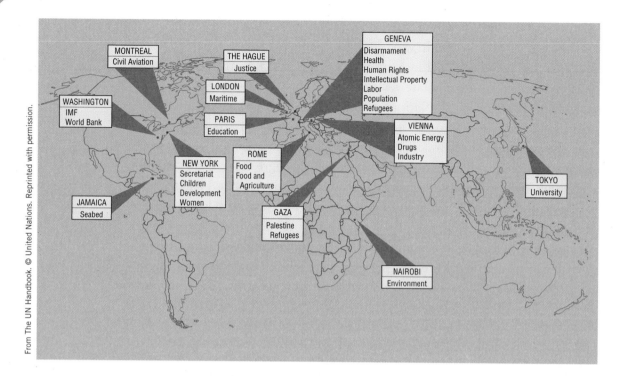

From The UN Handbook. © United Nations. Reprinted with permission.

MAP 5.2

THE UN's HEADQUARTERS AND GLOBAL NETWORK To reduce the gap between aspiration and accomplishment, the UN has spread its administrative arm to every corner of the globe in order to fulfill its primary purpose of spearheading international cooperation. "Although best known for peacekeeping, peace building, conflict prevention and humanitarian assistance, there are many other ways the United Nations and its System (specialized agencies, funds and programmes) affect our lives and make the world a better place. The Organization works on a broad range of fundamental issues, from sustainable development, environment and refugees protection, disaster relief, counter terrorism, disarmament and non-proliferation, to promoting democracy, human rights, governance, economic and social development and international health, clearing land mines, expanding food production, and more, in order to achieve its goals and coordinate efforts for a safer world for this and future generations" (United Nations, June 7, 2010).

Organizational Structure   The UN's limitations are perhaps rooted in the ways it is organized for its wide-ranging purposes. According to the Charter, the UN structure contains the following six major organs:

■ General Assembly. Established as the main deliberative body of the United Nations, all members are equally represented according to a one-state/one-vote formula. Decisions are reached by a simple majority vote, except on so-called important questions, which require a two-thirds majority. The resolutions it passes, however, are only recommendations.

■ Security Council. Given primary responsibility by the Charter for dealing with threats to international peace and security, the Security Council consists of five permanent members with the power to veto substantive decisions (the United States, the United Kingdom, France, Russia, and the People's Republic of China), and ten nonpermanent members elected by the General Assembly for staggered two-year terms.

- **Economic and Social Council.** Responsible for coordinating the UN's social and economic programs, functional commissions, and specialized agencies, its fifty-four members are elected by the General Assembly for staggered three-year terms. This body has been particularly active in addressing economic development and human rights issues.

- **Trusteeship Council.** Charged with supervising the administration of territories that had not achieved self-rule, the Trusteeship Council suspended operation in 1994, when the last remaining trust territory gained independence.

- **International Court of Justice.** The principal judicial organ of the United Nations, the International Court of Justice is composed of fifteen independent judges who are elected for nine-year terms by the General Assembly and Security Council (see Chapter 10). The competence of the Court is restricted to disputes between states, and its jurisdiction is based on the consent of the disputants. The Court may also give nonbinding advisory opinions on legal questions raised by the General Assembly, Security Council, or other UN agencies.

- **Secretariat.** Led by the Secretary-General, the Secretariat contains the international civil servants who perform the administrative and secretarial functions of the UN.

The founders of the UN expected the Security Council to become the organization's primary body, because it was designed to maintain peace and its permanent members were the victorious great powers that had been allied during World War II. It is exclusively permitted by the UN Charter to initiate actions, especially the use of force. The General Assembly can only make recommendations.

However, despite the intentions of the founders of the UN, the General Assembly has assumed wider responsibilities as countries in the Global South—seizing advantage of their growing numbers under the one-state/one-vote rules of the General Assembly—have guided UN involvement in directions of particular concern to them. Today, a coalition of Global South countries constituting three-fourths of the UN membership seeks to resist domination by the Global North. This coalition directs the UN to address economic and social needs and protests when it fails to respect the Global South's special interests.

The growth of the General Assembly's power may not be sufficient to ensure the Global South's control of the agenda, however, as the original five great powers in the Security Council continue to run the show—with the U.S. *hegemon* in a pivotal position of preeminent influence. The United States resisted the 2005 proposal to expand the Security Council to twenty-four members because it would dilute American power, and it announced that it would not support extension of the veto power held by the big five permanent members to other members. In a similar move to maintain power within the UN, in 2008 China surprised many with its refusal to support an Indian bid for a permanent seat.

Budget Blues Differences between the Global North and the Global South over perceived priorities are most clearly exhibited in the heated debate over the UN's budget. This controversy centers on how members should interpret the organization's Charter, which states that "expenses of the Organization shall be borne by the members as apportioned by the General Assembly."

The UN budget consists of three distinct elements: the core budget, the peace-keeping budget, and the budget for voluntary programs. States contribute to the voluntary programs and some of the peacekeeping activities as they see fit. The core budget and other peacekeeping activities are subject to assessments.

The precise mechanism by which assessments have been determined is com-plicated, but, historically, assessments have been allocated according to states' capacity to pay. Thus, the United States, which has the greatest resources, contributes 22 percent of the UN's regular budget, for a net contribution in

Ban Ki-Moon, 2007-present With a global reputation as someone who will do the right thing, he is one of the most popular leaders of the world.

Kofi Annan, 1996–2006 He had a quiet charisma, but the Iraq war and the oil-for-food scandal marred his second term.

Boutros Boutros-Ghali, 1992–1996 The United States dumped the acerbic and undiplomatic Egyptian after one turbulent term.

Javier Perez de Cuellar, 1982–1991 He quietly guided the organization out of Cold War paralysis and back into business.

Kurt Waldheim, 1972–1981 An effective bureaucrat, Waldheim is now remembered mainly for his Nazi past.

U Thant, 1961–1971 The placid Thant had a low profile but got flak for pulling U.N. peacekeepers from Sinai.

Dag Hammarskjold, 1953–1961 The U.N.'s most effective leader. Hammarskjold died on a peacekeeping mission to Congo.

Trygve Lie, 1946–1952 The gruff politician helped create the organization but accomplished little in office.

LEADERS OF THE UN The Secretary-Generals of the UN have had a big influence in shaping the UN's response to an array of global problems. Shown here is the present Secretary-General, Ban Ki-Moon, the seven Secretary-Generals who have preceded him, and a profile of their administrative philosophies while holding what U.S. President Franklin D. Roosevelt called "the most important job in the world."

2010 of almost $52 million. Yet, the poorest 28 percent of the UN's members, or a total of fifty-four member states, pay the minimum (0.001 percent), contributing only $24,363 annually, which accounts for less than 1 percent of the UN's 2010–2011 budget. In comparison, the richest 28 percent of states were assessed to pay more than 97 percent of the UN's 2010–2011 budget. Although this formula is under attack in many wealthy states, it still governs.

Resistance to this budgetary formula for funding UN activities has always existed. It has grown progressively worse in large part because when the General Assembly apportions expenses, it does so according to majority rule. The problem is that those with the most votes (the less developed countries) do not have the money, and the most prosperous countries do not have the votes. Wide disparities have grown—the largest contributors command only ten votes but pay 82 percent of the cost, while the poorest members pay only 18 percent of the UN budget but command 182 votes. This deep imbalance contributes to the *great powers*' concern about the UN's priorities, administrative efficiency, and expenses, and has led to many fierce disputes with the *small powers* over which issues should be the focus of the UN's attention and resources. The wealthy members charge that the existing budget procedures institutionalize a system of taxation without fair representation. The critics counter with the argument that, for fairness and justice, the great power members should bear financial responsibilities commensurate with their wealth and influence.

At issue, of course, is not simply money, which is paltry. By way of comparison, at the start of 2011, all the UN's programs had available only $4.00 to serve each of the world's 6.8 billion people; contrast this to $1.53 trillion in world military spending with an average global per capita cost of $225 (Global Policy Forum 2010, SIPRI 2010). Differences about what is important and which states should have political influence are the real issues. Poor states argue that need should determine expenditure levels rather than rich countries' interests, while major contributors do not want to pay for programs they oppose. For years, the United States has been the most vocal about its dissatisfaction and since 2000 has been in arrears, or behind in its payments, an average of $1.35 billion each year.

Of course, this must be viewed in light of the heavy portion of payments that the United States is assessed. At the start of 2010, the United States was paying 22 percent of the regular budget, and the four other permanent members of the Security Council were scheduled to pay proportionately less (Britain, 6.6 percent; France, 6.1 percent; China, 3.2 percent; and Russia, only 1.6 percent). Yet even this formula understandably upsets other major contributors who pay large sums but are still excluded from Security Council participation as permanent members, such as Japan, which paid 12.5 percent of the UN budget in 2010.

Future Challenges   The UN's future remains uncertain, and its persistent financial troubles leave it without the resources to combat global problems and carry out the responsibilities assigned to it. Doubts about its viability and value to the global community have been exacerbated by a string of scandals including charges of mismanagement in the 1990s Iraqi "Oil-for-Food" program, sexual abuse of women in the Congo by UN peacekeepers, and inaction until late 2007 in response to years of mass genocide in the Darfur region of Sudan.

However, given the UN's successful history of organizational adaptation to challenges, supporters have reasons to be optimistic about the organization's long-term prospects to live up to its creators' bold mandate to attack world problems. Despite some resistance by members of the Global South that feared that new Secretary General Ban Ki-Moon might bend to big-donor pressure and compromise the interests of small powers, since 2006 the UN has undertaken a series of reforms to change its management procedures and bring its recruitment, contracting, and training responsibilities into line with its vast new responsibilities. These reforms include protection for "whistleblowers" who report scandals, an antifraud and anticorruption policy, a unified standard of conduct for peacekeepers to prevent sexual abuse, and expanded financial disclosure requirements for senior officials. These massive reforms also cut the Secretariat's administrative costs by one-third, from 38 percent of the core budget to 25 percent, and put the savings into a development fund for poor countries.

The UN will likely remain an arena for heated jockeying among member states and hemispheric blocs, a fact bound to undermine its capacity to solve new global problems. The UN is frequently blamed unfairly for failures when the real failure belongs to its members, particularly those of the Global North (Power 2008). "Those powers are seldom willing to give it sufficient resources, attention and boots on the ground to accomplish the ambitious mandates they set for it" (Fukuyama 2008, p. 14). As one high-level UN civil servant, Brian Urquhart, argues, "Either the UN is vital to a more stable and equitable world and should be given the means to do the job, or peoples and government should be encouraged to look elsewhere."

In the final analysis, the UN can be no more than the mandates and power that the member states give to it. Yet as supporters point out, the UN remains "the forum of choice for regime negotiation and norm promotion for contested contemporary challenges" (Thakur and Weiss 2009, p. 18). From a *constructivist*

perspective, the legitimacy of the United Nations is based on its representation of the common will of states, and "in certain cases, the United Nations even claims to represent the collective will of humanity" (Ellis 2009, p. 4).

On this foundation, the UN is well positioned to formulate policies with global relevance and application, as seen in its success in shaming human rights violators through resolutions in the United Nations Commission on Human Rights (Lebovic and Voeten 2009), its efforts to combat global pandemics such as HIV/AIDS (Thakur and Weiss 2009), and its role in promoting confidence-building measures that do more than prevent conflict but have actually encouraged members to proactively discuss and work through their grievances (Shannon 2009). Though much maligned, the UN is very much needed. "Only a global organization is capable of meeting global challenges," observed former UN Secretary General Kofi-Annan. "When we act together, we are stronger and less vulnerable to individual calamity."

Other Prominent Global IGOs

Beyond the UN, literally hundreds of other IGOs are active internationally. We look briefly at three of the most prominent of these other IGOs, all of which are specialized in their focus on the international political economy: the World Trade Organization (WTO), the World Bank, and the International Monetary Fund (IMF).

Note that each of these IGOs was created by the great powers for the purposes of their sponsors in response to the great powers' need for a stable international economic order, even at the voluntary sacrifice of sovereignty. Why, one may ask, would states give up some of their own independent autonomy, when that surrender reduces some of their control over their destiny? The primary reason is that multilateral cooperation enables those cooperating states to receive benefits that they would not otherwise receive. The creation of international *regimes* (rules agreed to by a set of states to regulate cooperative ventures) as well as authoritative IGO institutions for global governance can pay dividends. Shared problems often cannot be managed without multilateral cooperation. Unilateral measures on many issues by even the most powerful great power acting independently simply will not work.

The World Trade Organization Remembering the hardships caused by the Great Depression of 1929, after World War II the United States sought to create international economic institutions that would prevent another depression by facilitating the expansion of world trade. One proposed institution was the International Trade Organization (ITO), first conceived as a specialized agency within the overall framework of the UN. While negotiations for the anticipated ITO were dragging on, many people urged immediate action. Meeting in Geneva in 1947, twenty-three states agreed to a number of bilateral tariff concessions between two states. These treaties were written into a final act called the General Agreement on Tariffs and Trade (GATT), which originally was thought of as a temporary arrangement until the ITO came into operation.

When a final agreement on the ITO proved elusive, GATT provided a mechanism for continued multilateral negotiations on reducing tariffs and other barriers to trade. Over the next several decades, eight rounds of negotiations were held to liberalize trade. Under the principle of nondiscrimination, GATT members were to give the same treatment to each other as they gave to their "most favored" trading partner.

On January 1, 1995, GATT was superseded by the World Trade Organization (WTO). Although it was not exactly what the ITO envisaged immediately following World War II, it nevertheless represents the most ambitious tariff-reduction undertaking yet. Unlike GATT, the WTO was and still is a full-fledged IGO with formal decision-making procedures. Mandated to manage disputes arising from its trading partners, the WTO was given authority to enforce trading rules and to adjudicate trade disputes.

The WTO now seeks to transcend the existing matrix of free-trade agreements between pairs of countries and within particular regions or free-trade blocs and replace them with an integrated and comprehensive worldwide system of liberal or free trade. This liberal agenda poses a threat to some states. At the heart of their complaint is the charge that the WTO undermines the traditional rule of law prohibiting interference in sovereign states' domestic affairs, including management of economic practices within the states' territorial jurisdiction. However, it should be kept in mind that the WTO developed as a result of voluntary agreements states reached to surrender some of their sovereign decision-making freedom, under the conviction that this pooling of sovereignty would produce greater gains than losses. Nonetheless, the WTO is criticized because "there is little evidence of democracy within the WTO operations" (Smith and Moran 2001). Many of its policies are orchestrated by its most powerful members during informal meetings that do not include the full WTO membership.

The World Bank Created in July 1944 at the United Nations Monetary and Financial Conference held in Bretton Woods, New Hampshire, with forty-four countries in attendance, the World Bank (or International Bank for Reconstruction and Development) was originally established to support reconstruction

Beth A. Keiser/AP Photo

RAGE AGAINST INSTITUTIONAL SYMBOLS OF GLOBALIZATION In the recent past, the meetings attended by finance ministers at such powerful IGOs as the World Bank and the IMF drew little interest or publicity. Now, with increasing criticism of the globalization of national economies, these meetings are convenient targets for protesters. Seen here is one recent outburst, when the meeting of the WTO mobilized a broad-based coalition of NGOs to criticize the impact of economic globalization.

efforts in Europe after World War II. Over the next decade, the Bank shifted its attention from reconstruction to developmental assistance. Because Global South countries often have difficulty borrowing money to finance projects aimed at promoting economic growth, the Bank offers them loans with lower interest rates and longer repayment plans than they could typically obtain from commercial banks. "From July 2008 through January 2010, the World Bank Group committed $89 billion to developing countries as the trade, finance, and investment that fueled their growth dropped precipitously, endangering several decades-worth of hard-won development gains" (World Bank 2010).

Administratively, ultimate decision-making authority in the World Bank is vested in a board of governors, consisting of a governor and an alternate appointed by each of the Bank's 185 member countries. A governor customarily is a member country's minister of finance or an equivalent official. The board meets annually in the Bank's Washington, DC, headquarters to set policy directions and delegate responsibility for the routine operations of the Bank to the twenty-four directors of its executive board. The five countries with the largest number of shares in the World Bank's capital stock (the United States,

Germany, Japan, France, and the United Kingdom) appoint their own executive directors, and the remaining executive directors are either appointed (Saudi Arabia), elected by their states (China, Russia, and Switzerland), or elected by groups of countries. This weighted voting system recognizes the differences among members' holdings system and protects the interests of the great powers that make more substantial contributions to the World Bank's resources. If a country's economic situation changes over time, its quota is adjusted and its allocation of shares and votes changes accordingly.

Over the years, both the self-image and operations of the World Bank have changed—from a strictly financial IGO to now assisting states' development planning and training. The World Bank's success in addressing poverty has been attributed in part to the introduction of Poverty Reduction Strategy (PRS) programs that include input from the poor themselves (Blackmon 2008). The World Bank also has participated increasingly in consortium arrangements for financing private lending institutions while insisting that democratic reforms are made a condition for economic assistance. Additionally, with charges of bribery, kickbacks, and embezzlement being levelled against World Bank projects from road building in Kenya to dam construction in Lesotho, the last three bank presidents (James Wolfensohn, Paul Wolfowitz, and Robert Zoellick) have insisted on anticorruption reforms as well.

Despite its intention to lend more than $40 billion to countries in the Global South in 2010, and more than another $55 billion by 2012, the World Bank is poorly prepared to meet all the needs for financial assistance of developing states. The repayment of loans in hard currencies has imposed serious burdens on impoverished and indebted Global South states. The deficiencies of the World Bank, however, have been partly offset by the establishment of another lending IGO, the International Monetary Fund.

The International Monetary Fund   Before World War II, the international community lacked institutional mechanisms to manage the exchange of money across borders. At the 1944 Bretton Woods Conference, the United States was a prime mover in creating the International Monetary Fund (IMF), a truly global IGO designed to maintain currency-exchange stability by promoting international monetary cooperation and orderly exchange arrangements and by functioning as a lender of last resort for countries experiencing financial crises.

The IMF is now one of the sixteen specialized agencies within the UN system. Each IMF member is represented on its governing board, which meets annually to fix general policy. Day-to-day business is conducted by a twenty-two-member executive board chaired by a managing director, who is also the administrative head of a staff of approximately two thousand employees.

The IMF derives its operating funds from its 185 member states. Contributions are based on a quota system set according to a state's national income, monetary reserves, and other factors affecting each member's ability to contribute. In this way, the IMF operates like a credit union that requires each participant to contribute to a common pool of funds from which it can borrow when the need arises. The IMF's voting is weighted according to a state's monetary contribution, giving a larger voice to the wealthier states.

The IMF attaches strict conditions to its loans, which has led to considerable criticism, as IMF loan programs have been linked to slower economic growth (Vreeland 2003) as well as increases in human rights violations (Abouharb and Cingranelli 2007). (See Controversy: The IMF, World Bank, and Structural Adjustment Policies: Is the "Cure" Worse than the "Disease"? in Chapter 12). Push for IMF reform has become prevalent following the Asian financial crisis in the late 1990s, as many argued that IMF intervention was counterproductive. It has also come under fire for implementing "cookie-cutter" solutions that did not take into account differences in the political and economic systems of individual countries (Stiglitz 2003).

REGIONAL INTERGOVERNMENTAL ORGANIZATIONS

The tug of war between individual states and groups of states within the UN, the WTO, the World Bank, and the IMF are reminders of an underlying principle that IGOs are run by the states that join them. This severely inhibits the IGOs' ability to rise above interstate competition and independently pursue their organizational purposes. Because they cannot act autonomously and lack the legitimacy and capability for independent global governance, universal IGOs are often viewed, from a *realist* perspective, more as instruments of their state members' foreign policies and arenas for debate than as independent nonstate actors. When states dominate universal international organizations like the UN, the prospects for international cooperation can decline because, as *realism* emphasizes, states are fearful of multilateral organizations that compromise their vital national interests. This limits IGOs' capabilities for multilateral decision making to engineer global change.

A rival hypothesis—that cooperation among powerful states is possible and that international organizations help produce it—emerges from *liberal* theory. From this perspective, the "reality of a world of interconnected and transnational threats is a simple one: you have to cooperate with others to get them

European Union (EU)
a regional organization created by the merger of the European Coal and Steel Community, the European Atomic Energy Community, and the European Economic Community (called the European Community until 1993) that has since expanded geographically and in its authority.

security community
a group of states whose high level of institutionalized or customary collaboration results in the settlement of disputes by compromise rather than by military force.

Third Way
an approach to governance advocated primarily by many European leaders who, while recognizing few alternatives to liberal capitalism, seek to soften the cruel social impact of free-market individualism by progressively allowing government intervention to preserve social justice and the rights of individuals to freedom from fear of the deprivations caused by disruptions in the global economy.

political integration
the processes and activities by which the populations of many or all states transfer their loyalties to a merged political and economic unit.

to cooperate with you" (Jones et al. 2009, p. 5). This viewpoint is pertinent to regional intergovernmental organizations, especially the *European Union (EU)*. The EU serves as a model for other regional IGOs to emulate as the globe's greatest example of peaceful cross-border cooperation producing an integrated *security community* with a single economy. In addition, the EU's dedication to liberal democratic governance and capitalist free markets, as well as its emphasis on the search for a *Third Way* to alleviate human suffering, is paving an approach that other regional IGOs are pursuing.

The European Union

The EU is not, strictly speaking, a freestanding supranational organization for the collective management of European domestic and foreign affairs. The EU coexists with a large number of other European IGOs, in which it is nested and with which it jointly makes decisions. Of these, the Organization for Security and Cooperation in Europe (OSCE) and the Council of Europe stand as regional institutions of equal European partners, free of dividing lines, designed to manage regional security and promote the human rights of minorities through democratization. In this overlapping network of European IGOs, the EU nonetheless is prominent as the primary example of a powerful organization that has transformed itself from a single- to a multiple-purpose nonstate actor.

EU Expansion and Political Integration   As *constructivism* argues, ideas have consequences. Big ideas often come from painful experiences and crises, such as devastating wars. And that is what happened after World War II. European leaders conceived of a bold plan to remove the curse of war by attacking the incentives for war. Their reform program aimed at the *political integration* of Europe to build a new supranational institution that transcended individual European states—to seek nothing less than the *transformation* of international relations from instruments *of states* to institutions *over* them.

The process of European integration began with the creation of the European Coal and Steel Community (ECSC) in 1951, the European Atomic Energy Community (Euratom) in 1957, and the European Economic Community (EEC) in 1957. These initiatives initially centered on trade development. Since the late 1960s, the three have shared a common organization, and, through successive steps, have enlarged the EU's mission as they came to be called "the European Community." Its membership grew, and its geographical scope broadened as the EU expanded in a series of waves to encompass fifteen countries by 1997: Belgium, France, Germany, Italy, Luxembourg, and the Netherlands (the original "six"); Denmark, Ireland, and the United Kingdom (which joined in 1973); Greece (1981); Portugal and Spain (1986); and Austria,

Finland, and Sweden (1995). In 2004, the EU reached a new milestone in its path toward enlargement when it formally admitted ten new members (the Czech Republic, Slovakia, Estonia, Hungary, Latvia, Lithuania, Malta, Poland, Slovenia, and the Greek-controlled part of Cyprus). This bold enlargement added seventy-five million people to create the globe's biggest free-trade bloc, and it transformed the face of Europe by ending the continent's division. And that enlargement process continued when Bulgaria and Romania joined in 2007, bringing the EU to twenty-seven members (see Map 5.3).

Further expansion is also conceivable because the admission procedures for possible new membership are currently under way for Croatia and Turkey, and other countries in the western Balkans are lobbying for future membership. Recently, on July 16, 2009, Iceland applied for membership with a targeted date of 2011 for acceptance into the bloc. Expansion remains controversial, however. In particular, the prospect of a populous Muslim Turkey joining the EU raises fundamental questions about Europe's identity. As constructivist theorists point out, identities shape how agents envision their interests and, in turn, how they act. The possible entry of Turkey and, perhaps, more remote and different countries would have major implications for the way many people, especially within the six Western founders of the EU, conceive of Europe. Nevertheless, the idea of a single, integrated Europe is compelling for those who are haunted by the specter of European nationalities and states that have been fighting each other ever since the Pax Romana collapsed eighteen hundred years ago.

EU enlargement through eastward expansion has presented the organization with a host of troublesome questions, compounded by the fact that the twelve newest members, whose combined economies are less than 10 percent of that of the entire EU, have poorer economies and smaller populations than the previous fifteen EU members. These new members, therefore, have different needs and interests that can make reaching agreement on policy decisions increasingly difficult. This was dramatically evident in Greece in May 2010, as the country negotiated with the EU and the IMF for a three-year economic bailout package—the first for a Eurozone state—in exchange for austerity measures, sparking the first deadly violent protests in Greece in twenty years. There are also concerns about weak economic conditions and rising government deficits in Spain and Hungary and the burden this may place on other members of the EU. If Germany, France, and the other Benelux countries join together to oppose the smaller, less developed new members, a "club within a club" could split the EU into two opposed coalitions. And if East–West frictions coincide with new tensions between the big and small EU members, collective decision making will be immeasurably more complicated. How is the EU organized to avoid this outcome?

The Evolutionary Development of European Union Expansion

Adapted from "Few to Many: The Expansion of the European Union, 1951–2005," *Wall St. Journal Europe*, May 3, 2004, p. A6. Reprinted by permission.

Belgium (1); France (2); Germany (3); Italy (4); Luxembourg (5); Netherlands (6)

Denmark (7); Ireland (8); United Kingdom (9)

Greece (10)

Portugal (11); Spain (12)

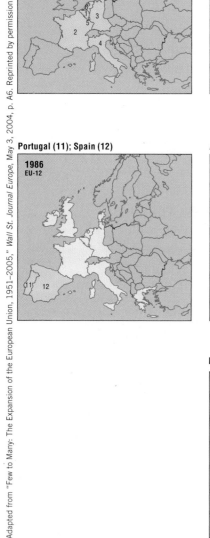

Austria (13); Finland (14); Sweden (15)

Cyprus (16); Czech Republic (17); Estonia (18); Hungary (19); Latvia (20); Lithuania (21); Malta (22); Poland (23); Slovakia (24); Slovenia (25)

Bulgaria (26); Romania (27)

MAP 5.3

FROM FEW TO MANY: THE EXPANSION OF THE EUROPEAN UNION, 1951–2010 The European Union is a premier example of the formation and integrative growth of a supranational regional IGO. It has grown in seven expansions from six members in 1951 to twenty-seven in 2010, as shown here, and waiting in the wings are Ukraine, Turkey, and others. Expansion has enabled the EU to position itself to become a true superpower (see Chapter 3).

EU Organization and Management   As the EU has grown and expanded its authority, its principal institutions for governance have changed. As shown in Figure 5.2, the EU organization includes a Council of Ministers, the European Commission, a European Parliament, and a Court of Justice.

The EU's central administrative unit, the Council of Ministers, represents the governments of the EU's member states and retains final authority over the policy making decisions. The council sets general policy guidelines for the *European Commission,* which consists of thirty-two commissioners (two each from Britain, France, Germany, Italy, and Spain, and one each from the other member states). Commissioners are nominated by EU member governments and must be approved by the European Parliament. Headquartered in

European Commission
the executive organ administratively responsible for the European Union.

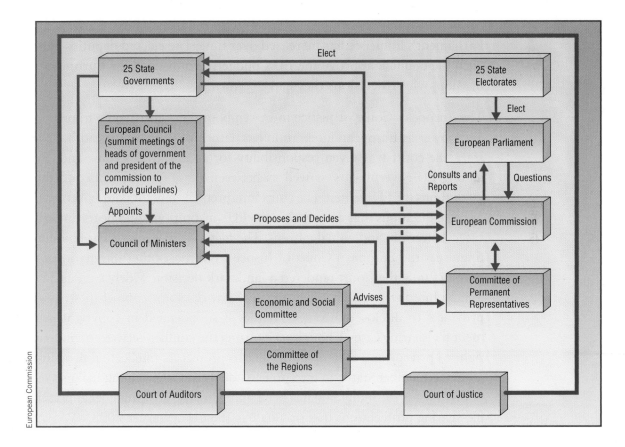

FIGURE 5.2

THE EVOLUTIONARY DEVELOPMENT OF THE EUROPEAN UNION'S GOVERNMENTAL STRUCTURE
The EU is a complex organization, with different responsibilities performed by various units. This figure illustrates the principal institutions and the relationships among them that collectively lead to EU decisions and policies.

Brussels, the primary functions of the European Commission are to propose new laws for the EU, oversee the negotiation of EU treaties, execute the European Council's decrees, and manage the EU's budget (which, in contrast with most international organizations, derives part of its revenues from sources not under the control of member states).

The European Parliament represents the political parties and public opinion within Europe. It has existed from the beginning of Europe's journey toward political unification, although at its creation this legislative body was appointed rather than elected and had little power. That is no longer the case. The European Parliament is now chosen in a direct election by the citizens of the EU's member states. Its more than six hundred deputies debate issues at the monumental glass headquarters in Brussels and at its lavish Strasbourg palace in the same way that democratic national legislative bodies do. The European Parliament shares authority with the Council of Ministers, but the Parliament's influence has increased over time. The elected deputies pass laws with the council, approve the EU's budget, and oversee the European Commission, whose decisions they can overturn.

The European Court of Justice in Luxembourg has also grown in prominence and power as European integration has gathered depth and breadth. From the start, the court was given responsibility for adjudicating claims and conflicts among EU governments as well as between those governments and the new institutions the EU created. The court interprets EU law for national courts, rules on legal questions that arise within the EU's institutions, and hears and rules on cases concerning individual citizens. The fact that its decisions are binding distinguishes the European Court of Justice from most other international tribunals. In 2008, the Court rendered a landmark decision widely seen as a victory for the Internet surfer in ruling that EU law does not compel Internet service providers to disclose customers' names if subpoenaed in copyright infringement file-sharing cases. Though recognizing the conflict between an individual's right to privacy and a company's right to protect its intellectual property, and allowing member states to interpret EU directives, the "ruling means the right of privacy for the individual has been upheld as the governing legal principle in file-sharing prosecutions that originate in the EU" (Warner 2008).

pooled sovereignty
legal authority granted to an IGO by its members to make collective decisions regarding specified aspects of public policy heretofore made exclusively by each sovereign government.

EU Decision-Making Challenges Disagreement persists over the extent to which the EU should become a single, truly united superstate, a "United States of Europe." Debate continues also over how far and how fast such a process of *pooled sovereignty* should proceed, and several efforts to further integrate the countries of Europe have met with resistance—the Danes rejected the Maastricht Treaty in 1992, the Irish rejected the Nice Treaty in 2001, and the French and Dutch rejected the EU Constitution in 2005. A final draft of the most recent initiative, the Lisbon Treaty, was agreed to by the leaders of the twenty-seven member states in October 2007. It was presented as an institutional treaty that would streamline the decision-making process for the EU by creating a full-time president and a single foreign policy chief to represent EU governments as a whole. It would also discard national vetoes in a number of areas, change members' voting weights, and give the European Parliament additional powers.

While proponents of the Lisbon Treaty argued that institutional reform is critical if expansion is to continue and Europe is to be a unified global power that can balance other major powers, resistance within the EU indicated that many were satisfied with the status quo. These detractors remained reluctant to pursue deeper political integration and further constrain the pursuit of individual national self-interest, and concerned about the extent to which EU decision making is democratic. Ratification was required by all twenty-seven member states for the treaty to go into force and was initially anticipated before the end of 2008. However, the Irish initially rejected the treaty in a national referendum, leading to speculation that there was not sufficient popular support for a federal Europe. This decision was reversed in a subsequent referendum in October 2009, and with the final ratification by the Czech Republic, the Lisbon Treaty became law on December 1, 2009. Herman Van Rompuy of Belgium became the EU's first full-time president and began his first official working day on January 4, 2010.

These issues will be debated in the future, and only time will tell how they will be resolved. That said, the EU represents a remarkable success story in international history. Who would have expected that competitive states that had spent most of their national experiences waging war against one another would put their clashing ideological and territorial ambitions aside and construct a "European-ness" identity built on unity and confederated decision making?

Other Regional IGOs

Since Europe's 1950s initiatives toward integration, more than a dozen regional IGOs have been created in various other parts of the world, notably among states in the Global East and Global South. Most seek to stimulate regional economic growth, but many have expanded from that original single purpose to pursue multiple political and military purposes as well. The major regional organizations include:

- The Asia Pacific Economic Cooperation (APEC) forum, created in 1989 as a gathering of twelve states without a defined goal. APEC's membership has grown to twenty-one countries (including the United

States). In June 2010, APEC held its fourteenth annual meeting in Sapporo, Japan, to further discuss how to promote regional economic integration, devise a new growth strategy, and enhance human security.

■ The Association of Southeast Asian Nations (ASEAN), established in 1967 by five founding members to promote regional economic, social, and cultural cooperation. In 1999, it created a free-trade zone among its ten Southeast Asian members as a counterweight outside the orbit of Japan, China, the United States, and other great powers so that ASEAN could compete as a bloc in international trade.

■ The Council of Arab Economic Unity (CAEU), established in 1964 from a 1957 accord to promote trade and economic integration among its ten Arab members.

■ The Caribbean Community (CARICOM), established in 1973 as a common market to promote economic development and integration among its fifteen country and territory members.

■ The Economic Community of West African States (ECOWAS), established in 1975 to promote regional economic cooperation among its fifteen members, with a much larger agenda today.

■ The Latin American Integration Association (LAIA), also known as Asociación Latinoamericana de Integración (ALADI), established in 1980 to promote and regulate reciprocal trade among its twelve members.

■ The North Atlantic Treaty Organization (NATO), a military alliance created in 1949 primarily to deter the Soviet Union in Western Europe. The security IGO has expanded its membership to twenty-six countries and broadened its mission to promote democratization and to police civil wars and terrorism outside its traditional territory within Europe. The United States and Canada are also members.

■ The South Asian Association for Regional Cooperation (SAARC), established in 1985 to promote economic, social, and cultural cooperation and respect for sovereign territorial independence and noninterference in states' internal affairs among its seven members.

■ The Southern African Development Community (SADC), established in 1992 to promote regional economic development and integration and to alleviate poverty among its fourteen members.

As these examples illustrate, most IGOs are organized on a regional rather than global basis. The governments creating them usually concentrate on one or two major goals (such as liberalizing trade or promoting peace within the region) instead of attempting to address at once the complete range of issues that they face in common, such as environmental protection, democratization, and economic and security cooperation. Africa illustrates this tendency at the regional level. Within strife-torn Africa, fragile states have created a complex network of regional IGOs, with multiple, cross-cutting memberships. Some are large multipurpose groups such as the Economic Community of Western African States (ECOWAS), the Common Market for Eastern and Southern Africa (COMESA), the Southern African Development Community (SADC), and the Arab Maghreb Union (AMU). Alongside these are many smaller organizations such as the Economic Community of the Great Lakes Countries and the Mano River Union.

It is hazardous to generalize about organizations so widely divergent in membership and purpose, yet no regional IGOs have managed to collaborate at a level that begins to match the institutionalized collective decision making achieved by the EU. The particular reasons why many regional IGOs sometimes fail and are often ineffective vary. Evidence suggests that the factors promoting successful integration efforts are many and their mixture complex. It is not enough that two or more countries choose to interact cooperatively. Chances of political integration wane without geographical proximity, steady economic growth, similar political systems, supportive public opinion led by enthusiastic leaders, cultural homogeneity, internal political stability, similar experiences in historical and internal social development, compatible economic systems with supportive business interests, a shared perception of a common external threat, bureaucratic compatibilities, and previous collaborative efforts (Deutsch 1957).

The substantial difficulty that most regions have experienced in achieving a level of institution building similar to that of the EU suggests the enormity of the obstacles to creating new political communities out of previously divided ones. At the root of the barriers is one bottom line: All IGOs are limited by national leaders' reluctance to make politically costly choices that would undermine their personal popularity at home and their governments' sovereignty. Nonetheless, regional ventures in cooperation demonstrate that many states accept the fact that they cannot individually manage many of the problems that confront them collectively.

Because the state is clearly failing to manage many transnational policy problems, collective problem solving through IGOs is likely to continue. In turn, IGOs' expanding webs of interdependence are infringing on the power of states and changing the ways in which they network on the global stage. This is why the thesis that the state is in retreat and its power to govern is eroding is so commonly voiced (Paul, Ikenberry, and Hall 2003). There are many good reasons to see the impact of IGOs as a threat to states' continuing domination of world politics (see Controversy: Will Global IGOs Replace States as the Primary Actors in World Politics?). As political scientist James N. Rosenau hypothesizes, "While states may not be about to exit from the political stage, and while they may even continue to occupy center stage, they do seem likely to become vulnerable and impotent."

IGOs are not the only nonstate actors leading the potential *transformation* of world politics. Another set of agents is nongovernmental organizations (NGOs). They include not only transnational humanitarian organizations such as Amnesty International but also multinational corporations, transnational religions and ethnic groups, and global terrorist networks. Such NGOs are growing in number and roaring in voices too loud to ignore, making them increasingly influential in world politics. We now evaluate their behavior and global impact.

> *No reason exists why—in addition to states—nationalities, diasporas, religious communities and other groups should not be treated as legitimate actors. . . . In the emerging global politics, however, state sovereignty and authority are withering and no alternative, such as some system of world government, is about to fill the vacuum.*
>
> —Samuel P. Huntington, realist theoretician

PROMINENT TYPES OF NONGOVERNMENTAL ORGANIZATIONS

Increasing numbers of people have found that through joining nongovernmental organizations (NGOs), they can lobby to influence international decision making. They have chosen to become international decision makers themselves by electing to join one or more NGOs, and these tens of thousands of "transitional activists" are influencing the policies of state governments and intergovernmental organizations (IGOs) through a variety of strategies. NGO activism is transcending the traditional distinctions between what is local and what is global (Tarrow 2006).

Today, a small subset of increasingly active and self-assertive NGOs receives the most attention and provokes the most controversy. To evaluate if and how NGOs are contributing to global changes, *World Politics* will ask you to examine only five of the most visibly active NGO nonstate actors: ***nonstate nations*** that include ethnic nationalities and indigenous peoples, transnational religious movements, transnationally active terrorist groups, and multinational corporations.

nonstate nations
national or ethnic groups struggling to obtain power and/or statehood.

CONTROVERSY:

WILL GLOBAL IGOs REPLACE STATES AS THE PRIMARY ACTORS IN WORLD POLITICS?

At the *global level of analysis*, the question at center stage is whether existing territorially defined states can cope with the many challenges they now face in the absence of creating powerful IGOs to manage those problems. The nineteenth-century French political philosopher Auguste Comte argued that all institutions form in order to address problems and meet human needs, and that when those IGOs are no longer able to perform these functions, they disappear. Today, the managerial capabilities of states are failing to inspire confidence. So a controversy has arisen: Do states have a future, and if not, will IGOs become the new primary actors in world politics?

That question has become a hot topic about which heated controversies now center. In formulating your assessment, consider not only what you have learned about IGOs and their power and limits in this chapter, but also the range of theoretical opinion percolating about this question. Consider the differences of opinions reflective of realist and liberal theorizing in this table:

Theoretical Perspective	
Realism	Liberalism
"Institutions are basically a reflection of the distribution of power in the world. They are based on the self-interested calculations of the great powers, and they have no independent effect on state behavior."—John Mearsheimer, political realist	"We are at present embarked on an exceedingly dangerous course, one symptom of which is the erosion of the authority and status of world and regional intergovernmental institutions. Such a trend must be reversed before once again we bring upon ourselves a global catastrophe and find ourselves without institutions effective enough to prevent it."—Javier Pérez De Cuéllar, UN Secretary General
"States retain many of their present functions [even if] effective governance of a partially—and increasingly—globalized world will require more extensive international institutions to promote cooperation and resolve conflict."—Robert O. Keohane, international relations scholar	"A wide variety of forces has made it increasingly difficult for any state to wield power over its peoples and address issues it once considered its sole prerogative."—The Stanley Foundation

The task of inquiry for you to face is to weigh the evidence behind these rival theoretical interpretations. Both perspectives cannot be equally valid. As former President of China Mao Zedong once counseled, "Seek truth through facts."

WHAT DO YOU THINK?

- Can IGOs assume a capacity for global governance?

- If so, would this usher into being a *transformation* in world politics of such proportions that future generations will conclude that one global system has ended and a new one has begun?

- How does the idea of IGOs as major actors in world politics fit with theories on conflict and peace, such as democratic peace theory or realism? Are they compatible? Why or why not?

Nonstate Nations: Ethnic Groups and Indigenous Peoples

Realists often ask us to picture the all-powerful state as an autonomous ruler of a unified nation, that is, as a *unitary actor*. But, in truth, that construction is misleading. Most states are divided internally and are highly penetrated from abroad, and few states are tightly unified and capable of acting as a single body with a common purpose.

ethnic nationalism
devotion to a cultural, ethnic, or linguistic community.

ethnic groups
people whose identity is primarily defined by their sense of sharing a common ancestral nationality, language, cultural heritage, and kinship.

ethnicity
perceptions of likeness among members of a particular racial grouping leading them to prejudicially view other nationality groups as outsiders.

Although the state unquestionably remains the most visible global actor, as constructivism emphasizes, ***ethnic nationalism*** (people's loyalty to and identification with a particular ethnic nationality group) reduces the relevance of the unitary state. Many states are divided, multiethnic and multicultural societies made up of a variety of politically active groups that seek, if not outright independence, a greater level of regional autonomy and a greater voice in the domestic and foreign policies of the state. Individuals who think nationalistically are very likely to pledge their primary allegiance not to the state and government that rules them but, rather, to a politically active ***ethnic group*** whose members identify with one another because they perceive themselves as bound together by kinship, language, and a common culture.

Ethnicity is socially constructed, in that members of an ethnic or racial group learn to see themselves as members of that group and accordingly perceive their identity as determined by their inherited membership at birth. That perception is likely to be strongly reinforced when recognized by other ethnic groups. Hence, ethnicity is in the eye of the beholder—a constructed identity. "A basic definition might be a group of humans who share significant elements of culture and who reproduce themselves socially and biologically" (T. Hall 2004, p. 140).

Three-fourths of the world's larger countries are estimated to contain politically significant minorities, and since 1998, 283 minority groups, comprising 18.5% (over one-sixth) of the world population, have been classified as "at risk" from persecution by the state in which they resided and had mobilized for collective defense against the government they perceived as perpetuating organized discriminatory treatment (Minorities At Risk, June 3, 2010). China came under intense international criticism for its crackdown on ethnic Tibetan groups following rioting in Lhasa, the Tibetan capital. Representing Tibetan interests, the Dalai Lama sought renewed talks with China in "the interest of stability, unity and harmony of all nationalities in the People's Republic of China." The Chinese, however, see him as a "splittist," with the spiritual leader having fled Tibet in 1959 following a failed armed uprising against Chinese communist rule (Drew 2008). Ethnic divisions such as these challenge the realist "billiard ball" conception

Gleison Miranda/Funai/AP Photo

PROTECTING INDIGENOUS PEOPLES Warriors from an isolated Amazon basin rainforest tribe on the Brazilian-Peruvian border prepare to defend their homes from the strange "bird" flying above. Dedicated to locating remote tribes and protecting them, this aerial picture was released in 2008 by activists with the *Brazilian Indian Protection Agency, Funai,* and *Survival International* in an effort to generate international concern for the threat posed by the logging industry to "uncontacted" indigenous tribes in the area. Through these actions, these NGOs claimed success in pressuring Peru to reexamine its logging policy.

of international relations as homogeneous interactions between unified states. "The multiethnic state is 'normal' in the statistical sense [and] this deepens the puzzle of the chimera of the ethnically homogeneous nation-state" (T. Hall 2004, p. 142).

Indigenous peoples are ethnic and cultural groups that are native populations to a particular area. In most cases, indigenous people were at one time politically sovereign and economically self-sufficient, but are now controlled by a state govenment. Today an estimated 350 million indigenous people, or about 5.3 percent of the world's population, are scattered in more than seventy countries (International Work Group for Indigenous Affairs, June 3, 2010; Office of the High Commissioner for Human Rights, June 3, 2010).

The number of distinct nonstate nations is usually measured by the number of known spoken languages because each language provides an ethnic and cultural identity (see Map 5.4). As Edward Sapir and Benjamin Lee Whorf hypothesized in the 1930s, different languages reflect different views of the

indigenous peoples
The native ethnic and cultural inhabitant populations within countries ruled by a government controlled by others.

Case Study:
International Law and Organization: Indigenous Peoples

world that predispose their speakers toward different ways of thought. By this index, indigenous cultures are disappearing. "Some experts maintain that 90 percent of the world's languages will vanish or be replaced by dominant languages by the end of this century" (*Vital Signs, 2006–2007*, p. 112). What this means is that indigenous peoples are at risk, with high percentages nearing extinction.

Though indigenous peoples are located *within* many of the globe's pluralistic states, they also display a transnational face because they are geographically spread *across* existing state boundaries. This dispersion has increased as indigenous peoples have migrated across borders from their ancestral homelands. For example, indigenous peoples such as the sizable Kurdish minorities of Turkey, Iraq, Iran, and Syria have members living in more than one of

MAP 5.4

ETHNOLINGUISTIC DIVISIONS **Differences in language often reflect differences in interests and attitudes. Where there is great diversity, state governments face a formidable challenge to reconcile these differences and generate common identity and goals—and "empirical cross-country studies suggest that linguistic fractionalization hurts economic performance" and quality of government (WDR 2009, p. 104). As shown here, the diversity of ethnic language groups in Africa is very high.**

the globe's existing independent states, but as yet there is no single sovereign country the Kurds can call their home.

As a result of divisions such as these, as many as eleven separate transnational cultural identities, or "civilizations," can be identified across the globe (see Map 5.5). The consequences are not certain, but some possibilities for world politics are alarming. Samuel P. Huntington (1996, 2001a) pessimistically predicts the most troubling outcome: that a *clash of civilizations* is probable between some of these universalistic civilizational identities and that armed conflict is especially likely between the West and Islam.

That prediction proved rather prophetic on September 11, 2001, when the Al Qaeda terrorist network attacked the United States to vent the anger of its extremist Islamic members against the West. "What recent events demonstrate is that ethnicity, and race [and cultural conflict] are issues that are not disappearing and becoming less important . . . Recent processes of global change, often glossed under the term globalization, are rapidly changing the contexts under which ethnic [and cultural] conflict arises [which] are no

Case Study:
*The End of History
or the Clash of
Civilizations?*

clash of civilizations
political scientist
Samuel Huntington's
controversial thesis that
in the twenty-first cen-
tury the globe's major
civilizations will conflict
with one another,
leading to anarchy and
warfare similar to that
resulting from conflicts
between states over
the past five hundred
years.

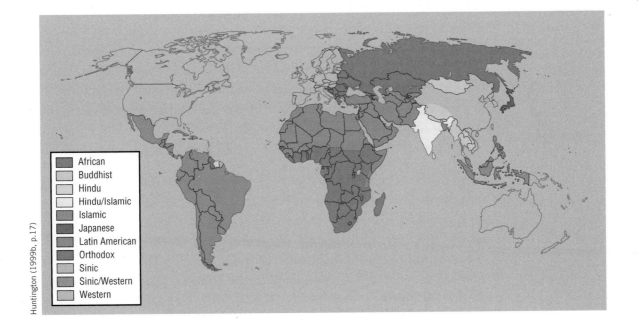

Huntington (1999b, p.17)

Legend:
- African
- Buddhist
- Hindu
- Hindu/Islamic
- Islamic
- Japanese
- Latin American
- Orthodox
- Sinic
- Sinic/Western
- Western

MAP 5.5

THE WORLD'S MAJOR CIVILIZATIONS: WILL THEIR CLASH CREATE GLOBAL DISORDER? **This map shows the location of the world's major civilizations according to the much-debated thesis of Samuel P. Huntington, who predicts that future global war is likely to result from a "clash of civilizations." Critics of this thesis point out that no "civilization" is homogeneous in language or beliefs, that the characteristics of any civilization fail to predict how individual people identified with it will act, and that even identity-creating groups such as distinct cultures have often learned to speak to one another across their differences and to coexist peacefully (Sen 2006; Appiah 2006).**

longer, if they ever were, entirely local" (T. Hall 2004, p. 150). For that reason, we now turn from ethnic group NGOs to an examination of the ways religious movements may operate as transnationally active NGOs as well.

Transnational Religious Movements

In theory, religion would seem a natural worldwide force for global unity and harmony. Yet millions have died in the name of religion. The Crusades, which took place between the eleventh and fourteenth centuries, originally were justified by Pope Urban II in 1095 to combat Muslim aggression, but the fighting left millions of Christians and Muslims dead and, "in terms of atrocities, the two sides were about even [as both religions embraced] an ideology in which fighting was an act of self sanctification" (Riley-Smith 1995). Similarly, the religious conflicts during the Thirty Years' War (1618–1648) between Catholics and Protestants killed nearly one-fourth of all Europeans.

transnational religious movements
a set of beliefs, practices, and ideas administered politically by religious organizations to promote the worship of their conception of a transcendent deity and its principles for conduct.

Many of the world's more than 6.8 billion people are affiliated at some level with *transnational religious movements*—politically active organizations based on strong religious convictions. At the most abstract level, a religion is a system of thought shared by a group that provides its members an object of devotion and a code of behavior by which they can ethically judge their actions. This definition points to commonalities across the great diversity of organized religions in the world, but it fails to capture that diversity. The world's principal religions vary greatly in the theological doctrines or beliefs they embrace. They also differ widely in the size of their followings, in the geographical locations where they are most prevalent (see Map 5.6), and in the extent to which they engage in political efforts to direct international affairs.

These differences make it risky to generalize about the impact of religious movements on world affairs (Haynes 2004). Those who study religious movements comparatively note that a system of belief provides religious followers with their main source of identity, and that this identification with and devotion to their religion springs from the natural human need to find a set of values with which to evaluate the meaning of life and the consequences of choices. This need sometimes leads believers of a religious creed to perceive the values of their own religion as superior to those of others, which sadly often results in intolerance. The proponents of most organized religious movements believe that their religion should be universal—that is, accepted by everyone throughout the world. To confirm their faith in their religious movement's natural superiority, many organized religions actively proselytize to convert nonbelievers to their faith, engaging in evangelical crusades to win over nonbelievers and followers of other religions. Conversion is usually

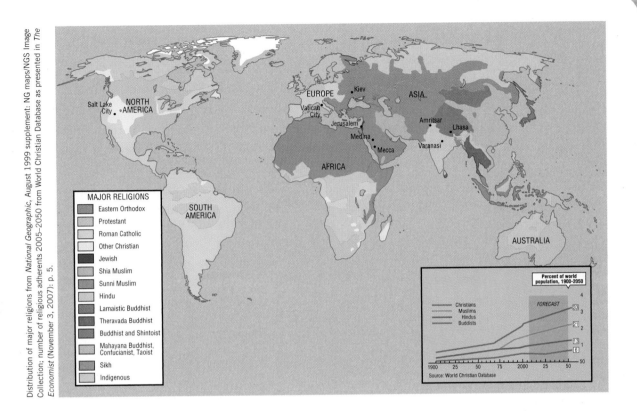

MAP 5.6

MAJOR RELIGIONS OF THE WORLD This map shows where the world's major religious affiliations have attracted a dominant following. The chart on the bottom right predicts the number of people who will adhere to the four largest religious groups by the year 2050.

Distribution of major religions from *National Geographic*, August 1999 supplement: NG maps/NGS Image Collection; number of religious adherents 2005–2050 from World Christian Database as presented in *The Economist* (November 3, 2007): p. 5.

achieved by persuasion through missionary activities. But at times conversion has been achieved by the sword, tarnishing the reputations of some international religious movements (see Controversy: Are Religious Movements Causes of War or Sources of Transnational Harmony?).

In evaluating the impact of religious movements on international affairs, it is important to distinguish carefully the high ideals of doctrines from the activities of the people who head these religious bodies. The two realms are not the same, and each can be judged fairly only against the standards they set for themselves. To condemn what large-scale religious movements sometimes do administratively when they abuse their own religion's principles does not mean that the principles themselves deserve condemnation. Consider the Hindu ideology of tolerance of different religions, which teaches that there are many paths to truth and accepts pluralism among diverse populations. Similarly, Buddhism preaches pacifism, as did early Christianity, which prohibited Christians from serving in the armies of the Roman Empire (later, by the fourth century, when church and state became allies, only Christians were allowed to join Roman military units).

The relationship between transnational religions and states' governments is a major issue in the global community. In some countries, the two realms are separate politically, with legal protection for freedom of religion and little or no state support for a particular established religion. But in many other countries, religion and state are tightly linked and almost indistinguishable. In such a country, that is, in a *theocracy*, religious institutions submissively subordinate their religion to state control in order to survive, grow, receive state subsidies, and cement political influence. In these countries, crown and church protect and preserve each other through an alliance.

theocracy
a country whose government is organized around a religious dogma.

Most troublesome, however, are radical religious movements that are enraged, militant, and fanatically dedicated to promote their cause globally, often through violence and terror (Kifner 2005). The leaders of extreme *militant religious movements* are convinced that those who do not share their convictions must be punished and that compromise is unacceptable. Underlying this perspective, radical religious movements hold some common beliefs and perceptions:

militant religious movements
politically active organizations based on strong religious convictions, whose members are fanatically devoted to the global promotion of their religious beliefs.

- They view existing government authority as corrupt and illegitimate because it is secular and not sufficiently rigorous in upholding religious authority or religiously sanctioned social and moral values.

- They attack the inability of government to address the domestic ills of society. In many cases the religious movement substitutes itself for the government at the local level and is involved in education, health, and other social welfare programs.

- They subscribe to a particular set of behaviors and opinions that they believe political authority must reflect, promote, and protect in all governmental and social activities. This generally means that government and all of its domestic and foreign activities must be in the hands of believers or subject to their close oversight.

- They are universalists: unlike ethnic movements, they tend to see their views as part of the inheritance of everyone who is a believer. This tends to give them a trans-state motivation, a factor that then translates their views on legitimacy of political authority into a larger context for action. In some cases, this means that international boundaries are not recognized as barriers to the propagation of the faith, even if this means they resort to violence.

- They are exclusionists: they relegate all conflicting opinions on appropriate political and social order to the margins—if they do not exclude them altogether. This translates as second-class citizenship for any nonbeliever in any society where such a view predominates (Shultz and Olson 1994, pp. 9–10).

CONTROVERSY:

ARE RELIGIOUS MOVEMENTS CAUSES OF WAR OR SOURCES OF TRANSNATIONAL HARMONY?

After 9/11, debate about the impact of religion on international conflict intensified because many believed that the terrorist attacks were motivated by religious fanatics in the Islamic Al Qaeda global terrorist organization. As a result, the "religious roots of terrorism" (Juergensmeyer 2003) and religious opposition to democracy in the Global South (Shah 2004) have received much attention, as have religions and religious bodies acting as NGO global actors more generally (Haynes 2004).

"To do harm, to promote violence and conflict in the name of religion," said Pope John Paul II in Egypt after fighting between Christians and Muslims led to bloodshed in 2000, "is a terrible contradiction and a great offense against God. But past and present history give us many examples of such misuse of religion." Yet it is difficult to understand the religious origins of violence because most people equate religion with peace, compassion, and forgiveness, not hatred or intolerance. Indeed, because high ideals inspire the believers of nearly all the world's major religious movements, many of the principles religions espouse are very similar and conducive to peaceful relations between people. They all voice respect and reverence for the sanctity of life and acceptance of all people as equal creations of a deity, regardless of race or color. These are noble ideals. Religions speak to universal principles, across time and place—to enduring values in changing times. Moreover, they recognize no boundaries for their eternal validity—no north, south, east, or west—but only true virtue wherever found and the relevance of moral precepts (e.g., the prohibition of killing and the value of working for the betterment of humankind throughout the world).

However, in an age of religious conflict and political violence, the role of religious NGOs in international affairs is controversial. Consider the view of sociologists of religion who contend that religious hostility results from the fact that universalistic religions are managed by organizations that often adopt a particularistic and dogmatic outlook (see Juergensmeyer 2003). The virtues that religions uphold ironically can become weapons against those who do not hold such views. Followers of a religion may conceive the world and history through an ideological lens that views one deity protecting a chosen people against inferior others. In an effort to believe in unshakable doctrines, they reject the attempt to separate what they wish to be true from what they or other religions think to be true. This constructed reality inspires an ethic that justifies violence, plunder, and conquest. In part, they tend to see outsiders as threatening rivals whose loyalty and allegiance to other deities represents a challenge to their own religion's claim of universal worldwide applicability. In a word, religious movements often practice intolerance—disrespect for diversity and the right of people to freely embrace another religion's beliefs. The next logical step is for fanatics to paint these imagined enemies as evil, unworthy of mercy, and to justify brutal violence against them.

Yet it is dangerous to accept stereotypes of religious groups as responsible for relentless barrages of terrorism. Paganistic and atheistic societies recognizing no higher deity have equally long histories of waging violent wars against external enemies and their own people. Meanwhile, many religions ably perform the mission of peace making, and in fact most religious bodies have historically coexisted peacefully for centuries. Thus, it is important for you to objectively weigh the evidence about the impact of religious NGOs on world affairs.

(continued)

ARE RELIGIOUS MOVEMENTS CAUSES OF WAR OR SOURCES OF TRANSNATIONAL HARMONY? (Continued)

WHAT DO YOU THINK?

- If all the world's great religious movements espouse universalistic ideals, why are those same religions increasingly criticized as sources of international conflict—of exclusivism, hatred, terror, and war?

- Given that many wars have been fought in the name of religion, how might realism view the impact of religious movements on world politics?

- Which global actors are better suited to address the challenges posed to the global community by violent NGOs? Can states respond more effectively, or IGOs? Why?

secession, or separative revolts
a religious or ethnic minority's efforts, often by violent means, to gain independent statehood by separating territory from an established sovereign state.

diasporas
the migration of religious or ethnic groups to foreign lands despite their continuation of affiliation with the land and customs of their origin.

international terrorism
the threat or use of violence as a tactic of terrorism against targets in other countries.

Militant religious movements tend to stimulate five specific types of international activities. The first is *irredentism*—the attempt by a dominant religion (or ethnic group) to reclaim previously possessed territory in an adjacent region from a foreign state that now controls it, often through the use of force. The second is *secession, or separative revolts*—the attempt by a religious (or ethnic) minority to revolt and break away from an internationally recognized state. Third, militant religions tend to incite migration, the departure of religious minorities from their countries of origin to escape persecution. Whether they move by force or by choice, the result, a fourth consequence of militant religion, is the same: the emigrants create *diasporas*, or communities that live abroad in host countries but maintain economic, political, and emotional ties with their homelands (Sheffer 2003). Finally, as we shall see, a fifth effect of militant religions is *international terrorism* in the form of support for radical coreligionists abroad (Homer-Dixon 2005; Sageman 2004).

Ahmed Jadallah/Reuters/CORBIS

PAPAL DIPLOMACY Religious groups are undeniably important nonstate actors on the global stage. Calling for compassion and peace, Pope Benedict lamented that "In a world where more and more borders are being opened up—to trade, to travel, to movement of peoples, to cultural exchanges—it is tragic to see walls still being erected." Pictured here, Pope Benedict is welcomed by Jordan's King Abdullah upon his arrival in Amman.

In sum, transnational religious movements not only bring people together but also divide them. Through globalization, religions are transforming social forces that create transnational communities of believers with "dual loyalties" to more than one country; immigration by adherents to religion brings more faiths into direct contact with one another and forges global networks transcending borders (Levitt 2007). This consequence notwithstanding, transnational religions compete with one another, and this tends to divide humanity and breed separatist efforts that can tear countries apart.

Transnational Terrorist Groups

Are terrorist groups correctly seen as a particular category of nonstate actors—as NGOs—on the global stage? Many people now think so, even if these groups can hardly be considered conventional NGOs, given their use of violence. Yet a word of caution is in order. Even if you recognize the existence of terrorist groups as a virulent type of NGO conducting its lethal trade across borders, it is very difficult to identify these terrorist groups, and you would make a big mistake if you lumped all terrorist movements together. Today, *terrorism* is a strategy practiced by a very diverse group of nonstate actors.

terrorism
premeditated violence perpetrated against noncombatant targets by subnational or transnational groups or clandestine agents, usually intended to influence an audience.

While terrorism has plagued world politics for centuries, with some historians placing the beginnings of terrorism in the first century BCE with the Sicarii Zealots (who violently targeted Jewish high priests, whom they saw as collaborating with the Romans in violation of Jewish religious law), terrorism today is arguably much different than in the past. Terrorism now is seen as:

- global, in the sense that with the death of distance, borders no longer serve as barriers to terrorism

- lethal, because now terrorists have shifted their tactics from theatrical violent acts seeking to alarm for publicity to purposeful destruction of a target's civilian noncombatants, to kill as many as possible for the purpose of instilling fear in as many people as possible

- waged by civilians without state sanction in ways and by means that erase the classic boundaries between terrorism and a declared war between states

- reliant on the most advanced technology of modern civilization, despite viewing sophisticated technological means of modern civilization as a threat to the terrorists' sacred traditions

- orchestrated by transnational nonstate organizations through global conspiratorial networks of terrorist cells located in many countries, involving unprecedented levels of communication and coordination (Sageman 2004)

postmodern terrorism
to Walter Laqueur, the terrorism practiced by an expanding set of diverse actors with new weapons "to sow panic in a society to weaken or even overthrow the incumbents and to bring about political change."

information age
the era in which the rapid creation and global transfer of information through mass communication contribute to the globalization of knowledge.

Renowned historian and terrorism expert Walter Laqueur sees a future of *postmodern terrorism* that poses great threat to technologically advanced societies, where terrorists tend to be less ideological, more likely to hold ethnic grievances, and increasingly difficult to distinguish from other criminals. So-called postmodern terrorism is likely to expand because the globalized international environment, without meaningful barriers separating countries, allows terrorists to practice their ancient trade by new rules and methods. The *information age* facilitates transnational networking among terrorists, and has made available a variety of new methods such as electronic "cyberterrorism" and "netwar" strategies.

Moreover, this new global environment encourages the rapid spread of new weapons and technology across borders, which provides unprecedented opportunities for terrorists to commit atrocities and to change their tactics in response to successes in countering them. The growing difficulty of detecting and deterring the attacks of disciplined globalized terrorist networks is further exacerbated by their ties to international organized crime (IOC) syndicates and internationally linked networks of thousands of gangs that facilitate their profit in the narcotics trade and provide resources to support terrorist activities.

The activities of nonstate terrorist organizations are likely to remain a troubling feature of world politics also because every spectacular terrorist act generates a powerful shock effect and gains worldwide publicity through the global news media. In an effort to diminish the capacity of terrorists to garner such world-wide attention, U.S. Senator Joe Lieberman called on Google and others to remove Internet video content that was produced by terrorist organizations: "Islamist terrorist organizations use YouTube to disseminate their propaganda, enlist followers, and provide weapons training . . . (and) YouTube also, unwittingly, permits Islamist terrorist groups to maintain an active, pervasive, and amplified voice, despite military setbacks."

Table 5.2 identifies some of the known terrorist NGOs. As you can see, there is diversity in the primary goals of various groups. Some, such as FARC and ETA, focus on secular nonreligious objectives such as ethnic self-determination or overthrow of a government. Others, most notably Al Qaeda, are driven by religious convictions and have more sweeping goals. There is also variation in the manner in which their organizations are structured, with some having a hierarchical structure and newer groups tending to favor a networked form with insulated cells dispersed across the globe.

Though terrorists are popularly portrayed as "madmen" bent on death and destruction, as terrorist expert Bruce Hoffman has noted, "Terrorism has a purpose. Writing it off as mindless and irrational is not useful" (Lemann

Table 5.2   Some Terrorist NGOs: Primary Location and Goals

Name	Primary Location	Goal
Al Qaeda	A global network with cells in a number of countries and tied to Sunni extremist networks. Bin Laden and his top associates are suspected to reside in Afghanistan or the border region in Pakistan, and the group maintains terrorist training camps there.	To establish pan-Islamic rule throughout the world by working with allied Islamic extremist groups to overthrow regimes it deems "non-Islamic" and expel Westerners and non-Muslims from Muslim countries.
Revolutionary Armed Forces of Colombia (FARC)	Colombia with some activities (extortion, kidnapping, logistics) in Venezuela, Panama, and Ecuador.	To replace the current government with a Marxist regime.
Hezbollah (Party of God), a.k.a. Islamic Jihad, Revolutionary Justice Organization, Organization of the Oppressed on Earth, and Islamic Jihad for the Liberation of Palestine	In the Bekaa Valley, the southern suburbs of Beirut, and southern Lebanon. Has established cells in Europe, Africa, South America, North America, and Asia.	To increase its political power in Lebanon, and opposing Israel and the Middle East peace negotiations.
Hamas (Islamic Resistance Movement)	Primarily the occupied territories, Israel.	To establish an Islamic Palestinian state in place of Israel, and gain international acceptance of its rule in Gaza.
Army for the Liberation of Rwanda (ALIR), a.k.a. Interahamwe, Former Armed Forces (ex-FAR)	Primarily in the Democratic Republic of the Congo and Rwanda, but a few may operate in Burundi.	To topple Rwanda's Tutsi-dominated government, reinstitute Hutu control, and, possibly, complete the genocide begun in 1994.
Revolutionary United Front (RUF)	Sierra Leone, Liberia, Guinea.	To topple the current government of Sierra Leone and retain control of the lucrative diamond-producing regions of the country.
Basque Fatherland and Liberty (ETA), a.k.a. Euzkadi Ta Askatasuna	Primarily in the Basque autonomous regions of northern Spain and southwestern France.	To establish an independent homeland based on Marxist principles in the Basque autonomous regions.
Al-Gama'a al-Islamiyya	Primarily southern Egypt, but has a worldwide presence, including Afghanistan, Yemen, Sudan, Austria, and the United Kingdom.	To overthrow the Egyptian government and replace it with an Islamic state; attack United States and Israeli interests in Egypt and abroad.
Liberation Tigers of Tamil Eelam	Sri Lanka.	To establish an independent Tamil state. On May 19, 2009, the Sri Lankan government declared an end to the 25-year civil war and a defeat of what had been characterized as the fiercest terrorist force in the world.
Aum Supreme Truth (Aum), a.k.a. Aum Shinrikyo, Aleph	Principal membership is located only in Japan, but a residual branch comprising an unknown number of followers has surfaced in Russia.	To take over Japan and then the world.
Sendero Luminoso (Shining Path)	Peru.	To destroy existing Peruvian institutions and replace them with a communist peasant revolutionary regime.
New People's Army (NPA)	Philippines.	To overthrow the government of the Philippines.

Source: Adapted from the Center for Defense Information, www.cdi.org, (June 5, 2010).

2001, p. 36). Take care to consider how your value judgments can affect your image and interpretation of the identity and purpose of any group you may believe belongs in this menacing category of NGO actors. Constructing a valid account will be a challenge especially in regard to such a controversial topic. The cliché "one person's terrorist is another person's freedom fighter" springs from the hold of prior and subjective perceptions on many people's definitions of objective realities.

The same obstacles to objective interpretation apply to the analysis of another type of NGO, multinational corporations (MNCs). Like transnational terrorist groups, MNCs are both praised and condemned because different people ascribe to them different attributes. In the information age of disappearing borders, money matters. This makes MNCs increasingly influential as nonstate actors—connecting cash flows and people globally in ways that may be eroding the sovereignty that states have previously taken as an unchanging fact.

Multinational Corporations

Multinational corporations (MNCs)—business enterprises organized in one society with activities in others growing out of direct investment abroad—are a fourth major type of NGO. MNCs have grown dramatically in scope and potential influence with the globalization of the world political economy since World War II (see Chapters 9 and 10). As a result of their immense resources and power, MNCs have provoked both acceptance and animosity. As advocates of liberal free trade and as active contributors to the globalization of world politics, MNCs generate both credit for the positive aspects of free trade and globalization as well as blame for their costs. This has made them highly controversial nonstate actors, especially in the Global South, where people frequently see MNCs as the cause of exploitation and poverty (see Chapter 4).

In the past, MNCs were headquartered almost exclusively in the United States, Europe, and Japan, and their common practice was to make short-term investments in the Global South's plants, sales corporations, and mining operations. At the start of the twenty-first century, about 80 percent of all MNCs' employees worked in the developing countries, where wages were lower, to bolster corporate profits at the parent headquarters in the Global North. But no longer. "More and more multinationals will shift the operation and control of key business functions away from their home office . . . A growing number of companies are setting up regional headquarters or relocating specific headquarter functions elsewhere" (Hindle 2004, pp. 97–98).

Such outsourcing of management to locations where wages and costs are lower but skills are substantial is likely to continue, accelerating the consolidation of the global economy into a seamless, integrated web. This outsourcing is now eagerly welcomed by the Global South's developing countries as a means to economic growth, where once MNC domination was resisted. Nonetheless, wealth and power remain highly concentrated; the big seem to get bigger and bigger. The assets controlled by the fifty largest MNCs from the Global South are less than 10 percent of the amount controlled by the fifty largest MNCs from the Global North (Oatley 2008, p. 175).

MNCs are increasingly influential NGOs because the world's giant producing, trading, and servicing corporations have become the primary agents of the globalization of production. Table 5.3 captures their importance in world politics, ranking firms by annual sales and states by GNI. The profile shows that of the world's top thirty-five economic entities, multinationals account for only five; but in the next thirty-five, they account for seventeen. Altogether, MNCs comprise almost a third of the top seventy economic entities, illustrating that MNCs' financial clout rivals or exceeds that of most countries.

In part due to their global reach and economic power, MNCs' involvement in the domestic political affairs of local or host countries is controversial. In some instances this concern has extended to MNCs' involvement in the domestic politics of their home countries, where they actively lobby their governments for more liberal trade and investment policies to enhance the profitability of their business. In turn, both host and home governments have sometimes used MNCs as instruments in their foreign policy strategies. Perhaps the most notorious instance of an MNC's intervention in the politics of a host state occurred in Chile in the early 1970s when International Telephone and Telegraph (ITT) tried to protect its interests in the profitable Chiltelco telephone company by seeking to prevent the election of Marxist-oriented Salvador Allende as president and, once Allende was elected, pressured the U.S. government to disrupt the Chilean economy. Eventually Allende was overthrown by a military dictatorship. More recently, the huge profits and activities of corporate giant Halliburton to rebuild the infrastructure of Iraq after the 2003 U.S. occupation provoked widespread complaints that this MNC was exploiting the circumstances to line its pockets, at U.S. taxpayers' expense. As a sign of the times, in 2007 the corporate giant Halliburton moved its headquarters from Texas to Dubai.

This global penetration positions the biggest MNCs to propel changes in relations between countries and within them, as well as in the global marketplace. For example, the MNCs have recently taken steps toward engineering

Table 5.3 Countries and Corporations: A Ranking by Size of Economy and Revenues

Rank	Country/Corporation	GNI/Revenues (billions of dollars)
1	United States	14,572.9
2	Japan	4,869.1
3	China	3,888.1
4	Germany	3,506.9
5	United Kingdom	2,827.3
6	France	2,695.6
7	Italy	2,121.6
8	Spain	1,454.8
9	Canada	1,453.8
10	Brazil	1,401.3
11	Russia	1,371.2
12	India	1,186.7
13	Mexico	1,062.4
14	South Korea	1,046.2
15	Australia	862.5
16	Netherlands	811.4
17	Turkey	666.6
18	Belgium	477.3
19	Sweden	469.4
20	ROYAL DUTCH SHELL	458.4
21	Poland	447.1
22	EXXON MOBIL	442.8
23	Saudi Arabia	440.5
24	Indonesia	426.8
25	Switzerland	424.5
26	Norway	416.4
27	WAL-MART STORES	405.6
28	Austria	382.7
29	BRITISH PETROLEUM	367.1
30	Denmark	323.0
31	Greece	319.2
32	Argentina	286.6
33	South Africa	283.2
34	CHEVRON	263.2
35	Finland	252.9
36	Iran	251.5
37	Thailand	247.2

Rank	Country/Corporation	GNI/Revenues (billions of dollars)
38	TOTAL	234.6
39	CONOCOPHILLIPS	230.8
40	ING GROUP	226.6
41	Ireland	220.3
42	Portugal	219.6
43	Hong Kong, China	219.3
44	Colombia	207.9
45	SINOPEC	207.8
46	TOYOTA MOTORS	204.4
47	JAPAN POST HOLDINGS	198.7
48	Malaysia	196.0
49	GENERAL ELECTRIC	183.2
50	CHINA NATIONAL PETROLEUM	181.1
51	Israel	180.6
52	Romania	178.1
53	Nigeria	177.4
54	Czech Republic	173.6
55	Philippines	170.4
56	Singapore	168.2
57	VOLKSWAGEN	166.6
58	STATE GRID	164.1
59	DEXIA GROUP	161.3
60	ENI	159.3
61	Chile	157.5
62	Pakistan	157.3
63	GENERAL MOTORS	149.0
64	Ukraine	148.6
65	Egypt	146.8
66	FORD MOTOR	146.3
67	Algeria	144.2
68	ALLIANZ	142.4
69	HSBC HOLDINGS	142.0
70	GAZPROM	141.5

Gross National Income (GNI), World Bank, 2010 *World Development Report*, pp. 32–34; MNC revenues, *Fortune*, http://money.cnn.com (June 3, 2010).

a "social responsibility revolution" by "making products and delivering services that generate profits and also help the world address challenges such as climate change, energy security, healthcare, and poverty. It's not just about public relations any more. Firms see big profits in green solutions" (Piasecki

2007). Consider Wal-Mart, with annual sales of more than $405 billion (larger than Austria's GDP) and nearly two million employees, which has unveiled its "Sustainability 360" initiative to sell environmentally friendly products in order to increase the 100 million customers throughout the world Wal-Mart currently attracts every week.

In the interest of corporate social responsibility, MNCs in many sectors are also increasingly sensitive to human rights conditions in potential host countries, as well as the impact MNCs themselves may have upon human rights. Developing business partnerships with countries in the Global South where there is greater respect for human rights tends to translate into reduced political risk and a more productive work force for investors (Blanton and Blanton 2009). Moreover, due to increased oversight by activist NGOs that monitor and publicize corporate involvement in human rights violations, multinational corporations are aware that too close of an association with human rights abusers may result in damage to corporate image—and potentially share values as well (Spar 1999).

MNCs assist in promoting free trade and are active participants in the process by which governments have reached agreements on rules liberalizing economic transactions in the global marketplace. Thus, as another consequence of their growing wealth and power, it is tempting to conclude that MNCs are a threat to state power. However, this interpretation overlooks the fact that, as MNCs have grown in size, the regulatory power of states has also grown.

> Only the state can defend corporate interests in international negotiations over trade, investment, and market access. Agreements over such things as airline routes, the opening of banking establishments, and the right to sell insurance are not decided by corporate actors who gather around a table; they are determined by diplomats and bureaucrats. Corporations must turn to governments when they have interests to protect or advance (Kapstein 1991–1992, p. 56).

Still, the blurring of the boundaries between internal and external affairs adds potency to the political role that MNCs unavoidably play as nonstate actors at the intersection of foreign and domestic policy. The symbolic invasion of national borders by MNCs can be expected to arouse the anger of many local nationalists who fear the loss of income, jobs, and control to foreign corporate interests. Because multinationals often make decisions over which leaders of states have little control (such as investments), MNCs' growing influence appears to contribute to the erosion of the global system's major organizing principle—that the state alone should be sovereign. MNCs' awesome financial resources are much greater than the official statistics suggest, and this is why many states fear that MNCs, which insist on freedom to compete internationally, are stripping away their sovereign control. And in fact, in some respects states *are* losing control of their national economies as MNCs merge with one another and, in the process, cease to remain tied to any one parent state or region.

"Who owns whom?" can no longer be answered. This is because many MNCs are now *globally integrated enterprises* that produce the same goods in different countries so that their horizontal organization no longer ties them to any single country. Consider this: "Half of Xerox's employees work on foreign soil, and less than half of Sony's employees are Japanese. More than 50 percent of IBM's revenues originate overseas; the same is true for Citigroup, ExxonMobil, DuPont, Procter & Gamble, and many other corporate giants. Joint ventures are no longer merely a domestic decision. Corning obtains one-half of its profits from foreign joint ventures with Samsung in Korea, Asahi Glass in Japan, and Ciba-Geigy in Switzerland" (Weidenbaum 2004, pp. 26–27). Business organizations today are better thought of as "global" than as "multinational."

globally integrated enterprises
MNCs organized horizontally, with management and production located in plants in numerous states for the same products they market.

Controlling the webs of corporate interrelationships, joint ventures, and shared ownership for any particular state purpose is nearly impossible. Indeed, 30 to 40 percent of world trade takes place *within* multinationals, from one branch to another (Oatley 2008, p. 170). This further undermines states' ability to identify the MNCs they seek to control, and contributes to the perception that MNCs are becoming "stateless." Thus, how can any single state manage such multinational giants when no country can claim that an MNC is "one of ours"?

In the past twenty years the number of MNCs has increased ninefold (Oatley 2008, p. 189) and MNCs are playing a correspondingly larger and larger role in world politics. This is forcing sovereign states to confront many challenges. How will they respond? Assessing the future requires a theoretical examination of contemporary thinking regarding MNCs and other types of NGOs.

Issue-Advocacy Groups

As citizens increasingly participate in NGOs in order to gain a voice in and influence over the institutions that shape the conditions in which they live, issue-advocacy group activity on the global stage has risen to unprecedented levels. "In its simplest form, issue advocacy is about three things: defining a problem (e.g., social, environmental, economic, etc.), identifying and advocating a specific solution, and motivating action" (Hannah 2009).

Greenpeace, Amnesty International, and Doctors Without Borders are just a few examples of nongovernmental issue-advocacy groups that actively seek to influence and change global conditions.

Many people now see NGOs as a vehicle empowering individuals to engineer transformations in international affairs. What is clear is that networks of transnational activists have formed NGOs at an accelerating rate, and through their leverage have performed an educational service that has demonstratively contributed to the emergence of a global *civil society*. The growth of transnational activism by NGOs "is leading to a diffusion of power away from central governments" (Nye 2007), and these networks

civil society
a community that embraces shared norms and ethical standards to collectively manage problems without coercion and through peaceful and democratic procedures for decision making aimed at improving human welfare.

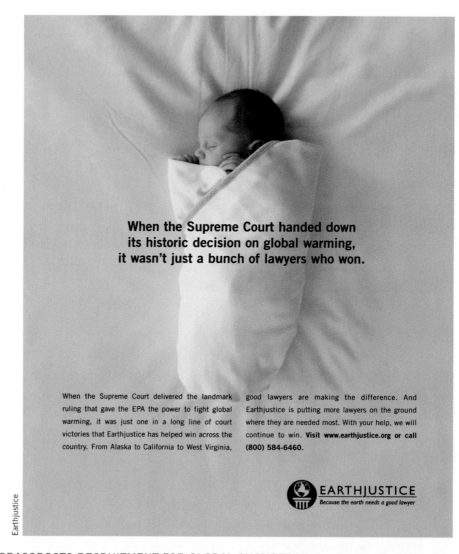

When the Supreme Court handed down
its historic decision on global warming,
it wasn't just a bunch of lawyers who won.

When the Supreme Court delivered the landmark ruling that gave the EPA the power to fight global warming, it was just one in a long line of court victories that Earthjustice has helped win across the country. From Alaska to California to West Virginia, good lawyers are making the difference. And Earthjustice is putting more lawyers on the ground where they are needed most. With your help, we will continue to win. **Visit www.earthjustice.org or call (800) 584-6460.**

EARTHJUSTICE
Because the earth needs a good lawyer

Earthjustice

GRASSROOTS RECRUITMENT FOR GLOBAL CHANGE NGOs are advocates of a wide variety of changes in the world. In this advertisement, the Earthjustice Legal Defense Fund promotes the fight against global warming.

of transnational social movements are altering international culture by reshaping values about international conduct (Barnett and Finnemore 2004; Heins 2008).

That said, studies of the impact of NGO pressure on global policy making suggest some conclusions that temper confidence in the expectation that NGO pressure can lead to far-reaching transformational reforms in the conduct of international relations:

- Interest group activity operates as an ever-present, if limited, constraint on global policy making. Single-issue NGO interest groups have more influence than large general-purpose organizations. However, the impact *varies with the issue*.

- As a general rule, issue-advocacy groups are relatively weak in the *high politics* of international security because states remain in control of defense policy and are relatively unaffected by external NGO pressures.

- Conversely, the clout of issue-advocacy groups is highest with respect to issues in *low politics*, such as protecting endangered species (e.g., whales) or combating climate change, which are of concern to great and small powers alike.

- The influence between state governments and NGOs is reciprocal, but it is more probable that government officials manipulate transnational interest groups than that NGOs exercise influence over governments' foreign policies.

- Issue-advocacy groups sometimes seek *inaction* from governments and maintenance of the status quo; such efforts are generally more successful than efforts to bring about major changes in international relations. For this reason NGOs are often generally seen as agents of policy continuities.

The foregoing characteristics of NGO efforts to redirect global policy suggest that the mere presence of such groups, and the mere fact they are organized with the intent of persuasion, does not guarantee their penetration of the global policy-making process. On the whole, NGOs have participation without real power and involvement without real influence, given that the ability of any *one* to exert influence is offset by the tendency for countervailing powers to materialize over the disposition of any major issue. That is, when any coalition of interest groups seeks vigorously to push policy in one direction, other nonstate actors—aroused that their established interests are being disturbed—are stimulated to push policy in the opposite direction. Global policy making consequently resembles a taffy pull: every nonstate actor attempts to pull policy in its own direction while resisting the pulls of others.

The result is often that the quest for consensus proves elusive, the capacity of a network to push history forward rapidly in a particular direction is constrained, and the international community's posture toward many global problems fails to move in any single direction. The result is usually a continuous battleground over the primary global issues from which no permanent resolution of the struggle materializes. The debate and contests between those wishing to make environmental protection a global priority and those placing economic growth ahead of environmental preservation provide one example among many.

> *We're not asking you to put your hand in your pockets, but we are asking people to put their fist in the air. This is your moment. Make history by making poverty history.*
>
> —Bono, lead singer of the rock band U2

NONSTATE ACTORS AND THE FUTURE OF WORLD POLITICS

As the world grows more interdependent and transactions across state borders increase through the movement of people, information, and traded products, it is likely that world politics nonetheless will be increasingly affected by the activities of both IGO and NGO nonstate actors. Even though nonstate actors are unlikely to join together in a common cause to pressure the international community for radical reforms, their activities (however divided) are likely to challenge the ironlike grip that sovereign states have exercised in determining the global system's architecture and rules ever since the 1648 Peace of Westphalia:

> The idea of sovereign equality reflected a conscious decision governments made 60 years ago that they would be better off if they repudiated the right to meddle in the internal affairs of others. That choice no longer makes sense. In an era of rapid globalization, internal developments in distant states affect our own well-being, even our security. That is what Sept. 11 taught us. Today respect for state sovereignty should be conditional on how states behave at home, not just abroad. Sovereignty carries with it a responsibility to protect citizens against mass violence and a duty to prevent internal developments that threaten others. We need to build an international order that reflects how states organize themselves internally (Daalder and Lindsay 2004).

Are transnational nonstate actors truly capable of flexing their muscles in ways that can directly challenge states' sovereign control over both their foreign and domestic policies? If so, are the pillars of the Westphalian state system beginning to crumble, as some predict (Falk and Strauss 2001; Kegley and Raymond 2002a)?

As you contemplate these questions, keep in mind one clear lesson: It is misleading to think that politics is only about territorial states in interaction with each other, exercising supreme authority within their own borders. Given their accountability and abuses of power (Grant and Keohane 2005), are there good reasons to see the challenges of IGOs and NGOs as a threat to states' continuing domination of world politics? Are nonstate actors integral to the construction of shared meanings that people use to define their identities and identify their interests? If that is the prevailing trend, as nonstate actors "multiply the channels of access to the international system," are they "blurring the boundaries between a state's relations with its own nationals and the recourse both citizens and states have to the international system" (Keck and Sikkink 2008, p. 222), and thus transforming the practice of state sovereignty?

The outlines of a future type of dual global system may be coming into view, driven simultaneously both by the continuing importance of relations between states and by the growing impact of multiple cross-border transactions and channels of communication among nonstate actors. Are the *liberal* and *constructivist* perspectives on the processes by which trends in world politics are set in motion correct? To be sure, transnational NGOs are putting increasing pressure on states and, in the process, may truly be paving the path for a possible *transformation* of world politics. This change would lead to a hybrid or two-tiered world in which the clout and authority of the governments that rule countries decline while the relative power of nonstate actors rises.

That said, skeptics counter that NGOs have failed to become "a serious rival to the power and processes of the state"; their goals of transforming the dominant processes of policy making and corporate capitalism have not met with success (Price 2003, p. 591). Indeed, it has been argued that it is inaccurate to accept the interpretation often pictured by *neoliberal theory* of NGOs weakening state sovereignty, because instead NGOs (some well-financed by states and IGOs) "have helped states retain—and in some instances even increase—their internal and external control, autonomy and legitimacy" (Weir 2007). Seen through *realist theory*, the critical choices that direct global destiny are ultimately made by the most powerful states.

These speculations by no means resolve the question of whether the era of state dominance is coming to an end as nonstate actors find their clout rising. Relations between global actors, as well as broader developments in world politics, are the consequence of innumerable decisions made by states, transnational organizations, and individuals. In the next chapter, we will look at the processes by which both state and nonstate actors make international decisions in an effort to further enhance your understanding of the challenges of world politics.

Take an Online Practice Quiz

www.cengagebrain.com/shop/ISBN/0495802204

Suggested Readings

Boehmer, Charles and Timothy Nordstrom. (2008) "Intergovernmental Organization Memberships: Examining Political Community and the Attributes of International Organizations," *International Interactions* 34: 282–309.

Heins, Volker. (2008) *Nongovernmental Organizations in International Society: Struggles over Recognition.* New York: Palgrave Macmillan.

Jones, Bruce, Carlos Pascual, and Stephen John Stedman. (2009) *Power & Responsibility: Building International Order in an Era of Transnational Threats.* Washington, D.C.: Brookings.

Milner, Helen V. and Andrew Moravcsik. (2009) *Power, Interdependence, and Nonstate Actors in World Politics.* Princeton, NJ: Princeton University Press.

Reimann, Kim D. (2006) "A View from the Top: International Politics, Norms and the Worldwide Growth of NGOs," *International Studies Quarterly* 50: 45–67.

Thakur, Ramesh and Thomas G. Weiss, eds. (2009) *The United Nations and Global Governance: An Unfinished Journey.* Bloomington: Indiana University Press.

CHAPTER 6
INTERNATIONAL DECISION MAKING

CHAPTER OUTLINE

FOREIGN POLICY MAKING IN INTERNATIONAL AFFAIRS

Transnational Actors and Decision Processes

Influences on the Making of Foreign Policy Decisions

DECISION MAKING BY TRANSNATIONAL ACTORS: THREE PROFILES

Decision Making as Rational Choice

The Bureaucratic Politics of Foreign Decision Making

The Leverage and Impact of Leaders

CONTROVERSY: Do Leaders Make a Difference?

THE GLOBAL AND DOMESTIC DETERMINANTS OF STATES' INTERNATIONAL DECISIONS

International Influences on Foreign Policy Choice

The Domestic Sources of Foreign Policy Decisions

CONTROVERSY: Are Democracies Deficient in Foreign Affairs?

Decisions and actions in the international arena can be understood, predicted, and manipulated only insofar as the factors influencing the decision can be identified and isolated.

—Arnold Wolfers, political scientist

"HOW ARE FOREIGN POLICY DECISIONS REACHED?" That was the question put to former U.S. Secretary of State Henry A. Kissinger in an interview with one of your text's authors, Charles Kegley. Kissinger has observed that "Much of the anguish of foreign policy results from the need to establish priorities among competing, sometimes conflicting, necessities."

Y ou have completed your higher education degrees in international studies. Next, you have embarked on your career. Your employment allowed you to apply your acquired knowledge to help make the world a better place. As a result of your wise and efficient use of your analytic capabilities in your work with the World Health Organization (WHO), you now find that you have earned a very important appointment: to head and lead an established nongovernmental organization (NGO) in your area of expertise. In that role, you are expected to construct your NGO's *foreign policy*. Your challenge is to make decisions, based on your organization's values, about the foreign policy goals your NGO should pursue as well as the means by which those international goals might best be realized.

Congratulations! You have unprecedented power. Now your task is to make critical choices that are destined to determine whether or not your foreign policies will succeed. How are you, as a governing authority of a transnational *actor* on the world stage, to make decisions that will best serve your organization's interest and the world at large?

As an international decision maker, your approach will partly depend on your preferences and priorities. But there is no sure path as to how to make foreign policy decisions that are workable, moral, and successful. You will face many obstacles and constraints on your ability to make informed choices. As former U.S. Secretary of State Henry Kissinger warns, foreign policy decisions are rarely made by people having all the facts: The policy maker "has to act in the fog of incomplete knowledge without the information that will be available later to the analyst." What is more, any choice you might make is certain to carry with it costs that compromise some values you hold dear and undermine some of the other goals you would like to pursue. So you now face the kind of challenge that throughout history has befuddled every decision maker who has had the power to make foreign policy decisions on behalf of the transnational actor he or she led.

FOREIGN POLICY MAKING IN INTERNATIONAL AFFAIRS

The purpose of this chapter is to introduce you to the lessons that history provides about the patterns, pitfalls, and payoffs that surround alternative approaches for making international decisions. This introduction opens a window to rival ways of describing the processes by which transnational actors make foreign policy decisions.

Case Study: *Foreign Policy*

Transnational Actors and Decision Processes

The chapter, which is derived from historical experience and *theories* of *international relations* that scholarship has constructed about this topic, will look at patterns of international decision making by all transnational actors—the individuals, groups, states, and organizations that play a role in world politics. Thus, it will not only cover countries (for example, Japan) but also take into view at the same time the decision-making practices of international organizations such as the Nordic Council; nongovernmental organizations (NGOs) such as the World Wildlife Federation; multinational corporations such as Wal-Mart; indigenous nationalities such as Kurds in Iran, Iraq, and Turkey; and terrorist networks such as Al Qaeda. In addition, it is important to reflect on how each and every one of us—all individual people—are part of the equation because we are all in a sense transnational actors capable of making free choices that contribute in countless ways to the direction of trends in world politics. When mobilized and inspired by a sense of agency, individuals can make a difference in the course of world history; indeed, the decisions that we make every day and the groups that we join are reflections of our own personal "foreign policy," whether or not we are aware of the consequences of our daily choices. Every person matters. As American anthropologist Margaret Mead advised, "Never doubt that a small group of thoughtful, committed citizens can change the world. Indeed, it is the only thing that ever has."

To stimulate your thinking about international decision making by all types of transnational actors, *World Politics* provides a framework for analyzing and explaining the processes by which foreign policies are made.

Influences on the Making of Foreign Policy Decisions

To structure theoretical thinking about international decision making, it is useful to think in terms of the factors or causes that influence the ways in which foreign policy decisions are made by all transnational actors. What variables or causal influences impact foreign policy decision making?

For starters, it would be an error to assume that international decisions and behaviors are influenced solely by the choices of global leaders. This kind of single-factor explanation will not work because no decision maker (not even the most authoritarian in a dictatorship) can act alone in terms of his or her whims and fancies. The leaders of all groups are constrained by various pressures and circumstances that restrict free choices. Speaking on the making of American foreign policy decisions, former U.S. Secretary of State Henry

Kissinger pointed out that "One of the most unsettling things for foreigners is the impression that our foreign policy can be changed by any new president on the basis of the president's personal preference." "To some extent," former U.S. presidential adviser Joseph A. Califano said, "a president is a prisoner of historical forces that will demand his attention whatever his preference in policy objectives."

No single category of causation can fully explain foreign policy decisions; rather, a number converge to codetermine the decisions that produce foreign policy "outputs." So to cut into the question of how international decision making unfolds, we must go beyond a single-factor explanation and think in terms of multiple causes.

For that, it is useful to identify the various clusters of variables that exert an influence on the choices that all types of transnational actors make when they formulate a foreign policy. Similar to the *level-of-analysis* distinction introduced in Chapter 1 (see Figure 1.1), we can construct an image of the determinants of decision making in the foreign-policy-making process by reference to three major sets of causal variables. These are the (1) global conditions that prevail at the time of decision, (2) the internal characteristics of the transnational actor making foreign policy choices, and (3) the leaders who head the transnational actor making the decision.

This three-part framework encourages you to think in causal terms about classes of phenomena that explain why particular decisions are made. Each category encompasses a large number of factors, which, together with the influences grouped in the other two categories, tell you what to observe when you construct an explanation as to why a particular decision by a particular transnational actor was made (see Figure 6.1).

Global conditions at the time of the decision color the degree to which both an actor's internal attributes and individual leader preferences can account for the choices made. The *internal characteristics* of the transnational actor heavily constrain the range of choice open to the individual decision maker. The characteristics of the *leaders* are important as well, because their individual values, personalities, beliefs, intelligence, and prior experiences not only define the kind of people they are but also predispose them to take certain kinds of positions on global issues. The three categories of influences serve as "inputs" that shape the policy-making process. They ultimately lead to foreign policy decisions and outcomes, or foreign policy "outputs," that in turn provide "feedback" that may subsequently affect the inputs themselves.

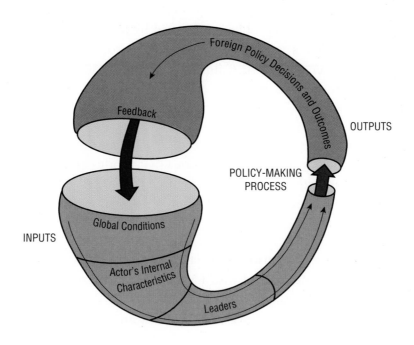

FIGURE 6.1

A "FUNNEL VISION" OF THE INFLUENCES ON INTERNATIONAL DECISION MAKING The determinants or the factors that influence the foreign policy choices of transnational actors are shown here as a "funnel of causality." This construction classifies three categories of influence in the foreign policy-making process, whereby policy "inputs" shape the decisions that produce policy "outputs."

Let's take a closer look at these three categories of causation, beginning with the most comprehensive, global conditions, and working to the most specific, individual leaders.

Global Conditions What is happening in world politics provides the setting for international decision making. The changing state of the world—everything that occurs beyond the actor—affects the decisions of transnational actors. The prevailing global circumstances define the decisional situation, provoking the need to make decisions and restricting policy options available to the actor. As John Quincy Adams noted while U.S. secretary of state, "I know of no change in policy, only of circumstances."

Take any global trend highlighted in *World Politics* and we can easily visualize how changes in the state of the world condition the issues on the global agenda: global warming, nuclear proliferation, international trade, the AIDS/HIV crisis, international terrorism, and civil wars—you name it. All shifts in global circumstances give rise to crucial decisions by transnational actors. The view that changes of global circumstances serve as a catalyst for international decision making was captured by U.S. President Richard Nixon when he declared, "The world has changed. Our foreign policy must change with it."

Internal Characteristics   As important as the global environment is, it would be mistaken to think it alone is the sole source driving international decision making. Every actor on the global stage is defined by their own attributes, which also act to determine the actor's foreign policy choices.

All transnational actors organized to take action abroad are composed of a collection of individuals. How these group actors are governed, and the processes and procedures they follow to reach foreign policy decisions, are forces of their own that structure and determine the *kinds* of decisions that are reached. The size of the organization, its power relative to the other actors with which it interacts, the financial resources, and the distribution of opinion within the actor all affect the capacity of the actor to make foreign policy choices in response to changes in global circumstances. With respect to states, for example, the rise of "bureaucratic politics" among competing agencies seeking to direct the course of a country's foreign policy now heavily influences the choices that will be made. This is illustrated by former U.S. Under Secretary of State George W. Ball's warning that the nature of the institutional machinery produced the decisions that led to America's failed war in Vietnam: "The process was the author of the policy." Choices about ends and means in foreign policies, therefore, are molded by transformations in international relations *and* by the impact of these global changes on the characteristics of transnational actors.

Actor Leadership   The personal characteristics of the leaders heading transnational actors assume great importance in the making of international decisions. Leaders are influential because "factors external to the actor can become determinants only as they affect the mind, the heart, and the will of the decision maker. A human decision to act in a specific way necessarily represents the last link in the chain of antecedents of any act of policy. A geographical set of conditions, for instance, can affect the behavior of a nation only as specific persons perceive and interpret these conditions" (Wolfers 1962, p. 50). Thus, changes in global conditions and actors' collective internal characteristics may influence the costs and benefits of particular foreign policy options and stimulate the need for choice. However, these are mediated by leaders' perceptions. As *constructivist theory* argues, ideas and expectations within the heads of leaders are the intellectual filters through which objective realities are interpreted. Therefore, in any explanation of why any international decision is made, it is imperative to take into account how leaders' ideas and images influence the choices taken.

Again inspect this threefold set of influences on international decision making in Figure 6.1. Note that this organization for interpretation is *explanatory*. The framework provides clues as to where to look when asking *why* a foreign policy decision has been reached. Each policy decision can be viewed as the result of the multiple prior causal events taking place in the funnel. Thus, the model stipulates the conditions that precede and promote policy decisions (bearing in mind that frequently it is difficult to distinguish decision making itself from its prior conditions). Policy outcomes depend on the prior conditions in the funnel and are explained by the combined impact of the input factors on the output or outcome (the policy decision).

Observe as well that our framework implies a temporal or time sequence in the transition from inputs to outputs in the foreign-policy-making process. That is, changes in the determinants of foreign policy occurring at time t produce decisions at a later time $(t + 1)$, which lead to policy outcomes that impact all the causal factors at a still later time $(t + 2)$. Moreover, these policy outcomes have consequences for the input factors themselves at a later time $(t + 3)$ because they exert "feedback" on these causal factors as the foreign policy decisions alter the conditions that influence subsequent $(t + 4)$ policy making. For example, a cluster of factors at some point in time (t) led the United States to make the decision in March 2003 $(t + 1)$ to invade Iraq

Gerald Herbert/AP Photo

CHOICE AND CONSEQUENCE The Bush Administration's March 2003 decision to invade Iraq generated a hostile public reaction on the four-year anniversary of that decision. Shown here on March 17, 2007, are thousands of protestors voicing their rage against the war near the Pentagon, the headquarters and symbol of U.S. military power.

($t + 2$), but this decision exerted a painfully negative "feedback" influence on public opinion within America and abroad when that invasion increased the level of international terrorism the invasion was designed to terminate, and this reaction in turn later ($t + 3$) transformed global conditions as well as attitudes within American society, which then began to galvanize revisions ($t + 4$) of the original policy decision. Thus, the model advanced here is dynamic. It can be used to account for past policy decisions and behaviors as well as for the effects of those outcomes on later policy decisions. This way of tracing the determinants and consequences of international decisions provides you, the analyst, with a lens with which to view and explain theoretically the foreign policy of transnational actors in historical perspective, because the model is not tied analytically to any one time period or actor.

With this analytic framework in mind, you are armed intellectually to probe international decision making in greater depth. Or are you? To better inform your analyses of the causes of international decision making, let us inspect three models of decision making formulated by scholars of this topic: rational choice, bureaucratic politics, and the political psychology of leaders and leadership.

In the episodic and visual comprehension of our foreign policy, there is serious danger that the larger significance of developments will be lost in a kaleidoscope of unrelated events. Continuities will be obscured, causal factors unidentified.

—George W. Ball, former U.S. Under Secretary of State

DECISION MAKING BY TRANSNATIONAL ACTORS: THREE PROFILES

Realism assumes that foreign policy making consists primarily of adjusting a *transnational actor* to the pressures of an anarchical global system whose essential properties will not vary. Accordingly, it presumes that all decision makers are essentially alike in their approach to foreign policy making:

> If they follow the [decision] rules, we need know nothing more about them. In essence, if the decision maker behaves rationally, the observer, knowing the rules of rationality, can rehearse the decisional process in his own mind, and, if he knows the decision maker's goals, can both predict the decision and understand why that particular decision was made (Verba 1969, p. 225).

Because realists believe that leaders' goals and their corresponding approach to foreign policy choices are the same, the decision-making processes of each

unitary actor
a transnational actor (usually a sovereign state) assumed to be internally united, so that changes in its domestic opinion do not influence its foreign policy as much as do the decisions that actor's leaders make to cope with changes in its global environment.

rational choice
decision-making procedures guided by careful definition of situations, weighing of goals, consideration of all alternatives, and selection of the options most likely to achieve the highest goals.

actor can be studied as though each were a *unitary actor*—a homogeneous or monolithic unit with few or no important internal differences that affect its choices. From this assumption can be derived the expectation that transnational actors can and do make decisions by rational calculations of the costs and benefits of different choices.

Decision Making as Rational Choice

The decision-making processes of unitary actors that determine national interests are typically described as rational. We define rationality or *rational choice* here as purposeful, goal-directed behavior exhibited when "the individual responding to an international event . . . uses the best information available and chooses from the universe of possible responses most likely to maximize his [or her] goals" (Verba 1969). Scholars describe rationality as a sequence of decision-making activities involving the following intellectual steps:

- ◼ Problem Recognition and Definition. The need to decide begins when policy makers perceive an external problem and attempt to define objectively its distinguishing characteristics. Objectivity requires full information about the actions, motivations, and capabilities of other actors as well as the character of the global environment and trends within it. The search for information must be exhaustive, and all the facts relevant to the problem must be gathered.

- ◼ Goal Selection. Next, those responsible for making foreign policy choices must determine what they want to accomplish. This disarmingly simple requirement is often difficult. It requires the identification and ranking of *all* values (such as security and economic prosperity) in a hierarchy from most to least preferred.

- ◼ Identification of Alternatives. Rationality also requires the compilation of an exhaustive list of *all* available policy options and an estimate of the costs associated with each alternative.

- ◼ Choice. Finally, rationality requires selecting the single alternative with the best chance of achieving the desired goal(s). For this purpose, policy makers must conduct rigorous means-ends, cost-benefit analysis guided by an accurate prediction of the probable success of each option.

Policy makers often describe their own behavior as resulting from a rational decision-making process designed to reach the "best" decision possible, which employs the logic of *consequentialism* to estimate the results that can be expected from the decision taken.

The quest for rational decision making was illuminated, for example, in the crises that the closed circle of President George W. Bush's U.S. advisers faced in September 2001. They claimed that they were faithfully following the rules for rational choice in their declared war against "global terrorism" following 9/11 and in their decision to attack the dictator Saddam Hussein's Iraq. The administration launched a campaign in public diplomacy to persuade all states that it was in their best interest to recognize the danger posed by the high probability that Iraq had illegally obtained weapons of mass destruction, and it took its argument to the UN. The message was clothed in the language of deliberate rational choice to convince skeptics that the costs and benefits of all options had been carefully weighed.

Simulation:
Explaining U.S. intervention in Iraq: Rational Actor, Organizational Process

However, like beauty, rationality often lies in the eye of the beholder, and reasonable, clear-thinking people can and often do disagree about the facts and about the wisdom of foreign policy goals. Republican Senator Chuck Hagel in 2002, for instance, worried that Bush failed to address important questions required of a rational choice: "If we invade Iraq, what allies will we have? Who governs after Saddam? What is the objective? Have we calculated the consequences, particularly the unintended consequences? . . . We must recognize there are no easy, risk-free options." Others charged the Bush Administration with engaging in *threat inflation,* where the beliefs and perceptions of key decision makers led them to create a concern for the threat of terrorism that went beyond the scope and urgency that an objective analysis would justify (Thrall and Cramer 2009). To many throughout the world, these critical concerns later proved prophetic, as the cost in lives and money mounted and public support for the U.S. intervention in Iraq declined (despite the dramatic capture of Saddam Hussein and the end of his tyranny).

threat inflation
the effort by elites to create concern for a threat that exceeds the scope and urgency that would be justified by an impartial analysis

This debate demonstrated that while rationality is a decision-making goal to which all transnational actors aspire, it is difficult to determine when the criteria for rational choice have been met. This raises the question: What are the barriers to rationality?

> *It is doubtful that decision makers hear arguments on the merits and weigh them judiciously before choosing a course of action.*
>
> —Daniel Kahneman and Jonathan Renshon, decision-making theorists

Impediments to Rational Choice   Despite the apparent application of rationality in these crises, rational choice is often more an idealized standard than an accurate description of real-world behavior. Theodore Sorenson—one of President Kennedy's closest advisers and a participant in the Cuban Missile

Crisis deliberations—has written not only about the steps that policy makers in the Kennedy Administration followed as they sought to follow the process of rational choice but also about how actual decision making often departed from it. He described an eight-step process for policy making that is consistent with the rational model we have described: (1) agreeing on the facts; (2) agreeing on the overall policy objective; (3) precisely defining the problems; (4) canvassing all possible solutions; (5) listing the consequences that flow from each solution; (6) recommending one option; (7) communicating the option selected; and (8) providing for its execution. But he explained how difficult it is to follow these steps, because:

> . . . each step cannot be taken in order. The facts may be in doubt or dispute. Several policies, all good, may conflict. Several means, all bad, may be all that are open. Value judgments may differ. Stated goals may be imprecise. There may be many interpretations of what is right, what is possible, and what is in the national interest (Sorensen 1963, pp. 19–20).

bounded rationality
the concept that decision maker's capacity to choose the best option is often constrained by many human and organizational obstacles.

Despite the virtues rational choice promises, the impediments to its realization in foreign policy making are substantial. In fact, ***bounded rationality*** is typical (Simon 1997; Kahneman 2003).

Some of the barriers that make errors in foreign policy so common are human, deriving from deficiencies in the intelligence, capability, and psychological needs and aspirations of foreign policy decision makers. Others are organizational, because most decisions require group agreement about the actor's best interests and the wisest course of action. Reaching agreement is not easy, however, as reasonable people with different values often disagree about goals, preferences, and the probable results of alternative options. Thus, the impediments to rational policy making are not to be underestimated.

Scrutiny of the actual process of decision making reveals other hindrances. Available information is often insufficient to recognize emergent problems accurately, resulting in decisions made on the basis of partial information and vague memories. As the U.S. commander in the Iraq war, General David H. Petraeus, quoted Charles W. Kegley and Eugene Wittkopf (1982) in his 1987 Princeton University Ph.D. dissertation, "Faced with incomplete information about the immediate problem at hand, it is not surprising that decision makers turn to the past for guidance" and rely on historical analogies. Moreover, the available information is often inaccurate because the bureaucratic organizations that political leaders depend upon for advice screen, sort, and rearrange it. Compounding the problem is decision makers' susceptibility to *cognitive dissonance*—they are psychologically prone to block out dissonant, or inconsistent, information and perceptions about their preferred choice and to look instead for information that conforms to their preexisting beliefs to justify their choice. On top of that, they are prone to make decisions on the basis of "first impressions, or intuition, or that amorphous blending of 'what is' with 'what could be' that we call imagination [even though] there is a great body of data suggesting that formal statistical analysis is a much better way of predicting everything . . . than the intuition even of experts" (Brooks 2005; but see also Gladwell 2005, who argues that snap judgments and "rapid cognition can be as good as decisions made cautiously and deliberately"). Those who see themselves as "political experts" are habitually mistaken in their judgments and forecasts (Tetlock 2006), and leaders are prone to place faith in their prior prejudices, to draw false analogies with prior events (Brunk 2008), and to make decisions on emotion (Westen 2007). As so-called "behavioral international relations" research on decision making and *game theory* shows (Mintz 2007), leaders are limited in their capacity to process information and avoid biases; preoccupied with preventing losses, leaders are also prone to "wishful thinking" and "shooting from the hip," which results in frequently making irrational decisions. These intellectual propensities explain why policy makers sometimes pay little heed to warnings, overlook information about dangers, and repeat their past intellectual mistakes.

ROAD-TRIP DIPLOMACY President Barack Obama has emphasized a willingness to engage in dialogue with leaders of all nations as a key component of his commitment to diplomacy, with a pledge to "personally lead a new chapter of American engagement." Pictured here are the leaders of the Group of 8 (G-8) in Canada on June 25, 2010. From left are Japanese Prime Minister Naoto Kan, European Commission President Jose Manuel Barroso, Italian Prime Minister Silvio Berlusconi, French President Nicolas Sarkozy, U.S. President Obama, Canadian Prime Minister Stephen Harper, Russian President Dmitry Medvedev, German Chancellor Angela Merkel, U.K. Prime Minister David Cameron, and European Council President Herman Van Rompuy.

To better capture the way most leaders make policy decisions, Robert Putnam coined the phrase *two-level games.* Challenging the assumptions of realism, he asserted that leaders should formulate policies simultaneously in both the diplomatic and domestic arenas and should make those choices in accordance with the rules dictated by the "game."

> At the national level, domestic groups pursue their interests by pressuring the government to adopt favorable policies, and politicians seek power by constructing coalitions among these groups. At the international level, national governments seek to maximize their own ability to satisfy domestic pressures, while minimizing the adverse consequences of foreign developments. Neither of the two games can be ignored by central decision makers so long as their countries remain interdependent, yet sovereign (Putnam 1988, p. 434).

Most leaders must meet the often incompatible demands of internal politics and external diplomacy, and it is seldom possible to make policy decisions that respond rationally to both sets of goals. Policies at home often have

game theory
mathematical model of strategic interaction where outcomes are determined not only by a single actor's preferences, but also by the choices of all actors involved.

two-level games
a concept referring to the growing need for national policy makers to make decisions that will meet both domestic and foreign goals.

many consequences abroad. Foreign activities usually heavily influence an actor's internal condition. This is why many leaders are likely to fuse the two sectors in contemplating policy decisions.

Yet critics suggest that the two-level game model does not go far enough and could be improved by incorporating insights from *constructivism*—that it still relies too heavily on rationalism in assuming "that international negotiators have clear self-interests, represent certain domestic and state interests, and seek to maximize these interests; how these interests are constituted is left unexplored" (Deets 2009, p. 39). "Are domestic divisions—those based on ideology, on competing interests, on the struggle for power across political institutions—so serious as to make rational decision making impossible" (Kanet 2010, p.127)? States are administered by individuals with varying beliefs, values, preferences, and psychological needs, and such differences generate disagreements about goals and alternatives that are seldom resolved through orderly, rational processes. Moreover, these individuals are greatly shaped by the socially accepted shared understandings within their own policy-making community and culture. In order to more fully understand international decision making, it is important to consider not only domestic interests and identities, but also the "interactive processes among domestic and international actors through which interests and identities are created and changed" (Deets 2009, p. 39; see also Houghton 2007).

Yet there seldom exists a confident basis for making foreign policy decisions. Decision making often revolves around the difficult task of choosing among values, so that the choice of one option means the sacrifice of others. Indeed, many decisions tend to produce negative unintended consequences—what economists call *externalities*. Especially in the realm of foreign policy where risk is high and there is much uncertainty, decision makers' inability to rapidly gather and digest large quantities of information constrains their capacity to make informed choices. Because policy makers work with an overloaded *policy agenda* and short deadlines, the search for policy options is seldom exhaustive. "There is little time for leaders to reflect," observed Henry Kissinger (1979). "They are locked in an endless battle in which the urgent constantly gains on the important. The public life of every political figure is a continual struggle to rescue an element of choice from the pressure of circumstance."

In the choice phase, then, decision makers rarely make value-maximizing choices. Instead of selecting the option with the best chance of success, they typically end their evaluation as soon as an alternative appears that seems superior to those already considered. Herbert Simon (1957) describes this as *satisficing* behavior. Because people frequently face difficult decisions where

externalities
the negative side effects that result from choices, such as inflation resulting from runaway government spending.

policy agenda
the changing list of problems or issues to which governments pay special attention at any given moment.

satisficing
the tendency for decision makers to choose the first satisfactory option rather than searching further for a better alternative.

it is not possible to make a choice without compromising competing preferences, they rarely "optimize" by seeking the best alternative. Rather, decision makers are prone to rapidly estimate whether rival options are good or bad, react to these hastily constructed classifications, and then are content to settle with the relatively good alternative as opposed to the best.

Rooted in the experiments of Amos Tversky and Daniel Kahneman, who won the 2002 Nobel Prize in economics, prospect theory similarly challenges the idea that decision makers behave rationally. *Prospect theory* looks at how people perceive and misperceive risks when making choices under conditions of uncertainty, and posits that there are consistent and predictable biases in the way that people depart from rational decision making. People perceive alternatives in terms of their sense of potential gains and losses—"those faced with gains tend to be risk averse, while those confronting losses become much more risk seeking" (McDermott et al. 2008, p. 335). Indeed, "evidence suggests that individuals value losses twice as much as they value gains" (Elms 2008, p. 245). One implication for decision making is that people tend to gravitate toward the "status quo" (Grunwald 2009). Like people everywhere, leaders tend to overvalue certainty and "peace of mind," even to their detriment. They do not calculate the consequence of choices, and are more concerned with the potential losses that may result from a change than with the potential gains. This problematic outcome is compounded by another common decision-making error—the tendency to myopically frame decisions by focusing on short-term choices rather than long-term ones (Elms 2008).

prospect theory
a social psychological theory explaining decision making under conditions of uncertainty and risk that looks at the relationship between individual risk propensity and the perceived prospects for avoiding losses and realizing big gains.

Another implication of prospect theory is that when leaders take risks to initiate bold new foreign policy directions, they will have great difficulty admitting and correcting those choices if they later prove mistaken. As critics lament of George W. Bush's refusal to acknowledge decision-making failures regarding the Iraq war (Draper 2008; Goldsmith 2008), leaders are prone to cling to failed policies long after their deficiencies have become apparent. Similar criticisms were also made regarding both the Johnson and Nixon administrations' decisions to keep the United States mired in the unpopular war in Vietnam (Polsky 2010).

The dilemma that prospect theory presents, of course, is that "if people can't be trusted to make the right choices for themselves, how can they possibly be trusted to make the right decisions for the rest of us?" (Kolbert 2008). Yet while decision making that departs from rationality can be problematic, irrationality can still produce "good" decisions. Along these lines, experimental literature indicates that people tend to incorporate a sense of fairness into their decision making even if it is contrary to their own rational self-interest.

Video: *Determining Foreign Policy*

Table 6.1 Foreign Policy Decision Making in Practice and Theory

Actual Common Practice	Ideal Rational Process
Distorted, incomplete information	Accurate, comprehensive information
Personal motivations and organizational interests shape choices about national goals	Clear definition of national interests
Limited number of options considered; none thoroughly analyzed	Exhaustive analysis of all options
Courses of action selected by political bargaining and compromise	Selection of optimal course of action for producing desired results
Confusing and contradictory statements of decision, often framed for media consumption	Effective statement of decision and its rationale to mobilize domestic support
Neglect of the tedious task of managing the decision's implementation by foreign affairs bureaucracies	Careful monitoring of the decision's implementation by foreign affairs bureaucracies
Superficial policy evaluation, uncertain responsibility, poor follow-through, and delayed correction	Instantaneous evaluation of consequences followed by correction of errors

As economic behaviorist Dan Ariely's (2008) work demonstrates, "People, it turns out, want to be generous and they want to retain their dignity—even when it doesn't really make sense" (Kolbert 2008, p. 79).

Despite the image that policy makers seek to project, often the degree of rationality "bears little relationship to the world in which officials conduct their deliberations" (Rosenau 1980). Yet while rational foreign policy making is more an ideal than a reality, we can still assume that policy makers aspire to rational decision-making behavior, which they may occasionally approximate. Indeed, as a working proposition, it is useful to accept rationality as a picture of how the decision process *should* work as well as a description of key elements of how it *does* work (see Table 6.1).

The Bureaucratic Politics of Foreign Policy Decision Making

To make the right choices, leaders must seek information and advice, and must see that the actions their decisions generate are carried out properly. Who can assist in these tasks?

In today's world, leaders must depend on large-scale organizations for information and advice as they face critical foreign policy choices. Both "institutions and individuals matter in the making and implementation of foreign policy" (Kanet 2010, p. 127). Even transnational actors without large budgets and complex foreign policy bureaucracies seldom make decisions without the advice and assistance of many individuals and administrative agencies to cope with changing global circumstances.

Bureaucratic Efficiency and Rationality   Bureaucracies, according to the theoretical work of the German social scientist Max Weber, are widely believed to increase efficiency and rationality by assigning responsibility for different tasks to different people. They define rules and standard operating procedures that specify how tasks are to be performed; they rely on record systems to gather and store information; they divide authority among different organizations to avoid duplication of effort; and they often lead to meritocracies by hiring and promoting the most capable individuals. Bureaucracies also permit the luxury of engaging in forward planning to determine long-term needs and the means to attain them. Unlike leaders, whose roles require attention to the crisis of the moment, bureaucrats are able to consider the future as well as the present. The presence of several organizations also can result in *multiple advocacy* of rival choices (George 1972), thus improving the chance that all possible policy options will be considered.

The Limits of Bureaucratic Organization   What emerges from our description of bureaucracy is another idealized picture of the policy-making process. Before jumping to the conclusion that bureaucratic decision making is a modern blessing, however, we should emphasize that the foregoing propositions tell us how bureaucratic decision making *should* occur; they do not tell us how it *does* occur. The actual practice and the foreign policy choices that result show that bureaucracy produces burdens as well as benefits.

Consider the 1962 Cuban Missile Crisis, probably the single most threatening crisis in the post–World War II era. The method that U.S. policy makers used in orchestrating a response is often viewed as having nearly approximated the ideal of rational choice. From another decision-making perspective, however, the missile crisis reveals how decision making by and within organizational contexts sometimes compromises rather than facilitates rational choice.

In Graham Allison's well-known book on the missile crisis, *Essence of Decision* (1971), he advanced what is widely known as the *bureaucratic politics model* (see also Christensen and Redd 2004; Allison and Zelikow 1999; Hermann 1988). This model of decision making highlights the constraints that organizations and coalitions of organizations in *policy networks* place on decision makers' choices and the "pulling and hauling" that occurs among the key participants and *caucuses* of aligned bureaucracies in the decision process.

multiple advocacy
the concept that better and more rational choices are made when decisions are reached in a group context, which allows advocates of differing alternatives to be heard so that the feasibility of rival options receives critical evaluation.

bureaucracies
the agencies and departments that conduct the functions of a central government or of a nonstate transnational actor.

bureaucratic politics model
a description of decision making that sees foreign policy choices as based on bargaining and compromises among competing government agencies.

policy networks
leaders and organized interests (such as lobbies) that form temporary alliances to influence a particular foreign policy decision.

caucuses
informal groups that individuals in governments and other groups join to promote their common interests.

standard operating procedures (SOPs) rules for reaching decisions about particular types of situations.

The bureaucratic politics model emphasizes how large-scale bureaucratic organizations contribute to the policy-making process by devising *standard operating procedures (SOPs)*—established methods to be followed in the performance of designated tasks. Not surprisingly, participants in the deliberations that lead to policy choices also often define issues and favor policy alternatives that serve their organization's needs. "Where you stand depends on where you sit" is a favorite aphorism reflecting these bureaucratic imperatives. Consider why professional diplomats typically favor diplomatic approaches to policy problems, whereas military officers routinely favor military solutions.

The consequence is that "different groups pulling in different directions produce a result, or better a resultant—a mixture of conflicting preferences and unequal power of various individuals—distinct from what any person or group intended" (Allison 1971). Rather than being a value-maximizing process, then, policy making is itself an intensely competitive game of *politics*. Rather than presupposing the existence of a *unitary actor,* "bureaucratic politics" shows why "it is necessary to identify the games and players, to display the coalitions, bargains, and compromises, and to convey some feel for the confusion" (Allison 1971).

Fighting among insiders and the formation of factions to carry on battles over the direction of foreign policy decisions are chronic in nearly every transnational actor's administration (but especially in democratic actors' accepting of participation by many people in the policy-making process). Consider the United States. Splits among key advisers over important foreign policy choices have been frequent. For example, under Presidents Nixon and Ford, Secretary of State Henry Kissinger fought often with James Schlesinger and Donald Rumsfeld, who headed the Department of Defense, over strategy regarding the Vietnam War; Jimmy Carter's national security adviser, Zbigniew Brzezinski, repeatedly engaged in conflicts with Secretary of State Cyrus Vance over the Iran hostage crisis; and under Ronald Reagan, Caspar Weinberger at Defense and George Shultz at State were famous for butting heads on most policy issues. Such conflicts are not necessarily bad because they force each side to better explain its viewpoint, and this allows heads of state the opportunity to weigh their competing advice before making decisions. However, battles among advisers can lead to paralysis and to rash decisions that produce poor results. That possibility became evident in the fall of 2002, when serious divisions within George W. Bush's administration developed over how and why the president's goal was to wage war against Saddam Hussein in Iraq. Fissures became apparent as key officials publicly debated the wisdom of diplomacy versus invasion, and then how best to conduct the invasion.

In addition to their influence on the policy choices of political leaders, bureaucratic organizations possess several other characteristics that affect decision making. One view proposes that bureaucratic agencies are parochial and that every administrative unit within a transnational actor's foreign-policy-making bureaucracy seeks to promote its own purposes and power. Organizational needs, such as large staffs and budgets, come before the actor's needs, sometimes encouraging the sacrifice of the actor's interests to bureaucratic interests.

Characteristically, bureaucratic agencies are driven to enlarge their prerogatives and expand the conception of their mission, seeking to take on other units' responsibilities and powers. Far from being neutral or impartial managers, desiring only to carry out orders from the leaders, bureaucratic organizations frequently take policy positions designed to increase their own influence relative to that of other agencies. Moreover, in contrast to rational choice theory, which sees decision made by a unitary actor, bureaucratic agencies and their staff may not agree with the leader's values and priorities. As former National Security Adviser Zbigniew Brzenski (2010, p. 18) cautions, an actor's foreign policy priorities may become diluted or delayed by unsympathetic bureaucrats as "officials who are not in sympathy with advocated policies rarely make good executors."

The tragic surprise terrorist attack on September 11, 2001, provides a telling example of these ascribed characteristics of bureaucratic politics. The attacks on 9/11 were regarded by many as the worst intelligence failure since Pearl Harbor. Alarmed U.S. citizens asked why, with an enormous army of agencies gathering intelligence, weren't the multitude of messages and warnings about the attack on the World Trade Center and the Pentagon translated in time to prevent the disaster? Why weren't those dots connected? Why were the warnings ignored?

The answer at first accepted by most analysts was that America's chaotic system of intelligence was paralyzed by the morass of cross-cutting bureaucracies responsible. They engaged in turf battles with one another and did not share the vital information that arguably could have identified the Al Qaeda plot and prevented it. The problem was miscommunication and noncommunication; the signals about the attack were not forwarded to the executive branch in time. Why? Morton Abramowitz (2002), a former assistant secretary of state in the Reagan Administration, voiced his explanation when he wrote "Three features pervade the making of foreign policy in Washington today: massive overload, internal warfare, and the short term driving out the long term." These problems exist in every administration, but are particularly problematic when intense ideological perspectives are in play.

As the horror of 9/11 persisted, so did interest in and concern about who did what prior to September 11, 2001, to disrupt the Al Qaeda terrorist network operation. A congressional bipartisan commission was created to investigate what had gone wrong, in order to make needed corrections in the way the U.S. government makes decisions for national security and counterterrorism. The 9/11 Commission (2004) produced a new set of explanations for why so many opportunities to head off the 9/11 disaster were missed.

The Commission did not center blame on the inadequacies and infighting of the country's "alphabet soup" of agencies fighting terror, such as the CIA and FBI. Instead, the Commission pointed its criticism at the growing complaints (Mann 2004; Woodward 2004) about the White House's inaction and pre-9/11 downplaying or ignoring of the loud and clear warnings submitted by U.S. intelligence bureaucracies of the true, imminent dangers of a likely terrorist attack. In this case, the failure of the U.S. government to protect its citizens might have been more due to the unwillingness of American leadership to listen to the warnings of its national security bureaucracies than to the crippling effects of bureaucratic struggles.

Still, consider the problems faced by every U.S. president who must seek to manage hundreds of competing agencies and subagencies, each of which are habitually loath to share information with one another for fear of compromising "sources and methods." Each agency competes with its rivals and engages in finger-pointing and scapegoating as a blood sport. Moreover, as FBI Special Agent Coleen Rowley testified, "There's a mutual-protection pact in bureaucracies. Mid-level managers avoid decisions out of fear a mistake will sidetrack their careers while a rigid hierarchy discourages agents from challenging superiors. There is a saying: 'Big cases, big problems; little cases, little problems; no cases, no problems.' The idea that inaction is the key to success manifests itself repeatedly" (Toner 2002).

groupthink
the propensity for members of a group to accept and agree with the group's prevailing attitudes, rather than speaking out for what they believe.

We can discern still another property of bureaucratic politics: the natural inclination of professionals who work in large organizations is to adapt their outlook and beliefs to those prevailing where they work. As *constructivist theory* explains, every bureaucracy develops a shared mind-set, or dominant way of looking at reality, akin to the *groupthink* characteristic that small groups often manifest (Janis 1982). Groupthink is often also cited by scholars as a process governing policy decision making that leads to riskier choices and more extreme policies (that ultimately fail miserably) than likely would have been made by individuals without the pressures in peer groups. An institutional mind-set, or socially constructed consensus, also discourages creativity, dissent, and independent thinking: it encourages reliance on standard operating procedures and deference to precedent rather than the exploration of new options to meet new challenges. This results in policy decisions that rarely deviate from conventional preferences.

This accounts for why "organizational routines favor continuity over change because information is processed in certain ways and certain sources of information are privileged" (Garrison 2006, p. 291). These propensities in bureaucratic decision making suggest why "social scientists have in an increasing degree considered indifference and not rationality as the hallmark of bureaucracy" (Neumann 2007, p. 197).

In your future employment, you are likely to directly observe the efforts of your employer to make rational decisions. You also are bound to notice firsthand within your organization both the advantages of bureaucratic administration and its liabilities. Many students before you have entered the workforce and found that the payoffs of rational choice and the pitfalls of bureaucratic politics surrounding actual practice described here were *not* figments of scholars' imagination. Rather, these properties and propensities of decision making speak to the real experiences of professionals who have entered into policy-making positions. (Many a student reader of previous editions of *World Politics* has later reported that these interpretations prepared them well for what they encountered later in their careers and helped

COLLECTIVE DECISION MAKING Policy decisions are often made in small groups. Pictured here is U.S. President Barack Obama meeting with his cabinet to discuss the global economic crisis and recovery efforts in the United States. From left are Chairman of the Recovery Act Earl Devaney, U.S. Vice President Joe Biden, Obama, U.S. Attorney General Eric Holder, and U.S. Secretary for Housing and Urban Development Shaun Donovan.

them overcome some naïve expectations that governments, and nonstate actors, stand united, when most of the effort *within* them centers on debate and dispute among participating factions within their decision-making unit.) And keep in mind that Harvard University's John F. Kennedy School of Government bases its entire curriculum on the conviction that the essence of national and international service requires awareness of interagency bureaucratic bargaining and the contributions and impediments that competition makes to rational decision making.

The Leverage and Impact of Leaders

The course of history is determined by the decisions of political elites. Leaders and the kind of leadership they exert shape the way in which foreign policies are made and the consequent behavior of the actors in world politics. "There is properly no history, only biography" is how Ralph Waldo Emerson encapsulated the view that individual leaders move history.

history-making individuals model
an interpretation that sees foreign policy decisions that affect the course of history as products of strong-willed leaders acting on their personal convictions.

Bush Doctrine
the unilateral policies of the George W. Bush Administration proclaiming that the United States will make decisions to meet America's perceived national interests, not to concede to other countries' complaints or to gain their acceptance.

roles
the constraints written into law or custom that predispose decision makers in a particular governmental position to act in a manner and style that is consistent with expectations about how the role is normally performed.

Leaders as Movers of World History   This *history-making individuals model* of policy decision making perceives world leaders as the people whose initiatives create global changes. We expect leaders to lead, and we assume new leaders will make a difference. We reinforce this image when we routinely attach the names of leaders to policies—as though the leaders were synonymous with major international developments—as well as when we ascribe most successes and failures in foreign affairs to the leaders in charge at the time they occurred. The equation of U.S. foreign policy with the **Bush Doctrine** in the 2000s is a recent example.

Citizens are not alone in thinking that leaders are the decisive determinants of states' foreign policies and, by extension, world history. Leaders themselves seek to create impressions of their own self-importance while attributing extraordinary powers to other leaders. The assumptions they make about the personalities of their counterparts, consciously or unconsciously, in turn influence their own behavior (Wendzel 1980), as political psychologists who study the impact of leaders' perceptions and personalities on their foreign policy preferences demonstrate (see, for example, the journal *Political Psychology*). Moreover, leaders react differently to the positions they occupy. All are influenced by the *roles* or expectations that by law and tradition steer the decision maker to behave in conformity with prevailing expectations about how the role is to be performed. Most people submissively act in accordance with the customary rules that define the positions they hold, behaving as their predecessors tended to behave when they held the same position.

Others, however, are by personality or preference more bold and ambitious, and they seek to decisively escape the confines of their new role by redefining how it will be performed.

One of the difficulties of leader-driven explanations of international decision making is that history's movers and shakers often pursue decidedly irrational policies. The classic example is Adolf Hitler, whose ruthless determination to seek military conquest of the entire European continent proved disastrous for Germany. How do we square this kind of behavior with the logic of realism? That theory says that survival is the paramount goal of all states and that all leaders engage in rational calculations that advance their countries' aspirations for self-advantage. But this theory cannot account for the times when the choices leaders make ultimately prove counterproductive. If the realists are correct, even defects in states' foreign-policy-making processes cannot easily explain such wide divergences between the decisions leaders sometimes make and what cold cost-benefit calculations would predict.

Realism discounts leaders by assuming that global constraints "limit what leaders can do. Because the [global] systemic imperatives of anarchy or interdependence are so clear, leaders can only choose from a limited range of alternatives. If they are to exercise rational leadership and maximize their state's movement toward its goals, only certain actions are feasible" (Hermann and Hagan 2004). However, so-called *instrumental rationality* is another matter. It pictures leaders as powerful decision makers who are able, "based on their perceptions and interpretations, [to] build expectations, plan strategies, and urge actions on their governments about what is possible" (Hermann and Hagan 2004). In this respect, leaders do actually lead and are important. They are instrumentally rational because they have preferences on which they choose. When faced with two or more alternative options, they can rationally make the choice that they believe will produce their preferred outcome.

instrumental rationality
a conceptualization of rationality that emphasizes the tendency of decision makers to compare options with those previously considered and then select the one that has the best chance of success.

The idea of instrumental rationality demonstrates that rationality does not "connote superhuman calculating ability, omniscience, or an Olympian view of the world," as is often assumed when the rational-actor model we have described is applied to real-world situations (Zagare 1990, p. 243). It also suggests that an individual's actions may be rational even though the process of decision making and its product may appear decidedly irrational. Why did Libya's leader, the mercurial Muammar Qaddafi, repeatedly challenge the United States, almost goading President Ronald Reagan into a military strike in 1986? Because, we can postulate, Qaddafi's actions were consistent with his preferences, regardless of how "irrational" it was for a fourth-rate military power to take on the world's preeminent superpower. This and many other examples serve as a reminder of the importance of the human factor in understanding how decisions are made. Temptation, lack of self-control, anger, fear of getting hurt, religious conviction, bad habits, and overconfidence all play a part in determining why people make the kinds of decisions they do.

Factors Affecting Leadership   Despite the popularity of the *history-making individuals model,* we must be wary of ascribing too much importance to individual leaders. Their influence is likely to be subtler, a probability summarized by U.S. President Bill Clinton in 1998 when he observed, "Great presidents don't do great things. Great presidents get a lot of other people to do great things." Former Secretary of State Henry Kissinger urged against placing too much reliance on personalities:

> [There is] a profound American temptation to believe that foreign policy is a subdivision of psychiatry and that relations among nations are like relations among people. But the problem [of easing protracted conflicts] is not so simple. Tensions . . . must have some objective causes, and unless we can remove these causes, no personal relationship can possibly deal with them. We are [not] doing . . . ourselves a favor by reducing the issues to a contest of personalities. (University of South Carolina Commencement Address, 1985)

Most leaders operate under a variety of political, psychological, and circumstantial constraints that limit what they can accomplish and reduce their control over events. In this context, Emmet John Hughes (1972), an adviser to President Dwight D. Eisenhower, concluded that "all of [America's past presidents] from the most venturesome to the most reticent have shared one disconcerting experience: the discovery of the limits and restraints—decreed by law, by history, and by circumstances—that sometimes can blur their clearest designs or dull their sharpest purposes."

The question at issue is not whether political elites lead or whether they can make a difference. They clearly do both. But leaders are not in complete control, and their influence is severely constrained. Thus, personality and personal political preferences do not determine foreign policy directly. The relevant question, then, is not whether leaders' personal characteristics make a difference, but rather under what conditions their characteristics are influential. As Margaret G. Hermann has observed, the impact of leaders is modified by at least six factors:

(1) what their world view is, (2) what their political style is like, (3) what motivates them to have the position they do, (4) whether they are interested in and have any training in foreign affairs, (5) what the foreign policy climate was like when the leader was starting out his or her political career, and (6) how the leader was socialized into his or her present position. World view, political style, and motivation tell us something about the leader's personality; the other characteristics give information about the leader's previous experiences and background (Hermann 1988, p. 268).

The impact of leaders' personal characteristics on foreign policy decisions generally increases when their authority and legitimacy are widely accepted or when leaders are protected from broad public criticism. Moreover, certain circumstances enhance individuals' potential influence. Among them are new situations that free leaders from conventional approaches to defining the situation; complex situations involving many different factors; and situations without social sanctions, which permit freedom of choice because norms defining the range of permissible options are unclear (DiRenzo 1974).

I have not controlled events, events have controlled me.

—Abraham Lincoln, U.S. president

A leader's **political efficacy** or self-image—that person's belief in his or her own ability to control events politically—combined with the citizenry's relative desire for leadership, will also influence the degree to which personal values and psychological needs govern decision making (DeRivera 1968). For example, when public opinion strongly favors a powerful leader, and when the head of state has an exceptional need for admiration, foreign policy will more likely reflect that leader's inner needs. Thus, Kaiser Wilhelm II's narcissistic personality allegedly met the German people's desire for a symbolically powerful leader, and German public preferences in turn influenced the foreign policy that Germany pursued during Wilhelm's reign, ending in World War I (Baron and Pletsch 1985).

political efficacy
the extent to which policy makers' self-confidence instills in them the belief that they can effectively make rational choices.

Leaders' gender may also influence their decision making. *Feminism* suggests that men and women tend to see issues such as war, peace, security, and the use of military force in different ways, and this may influence the way in which they make decisions and interact with the world around them. Similarly, *social constructivism* considers the existence of different values and views between women and men as a product of distinct socialization experiences. "Because women tend to define themselves more through their relationships than do men, their actions and rhetoric. . . may be more oriented toward maintaining and protecting these relationships.

In contrast, men tend to focus on end gains, making the achievement of personal preferences and goals" central to their decision making (Boyer et al. 2009, p. 27). It is likely, therefore, that gender influences the decision-making process, even if it does not make a difference in terms of the final decision outcome.

Other factors undoubtedly influence how much leaders can shape their states' choices. For instance, when leaders believe that their own interests and welfare are at stake, they tend to respond in terms of their private needs and psychological drives. When circumstances are stable, however, and when leaders' egos are not entangled with policy outcomes, the influence of their personal characteristics is less apparent.

The timing of a leader's assumption of power is also significant. When an individual first assumes a leadership position, the formal requirements of that role are least likely to restrict what he or she can do. That is especially true during the "honeymoon" period routinely given to newly elected leaders, during which time they are relatively free of criticism and excessive pressure. Moreover, when a leader assumes office following a dramatic event (a landslide election, for example, or the assassination of a predecessor), he or she can institute policies almost with a free hand, as "constituency criticism is held in abeyance during this time" (Hermann 1976).

A national crisis is a potent circumstance that increases a leader's control over foreign policy making. Decision making during crises is typically centralized and handled exclusively by the top leadership. Crucial information is often unavailable, and leaders see themselves as responsible for outcomes. Not surprisingly, great leaders (e.g., Napoleon Bonaparte, Winston Churchill, and Franklin D. Roosevelt) customarily emerge during periods of extreme tumult. A crisis can liberate a leader from the constraints that normally would inhibit his or her capacity to control events or engineer foreign policy change.

History abounds with examples of the seminal importance of political leaders who emerge in different times and places and under different circumstances to play critical roles in shaping world history. Mikhail Gorbachev dramatically illustrates an individual's capacity to change the course of history. Many experts believe that the Cold War could not have been brought to an end, nor Communist Party rule in Moscow terminated and the Soviet state set on a path toward democracy and free enterprise, had it not been for Gorbachev's vision, courage, and commitment to engineering these revolutionary, system-transforming changes.

CONTROVERSY:

DO LEADERS MAKE A DIFFERENCE?

Some theorists, such as proponents of *neorealism,* embrace the assumption of rationality and assume that any leader will respond to a choice in the same way: the situation structures the reaction to the existing costs and benefits of any choice. But does this assumption square with the facts? What do we know about the impact of people's perceptions and values on the way they view choices? Political psychology and constructivism tell us that the same option is likely to have different value to different leaders. Does this mean that different leaders would respond differently to similar situations?

Consider the example of Richard Nixon. In 1971, Americans took to the streets outside the White House to protest the immorality of Nixon's massive bombing of Vietnam. His reaction to this perceived threat was to shield himself from the voice of the people, without success, as it happened. Nixon complained that "nobody can know what it means for a president to be sitting in that White House working late at night and to have hundreds of thousands of demonstrators charging through the streets. Not even earplugs could block the noise."

Earlier, on a rainy afternoon in 1962, John F. Kennedy faced a similar citizen protest. Americans had gathered in front of the White House for a "Ban the Bomb" demonstration. His response was to send out urns of coffee and doughnuts and invite the leaders of the protest to come inside to state their case, believing that a democracy should encourage dissent and debate.

Nixon saw protesters as a threat; Kennedy saw them as an opportunity. This comparison suggests that the type of leader can make a difference in determining the kinds of choices likely to be made in response to similar situations. More important than each president's treatment of the protesters, however, was whether he actually changed his policy decisions based on the protests.

Although Kennedy was hospitable to protesters, he did not ban nuclear weapons; in fact, military spending under Kennedy grew to consume half of the federal budget. Many would protest that Kennedy alone could not be expected to eliminate nuclear weapons—that the *zeitgeist* was dominated by fear of the Soviet Union and intense concern for national security. The protesters in 1971, however, were more in keeping with the spirit of the times. Although they alone may not have persuaded Nixon to alter his policies in Vietnam, widespread protest and discontentment with the war, as well as America's inability to win, eventually prompted Nixon to order the gradual withdrawal of

AP Photo

(*continued*)

DO LEADERS MAKE A DIFFERENCE? (Continued)

U.S. troops, ending American participation in the Vietnam war. These outcomes suggest that leaders are captive to *zeitgeist,* or larger forces that drive international relations in their times.

WHAT DO YOU THINK?

- Did Kennedy and Nixon choose courses of action that reflected who they were as individuals? Or would any president in their respective eras have made similar choices?

- How would rational choice theorists understand the behavior of Nixon? Of Kennedy? What are limitations of the rational choice approach for explaining their decisions?

- Thinking ahead, what are some other factors, domestic or international, that could have affected Kennedy and Nixon's decisions regarding their respective military engagements, beyond *zeitgeist?*

zeitgeist
the "spirit of the times," or the dominant cultural norms assumed to influence the behavior of people living in particular periods.

Having said that the history-making individuals model may be compelling, we must be cautious and remember that leaders are not all-powerful determinants of states' foreign policy behavior. Rather, their personal influence varies with the context, and often the context is more influential than the leader (see Controversy: Do Leaders Make a Difference?). The "great person" versus *zeitgeist* ("spirit of the times") debate is pertinent here, as constructivist theorists like to observe. At the core of this enduring controversy is the question of whether certain times are conducive to the emergence of leaders or whether famous leaders would have an impact whenever and wherever they lived (see Greenstein 1987). That question may be unanswerable, but at least it reminds us that multiple factors affect states' foreign policy decisions. The history-making individuals model alone appears too simple an explanation of how transnational actors react to external challenges.

THE GLOBAL AND DOMESTIC DETERMINANTS OF STATES' INTERNATIONAL DECISIONS

We have discussed alternative ways of thinking about international decision making, and it is very important now to look at the factors that apply exclusively to the most important actors—states. States have the most power, and by international law are the only transnational actors with the capacity to possess territory, to exercise control over activities within borders, and to monopolize the use of military force. States comprise a special category of player on the world stage and respond to global trends and transformations in ways that are arguably unique. States' foreign policy decisions are the most consequential, and the factors that influence their capacity to make decisions to adapt to changes in world politics are different from many of those that impact other transnational actors' decisions. Therefore, to place states' decision making into proper perspective, this chapter will conclude with insights from "the comparative study of foreign policy" (see Hermann 2008) that help us better appreciate how foreign policy decision making by states is shaped.

Geostrategic location, military might, economic prowess, and system of government are all variables that affect state foreign policy choices. Still, because of the diversity of states as well as their different locations and positions within the contemporary global system, it is difficult to generalize about the influence of any one factor or combination of factors. In classifying the determinants not only of states' foreign policies but also of trends in world politics generally, *the* levels-of-analysis framework introduced in Chapter 1 (see Figure 1.2) helps to describe the multiple influences on decision-making processes. Recall that states and the global system make up two distinct levels: the state level encompasses domestic characteristics, and the global or international system level encompasses all actors' relationships and the changes in these relations over time.

Global or "external" influences on foreign policy include all activities occurring beyond a state's borders that affect the choices its officials and the people they govern make. Such factors as the number of military alliances and the changing levels of international trade sometimes profoundly affect the choices of decision makers. Internal or "domestic" influences, on the other hand, are those that exist at the level of the state, not the global system. Here, attention focuses on variations in *states' attributes*, such as military capabilities, level of economic development, and types of government, that may influence different countries' foreign policy choices. Examples of both types of influences are discussed in the sections that follow.

states' attributes
state characteristics that shape foreign policy behavior, such as its size, wealth, and the extent to which its leaders are accountable to its citizens in comparison with other states.

International Influences on Foreign Policy Choice

The global environment within which states operate shapes opportunities for action. It sets an ecological context that limits some foreign policy choices but facilitates others (Sprout and Sprout 1965; Starr 1978). Among the most significant factors of the international environment that make possible certain courses of action but not others are the distribution of power among states and the pattern of the alliances around the most powerful.

Polarity and Polarization   Power can be distributed in many ways. It can be concentrated in the hands of one preponderant state, as in the ancient Mediterranean world at the zenith of the Roman Empire, or it may be diffused among several rival states, as it was at the birth of the state system in 1648 following the Thirty Years' War, when a handful of great power rivals possessed approximately equal strength. Scholars use the term *polarity* to describe the distribution of power among members of the global system. As explained in Chapter 3, unipolar systems have one dominant power center, bipolar systems contain two centers of power, and multipolar systems possess more than two such centers.

Closely related to the distribution of power is the pattern of alignments among states. *Polarization* refers to the degree to which states cluster around the powerful. For instance, a highly bipolarized system is one in which small and medium-size states form alliances with one of the two dominant powers. The network of alliances around the United States and Soviet Union during the Cold War exemplified such a system. Today, the "nature of the international system . . . will have to be rethought as new powers rise, old ones continue to fade, and attention shifts from the Atlantic to the Pacific" (Mead 2010, p. 64).

Polarity and alliance polarization influence foreign policy by affecting the decision latitude possessed by states. For example, as seen in Chapters 3 and 9, when power is concentrated in the hands of a single state in a unipolar system, it can more easily choose to use military force and intervene in the affairs of others than it would in a system characterized by a distribution of shared power, where rivals might obstruct its actions. However, when alliances are tight military blocs, the small state members of each alliance will feel compelled to conform to the dictates of the alliance's leader.

Conversely, when alliances are loosely shifting with fluid membership, smaller states can more readily choose to craft foreign policies that are independent of the wishes of the powerful. Of course, you could think of other examples to show how the structural properties of the global system affect decision latitude. What they would show is that the foreign policy impact of polarity and polarization hinges on the geostrategic position of a given state.

Geostrategic Position   Some of the most important influences on a state's foreign policy behavior are its location and physical terrain. The presence of natural frontiers, for example, may profoundly guide policy makers' choices (see Map 6.1). Consider the United States, which was secure throughout most of its early history because vast oceans separated it from potential threats

polarity
the degree to which military and economic capabilities are concentrated in the global system that determines the number of centers of power, or "poles."

polarization
the formation of competing coalitions or blocs composed of allies that align with one of the major competing poles, or centers, of power.

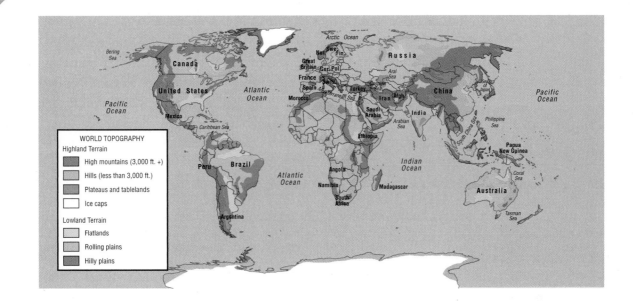

MAP 6.1

GEOGRAPHIC INFLUENCES ON FOREIGN POLICY How countries act toward others is shaped by the number of neighboring states on their borders and whether they are protected from invasion by natural barriers such as mountains and oceans. This map suggests how, until recently, the separation of the United States from Eurasia encouraged an isolationist policy during many periods in U.S. history. Note also how topography, location, and other geopolitical factors may have influenced the foreign policy priorities of Great Britain, Germany, China, Finland, and states in South America—hypotheses advanced by the geopolitics approach to international politics.

in Europe and Asia. The advantage of having oceans as barriers to foreign intervention, combined with the absence of militarily powerful neighbors, permitted the United States to develop into an industrial giant and to practice safely an isolationist foreign policy for more than 150 years. Consider also mountainous Switzerland, whose easily defended topography has made neutrality a viable foreign policy option.

Similarly, maintaining autonomy from continental politics has been an enduring theme in the foreign policy of Great Britain, an island country whose physical detachment from Europe long served as a buffer separating it from entanglement in major power disputes on the Continent. Preserving this protective shield has long been a priority for Britain, and it helps to explain why London has been so hesitant in the past twenty years to accept full integration in the European Union (EU).

Most countries are not insular, however; they have many states on their borders, denying them the option of noninvolvement in world affairs. Germany, which sits in the geographic center of Europe, historically has found its domestic political system and foreign policy preferences shaped by its geostrategic position. In the twentieth century, for example, Germany struggled through no less than six major radical changes in governing institutions, each of which pursued very different foreign policies: (1) the empire of Kaiser Wilhelm II; (2) the Weimar Republic; (3) Adolf Hitler's dictatorship; its two post–World War II successors, (4) the capitalist Federal Republic in West Germany and (5) the communist German Democratic Republic in East Germany; and, finally, (6) a reunited Germany after the end of the Cold War, now committed to liberal democracy and full integration in the EU. Each of these governments was preoccupied with its relations with neighbors but responded to the opportunities and challenges presented by Germany's position in the middle of the European continent with very different foreign policy goals. In no case, however, was isolationistic withdrawal from involvement in continental affairs a practical geostrategic option.

geopolitics
the theoretical postulate that states' foreign policies are determined by their location, natural resources, and physical environment.

History is replete with other examples of geography's influence on states' foreign policy goals. This is why geopolitical theories are valuable. The *geopolitics* school of realist thought and political geography generally stresses the influence of geographic factors on state power and international conduct (Cohen 2003). Illustrative of early geopolitical thinking is Alfred Thayer Mahan's *The Influence of Sea Power in History* (1890), which maintains that control of the seas shaped national power and foreign policy. States with extensive coastlines and ports enjoyed a competitive advantage. Later geopoliticians, such as Sir Halford Mackinder (1919) and Nicholas Spykman (1944), argued that not only location but also topography, size (territory and population), climate, and distance between states are powerful determinants of individual countries' foreign policies. The underlying principle behind the geopolitical perspective is self-evident: leaders' perceptions of available foreign policy options are influenced by the geopolitical circumstances that define their state's place on the world stage.

Geopolitics is only one aspect of the *global* environment that may influence foreign policy. In later chapters, we will discuss additional global factors. Here, we comment briefly on three *internal* attributes of states that influence their foreign policies: military capabilities, economic conditions, and type of government.

The Domestic Sources of Foreign Policy Decisions

Various domestic factors and national attributes affect the capacity of states to act when foreign policy decisions must be made. To illustrate the impact of internal factors, consider next the three regarded by scholars as the most influential.

Military Capabilities   The realist proposition that states' internal capabilities shape their foreign policy priorities is supported by the fact that states' preparations for war strongly influence their later use of force (Levy 2001). Thus, although most states may seek similar goals, their ability to realize them will vary according to their military capabilities.

Because military capabilities limit a state's range of prudent policy choices, they act as a mediating factor on leaders' national security decisions. For instance, in the 1980s, Libyan leader Muammar Qaddafi repeatedly provoked the United States through anti-American and anti-Israeli rhetoric and by supporting various terrorist activities. Qaddafi was able to act as he did largely because neither bureaucratic organizations nor a mobilized public existed in Libya to constrain his personal whims. However, Qaddafi was doubtlessly more highly constrained by the outside world than were the leaders in the more militarily capable countries toward whom his anger was directed. Limited military muscle compared with the United States precluded the kinds of belligerent behaviors he threatened to practice.

Conversely, Saddam Hussein made strenuous efforts to build Iraq's military might and by 1990 had built the world's fourth-largest army. Thus, invading Kuwait to seize its oil fields became a feasible foreign policy option. In the end, however, even Iraq's impressive military power proved ineffective against a vastly superior coalition of military forces, headed by the United States. The 1991 Persian Gulf War forced Saddam Hussein to capitulate and withdraw from the conquered territory. Twelve years later, the United States invaded Iraq and finally ousted Saddam Hussein from office. The lessons: what states believe about their own military capabilities and those of their adversaries (and their enemies' intentions) guide their decisions about war and peace.

Economic Conditions   The level of economic and industrial development a state enjoys also affects the foreign policy goals it can pursue. Generally, the more economically developed a state, the more likely it is to play an activist role in the global political economy. Rich states have interests that extend far beyond their borders and typically possess the means to pursue and protect them. Not coincidentally, states that enjoy industrial capabilities and extensive involvement in international trade also tend to be militarily powerful—in part because military might is a function of economic capabilities.

Although economically advanced states are more active globally, this does not mean that their privileged circumstances dictate adventuresome policies. Rich states are often "satisfied" states that have much to lose from revolutionary change and global instability (Wolfers 1962). As a result, they usually perceive the status quo as serving their interests and often forge international economic policies to protect and expand their envied position at the pinnacle of the global hierarchy.

Levels of productivity and prosperity also affect the foreign policies of the poor states at the bottom of the global hierarchy. Some economically weak states respond to their situation by complying subserviently with the wishes of the rich on whom they depend. Others rebel defiantly, sometimes succeeding (despite their disadvantaged bargaining position) in resisting the efforts by great powers and powerful international organizations to control their behavior.

Thus, generalizations about the economic foundations of states' international political behavior often prove inaccurate. Although levels of economic development vary widely among states in the global system, they alone do not determine foreign policies. Instead, leaders' perceptions of the opportunities and constraints that their states' economic resources provide may more powerfully influence their foreign policy choices.

constitutional democracy
government processes that allow people, through their elected representatives, to exercise power and influence the state's policies.

autocratic rule
a system of authoritarian or totalitarian government in which unlimited power is concentrated in a single leader.

Video: *Influencing Foreign Policy in Darfur*

Type of Government   A third important attribute affecting states' international behavior is their type of political system. Although realism predicts that all states will act similarly to protect their interests, a state's type of government demonstrably constrains important choices, including whether threats to use military force are carried out. Here the important distinction is between *constitutional democracy* (representative government), at one end of the spectrum, and *autocratic rule* (authoritarian or totalitarian) at the other.

In neither democratic (sometimes called "open") nor autocratic ("closed") political systems can political leaders survive long without the support of organized domestic political interests, and sometimes the mass citizenry. But in democratic systems, those interests are likely to spread beyond the government itself. Public opinion, interest groups, and the mass media are a more visible part of the policy-making process in democratic systems. Similarly, the electoral process in democratic societies more meaningfully frames choices and produces results about who will lead than the process used in authoritarian regimes, where the real choices are made by a few elites behind closed doors. In a democracy, public opinion and preferences may matter, and therefore differences in who is allowed to participate and how much they exercise their right to participate are critical determinants of foreign policy choices.

The proposition that domestic stimuli, and not simply international events, are a source of foreign policy is not novel. In ancient Greece, for instance, the realist historian Thucydides observed that what happened within the Greek city-states often did more to shape their external behavior than did the interactions between them. He added that Greek leaders frequently concentrated their efforts on influencing the political climate within their own polities. Similarly, leaders today sometimes make foreign policy decisions for domestic political purposes—as, for example, when bold or aggressive acts abroad are intended to influence election outcomes at home or to divert public attention from economic woes. This is sometimes called the "scapegoat" phenomenon or the *diversionary theory of war* (Levy 1989b; DeRouen and Sprecher 2006).

diversionary theory of war
the hypothesis that leaders sometimes initiate conflict abroad as a way of increasing national cohesion at home by diverting national public attention away from controversial domestic issues and internal problems.

The impact of government type on foreign policy choice has taken on great significance following the rapid conversion of many dictatorships to democratic rule. These liberal government conversions have occurred in three successive "waves" since the 1800s (Huntington 1991). The first wave occurred between 1878 and 1926, and the second between 1943 and 1962. The third wave began in the 1970s when a large number of nondemocratic countries began to convert their governments to democratic rule. In a remarkable global *transformation* from past world history, the once radical idea that democracy is the ideal form of decision making has triumphed. According to Freedom House, three-fourths of the world's countries are now fully or partially democratic (see Map 6.2).

democratic peace
the theory that although democratic states sometimes wage wars against nondemocratic states, they do not fight one another.

This recent growth of democracy has emboldened many liberals to predict that the twenty-first century will be safer than its predecessor. Their reasons for predicting the onset of a *democratic peace* vary, but rely on the logic that Immanuel Kant outlined in his 1795 treatise *Perpetual Peace*. Kant believed that because democratic leaders are accountable to the public, and that because ordinary citizens have to supply the soldiers and bear the human and financial cost of aggressive policies, they would constrain leaders from initiating foreign wars (especially against other liberal democracies similarly constrained by norms and institutions that respect compromise and civil liberties).

Jason Reed/Reuters/Landov

THE BURDEN OF FOREIGN POLICY CHOICE FOR GLOBAL LEADERSHIP The United States is called upon to provide visionary leadership for the world, and this entails a careful assessment of priorities and strategies. Barack Obama declared that "I will strengthen our common security by investing in our common humanity. Our global engagement cannot be defined by what we are against; it must be guided by a clear sense of what we stand for. We have a significant stake in ensuring that those who live in fear and want today can live with dignity and opportunity tomorrow."

A considerable body of empirical evidence supports the proposition that democracies do not wage war against each other (Rasler and

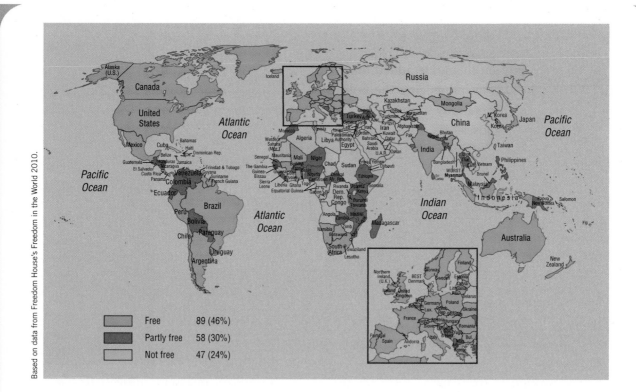

Free	89	(46%)
Partly free	58	(30%)
Not free	47	(24%)

MAP 6.2

HOW FREE IS YOUR COUNTRY? Liberal democratic peace theory predicts that as freedom across countries increases, so will peaceful relations among these democracies. Though improvements occurred in Asia, Freedom House's annual survey found that at the start of 2010, the number of electoral democracies had declined to the lowest level since 1995. According to Arch Puddington, Freedom House Director of Research, the "decline is global, affects countries with military and economic power, affects countries that had previously shown signs of reform potential, and is accompanied by enhanced persecution of political dissidents and independent journalists."

Thompson 2005; Russett 2001; Ray 1995). The type of government and, more specifically, whether leaders are accountable to opposition groups through multiparty elections strongly influence foreign policy goals. Political scientists David Lektzian and Mark Souva (2009, p. 35) attribute the democratic peace to democracies' "greater ability to more credibly reveal information" than other regime types. Although liberals generally emphasize the pacifying effects of democracy, research findings on democratic peace have led some political conservatives to advocate a policy called "democratic realism" (Yang 2005), which would promote democracy through targeted interventions into regions where the advance of freedom is deemed critical in the struggle against Al Qaeda and other radical groups that threaten the United States (Krauthammer 2004).

Some see the intrusion of domestic politics into foreign policy making as a disadvantage of democratic political systems that undermines their ability to deal decisively with crises or to bargain effectively with less

CONTROVERSY:

ARE DEMOCRACIES DEFICIENT IN FOREIGN AFFAIRS?

History suggests that democracies enjoy faithful allies and lose fewer wars than do nondemocracies, but, despite these achievements, democracies may make foreign policy choices in ways that are less rational and efficient than autocracies (Siverson and Emmons 1991). One realist thesis argues that democracies are decidedly inferior to nondemocratic governance. Dictators and despots such as Adolf Hitler, Joseph Stalin, and Mao Zedong can embark as warmongers on grand international missions and be hailed as great unifiers and the builders of grandiose projects, whereas democratic politicians are "by nature mediocre. The great dictators . . . give the people a destiny, whereas democrats can only promise happiness. [Some realists fall] under the spell of absolute power. It is a fatal romanticism that justifies unlimited murder" (Buruma 2005). Because classical realism follows Machiavelli by honoring strong rulers who are able to convince subjects of their need to be ruled by them for the glory of the state, these realists prefer the capacity of nondemocratic governments to forge foreign policies freely in pursuit of national interests.

Does the nature of democratic rule help or hinder those governments' capacities to realize their goals under anarchy? In evaluating this controversy, consider that view by a leading realist American policy maker, George F. Kennan, who advanced the following thesis:

> I sometimes wonder whether a democracy is not uncomfortably similar to one of those prehistoric monsters with a body as long as this room and a brain the size of a pin. He lies there in his comfortable primeval mud and pays little attention to his environment; he is slow to wrath—in fact, you practically have to whack his tail off to make him aware that his interests are being disturbed; but, once he grasps this, he lays about him with such blind determination that he not only destroys his adversary but largely wrecks his native habitat. You wonder whether it would not have been wiser for him to have taken a little more interest in what was going on at an earlier date and to have seen whether he could not have prevented some of these situations from arising instead of proceeding from an undiscriminating indifference to a holy wrath equally undiscriminating (Kennan 1951, p. 59).

Against this criticism of democratic governments' tendency to react without foresight or moderation in foreign policy, defenders of liberal democratic governance such as Immanuel Kant, Thomas Jefferson, and Woodrow Wilson have argued just the opposite: that giving people power through the ballot and a voice in the making of foreign policy decisions restrains leaders in those countries from extreme or excessive choices, such as initiating a war of choice rather than necessity on a whim. To liberals, democratization also enables the leader of a democracy to bargain successfully with nondemocracies, because nondemocratic states know that democratic governments are likely to have the support of their people and to honor their agreements.

(*continued*)

ARE DEMOCRACIES DEFICIENT IN FOREIGN AFFAIRS?
(Continued)

WHAT DO YOU THINK?

- Are democratic procedures for making foreign policy decisions an aid or a handicap? What arguments and evidence can you provide to support your general conclusion about this timeless controversy?

- How does the role of presidential personalities in decision making engage with the supports for and criticisms of the democratic peace theory? Is there room for an individual level of analysis in a systemic theory?

- Thinking ahead, how does this discussion on the deficiency of democracies in foreign affairs change in light of the fact that the Global South, home of chronic poverty, war, tyranny, and anarchy, consists mainly of nondemocracies?

Case Study:
*Democracy and
Peace*

democratic adversaries and allies (see Controversy: Are Democracies Deficient in Foreign Affairs?). Democracies are subject to inertia. They move slowly on issues, because so many disparate elements are involved in decision making and because officials in democracies are accountable to public opinion and must respond to pressure from a variety of domestic interest groups (groups mobilized to exercise influence over the future direction of their country's foreign policies, especially on issues highly important to them). A crisis sufficient enough to arouse the attention and activity of a large proportion of the population may need to erupt in order for large changes in policy to come about. As French political sociologist Alexis de Tocqueville argued in 1835, democracies may be inclined to "impulse rather than prudence" because they overreact to perceived external dangers once they recognize them. "There are two things that a democratic people will always find difficult," de Tocqueville mused, "to start a war and to end it." In contrast, authoritarian governments can "make decisions more rapidly, ensure domestic compliance with their decisions, and perhaps be more consistent in their foreign policy" (Jensen 1982). But there is a cost: nondemocracies "often are less effective in developing an innovative foreign policy because of subordinates' pervasive fear of raising questions." In short, the concentration of power and the suppression of public opposition can be both advantageous and disadvantageous.

Can global actors, whether state or nonstate, respond to the demands that external challenges and internal politics simultaneously place on their leaders?

Foreign policy choice takes place in an environment of uncertainty and multiple competing interests. On occasion, it is also made in situations where policy makers are caught by surprise and a quick decision is needed. For those and many other reasons covered in this chapter, the decision-making capability of global actors is increasingly strained.

The trends and transformations currently unfolding in world politics are the products of countless decisions made daily throughout the world, and in Part III we will look more closely at some of the issues facing international decision makers today. Specifically, we will consider the concerns that decision makers must wrestle with in confronting armed aggression. In Chapter 7, you will have an opportunity to examine the global character and consequences of violent threats to security. In Chapters 8 through 11, we will weigh the rival ideas presented by the realist road to security and the liberal path to peace. You will also be invited to consider the insights that alternative constructivist, radical, and feminist theories provide in grappling with the challenge of finding solutions to the grave threat of armed aggression.

Take an Online Practice Quiz

www.cengagebrain.com/shop/ISBN/0495802204

| *Suggested Readings* |

Hermann, Margaret G., ed. (2007) *Comparative Foreign Policy Analysis: Theories and Methods*. Upper Saddle River, NJ: Prentice Hall.

Hudson, Valerie M. (2007) *Foreign Policy Analysis: Classic and Contemporary Theory*. Lanham, MD: Rowman & Littlefield Publishers.

Kaarbo, Juliet. (2008) "Coalition Cabinet Decision Making: Institutional and Psychological Factors," *International Studies Review* 10: 57−86.

Knetch, Thomas and M. Stephen Weatherford. (2006) "Public Opinion and Foreign Policy: The Stages of Presidential Decision Making," *International Studies Quarterly* 50: 705−727.

Renshon, Jonathan and Stanley A. Renshon. (2008) "The Theory and Practice of Foreign Policy Decision Making," *Political Psychology* 29: 509−536.

Wittkopf, Eugene R., Christopher Jones, and Charles W. Kegley, Jr. (2007) *American Foreign Policy: Pattern and Process*, 7th ed. Belmont, CA: Thomson Wadsworth.

Part 3
CONFRONTING
ARMED AGGRESSION

"What can war beget except war? But good will begets goodwill, equity, equity."
—Erasmus of Rotterdam, Renaissance moral philosopher and theologian

Roger Ressmeyer/CORBIS

NUCLEAR TESTING **Pictured here is a French atomic test in the South Pacific of a nuclear bomb smaller than the U.S. hydrogen bomb that, in 1952, created a three-mile fireball 1,000 times more powerful than each of the bombs the United States dropped on Hiroshima and Nagasaki. More than 2,000 nuclear weapons tests have occurred since 1945.**

WHEN YOU THINK ABOUT WORLD POLITICS, WHAT IS THE FIRST IMAGE THAT RACES TO YOUR MIND? For many people, world politics is about arms, alliances, and the exercise by military means of political influence over rivals and other actors on the global stage. Indeed, many people equate world politics with war and its threat to their nation, city, and the world at large. This preoccupation is as old as recorded history itself. And for understandable reasons: An attack by an enemy is the most danger-ous direct threat to survival, and preventing such death and destruction is a precondition for the attainment of all other important values, such as food, water, freedom, and the possession of a territory on which to live safely and without foreign domination. Yet war is a problem, and changes are required in the practices of states toward one another if we are to con-trol armed aggression and reduce its frequency and destructiveness.

In Part 3 of *World Politics*, you will have the opportunity to explore the many contending ideas and theoretical perspectives about how to best confront armed aggression. Chapter 7 looks at the military threats to international security posed by wars between states, wars within states, and international terrorism. In Chapter 8, the pursuit of national interest defined in terms of military power is examined through the lens of realist approaches to national and international security, with consideration of trends in weapons of war and alternative military methods. Chap-ter 9 provides an overview of the various roles that realists envision for alliances in international politics, including the attractive purposes that realists ascribe to alli-ances as a method for increasing the power of a state against its competitors and their allies, as well as an account of the risk and costs that realists warn can result from the formation of alliances. In Chapter 10, you will look at liberal ideas for negotiating at the bargaining table rather than fighting on the battlefield to settle international disputes, as well as subjecting inter-state relations to a true system of international law with strong sanctions for noncompliance with rules. Chapter 11 introduces the liberal proposal to "beat swords into plowshares" through disarma-ment of the weapons of war, empowering international organizations for maintain-ing the collective security of all countries, and the use of economic sanctions as a nonmilitary method of punishment for aggressors.

CHAPTER 7
THE THREAT OF ARMED AGGRESSION TO THE WORLD

CHAPTER OUTLINE

CHANGES IN INTERSTATE WAR AND ARMED AGGRESSION

CHANGING FREQUENCY AND TYPE OF ACTS OF ARMED AGGRESSION

ARMED AGGRESSION WITHIN STATES

Intrastate Conflict

The International Dimensions of Internal Conflict

TERRORISM

The New Global Terrorism

Counterterrorism

CONTROVERSY: Can The War Against Global Terrorism Be Won?

WHAT CAUSES ARMED AGGRESSION?

The First Level of Analysis: Individuals' Human Nature

The Second Level of Analysis: States' Internal Characteristics

The Third Level of Analysis: The Global System

ARMED AGGRESSION AND ITS FUTURE

Mankind must put an end to war or war will put an end to mankind.
—John F. Kennedy, U.S. President

THE CHANGING NATURE OF WAR The asymmetric struggle in Afghanistan between the world's most powerful military and insurgents has raised questions about the conventional understanding of war; in particular, how it is conducted and what constitutes "victory." In the first half of 2010, the number of civilian deaths was up 31 percent from the prior year - attributed primarily to the Taliban and other insurgents, who are responsible for 76 percent of civilian deaths. "We must continue our emphasis on reducing the loss of innocent civilian life to an absolute minimum," said U.S. Army General David Petraeus. "Every Afghan death diminishes our cause." Pictured here is the aftermath of an attack by Islamic militants on October 6, 2010 on tankers carrying oil for NATO forces in Afghanistan.

In the calm summer of 2001, complacency had taken hold in the zone of peace and prosperity in the Global North, where many thoughtful observers, noting the disappearance of interstate war among the economic giants, began to ask if war was becoming obsolete. That mood and conclusion were shattered shortly thereafter on September 11, 2001, when international terrorists destroyed New York's World Trade Center. The 9/11 attack and the U.S. war in Afghanistan, the terrorist attacks in Madrid in 2004 and London in 2005, the continuing U.S.-led military struggle against insurgents in Iraq, the 2006 Israeli-Hezbollah War in Lebanon, and a wave of civil wars dashed all prior hopes for peace. Violence seemingly could hurt anyone, anywhere, anytime.

It is understandable why so many people think that armed aggression is the essence of world politics. In *On War*, Prussian strategist Karl von Clausewitz advanced his famous dictum that war is merely an extension of diplomacy by other means, albeit an extreme form. This insight underscores the realist belief that *war* is a policy instrument transnational actors use to resolve their conflicts. War, however, is the deadliest instrument of conflict resolution, and its onset usually means that persuasion and negotiations have failed.

war
a condition arising within states (civil war) or between states (interstate war) when actors use violent means to destroy their opponents or coerce them into submission.

In international relations, *conflict* regularly occurs when actors interact and disputes over incompatible interests arise. In and of itself, conflict (like *politics*—activities aimed at getting another actor to do something it would not otherwise do) is not necessarily threatening, because war and conflict are different. Conflict may be seen as inevitable and occurs whenever two parties perceive differences between themselves and seek to resolve those differences to their own satisfaction. Some conflict results whenever people interact and may be generated by religious, ideological, ethnic, economic, political, or territorial issues; therefore, we should not regard it as abnormal. Nor should we regard conflict as necessarily destructive. Conflict can promote social solidarity, creative thinking, learning, and communication—all factors critical to the resolution of disputes and the cultivation of cooperation (Coser 1956). However, the costs of conflict do become threatening when the parties take up arms to settle their perceived irreconcilable differences or use force to settle old scores. When that happens, violence occurs, and we enter the separate sphere of warfare.

conflict
discord, often arising in international relations over perceived incompatibilities of interest.

This chapter presents information and ideas so you can explore the nature of *armed aggression* in your world—its types, frequency, and changing characteristics and causes. And you will be forced to confront the ethical dilemmas that these military threats create—about when it is moral or immoral to take up arms. *World Politics* puts into the spotlight three primary ways that

armed aggression
combat between the military forces of two or more states or groups.

USAF/Landov Media

THE SACRIFICE OF WAR In the war between the United States and Iraq, thousands of American soldiers and tens of thousands of Iraqi civilians have paid the ultimate sacrifice. As words are never enough, on February 26, 2009, Defense Secretary Robert Gates announced that the ban on taking pictures of service members' coffins returning home would be lifted, with their families' consent. Though the impact of such photos is of recurring debate, "pictures of the sacrifices made for a justified war don't make people turn their back on it—just as prohibiting images of an ill-advised conflict cannot guarantee public support" (Lacayo 2009, p. 19).

armed aggression today most often occurs: wars between states, wars within states, and terrorism. You will have the opportunity to review the leading theories that explain the causes of these three types of armed aggression in world politics.

> *Wars occur because people prepare for conflict, rather than for peace.*
>
> —Trygve Lie, former UN Secretary General

CHANGES IN INTERSTATE WAR AND ARMED AGGRESSION

In a world seemingly experiencing constant change, one grim continuity stands out: war and violence, or, in the words of former UN Secretary-General Boutros Boutros-Ghali, a "culture of death." The description remains apt. Since 1900, at least 750 armed conflicts have been waged, killing millions, creating hordes of refugees, and costing trillions of dollars of lost revenues as well as untold human misery. The belief that "only the dead will see the end of war" is based on the fact that warfare has been an ugly, almost constant factor in a changing world. In the past thirty-four hundred years, Chris Hedges (2003) calculates, "humans have been entirely at peace for 268 of them, or just 8 percent of recorded history."

Scientists who study war quantitatively through the scientific methodologies of *behavioralism* have attempted to estimate the frequency of armed conflicts and to measure trends and cycles in the global system's level of violent conflicts. Different definitions and indicators produce somewhat different pictures of variations over time (as *constructivism* emphasizes they will; see Gleditsch 2004). Nonetheless, various measures converge on the basic trends and patterns, from different periods of measurement. In the long term (over the past six hundred years), armed aggression has been continual, with a general trend toward rising incidence. In the relative short term (since 1950), however, the pattern has shown fewer, but more deadly, armed conflicts. These inventories report in different ways what the mass media tell us—that violence and global insecurity are entrenched properties of world politics. The armed aggression in 2010 in Afghanistan, Iraq, Somalia, and Thailand cast a dark shadow.

Video: *No End in Sight*

In the past, when people thought about armed conflicts, they thought primarily about wars *between* states and secondarily about civil wars *within* existing sovereign states. Both types of wars were frequently under way at similar rates each year between 1816 and World War II. However, that began to change thereafter, with internal wars increasingly defining the global landscape.

Figure 7.1 records the changes in both the number of conflicts over the past half century as well as the type of conflict. This new pattern of civil wars and armed conflicts that does not involve government forces on at least one side has become especially entrenched since 1990. Indeed, between 1989 and 2010, only eight of all 131 active armed conflicts worldwide, or 6 percent, were interstate wars between countries. The conflicts between Eritrea–Ethiopia (1998–2000) and India–Pakistan (1997–2003) concerned territory, while the war between Iraq and the United States and its allies (2003) was fought over governmental power. In 2009, all thirty-six armed conflicts were waged within states, with eighteen involving disputes over territory and eighteen over government. Seven of the major intrastate armed conflicts were internationalized, where troops from states that were not primary parties to the conflict aided the side of the government. These included the conflict between the United States and Al Qaeda, as well as those involving Afghanistan, Algeria, Iraq, Somalia, Rwanda, and Uganda (Harbom and Wallensteen 2010).

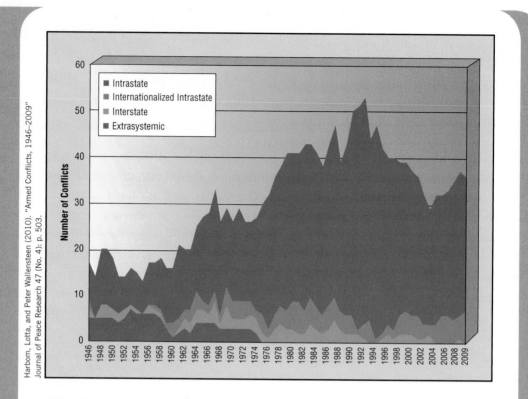

Harborn, Lotta, and Peter Wallensteen (2010). "Armed Conflicts, 1946–2009." Journal of Peace Research 47 (No. 4): p. 503.

FIGURE 7.1

CHANGING FREQUENCY AND TYPE OF ACTS OF ARMED AGGRESSION **Measuring the frequency of armed conflicts each year since 1946, the figure depicts a gradual increase in the frequency of conflicts until the peak in 1992, after which a decline transpired that lasted roughly a decade before, in 2003, the number of conflicts again began to rise. Throughout this period, the type of conflict has changed, with extrasystemic armed aggression becoming, it is hoped, extinct and interstate conflict between countries becoming very rare. At the same time, however, the occurrence of armed conflict within states has grown, as has the number of internal conflicts where there is intervention from third-party states on one side or the other.**

civil wars
wars between opposing groups within the same country or by rebels against the government.

Until 9/11, most security analysts expected *civil wars* to remain the most common type of global violence. However, they have had to revise their strategies and thinking to accommodate changing realities. Today, military planners face two unprecedented security challenges. As described by Henry Kissinger, these challenges are "terror caused by acts until recently considered a matter for internal police forces rather than international policy, and scientific advances and proliferation that allow the survival of countries to be threatened by developments entirely within another state's territory." This suggests that many future acts of armed aggression are probable, fought by irregular militia and private or semiprivate forces (such as terrorist networks) against the armies of states, or by "shadow warriors" commissioned by states as "outsourced" mercenaries or paid militia.

The characteristics of contemporary warfare appear to be undergoing a major *transformation*, even though many of the traditional characteristics of armed conflict continue. The general trends show the following:

- The proportion of countries throughout the globe engaged in wars has declined.

- Most wars now occur in the Global South, which is home to the highest number of states, with the largest populations, the least income, and the least stable governments.

- The goal of waging war to conquer foreign territory has ceased to be a motive.

- Wars between the great powers are becoming obsolete; since 1945 the globe has experienced a *long peace*—the most prolonged period in modern history (since 1500) in which no wars have occurred between the most powerful countries.

long peace
long-lasting periods of peace between any of the militarily strongest great powers.

Although the disappearance of armed aggression *between* states may be possible in the long-term future, armed aggression and violence persist, and their frequency is growing *inside* established states. Next we examine this second face of military threats to the world: armed aggression *within* states.

ARMED AGGRESSION WITHIN STATES

Large-scale civil strife is bred by the failure of state governments to effectively govern within their territorial borders. Mismanagement by governments lacking authority and unable to meet the basic human needs of their citizens is a global trend. Governmental incompetence has led to an epidemic of *failed states* throughout the globe. Today as many as 129 state governments are under stress and vulnerable to civil war (see Map 7.1). Sometimes the armed aggression is confined to local regions that seek secession and independence, and other times failing states are victims of widespread but episodic fighting by insurgents and warlords. Within five years after a fragile state succeeds in restoring domestic order, more than half collapse, and civil unrest resumes (*Foreign Policy*, July/August 2005, p. 58). The proliferation of failing states is a growing global danger, because the civil wars percolated by state failure lead to waves of immigrants, famine, disease, drug trafficking, environmental degradation, and terrorism.

failed states
countries whose governments have so mismanaged policy that their citizens, in rebellion, threaten revolution to divide the country into separate independent states.

The causes of state failure and civil disintegration are multiple, but failed states share some key characteristics that make them vulnerable to

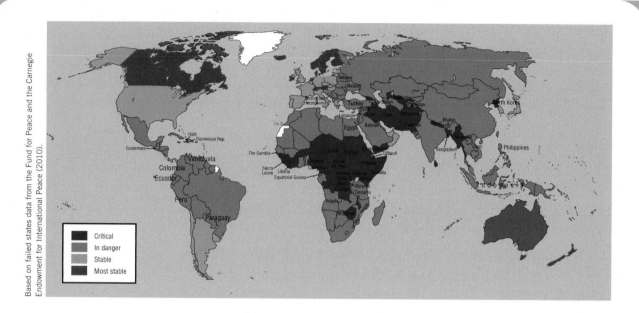

Based on failed states data from the Fund for Peace and the Carnegie Endowment for International Peace (2010).

MAP 7.1

THE THREAT OF FAILED STATES This map identifies the world's thirty-seven weakest countries whose governments are most critically in danger of failing and most likely to collapse in civil war and anarchy. Also identified are an additional ninety-two countries that are "in danger," where some significant element of their societies and institutions are vulnerable to failure. These potential "failed states" threaten the progress and stability of the other sustainable countries. State failure and civil war are particularly evident in the high-risk, weak, and impoverished states in Africa. In a ranking of state failure among 177 countries in 2010, Somalia topped the list, followed by Chad, Sudan, Zimbabwe, the Democratic Republic of the Congo, Afghanistan, and Iraq.

disintegration, civil war, and terrorism. In general, studies of this global trend suggest the following (Collier 2007; *Foreign Policy*, July/August 2010; Piazza 2008):

- A strong predictor of state failure is poverty, but extreme income and gender inequality within countries are even better warning signs.

- The failing states most vulnerable to internal rebellion are ruled by corrupt governments widely regarded as illegitimate and ineffective.

- Democracy, particularly with a strong parliament, generally lowers the risk of state failure; autocracy increases it.

- Poor democracies, however, are more unstable than either rich democracies or poor nondemocracies, and poor democracies that do not improve living standards are exceptionally vulnerable.

- Population pressures, exacerbated by internally displaced people, refugees, and food scarcity, contribute to state failure and civil unrest.

- Governments that fail to protect human rights are especially prone to fail.

■ So-called petrostates relying on oil and gas for income are shaky, especially if the governing authority is weak and permissive of huge gaps in the distribution of political power and wealth.

■ States with governments that do not protect freedom of religion are especially likely to fail.

■ States that have strong rules protecting free international trade gain stability; states with high inflation are prone to fail.

■ The stronger a country's capacity to prevent environmental deterioration, the more likely it is to remain stable.

■ The existence of a "youth bulge"—a large proportion of young adults in the population—increases the risk of state failure through war because large pools of underemployed youths are easily mobilized into military action.

Inasmuch as most of the sovereign states in the world have one or more of these attributes, it is likely that failed states will grow as a problem in the globalized twenty-first century. The globe is speckled with many dangerous flash points where countries are highly vulnerable to dissolution as a result of state failure, mismanagement, civil revolt, and violent government takeovers. To add to the grim picture, there are a number of disputed regions poised to declare independence. Among them are the Kurdish region of Turkey on the Iraqi border, Nagaland in India, the Cabinda exclave in Angola, and Baida in southern Somalia. In 2008, Kosovo declared its independence from Serbia. In a foreshadowing of the war to come between Russia and Georgia, Russia's Vladimir Putin asked of Georgia's two breakaway enclaves, "If people believe that Kosovo can be granted full independence, why then should we deny it to Abkhazia and South Ossetia?"

Intrastate Conflict

Armed conflicts within states have erupted far more frequently than have armed conflicts between states. Between 1989 and 2010, internal armed conflict over government or territory has been the most common by far. In this period, 123 armed conflicts within states took place in comparison to only eight between states. During 2009 alone thirty-six armed conflicts were raging in twenty-seven locations around the world. All were intrastate conflicts involving a government fighting with, in some cases, more than one rebel group at a time (Harbom and Wallensteen 2010).

Civil war, where the intensity of internal armed conflict reached at least one thousand battle-related deaths per year, occurred 153 times between 1816 and 2010 (Harbom and Wallensteen 2010; J. Singer 1991, pp. 66–75; Small and Singer 1982). Their outbreak has been somewhat irregular, with over 60 percent erupting after 1946 with the frequency steadily climbing each decade (see Table 7.1). However, this accelerating trend is, in part, a product of the increased number of independent states in the global system, which makes the incidence of civil war statistically more probable. Moreover, while the number of internal armed conflicts has risen by almost twenty-five percent since 2003, the number of civil wars with more than 1000 battle-related deaths is comparatively modest, with six taking place in 2009 (Harbom and Wallensteen 2010).

enduring internal rivalry (EIR)
protracted violent conflicts between governments and insurgent groups within a state.

Civil wars dominate the global terrain because they start and re-ignite at a higher rate than they end, and they last longer (Alley 2004; Hironaka 2005). There is a tendency for countries that have experienced one civil war to undergo two or more subsequent civil wars (Quinn, Mason, and Gurses 2007), and this pattern is even more pronounced for conflicts characterized by an *enduring internal rivalry (EIR)*. Empirical evidence shows that "76% of all civil war years from 1946 to 2004 took place in the context of EIRs," and that such civil wars were more likely to recur and to be followed by shorter peace spells (DeRouen and Bercovitch 2008, p. 55). Moreover, the average duration of civil wars once they erupt has increased; one study estimates that 130 civil wars fought worldwide since World War II lasted an average of eleven years (Stark 2007). Consider examples of long-lasting and

Table 7.1 Civil Wars, 1816–2010

Period	Key System Characteristics	System Size (average number of states)	Number of Civil Wars Begun
1816–1848	Monarchies in Concert of Europe suppress democratic revolutions	28	12
1849–1881	Rising nationalism and civil wars	39	20
1882–1914	Imperialism and colonialization	40	18
1915–1945	World wars and economic collapse	59	14
1946–1988	Decolonialization and independence for emerging Global South countries during Cold War	117	65
1989–2010	Age of failed states and civil wars	198	24
1816–2010			153

Data for 1816–1945 courtesy of the Correlates of War project under the direction of J. David Singer and Melvin Small; data from 1946 to 2010 for intrastate armed conflicts with one thousand or more battle-related deaths drawn from the Uppsala Conflict Data Program Dyadic Dataset v.1-2010 (see Harbom and Wallensteen 2010).

resumed civil wars in Afghanistan, Burundi, Chad, Colombia, Congo, Indonesia, Iran, Iraq, Ivory Coast, Lebanon, Liberia, Myanmar, Peru, the Philippines, Rwanda, Somalia, Sri Lanka, Sudan, Turkey, and Uganda.

Another noteworthy characteristic of civil wars is their severity. The number of lives lost in civil violence has always been very high, and casualties from civil wars since World War II have increased at alarming rates. Children are major participants and victims caught in the crossfire. The most lethal civil wars in history have erupted recently. The cliché that "the most savage conflicts occur in the home" captures the ugly reality, as genocide and mass slaughter aimed at depopulating entire regions have become commonplace in recent civil wars.

That grim reality was illustrated in Rwanda, where the Hutu government orchestrated a genocidal slaughter resulting in the murder of about eight hundred thousand predominantly Tutsi and moderate Hutu people in a matter of weeks. Sudan provides another horrifying example of the mass slaughter of civilians that often occurs when governments seek to keep power by destroying minority opposition groups. The Arab-controlled Sudanese government (and government-backed Janjaweed militia) that seized power in 1989 suspended democracy and undertook a divide-and-destroy campaign of *state-sponsored terrorism* against the black Christian and animist peoples living in the southern Darfur region. By February 2010, when the Sudanese government signed a ceasefire agreement with the JEM, the largest rebel group in Darfur, United Nations' estimates put the death toll at roughly 300,000 people, with 2.5 million having fled their homes. The bloodbath and mass exodus made this tragic place of death the worst since World War II, but the great powers—preoccupied with the Iraq and Afghanistan wars— were very late in authorizing UN or African peacekeepers in late 2007 to intervene to stop the killing.

state-sponsored terrorism formal assistance, training, and arming of foreign terrorists by a state in order to achieve foreign policy goals.

Another salient characteristic of civil wars is their resistance to negotiated settlement. Making peace is difficult among rival factions that are struggling for power, driven by hatred and poisoned by the inertia of prolonged killing that has become a way of life. Few domestic enemies fighting in a civil war have succeeded in ending the combat through negotiated compromise at the bargaining table. Most civil wars end on the battlefield (Walter 1997) but rarely with a decisive victory of one faction over another. This is why fighting often resumes after a temporary cease-fire. Evidence shows that "the longer peace can be sustained, the less likely civil war is to recur," and that the prospects for lasting peace improve when peace agreements are supported by external peacekeeping forces and post-war economic development (Quinn, Mason and Gurses 2007, p. 167).

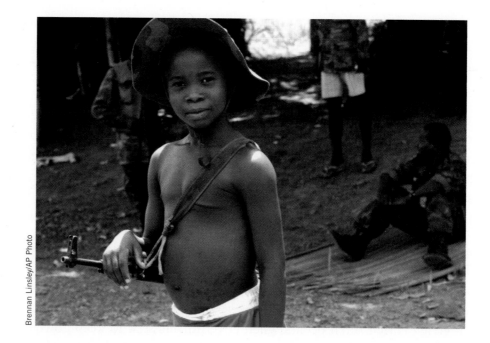

WARFARE AND CHILDREN Children have often been the major victims of civil strife, and even active participants as child soldiers. They join for many reasons—some are kidnapped and forced to join, others are lured by promises of money, others have lost loved ones and seek vengeance. After putting down arms, says Philippe Houdard, the founder of Developing Minds Foundation, the "biggest challenge is making them emotionally whole again... to get them from being killing machines to normal human beings" (Drost 2009, p. 8). Here we see an eleven year old boy standing on the roadside at a Sierra Leone military checkpoint.

The International Dimensions of Internal Conflict

The rise of failing states and their frequent fall into intrastate conflict may make it tempting for you to think of armed aggression within states as stemming exclusively from conditions within those countries. However, "every war has two faces. It is a conflict both between and within political systems; a conflict that is both external and internal. [It is undeniable that] internal wars affect the international system [and that] the international system affects internal wars" (Modelski 1964, p. 41).

Take, for example, the consequence of violent government takeover through a *coup d'etat*. Historically, successful coups tended to result in authoritarian regimes seizing power, such as Pinochet in Chile or Suharto in Indonesia. Between 1960 and 1990, an average of six coups occurred somewhere around the globe every year and 80 percent of the leaders held onto power for at least five years. While coups continue to occur—on February 18, 2010, a military junta overthrew the president of Niger, Mamadou Tandga, who had become widely unpopular in the past year as he turned toward autocracy—since the end of the Cold War, the frequency of coups has

coup d'etat
a sudden, forcible take-over of government by a small group within that country, typically carried out by violent or illegal means with the goal of installing their own leadership in power.

declined by almost half, and the resulting governments have permitted competitive elections within five years. Political scientists Hein Groemans and Nikolay Marinov attribute this changed pattern, in part, to an external factor: "Since the end of Cold War rivalry for spheres of influence, Western powers have become less willing to tolerate dictatorships—and more likely to make aid contingent upon holding elections" (Keating 2009b, p. 28).

Because the great powers have global interests, they have played roles "behind the scenes," not only in the occurrence of coup d'etats, but also militarily in intrastate conflict to support friendly governments and to overthrow unfriendly ones. On these occasions, wars within states became internationalized. But today it is often difficult to determine where an internal war ends and another begins. Outside intervention in intrastate conflict has been fairly common, and has occurred in over a fourth (31 of 114) of all intrastate armed conflicts since 1989 (Harbom and Wallensteen 2010).

In the aftermath of external intrusions, the targets' domestic societies have been transformed. At times, external actors (states and IGOs) have sent interventionary armed forces into failed states to contain and control the civil conflict causing violence and attempt to reestablish governing authority. A recent exception to the usual tendency for intrastate wars to become internationalized by foreign intervention is the U.S.-led invasion of Iraq: "In a reversal of the classic spillover of conflict from intra- to interstate, developments in Iraq during 2004 raised the prospect of an international conflict creating a fully fledged civil war" rather than restoring peace (SIPRI 2009).

There is another dimension to the internationalization of intrastate conflict. Many analysts believe that domestic insurrections become internationalized when leaders experiencing internal opposition within their state intentionally seek to provoke an international *crisis* in the hope that their citizens will become less rebellious if their attention is diverted to the threat of aggression from foreign countries. This proposition has become known as the ***diversionary theory of war***. This theory draws a direct connection between civil strife and foreign aggression. It maintains that when leaders sense their country is suffering from conflict at home, they are prone to attempt to contain that domestic strife by waging a war against foreigners—hoping that the international danger will take citizens' attention away from their dissatisfaction with their home leadership. "To put it cynically, one could say that nothing helps a leader like a good war. It gives him his only chance of being a tyrant and being loved for it at the same time. He can introduce the most ruthless forms of control and send thousands of his followers to their deaths and still

diversionary theory of war
the hypothesis that leaders initiate conflict abroad as a way of increasing their citizens' approval of them and national cohesion at home.

be hailed as a great protector. Nothing ties tighter the in-group bonds than an out-group threat" (Morris 1969, p. 32).

It is logical for leaders to assume that national unity will rise when a foreign rivalry exists (Lai and Reiter 2005; Mitchell and Prins 2004). This creates strong temptations for them to seek to manage domestic unrest by initiating foreign adventures and demonstrating their competence (Tarar 2006). Indeed, many political advisers have counseled this strategy, as realist theorist Niccolò Machiavelli did in 1513 when he advised leaders to undertake foreign wars whenever turmoil within their state became too great. He was echoed by Hermann Goering, the Nazi adviser to German dictator Adolf Hitler, who asserted "voice or no voice, the people can always be brought to do the bidding of the leaders. That is easy. All you have to do is tell them they are being attacked and denounce the pacifists for lack of patriotism." Similarly, in 1939, John Foster Dulles recommended before he became U.S. Secretary of State that "the easiest and quickest cure of internal dissension is to portray danger from abroad."

Whether leaders actually start wars to offset domestic conflict and heighten public approval remains a subject of debate. We cannot demonstrate that many leaders intentionally undertake diversionary actions to defend themselves against domestic opposition, even in democracies during bad economic times, or to influence legislative outcomes (Oneal and Tir 2006).

Unpopular leaders may instead be highly motivated to exercise caution in foreign affairs and to avoid the use of force overseas in order to cultivate a reputation as a peacemaker. It may be better for leaders facing opposition to avoid further criticism that they are intentionally manipulative by addressing domestic problems rather than engaging in reckless wars overseas—especially unpopular wars that trigger protest demonstrations and reduce leaders' public opinion approval ratings.

Mohammad Sajjad/AP Photo

ARMED AGGRESSION'S PAINFUL LEGACY Armed struggles within countries occur more frequently than those between states, though many have repercussions for world politics more broadly. Pictured here are residents of the Pakistani district of Dir fleeing the fighting between Taliban militants and government in April 2009. Many in the Global North fear "that Pakistan, a nuclear-armed country, lacks the will to fight extremists in the northwest, where the leader of Al Qaeda, Osama bin Laden, is thought to be hiding" (IHT, April 29, 2009, p. 1).

Hence, there is reason to question the link between civil unrest and the initiation of interstate war. As Jack Levy (1989b, p. 271) observes, the linkage depends on "the kinds of internal conditions that commonly lead to hostile external actions for diversionary purposes."

Diversionary wars are undertaken by desperate leaders in desperate times, such as in an economic recession or a reelection that the opposition appears likely to win. In noncrisis times, however, when people take to the streets to protest a leader's domestic policies, most leaders are more inclined to concentrate on the internal disturbances than to manufacture threats of a foreign war.

Intrastate conflict can become internationalized through both the tendency for them to incite external intervention as well as the propensity for leaders of governments that are failing to wage wars abroad in order to try to control rebellion at home. These two trends both are making for the globalization of armed aggression. And that globalization is evident in yet another, third type of armed aggression that brings violence to world politics: the threat of global terrorism that knows no borders and that is spreading worldwide.

TERRORISM

Since the birth of the modern state system some three and a half centuries ago, national leaders have prepared for wars against other countries. Throughout this period, war has been conceived as large-scale organized violence between the regular armies of sovereign states. Although leaders today still ready their countries for such clashes, increasingly they are faced with the prospect of *asymmetric warfare*—armed conflict between terrorist networks and conventional military forces.

Terrorism was well known even in ancient times, as evident in the campaign of assassinations conducted by the Sicarii (named after a short dagger, or sica) in Judea during the first century BCE. Today it is practiced by a diverse group of movements. In 2011 the U.S. National Counterterrorism Center (NCTC) identified dozens of different transnational actors as worldwide terrorist groups. Political terrorism is "the premeditated use or threat to use violence by individuals or subnational groups to obtain a political or social objective through the intimidation of a large audience beyond that of the immediate victims" (Sandler 2010, p. 205). Because perpetrators of terrorism often strike symbolic targets in a horrific manner, the psychological impact of an attack can exceed the physical damage. A mixture of drama and dread, terrorism is not senseless violence; it is a premeditated political strategy that threatens people with a coming danger that seems ubiquitous, unavoidable, and unpredictable.

asymmetric warfare armed conflict between belligerents of vastly unequal military strength, in which the weaker side is often a nonstate actor that relies on unconventional tactics.

Consider estimates of the growing intensity of terrorism's threat. According to the U.S. Department of State's Office of the Coordinator for Counterterrorism, the yearly number of acts of international terrorism increased

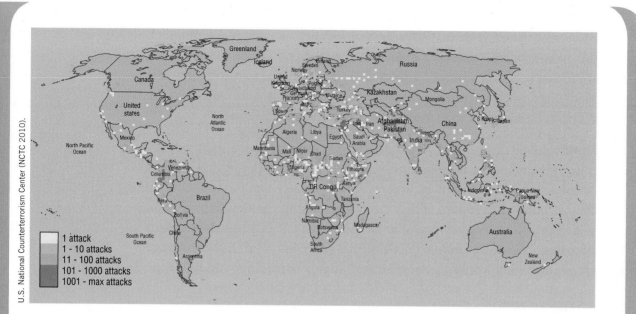

U.S. National Counterterrorism Center (NCTC 2010).

MAP 7.2

THE PERSISTENT THREAT OF GLOBAL TERRORISM Shown here are the locations of terrorist attacks that occurred from 2005 until the start of 2010, with incidents most heavily concentrated in the Near East, South Asia, and Africa. Reflecting upon initiatives to combat terrorism, on June 7, 2010, UN Secretary-General Ban Ki-moon noted that the "complexity and interdependence of these issues mean that no single country or organization can provide solutions alone. Dialogue and cooperation are critical."

steadily from 174 in 1968 to a peak of 666 in 1987, but then began to decline just as steadily to 200 acts in 2002. After the United States broadened its definitional criteria to include the deaths of civilian victims in Iraq, the estimates of the number of global terrorist acts rose dramatically (see Map 7.2 and Figure 7.3). Many experts believe that the presence of U.S. soldiers on Islamic soil in Iraq counterproductively ignited a new wave of deadly terrorist activity throughout the world; as of 2008, 70 percent of the most respected terrorist experts believe that the world is becoming increasingly dangerous for Americans and the United States and that the globe is growing more dangerous, though this represents a drop from 91 percent the previous year (*Foreign Policy*, September/October 2008, p. 80).

Terrorism can be employed to support or to change the political status quo. Repressive terror, which is wielded to sustain an existing political order, has been utilized by governments as well as by vigilantes. From the Gestapo (secret state police) in Nazi Germany to the "death squads" in various countries, establishment violence attempts to defend the prevailing political order by eliminating opposition leaders and by intimidating virtually everyone else.

Dissidents who use terrorism to change the political status quo vary considerably. Some groups, like the MPLA (Popular Movement for the Liberation of Angola), used terrorism to expel colonial rulers; others, such as ETA (Basque Homeland and Liberty), adopt terrorism as part of an ethnonational separatist struggle; still others, including the Islamic Jihad, the Christian Identity Movement, the Sikh group Babbar Khalsa, and Jewish militants belonging to Kach, place terror in the service of what they see as religious imperatives. Finally, groups such as the Japanese Red Army and Italian Black Order turn to terrorism for left- or right-wing ideological reasons. Dissident terror may be grounded in anticolonialism, separatism, religion, or secular ideology.

To accomplish these objectives, terrorists use a variety of tactics, including bombing, assault, hijacking, and taking hostages (see Figure 7.2). Bombing alone accounts for over one-third of all recorded terrorist incidents. Hijacking and hostage taking generally involve more complex operations than planting a bomb in a crowded department store or gunning down travelers in a train station. An example of such careful planning can be seen in the September 1970 coordinated hijacking of five airliners by

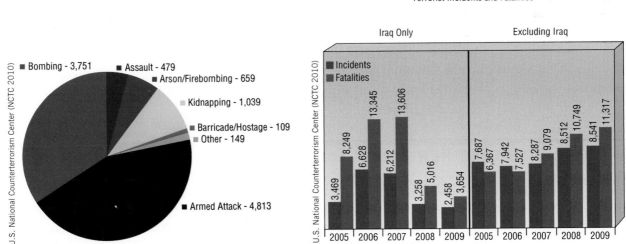

FIGURES 7.2 & 7.3

TOOLS OF TERRORIST WARFARE The figure on the left records the major methods used by terrorists worldwide in 2009, and the number of attacks associated with each. As the second most frequently used tactic, bombings included all of the 299 suicide attacks committed in 2009. The figure on the right depicts the number of incidents and fatalities across the world, as well as in Iraq alone.

Palestinians, which eventually led to one airliner being blown up in Cairo and three others in Jordan. To be successful, these kinds of seizures require detailed preparation and the capacity to guard captives for long periods of time. Among the payoffs of such efforts is the opportunity to articulate the group's grievances. The Lebanese group behind the 1985 hijacking of TWA Flight 847, for instance, excelled at using U.S. television networks to articulate its grievances to the American public, which reduced the options that the Reagan administration could consider while searching for a solution to the crisis.

Beyond the conventional tactics of bombings, assaults, hijacking, and hostage taking, two other threats could become part of the terrorist repertoire. First, dissidents may acquire weapons of mass destruction to deliver a mortal blow against detested enemies. Nuclear armaments are the ultimate terror weapons, but radiological, chemical, and biological weapons also pose extraordinary dangers. Crude radiological weapons can be fabricated by combining ordinary explosives with nuclear waste or radioactive isotopes, stolen from hospitals, industrial facilities, or research laboratories. Rudimentary chemical weapons can be made from herbicides, pesticides, and other toxic substances that are available commercially. Biological weapons based on viral agents are more difficult to produce, although the dispersal of anthrax spores through the mail during the fall of 2001 illustrated that low-technology attacks with bacterial agents in powder form are a frightening possibility.

The second tactical innovation on the horizon is cyberterrorism. Not only can the Internet be used by extremists as a recruiting tool and a means of coordinating their activities with like-minded groups, but it also allows them to case potential targets by hacking into a foe's computer system. Viruses and other weapons of *information warfare* could cause havoc if they disable financial institutions.

information warfare attacks on an adversary's telecommunications and computer networks to degrade the technological systems vital to its defense and economic well-being.

The New Global Terrorism

The conventional view of terrorism as a rare and relatively remote threat was challenged by the events of September 11, 2001. The horrors visited on the World Trade Center, the Pentagon, and the crash victims in Pennsylvania forced the world to confront a grim new reality: Terrorists were capable of executing catastrophic attacks almost anywhere, even without an arsenal of sophisticated weapons. Not only did groups like Al Qaeda have global reach, but stealth, ingenuity, and meticulous planning could compensate for their lack of firepower. "America is full of fear," proclaimed a jubilant Osama bin Laden. "Nobody in the United States will feel safe."

What arguably made 9/11 a symbolic watershed was that it epitomized a deadly new strain of *terrorism*. Previously, terrorism was regarded as political theater, a frightening drama where the perpetrators wanted a lot of people watching, not a lot of people dead. Now there seems to be a desire to kill as many people as possible. Driven by searing hatred, annihilating enemies appears more important to global terrorists than winning sympathy for their cause.

Another feature of this new strain of terrorism is its organizational form. Instead of having a hierarchical command structure, for example, Al Qaeda possesses a decentralized horizontal structure. Loosely tied together by the Internet, e-mail, and cellular telephones, Al Qaeda originally resembled a hub-and-spoke organization: Osama bin Laden and a small core of loyalists provided strategic direction and aid to a franchise of affiliated terrorist cells. Rather than serving as a commander, bin Laden functioned as a coordinator who, in addition to planning dramatic, high-casualty attacks, provided financial and logistical support to extremist groups fighting those whom he perceived as archenemies.

Following the demise of the Taliban regime in Afghanistan after the U.S.-led military intervention, Al Qaeda underwent a structural change. Combined with its loss of a safe haven in Afghanistan, the killing or capture of roughly one-third of Al Qaeda's leadership transformed the organization into an entity that resembled a chain. Bin Laden and his close associates continued offering ideological inspiration to small, disparate cells scattered around the world, but they no longer were directly involved in the planning and execution of most of the attacks undertaken in Al Qaeda's name. Operating independently, without the training, financing, and logistical infrastructure previously available through a central headquarters, Al Qaeda's diffuse underground cells began to concentrate on "soft" targets, sometimes attacking in conjunction with sympathetic local forces. Though Al Qaeda did not claim responsibility, some point to the December 2007 assassination of former Pakistan Prime Minister Benazir Bhutto as illustration of this pattern of activity (though others blamed the attack on political rival Pervez Musharraf).

What makes the new breed of terrorists who belong to organizations such as Al Qaeda more lethal than previous terrorists is their religious fanaticism, which allows them to envision acts of terror on two levels. At one level, terrorism is a means to change the political status quo by punishing those culpable for felt wrongs. At another level, terrorism is an end in itself, a sacrament performed for its own sake in an eschatological confrontation between good and evil (Juergensmeyer 2003). Functioning only on the first

TERRORISTS BEHIND MASKS Shown here is the faceless militia that targets armies in uniforms: Looking like self-funded criminal gangs with no ranks and uncertain allegiances, many terrorist groups hide their identity and report to no superiors.

level, most secular terrorist groups rarely employ suicide missions. Operating on both levels, religious terrorist groups see worldly gain as well as transcendent importance in a martyr's death (Bloom 2005; Pape 2005). Ramadan Shalah of the Palestinian Jihad explained the military logic of suicide tactics through asymmetric warfare by asserting: "Our enemy possesses the most sophisticated weapons in the world.... We have nothing...except the weapon of martyrdom. It is easy and costs us only our lives."

Counterterrorism

The threat facing civilization after September 11, 2001, was described by then U.S. President George W. Bush as a network of terrorist groups and rogue states that harbored them. Efforts to combat this threat, he insisted, "will not end until every terrorist group of global reach has been found, stopped, and defeated." In what was subsequently called the *Bush Doctrine*, the president declared that each nation had a choice to make: "Either you are with us, or you are with the terrorists."

Bush Doctrine
the declaration that the United States intended to behave globally in terms of its perceived national self-interests, without the necessary approval of others, and, as a corollary, would consider taking unilateral preemptive military action against any perceived security threat (such as Iraq) to defeat it before it could attack the United States.

As you learned in Chapter 5, terrorist groups are a type of transnational non-state actor (or global NGO), distinguished by the fact that they use violence as their primary method of exercising influence. States have often financed, trained, equipped, and provided sanctuary for terrorists whose activities serve their foreign policy goals. The practice of such *state-sponsored terrorism* is among the charges that the United States leveled against Iraq prior to toppling Saddam Hussein in 2003, and continues to apply to Cuba, Iran, Sudan, and Syria. However, disagreement about the character and causes of global terrorism remain pronounced, and, without agreement on these preliminaries, a consensus on the best response is unlikely. Much like a disease that cannot be treated until it is accurately diagnosed, so the plague of the new global terrorism cannot be eradicated until its sources are understood. Those persuaded by one image of terrorism are drawn to certain counterterrorism policies, whereas those holding a different image recommend contrary policies. As constructivist theorists remind us, what we see depends on what we expect, what we look at, and what we wish to see.

Consider the diametrically opposed views of whether repression or conciliation is the most effective counterterrorist policy. Those advocating repression see terrorism springing from the cold calculations of extremists who should be neutralized by preemptive surgical strikes. In contrast to this coercive counterterrorism approach, those who see terrorism rooted in frustrations with a society lacking in civil liberties and human rights (Krueger 2007) or widespread poverty and poor education (Azios 2007) urge negotiation and cooperative nonmilitary approaches (Cortright and Lopez 2008). Rather than condoning military strikes aimed at exterminating the practitioners of terrorism, they endorse conciliatory policies designed to reduce terrorism's appeal.

The debate about how to deal with the new global terrorism has provoked serious concerns about strategies for combating this global threat (see Controversy: Can the War against Global Terrorism Be Won?). The debate revolves around a series of interconnected issues: Are repressive counterterrorist policies ethical? Are they compatible with democratic procedures? Do they require multilateral (international) backing to be legal, or can they be initiated unilaterally? Is conciliation more effective than military coercion? What are the relative costs, risks, and benefits of these contending approaches to combat terrorism?

Although most experts would agree that while "it is not possible to extirpate terrorism from the face of the globe," they share faith in the more modest goal—that "it should be possible to reduce the incidence and effectiveness of terrorism" (Mentan 2004, p. 364) and contain it (Shapiro 2007). Accomplishing this goal while maintaining a proper balance between undertaking resolute action and upholding civil liberties will be difficult for multiple reasons:

- Today's borderless world makes terrorism easy to practice.

- Numerous *failed* states offer out-of-the-way places for terrorist groups to locate and train.

- The growing possibility that terrorists will obtain weapons of mass destruction will create unprecedented opportunities for them to commit unspeakable atrocities.

- "Technology allows modern-day terrorism to assume insidious forms" (Sandler and Enders 2007, p. 301), and the tolerant virtual environment of the Internet provides an online breeding ground for a new generation of terrorists—essentially a self-recruited leaderless jihad, inspired by Al Qaeda's ideology, but lacking any formal connections. It is composed largely of young people seeking an outlet for their frustrations and a sense of significance and belonging in their lives (Sageman 2008).

- Finally, contemporary terrorists have become extremely violent, holding few reservations about inflicting heavy casualties and causing enormous physical destruction.

The history of terrorism indicates that there is no single counterterrorist ortho-doxy on strategic questions, no canon with strict guidelines running from ultimate goals to intermediate objectives to specific tactics. Though "groups whose attacks on civilian targets outnumbered attacks on military targets systematically failed to achieve their policy objectives" (Abrahms 2008, p. 424), strategic thinking about the use of terrorism in asymmetric warfare has evolved in response to new technologies, new targets of opportunity, and new counterterrorist policies. The perpetrators of terrorism are not mindless; they have shown that they have long-term aims and rationally calculate how different operations can accomplish their purposes. Indeed, it is their ability to plan, execute, and learn from these operations that makes today's terror-ists so dangerous. Moreover, exposure to terrorism can encourage political exclusionism and threaten the principles of democratic governance.

> Alongside the heavy losses and fear, terror creates an enormous challenge to the fabric of democratic societies. In many cases, there is a difficult inner tension between the fundamental need to feel secure and the aspiration to sustain democratic values and preserve democratic culture. More specifi-cally, in times of terrorist threat and severe losses, when direct confrontation with the perpetrators of terrorism is either impossible or does not guarantee public safety, rage is frequently aimed at minority groups and their members. This rage can be easily translated into support for nondemocratic practices in dealing with minorities. Hence, one of the key psychosocial-political con-sequences of terrorism is the development of hostile feelings, attitudes, and behaviors toward minority groups (Canetti-Nisim et al. 2009, p. 364).

Armed aggression poses a threat of huge proportions to the global future. Having examined trends in the frequency and changing character of armed aggression between states, within them, and in global terrorism, it is difficult not to recognize that warfare in all its forms is an extremely dangerous threat to the world. The magnitude of armed aggression raises questions about why wars occur. What ends motivate human beings to continue to resort to armed aggression, given the unspeakable casualties? The question provokes a more fundamental set of related questions about the causes of aggression generally. Accordingly, consider some of the major contending hypotheses and theories about the sources from which armed conflicts arise.

Case Study:
Terrorism

> *There's nothing quite like a protracted war to shift the landscape of existence. When policy makers start a war, do they realize they have dragged heavy hands across the map of the world and altered the details of daily life?*
>
> —Anna Quindlen, political journalist

CONTROVERSY:

CAN THE WAR AGAINST GLOBAL TERRORISM BE WON?

In the wake of 9/11, a new conventional wisdom arose—as then U.S. Secretary of Defense Donald Rumsfeld put it, "if the [United States] learned a single lesson from 9/11, it should be that the only way to defeat terrorists is to attack them. There is no choice. You simply cannot defend in every place at every time against every technique. All the advantage is with the terrorist in that regard, and therefore you have no choice but to go after them where they are." This statement reflects the view that even if appeasement is tempting, the only way to respond is relentlessly and thoroughly.

Others argue that to truly undermine terrorism, we must address the underlying conditions that give it appeal. Efforts to defeat Al Qaeda in Afghanistan must include the establishment of a government that can meet the needs of the people, and jobs that provide security and an alternative to fighting. Assessing the prospects of winning the war on terror in Afghanistan, Lieutentant Colonel Brett Jenkinson, commander of the U.S. battalion in the Korengal Valley, explains that "We are not going to kill our way out of this war ... What we need is a better recruiting pitch for disaffected youth. You can't build hope with military might. You build it through development and good governance" (Baker and Kolay 2009, p. 27).

Exactly what approach to take to control the new global terrorism remains controversial. Many experts question the U.S. characterization of the problem and the ambitious crusade it undertook, including skeptical allies on whom the United States depends if the antiterror war is to be won. To conduct a worldwide war requires an enduring commitment at high costs. That is why proposals for an effective and just response to the new global terrorism differ, as do recommendations about how the world can most effectively reduce the probability that 9/11 will be repeated.

What makes counterterrorism so problematic is that strategists often fail to distinguish different types of terrorist movements and their diverse origins. Therefore they construct counterterrorist strategies in the abstract—with a single formula—rather than tailoring approaches for dealing with terrorism's alternate modes. As one expert advises, "One lesson learned since 9/11 is that the expanded war on terrorism has created a lens that tends to distort our vision of the complex political dynamics of countries" (Menkhaus 2002, p. 210).

In evaluating proposed controls in the fight against the latest wave of global terrorism, you will need to confront a series of incompatible clichés and conclusions: "concessions only encourage terrorists' appetite for further terrorism," as opposed to "concessions can redress the grievances that lead to terrorism"; or "terrorism requires a long-term solution" as opposed to the claim that "terrorism cannot be cured but it can be prevented by preemption." Your search for solutions will necessarily spring from incompatible assumptions you make about terrorism's nature and sources, and these assumptions will strongly affect your conclusions about the wisdom or futility of contemplated remedies.

Keep in mind that what may appear to be policy around which an effective counterterrorist program might be constructed could potentially only make the problem worse by provoking the very result your preferred plan was

(*continued*)

CAN THE WAR AGAINST GLOBAL TERRORISM BE WON? (Continued)

designed to solve: future terrorist actions. Counterterrorism is controversial because one person's solution is another person's problem, the answers are often unclear, and the ethical criteria for applying just-war theory to counterterrorism need clarification (Patterson 2005). A counterterrorist program that may succeed in one location may backfire in another.

WHAT DO YOU THINK?

- How does armed aggression, such as terrorism, by nonstate actors change the circumstances of war for policy makers? How does it change the circumstances of intervention for policy makers?

- Because promise and/or peril may result when the same countermeasure is deployed, what would you advise governments about the best methods of fighting terrorism?

- How might intergovernmental organizations such at the UN complement states' abilities to fight terrorism? How might they hinder a state's efforts at counterterrorism?

WHAT CAUSES ARMED AGGRESSION?

Video: *A Long-Term Decision*

Animated Learning Module: *Threats*

Throughout history, efforts have been made to explain why people engage in organized violence. Inventories of war's origins (see Cashman and Robinson 2007; Midlarsky 2000; Vasquez 2000) generally agree that hostilities are rooted in multiple sources found at various *levels of analysis* (recall Chapters 1 and 6). Some causes directly influence the odds of war; others are remote and indirect, creating explosive background conditions that enable any one of a number of more proximate factors to trigger violence. The most commonly cited causes of armed aggression are customarily classified by three broad categories: (1) aggressive traits found in the human species, (2) detrimental national attributes that make some states likely to engage in aggression, and (3) volatile conditions within the global system that encourage disputes to become militarized.

The First Level of Analysis: Individuals' Human Nature

"At a fundamental level, conflict originates from individuals' behavior and their repeated interactions with their surroundings" (Verwimp et al. 2009, p. 307). Likewise, in a sense, all wars originate from the decisions of the leaders of states or transnational nonstate actors such as terrorist organizations. Leaders' choices ultimately determine whether armed aggression will occur (see Chapter 6). So a good starting point for explaining why warfare occurs is to consider the relationship of armed aggression to the choices of individual leaders. For this *level of analysis*, questions about human nature are central.

The repeated outbreak of war has led some, such as psychiatrist Sigmund Freud, to conclude that aggression is an instinctive part of human nature that stems from humans' genetic psychological programming. Identifying *Homo sapiens* as the deadliest species, ethologists (those who study animal behavior) such as Konrad Lorenz (1963) similarly argue that humans are one of the few species practicing *intraspecific aggression* (routine killing of their own kind), in comparison with most other species that practice *interspecific aggression* (killing only other species, except in the most unusual circumstances—cannibalism in certain tropical fish being one exception). Ethologists are joined in their interpretation by adherents of realist theory who believe that all humans are born with an innate drive for power that they cannot avoid, and that this instinct leads to competition and war. They therefore accept the sociological premise suggested by Charles Darwin's theories of evolution and natural selection. Life entails a struggle for survival of the fittest, and natural selection eliminates the traits that interfere with successful competition. To realists, *pacifism* is counterproductive because it is contrary to basic human nature, which they see as aggressive and power seeking. Additionally, by ruling out military action, pacifism rejects the primary realist policy instrument for ensuring state security.

intraspecific aggression
killing members of one's own species.

interspecific aggression
killing others that are not members of one's own species.

pacifism
the liberal idealist school of ethical thought that recognizes no conditions that justify the taking of another human's life, even when authorized by a head of state.

Many question these theories on both empirical and logical grounds. If aggression is truly an inevitable impulse deriving from human nature, then should not all humans exhibit this genetically determined behavior? Most people, of course, do not on ethical grounds, rejecting killing as evil, and neither murdering nor accepting others' killing on behalf of the state or any other cause. In fact, at some fundamental genetic level, human beings are wired to seek consensus, not conflict. Argues international theorist Francis Fukuyama (1999a), "people feel intensely uncomfortable if they live in a society that doesn't have moral rules."

In addition, liberal theory and behavioral social science research suggest that genetics fails to explain why individuals may be belligerent only at certain times. Social Darwinism's interpretation of the biological influences on human behavior can be countered by examining why people cooperate and act morally. As James Q. Wilson (1993, p. 23) argues, Darwinian *survival of the fittest* realist theory overlooks the fact that "the moral sense must have adaptive value; if it did not, natural selection would have worked against

survival of the fittest
a realist concept derived from Charles Darwin's theory of evolution that advises that ruthless competition is ethically acceptable to survive, even if the actions violate moral commands not to kill.

nature versus nurture
the controversy over whether human behavior is determined more by the biological basis of "human nature" than it is nurtured by the environmental conditions that humans experience.

socialization
the processes by which people learn to accept the beliefs, values, and behaviors that prevail in a given society's culture.

national character
the collective characteristics ascribed to the people within a state.

ecological fallacy
the error of assuming that the attributes of an entire population—a culture, a country, or a civilization—are the same attributes and attitudes of each person within it.

people who had such useless traits as sympathy, self-control, or a desire for fairness in favor of those with the opposite tendencies."

Although the **nature versus nurture** debate regarding the biological bases of aggression has not been resolved (Kluger 2007; Ridley 2003), most social scientists now strongly disagree with the realist premise that because humans are essentially selfish, they are also aggressive and murder and kill because of their innate genetic drives to act aggressively. Instead, they interpret war as a learned cultural habit. Aggression is a propensity acquired early in life as a result of *socialization*. Therefore, aggression is a learned rather than a biologically determined behavior, and "violent human nature is a myth" (Murithi 2004).

Individuals' willingness to sacrifice their lives in war out of a sense of duty to their leaders and country is one of history's puzzles. "The fog of war" is what Russian author Leo Tolstoy and others have called the fact that people will give their lives in struggles, large and small, even when the importance and purpose of those struggles are not understood. Clearly, this self-sacrifice stems from learned beliefs that some convictions are worth dying for, such as loyalty to one's own country. "It has been widely observed that soldiers fight—and noncombatants assent to war—not out of aggressiveness but obedience" (Caspary 1993). But this does not make human nature a cause of war, even if learned habits of obedience taught in military training are grounds for participation in aggression authorized by others, and even if at times the mass public's chauvinistic enthusiasm for aggression against foreign adversaries encourages leaders to start wars.

This suggests that factors beyond **national character** (the inborn collective traits of particular peoples) better explain why certain countries tend to engage in organized violence. Rather, armed aggression occurs most often as a result of the choices leaders make, and not because of the popular preferences of their entire societies. As English statesman Saint Thomas More (1478–1535) put this hypothesis, "The common people do not go to war of their own accord, but are driven to it by the madness of kings." Similarly, U.S. diplomat Ralph Bunche argued before the UN that "there are no warlike people—just warlike leaders."

This idea introduces an important analytic problem. Can the characteristics of cultures and populations within countries in the aggregate, the sum of the parts, predict the behaviors of the individuals within those groups? No. To generalize from the whole to the part is to commit what demographers and statisticians call a logical *ecological fallacy*. Why? Because, unless all members of the same group are exactly alike, the characteristics of the collectivity (the entire state or culture, for example) do not safely predict the beliefs and behaviors of the individuals in the grouping. Do all Americans think alike? All Muslims? All Japanese or Chinese? Hardly. This is racial and cultural stereotyping at its worst. Rarely can we safely generalize from groups to individuals. Likewise, the opposite, what logicians call the *individualistic fallacy*, is also a mental error. We cannot generalize safely about the beliefs or behavior of individual leaders (Adolf Hitler of Nazi Germany, Joseph Stalin of the Soviet Union, Barack Obama of the United States, Gordon Brown of Great Britain, or Dmitry Medvedev of Russia) and ascribe them to the prevailing preferences of the collective cultures and states that each of them headed.

What should be obvious is that some of the foreign policy decisions by leaders are immoral. Moreover, many of those decisions by countries' leaders are the outcome of flawed decision-making processes; they fail to form to the *rational choice* model of foreign policy decision making that operates from the assumption that decision makers make choices through cool-headed calculations of cost and benefits in order to select the option that has the best chance of accomplishing preferred goals. In addition, even intelligent and moral leaders are sometimes prone to make unnecessarily high-risk decisions to wage war because they are pressured through *groupthink* by influential advisers within their decision-making group rather than acting on what they personally believe would be the most rational choice.

This observation about the determinants of leaders' choices about war and peace directs attention to the domestic factors that encourage some states to engage in foreign aggression.

individualistic fallacy the logical error of assuming that an individual leader, who has legal authority to govern, represents the people and opinions of the population governed, so that all citizens are necessarily accountable for the vices and virtues (to be given blame or credit) of the leaders authorized to speak for them.

The Second Level of Analysis: States' Internal Characteristics

Conventional wisdom holds that variations in states' governments, sizes, ideologies, geographical locations, population dynamics, ethnic homogeneity, wealth, economic performance, military capabilities, and level of educational attainment influence whether they will engage in war. We next examine some theories about the internal characteristics of states that influence leaders' choices regarding the use of force.

Implicit in this approach to explaining armed aggression at the *state level of analysis* is the assumption that differences in the types or categories of states determine whether they will engage in war. Arguing that the prospects for war are influenced most heavily by national attributes and the types of leaders making policy decisions for states challenges the premise of *neorealism* that war is inevitable and that global circumstances, not domestic factors, are the most important determinants of warfare.

Duration of Independence Armed aggression has often been an instrument through which states have been given—or denied—birth. However, statehood does not guarantee peace. New states, not long-lasting ones, are the most likely to experience civil wars and also to initiate foreign wars. Newly independent countries usually go through a period of political unrest following their acquisition of sovereignty and independence as members in the community of states. They then are likely to seek to resolve long-standing internal grievances and take up arms over contested territories with their neighboring enemies (Rasler and Thompson 2006). Such foreign disputes frequently expand into larger wars because throughout history they have frequently provoked great power *intervention*, or external interference by other states or nonstate IGOs into the opposed countries' internal affairs. The high levels of civil wars and wars between neighboring states throughout the Global South may be explained by the fact that nearly all of these less developed countries have recently gained independence from colonialism, many through revolutions.

Cultural Traditions and Nationalism   Countries' behavior is strongly influenced by the cultural and ethical traditions of their peoples. In the state system, governed by the rules championed by realism, moral constraints on the use of force do not command wide acceptance (Hensel 2006). Instead, most governments encourage their populations to glorify the state and to accept whatever decisions their leaders claim are necessary for national security, including warfare against adversaries. Advocates of the cultural origins of war argue that most people in most societies live an everyday experience of disengagement, or "numbness," that disinclines them to oppose their leaders' decisions to wage war. The modern state thus organizes its society to accept war and "builds a culture that affirms death" and accepts senseless carnage (Caspary 1993).

As a natural extension of unerring loyalty to a nation, *nationalism* is widely believed to be the cauldron from which wars often spring (Van Evera 1994). It began as a serious force in Europe 350 years ago when monarchical rulers such as Ferdinand and Isabella of Spain engaged in "state building" by forcibly constructing nationalism to mobilize and manage the population, which bred religious and political intolerance, the repression of minorities, and war

(Marx 2003). English essayist Aldous Huxley saw nationalism as "the religion of the twentieth century"—when history's most destructive interstate wars were fought—and the linkage between nationalism and war has since grown over time (Woodwell 2008).

"The tendency of the vast majority of people to center their supreme loyalties on the nation-state," Jack Levy explains, is a powerful catalyst to war. When people "acquire an intense commitment to the power and prosperity of the state [and] this commitment is strengthened by national myths emphasizing the moral, physical, and political strength of the state and by individuals' feelings of powerlessness and their consequent tendency to seek their identity and fulfillment through the state, … nationalism contributes to war" (Levy 1989a). This leads many to critique nationalism, although many defend it as a virtue that makes for unity and solidarity within a country. Whatever its consequences, nationalism is widely seen as perhaps the most powerful force in today's world, an idea and *ideology* that animates the constructed images of many.

In contrast, critics operating from the perspective of feminist theories of international relations argue that the foundation of war worldwide, alongside cultural numbing, is rooted in the masculine ethos of realism, which prepares people to accept war and to respect the warrior as a hero (see Enloe 2000

Case Study:
Hitler's Rise to Power and Its Lessons

NATIONALISM'S DARK AND DEADLY PAST Under the fascist dictatorship of Adolf Hitler (left), the Nazi government glorified the state and claimed that the German people were a superior race. What followed from this extreme form of nationalism was a ruthless German world war and campaign of genocide that exterminated six million Jews and other ethnic minorities. U.S. troops under the command of General George Patton (right) liberated the concentration camp at Buchenwald in May 1945, but not in time to save the lives of the prisoners whom the Nazi guards had put to death in the gas chambers.

and 2004; Tickner 2002). Gender roles supported by realist values, feminist theory contends, contribute to the prevalence of militarism and warfare. To feminists and other constructivist theorists who embrace a cultural interpretation, the penchant for warfare does not evolve in a vacuum but is produced by the ways in which societies shape their populations' beliefs and norms. Many governments, through the educational programs they fund in schools and other institutions, indoctrinate militaristic values in their political culture that condone the practice of war. Ironically, in a world of diverse national cultures, the messages of obedience and of duty to make sacrifices to the state through such **cultural conditioning** are common. States disseminate the belief that their right to make war should not be questioned and that the ethical principles of religious and secular philosophies prohibiting violence should be disregarded. Consequently, critics stress the existence of powerful institutions that prepare individuals to subconsciously accept warfare as necessary and legitimate.

cultural conditioning
the impact of national traditions and societal values on the behavior of states, under the assumption that culture affects national decision making about issues such as the acceptability of aggression.

Feminist theory extends this explanation of armed aggression. It accounts for the fact that the probability of violence increases in cultures in which gender discrimination, inequality, and violence toward women are an accepted way of life. Where cultural norms condone the mistreatment of women and deny them opportunities for education and employment, the outbreak of civil war is high (Caprioli 2005; Melander 2005).

Poverty and Relative Deprivation A country's level of economic development affects the probability of its involvement in war and armed revolution. Indeed, "underdevelopment is a statistically significant predictor of war" (Lemke 2003, p. 58), and discontent with globalization and foreign economic liberalization can result in violent protest and civil war (Bussmann and Schneider 2007).

relative deprivation
inequality between the wealth and status of individuals and groups, and the outrage of those at the bottom about their perceived exploitation by those at the top.

Armed aggression, often an angry response to frustration, is a product of **relative deprivation**—people's perception that they are unfairly deprived of the wealth and status that they rightly deserve in comparison with advantaged others. Violence erupts so frequently because hundreds of millions "belong to groups that face some form of cultural exclusion and are disadvantaged or discriminated against relative to others in their country," the United Nations observes. The same is true for national images of relative deprivation between countries. This is why the probability of armed aggression is the highest in the Global South, where peoples' expectations of what they deserve are rising more rapidly than their material rewards, and the existing gap in the distribution of wealth and opportunities is widening.

Popular support is critical to the success of armed rebellions, and poverty is a great motivator for allegiance to armed groups that promise security and an improved standard of living. Families "in conflict areas draw on local armed groups to protect their economic status when anticipating violence and... the poorer the household is at the start of the conflict, the higher is the probability of the household participating and supporting an armed group" (Justino 2009, p. 315). This relationship between poverty and armed aggression is all the more pronounced in countries where there is a "youth bulge," where a large portion of the population is young and cannot secure jobs, provide for families, and achieve economic security. This is pointed to as one, among many, of the factors that will continue to contribute to unrest in Gaza as the unemployment rate continues to hover around 50 percent, and the demand for jobs will soar as 45 percent of the population is under 15 and will begin to enter the workforce over the coming years (McGirk 2009, p. 28).

Before concluding that poverty always breeds armed aggression, note that the *most* impoverished countries have been the least prone to start wars with their neighbors. The poorest countries cannot vent their frustrations aggressively because they lack the military or economic resources to do so. This does not mean that the poorest countries will always remain peaceful. If the past is a guide to the future, then impoverished countries that develop economically will be the most likely to acquire arms and engage in future external wars. In particular, states are likely to initiate foreign wars *after* sustained periods of economic growth—that is, during periods of rising prosperity, when they can afford them (Cashman and Robinson 2007). This signals looming dangers if the most rapidly growing Global South economies direct their growing resources toward armaments rather than investing in sustainable development. The decision in 1998 by both Pakistan and India to acquire nuclear weapons could be followed by other restless countries, such as Iran and Syria.

Geopolitical Environmental Factors "Location, location, location"—the geographical roots of armed aggression are now increasingly recognized as a powerful influence on the probability of instability and warfare (Flint 2004). Territorial issues and the stability of international borders are important because the setting and location of states and their distances from one another influence the likelihood of disputes and war (Gibler 2007; Starr 2006). Indeed, the likelihood that a country will undergo armed aggression is strongly affected by key characteristics of its geographic circumstances, such as low supplies of cropland, fresh water, and treasured natural resources such as oil and gas reserves. In addition, topography was signaled as a primary cause of war in 2002 when the UN designated that year as the *International Year*

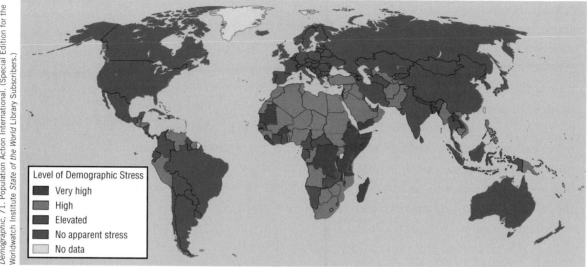

Cincotta Richard, Robert Engelman, and Daniele Anastasion, 2003. "Population and Civil Conflict After the Cold War," In *The Security Demographic*, 71. Population Action International. (Special Edition for the Worldwatch Institute *State of the World* Library Subscribers.)

MAP 7.3

DEMOGRAPHIC STRESS AND THE LIKELIHOOD OF CIVIL WAR Where there are large numbers of unemployed youth concentrated in large cities and a lack of environmentally sustainable growth, the odds of civil war increase dramatically. Shown here are the projected locations of such demographic stress where the likelihood of civil war is expected to be high through the year 2010.

of the Mountains because twenty-three of the twenty-seven armed conflicts under way then were fought in mountainous areas. In particular, "if a country is mountainous and has a large, lightly populated hinterland, it faces an enhanced risk of rebellion [and] when valuable natural resources are discovered in a particular region of a country, the people living in such localities suddenly have an economic incentive to succeed violently if necessary... conflict is also more likely in countries that depend heavily on natural resources for their export earnings, in part because rebel groups can extort the gains from this trade to finance their operations" (Collier 2003, p. 41).

Demographic Stress A number of demographic factors contribute to the onset of armed aggression. Map 7.3 shows that the risk of civil war is the greatest in those countries in which population dynamics impact heavily on living conditions. For example, such variables as the rate of urban population growth and the rate of death among working-age adults are predictors of the outbreak of armed rebellion. Particularly influential as a demographic catalyst to civil war is the presence of a large proportion of young males in the population: "young men—out of school, out of work, and charged with hatred—are the lifeblood of deadly conflict. Countries with a high proportion of adults under thirty have two and a half times the probability of experiencing a new outbreak of civil conflict as do those more mature age structures relative to population size" (Cincotta and Engleman 2004, p. 18). So the future faces an increasing threat—"a clash of generations"—as youth bulges increase the risk of internal armed conflict and political violence (Urdal 2006).

Militarization "If you want peace, prepare for war," realism counsels. It is questionable whether the acquisition of military power leads to peace or to war, but clearly most Global South countries agree with the realists' thesis that weapons contribute to their security. They have been among the biggest customers in the robust global trade in arms and have built huge armies to guard against their neighboring states' potential aggression and to control their own citizens (see Blanton and Nelson 2012; and Chapter 8).

As Global South countries concentrate their budgets on equipping their militaries, many worry that war will become more frequent before it becomes less so. Militarization has *not* led to peace in the Global South. Will the curse of violence someday be broken there?

One clue comes from examination of the relationship between changes in military capabilities and war that occurred over centuries in Europe. During its transition to the peak of development, Europe was the location of the world's most frequent and deadly wars. The major European states armed themselves heavily and were engaged in warfare about 65 percent of the time in the sixteenth and seventeenth centuries (Wright 1942). Between 1816 and 1945, three-fifths of all interstate wars took place in Europe, with one erupting about every other year (J. Singer 1991, p. 58). Not coincidentally, this happened when the developing states of Europe were most energetically arming in competition with one another. Perhaps as a consequence, the great powers—those with the largest armed forces—were the most involved in, and most often initiated, war. Since 1945, however, with the exception of war among the now-independent units of the former Yugoslavia and between Russia and Georgia, interstate war has not occurred in Europe. As the European countries moved up the ladder of development, they moved away from war with one another.

In contrast, the developing countries now resemble Europe before 1945. If, in the immediate future, the Global South follows the model of Europe before 1945, we are likely to see a sea of Global South violence surrounding a European (and Global North) island of peace and prosperity.

Economic System Does the character of states' economic systems influence the frequency of warfare? The question has provoked controversy for centuries. Particularly since Marxism took root in Russia following the Bolshevik

Revolution in 1917, communist theoreticians claimed that capitalism was the primary cause of imperialistic wars and colonialism. They were fond of quoting Vladimir Lenin's 1916 explanation of World War I as a war caused by imperialistic capitalists' efforts "to divert the attention of the laboring masses from the domestic political crisis" of collapsing incomes under capitalism. According to the ***communist theory of imperialism***, capitalism produces surplus capital. The need to export it stimulates wars to capture and protect foreign markets. Thus *laissez-faire economics*—based on the philosophical principle of free markets with little governmental regulation of the marketplace—rationalized militarism and imperialism for economic gain. Citing the demonstrable frequency with which wealthy capitalist societies militarily intervened on foreign soil for capital gain, Marxists believed that the best way to end international war was to end capitalism.

communist theory of imperialism
the Marxist-Leninist economic interpretation of imperialist wars of conquest as driven by capitalism's need for foreign markets to generate capital.

Contrary to Marxist theory, ***commercial liberalism*** contends that free-market systems promote peace, not war. Defenders of capitalism have long believed that free-market countries that practice free trade abroad are more pacific. The reasons are multiple, but they center on the premise that commercial enterprises are natural lobbyists for world peace because their profits depend on it. War interferes with trade, blocks profit, destroys property, causes inflation, consumes scarce resources, and necessitates big government, counterproductive regulation of business activity, and high taxes. By extension, this reasoning continues, as government regulation of internal markets declines, prosperity increases and fewer wars will occur.

commercial liberalism
an economic theory advocating free markets and the removal of barriers to the flow of trade and capital as a locomotive for prosperity.

The evidence for these rival theories is, not surprisingly, mixed. Conclusions depend in part on perceptions regarding economic influences on international behavior, in part because alternative perspectives focus on different dimensions of the linkage. This controversy was at the heart of the ideological debate between East and West during the Cold War, when the relative virtues and vices of two radically different economic systems—communism and capitalism—were uppermost in people's minds.

The end of the Cold War did not end the historic debate about the link between economics and war. This basic theoretical question commands increasing interest, especially given the "shift in the relevance and usefulness of different power resources, with military power declining and economic power increasing in importance" (Huntington 1991b, p. 5).

Type of Government Realist theories discount the importance of government type as an influence on war and peace. Not so with liberalism. As noted in Chapter 2, *liberal theory* assigns great weight to the kinds of political institutions that states create to make policy decisions, and it predicts that the spread of "free" democratically ruled governments will promote peaceful interstate relations. As Immanuel Kant in 1795 argued in *Perpetual Peace*, when citizens are given basic human rights such as choosing their leaders through ballots as well as civil liberties such as free speech and a free press, these democracies would be far less likely to initiate wars than would countries ruled by dictators and kings. This is because a government accountable to the people would be constrained by public opinion from waging war. Kant was joined by other liberal reformers, such as Thomas Jefferson, James Madison, and Woodrow Wilson in the United States. They all believed that an "empire of liberty" (as Madison pictured a growing community of liberal democracies) would be one freed of the curse of war and that, if democratic institutions spread throughout the world, the entire past pattern of belligerent international relations would be replaced by a new pacific pattern.

These liberal predictions have been fulfilled by the passage of time since they were first advanced. "We now have solid evidence that democracies do not make war on each other" (Dahl et al. 2003, p. 492). Much research demonstrates that democracies resolve their differences with one another at the bargaining table rather than the battlefield, and that they are more likely to win wars than nondemocracies (Choi 2004; Souva 2004). This pattern provides the cornerstone for the *democratic peace* proposition (Ray 1995; Sobek 2005) holding that, as Bruce Russett summarizes:

> Democracies are unlikely to engage in any kind of militarized disputes with each other or to let any such disputes escalate into war. They rarely even skirmish. Pairs of democratic states have been only one-eighth as likely as other kinds of states to threaten to use force against each other, and only one-tenth as likely actually to do so. Established democracies fought no wars against one another during the entire twentieth century.
>
> The more democratic each state is, the more peaceful their relations are likely to be. Democracies are more likely to employ "democratic" means of peaceful conflict resolution. They are readier to reciprocate each other's behavior, to accept third-party *mediation* or *good offices* in settling disputes, and to accept binding third-party *arbitration* and *adjudication*. Careful statistical analyses of countries' behavior have shown that democracies' relatively peaceful relations toward each other are not spuriously caused by some other influence such as sharing high levels of wealth, or rapid growth, or ties of alliance. The phenomenon of peace between democracies is not limited just to the rich industrialized states of the Global North. It was not maintained simply by pressure from a common adversary in the Cold War, and it has outlasted that threat (Russett 2001, p. 235; see also Russett 2005).

The growing recognition that ballots serve as a barrier against the use of bullets and bombs by one democracy against another has been inspired by the growth of democratic governance over the past three centuries (see Figure 7.4). Yet there is no certainty that liberal democracy will become universal or that the continued growth of democracy will automatically produce a peaceful world order (Rasler and Thompson 2005). Emerging democracies in fact are prone to fight wars (Mansfield and Snyder 2005a). The fact that leaders in elective democracies are accountable to public approval and electoral rejection does not guarantee that they will not use force to settle disputes with other democracies.

The fragility of democratic institutions was illustrated by the sham reelection of President Mahmoud Ahmadinejad in Iran. Though analysts had predicted a close race between Ahmadinejad and challenger Mir Hosein Mousavi, the official result claimed a margin of 63 percent for the incumbent. Most Iranians believe that electoral fraud occurred on an enormous scale, and three days after the election, on June 15, 2009, hundreds of thousands of Iranians took to the street in protest. The pillars of the Islamic Republic's pretensions of democracy were shaken as the government responded with a brutal crackdown that crushed dissent and restricted the opposition. After more than two weeks of protest, the government succeeded in largely quelling the massive demonstrations that challenged Ahmadinejad's legitimacy, with hardliners calling for demonstrators to be shown no mercy for their defiance. Ahmad Khatami, an Assembly of Experts member, said, "I want the judiciary to punish rioters without mercy, to teach everyone a lesson." Yet despite government repression, protests continued. A massive demonstration took place again in December 2009, and opposition continued on into 2010 with dissidents using

FIGURE 7.4

THE ADVANCE OF ELECTORAL DEMOCRACY, 1700–2010 For 250 years since 1700, most choices about war were made by monarchs, despots, dictators, and autocrats. That has changed in a major global *transformation*, occurring in three "waves" in the growth of "electoral democracy" worldwide, with competitive and regular multi-party elections conducted openly without massive voting fraud (see Cederman and Gleditsch 2004), as this figure shows. In 1974 only one in four countries were electoral democracies; today, the number has grown to 116 countries, or approximately 60 percent, reflecting a slight decline from 119 electoral democracies in the year prior (Freedom House 2010). Whether this long-term transformation will produce peace is being tested.

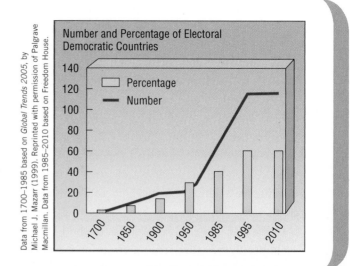

Data from 1700–1985 based on *Global Trends 2005*, by Michael J. Mazarr (1999). Reprinted with permission of Palgrave Macmillan. Data from 1985–2010 based on Freedom House.

Ben Curtis/AP Photo

DISILLUSIONMENT AND CIVIL UNREST In reaction to the disputed outcome of the presidential election in Iran on June 12, 2009, the country witnessed the largest street demonstrations since the Islamic Revolution in 1979. Shown here are supporters of leading opposition presidential candidate Mir Hossein Mousavi protesting at a mass rally in Azadi (Freedom) square in Tehran. The government enacted a clampdown on protesters by the army and police, leaving the opposition with few options and widespread discontent. Said one Iranian citizen, "People are depressed, and they feel they have been lied to, robbed of their rights and now are being insulted ... It is not just a lie; it's a huge one. And it doesn't end" (Fathi 2009, p.A6).

the internet and mobile phones to oppose Iran's ruthless rulers and reach out to the global community.

This discussion of the characteristics of states that influence their proclivity for war does not exhaust the subject. Many other potential causes internal to the state exist. But, however important domestic influences might be as a source of war, many believe that the nature of the *global system* is even more critical.

The Third Level of Analysis: The Global System

Realism emphasizes that the roots of armed conflict rest in human nature. In contrast, *neorealism* sees war springing from changes at the global level of analysis, that is, as a product of the decentralized character of the global system that requires sovereign states to rely on *self-help* for their security:

> Although different realist theories often generate conflicting predictions, they share a core of common assumptions: The key actors in world politics

are sovereign states that act rationally to advance their security, power, and wealth in a conflictual international system that lacks a legitimate governmental authority to regulate conflicts or enforce agreements.

For realists, wars can occur not only because some states prefer war to peace, but also because of unintended consequences of actions by those who prefer peace to war and are more interested in preserving their position than in enhancing it. Even defensively motivated efforts by states to provide for their own security through armaments, alliances, and deterrent threats are often perceived as threatening and lead to counteractions and conflict spirals that are difficult to reverse. This is the *security dilemma*—the possibility that a state's actions to provide for its security may result in a decrease in the security of all states, including itself (Levy 1998b, p. 145).

International *anarchy*, or the absence of institutions for global governance, may promote war's outbreak. However, anarchy fails to provide a complete explanation of changes in the levels of war and peace over time or why particular wars are fought. To capture war's many global determinants, consider also how and why global systems change. This requires exploring the impact of such global factors as the distribution of military capabilities, balances (and imbalances) of power, the number of alliances and international organizations, and the rules of international law. At issue is how the system's characteristics and institutions combine to influence changes in war's frequency. You can examine many of these factors in Chapters 8, 9, 10, and 11. Here you can focus on cycles of war and peace at the global level.

Does Violence Breed Violence? Many interpreters of world history have noted that the seeds of future wars are often found in past wars (see Walter 2004). In his acceptance speech of the 2002 Nobel Peace Prize, former U.S. President Jimmy Carter sadly observed that "violence only begets conditions that beget future violence." For example, World War II was an outgrowth of World War I, the U.S. attack of Iraq in 2003 was an extension of the 1990 Persian Gulf War, and the successive waves of terrorism and war in the Middle East were little more than one war, with each battle stimulated by its predecessor. Because the frequency of past wars is correlated with the incidence of wars in later periods, war appears to be contagious and its future outbreak inevitable. If so, then something within the dynamics of global politics—its anarchical nature, its weak legal system, its uneven distribution of power, inevitable destabilizing changes in the principal actors' relative power, or some combination of structural attributes—makes the global system that is centered on states a "war system."

Those believing in war's inevitability often cite the historical fact that war has been so repetitive. Armed conflicts typically have "a history, many of them a long one. In such entrenched conflicts, the warring parties are more likely to show little interest in negotiation" (Harbom and Wallensteen 2007, p. 625). However, it is not safe to infer that past wars *cause* later wars. The fact that a war precedes a later one does not mean that it caused the one that followed. Thus, many scholars reject the deterministic view that history is destiny, with outcomes caused by previous events. Instead, they embrace the *bargaining model of war*, which sees war as a product of rational choice weighing antici- pated costs against benefits. The decision to engage in warfare is part of the bargaining process that occurs between adversaries to settle disputes and dis- agreements "over scarce goods, such as the placement of a border, the com- position of a national government, or control over national resources" (Reiter 2003, p. 27; see also Filson and Werner 2002; Smith and Stam 2004).

bargaining model of war an interpretation of war's onset as a choice by the initia- tor to bargain through aggression with an enemy in order to win on an issue or to obtain things of value, such as territory or oil.

War's recurrence throughout history does not necessarily mean we will always have it. War is not a universal institution; some societies have never known war and others have been immune to it for prolonged periods. More- over, since 1945 the outbreak of armed aggression *between* states has greatly declined, despite the large increase in the number of independent countries. This indicates that armed conflict is not necessarily inevitable and that his- torical forces do not control people's freedom of choice or experiences.

Power Transitions These trends notwithstanding, when changes have occurred in the major states' military capabilities, war has often resulted. Although not inevitable, war has been likely whenever competitive states' power ratios (the differentials between their capabilities) have narrowed. As Monica Toft (2007, pp. 244–246) concludes "Peace is clearly a value most states share, but not always, and not always above all other values.... Shifts in the distribu- tion of power go a long way toward explaining the likelihood of violence."

This hypothesis is known as the *power transition theory*. This theoretical explanation of armed aggression is a central tenant of structural realism— the neorealist theory that emphasizes that change in the great powers' mili- tary capabilities relative to their closest rivals is a key determinant of the behavior of states within the global system and of the probability of warfare (see Palmer and Morgan 2007, Zagare 2007). As Michelle Benson (2007) explains, "this theory has proven itself to be the most successful structural theory of war [suggesting] that three simple conditions—power transition, relative power parity, and a dissimilarity of preferences for the status quo— are necessary for great power war."

power transition theory the theory that war is likely when a domi- nant great power is threatened by the rapid growth of a rival's capa- bilities, which reduces the difference in their relative power.

During the transition from developing to developed status, emergent challengers can achieve through force the recognition that their newly formed military muscles allow them. Conversely, established powers ruled by risk-acceptant leaders are often willing to employ force to put the brakes on their relative decline. Thus, when advancing and retreating states seek to cope with the changes in their relative power, war between the rising challenger(s) and the declining power(s) has become especially likely. For example, the rapid changes in the power and status that produced the division of Europe among seven great powers nearly equal in military strength are often (along with the alliances they nurtured) interpreted as the tinderbox from which World War I ignited.

Rapid shifts in the global distribution of military power *have* often preceded outbursts of aggression, especially when the new distribution nears approximate equality and thereby tempts the rivals to wage war against their hegemonic challengers. According to the power transition theory, periods in which rivals' military capabilities are nearly balanced create "the necessary conditions for global war, while gross inequality assures peace or, in the worst case, an asymmetric, limited war" (Kugler 2001). Moreover, transitions in states' relative capabilities can potentially lead the weaker party to start a war in order to either overtake its rival or protect itself from domination. Presumably, the uncertainty created by a rough equilibrium prompts the challenger's effort to wage war against a stronger opponent. Though the challenger tends to be unsuccessful in its bid for victory, there are notable exceptions where the initiator had advantages (such as the Vietnam, the Six-Day, Bangladesh, Yom Kippur/Ramadan, Falklands, and Persian Gulf wars).

Cyclical Theories If war is recurrent though not necessarily inevitable, are there other global factors besides power transitions that might also explain changes over time in its outbreak? The absence of a clear trend in its frequency since the late fifteenth century, and its periodic outbreak after intermittent stretches of peace, suggests that world history seesaws between long cycles of war and peace. This provides a third global explanation of war's onset.

Long-cycle theory seeks to explain how an all-powerful invisible hand built into the global system's dynamics causes peaks and valleys in the frequency with which major wars have erupted periodically throughout modern history. As noted in Chapter 3, its advocates argue that cycles of world leadership and global war have existed over the past five centuries, with a "general war" erupting approximately once every century, although at irregular intervals (Modelski and Thompson 1996; Wallerstein 2005; Ferguson 2010).

Long-cycle theory draws its insights from the observation that a great power has risen to a hegemonic position about every eighty to one hundred years. Using

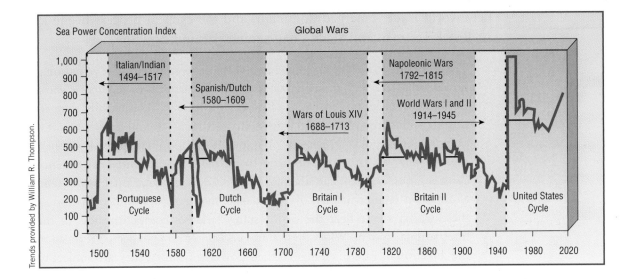

FIGURE 7.5

THE LONG CYCLE OF GLOBAL LEADERSHIP AND GLOBAL WAR, 1494–2020 Over the past five hundred years, five great powers have risen to control the global system, but in time each former hegemonic leader's top status eventually slipped and a new rival surfaced and waged a global war in an effort to become the next global leader. The troubling question is whether this long cycle of war can be broken in the future when U.S. leadership is eventually challenged by a rising military rival such as China.

as a measure of dominance the possession of disproportionate sea power, we observe the rise of a single hegemon regularly appearing after particular hegemonic wars (see Figure 7.5). Portugal and the Netherlands rose at the beginning of the sixteenth and seventeenth centuries, respectively; Britain climbed to dominance at the beginning of both the eighteenth and nineteenth centuries; and the United States became a world leader at the end of World War II and regained its position of global supremacy after the Cold War ended in 1991.

During their reigns, these hegemonic powers monopolized military power and trade and determined the system's rules. Yet no previous hegemonic power has retained its top-dog position perpetually (see Table 3.1). "The best instituted governments," observed British political philosopher Henry St. John in 1738, "carry in them the seeds of their destruction: and, though they grow and improve for a time, they will soon tend visibly to their dissolution. Every hour they live is an hour the less that they have to live." In each cycle, overcommitments, the costs of empire, and ultimately the appearance of rivals led to the delegitimation of the hegemon's authority and to the deconcentration of power globally. As challengers to the hegemon's rule grew in strength, a "global war" has erupted after a long period of peace in each century since 1400. At the conclusion of each previous general war, a new world leader emerged dominant, and the cyclical process began anew. As Brock Tessman and Steve Chan summarize and explain:

> The theory of power cycles contends that the growth and decline of national power holds the key to understanding the occurrence of extensive wars. Certain critical points in a state's power trajectory are especially dangerous occasions for such armed clashes [from which we can] derive expectations about the risk propensity of states during different periods in their power cycle....Critical points tend to incline states to initiate deterrence confrontations and escalate them to war....Changes in national power tend to follow a regular pattern of ascendance, maturation, and decline and... these trajectories reflect the major states' relative competitiveness in the international system. When these states encounter an unexpected reversal in the direction or rate of change in their power trajectory, they are subject to various psychological impulses or judgmental challenges that increase the danger of extensive wars (Tessman and Chan 2004, p. 131).

Such deterministic theories have intuitive appeal. It seems plausible, for instance, that just as long-term downswings and recoveries in business cycles profoundly affect subsequent behaviors and conditions, wars will produce after effects that may last for generations. The idea that a country at war will become exhausted and lose its enthusiasm for another war, but only for a time, is known as the *war weariness hypothesis* (Blainey 1988). Italian historian Luigi da Porto expresses one version: "Peace brings riches; riches bring pride; pride brings anger; anger brings war; war brings poverty; poverty brings humanity; humanity brings peace; peace, as I have said, brings riches, and so the world's affairs go round." Because it takes time to move through these stages, alternating periods of enthusiasm for war and weariness of war appear to be influenced by learning and forgetting over time.

war weariness hypothesis
the proposition that fighting a major war is costly in terms of lost lives and income, and these costs greatly reduce a country's tolerance for undertaking another war until enough time passes to lose memory of those costs.

ARMED AGGRESSION AND ITS FUTURE

You have now inspected three trends in the major types of armed aggression in the world: wars between states, civil wars within states, and global terrorism. Some of these trends, you have noticed, are promising. War between states is disappearing, and this inspires hope among optimists that it will vanish from human history. As security studies experts hopefully predict, "Unlike breathing, eating or sex, war is not something that is somehow required by the human condition or by the forces of history. Accordingly, war can shrivel up and disappear, and it seems to be in the process of doing so" (Mueller 2004, p. 4).

However, that threat remains, and because another major war between states could occur again, all of humanity is endangered. War inside states is increasing in frequency and death rates, and this trend in the growth and expansion of civil wars threatens everyone in the borderless globalized world. And, of course, the specter of international terrorism casts a very dark shadow over the world's future.

There is no sure guide to what the future will hold. But the sad news is that your life and livelihood are certain to be threatened by the continuing onset of armed aggression. That threat imperils the future and affects *all* other aspects of world politics—which is why much of world history is written about the causes and consequences of armed aggression from the vantage point of all peoples' and professions' perspectives. As British poet Percy B. Shelley framed it:

> War is the statesman's game, the priest's delight,
> The lawyer's jest, the hired assassin's trade,
> And, to those royal murderers, whose mean thrones
> Are brought by crimes of treachery and gore,
> The bread they eat, the staff on which they lean.

Lucius Annaeus Seneca, a Roman statesman and philosopher in the first century CE, wryly noted that "Of war men ask the outcome, not the cause." Yet in order for us to reduce and possibly eliminate, the plague of armed aggression in the world, it is necessary for us to first understand what drives the occurrence of violent conflict. The correlates of war speak to the correlates of peace. Thus, in this chapter you also have been given the opportunity to examine the many leading causes of armed aggression that theorists have constructed to explain why armed aggression in its various forms erupts.

It is the alternative potential paths to peace, security, and world order that you will next consider. In Chapters 8 and 9, we examine the vision realism advances about dealing with the threat of war, specifically as it deals with arms, military strategy, alliances and the balance of power.

> *Peace, like war, can succeed only where there is a will to enforce it
> and where there is available power to enforce it.*
> —Franklin D. Roosevelt, U.S. President

Take an Online Practice Quiz

www.cengagebrain.com/shop/ISBN/0495802204

Suggested Readings

Bennett, Scott and Allan C. Stam. (2004) *The Behavioral Origins of War*. Ann Arbor: University of Michigan Press.

Combs, Cynthia C. (2010) *Terrorism in the Twenty-First Century*. 6th edition. Upper Saddle River, NJ: Prentice Hall.

Harbom, Lotta & Peter Wallensteen. (2010) "Armed Conflicts, 1946–2009" Journal of Peace Research 47 (No. 4): 501–509.

Kegley, Charles W., ed. (2003) *The New Global Terrorism: Characteristics, Causes, Controls*. Upper Saddle River, NJ: Prentice Hall.

Lemke, Douglas. (2008) "Power Politics and Wars without States" *American Journal of Political Science* 52: 774–786.

Piazza, James A. (2008) "Incubators of Terror: Do Failed and Failing States Promote Transnational Terrorism?" *International Studies Quarterly* 52: 469–488.

Rasler, Karen and William R. Thompson. (2005) *Puzzles of the democratic peace: theory, geopolitics, and the transformation of world politics*. London: Palgrave Macmillan.

CHAPTER 8
THE MILITARY PURSUIT OF POWER THROUGH ARMS AND MILITARY STRATEGY

Throughout history, the decisive factor in the fates of nations has usually been the number, efficiency, and dispositions of fighting forces. Military influence bears a direct relationship to gross national strength; without that, the most exquisite statesmanship is likely to be of limited use.

—F. Clifton German, social scientist

CHAPTER OUTLINE

REALIST APPROACHES TO WAR AND PEACE

POWER IN WORLD POLITICS

The Elements of State Power

Trends in Military Spending

The Changing Character of Power

CONTROVERSY: Does High Military Spending Lower Human Security?

CHANGES IN MILITARY CAPABILITIES

Trends in the Weapons Trade

Trends in Weapons Technology

Military Strategies

COERCIVE DIPLOMACY THROUGH MILITARY INTERVENTION

RIVAL REALIST ROADS TO SECURITY

U.S. Air Force, HO/AP Photo

BULLETS AND BOMBS TO BULLY. Throughout history, countries have been beguiled by bombs as a method for backing their enemies into surrender. Realists regard the prudent use of armed force as a powerful instrument for waging war and projecting military power in world politics. Shown here is one example: the use of air power to compel an adversary without waging a ground war. This method was successfully used by the United States and NATO against Serbia in 1999 and unsuccessfully by Israel in its 2006 war against Hezbollah terrorists in Lebanon.

Imagine yourself someday becoming the next Secretary-General of the United Nations. You would face the awesome responsibility for fulfilling the UN's Charter to preserve world peace. But looking at the globe, you would likely see that many countries are experiencing armed aggression, and that those wars are highly destructive of life and property. Moreover, you undoubtedly would be distressed by the fact that many countries and possibly some transnational terrorist groups now have the capacity to annihilate their enemies with new weapons of mass destruction. And you shudder at the realization that many states are living in constant fear of threats to their security while at the same time these armed actors are increasing the military power in their arsenals.

As a result of the escalating destructive power of modern weapons, you cannot help but to wonder about a globe in which the UN members that are most feverishly arming to increase their capacity to resist external and internal threats to their physical survival and core values are the same countries whose *national security,* or psychological freedom from fear of foreign aggression, seems to be the most rapidly declining. Taking a picture of the pregnant fears circulating the globe, you conclude that as a consequence a true *security dilemma* has been created: The armaments amassed by each state for what they claim to be defensive purposes are seen by others as threatening, and this has driven the alarmed competitors to undertake, as counter-measures, additional military buildups—with the result that the arming states' insecurities are increasing even though their arms are increasing. What course should you counsel the UN's members to pursue in order to escape the dilemma of rising insecurity in which they have imprisoned themselves?

Alas, your options may be limited and your advice ignored. Why? Because when the topic of war and peace is debated, and in periods when international tension is high, policy makers (and theorists) turn to realist theory for guidance.

> *The adversaries of the world are not in conflict because they are armed.*
> *They are armed because they are in conflict and have not yet learned*
> *peaceful ways to resolve their conflicting interests.*
>
> — Richard M. Nixon, U.S. President

REALIST APPROACHES TO WAR AND PEACE

Nearly all states continue to conclude that the anarchical global system requires them, of necessity, to rely on *self-help* to depend only on themselves for security. They have been schooled in the lessons constructed from *realism*—the school of thought that teaches that the drive for power and the domination of others for self-advantage is a universal and permanent motive throughout world history. For this reason, most states follow the realist roads to national and international security. This worldview or *paradigm* for organizing perceptions pictures the available and practical choices for states primarily among three time-honored options: (1) arming themselves, (2) forming or severing alliances with other countries, or (3) constructing strategies for controlling their destinies through military approaches and *coercive diplomacy,* such as acts of military intervention that target their enemies.

coercive diplomacy
the use of threats or limited armed force to persuade an adversary to alter its foreign and/ or domestic policies.

In this chapter, you will explore states' efforts to follow the realist recipes for reducing threats to their national security. In the spirit of seventeenth-century English philosopher Thomas Hobbes, who viewed the natural human condition as one of "war of all against all" and advised that successful states are those that hold the "posture of Gladiators; having their weapons pointing, and their eyes fixed on one another," this chapter introduces the major trends in military spending, the arms trade, and weapons technology that countries are relying on to militarily exercise influence and deter attacks from potential enemies.

The place to begin is to underscore the high place of *power* that realists put in the equation that they believe has, throughout history, driven world politics. National security is truly a paramount priority for the policy makers responsible for constructing their country's foreign policy agendas. Because the threat of armed aggression is ever present, realism recommends that war be placed at the very top of a state's concerns, and that to contain dangers, the pursuit of power must be prioritized above all others. As Table 8.1 demonstrates, this emphasis is part and parcel of a much broader range of foreign policy recommendations realists embrace to chart what this theoretical tradition believes to be the safest routes to national and international security. Keep this larger menu for choice and the premises on which it rests in mind as you consider the military methods that realists emphasize in this chapter (and the premium adherence that realists place on alliances and the balance of power considered in Chapter 9).

POWER IN WORLD POLITICS

Realist theorists far back in antiquity have based their thinking and policy recommendations on the belief that all people and states seek power. Even texts such as the Bible seem to reflect this assumption, as it observes and warns that people seem born to sin, and one of their inalterable compulsions

Table 8.1   Realist Roads to Security: Premises and Policy Recommendations

Premises	Policy Prescriptions
If you want peace, prepare for war.	Prepare for war
No state is to be trusted further than its national interest.	Remain vigilant
Standards of right and wrong apply to individuals but not states; in world affairs amoral actions are sometimes necessary for security.	Avoid moralism
Isolationism is not an alternative to active global involvement.	Remain involved and actively intervene
Strive to increase military capabilities and fight rather than submit to subordination.	Protect with arms
Do not let any other state or coalition of states become predominant.	Preserve the balance of power
Negotiate agreements with competitors to maintain a favorable military balance.	Prevent arms races from resulting in military inferiority with rivals

Realist Picture of the Global Environment

Primary global condition: Anarchy; or the absence of authoritative governing institutions

Probability of system change/reform: Low, except in response to extraordinary events such as 9/11

Primary transnational actors: States, and especially great powers

Principal actor goals: Power over others, self-preservation, and physical security

Predominant pattern of actor interaction: Competition and conflict

Pervasive concern: National security

Prevalent state priorities: Acquiring military capabilities

Popular state practice: Use of armed force for coercive diplomacy

is the drive for power to dominate those with whom they come into contact. That said, this abstraction called *power,* which realists assume to be humans' and states' primary objective, defies precise definition. Constructivists recognize that in the broadest sense, power is usually interpreted as the political capacity of one actor to exercise influence over another actor to the first actor's benefit.

Most leaders follow *realpolitik* and operate from the traditional construction that conceives of power as a combination of factors that gives states the capability to promote national interests, to win in international bargaining, and to shape the rules governing interaction in the global system. However, beyond the semantic definition of power as *politics*—the exercise of influence to control others—power is an ambiguous concept (see Kadera and Sorokin 2004), and difficult to measure. A dictionary definition begs the question: What factors most enable an actor to control or coerce another?

If we view power as the means to control when *conflicts* or disputes over incompatible interests occur, it is reasonable to ask: Who is stronger and who is weaker? The answer to this question may predict which party will get its way and which will be forced to make concessions. These considerations invite the more fundamental question, "What empowers states to achieve their goals?"

The Elements of State Power

To estimate the comparative power of states, analysts usually rank countries according to the capabilities or resources presumed necessary to achieve influence over others. As former Secretary of State Condolezza Rice observed, "Power is nothing unless you can turn it into influence." For such purposes, multiple factors (most significantly, military and economic capability) measure countries' relative *power potential*. If we could compare each state's total capabilities, according to this logic, we could then rank them by their relative ability to draw on these resources to exercise influence. Such a ranking would reveal the global system's hierarchy of power, differentiating the strong from the weak, the great from the marginal.

power potential
the capabilities or resources held by a state that are considered necessary to its asserting influence over others.

Of all the components of state power potential, realists see military capability as the central element. Realist theory maintains that the ability to coerce militarily is more important than the ability to reward favors or to buy concessions. Realists therefore reject the view of liberal strategic thinkers who maintain that under conditions of *globalization* linking countries economically, politically, and culturally in webs of interdependence, economic resources are increasingly more critical to national strength and security than are military capabilities (Nye 2008).

Following traditional thinking, one way to estimate the power potential of states is to compare the extent to which they spend money on acquiring military capabilities. On this index, the United States is the undisputed military powerhouse in the world, spending for defense at a feverish pace that is leaving all other countries far behind. Figure 8.1 shows the trend in U.S. defense budgets over six decades that has made America unsurpassed in military spending: The United States' military spending accounted for 43 percent of the world total in 2009, followed by China with 6.6 percent, France with 4.2 percent, and the United Kingdom with 3.8 percent (SIPRI 2010).

Power potential also derives from factors other than military expenditures. Among the so-called elements of power, analysts also consider such capabilities as the relative size of a state's economy, its population and territorial size,

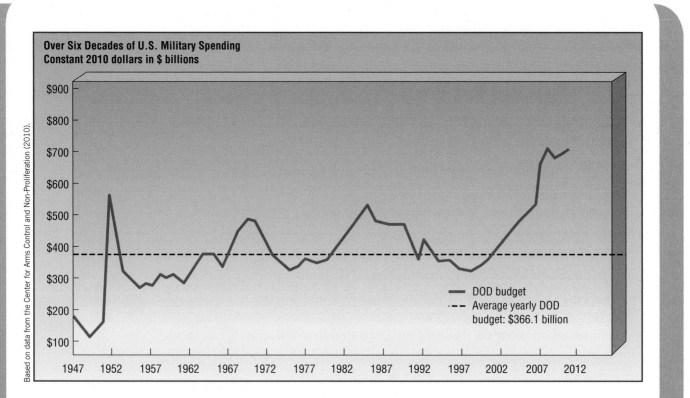

Based on data from the Center for Arms Control and Non-Proliferation (2010).

FIGURE 8.1

OVER SIX DECADES OF U.S. MILITARY SPENDING America's military expenditures have been rising rapidly since 1999, and are at the highest level in real terms since World War II. This commitment to militarization is the principal reason the United States is regarded as a true hegemonic superpower, without rival. In 2011, U.S. military spending is scheduled to climb again and includes $548.9 billion in base budget, which excludes nuclear expenditures, plus $159.3 billion in Overseas Contingency Operations to fight the wars in Afghanistan and Iraq. This brings the U.S. defense budget to $708.3 billion in 2011, a 2.1 percent increase over the prior year (Olson 2010).

geographic position, raw materials, technological capacity, political culture and values, efficiency of governmental decision making, volume of trade, educational level, national morale, and internal solidarity. For example, if power potential is measured by territorial size, Russia, which is twice as large as its closest rivals (Canada, China, the United States, Brazil, and Australia, in that order), would be the globe's most powerful country. Likewise, if power is measured by the UN's projections for countries' populations by the year 2025, China, India, the United States, Indonesia, Pakistan, Nigeria, and Brazil, in that order, would be the most powerful. In a similar comparison, the rankings of countries' expenditures on research and development (as a percentage of GDP) to fund future economic growth and military strength would rank Israel, Sweden, Finland, Japan, Switzerland, the United States,

Denmark, Germany, Austria, Australia, and Canada as the countries with the brightest future (WDI 2010, pp. 340–342). Clearly, strength is relative. The leading countries in some dimensions of power potential are not leaders in others because power comes in many forms.

Thus, there is little consensus on how best to weigh the various factors that contribute to military capability and national power. That is, there is no agreement as to what their relative importance should be in making comparisons, or what conditions affect the power potential of each factor. Consider the divergent pictures of the global hierarchy that emerge when the great powers' relative capabilities are ranked in other categories that realists also define as especially important, such as the size of each state's economy and/or armed forces (see Maps 8.1 and 8.2).

Part of the difficulty of defining the elements of power is that their potential impact depends on the circumstances (in a bargaining situation between conflicting actors, for example) and especially on how leaders perceive those circumstances. Such judgments are subjective, as power ratios are not strictly products of measured capabilities. Perceptions also matter (see Chapter 6).

In addition, power is not a tangible commodity that states can acquire. It has meaning only in relative terms. Power is relational: A state can have power over some other actor only when it can prevail over that actor. Both actual and perceived strength determine who wins a political contest. To make a difference, an adversary must know its enemy's capabilities and its willingness to mobilize those capabilities for coercive purposes. Intentions—especially perceptions of them—are critically important when making threats. The mere possession of weapons does not increase a state's power if its adversaries do not believe it will use them or if they are willing to suffer huge damages to prevail.

Historically, those with the largest arsenals have not necessarily triumphed in political conflicts. Weaker states often successfully resist pressure from their military superiors. In fact, since 1950 weak states have won more than half of all *asymmetric wars* between belligerents of vastly unequal military strength. This is in part because the weaker party has a greater interest in surviving, and that greater interest, rather than relative military capabilities, is the major deciding factor in wars between the strong and weak (Arreguín-Toft 2006).

There are many examples of weak transnational actors prevailing in armed conflicts with significantly stronger opponents. Although Vietnam was weak in the conventional military sense, it succeeded against a vastly stronger France and, later, the United States. Similarly, United States' superior military power did not prevent North Korea's seizure of the USS *Pueblo* in 1968, Iran's taking

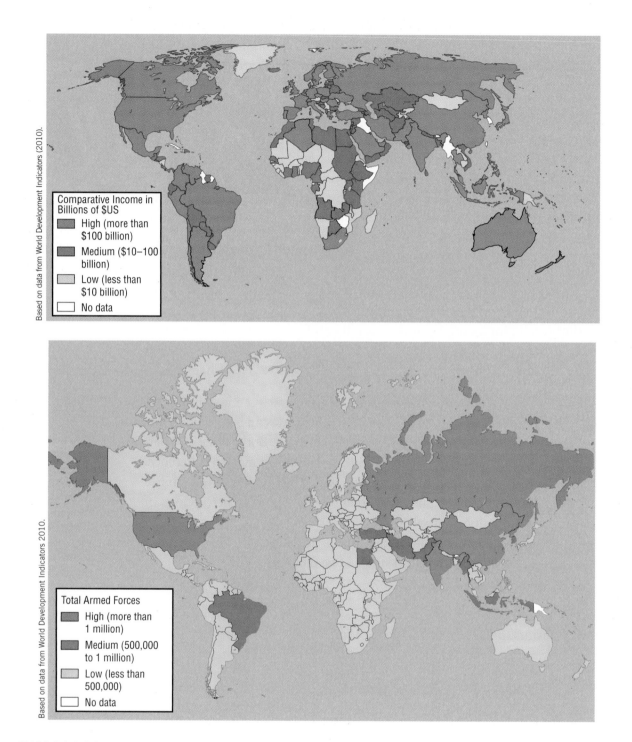

Based on data from World Development Indicators (2010).

Comparative Income in Billions of $US
- High (more than $100 billion)
- Medium ($10–100 billion)
- Low (less than $10 billion)
- No data

Based on data from World Development Indicators 2010.

Total Armed Forces
- High (more than 1 million)
- Medium (500,000 to 1 million)
- Low (less than 500,000)
- No data

MAPS 8.1 & 8.2

TWO MEASURES OF POWER POTENTIAL: STATE WEALTH AND SIZE OF NATIONAL ARMIES **The map on top measures gross national income (GNI) across countries to estimate the differences in national wealth that contribute to state power, and the distribution categorizes differences in the size of states' economies that separate the rich from the poor (and the strong from the weak). Another measure of power projection is the number of uniform personnel in states' armies, navies, and air forces. The map on the bottom classifies the varying size of each country's armed forces available for military operations.**

of American diplomats as hostages a decade later, or the Al Qaeda terrorist network's 9/11 attack. Indeed, after June 2004, the capacity of a quasi-sovereign Iraq to move in directions that the U.S. superpower objected to but could not control underscored the weakness of superior military force in interstate bargaining (L. Diamond 2005). The Soviet Union's inability, prior to its disintegration, to control political events in Afghanistan, Eastern Europe, or even among its own constituent republics (despite an awesome weapons arsenal) shows that the impotence of military power is not particular to the United States. History is replete with examples of small countries that won wars or defended their independence against much more militarily powerful enemies. Consider the seventeenth century, for example, with Switzerland against the Hapsburg Empire, the Netherlands against Spain, and Greece against the Ottomans. In each case, intangible factors such as the will of the target population to resist a more powerful army and their willingness to die to defend the homeland were key elements in the capacity of each of these weaker countries to defend itself against a much stronger military force. Great Britain reluctantly recognized this factor in 1781 when it concluded that the price of reclaiming the far-weaker American colonies was too great.

Nonetheless, the quest for security through arms and the realist belief in military force remain widespread. Most security analysts believe that this is because military capability is a prerequisite to the successful exercise of coercive diplomacy through the threat of limited force. Perhaps this conviction is what inspired former U.S. President George W. Bush to assert that "a dangerous and uncertain world requires America to have a sharpened sword."

Trends in Military Spending

Military power is central in leaders' concepts of national security, and even though the end of the Cold War reduced tensions worldwide and therefore the need for military preparations, world military spending has risen to $1.53 trillion in 2009, which represents a 6 percent increase since 2008 and a 49 percent increase since 2000. This staggering all-time high is equal to 2.7 percent of global gross domestic product, or $224 for each person in the world (SIPRI 2010). The world is spending over $2,912,861 each *minute* for military preparations.

Historically, rich countries have spent the most money on arms acquisitions, and this pattern has continued. As 2010 began, the Global North was spending $1125 billion for defense, in contrast with the developing Global South's $345 billion. Thus, the high-income developed countries' share of the world total was about 77 percent. However, when measured against other factors, the differences became clearer. The Global North's average military expenditure constituted 2.6 percent of GDP, whereas the Global South spent an average 2.0 percent—at a relatively greater sacrifice of funding to promote human development and economic growth among the poor (WDI 2010, p. 232, 318).

In addition, these two groups' military spending levels are converging over time. Figure 8.2 reveals that the Global South's military expenditure in 1961 was about 7 percent of the world total, but by 2010 its share had increased to 23 percent (WDI 2010, p. 318). This trend indicates that poor states are copying the past costly military budget habits of the wealthiest states.

Since 1945, only a handful of states have borne crushing military costs. The others have gained a relative competitive edge by investing in research on the development of goods to export abroad, while conserving resources by relying on allies and global institutions to provide defense against potential threats. The United States is an exception. While accounting for 42 percent of world military expenditures in 2009 the United States has also been the dominant investor in research and development funding, with its military preparation funding "accounting for the majority of U.S. federal R&D

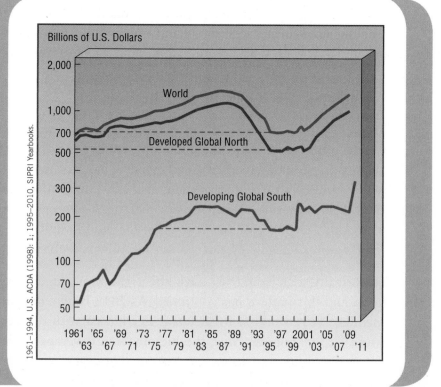

FIGURE 8.2

CHANGES IN THE LEVEL OF MILITARY EXPENDITURES SINCE 1960 Global military budgets have fluctuated since 1960, with total expenditures worldwide peaking in 1987, after which they fell about a third until the 9/11 terrorist attacks. As the trend shows, the military budget of the Global South's developing countries peaked in a 1982–1986 plateau, then declined before rising again to about 23 percent of the world total by the start of 2010.

spending" (Battelle 2009, p. 16; WDI 2010). In contrast, European countries invest heavily in the development of new technologies for consumers and civilians at home and abroad, and Japan concentrates almost all of its research expenditures on the development of products that have very little to do with military capabilities (SIPRI 2007). In comparative terms, the United States is slipping by not keeping up with its great power competitors and is now facing a "creativity crisis" (Florida 2007; Friedman 2005b) in education and science.

The Changing Character of Power

Military expenditures incur *opportunity costs*—when what is gained for one purpose is lost for other purposes—so that any particular choice means that the cost of some lost opportunity must be paid. Military spending, for example, retards economic growth and creates fiscal deficits. The substantial costs of defense can erode national welfare—what policy makers hope to defend with military might. As political scientist Richard Rosecrance notes, "States can afford more 'butter' if they need fewer 'guns.' The two objectives sometimes represent trade-offs: The achievement of one may diminish the realization of the other" (see Controversy: Does High Military Spending Lower Human Security?).

opportunity cost
the sacrifices that sometimes results when the decision to select one option means that the opportunity to realize gains from another options is lost.

Many analysts now argue that "the sources of power are, in general, moving away from the emphasis on military force and conquest that marked earlier eras. In assessing international power today, factors such as technology, external respect and reputation, education, and economic growth are becoming more important" (Nye 2005, p. 55). In part, this shift is because military force has often proven ineffectual, notably against revisionist states and violent transnational terrorist groups resisting pressure from abroad. Arguably, intelligence and communications are more critical in fighting counterterrorism than are a country's military capabilities. Moreover, awareness of the importance of economic competitiveness, environmental protection, and human development to a country's standing in the world has directed increased attention to the nonmilitary underpinnings of national security.

soft power
the capacity to command global influence when a country's culture, ideas, and institutions are valued by most other countries.

These resources provide what is known as *soft power*—the ability to exercise international influence that is increased when a country's values and conduct are respected throughout the world. Unlike so-called *hard power* associated with military capabilities, soft power is "the ability to achieve goals through attraction rather than coercion . . . by convincing others to follow or getting them to agree to norms and institutions that produce the desired behavior"

hard power
the ability to exercise international influence by means of a country's military capabilities.

CONTROVERSY:

DOES HIGH MILITARY SPENDING LOWER HUMAN SECURITY?

Politics requires making hard choices about priorities and about how public funds should be spent. One such difficult choice is between "guns versus butter"—how to allocate scarce finances for military preparedness as opposed to meeting the human needs of citizens and enabling them to live a secure and long life. The former category looks to arms for *national security,* and the latter stresses *human security.* Neither goal can be pursued without making some sacrifice for the realization of the other.

"Guns versus butter" is a serious controversy in every country, and different countries deal with it in different ways. That difference is captured by the range in states' willingness to pay a heavy burden for defense—by grouping states according to the share of gross domestic product (GDP) they devote to the military and then juxtaposing this relative burden with their GDP. The ***relative burden of military spending,*** the ratio of defense spending to GDP, is the customary way to measure the sacrifices required by military spending. The global trend shows that the share of resources used for military purposes has increased steadily since 2000, and, on average, the military burden now corresponds to 2.7 percent of world GDP (SIPRI 2010). As the map shows, wide variations exist, with many countries allocating high proportions of their total GDP to defense and others spending their wealth to enhance human security.

Indeed, some comparatively wealthy states (Kuwait, Israel, and Brunei) bear a heavy burden, whereas other states that provide a high average income for their citizens (Japan, Austria, and Luxembourg) have a low

Based on data from the World Development Indicators (2010).

Military Expenditures as a Percentage of GDP

- High (more than 5%)
- Medium (2% to 5%)
- Low (less than 2%)
- No data

MAP 8.3

Military Expenditures as a Percentage of GDP

DOES HIGH MILITARY SPENDING LOWER HUMAN SECURITY?
(Continued)

defense burden. Likewise, the citizens of some very poor countries (Sierra Leone, Mozambique, and Chad) are heavily burdened, whereas those of others (Bhutan and Zaire) are not. It is therefore difficult to generalize about the precise relationship between a country's defense burden and its citizens' standard of living, human development, or stage of development. That said, a simple look at this map reveals that the majority of the countries with the highest military burden are also the countries that are experiencing the highest levels of armed aggression, or are located in regions with huge security problems, such as the Middle East and Africa (recall Chapter 7).

How much should a country sacrifice for national security? To many realists, the price is never too high. However, others caution that leaders should take heed of U.S. President Dwight Eisenhower's warning: "The world in arms is not spending money alone. It is spending the sweat of its children." These skeptics of high military spending believe the high costs can easily reduce citizens' human security. "It is important to remember that every defense dollar spent to over-insure against a remote or diminishing risk," cautions U.S. Secretary of Defense Robert Gates, "is a dollar not available to take care of our people, reset the force, win the wars we are in, and improve capabilities in areas where we are underinvested and potentially vulnerable." The consequences for the United States are not encouraging. Consider how, given the U.S. choice to prioritize military spending, the United States ranks on various nonmilitary measures of human security.

How the U.S. Ranks in the World	
Indicator	Rank
GNI for each person	1
Unemployment rate (% of labor force)	37
Female economic activity rate (aged 15 and older)	48
Human development (HDI)	4
Gender inequality	37
Life expectancy	28
Carbon dioxide emissions	2
Under five mortality rate	30
Number of physicians per person	37
Primary public education expenditures for each student	16
Total health expenditures (% of GDP)	1

Source: World Development Indicators (2010); Human Development Report (2010).

(continued)

DOES HIGH MILITARY SPENDING LOWER HUMAN SECURITY?
(Continued)

These rankings raise serious questions about the true costs of national security. The choices in balancing the need for defense against the need to provide for the common welfare are difficult because they entail a necessary trade-off between competing values. For this reason, military-spending decisions are highly controversial everywhere.

WHAT DO YOU THINK?

- If you were a head of state, what budget priorities would you propose for your country's national security and your citizens' human security?

- How would you reconcile the need for defense with the need to provide for the common welfare?

- What insights do realism, liberalism, and constructivism each give for defining the concept of security? What definition of security might feminist theory provide?

relative burden of military spending
a measure of the economic burden of military activities calculated by the share of each state's gross domestic product allocated to military expenditures.

(Keohane and Nye 1998, p. 86). In today's so-called information age, the relative importance of soft power is growing.

How people spend their money reveals their values. Similarly, how governments allocate their revenues reveals their priorities. Examination of national budgets discloses an unmistakable pattern: Although the sources of global political power may be changing, many states continue to seek security by spending substantial portions of their national treasures on arms.

> *The problem in defense spending is to figure out how far you should go without destroying from within what you are trying to defend from without.*
>
> —Dwight D. Eisenhower, U.S. President

CHANGES IN MILITARY CAPABILITIES

The growing militarization of the United States, the other great powers, and now mobilized nonstate terrorist movements has altered the global distribution of military capabilities. Part of the reason is that weapons production capabilities are more widespread than ever, with even Global South countries and terrorist organizations participating in the business of manufacturing modern aircraft, tanks, and missiles. A parallel change in the open and clandestine (secret) arms market and in the destructiveness of modern weapons has accelerated the spread of military capabilities around the world. Furthermore, as a trend in the arms industry, which has increased dramatically as a result of the Iraq war, the growth of *private military services* enhances military capabilities, as it allows governments to conduct operations with fewer troops than would otherwise be needed.

Trends in the Weapons Trade

During the Cold War, many states sought to increase their security through the purchase of arms produced by suppliers eagerly seeking allies and profits from exports. In 1961, the world arms trade was valued at $4 billion. Thereafter, the traffic in arms imports climbed rapidly and peaked in 1987 at $82 billion (U.S. ACDA 1997, pp. 10, 100). The end of the Cold War did not end the arms trade, however. Since 1991, when the Cold War ended, and continuing throughout the era of global terrorism that began on 9/11, the total value of all international arms transfers was over $438 billion (SIPRI 2010).

The global arms trade has fueled the dispersion of military capability worldwide. Weapons delivered in 2009 included 3,057 armored vehicles, 445 artillery pieces, 10,325 combat aircraft, 2,742 missiles, 667 air defense systems, and a large number of warships, submarines, and other technologically advanced weapons systems (SIPRI 2010).

The major recipients of all global arms shipments remain heavily concentrated in a subset of Global South and Global East arms purchasers. Between 2005 and 2009, China, India, South Korea, the United Arab Emirates, Singapore, Algeria, and Pakistan were seven of the top ten arms recipients. China was the largest recipient of global weapons transfers, importing $10.9 billion in arms during that period (SIPRI 2010). The stream of weapons to these insecure and eager buyers with money to spend is not likely to end soon. To promote what it called a "security dialogue" in the Persian Gulf, the United States proposed transferring $63 billion in new arms sales to the Middle East over the next ten years (*The Nation*, September 10-17, 2007, p. 8).

The regional distribution of arms deliveries seems to follow trends in the location of the world's flash points. Countries in the Middle East accounted for 12 percent of world arms imports in 2009 (WDI 2010). The increasing arms shipments this area has received are due in part to the heightened fears about national security throughout the troubled region, as reflected by the United States' devotion of 30 percent of its deliveries to this region. Significantly, the United Arab Emirates (UAE) has increased its demand for conventional weapons, tying with South Korea as the third largest arms recipient and commanding a 6 percent share of global arms imports. However, the Middle East is not alone as a troubled and insecure region. Asia is also living in a shadow of fear, and it again ranks first in the value of arms imports. China, India, and

private military services
the outsourcing of activities of a military-specific nature to private companies, such as armed security, equipment maintenance, IT services, logistics, and intelligence services.

South Korea—all Asian countries—are three of the five largest importers for the 2005–2009 period (SIPRI 2010).

Each state's proportionate share of total weapons purchases is likely to change, depending on the location of the globe's next hot spots and each country's involvement in them. Similarly, aggregate levels of world arms imports are likely to be influenced by the performance of each state in the global economy. Weapon imports fluctuate sharply from year to year—not only in unstable regions where the risks of civil war and terrorism are high and where pairs of enemy states are engaged in arms races, but also in countries where periods of economic growth make financial resources available for arms purchases.

Along with changing demands of arms importers, changes in the activities of arms suppliers are also important. During the Cold War, the superpowers dominated the arms export market. Between 1975 and 1989, the United States-Soviet share of global arms exports varied between one-half and three-fourths, and the United States alone had cornered 40 percent of the world arms export market when the Cold War ended (U.S. ACDA 1997). In that period, the two superpowers together "supplied an estimated $325 billion worth of arms and ammunition to the Third World" (Klare 1994, p. 139). In the post-9/11 global war on terrorism, the United States increased its worldwide supply of weapons to countries that agreed to be partners in the "coalition of the willing" in wars in Afghanistan and Iraq. Interestingly, it is still these two superpowers, the United States and Russia, that dominate the arms export market, supplying 30 and 23 percent of all conventional weapons exports, respectively, between 2005 and 2009 (SIPRI 2010). Yet while countries themselves are typically identified as global suppliers of arms, in some countries private companies are major producers of weapons and compete in the profitable arms marketplace (see Table 8.2). The 2008 arms sales of BAE Systems, a British-based company, were greater than the GDPs of 105 countries that same year. The sales of weapons by Lockheed Martin (at almost $30 billion) exceeded by $4 billion the total U.S. development assistance budget.

Another development in the post–Cold War era, which has been likened to modern-day mercenaries, is the growth in companies that provide private military services for hire on the global market. While the outsourcing of military-like activities enables governments "to maintain high levels of military operations with relatively small numbers of troops," relying on private contractors in war zones may compromise democratic accountability and the state's monopoly on the use of force, and it may also raise issues about legal status (SIPRI 2008). This dilemma was evident during the war in Iraq when

Table 8.2   Sellers of Security or Merchants of Death? Top 20 Arms-Producing Companies

Rank		Arms Sales ($billions)		
2008	2007	Company (Country)	2008	2007
1	2	BAE Systems (UK)	32.4	29.9
2	3	Lockheed Martin (USA)	29.8	29.4
3	1	Boeing (USA)	29.2	30.5
4	4	Northrop Grumman (USA)	26.1	24.6
5	5	General Dynamics (USA)	22.8	21.5
6	6	Raytheon (USA)	21.3	19.5
7	7	EADS (W.Europe)	17.9	13.1
8	9	Finmeccanica (Italy)	13.0	9.9
9	8	L-3 Communications (USA)	12.2	11.2
10	10	Thales (France)	10.8	9.4
11	11	United Technologies (USA)	9.9	8.8
12	12	SAIC (USA)	7.4	6.3
13	16	KBR (USA)	5.7	5.0
14	13	Computer Sciences Corp. (USA)	5.7	5.4
15	15	Honeywell (USA)	5.3	5.0
16	19	ITT Corporation (USA)	5.2	3.9
17	17	Rolls Royce (UK)	4.7	4.6
18	23	Almaz-Antei (Russia)	4.3	2.8
19	25	AM General (USA)	4.1	2.7
20	N	Navistar (USA)	3.9	3.7

Data Source: SIPRI 2010

employees of the Blackwater security firm killed seventeen Iraqi civilians and did not appear to be subject to either Iraqi, U.S., civilian, or military law.

Motives for the Arms Trade   As Assistant Defense Secretary during the Reagan administration, Lawrence Korb lamented that "The brakes are off. . . . There is no coherent policy on the transfer of arms. It has become a money game; an absurd spiral in which [the United States] exports arms only to have to develop more sophisticated ones to counter those spread out all over the world. . . . It is a frightening trend that undermines American moral authority." Economic gain continues to be an important rationale for foreign military sales because

Li Zhiping/XinHua/Xinhua Press/CORBIS

A WORLD AWASH WITH GUNS The sale of arms is a big trans-border business. Part of its growth is because the line between legal and illegal trades is blurred—there is a vibrant black market for the sale of arms to illicit groups, though "almost every firearm on the black market was originally traded legally" (de Soysa et al. 2009, p. 88). Shown here is an example of the thriving international trade in weapons: buyers at one of the many "arms bazaars" in the global weapons marketplace. There are over 875 million firearms in circulation, and as Nobel Laureate Oscar Arias Sanchez sadly noted, "the greatest percentage of violent deaths occurs from the use of light weapons and small arms."

military-industrial complex
a combination of defense establishments, contractors who supply arms for them, and government agencies that benefit from high military spending, which acts as a lobbying coalition to pressure governments to appropriate large expenditures for military preparedness.

producers sell arms abroad to subsidize their arms production at home. For example, the United States uses arms exports to offset its chronic balance-of-trade deficits and to ensure its lead in the lucrative arms business. The U.S. government routinely assigns thousands of full-time federal employees to promote U.S. arms deals, spending half a billion dollars annually to assist U.S. arms dealers. To cement its share of the arms trade, one-fourth "of all U.S. foreign aid goes to helping the recipients buy United States-produced weapons, equipment, or services" (*Harper's*, October 2005, p. 11). The *military-industrial complex* is widely believed to exercise enormous power over U.S. defense budgets and arms sales agreements. One symptom of the influence of defense contractors is their ability to charge the Pentagon inflated prices for their products. The U.S. government is estimated to overpay by 20 percent for military goods through the Pentagon's prime vendor procurement program, which greased the sale of a deep fat fryer for $5,919, a waffle iron for $1,781, and a toaster for $1,025 (Borenstein 2006; Markoe and Borenstein 2005). It is hardly surprising that arms manufacturers seek to increase their profits, but their corporate greed alarms critics, who worry about the manufacturers' success in lobbying Congress and the Pentagon for high military spending to gain government permission to sell new weapons worldwide.

The same kinds of pressures from military-industrial coalitions are operative in many other countries, and globalization has not weakened established national security practices (Ripsman and Paul 2005). What is more, as a sign of the globalization of arms transfers, defense contractors increasingly sell their products everywhere and push their production into other countries' markets as they consolidate their operations and ownership. As an example, the world's second largest aerospace firm, which sells everything from ballistic missiles to mobile medical units (the European Aeronautic Defense and Company), operates from Columbus, Mississippi, to penetrate the U.S. military market. Another example: *Marine One,* the U.S. president's helicopter, is produced in Britain and Italy in partnership with Lockheed Martin (Donnelly 2005).

The Strategic Consequences of Arms Sales The transfer of arms across borders has produced some unintended and counterproductive consequences. For example, during the Cold War the United States and the Soviet Union thought they could maintain peace by spreading arms to pivotal recipients. Between 1983 and 1987, the United States provided arms to fifty-nine Global South countries, whereas the Soviet Union supplied arms to forty-two (Klare 1990, p. 12). Yet many of the recipients went to war with their neighbors or experienced internal rebellion. Of the top twenty arms importers in 1988, more than half "had governments noted for the frequent use of violence" (Sivard 1991, p. 17). The toll in lives from the wars in the Global South since 1945 exceeds tens of millions of people.

Undoubtedly, the import of such huge arsenals of weapons aided this level of destruction. As the arms exporters "peddle death to the poor," they seldom acknowledge how this scouting for customers contradicts other proclaimed foreign policy goals. For example, while seeking to promote democratization, less democratic countries receive the greatest amounts of U.S. arms (Blanton 2005). Since 2001, less than three-fifths of U.S. arms have been exported to governments classified by Freedom House as "free" (O'Reilly 2005, p. 11), and now four-fifths of the countries that receive U.S. arms are classified by the U.S. State Department as either being undemocratic or having a poor human rights record (Jackson 2007, p. A9).

The inability of arms suppliers to control the uses to which their military hardware will be put is troubling. Friends can become foes, and supplying weapons can backfire—generating what the CIA calls *blowback* to describe what can happen when foreign activities such as covert shipments of arms are

blowback
the propensity for actions undertaken for national security to have the unintended consequence of provoking retaliatory attacks by the target when relations later sour.

THE PROBLEM IS PLANE: THE "FLYING SHAME" IN WEAPONS ACQUISITIONS The United States has increased its weapons acquisition plans, from seventy-one major programs costing $790 billion in 2001 to ninety-five new programs costing over $1.6 trillion in 2007 (Charette 2008). The concern: Who benefits—the American military, the corporate profits of weapons manufacturers, or American taxpayers? Shown here is one widely cited example of weapons procurement abuse. "In March 2008, the V-22 program signed a $10.4 billion multiyear production contract with Bell Boeing for the production of 167 aircraft through 2012, even though aircraft continue to be conditionally accepted with deviations and waivers relating to components such as brakes, landing gear, hydraulic hoses, de-icing systems, and radar altimeters" (O'Rourke 2009, p. 8).

later used in retaliations against the supplier (C. Johnson 2004). The United States learned this painful lesson the hard way. The weapons it shipped to Iraq when Saddam Hussein was fighting Iran in the 1980s were later used against U.S. forces in the Persian Gulf War (Timmerman 1991). This also happened when the Stinger missiles the United States supplied to Taliban forces resisting the Soviet Union's 1979 invasion in Afghanistan fell into the hands of terrorists later opposing the United States. Likewise, in 1982 Great Britain found itself shipping military equipment to Argentina just eight days before Argentina's attack on the British-controlled Falkland Islands; and in 1998 U.S. military technology sold to China was exported to Pakistan, making possible its nuclear weapons test.

Such developments have long-term consequences and are particularly alarming, as in the case of Pakistan, where there is grave concern about the ability of the state to ensure the security of nuclear material. According to Graham Allison, a leading nuclear expert, "The nuclear security of the arsenal is now a lot better than it was. But the unknown variable here is the future of Pakistan itself, because it's not hard to envision a situation in which the state's authority falls apart, and you're not sure who's in control of the weapons, the nuclear labs, the materials" (Sanger 2009b).

Trends in Weapons Technology

The widespread quest for armaments has created a potentially "explosive" global environment. The description is especially apt when we consider not only trends in defense expenditures and the arms trade but also in the destructiveness of modern weapons.

Nuclear Weapons Technological research and development has radically expanded the destructive power of national arsenals. Albert Einstein, the Nobel Prize–winning physicist whose ideas were the basis for the development of nuclear weapons, was alarmed by the threat they posed. He professed uncertainty about the weapons that would be used in a third world war but was confident that in a fourth war they would be "sticks and stones." He warned that inasmuch as "the unleashed power of the atom has changed everything save our modes of thinking we thus drift toward unparalleled catastrophe."

The use of such weapons could not only destroy entire cities and countries but also, conceivably, the world's entire population. The largest "blockbuster" bombs of World War II delivered the power of ten tons of TNT. The atomic bomb that leveled Hiroshima had the power of over 15,000 tons of TNT. Less than twenty years later, the Soviet Union built a nuclear bomb with the explosive force of 57,000,000 tons of TNT. Since 1945, more than 130,000 nuclear warheads had been built, all but 2 percent by the United States (55 percent) and the Soviet Union (43 percent). Most have been dismantled since the 1986 peak, but about 8,500 worldwide remained operational in 2010—with a combined explosive force of at least 1,300,000 Hiroshima atomic bombs. The United States possessed 2,700 deployed warheads; Russia, 4,850; France, 300; China, 240; Britain, 180; Israel, 80–100; Pakistan, 70–90; and India, 60–80. The size of North Korea's nuclear weapons inventory remains uncertain (Bernstein 2010; Norris and Kristensen 2009).

In addition, as many as twenty-one other states (such as Iran and Brazil) or NGO terrorist organizations are widely believed to be seeking to join the nuclear club. The *proliferation* of arms is a serious global concern, because the so-called *Nth country* problem (the addition of new nuclear states) is expected to become an increasing likelihood. Both *horizontal nuclear proliferation* (the increase in the number of nuclear states) and *vertical nuclear proliferation* (increases in the capabilities of existing nuclear powers) are probable.

Consider the successful acquisition of nuclear weapons by India and Pakistan, the conduct of nuclear tests by North Korea, and Iran and Syria's self-proclaimed aims to acquire nuclear weapons. Nuclear proliferation is likely to continue as the incentives to join the nuclear club and acquire missiles and

proliferation
the spread of weapon capabilities from a few to many states in a chain reaction, so that increasing numbers of states gain the ability to launch an attack on other states with devastating (e.g., nuclear) weapons.

Nth country problem
the expansion of additional new nuclear weapon states.

horizontal nuclear proliferation
an increase in the number of states that possess nuclear weapons.

vertical nuclear proliferation
the expansion of the capabilities of existing nuclear powers to inflict increasing destruction with their nuclear weapons.

bombers for their delivery are strong, which is why the threat remains that Argentina, Brazil, Libya, and Taiwan, which once had active nuclear weapons programs, could revive these capabilities to manufacture nuclear weapons. Likewise, there is widespread international concern regarding a previously undisclosed uranium enrichment site in Iran that was revealed in 2009. Though Iran professes that it is pursuing a peaceful nuclear program, the ability for uranium to be enriched from a low level nuclear fuel to one that provides weapons-grade material is seen by many as a serious threat to global and regional security. "Grounded in the tradition of realist and security-based approaches to nuclear proliferation and nuclear deterrence," the rationale behind the decision to acquire nuclear weapons is clear as "nuclear weapons on average and across a broad variety of indicators enhance the security and diplomatic influence of their possessors" (Gartzke and Kroenig 2009, p. 152).

The strong incentive of nonnuclear states to develop weapons similar to those of the existing nuclear club was reflected in the complaint of former French President Charles de Gaulle, who argued that without an independent nuclear capability France could not "command its own destiny." Similarly, in 1960 Britain's Aneurin Bevan asserted that without the bomb Britain would go "naked into the council chambers of the world." This sentiment continues to be reflected today by aspiring nuclear powers. Despite the tightening of sanctions by the United Nations Security Council in reaction to its nuclear and missile tests conducted on May 25, 2009, North Korea resolutely responded that "It has become an absolutely impossible option for (North Korea) to even think about giving up its nuclear weapons" (Fackler 2009, p. A12).

Because of the widespread conviction rooted in realism that military power confers political stature, many countries, such as Iran and North Korea, regard the *Nuclear Nonproliferation Treaty (NPT)* as hypocrisy because it provides a seal of approval to the United States, Russia, China, Britain, and France for possessing nuclear weapons while denying it to all others. The underlying belief that it is acceptable to develop a nuclear capacity for deterrence, political influence, and prestige was expressed in 1999 by Brajesh Mishra, India's national security adviser, when he justified India's acquisition of nuclear weapons by asserting that "India should be granted as much respect and deference by the United States and others as is China today."

Nuclear Nonproliferation Treaty (NPT)
an international agreement that seeks to prevent horizontal proliferation by prohibiting further nuclear weapons sales, acquisitions, or production.

Video: *Shifting Alliances in Iran*

While the underlying demand for nuclear weapons is rather straightforward, aside from economic motivations, it is less clear why nuclear-capable states themselves have contributed to the global spread of nuclear weapons by providing sensitive nuclear assistance to other non-nuclear states. Consider, for example, that Israel built its first nuclear weapon just two years after receiving sensitive nuclear assistance from France in the early 1960s. Similarly, after receiving assistance from China in the early 1980s with its nuclear program, Pakistan constructed its first nuclear weapon. Pakistani scientist A.Q. Khan operated a black market nuclear proliferation ring in the late 1990s, and this is thought to have aided Libya, Iran, and North Korea in their efforts to develop nuclear weapons. Focusing on the supply side of nuclear proliferation, political scientist Matthew Kroenig identifies three basic conditions under which states are likely to share sensitive nuclear assistance:

> First, the more powerful a state is relative to a potential nuclear recipient, the less likely it is to provide sensitive nuclear assistance. Second, states are more likely to provide sensitive nuclear assistance to states with which they share a common enemy. Third, states that are less vulnerable to superpower pressure are more likely to provide sensitive nuclear assistance (Kroenig 2009, p. 114).

Video: *Shifting Alliances in Iran*

Animated Learning Module: *Nonproliferation Treaty*

These strategic characteristics of the supplier provide some insight into the nuclear proliferation problem, which is also exacerbated by the widespread availability of materials needed to make a nuclear weapon. This is partly because of the widespread use of nuclear technology for generating electricity. Today, almost 450 nuclear-power reactors are in operation in seventy countries throughout the world. The number of new operational nuclear reactors is certain to increase because almost eighty new nuclear reactors are now under construction or planned.

In addition to spreading nuclear know-how, states could choose to reprocess the uranium and plutonium, which power plants produce as waste, for clandestine nuclear weapons production. Commercial reprocessing reactors are producing enough plutonium to make as many as 40,000 nuclear weapons. Conversion of peacetime nuclear energy programs to military purposes can occur either overtly or, as in the case of India and Pakistan, covertly.

KRT TV/AP Photo

A ROGUE NUCLEAR POWER Shown here is the launch of a missile in Musudan-ri, North Korea on April 5, 2009. A few weeks later, on May 25, North Korea conducted its second nuclear test in defiance of the United Nations. The United States, along with Russia, China, and other leading nations, called on North Korea to resume the so-called six-party talks that aimed to provide fuel and other benefits to North Korea if it dismantled its nuclear program. North Korea responded by threatening that "If the U.S. and its followers infringe upon our republic's sovereignty even a bit, our military and people will launch a 100- or 1,000-fold retaliation with merciless military strike."

nonproliferation regime
rules to contain arms races so that weapons or technology do not spread to states that do not have them.

The safeguards built into the *nonproliferation regime* are simply inadequate to detect and prevent secret nuclear weapons development programs.

It is very unlikely that the nuclear threat will disappear (see Figure 8.3). As Matthew Bunn, editor of *Arms Control Today* explains, "There's not a snow-ball's chance in hell we'll eliminate all nuclear weapons from the face of the earth. That genie is long since out of the bottle and there's no chance of ever getting him back in."

The Revolution in Military Technology and Weapons Delivery Capabilities   Another trend that is making the weapons of war increasingly deadly has been the rapidity of technological refinements that increase the capacity of states to send their weapons great distances with ever-greater accuracy. Missiles can now send

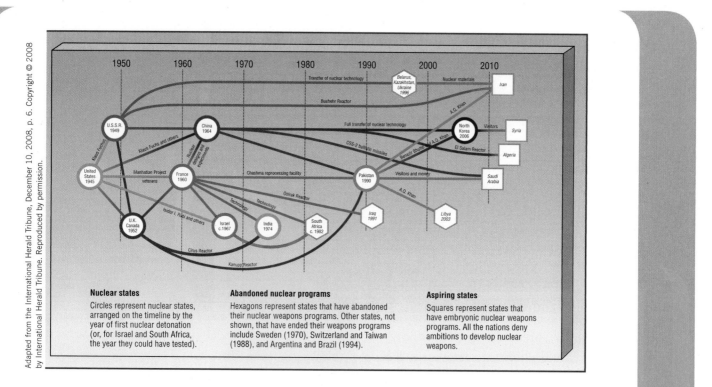

FIGURE 8.3

A CHAIN REACTION OF PROLIFERATION   Since the dawn of the nuclear age, the secrets for making nuclear weapons have spread through either intended transfer, leak, or espionage. The connections depicted above indicate the flow of information and technology, through either one-way or two-way transfers. Today there are five official nuclear states (the United States, Russia, the United Kingdom, China, and France) and four additional defacto nuclear states (India, Pakistan, North Korea, and Israel). Many others are poised to join the club of nuclear weapon powers, as this figure shows. Halting nuclear proliferation continues to be seen as one of the most urgent challenges facing the world, the importance of which was unanimously reaffirmed by the 189 members of the Nuclear Non-Proliferation Treaty at their five-yearly meeting in May 2010.

weapons from as far away as 11,000 miles to within 100 feet of their targets in less than thirty minutes. One example was the development by the United States and Russia of the ability to equip their ballistic missiles with *multiple independently targetable reentry vehicles (MIRVs)*. This allows these Cold War enemies to launch many warheads on a single missile toward different targets simultaneously and accurately. One MIRV U.S. MX Peacekeeper missile could carry ten nuclear warheads—enough to wipe out a city and everything else within a fifty-mile radius. Because the superpowers achieved MIRV capability before completing the START II treaty to ban them, the world's combined nuclear inventory grew nearly three times larger than the number of nuclear warheads previously in existence in spite of ongoing efforts to limit it.

Other technological improvements have led to steady increases in the speed, accuracy, range, and effectiveness of weapons. Laser weapons, nuclear-armed tactical air-to-surface missiles (TASMs), stealth air-launched cruise missiles (ACMs), and antisatellite (ASAT) weapons that can project force in and wage war from outer space have become a part of the military landscape.

For decades, a *firebreak* separated conventional and nuclear wars. The term comes from the barriers of cleared land that firefighters use to keep forest fires from racing out of control. In the context of modern weaponry, it is a psychological barrier whose purpose is to prevent even the most intensive forms of conventional combat from escalating into nuclear war. The danger is growing that the firebreak is being crossed from both directions—by a new generation of near-nuclear conventional weapons capable of levels of violence approximating those of a limited nuclear warhead and by a new generation of near-conventional *strategic weapons* capable of causing destruction similar to that of the most powerful weapons of mass destruction.

The global terrain is being transformed by another sea change in the kinds of arms being developed to wage war: the new high-tech *nonlethal weapons (NLWs)* made possible by the *revolution in military technology (RMT)*. The new generation includes sounds, shocks, and stinks to disperse or incapacitate crowds. One example is the Long Range Acoustic Device (LRAD) that blasts sounds at a deafening 150 decibels to incapacitate everyone within 300 meters by giving them an instant headache. Another example is the U.S. Air Force's "active denial technology" using electromagnetic radiation that penetrates clothing, causing water molecules to vibrate and burn skin tissue. And it's humorous, but true, that the Pentagon has considered various nonlethal chemical weapons to disrupt enemy discipline and morale, including an aphrodisiac chemical weapon "that would make enemy soldiers sexually irresistible to one another" (Hecht 2007).

---

multiple independently targetable reentry vehicles (MIRVs)
a technological innovation permitting many weapons to be delivered from a single missile.

firebreak
the psychological barrier between conventional wars and wars fought with nuclear weapons as well as weapons of mass destruction.

strategic weapons
weapons of mass destruction that are carried on intercontinental ballistic missiles (ICBMs), submarine-launched ballistic missiles (SLBMs), or long-range bombers and are capable of annihilating an enemy state.

nonlethal weapons (NLWs)
the wide array of "soft kill," low-intensity methods of incapacitating an enemy's people, vehicles, communications systems, or entire cities without killing either combatants or noncombatants.

revolution in military technology (RMT)
the sophisticated new weapons technologies that make fighting war without mass armies possible.

More seriously, NLWs already now deploy information-warfare squadrons to protect military computer networks from electronic sneak attacks; energy pulses to knock out or take down enemies without necessarily killing them; biofeedback, beamed electromagnetic and sonic wavelengths that can modify the human behavior of targets (for example, putting people to sleep through electromagnetic heat and magnetic radiation); and underground *smart bombs*, which at a speed of 1,000 feet per second can penetrate a buried bunker and, at the proper millisecond, detonate five hundred pounds of explosive to destroy an adversary's inventory of buried chemical and biological weapons.

The precision and power of today's conventional weapons have expanded exponentially, at precisely the moment when the revolution in military technology is leading to "the end of infantry" in the computer age. Even as the nuclear powers retain the capacity to turn cities into glass, they (and now, terrorist groups) increasingly rely on a variety of new cyberstrategies using information technological innovation to deter and demobilize enemies (see Dombrowski and Gholz 2007). They are turning to *virtual nuclear arsenals* for *deterrence* of an adversary's attack. Examples include such futuristic weapons as the electromagnetic pulse (EMP) bomb, which can be hand-delivered in a suitcase and can immobilize an entire city's computer and communications systems; computer viruses of electronic-seating microbytes that can eliminate a country's telephone system; and logic bombs that can confuse and redirect traffic on the target country's air and rail system. Also planned are *infowar tactics* that deploy information-age techniques "to disrupt the enemy's economy and military capabilities without firing a shot." One example of these is the U.S. Air Force's Commando Solo psychological operations plane, which can disrupt signals and insert in their place a "morphed" TV program, in which the enemy leader makes unpopular announcements on the screen to alienate the leader from the population.

A revolution in robotic military technology is also already under way, with new unmanned systems such as the forty-two-pound PackBot used to detect improvised explosive devices already in use in the wars in Iraq and Afghanistan. "When U.S. forces went into Iraq in 2003, they had zero robotic units on the ground. By the end of 2004, the number was up to 150. By the end of 2005 it was 2,400 and it more than doubled the next year" (Singer 2009b). By the start of 2011, the U.S. military had more than 12,000 (Singer 2010). All together, twenty-two different robot systems are now in use on the ground, with prototypes for a variety of others from automated machine guns to robotic stretcher bearers to lethal robots the size of insects. Robot

smart bombs
precision-guided military technology that enables a bomb to search for its target and detonate at the precise time it can do the most damage.

virtual nuclear arsenals
the next generation of "near nuclear" military capabilities produced by the revolution in military technology that would put strategic nuclear weapons of mass destruction at the margins of national security strategies by removing dependence on them for deterrence.

deterrence
preventive strategies designed to dissuade an adversary from doing what it would otherwise do.

infowar tactics
attacks on an adversary's telecommunications and computer networks to penetrate and degrade an enemy whose defense capabilities depend heavily on these technological systems.

soldiers that can think, see, and react like humans are based on nanotechnology (the science of very small structures), and, predicts Robert Finkelstein, a veteran engineer who leads Robotic Technologies Inc., by "2035 we will have robots as fully capable as human soldiers on the battlefield."

The Pentagon is enthusiastic, in part because weapons that are symbols of military might like stealth bombers and nuclear submarines are of little use in today's "asymmetric" conflicts, in which individual soldiers equipped with the latest technologies are needed for search-and-destroy missions against guerrilla militias. Moreover, robotic forces are not vulnerable to human frailties. Gordon Johnson, of the Pentagon's Joint Forces Command, notes the appeal of robotic forces, "They're not afraid. They don't forget their orders. They don't care if the guy next to them has just been shot. Will they do a better job than humans? Yes." Technological advances thus may make obsolete orthodox ways of classifying weapons systems as well as prior equations for measuring power ratios.

At the same time, while the creation of a whole range of robotic armed forces to carry out dangerous missions and do the fighting without risk of soldiers being killed is heralded as a breakthrough in the way weapons are being used, there are concerns about long-term implications. General Robert E. Lee famously observed "It is good that we find war so horrible, or else we would become fond of it." Some worry that times are changing, and that war waged by remote control will become too easy and irresistibly tempting as a means to resolve conflicts. Lee "didn't contemplate a time when a pilot could 'go to war' by commuting to work each morning in his Toyota to a cubicle where he could shoot missiles at an enemy thousands of miles away and then make it home in time for his kids soccer practice" (Singer 2009a).

Biological and Chemical Weapons   Biological and chemical weapons pose a special and growing threat, particularly in the hands of terrorists aiming for mass destruction rather than influencing public opinion. These unconventional weapons of mass destruction (WMD) are sometimes regarded as a "poor man's atomic bomb" because they can be built at comparatively little cost and cause widespread injury and death. Chemical weapons proliferation is of worldwide concern. In addition to the American hegemon, which led the way in building these weapons, twelve other states have declared past production of chemical weapons, still others are suspected of secret production, and many terrorists claim they intend to acquire and use them. Following the 9/11 terrorist attacks on the United States, for example, there were fears that the spread of anthrax through the U.S. mail system was the first step in an endless series of future biological warfare by terrorist networks.

Case Study: *Science and the Future*

Wally Santana/AP Photo

REMOTE-CONTROL WARFARE? The United States is building a new generation of technologically sophisticated weapons. Shown here, U.S. soldiers with land mine detectors wait as another soldier maneuvers a robot into a cave to check for mines, traps, and other weapons that may have been hidden by Taliban or Al Qaeda fugitives in the eastern border town of Qiqay, Afghanistan. The war in Afghanistan is the first time that robots have been used by the U.S. military for combat purposes. They are intended to help prevent U.S. casualties.

International law prohibits the use of chemical weapons. The 1925 Geneva Protocol banned the use of chemical weapons in warfare, and the Chemical Weapons Convention, ratified by 188 (96 percent) of the world's countries, requires the destruction of existing stocks. Israel and Myanmar signed the treaty in 1993, but as of October 26, 2010, have yet to ratify it. Only Syria, North Korea, Angola, Egypt, and Somalia declined to sign or accede to the Chemical Weapons Convention. However, Iran and Iraq's use of gas in their eight-year 1980s war against each other, and Iraq's 1989 use of chemical weapons against its own Kurdish population, demonstrate the weaknesses of these legal barriers. In addition, many radical extremists, often beyond the control of weak state governments, see chemical and biological weapons as a cheaper and efficient terrorist method. The firebreak has been breached.

Pervasive insecurity haunts much of the world because there do not exist real supranational controls over the proliferation of biological and chemical weapons. The twenty-first century has not become the peaceful and prosperous period many people expected. In October 2010, the famous "Doomsday Clock" estimated that the world was only six minutes from nuclear Armageddon—one minute closer than when the clock was originally set in 1947 when the threat of the end of the world loomed large. From an antiwar feminist perspective, which sees war as a gendered identity construct and seeks to change the specific social processes that associate manliness with militarized violence, "State security may sometimes be served by war, but too often human security is not" (Cohn and Ruddick 2008, p. 459).

The world is *not* a safer place. In response to military dangers, many leaders today still adhere to the realist axiom that "if you want peace prepare for war." Security, realists insist, requires military capabilities. However, because the possession of overpowering military capabilities does not automatically result in their wise use, realists council that what matters greatly in the pursuit of national security are the *methods* on which states rely to use the capabilities they have acquired. How can weapons most effectively be used to promote national interests and exercise international influence? This question underscores the vital importance of choices about the types of military strategies employed.

Military Strategies

The dropping of the atomic bomb on Japan on August 6, 1945, is the most important event distinguishing pre– from post–World War II world politics. In the blinding flash of a single weapon and the shadow of its mushroom cloud, the world was transformed from a "balance of power" to a "balance of terror" system. In the following decades, policy makers in the nuclear states had to grapple with two central policy questions: (1) whether they should use nuclear weapons, and (2) how to prevent others from using them. The search for answers was critical because the immediate and delayed effects of a nuclear war were terrifying to contemplate. Even a short war using a tiny fraction of any great power's nuclear arsenal would destroy life as we know it. The planet would be uninhabitable, because a *nuclear winter* would result, with devastating consequences: "Fires ignited in such a war could generate enough smoke to obscure the sun and perturb the atmosphere over large areas, [lowering] average planetary temperatures [and darkening] the skies sufficiently to compromise green plant photosynthesis" (Sagan and Turco 1993, p. 396). It has been estimated that "the missiles on board a single [U.S.] SLBM submarine may be enough to initiate nuclear winter" (Quester 1992, p. 43)—enough to end human existence.

nuclear winter
the expected freeze that would occur in the Earth's climate from the fallout of smoke and dust in the event nuclear weapons were used, blocking out sunlight and destroying the plant and animal life that survived the original blast.

Weapons of mass destruction have grown since World War II, and strategies have changed with changes in technologies, defense needs, capabilities, and global conditions. For analytical convenience, those postures can be divided into three periods: compellence, deterrence, and preemption. The first began at the end of World War II and lasted until the 1962 Cuban Missile Crisis. U.S. nuclear superiority was the dominant characteristic of this period. The second then began and lasted until the 1991 collapse of the Soviet Union. Growing Soviet military capability was the dominant characteristic of this period, which meant that the United States no longer stood alone in its ability to annihilate another country without fear of its own destruction. The third phase began after the breakup of the Soviet Union that ended the Cold War, after which the great powers began to revise their strategic doctrines in the light of new global threats.

Compellence   Countries that possess military preeminence often think of weapons as instruments in diplomatic bargaining. The United States, the world's first and for many years unchallenged nuclear power, adopted the strategic doctrine of *compellence* (Schelling 1966) when it enjoyed a clear-cut superiority over the Soviet Union. Military capabilities did not have to be used for them to be useful; the United States could exercise influence over enemies simply by demonstrating the existence of its powerful weapons and signalling its willingness to use those weapons. The U.S. doctrine of compellence used nuclear weapons as tools of political influence, not for fighting but for convincing others to do what they might not otherwise do.

The United States sought to gain bargaining leverage by conveying the impression that it would actually use nuclear weapons. This posture was especially evident during the Eisenhower administration, when Secretary of State John Foster Dulles practiced *brinkmanship*, deliberately threatening U.S. adversaries with nuclear destruction so that, at the brink of war, they would concede to U.S. demands. Brinkmanship was part of the overall U.S. strategic doctrine known as *massive retaliation*. To contain communism and Soviet expansionism, this doctrine called for a *countervalue targeting strategy*, that is, aiming U.S. nuclear weapons at what the Soviets most valued—their population and industrial centers. The alternative is a *counterforce targeting strategy*, which targets an enemy's military forces and weapons, thus sparing civilians from immediate destruction.

Massive retaliation heightened fears in the Kremlin that a nuclear exchange would destroy the Soviet Union but permit the survival of the United States. In addition to responding by increasing their nuclear capabilities, Soviet leaders accelerated their space program and successfully launched the world's first space satellite (*Sputnik*). This demonstrated Moscow's ability to deliver nuclear weapons beyond the Eurasian landmass. Thus, the superpowers'

compellence
a method of coercive diplomacy usually involving an act of war or threat to force an adversary to make concessions against its will.

brinkmanship
the intentional, reckless taking of huge risks in bargaining with an enemy, such as threatening a nuclear attack, to compel its submission.

massive retaliation
the Eisenhower administration's policy doctrine for containing Soviet communism by pledging to respond to any act of aggression with the most destructive capabilities available, including nuclear weapons.

countervalue targeting strategy
a bargaining doctrine that declares the intention to use weapons of mass destruction against an enemy's most valued nonmilitary resources, such as the civilians and industries located in its cities.

counterforce targeting strategy
targeting strategic nuclear weapons on particular military capabilities of an enemy's armed forces and arsenals.

strategic competition took a new turn, and the United States for the first time faced a nuclear threat to its homeland.

Deterrence   As U.S. nuclear superiority eroded, American policy makers began to question the usefulness of weapons of mass destruction as tools in political bargaining. They were horrified by the destruction that could result if compellence should provoke a nuclear exchange. The nearly suicidal Cuban Missile Crisis of 1962 brought about a major change in American strategic thought, shifting strategic policy from compellence to *nuclear deterrence*.

Whereas *compellence* relies on an offensive coercive threat aimed at persuading an adversary to relinquish something without resistance, *deterrence* seeks to dissuade an adversary from undertaking some future action. At the heart of deterrence theory is the assumption that the defender has the ability to punish an adversary with unacceptably high costs if it launches an attack. The key elements of deterrence are: (1) *capabilities*—the possession of military resources that signal to the adversary that threats of military retaliation are possible; (2) *credibility*—the belief that the actor is willing to act on its declared threats; and (3) *communication*—the ability to send a potential aggressor the clear message that the threat will be carried out. Ironically, the shift from a strategy of compellence to deterrence sped rather than slowed the arms race. A deterrent strategy depends on obtaining the unquestionable ability to inflict intolerable damage on an opponent. This means that an arming state seeking to deter an enemy must build its weapons to acquire a *second-strike capability*—sufficient destructive weapons to ensure that the country can withstand an adversary's first strike and still retain the capacity to retaliate with a devastating counterattack. To guarantee that an adversary was aware that a second-strike capability existed, deterrence rationalized an unrestrained search for sophisticated retaliatory capabilities. Any system that could be built was built because, as President Kennedy explained in 1961, "only when arms are sufficient beyond doubt can we be certain without doubt that they will never be employed."

The phrase *mutual assured destruction (MAD)* was coined to describe the strategic balance that emerged between the United States and the Soviet Union after the Cuban Missile Crisis. Regardless of who struck first, the other side could destroy the attacker. Under these circumstances, initiating a nuclear war was not a *rational choice;* the frightening costs outweighed any conceivable benefits. As Soviet leader Nikita Khrushchev put it, "If you reach for the push button, you reach for suicide." Safety, in former British Prime Minister Winston Churchill's words, was "the sturdy child of terror and survival the twin brother of annihilation."

nuclear deterrence dissuading an adversary from attacking by threatening retaliation with nuclear weapons.

second-strike capability a state's capacity to retaliate after absorbing an adversary's first-strike attack with weapons of mass destruction.

mutual assured destruction (MAD) a condition of mutual deterrence in which both sides possess the ability to survive a first strike with weapons of mass destruction and launch a devastating retaliatory attack.

WEAPONS FOR WAR AND PEACE Shown here is a U.S. test of a nuclear bomb in 1954, when only the United States and the Soviet Union had nuclear capabilities. Today the capacity to wage war with weapons of mass destruction has spread to many countries, and the diffusion is transforming the global balance of power. What to do with such weapons for war and for peace is the central concern of realist theorizing, which looks on the acquisition of military power and its consequences as the most important dimension of world politics.

Strategic Defense Initiative (SDI)
the so-called Star Wars plan conceived by the Reagan administration to deploy an antiballistic missile system using space-based lasers that would destroy enemy nuclear missiles before they could enter Earth's atmosphere.

As United States-Soviet relations evolved, another shift in strategic thinking occurred in 1983 when U.S. President Reagan proposed building a space-based defensive shield against ballistic missiles. The ***Strategic Defense Initiative (SDI),*** or "Star Wars" as it is now labeled, called for the development of a defense against ballistic missiles using advanced space-based lasers to destroy weapons launched in fear, anger, or by accident. The goal, as President Reagan defined it, was to make nuclear weapons "impotent and obsolete." Thus, SDI sought to shift U.S. nuclear strategy away from mutual assured destruction, which President Reagan deemed "morally unacceptable."

However, the United States never managed to build a reliable ballistic missile defense, which Reagan's own Secretary of State George Shultz called "lunacy." As Philip Coyle, former director of Operational Test and Evaluation for the Department of Defense, noted in 2006, there has been "no demonstrated capability to defend the United States against enemy attack under realistic conditions." Nevertheless, the United States continues to aggressively pursue antiballistic missile defense, having spent by 2010 more than $170 billion—with a 2011 budget request of $9.9 billion (Olson 2010). Despite protest from Russia, where President Medvedev threatened to point missiles at Europe in retaliation for the further development of the U.S. system, in 2008 the United States moved forward with a controversial plan in which Poland agreed to host ten U.S. two-stage ground-based missile defense interceptors and the Czech Republic agreed to host a ballistic missile defense radar site. However, in September 2009, the United States reversed course with its decision to scrap the missile defense shield program in Eastern Europe. Citing advances in missile technology and new evidence regarding Iranian missile capabilities as reasons for the change in policy, it was also widely seen as an effort by the United States to improve relations with Russia.

Threats and fears animate realists' preoccupation with strategies based on weapons. The strategy of compellence conceived of arms as a means for putting enemies in a defensive position and pushing them to make changes in their policies that they did not want to undertake; the strategy of deterrence conceived of using weapons for defense to prevent an attack. Both strategies worked in some ways but failed in others, and both dealt with the problem

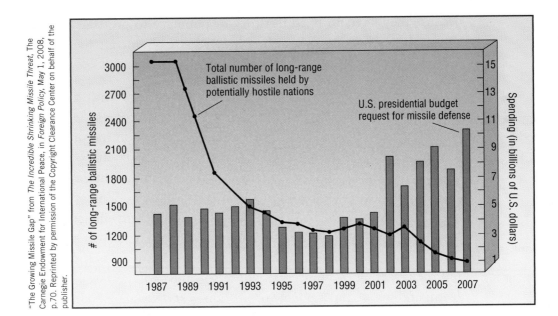

"The Growing Missile Gap" from *The Incredible Shrinking Missile Threat*, The Carnegie Endowment for International Peace, in *Foreign Policy*, May 1, 2008, p.70. Reprinted by permission of the Copyright Clearance Center on behalf of the publisher.

FIGURE 8.4

AN EXPANDING MISSILE GAP By 2012, the United States will have spent in excess of $180 million on missile defense. This is an enormous sum, the wisdom of which is questionable as the direct threat of ballistic missiles is limited and far less than it was twenty years ago. "The number of long-range missiles fielded by China and Russia has decreased 71 percent since 1987. The number of medium-range ballistic missiles pointed at U.S. allies in Europe and Asia has fallen 80 percent. Most of the twenty-eight countries that have any ballistic missiles at all have only short-range Scud missiles—which travel less than 300 miles and are growing older and less reliable every day" (Cirincione 2008, p. 68). On April 8, 2010, Obama and Medvedev signed a treaty to further reduce long-range missile stockpiles of both the United States and Russia to 700 missiles each, with a limit of no more than 1550 warheads.

of armed force by preserving the reliance on arms rather than trying to eliminate the threat. This is why the search continues for ways to move beyond compellence and deterrence in order "to counteract as well as reduce the negative effects of miscalculation and misperception, practices that are partially responsible for unpredicted and unwanted outcomes in international politics" (Sperandei 2006, p. 253).

Preemption   The end of the Cold War and with it the huge reduction in the total number of nuclear warheads today has not spelled a relaxation of tension. Strategic planning continues to find new ways of dealing with the constant danger of emergent military threats. As in the past, the U.S. hegemon has led the way in forging new strategies to deal with the post-9/11 threats of global terrorism and belligerent enemies. From that threat has come the radical new strategy of preemptive warfare.

"We face a threat with no precedent," President George W. Bush insisted in 2002. On the one hand, modern technology allows shadowy terrorist networks to launch catastrophic attacks against the United States. On the other hand, these networks cannot be dissuaded by the threat of punishment because they have no fixed territory or populace to protect. "We must take the battle to the enemy," Bush exhorted, "and confront the worst threats before they emerge."

Bush's call for acting preemptively against terrorists and the rogue states that harbor them became the major and most controversial cornerstone of the *U.S. National Security Strategy* (NSS). Building on the proposition that "nations need not suffer an attack before they can lawfully take action to defend themselves against forces that present an imminent danger," the strategic document argued that the acquisition of weapons of mass destruction by global terrorists provided the United States with a compelling case for engaging in anticipatory self-defense. "Traditional concepts of deterrence will not work against a terrorist enemy whose avowed tactics are wanton destruction and the targeting of innocents; whose so-called soldiers seek martyrdom in death; and whose most potent protection is *statelessness*." This requires, the 2002 NSS security strategy affirmed, the case for *preemptive war*—to coerce rather than deter enemies. The strategy called for striking a potential enemy before it undertakes armed aggression, either with or without the support of allies and international institutions.

The 2002 national security strategy was the most sweeping reformulation of U.S. defense policy since the 1947 National Security Act at the start of the Cold War. Although under international law states have a legal right

statelessness
the growing band of people who have no citizenship rights in any country and are forced out of one country and not accepted in any other.

preemptive war
a quick first-strike attack that seeks to defeat an adversary before it can organize an initial attack or a retaliatory response.

to defend themselves against aggression as well as imminent attacks, critics charge that beneath the language of military preemption lies a more radical policy of preventive war. A *preemptive* military attack entails the use of force to quell or mitigate an impending strike by an adversary. A *preventive* attack entails the use of force to eliminate any possible future strike, even if there is no reason to believe that the capacity to launch an attack currently exists. Whereas the grounds for preemption lie in evidence of a credible, imminent threat, the basis for prevention rests on the suspicion of an incipient, contingent threat (Kegley and Raymond 2004). Indeed, ethicists and legal experts, ever mindful of *just war theory*, question the morality and legality of preemptive war for preventive purposes. The U.S. posture has generated a heated debate.

just war theory
the theoretical criteria under which it is morally permissible, or "just," for a state to go to war and the methods by which a just war might be fought.

According to critics, preventive uses of military force set a dangerous precedent. Predicting an adversary's future behavior is difficult because its leadership's intentions are hard to discern, information on long-term goals may be shrouded in secrecy, and signals of its policy direction may be missed in an oversupply of unimportant intelligence information. If suspicions about an adversary become a justifiable cause for military action, then every truculent leader would have a rough-and-ready pretext for ordering a first strike.

In 2009, President Barack Obama signaled a shift from the "unapologetic and implacable demonstrations of will" (Krauthammer 2001) that had characterized the preemptive and unilateral policies of the prior administration. Instead, he called for an approach that maintained America's military strength but also sought to move beyond a single-minded focus on Iraq and broaden engagement with the global community. Among his priorities are reducing the threat of nuclear proliferation, securing all nuclear weapons and materials from terrorists and rogue states, and developing new defenses to protect against the threat of cyberterrorism and biological weapons. Calling nuclear proliferation and nuclear terrorism "a threat that rises above all others in urgency," he pledged to renew American diplomacy, with a willingness to engage in dialogue with friend and foe without precondition in order to advance U.S. interests (Ferguson 2010; Allison 2010).

The ever present threat of nuclear aggression raises anew timeless questions about the conditions under which, and the purposes for which, military force is justifiable. What does prudent precaution require when ruthless countries and nameless, faceless enemies pursue indiscriminate, suicidal attacks against innocent noncombatants? How can force be used to influence an adversary's decision-making calculus? What conditions affect the success of coercive diplomacy?

COERCIVE DIPLOMACY THROUGH MILITARY INTERVENTION

The strategy of coercive diplomacy is used in international bargaining to threaten or use limited force to persuade an opponent to stop pursuing an activity it is already undertaking. Often, threats to use arms are made to force an adversary to reach a compromise or, even better, to reverse its policies. The goal is to alter the target state's calculation of costs and benefits, so that the enemy is convinced that acceding to demands will be better than defying them. This result may be accomplished by delivering an ultimatum that promises an immediate and significant escalation in the conflict, or by issuing a warning and gradually increasing pressure on the target (Craig and George 1990).

gunboat diplomacy
a show of military force, historically naval force, to intimidate an adversary.

Coercive diplomacy's reliance on the threat of force is designed to avoid the bloodshed and expense associated with traditional military campaigns. Orchestrating the mix of threats and armed aggression can be done in various ways. The methods range from traditional *gunboat diplomacy* to threaten an enemy by positioning navies and/or armies near its borders to "tomahawk diplomacy" by striking an adversary with precision-guided cruise missiles. These are among the instruments of coercive diplomacy in the arsenal of military options envisioned by realist policy makers to pursue power. To explore this strategy, this chapter looks next at military intervention, the oldest and most widely used approach to military coercion.

covert operations
secret activities undertaken by a state outside its borders through clandestine means to achieve specific political or military goals with respect to another state.

Intervention can be practiced in various ways. States can intervene physically through direct entry of their armies into another country, indirectly by broadcasting propaganda to the target's population, or through *covert operations*. States also can intervene either alone or in league with other states. Overt military intervention is the most visible method of interference inside the borders of another country. For that reason, it is also the most controversial and costly.

Altogether, nearly 1,000 individual acts of military intervention were initiated between 1945 and 2001, resulting in 2.4 million fatalities (Tillema 2006). Interventionary acts have been frequently if episodically occurring since World War II (see Figure 8.5). This fluctuation in the rate of intervention suggests that military interventions rise and fall in response to both changing global circumstances and also in response to shifting perceptions of the advantages and disadvantages of intervention as an effective method of coercive diplomacy.

Each act of military intervention had a different rationale and produced different results. Past cases raise tough questions about the use of military intervention for coercive diplomacy. Does the record show that the actions met

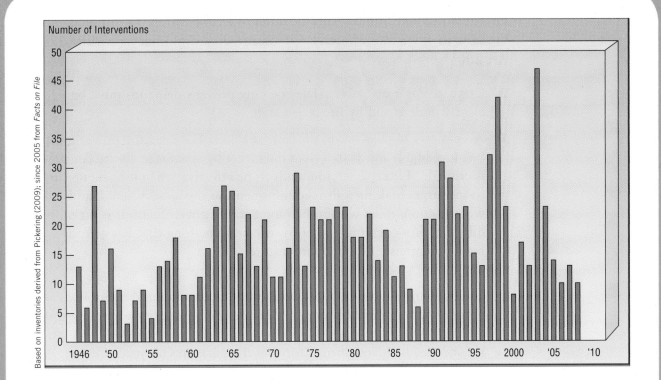

FIGURE 8.5

THE CHANGING INCIDENCE OF UNILATERAL MILITARY INTERVENTION FOR COERCIVE DIPLOMATIC PURPOSES SINCE 1945 As this evidence shows, states have frequently sent their troops into the sovereign territory of other states in order to influence the target, even though military intervention has been traditionally prohibited by international law. The frequency of this forceful coercive diplomacy fluctuates from year to year, and suggests that the fluctuations are dependent on the personal choices of the leaders authorizing their country's use of national armed forces for military engagement outside their borders.

the goals of the intervening states, such as successfully punishing countries so that they no longer violated their citizens' human rights? Have they for the most part restored order to war-torn societies? Or, on the whole, have they made circumstances worse?

These questions are hotly debated international issues now because of the wave of failed states. The great powers have not reached a consensus about the need to intervene in sovereign states when innocent civilians are victimized by tyrants. Why? Primarily because such interventions undercut the principles of state sovereignty and the *nonintervention norm* in international law. The UN's call for a "new commitment to intervention" stirred up the percolating existing debate about military intervention, even in the name of morality, justice, and human rights.

nonintervention norm
a fundamental international legal principle, now being challenged, that traditionally has defined interference by one state in the domestic affairs of another as illegal.

Today, policy makers disagree about the appropriate use of military coercion. Research on coercive diplomacy suggests that its success depends upon the context of each specific situation. The following conditions are thought to favor the effective use of coercive diplomacy (George 1992; Art 2005):

- **Clarity of user objectives.** The coercing power's demands must be clearly understood by the target state.

- **Asymmetry of motivation favoring the user.** The coercing power must be more highly motivated than the target by what is at stake. Timing is critical. Military coercion tends to be effective when it occurs prior to the target making a firm commitment on the issue at hand, and when factions exist within the target state's government. It is far more difficult for a coercing power to reverse something that has already been accomplished by the target state.

- **Opponent's fear of escalation and belief in the urgency for compliance.** The coercing power must create in the adversary's mind a sense of urgency for compliance with its demand. Two factors are important in affecting an adversary's perceptions: (1) the coercing power's reputation for successfully using armed force in the past, and (2) its capability to increase pressure to a level that the target would find intolerable. Coercion generally fails when the target has the ability to absorb the punishment delivered by the coercing state.

- **Adequate domestic and international support for the user.** In addition to having political support at home, the coercing power is helped when it can also count on support from key states and international organizations.

- **Clarity on the precise terms of settlement.** The coercing power must be able to articulate the specific conditions for ending the crisis, as well as to give assurances that it will not formulate new demands for greater concessions once the target capitulates.

Although these conditions improve the odds of successful coercive diplomacy, they do not guarantee success. History teaches that leaders who rely on military intervention for coercive diplomacy often start a process that they later find they cannot control.

Given the uncertainties surrounding the use of armed force, many a state that has ventured down this military path has come to regret it. Even the meaning of victory in war (especially against terrorists and desperadoes) befuddles politicians and military commanders (Martel 2008). In the aftermath of unsuccessful interventions, confidence in this military method of coercive diplomacy has frequently vanished, and the search for other means to exercise power in world politics has intensified.

RIVAL REALIST ROADS TO SECURITY

Since the beginning of history, preparations for war often have been chosen as a path to security. The realist call for "peace through strength" is certainly understandable in a world where fear of national vulnerability in an anarchic, self-help environment requires defense planners to assume the worst about other states' capabilities and intentions. Even if the military capabilities accumulated by an enemy are defensively motivated, they usually trigger a strong reaction. The state "always feels itself weak if there is another that is stronger," observed eighteenth-century French political philosopher Jean-Jacques Rousseau. "Its security and preservation demand that it make itself more powerful than its neighbors. It can increase, nourish, and exercise its power only at their expense.... It becomes small or great, weak or strong, according to whether its neighbor expands or contracts, becomes stronger or declines."

State power, Rousseau reminds us, is relative. Efforts to obtain absolute security by one state tend to be perceived as creating absolute insecurity for others, with the result that everyone becomes locked into an upward spiral of countermeasures that diminishes the security of all. Scholars refer to this as a *security dilemma,* a condition that results when each state's increase in military capabilities is matched by the others, and all wind up with no more security than when they began arming.

Many scholars (Jervis 1976; Snyder 1984) also describe the dynamics of this arms competition as the ***spiral model***. The imagery captures the tendency of defense-enhancing efforts to result in escalating arms races that diminish the security of all. Sir Edward Grey, British foreign secretary before World War I, described this process well:

spiral model
a metaphor used to describe the tendency of efforts to enhance defense to result in escalating arms races.

> The increase in armaments, that is intended in each nation to produce consciousness of strength and a sense of security, does not produce these effects. On the contrary, it produces a consciousness of the strength of other nations and a sense of fear. Fear begets suspicion and distrust and evil imaginings of all sorts, 'til each government feels it would be criminal and a betrayal of its own country not to take every precaution, while every government regards every precaution of every other government as evidence of hostile intent (Wight 2002, p. 254).

Although the security dilemma confronts all states' decisions, most leaders still refuse to accept vulnerability. Searching for strength, they often proceed from the assumptions that: (1) security is a function of power; (2) power is a function of military capability; and (3) military might is a measure of national greatness. Each of these suppositions is, of course, consistent with *realpolitik*.

Most realists and many others continue to put lasting faith in the realist premise that it is safer to rely on the force of arms than on the force of arguments to successfully resolve disputes. Yet security may depend as much on the control of force as on its pursuit. At issue is whether traditional realist emphasis on arms and military strategies that require either the threat or actual use of weapons for coercive diplomacy is the best and safest route to national and international security. To be sure, the traditional realist reliance on military capabilities to increase national security continues to resonate in world capitals. However, other realists recommend an alternative path—one that sees national interests served most, not by the acquisition and use of arms, but rather by the acquisition of allies in order to maintain a balance of power among rivals that will prevent any transnational actor from the temptation to use force against the others. This, these other realists believe, provides the safest path to security. Are they right? The next chapter reviews realist ideas about alliances, arms control, and their impact in creating a balance of power to keep the peace. Thus you can evaluate next the prospects, payoffs, and pitfalls of this other primary realist road to international and national security.

> *Until war is eliminated from international relations, unpreparedness for it is well nigh as criminal as war itself.*
>
> —Dwight Eisenhower, U.S. President

Take an Online Practice Quiz

www.cengagebrain.com/shop/ISBN/0495802204

Suggested Readings

Allison, Graham. (2010) "Nuclear Disorder: Surveying Atomic Threats," *Foreign Affairs* 89: 74–85.

Caldwell, Dan, and Robert E. Williams. (2006) *Seeking Security in an Insecure World*. Lanham, MD: Rowman & Littlefield.

Dombrowski, Peter, and Eugene Gholz. (2007) *Buying Military Transformation: Technological Innovation and the Defense Industry*. New York: Columbia University Press.

Gartzke, Erik and Matthew Kroenig. (2009) "A Strategic Approach to Nuclear Proliferation," *Journal of Conflict Resolution* 53: 151–160.

Kroenig, Matthew. (2009) "Exporting the Bomb: Why States Provide Sensitive Nuclear Assistance," *American Political Science Review* 103: 113–133.

Singer, P. W. (2009) *Wired for War: The Robotics Revolution and Conflict in the 21st Century*. New York: The Penguin Press.

CHAPTER 9
ALLIANCES AND THE BALANCE OF POWER

CHAPTER OUTLINE

REALIST INTERPRETATIONS OF ALLIANCES IN WORLD POLITICS

CONTROVERSY: Do the Advantages of Alliances Outweigh the Disadvantages?

REALISM AND THE BALANCING OF POWER

Rules for Rivals in the Balancing Process

Difficulties with the Maintenance of a Balance of Power

BALANCING POWER IN THE CONTEMPORARY GLOBAL SYSTEM

Models of the Balance of Power—Past and Present

What Lies Ahead?

CONTROVERSY: Is a Unipolar, Bipolar, or Multipolar System the Most Stable?

It is the existence of an enemy that gives rise to the need for allies, and it is for the advantageous conduct of fighting that alliances are formed.
—Steven Rosen, realist policy maker

Vladimir Rodionov/UPPA/Photoshot, Inc.

A NEW GLOBAL DANCE CARD? In June 2010, the BRICs (Brazil, Russia, India, and China) held their second annual summit to discuss, among other things, a greater say in global policy making. Seen as a balancing maneuver, this cooperative venture by the BRICs is a product of the rapid economic recovery of emerging markets and their growing sense that the global recession provides an opening for emerging market economies and developing countries to have greater influence in shaping the global economy. "Brazil, Russia, India and China have a fundamental role in the construction of a fairer international order that is more representative and safe," declared Brazilian President Luiz Inacio Lula da Silva. This picture shows, from left, Brazil's President Luiz Inacio da Silva, Russia's President Dmitry Medvedev, Chinese President Hu Jintao, and India's Prime Minister Manmohan Singh.

D o you know who your true friends are? Is there anyone who seems to dislike you and act in opposition to you? What if this foe happens to be a friend of your best friend? How should you then behave toward this individual?

Now stretch the scenario. What if there is a real bully who likes to push and shove you around? But what if that stronger person also chooses to pick on your foe, and that otherwise troublesome enemy asks you to join him for mutual protection? Are your interests served by such an unlikely alliance? Is an enemy of your biggest enemy now a possible friend? If so, can you count on that former adversary to stand by you, as promised, if the going gets tough? Or might you be deserted?

Complicate this situation still further. You make the sad discovery that the person you thought was your best friend has been flirting with your girlfriend or boyfriend. But given the bully's threat, should you overlook this insult and call upon your "friend" for support? What if your request is denied? And you are aware that it might be. You recall hearing "a friend in need is a friend indeed," but a self-serving and fearful so-called friend may reject you because when friendship is tested he concludes that "a friend in need is a pest!" Some friend!

Strange as it may seem, these kinds of hypothetical circumstances and choices for people have a powerful parallel in the real world of international politics. Countries, like individuals, make decisions that create friends and enemies. These decisions are based on converging and clashing interests and values. As realist theoretician Thucydides counseled, "One has to behave as friend or foe according to the circumstances," and these choices are made on a complex geo-strategic playing field in which today's enemy may be tomorrow's ally and where fears of entrapment, abandonment, or betrayal are ever present. Moreover, the game is played by actors unequal in strength, but with similar needs: to find allies as a means to self-protection when threats from another actor or opposed coalition appear on the scene. Alliances, like some personal friendships, are often *against* rather than *for* someone or something. And when relationships and conditions change, new alliances form and established alliances dissolve as transnational actors—all obsessed with the power of their rivals—realign.

Alliances in world politics require agreements between parties in order for them to cooperate. For that reason, it may seem that *liberal theory,* with its emphasis on the possibility of self-sacrifice for mutual gain, might provide a key to understanding why and how states join together in alliances. According to liberal theory, states form alliances even if their immediate interest is not realized, in order to maximize their long term collective interest. However, realism provides the dominant lens through which the dynamics of alliance formation and decay, and the impact of these dynamics on global security, are most often interpreted. Realism, you have learned, portrays world politics as a struggle for power under conditions of anarchy by competitive rivals pursuing only their own self-interests (and *not* for moral principles and global ideals such as improving the security and welfare of *all* throughout the globe). International politics, to realism, is a war of all against all, fought to increase national power and national security by preparing for war and seeking advantages over rivals such as by acquiring superior military capabilities.

Realists picture alliances as temporary, opportunistic agreements to cooperate. Participating parties join together in order to compete with and hold in check the dangerous ambitions of others. Realism provides the most compelling explanation of the coldly calculating motives underlying decisions about alliances, which realists see driven first and foremost as a method for protecting allies from threats posed by predatory common enemies. Most policy makers find this convincing because it speaks to their own experiences (just like the hypothetical scenario about friendships and foes that introduced the basic politics of human interaction and the factors that may influence such personal choices about with whom to ally and whom to regard as an adversary). Realist theory is the best paradigm for thinking about the calculations actors make regarding their security and how it might be maximized. Moreover, realism advances a rational choice account of alliance decisions, based on the observation that military partnerships have rarely been built to express friendship or agreements about ideas and ideals (Owen 2005). Instead, realist theory posits that military alliances are forged when the parties perceive that the advantages of an alliance outweigh the disadvantages.

This chapter looks at alliances in world politics from the account of realist theory, because realism is above all an interpretation of the preconditions for global security, or how military threats to international stability are best managed. As you shall see, realism maintains that alliances are the mechanism by which a "balance of power" can be maintained to prevent an aspiring hegemon from waging imperial wars to achieve world domination.

You might have already guessed that the basis for international stability and security is more complicated than this introduction implies. *Realpolitik* may be the most compelling theory of alliances discussed in government chambers, but the realist perspective has within its adherents disagreements about the role of alliances in world politics. So take a look at the leading hypotheses before considering the balance of power that is affected by alliance politics in theory and how that theory applies to trends in contemporary global circumstances.

> *Warfare is not a question of brute strength, but rather*
> *of winning and losing friends.*

—Count Diego Sarmiento Gondomar, Spanish Ambassador to London in 1618

REALIST INTERPRETATIONS OF ALLIANCES IN WORLD POLITICS

When threats to international peace surface, policy makers adhering to the liberal theoretical tradition recommended, almost as a knee-jerk reaction, that the disputants open negotiations to settle their differences at the bargaining table. To liberals, war represents the failure of diplomacy, the failure of countries to resolve their differences through cooperative negotiations to reach compromises (see Chapter 10). However, those abiding by realist foreign policy recommendations see countries' interests as best served by either unilaterally arming themselves sufficiently to contain an emergent threat (recall Chapter 8) or combining their strength with the other threatened states in an alliance to contain and combat the common danger.

To the realist frame of mind, *alliances* predictably come into being when two or more states face a common security threat. "An alliance (or alignment) is a formal (or informal) commitment for security cooperation between two or more states, intended to augment each member's power, security, and/or influence" (Walt 2009, p. 86). By acquiring allies, states increase their mutual military capabilities. When facing a common threat, alliances provide their members with the means of reducing their probability of being attacked (*deterrence*), obtaining greater strength in case of attack (defense), and precluding their allies from alliance with the enemy (Snyder 1991).

alliances
coalitions that form when two or more states combine their military capabilities and promise to coordinate their policies to increase mutual security.

These advantages notwithstanding, realists often see a downside and counsel against forming alliances, as Britain's Lord Palmerston did in 1848 when he advised that states "should have no eternal allies and no perpetual enemies." Their only duty is to follow their interests and whenever possible to rely on *self-help* by depending only on their own state for defense, because under anarchy no state can really count on allies to come to its defense if attacked.

Yuri Gripas/AFP/Getty Images

PARTNERSHIPS FOR SECURITY In a speech to graduating cadets at West Point in May 2010, President Obama highlighted alliances as a critical element of his administration's national security strategy. "The burdens of this century cannot fall on American shoulders alone," Obama said. "We will be steadfast in strengthening those old alliances that have served us so well . . . As influence extends to more countries and capitals, we must also build new partnerships, and shape stronger international standards and institutions." Pictured here, Obama presents a diploma during the graduation and commissioning ceremony.

The greatest risk to forming alliances is that they bind a state to a commitment that may later become disadvantageous. This is why "wise and experienced statesmen usually shy away from commitments likely to constitute limitations on a government's behavior at unknown dates in the future in the face of unpredictable situations" (Kennan 1984a, p. 238). Because conditions are certain to change sooner or later and the usefulness of all alliances is certain to change once the common threat that brought the allies together declines, the realist tradition advises states not to take a fixed position on temporary convergences of national interests and, instead, to forge alliances only to deal with immediate threats.

When considering whether a new alliance is a *rational choice* in which the benefits outweigh the costs, heads of state usually recognize that allies can easily do more harm than good (see Controversy: Do the Advantages of Alliances Outweigh the Disadvantages?). Many realists advise states against forming alliances for defense, basing their fears on five fundamental flaws:

- Alliances enable aggressive states to combine military capabilities for war.

- Alliances threaten enemies and provoke the creation of counteralliances, which reduces the security for both coalitions.

CONTROVERSY:

DO THE ADVANTAGES OF ALLIANCES OUTWEIGH THE DISADVANTAGES?

When states make decisions about forging alliances, they must keep in mind the many risks of sharing their fate with other states. Although realists generally see alliances as potentially beneficial, they caution that making a defense pact with an ally will also carry a heavy price (Weitsman 2004). Creating alliances will:

The Granger Collection

- foreclose options

- reduce the state's capacity to adapt to changing circumstances

- weaken a state's capability to influence others by decreasing the number of additional partners with which it can align

- eliminate the advantages in bargaining that can be derived from deliberately fostering ambiguity about one's intentions

- provoke the fears of adversaries

- entangle states in disputes with their allies' enemies

- interfere with the negotiation of disputes involving an ally's enemy by preventing certain issues from being placed on the agenda

- preserve existing rivalries

- stimulate envy and resentment on the part of friends who are outside the alliance and are therefore not eligible to receive its advantages

These potential dangers explain why alliance decisions are so controversial, even when advocates enthusiastically propose that another state be sought as an ally for mutual defense. The posture of leaders about the advantage or disadvantage of alliances has depended on their personal philosophy and the country's circumstances.

Consider the perspective of George Washington, the first president of the United States, advising other leaders in American government that it should be the foreign policy of the United States to "steer clear of permanent alliances." He felt that whereas a state "may safely trust to temporary alliances for extraordinary emergencies" it is an "illusion . . . to expect or calculate real favors from nation to nation." Yet, almost every state is insecure in one way or another and is tempted to recruit allies to bolster its defense capabilities and protect its power in a united coalition opposed to adversaries that threaten it.

(*continued*)

DO THE ADVANTAGES OF ALLIANCES OUTWEIGH THE DISADVANTAGES? (Continued)

WHAT DO YOU THINK?

- What are the advantages of having alliance partners, and how can a country bolster such partnerships?

- Imagine you are a policy maker for your government today. What countries would you seek an alliance with, and which would you avoid? Why?

- How might the rise of international organizations (IOs) as global actors shape the nature of alliances in the future? Do you think that IOs will begin to render alliances irrelevant?

- Alliance formation may draw otherwise neutral parties into opposed coalitions.

- Once states join forces, they must control the behavior of their own allies to discourage each member from reckless aggression against its enemies, which would undermine the security of the alliance's other members.

- The possibility always exists that today's ally might become tomorrow's enemy.

Despite their uncertain usefulness, many states throughout history have chosen to ally because, the risks notwithstanding, the perceived benefits to security in a time of threat justified that decision.

To best picture how alliances affect global security, it is instructive to move from the state level of analysis, which views alliance decisions from the perspective of an individual state's security, to the global level of analysis (recall Chapter 1) by looking at the impact of alliances on the frequency of interstate war. This view focuses attention on the possible contribution of alliance formation to maintaining the balance of power.

REALISM AND THE BALANCING OF POWER

The concept of a balance of power has a long and controversial history. Supporters envision it as an equilibrating process that maintains peace by counterbalancing any state that seeks military superiority, distributing global power evenly through *alignments* or shifts by nonaligned states to one or the other opposed coalitions. Critics deny the effectiveness of the balance of power, arguing that it breeds jealousy, intrigue, and antagonism. Part of the difficulty in evaluating these rival claims lies in the different meanings attributed to the concept (see Vasquez and Elman 2003). Whereas "balance of power" may be widely used in everyday discourse, there is confusion over precisely what it entails.

At the core of nearly all the various meanings of "balance of power" is the idea that national security is enhanced when military capabilities are distributed so that no one state is strong enough to dominate all others. If one state gains inordinate power, balance-of-power theory predicts that it will take advantage of its strength and attack weaker neighbors, thereby giving compelling incentive for those threatened to align and unite in a defensive coalition. According to the theory, the threatened states' combined military strength would deter (or, if need be, defeat) the state harboring expansionist aims. Thus, for realists, laissez-faire competition among states striving to maximize their national power yields an international equilibrium, ensuring the survival of all by checking hegemonic ambitions.

Balance-of-power theory is also founded on the realist premise that weakness invites attack and that countervailing power must be used to deter potential aggressors. Realists assume that the drive for expanded power guides every state's actions. It follows that all countries are potential adversaries and that each must strengthen its military capability to protect itself. Invariably, this reasoning rationalizes the quest for military superiority, because others pursue it as well. The reasons spring from the realist belief that a system revolving around suspicion, competition, and anarchy will breed caution; uncertainty creates restraints on the initiation of war.

Why? As President George Washington once noted, "It is a maxim founded on the universal experience of mankind that no nation is to be trusted farther than it is bound by its interest." When all states are independent and, as sovereign actors, free to make rational choices designed to protect their national security interests in a climate of fear and mistrust, they have powerful incentives to realign and form coalitions that would lead to an approximately even distribution of power, curbing the natural temptation of any great power to imperialistically attempt to conquer the others. In classic balance-of-power theory, fear of a third party will encourage alignments, because those threatened would need help to offset the power of the common adversary. An alliance would add the ally's power to the state's own and deny the addition of that power to the enemy. As alliances combine power, the offsetting

alignments
the acceptance by a neutral state threatened by foreign enemies of a special relationship short of formal alliance with a stronger power able to protect it from attack.

coalitions would give neither a clear advantage. Therefore, aggression would appear unattractive and would be averted.

To deter an aggressor, counteralliances are expected to form easily, because *free riders*, states sitting on the sidelines, cannot, as rational actors, risk *nonalignment*. If they refuse to ally, their own vulnerability will encourage an expansionist state to attack them sooner or later. To balance power against power in opposed coalitions approximately equal in strength, realists recognize that what is required is for national actors to see the value of rapidly shifting alliances. This requires adherence to decision rules.

Rules for Rivals in the Balancing Process

Although balancing is occasionally described as an automatic, self-adjusting process, most realists see it as the result of deliberate choices undertaken by national leaders to maintain an equilibrium among contending states. It is necessary for all leaders to constantly monitor changes in states' relative capabilities so policies about arms and allies can be adjusted to rectify imbalances of power. Choices must be made by rational, self-interested actors that recognize the trade-off of costs and benefits between strategic options. For example, some options, such as expanding military capabilities through armaments and alliances, attempt to add weight to the lighter side of the international balance. Others, such as negotiating limits on weaponry and on a great power's sphere of influence to reduce the size of the geographical region under the domination of a great power, attempt to decrease the weight of the heavier side.

Various theorists have attempted to specify a set of rules that must be heeded in this constructed *security regime* in order for the balancing process to function effectively. These rules include:

- **Stay vigilant.** Constantly watch foreign developments in order to identify emerging threats and opportunities. Because international anarchy makes each state responsible for its own security and because states can never be sure of one another's intentions, self-interest encourages them to maximize their relative power. As Morton Kaplan (1957, p. 35) wrote: "Act to increase capabilities but negotiate rather than fight. . . . [At the same time, states should] fight rather than pass up an opportunity to increase capabilities."

- **Seek allies whenever your country cannot match the armaments of an adversary.** States align with each other when they adopt a common stance toward some shared security problem. An alliance is produced when they formally agree to coordinate their behavior under certain specified circumstances.

free riders
those who obtain benefits at others' expense without the usual costs and effort.

nonalignment
a foreign policy posture in which states do not participate in military alliances with either of two rival blocs for fear that alliance will lead to involvement in an unnecessary war.

- **Remain flexible in making alliances.** Formed and dissolved according to the strategic needs of the moment, alliances must be made without regard to similarities of culture or ideological beliefs (Owen 2005). Because alliances are instrumental, short-term adjustments aimed at rectifying imbalances in the distribution of military capabilities, past experiences should not predispose states to accept or reject *any* potential partner.

    Nowhere is this better seen than in the *balancer* role Great Britain once played in European diplomacy. From the seventeenth through the early twentieth centuries, the British shifted their weight from one side of the continental balance to the other, arguing that they had no permanent friends and no permanent enemies, just a permanent interest in preventing the balance from tipping either way (Dehio 1962). As described by Winston Churchill, Britain's goal was to "oppose the strongest, most aggressive, most dominating power on the continent. . . . [It] joined with the less strong powers, made a combination among them, and thus defeated and frustrated the continental military tyrant whoever he was, whatever nation he led."

balancer
under a balance-of-power system, an influential global or regional great power that throws its support in decisive fashion to a defensive coalition.

- **Oppose any state that seeks hegemony.** The purpose of engaging in balance-of-power politics is to survive in a world of potentially dangerous great powers. If any state achieves absolute mastery over everyone else, it will be able to act freely. Under such circumstances, the territorial integrity and political autonomy of other states will be in jeopardy. By joining forces with the weaker side to prevent the stronger side from reaching preponderance, states can preserve their independence. As Joseph Nye (2008) phrased it, "Balance of power is a policy of helping the underdog because if you help the top dog, it may eventually turn around and eat you."

    For this reason, when a single superpower attains preponderant status, the usual reaction at first of other major powers is to engage in "soft balancing" by using "nonmilitary tools to delay, frustrate, and undermine" the hegemon's "military policies. Soft balancing using international institutions, economic statecraft, and diplomatic arrangement," Richard A. Pape (2005b, p. 10) observes, was "a prominent feature of the international opposition to the U.S. war against Iraq."

- **Be charitable in victory.** In the event of war, the winning side should not eliminate the defeated. Looking forward rather than backward, it should do as little damage as possible to those it has vanquished because yesterday's enemy may be needed as tomorrow's ally. Victors that couple firmness regarding their own interests with fairness toward the interests of others encourage defeated powers to work within the postwar balance of power. Similarly, states that win at the bargaining table can stabilize the balance of power by granting the other side compensation in return for its concessions.

These realist policy prescriptions urge states to check the ambitions of any great power that threatens to amass overwhelming power, because aspiring hegemons are a potential threat to everyone. Human beings and states, they argue, are by nature selfish, but balancing rival interests stabilizes their interactions. Weakness, realists insist, invites aggression. Thus, when faced with unbalanced power, leaders of states should mobilize their domestic resources or ally with others to bring the international distribution of power back into equilibrium (Schweller 2004; Waltz 1979).

The resistance of Germany, France, and many other countries to the 2003 U.S. decision to launch a war of preemption to prevent Iraq from acquiring and using weapons of mass destruction—especially as evidence of Iraq's possession of such weapons, ties to the 9/11 terrorist attacks, or intention to wage war were highly questionable—illustrates the balancing process. Also illustrative is the alarm of countries in the Baltic, such as Estonia, Latvia and Lithuania, to France's decision to sell Mistral-class assault ships to Russia that would enter service in 2015. Kaarel Kaas, a policy analyst with the International Center for Defense Studies in Talinn Estonia, cautions that such ships would "transform the power balance" on Russia's borders (The Economist, February 13, 2010, p.54).

Difficulties With the Maintenance of a Balance of Power

Can balancing power help to preserve world order, as most realists believe? Critics of balance-of-power theory raise several objections to the proposition that balancing promotes peace:

bandwagoning
the tendency for weak states to seek alliance with the strongest power, irrespective of that power's ideology or type of government, in order to increase their security.

- Scholars argue that the theory's rules for behavior are contradictory (Riker 1962). On the one hand, states are urged to increase their power. On the other hand, they are told to oppose anyone seeking preponderance. Yet sometimes *bandwagoning* with (rather than balancing against) the dominant state can increase a weaker country's capabilities by allowing it to share in the spoils of a future victory. History suggests that states that are most content with the status quo tend to balance against rising powers more than do dissatisfied states.

- Balance-of-power theory assumes policy makers possess accurate, timely information about other states. As discussed in the previous chapter, the concept of "power" has multiple meanings. Tangible factors are hard to compare, such as the performance capabilities of the different types of weapons found in an adversary's arsenal. Intangible factors, such as leadership skills, troop morale, or public support for adventuresome or aggressive foreign policies, are even more difficult to gauge. Without a precise measure of relative strength, how can policy makers know when power is becoming unbalanced? Moreover, in an environment of secret alliances, how can they be sure who is really in league with whom? An ally who is being counted on to balance the power of an opponent may have secretly agreed to remain neutral in the event of a showdown. Consequently, the actual distribution of power may not resemble the constructed distribution imagined by one side or the other.

- The uncertainty of power balances due to difficulties in determining the strength of adversaries and the trustworthiness of allies frequently causes defense planners to engage in worst-case analysis, which can spark an arms race. The intense, reciprocal anxiety that shrouds balance-of-power politics fuels exaggerated estimates of an adversary's strength. This, in turn, prompts each side to expand the quantity and enhance the quality of its weaponry. Critics of realism warn that if a serious dispute occurs between states locked in relentless arms competition under conditions of mutually assured suspicions, the probability of war increases.

- Balance-of-power theory assumes that decision makers are risk averse—when confronted with countervailing power, they refrain from fighting because the dangers of taking on an equal are too great. Yet, as *prospect theory* (see Chapter 6) illuminates, national leaders evaluate risks differently. Some are risk-acceptant. Rather than being deterred by equivalent power, they prefer gambling on the chance of winning a victory, even if the odds are long. Marshaling comparable power against adversaries with a high tolerance for risk will not have the same effect as it would on those who avoid risks.

- The past performance of balance-of-power theory is checkered. If the theory's assumptions are correct, historical periods during which its rules were followed should also have been periods in which war was less frequent. Yet a striking feature of those periods is their record of warfare. After the 1648 Peace of Westphalia created the global system of independent territorial states, the great powers participated in a series of increasingly destructive general wars that threatened to engulf and destroy the entire multistate global system. As Inis L. Claude (1989) soberly concludes, it is difficult to consider these wars "as anything other than catastrophic failures, total collapses, of the balance-of-power system. They are hardly to be classified as stabilizing maneuvers or equilibrating processes, and one cannot take seriously any claim of maintaining international stability that does not entail the prevention of such disasters." Indeed, the historical record has led some theorists to construct *hegemonic stability theory* as an alternative to the balance of power. This theory postulates that a single, dominant hegemon can guarantee peace better than a rough equality of military capabilities among competing great powers (Ferguson 2004; Mandelbaum 2006a).

A significant problem with the balance-of-power system is its haphazard character. To bring order to the global system, the great powers have occasionally tried to institutionalize channels of communication. The Concert of Europe that commenced with the Congress of Vienna in 1815 exemplified this strategy. In essence, it was a club exclusively for the great powers.

concert
a cooperative agreement in design and plan among great powers to manage jointly the global system.

The idea behind a *concert* is "rule by a central coalition" of great powers (Rosecrance 1992). It is predicated on the belief that the leading centers of power will see their interests advanced by collaborating to prevent conflict from escalating into war in those regions under their collective jurisdiction. Although it is assumed that the great powers share a common outlook, concerts still allow "for subtle jockeying and competition to take place among them. Power politics is not completely eliminated; members may turn to internal mobilization and coalition formation to pursue divergent interests. But the cooperative framework of a concert, and its members' concern about preserving peace, prevent such balancing from escalating to overt hostility and conflict" (Kupchan and Kupchan 2000, p. 224).

A common sense of duty is the glue that holds great-power concerts together. When belief in mutual self-restraint fades, concerts unravel. "Friction tends to build as each state believes that it is sacrificing more for unity than are others," notes Robert Jervis (1985, p. 61), adding that "Each will remember the cases in which it has been restrained, and ignore or interpret differently cases in which others believe they acted for the common good." Overcoming this friction requires continuous consultation in order to reinforce expectations of joint responsibilities. Concert members should not be challenged over their vital interests, nor should they suffer an affront to their prestige and self-esteem (Elrod 1976). A "just" equilibrium among contending great powers bound together in a concert means more than an equal distribution of military capabilities; it includes recognition of honor, rights, and dignity (Schroeder 1989).

Although a concert framework can help manage relations among counterpoised great powers, the normative consensus underpinning this arrangement is fragile and can erode easily. And this potential for great power harmony to be replaced by great power rivalry is what alarms many realist observers. A dangerous power vacuum could result if the world witnesses "the end of alliances," when formal military ties fade away and are replaced by informal shifting alignments among the competitors (Menon 2007).

These difficulties in preserving the balance of power lead most realists to conclude that international conflict and competition is permanent in world politics and, therefore, that the best hope is to count on the emergence of a stable balance of power to preserve peace. Next, take a look at trends in the historical record and projections for the future about how the balance of power is likely to function.

BALANCING POWER IN THE CONTEMPORARY GLOBAL SYSTEM

The use of alliances to balance power has shifted over time in a series of redistributions. At one extreme have been periods in which a powerful state has tried to prevail over another state, which in response usually has built additional arms or sought allies to offset its adversary's strength. At the other extreme, at times a more fluid competition has emerged, with encroachments by one state against another also precipitating a quest for arms and allies. But rather than resulting in the formation of rigid, counterbalanced blocs, this kind of military confrontation has triggered many shifts by others to produce a kaleidoscope of overlapping alliances—a checkerboard of multiple great powers competing in balance-of-power politics.

Having examined how the balance of power is supposed to operate, the chapter next considers how it actually has functioned in world politics. To visualize these potential types of *global structure* and their causes and consequences, the chapter now considers several models of balance-of-power distributions that have arisen since World War II, with an eye to the kinds of power divisions that may develop in the twenty-first century's age of globalization now dominated by American military supremacy.

global structure
the defining characteristics of the global system—such as the distribution of military capabilities —that exist independently of all actors but powerfully shape the actions of every actor.

Models of the Balance of Power—Past and Present

Military power can be distributed around one or more power centers in different ways—an idea scholars call *polarity* (recall Chapter 3). Historically, these have ranged from highly concentrated power on one end of the continuum to highly dispersed power distributions on the other. The former has included regional empires (e.g., the Roman Empire), and an example of the latter is the approximate equality of power held by the European powers at the conclusion of the Napoleonic Wars in 1815. Using the conventional means by which historians separate turning points from one type of balance-of-power system to another, four distinct periods of polarity are observable in recent history. Balance-of-power systems evolve in a cyclical fashion—after four transformations, the system concludes the same way it began: (1) unipolarity, 1945–1949; (2) bipolarity, 1949–1991; (3) multipolarity 1991–2001; and (4) another unipolar system today with the United States again an unchallenged hegemon.

Unipolarity—The United States Most countries were devastated by World War II. The United States, however, was left in a clearly dominant position, with its economy accounting for about half the world's combined gross national product (GNP). The United States was also the only country with the atomic bomb and had demonstrated its willingness to use the new weapon. This underscored to others that it was without rival and incapable of being counterbalanced. The United States was not just stronger than *anybody*—it was stronger than *everybody*.

In the period immediately following World War II, a unipolar distribution of power materialized, because power was concentrated in the hands of a single hegemon able to exercise overwhelming influence over all other states, either through leadership or through domination. So supremely powerful was the United States at that time that people spoke of a new "American Empire" ruling over an impoverished world ravaged by war. That hegemonic status was short lived, however, as an ascendant challenger to U.S. preponderance, the Soviet Union, soon began to undermine America's supremacy and hegemonic status.

The U.S. capacity to act unilaterally in pursuit of its interests and ideals underwent a decline over the next four decades, as the U.S. grip on global developments and its ability to influence others eroded.

Bipolarity—The United States and Russia The recovery of the Soviet economy, the growth of its military capabilities, its maintenance of a large army, and growing Soviet-U.S. rivalry less than five years after the end of World War II gave rise to a new distribution of world power. The Soviets broke the U.S. monopoly on atomic weapons in 1949 and exploded a thermonuclear device in 1953, less than a year after the United States. This achievement symbolized the creation of global *bipolarity*—the division of the balance of power into two coalitions headed by rival military powers, each seeking to contain the other's expansion. Military capabilities became concentrated in the hands of two competitive "superpowers," whose capacities to massively destroy anyone made comparisons with the other great powers meaningless.

These superpowers drove the formation of two opposing blocs or coalitions through *polarization* when states joined counterbalanced alliances. In interpreting these dynamics, it is important not to use the concepts of polarity and polarization interchangeably. They refer to two distinct dimensions of the primary ways in which military power is combined (or divided) at any point in time in the global system. When states independently build arms at home, their differential production rates change the global system's *polarity*, or the number of power centers (poles). In contrast, when states combine their arms through alliance formation, the aggregation of power through *polarization* changes the system's balance of power. A system with multiple power centers can be said to be moving toward a greater degree of polarization if its members form separate blocs whose external interactions are characterized by increasing levels of conflict while their internal interactions become more cooperative (Rapkin and Thompson with Christopherson 1989). Polarization increases when the number of cross-cutting alignments declines. The concept of polarization is especially apt in this context because a *pole* suggests the metaphor of a magnet—it both repels and attracts.

polarization
the degree to which states cluster in alliances around the most powerful members of the global system.

The formation of the *North Atlantic Treaty Organization (NATO)*, linking the United States to the defense of Western Europe, and the Warsaw Pact, linking the former Soviet Union in a formal alliance with its Eastern European clients, occurred due to this polarization process. The opposing blocs formed in part because the superpowers competed for allies and in part because the less powerful states looked to one superpower or the other for protection. Correspondingly, each superpower's allies gave it forward bases from which to carry on the competition. In addition, the involvement of most other states in the superpowers' struggle globalized the East–West conflict. Few states remained outside the superpowers' rival alliance networks as neutral or nonaligned countries.

North Atlantic Treaty Organization (NATO)
a military alliance created in 1949 to deter a Soviet attack on Western Europe that since has expanded and redefined its mission to emphasize not only the maintenance of peace but also the promotion of democracy.

By grouping the system's states into two blocs, each led by a superpower, the Cold War's bipolar structure bred insecurity among all. The balance was constantly at stake. Each bloc leader, fearing that its adversary would attain hegemony, viewed every move, however defensive, as the first step toward world conquest. Zero-sum conflict prevailed as both sides viewed what one side gained as a loss for the other. Both superpowers attached great importance to recruiting new allies. Fear that an old ally might desert the bloc was ever present. Bipolarity left little room for compromise or maneuver and worked against the "normalization" of cooperative superpower relations (Waltz 1993).

Bipolarity first began to disintegrate in the 1960s and early 1970s when the opposed coalitions' internal cohesion eroded and new centers of power emerged. At the same time, weaker alliance partners were afforded more room for maneuvering, as illustrated by the friendly relations between the United States and Romania and between France and the Soviet Union. The superpowers remained dominant militarily, but this less rigid system allowed other states to act more independently.

doctrines
the guidelines that a great power or an alliance embraces as a strategy to specify the conditions under which it will use military power and armed force for political purposes abroad.

Rapid technological innovation in the superpowers' major weapons systems was a catalyst in the dissolution of the Cold War blocs and the national strategic *doctrines* that the adversaries had constructed. Intercontinental ballistic missiles (ICBMs), capable of delivering nuclear weapons through space from one continent to another, lessened the importance of forward bases on allies' territory for striking at the heart of the adversary. Furthermore, the narrowed differences in the superpowers' arsenals loosened the ties that had previously bound allies to one another. The European members of NATO in particular began to question whether the United States would, as it had pledged, protect Paris or London by sacrificing New York. Under what conditions might Washington or Moscow be willing to risk a nuclear holocaust? The uncertainty became pronounced as the pledge to protect allies through *extended deterrence* seemed increasingly insincere.

extended deterrence
the protection received by a weak ally when a heavily militarized great power pledges to "extend" its capabilities to it in a defense treaty.

The movement toward democracy and market economies by some communist states in the late 1980s further eroded the bonds of ideology that had formerly helped these countries face their security problems from a common posture. The 1989 dismantling of the Berlin Wall tore apart the Cold War architecture of competing blocs. With the end of this division, and without a Soviet threat, the consistency of outlook and singularity of purpose that once bound NATO members together disappeared. Many perceived the need to replace NATO.

Video: *Shifting Alliances in Iran*

However, NATO has proven itself to be an adaptive alliance (see Chapter 11). For example, in 2002 the NATO-Russia Council (NRC) was established to provide a framework for consultation and cooperation between the twenty-eight allies and Russia on current security issues and a wide range of issues of mutual interest. There have been setbacks, such as the freezing of relations in late 2008 during Russia's war with Georgia and a proposal by Russia in November 2009 for a new European security treaty that places Moscow at the center of a pan-European institution rather than NATO. Nonetheless, there are renewed calls to include Russia in NATO expansion as "including former adversaries in a postwar order is critical to the consolidation of great-power peace. Anchoring Russia in an enlarged Euro-Atlantic order, therefore, should be an urgent priority for NATO today" (Kupchan 2010, p. 100).

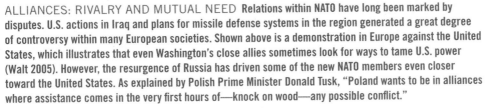

ALLIANCES: RIVALRY AND MUTUAL NEED Relations within NATO have long been marked by disputes. U.S. actions in Iraq and plans for missile defense systems in the region generated a great degree of controversy within many European societies. Shown above is a demonstration in Europe against the United States, which illustrates that even Washington's close allies sometimes look for ways to tame U.S. power (Walt 2005). However, the resurgence of Russia has driven some of the new NATO members even closer toward the United States. As explained by Polish Prime Minister Donald Tusk, "Poland wants to be in alliances where assistance comes in the very first hours of—knock on wood—any possible conflict."

The United States: Dominant Superpower or Hobbled Hegemon? Following the collapse of the Soviet Union in 1991, a *power transition*—a change in the ratio of military capabilities between great power rivals that produces tensions and increases the probability of war between them—occurred. This prompted many analysts to conclude that a new era of unipolarity had arisen, with the United States emerging as the world's only superpower. A decade after the collapse of communism in Europe, columnist Charles Krauthammer (2002) proclaimed that "no country has been as dominant culturally, economically, technologically, and militarily in the history of the world since the Roman Empire." Others, however, perceived the emergence of a hybrid "uni-multipolar" system with the United States as the sole superpower, but with other states not easily dominated, though still requiring collaboration for the resolution of key international issues (Huntington 2005).

The question remains as to whether U.S. predominance will prove beneficial or damaging. Recall that to hegemonic stability theorists, a unipolar concentration of power allows the global leader to police chaos and maintain international peace. Their faith in America as a well-intentioned peacekeeper was bolstered by then President George W. Bush's pledge in 2001 that the U.S. role in the world would be "the story of a power that went into the world to protect but not possess, to defend but not to conquer."

Against this optimistic view runs a strong suspicion about the future stability of a unipolar world under U.S. management. Fears rose in reaction to the assertive *Bush Doctrine* pledging that the United States would unilaterally act however it wishes abroad, without the approval of others. As one critic warned, "It is virtually universal in history that when countries become hegemons…they tend to want everything their own way, and it never works" (Mathews 2000). Throughout the world, U.S. leadership was condemned for its shortsightedness and willingness to put narrow self-interests ahead of ideals by seeking to preserve America's position as world leader without working through multilateral cooperation with others for peace and prosperity. However, there may be winds of change. As "our first global president," opines historian Douglas Brinkley, President Barack Obama is a transformational leader abroad and "is playing to the world right out of the gates, whereas most presidents have not" (Raasch 2009). In 2010, a survey by the Pew Research Center found that the global public remained broadly positive (in most non-Muslim nations) about U.S. relations with the rest of the world under Obama's leadership. The national median confidence in Obama to do the right thing in world affairs was 71 percent, and overall approval of his policies was 64 percent. In particular, huge percentages in key allies—Germany (88 percent), France (84 percent), Spain (76 percent), and Britain (64 percent)—said that they back the U.S. president's policies.

Constructivists suggest that resistance faced by the United States, particularly with regard to premises such as those embodied by the Bush Doctrine, is not surprising as a unipolar system depends heavily upon the social system in which it is embedded. Instead of through material capabilities that are considered important by realists, constructivists argue that by leading the way as the champion of universal values with widespread appeal and by investing in the development of norms or institutions from which they benefit, a dominant state can greatly enhance its power and induce cooperation or acquiescence from others. The United States had great success at this in the period following World War II when it was an ardent promoter of democracy, human rights, and freedom and was the primary architect behind an array of international institutions that reflected its values and shaped world politics. However, creating a social system that legitimates popular values

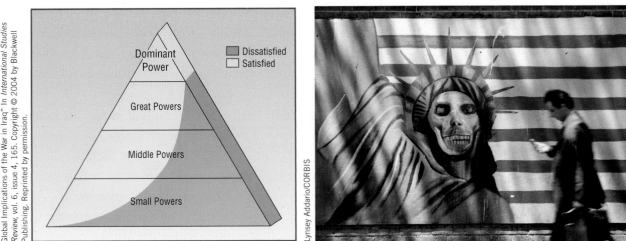

Kugler J, R. Tammen, and B. Efird, "Integrating Theory and Policy: Global Implications of the War in Iraq" In *International Studies Review*, vol. 6, issue 4, 165. Copyright © 2004 by Blackwell Publishing. Reprinted by permission.

Lynsey Addario/CORBIS

FIGURE 9.1

A POWER TRANSITION IN THE GLOBAL HIERARCHY Where countries sit in the world pyramid of power predicts their posture toward global change. As this figure suggests, the more favorable a country's position is in the world hierarchy, the more satisfied it is with the international status quo; conversely, states lower in the hierarchy are more dissatisfied and therefore promote change. As the figure on the left suggests, the power transition theory provides leverage for "anticipating when and where great power and regional wars most likely will occur. With a warning well ahead of time comes the opportunity to construct current policies that can manage the events that lead to future disputes" (Kugler, Tammen, and Efired 2004). The photo on the right captures the cross-cutting combination of anger and allegiances that surfaces during power transitions—a mural with a ghostly Statue of Liberty on a wall facing the U.S. Embassy in Tehran.

can in turn constrain a unipole by creating resistance to policies deemed illegitimate (Finnemore 2009).

Will the optimists, or the pessimists, be proved more accurate in their predictions about the future consequences of the hierarchical structure of world power? Time will tell, but one trend is certain to influence what unfolds: the eventual erosion of today's U.S. preponderance. That unipolar distribution is unlikely to last long. The toll of imperial overstretch from the extraordinary costs of global management in conjunction with the inevitability of differential economic growth rates that favor fast-growing challengers assures that China and India as well as the European Union will challenge U.S. supremacy economically. As Figure 9.1 suggests, power transitions breed turmoil and global instability when rising powers, dissatisfied with their subordination by the reigning hegemon, are prone to disrupt the prevailing global hierarchy in their favor. This power transition will occur sooner rather than later (Ikenberry 2008) if the United States fails to reduce the heavy financial burden of the American global empire. Continuing U.S. dominance in a unipolar distribution of world power is certain to breed resistance if America mismanages its special opportunity to lead and fails to alter the course of history for the benefit of all humanity (Chua 2008; Haass 2005).

What Lies Ahead?

Sooner or later, America's unipolar period in the sun will inevitably fade, and some new distribution of power will develop. The probable consequences of such a transformation in world politics are not clear. Some forecast the return of a bipolar pattern of direct opposition, with a new Sino-Russian bloc, European-Russian entente, or Sino-Japanese alliance countering the United States (Brzezinski 2004). Others see the emergence of a more complex multipolar pattern of balance-of-power competition, where the United States, China, Japan, Russia, India, and the European Union would constitute six centers of global power. According to this image of the future, as power becomes more equally distributed, each player will be increasingly assertive, independent, and competitive, leading to confusion about the identity of friends and foes.

The search for the capacity to compete on an equal footing with the other centers of power is characteristically strong when power becomes spread across three or more poles. With the effort by the European Union to enter the playing field alongside the United States, China, Japan, Russia, and other regional players like Brazil and India, the game of rivalry and balancing is becoming much different from the strategies and alignments that tend to materialize in unipolar and bipolar systems. As power becomes increasingly equally distributed, each leading power suspiciously confronts the other; diplomacy displays a nonideological, chesslike character; and conflict intensifies as each contender fears the power of its rivals. An enlarged global chessboard of multiple geostrategic relationships develops. A congested landscape leads to uncertainty about other's allegiances. To make this setting even more confusing, in multipolar systems, the interplay takes place simultaneously on two playing fields—the first military and the second economic (recall Table 3.2). The major players align together against others on particular issues, as their interests dictate. Behind the diplomatic smiles and handshakes, one-time friends and allies begin to grow apart, formally "specialized" relations begin to dissolve, and former enemies forge friendly ties and begin making a common cause against other centers of power that threaten them.

This competition under conditions of multipolarity is already unfolding. It is evident in the growing trade-bloc rivalry on the economic battlefield between the United States, the European Union, and China and Japan in the Far East (see Chapter 13). The largest emerging markets are also vying for economic power. At the start of 2010, Brazil commanded 2.6 percent, India 1.9 percent, and Mexico 1.8 percent of global economic output, with developing countries accounting for almost 30 percent of global economic output overall (WDI 2010).

Much counterbalancing and shifting in flexible and fluid alliances is occurring. For example, friction grew between the United States and its closest allies over how to pursue the war on terrorism, particularly with regard to the Iraq War. As a measure of how sensitive particular issues can be among great powers, both the European Union's foreign affairs commissioner, Christopher Pattern, and the German foreign minister, Joschka Fischer, castigated President Bush for treating America's coalition partners as subordinate "satellites," and Russia's Vladimir Putin quickly joined their criticism of unilateral U.S. disregard of the interests of America's would-be partners in the antiterrorist coalition.

In an effort to renew partnerships that had been strained because of the Iraq War, U.S. President Barack Obama acknowledged that "there have been times where America's shown arrogance and been dismissive, even derisive" toward Europe. "We must be honest with ourselves," President Obama said. "In recent years, we've allowed our alliance to drift." At a NATO summit marking the sixtieth anniversary of the alliance, he called for all countries to play a part in the fight against Al Qaeda, reminding the leaders of the twenty-eight countries that "we have a mutual interest in ensuring that organizations like Al Qaeda cannot operate."

Another indicator of continuing balance-of-power jockeying for global position and independence typical of emergent multipolarity is the renewed emphasis on the geopolitics of the Eurasian region of the world. In the spirit of Alfred Thayer Mahan, a U.S. naval captain who thought that naval power was the decisive factor in global political struggles and in 1902 coined the term "Middle East" to designate the area between India and Arabia that was of particular naval strategic importance, many anticipate that "the Indian Ocean will be the heart of geopolitical competition in the twenty-first century" (Kaplan 2009a, p. 99). It is anticipated that a dynamic great power rivalry will develop between India and China in the area, and that the role of the United States will be to serve as a stabilizing power with the goal of "indispensability" as opposed to dominance (Gelb 2009; Kaplan 2009b).

At times, the United States has also cast itself in the role of *balancer*, positioned in the middle of disputes between China and Russia. At other times, the United States has found itself opposed by these two neighboring great powers. Over the last few years, China and Russia have sought to put their

Bela Szandelszky/AP Photo

A SHIFTING BALANCE OF POWER? The Caucasus region is an area of geopolitical significance that "has become the arena for competition between the Americans and Europeans on one hand, and Russia on the other, over how to bring these countries into their respective spheres of influence" (Dempsey 2008, p. 3). Shown here are blindfolded Georgians atop a Russian personnel carrier. With Russia's show of strength in Georgia in 2008, its opposition to the expansion of NATO, and its resistance to the development of U.S. missile defense in the region, many have felt a Cold War chill in the air and speculated about a changing tide of strength and strategic interest. At the very least, as Ukrainian Prime Minister Hryhoriy Nemyria observed, "This crisis makes crystal clear that the security vacuums that have existed in the post-Soviet space remain dangerous."

Cold War rivalries behind them, strengthen bilateral ties, and rise as a counterbalance to U.S. global dominance. In a meeting with Russian Prime Minister Vladimir Putin in March 2010, Chinese Vice President Xi Jinping expressed his view that "China and Russia should in the future facilitate the establishment of a multipolar world and democratization of international relations."

However, it is difficult to confidently predict what the twenty-first century will look like and whether it will be chaotic or stable. Should a new multipolar world develop in the mid-twenty-first century, the probable consequences are unclear. Three different schools of thought on the relationship between polarity and global stability contend with one another (see Controversy: Is a Unipolar, Bipolar, or Multipolar System the Most Stable?). Because there is no real consensus on whether systems with a certain number of poles are

CONTROVERSY:

IS A UNIPOLAR, BIPOLAR, OR MULTIPOLAR SYSTEM THE MOST STABLE?

In the early twenty-first century, a long-standing debate has intensified about which type of polarity distribution—unipolar, bipolar, or multipolar—is the most capable of preventing large-scale war. Consider the divided opinions about this issue, as represented by the arguments in three contending schools of thought.

One interpretation holds that peace will occur when one hegemonic state acquires enough power to deter others' expansionist ambitions. This view maintains that the concentration of power reduces the chances of war because it allows a single superpower to maintain peace and manage the global system. The long peace under Britain's leadership in the 1800s (the Pax Britannica) and earlier, under the Roman Empire (the Pax Romana), offered support for the idea that unipolarity brings peace, and therefore inspires the hope that the twenty-first century under a Pax Americana will be stable as long as U.S. dominance prevails (Ferguson 2006; Mandelbaum 2006b).

In contrast, a second school of *neorealist* thought (e.g., Waltz 1964) maintains that bipolar systems are the most stable. According to this line of reasoning, stability, ironically, results from "the division of all nations into two camps [because it] raises the costs of war to such a high level that all but the most fundamental conflicts are resolved without resort to violence" (Bueno de Mesquita 1975, p. 191). Under such stark simplicities and balanced symmetries, the two leading rivals have incentives to manage crises so that they do not escalate to war.

Those who believe that a bipolar world is inherently more stable than either its unipolar or multipolar counterparts draw support from the fact that in the bipolar environment of the 1950s, when the threat of war was endemic, major war did not occur. Extrapolating, these observers (e.g., Mearsheimer 1990) reason that because a new multipolar distribution of global power makes it impossible to run the world from one or two centers, disorder will result:

> It is rather basic. So long as there [are] only two great powers, like two big battleships clumsily and cautiously circling each other, confrontations—or accidents—[are] easier to avoid. [With] the global lake more crowded with ships of varying sizes, fueled by different ambitions and piloted with different degrees of navigational skill, the odds of collisions become far greater (House 1989, p. A10).

A third school of thought argues that multipolar systems are the least war prone. Although the reasons differ, advocates share the belief that polarized systems that either concentrate power, as in a unipolar system, or that divide the world into two antagonistic blocs, as in a bipolar system, promote struggles for dominance (Morgenthau 1985; Thompson 1988). The peace-through-multipolarity school perceives multipolar systems as stable because they encompass a larger number of autonomous actors, giving rise to more potential alliance partners. This is seen as pacifying because it is essential to counterbalancing a would-be aggressor, as shifting alliances can occur only when there are multiple power centers (Deutsch and Singer 1964). Also, multipolar distributions of world power reduce the temptations of a great power to pursue a global imperial empire, because the effort to do so is likely to make it weaker and less secure as it becomes encircled by the threatened states (Kennedy 2006), and because multipolarity limits the usefulness of self-help strategies to expand global influence (Rosecrance 2005).

(continued)

IS A UNIPOLAR, BIPOLAR, OR MULTIPOLAR SYSTEM THE MOST STABLE? (Continued)

Abstract deductions and historical analogies can lead to contradictory conclusions, as the logic underlying these three inconsistent interpretations illustrates. The future will determine which of these rival theories is the most accurate.

WHAT DO YOU THINK?

- Based on your estimates of the possibilities of war and peace, which rival theory do you predict to be most accurate?

- Given the ever-present possibilities of nuclear proliferation among a broad variety of countries, the distribution of economic power across many countries, as well as the increasing importance of soft power, can there ever really be a strictly unipolar or bipolar world? Can these theories be expanded or combined to account for these types of "power"?

- What would be the Marxist and constructivist critiques of these theories of world system polarity?

Case Study:
*International
Security:
Nonproliferation*

more war prone than others, it would be imprudent to conclude that a new multipolar system will necessarily produce another period of warfare or of peace. But if the past is truly a reliable guide to the future, the distribution of global power will exert a strong influence on what kind of global system the world will experience.

Realists insist that the tragic struggle for security among great powers will continue (Mearsheimer 2001). Their expectations have been strengthened by China's rapid rise toward becoming the globe's biggest economy and the growing fears that this coming financial primacy will translate into Chinese *hard power* and a military threat, possibly even a new Chinese unipolar period. If the future belongs to China, counterbalancing by the other great powers in an anti-Chinese coalition is likely (Kugler 2006), possibly culminating in plans to contain and fight China (Kaplan 2005a). Likewise, realists think that great power competition will continue because the American military giant is unlikely to gracefully accept a reduction of its stature. Thus, realists believe that the U.S. quest to run a global empire will guarantee efforts to counterbalance American domination in hostile reaction (Walt 2005).

Charles Dharapak/AP Photo

MAKE NEW FRIENDS BUT KEEP THE OLD Global summits provide foreign leaders an opportunity to meet and listen to each other and strengthen alliances. "It's an opportunity," explained Denis McDonough, U.S. Deputy National Security Adviser, "to re-energize our alliances to confront the looming threats of the twenty-first century." Pictured here are leaders from around the world at the Nuclear Security Summit held in Washington D.C. on April 13, 2010. Leaders gathered to discuss ways to foil the threat of nuclear terrorism.

Other realists anticipate rising great power competition if, as they expect, the European Union grows to superpower status and begins flexing its muscles to counterbalance U.S. supremacy (Leonard 2005; McCormick 2007). In that scenario, the trans-Atlantic divide will widen, and so will economic struggles with China, India, and Japan as those rising powers begin to exert external pressure to contain European hegemony (Van Oudernaren 2005). A global shift is clearly in the making, although the trajectories in the rise and fall of the great powers' relative position in the global hierarchy are much in doubt.

As realists warn, if the past history of power transitions in the global balance of power is prologue, the global future may be a very dangerous future. "Major shifts of power between states," James Hoge (2006) warns, "occur infrequently and are rarely peaceful." When American primacy does wane, the American "hobbled hegemon" will no longer remain in position to play its self-described role of global peacekeeper. This power transition will create a new multipolar system (Palmer and Morgan 2007). The probable consequences are certain to prove disquieting.

Let us hope that these kinds of conditions will not materialize. But whatever ensues, a crucial question is certain to command attention at the center of

Simulation:
International
Relation Post 9/11

debate: whether international security is best served by states' military search for their own national security or whether, instead, the military pursuit of security through arms, alliances, and the balance of power will sow the seeds of the world's destruction. In the next two chapters of *World Politics*, turn your attention away from the balance-of-power politics of realism to examine proposals by liberal theorists to engineer institutional reforms in order to create a more orderly world order.

> *Those who scoff at "balance-of-power diplomacy" should recognize that the alternative to a balance of power is an imbalance of power—and history shows us that nothing so drastically escalates the danger of war as such an imbalance.*
>
> —Richard M. Nixon, U.S. President

Take an Online Practice Quiz

www.cengagebrain.com/shop/ISBN/0495802204

Suggested Readings

Brooks, Stephen G. and William C. Wohlforth. (2008) *World Out of Balance: International Relations and the Challenge of American Primacy.* Princeton, NJ: Princeton University Press.

Finnemore, Martha. (2009) "Legitimacy, Hypocrisy, and the Social Structure of Unipolarity: Why Being a Unipole Isn't All It's Cracked Up to Be," *World Politics* 61 (1): 58–85.

Haass, Richard N. (2008) "The Age of Nonpolarity," *Foreign Affairs* 87 (May/June): 44–56.

Kaplan, Robert D. (2009a) "The Revenge of Geography" *Foreign Policy* (May/June): 96–105.

Snyder, Glenn H. (2007) *Alliance Politics.* Ithaca: Cornell University Press.

Walt, Stephen M. (2009) "Alliances in a Unipolar World," *World Politics* 61 (1): 86–120.

CHAPTER 10
NEGOTIATED CONFLICT RESOLUTION AND INTERNATIONAL LAW

CHAPTER OUTLINE

LIBERAL AND CONSTRUCTIVIST ROUTES TO INTERNATIONAL PEACE

INTERNATIONAL CRISES AND THE NEGOTIATED SETTLEMENT OF DISPUTES

CONTROVERSY: Can Women Improve Global Negotiations and the Prospects for World Peace?

LAW AT THE INTERNATIONAL LEVEL

THE CHARACTERISTICS OF INTERNATIONAL LAW

Core Principles of International Law Today

Limitations of the International Legal System

The Abiding Relevance of International Law

THE LEGAL CONTROL OF ARMED AGGRESSION

Just War Doctrine: The Changing Ethics Regarding the Use of Armed Force

CONTROVERSY: Was the War in Iraq a Just War?

New Rules for Military Intervention

THE JUDICIAL FRAMEWORK OF INTERNATIONAL LAW

Law's Contribution to Peace and Justice

Although a more assertive world means more antagonists and demagogues, it also means more negotiators and regional leaders with a stake in keeping the peace. If that impulse can be organized and encouraged, the world will be a better place for it.
—Fareed Zakaria, international journalist

FDR Library: Wally McNamee/Historical/CORBIS; Dirck Halstead/Time & Life Pictures/Getty Images; Sergei Guneyev/Time Life Pictures/Getty Images; Larry Downing/Reuters/Landov; RIA-Novosti, Vladimir Rodionov, Presidential Press Service/AP Photo

Winston Churchill, Franklin D. Roosevelt, and Joseph Stalin, 1945

Richard Nixon and Leonid Brezhnev, 1972

Ronald Reagan and Mikhail Gorbachev, 1988

Boris Yeltsin and Bill Clinton, 1994

Vladimir Putin and George W. Bush, 2002

Dmitri Medvedev and Barack Obama, 2009

DIPLOMACY DIALOGUES To liberal reformers, direct negotiations between adversaries are a crucial step on the path to make peace a possibility. Talks allow both sides to put their interests on the bargaining table and discuss issues openly—far better than resolving them on the battlefield. As shown here, despite times of open hostility and opposing interests, diplomatic summits between the United States and Russia help to keep conflicts between the two great military powers "cold." While tensions persist, diplomacy is "worth a try. For this truth hasn't changed since the Cold War: when Russia and the United States don't get along, the rest of the world has every right to feel uneasy" (Ghosh 2009, p. 14).

Y ou overlook the incredibly low chances, purchase a lottery ticket, and hit an enormous jackpot. You are now very, very rich! What next? Remembering your pledge to try to make the world a better place before you die, you decide to put your ethical principles above power. To make a difference, you decide to invest your newfound wealth in projects that will "give peace a chance." Congratulations! You are joining Andrew Carnegie, Bill Gates, Warren Buffet, and other exceptionally wealthy philanthropists who generously chose to give large portions of their fortunes to causes that try to change the world for the better. You and they are following Carnegie's motto: "Private money for public service."

On what ventures should you prioritize the distribution of your fortune? The menu for choice is large. You could seek, for example, to strengthen human rights law, provide humanitarian relief for refugees, fight worldwide poverty and disease, join others in seeking to stem the threat of global warming, or subsidize a global campaign to educate all youth throughout the world. The needs are endless. Sorting through your moral values, however, you conclude that the greatest threat to the world is the awesome danger of armed aggression. Acting on this conviction, you see your mission to be helping others find better ways than military methods for preventing war. Reliance on weapons of war and balances of power has been tried since the beginning of time, but never with lasting success. So now you have found your cause—finding peaceful methods for controlling armed aggression. Alas, you must now go another difficult step in your attempt to clarify your values.

It is time for you to do some homework and draw lessons from policy makers and philosophers who have spent their lifetimes probing the same question you are now asking yourself—how to do good in a wicked world. Your Internet search directs you to thinkers who have values compatible with your own and who see ideas as powerful forces that shape our reality. The search engine directs you for insight to the knowledge of theorists from both liberal and constructivist perspectives.

To win without fighting is best.

—Sun Tzu, strategist in ancient China

LIBERAL AND CONSTRUCTIVIST ROUTES TO INTERNATIONAL PEACE

Scanning a long list of great books and then consulting them, you digest a vast literature and then reconstruct the principal approaches to the control of armed aggression. As Kimberly Hudson summarizes:

> Changing attitudes toward sovereignty are evident in the emerging norms of "sovereignty as responsibility," the "responsibility to protect," and the "responsibility to prevent," as well as in the work of international relations theorists in the liberal and constructivist schools. Unlike the realists, . . . who tend to view international relations as the a-moral, rational pursuit of narrow self-interest by rational unitary sovereign states, liberals emphasize interdependence and the possibility of cooperation, while constructivists stress the centrality of ideas as important for explaining and understanding international relations (Hudson 2009, p. 1).

The paths to peace that are depicted by various liberal thinkers differ greatly in their approach to world order, but they all share your great fear of states' historic propensity to wage war. You are drawn in particular to those sets of premises and perspectives that focus on diplomacy and international law as a means of resolving conflict. Resting on the liberal premises that principled moral behavior ultimately reaps higher rewards for all because fair treatment toward others promotes their fair behavior, and interstate cooperation can be encouraged by creating rules for peaceful interaction, liberal theory leads us to place emphasis on the role of collaboration and rule-making in shaping behavior in world politics.

To understand how international rules are created, *constructivism* informs us that leading ideas have meaningful consequences, and that when a favorable climate of opinion crystallizes about the preferred conduct for relations between states, those constructed images influence perceptions about the rules by which the game of nations should be played. Diplomatic negotiations and international law communicate the prevailing international consensus about the rules to govern international relations. For this reason, consistent with constructivist theory, many experts see international law mirroring changes in the most popular constructions of images about the ways in which states are habitually acting or should act toward one another in any particular period of history.

Keep these perspectives in mind as you contemplate the benefits and liabilities of alternative roads to peace. Here, rivet your focus on the hypotheses that the best way to prevent armed aggression is to either (1) settle, through

NEGOTIATING WITH A NEGOTIATOR ABOUT NEGOTIATION U.S. President George H. W. Bush meets with Charles Kegley, one of the authors of *World Politics*. The major topics they discussed: the uses and limits of methods of dispute settlement without the use of military force. These include diplomatic negotiations, international courts, collective security, and other methods of conflict resolution that are advocated by policy makers whose image of world politics is informed by liberal and constructivist theories.

diplomatic negotiations, international disputes before they escalate to warfare or (2) bring the use of armed force under meaningful legal controls that restrict the purposes for which armed aggression can be legally conducted, so that the likelihood of taking up arms will decline.

INTERNATIONAL CRISES AND THE NEGOTIATED SETTLEMENT OF DISPUTES

Recall the strategy realism strongly recommended: *coercive diplomacy*—a method of bargaining between states in which threats to use arms or the actual use of limited armed force are made to persuade an opponent to change its foreign policy and force it to make undesired concessions and compromises. The goal here is political—to exercise influence over an enemy in order to convince that enemy that acceding to an opposing state's demands will be less costly than defying those demands. This result, realists advise, can be accomplished by delivering an ultimatum that threatens the target with an immediate threat in order to increase pressure and make it comply with the coercive state's request.

The major problem with coercive diplomacy's reliance on the threat of armed force is that such acts usually create a crisis that escalates to war. And crises have been very frequent in modern history, and now "talk of crisis is everywhere in contemporary international relations" (Clark and Reus-Smit 2007) (see Figure 10.1). The problem that liberal reformers identify is that these crises and armed conflicts could potentially have been settled by diplomatic negotiations had that avenue for dispute settlement been attempted.

When a crisis erupts, the capacity for reaching coolheaded rational decisions is reduced. The threat to use force causes stress and reduces the amount of time available to reach decisions that might successfully end the *crisis* peacefully. Consider the 1962 Cuban Missile Crisis, which occurred when the Soviet Union installed medium-range nuclear missiles in Cuba and the United States responded to the emergent threat with a naval blockade. The danger of a total nuclear war quickly rose; in the aftermath U.S. President John F. Kennedy estimated that the odds were 50-50 that a nuclear exchange could have destroyed the entire world. And, often, such crises resulting from coercive military diplomacy *have* escalated to the use of force when bargaining failed and the adversaries took up arms. The Suez Crisis of 1956 is an often-cited example of the inherent dangers.

crisis
a situation in which the threat of escalation to warfare is high and the time available for making decisions and reaching compromised solutions in negotiations is compressed.

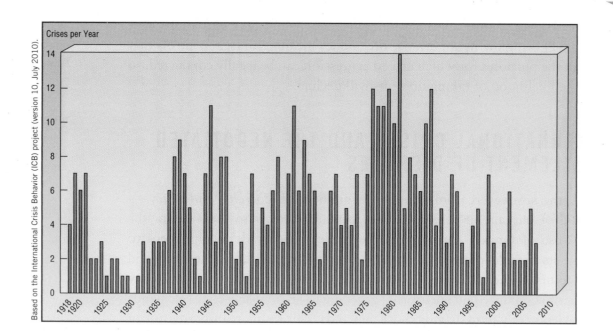

FIGURE 10.1

THE ANNUAL FREQUENCY OF NEW INTERNATIONAL CRISES SINCE WORLD WAR I More than a 1000 actors have been involved in over 455 international crises between 1918 and 2010. The frequency has varied over time, but its recurrence attests to states' compulsion to make threats to use military force to get their way and demonstrates that efforts to resolve disputes through negotiations have frequently either failed or were not pursued.

To liberals, it is always better to talk about percolating divisive issues at a negotiating table than to let anger and anxieties sizzle and tempt the disputants to take up arms. Only through discussion and bargaining can positions be clarified and, possibly, concession and compromises be reached that terminate the threat of warfare. *Negotiation* is a process of bargaining between two or more actors in an effort to deal with an issue or situation in order to reach an agreement that settles the dispute. At a basic, elementary level, negotiation entails an exchange of communications, with discussion flowing back and forth between the bargaining parties. As an approach to conflict management, the goal is to facilitate communication between the parties regarding their intentions and goals, and produce options that address the interests of those involved. In the give-and-take required to negotiate a compromised solution, there is a strong propensity for some level of *reciprocity* to emerge from the action-and-reaction sequence of communications—to return in kind or degree the kind of friendly or hostile communication received from the other party.

negotiation
diplomatic dialogue and discussion between two or more parties with the goal of resolving through give-and-take bargaining perceived differences of interests and the conflicts they cause.

reciprocity
the return of favors for favors or punishment for punishment between parties in a mutual exchange relationship.

Note that, for this reason, reciprocated communications can produce greater cooperation or greater conflict. The Chinese translation of the word "crisis" means both "opportunity" and "danger," and efforts to negotiate compromises provide an opportunity to produce a positive agreement or to produce a dangerous negative outcome that heightens threats and tensions. That is why negotiation is not a sure cure-all for the resolution of interstate conflicts and crises. Still, negotiations make possible the settlement of disputes, providing the offers of concessions freely given are reciprocated by the target with the same level of similar concessions. Vladimir Putin, Russia's Prime Minister, offered wise counsel saying that "Today to be successful, one must be able to reach agreements. The ability to compromise is not a diplomatic politeness but rather taking into account and respecting your partner's legitimate interests."

Reciprocated gestures of goodwill and empathy for the opponent's situation pave the way for a compromised agreement. Indeed, a common bargaining approach to induce the other party to reach agreements is through a *tit-for-tat strategy* that responds to any cooperative offer by immediately reciprocating it with an equal offer; the reward through repetitive concessions can facilitate a mutually satisfactory agreement.

tit-for-tat strategy
a bargaining approach that consistently reciprocates in kind the offers or threats made by the other party in a negotiation, with equivalent rewards returned and equivalent punishing communications returned in retaliation.

British diplomatic historian Sir Harold Nicolson defined diplomacy as "the management of the relations between independent states by the process of negotiation." Diplomacy is aimed at resolving international disputes peacefully, which is why diplomacy is favored by liberals. Conversely, realists, for whom states' primary interest is the pursuit of power, believe that threats of war preserve peace better than diplomatic efforts. Marxism takes a similarly pessimistic view of diplomatic approaches to peace, declaring that "when equal rights collide, force decides" (Carty 2008, p.122). Chinese Foreign Minister Zhou Enlai spoke to this view when he stated his cynical conviction that "all diplomacy is the continuation of war by other means."

Even when pursued for the prevention of armed aggression and the peaceful settlement of conflicts, diplomacy requires great intelligence, information, imagination, flexibility, ingenuity, and honesty to successfully maintain peaceful negotiations. To quell controversies, manage quarrels without resort to force, and lessen tensions and promote mutual understanding between rivals is a huge challenge in world politics. Convincing adversaries that their interests are served by forging cordial and durable relations and engaging them in a web of mutual interests is fraught with difficulties and as a result, negotiations between disputants often fail.

Compounding the challenge is the common liability that while diplomats are sent to negotiate for his or her country, no matter what their skill or sincerity, they cannot succeed unless they have the full backing of their government's authority. Diplomats must possess the authority to compromise and their leadership must accept the potential for public criticism for partially backing down to an adversary. Indeed, public scrutiny can cripple negotiations. Sometimes secrecy is necessary to make concessions and reach compromises without losing face; "unless covenants are arrived at secretly," warned U.S. President Richard M. Nixon, "there will be none to agree to openly." Dag Hammarskjöld, as UN Secretary General, similarly cautioned that "The best results of negotiation cannot be achieved in international life any more than in our private world in the full glare of publicity with current debate of all moves, unavoidable misunderstandings, inescapable freezing of positions due to considerations of prestige and the temptation to utilize public opinion as an element integrated into the negotiation itself." These problems, potholes, and pitfalls notwithstanding, liberals regard negotiation as a preferred method for fostering international peace. The alternative—the coercive use of military power—is ethically unacceptable to people seeking to avoid war.

Fortunately, those playing the game of international politics have been inventive in creating supplementary methods to enable negotiations to reduce the threat of war. Several types of approaches are available for opponents facing dangerous relations and the threat of war. All are now nested in the laws of nations accepted by the global community. Among such conflict resolution procedures, *mediation* by third-party intermediaries to assist in negotiated settlements displays a strong track record in terminating international crises (Bercovitch and Gartner 2008; Frazier and Dixon 2006). Mediation occurs

mediation
a conflict-resolution procedure in which a third party proposes a nonbinding solution to the disputants.

when an outside actor, either another state or a group of states in an intergovernmental organization (IGO), participate directly in negotiations between the parties to a dispute to aid them in recognizing their shared interests and proposing solutions based on these common interests. Three modes of mediation are practiced: "manipulation (in which the third party employs leverage in a carrot-and-stick approach to manipulate the parties toward a particular conclusion), facilitation (in which the third party takes on the noncoercive, facilitative role of communicator), and formulation (in which the mediator makes substantive suggestions as to what solutions might be possible)" (Wilkenfeld et al. 2005). Mediation works best, history shows, when democracies or international institutions perform the negotiating service, due in part to the influence of democratic social norms of conflict resolution (Mitchell et al. 2008; Shannon 2009). Greater involvement of women in international negotiations may also enhance the prospects for dispute resolution (see Controversy: Can Women Improve Global Negotiations and the Prospects for World Peace?). More pessimistically, the mediation of international crises has proven less successful when ethnic groups have been a player in the crisis that led to armed aggression (Ben-Yehuda and Mishali-Ran 2006).

Video: *Protecting Our Citizens*

CONTROVERSY:

CAN WOMEN IMPROVE GLOBAL NEGOTIATIONS AND THE PROSPECTS FOR WORLD PEACE?

Feminist theory stresses the importance of gender in studying world politics, and explores the extent to which a "masculine" conceptualization of key ideas—such as power, interest, and security—shapes the conduct of foreign affairs. While recognizing the influence of a masculine tradition of thought in world politics, some feminist scholarship posits that in practice there is on average no significant difference in the capabilities of men and women. Others, however, claim that differences exist and are contextual, with each gender being more capable than the other in certain endeavors. Does this apply to international negotiation? Do women bring strengths to the bargaining table and enhance the prospects for conflict resolution? Or are men better suited to the management of conflict?

Since the 1990s, feminist scholars have pointed to the different ways in which gender identity shapes international decision making (Ackerly and True 2008; Bolzendahl 2009; Peterson and Runyan 2009). With its emphasis on the role of power in an amoral pursuit of narrow self-interest by rational actors, realism portrays a competitive world with a preference for an instrumental masculine orientation to decision making. Power is typically viewed as the ability to influence another to do what you want them to do, and in this context the accumulation of power is achieved through greater strength and authority, and at the expense of others. Men tend to have independent self-schemas that lead

(continued)

CAN WOMEN IMPROVE GLOBAL NEGOTIATIONS AND THE PROSPECTS FOR WORLD PEACE? (Continued)

them to define themselves in distinction from others, and in decision making "tend to focus on end gains, making the achievement of personal preferences and goals the primary negotiation objective" (Boyer et al. 2009, p. 27). Thus men are often comfortable negotiating in situations in which controlled conflict is expected.

Some argue, however, that as a product of their traditional social roles, the tendency of women to have interdependent self-schemas and a nurturing orientation provides them with valuable perspectives that are an asset to conflict negotiation and mediation. How women frame and conduct negotiations is influenced by "a relational view of others, an embedded view of agency, an understanding of control through empowerment, and problem-solving through dialogue" (Kolb 1996, p. 139). As women are likely to "define themselves more through their relationships than do men, their actions and rhetoric within the negotiation process may be more oriented toward maintaining and protecting these relationships" (Boyer et al. 2009, p. 27). Moreover, women understand events in terms of a context that takes into account relationships as well as evolving situations. Eschewing the realist perspective of power achieved through competition, women tend to be more inclined to a liberal view of mutual empowerment achieved through cooperative interactions that construct connections and understanding. Not only are women more likely to cooperate with one another, "increasing the flow of information between the negotiators is essential to achieving a superior solution in an integrative bargain . . . and women are more likely to use these methods" (Babcock and Laschever 2003, pp. 169–170).

If gender differences produce different processes and outcomes in international negotiation, then many hypothesize that increasing the number of women involved in decision making may bring a fresh perspective to conflict management (Anderlini 2007). Rooted in the premise that women bring certain values to negotiation and mediation that are derived from their gendered socialization experiences, and that these insights and policy prescriptions have been absent due to the exclusionary nature of international negotiations (Hudson 2005), such is the intent of UN Resolution 1325, which seeks to "increase the participation of women at decision making levels in conflict resolution and peace processes" in the interest of generating new perspectives and options for lasting conflict resolution.

For social constructivists, "men and women's roles are not inherent or predetermined, but rather a social fact that can change through practice, interaction, and the evolution of ideas and norms" (Boyer et al. 2009, p. 26). Perhaps as greater numbers of women are included in international negotiations where men have traditionally dominated, both will benefit from the perspectives of the other and the role of diplomacy in preventing and resolving conflict will be enhanced.

WHAT DO YOU THINK?

- As a lead mediator trying to resolve an intractable conflict between two countries, what value would you place on having women at the bargaining table?

- Might the role of women in negotiation vary across different regions of the world? Will the negotiating styles of women be received differently across different cultures?

- Consider two current U.S. foreign policy figures: Secretary of State Hillary Clinton and President Barack Obama. How would you categorize their negotiating tendencies? Do they fit the gender mold as described here? Why or why not? What lessons for conflict resolution do they have to offer?

In addition, to reach agreements and settle disputes peacefully, several other conflict management procedures are practiced. They include:

- *Good offices*—when two conflicting parties have a history of relatively peaceful negotiations, often a "good office" will be provided by a third party as neutral ground for negotiation. In these circumstances, the good office provider does not participate in the actual negotiations

- *Conciliation*—when two or more conflicting parties wish to negotiate a dispute resolution but wish to maintain control over the final compromise, often a third party will assist both sides during the negotiations and attempt to offer unbiased opinions and suggestions to help achieve a solution while remaining neutral and refraining from proposing a solution

- *Arbitration*—when disputing parties are willing to allow a third party to make a binding decision to resolve their dispute, a temporary ruling board considers both opposing arguments and reaches a decision

- *Adjudication*—perhaps the most formal of the dispute resolution options, this approach is roughly the equivalent of arguing a case in court and accepting a binding decision or ruling by a judge

All of these methods for crisis management and dispute settlement are embedded in the international laws pertaining to negotiation. Liberals have long advocated that international law be strengthened in order to police armed aggression between states and to more capably provide for world order. Next the chapter will consider the place of international law in world politics and the rules that have been fashioned to control by legal methods armed international aggression.

good offices
provision by a third party to offer a place for negotiation among disputants but third party does not serve as a mediator in the actual negotiations.

conciliation
a conflict-resolution procedure in which a third party assists both parties to a dispute but does not propose a solution.

arbitration
a conflict-resolution procedure in which a third party makes a binding decision between disputants through a temporary ruling board created for that ruling.

adjudication
a conflict-resolution procedure in which a third party makes a binding decision about a dispute in an institutional tribunal.

LAW AT THE INTERNATIONAL LEVEL

When you think about law, it is very likely that you construct an image of how law functions within the country in which you are residing. In this constructed image, when a society perceives a particular type of behavior to be harmful, a law is predictably passed to prohibit it. The emergent consensus in many countries that underage drinking and smoking in public places are harmful led, for example, to new laws to regulate and prohibit these practices. So war—one state's attack, by choice, of another state, without imminent threat and therefore not in self-defense—would seem to likewise be an evil and dangerous practice that the global community would automatically prohibit, right? Actually, no, or at least not until relatively recently in the modern saga of world history.

International law has been conceived by and written mostly by realists, who place the privileges of the powerful as their primary concern and have historically advocated that war should be an acceptable practice to protect a dominant state's position in the global hierarchy. As William Bishop (1902) wrote, international law is not violated "when a state resorts to war for any reason it felt proper." This view then echoed the opinion of Henry Wheaton (1846), that "every state has a right to force." If murder and killing have been condemned in the precepts of your religion and prohibited by the laws of your country, you may be shocked to learn that the military drive for power has been legal in most historical phases of international law. Next, the chapter will look at the evolution of international law and how that situation came to be.

THE CHARACTERISTICS OF INTERNATIONAL LAW

In 1984, the United States announced that it would unilaterally withdraw from the jurisdiction of the International Court of Justice, or the World Court. This move followed Nicaragua's accusation that the U.S. Central Intelligence Agency (CIA) had illegally attempted to "overthrow and destabilize" the elected Sandinista government. Nicaragua charged that the United States had illegally mined its ports and supplied money, military assistance, and training to the rebel *contra* forces. The United States denied the tribunal's authority. In so doing, however, it was not acting without precedent; others had done so previously. Nonetheless, by thumbing its nose at the court and the rule of law it represents, had the United States, as some claimed, become an "international outlaw"? Or, as others asserted, had it acted within its rights?

The World Court supported the former view. In 1984, the court ruled against the United States as follows:

> The right to sovereignty and to political independence possessed by the Republic of Nicaragua, like any other state of the region or of the world, should be fully respected and should not in any way be jeopardized by any military and paramilitary activities which are prohibited by the principles of international law, in particular the principle that states should refrain in their international relations from the threat or the use of force against the territorial integrity or the political independence of any state, and the principle concerning the duty not to intervene in matters within the domestic jurisdiction of a state (*New York Times,* May 11, 1984, p. 8).

Yet this ruling had little effect, as neither the court nor Nicaragua had any means to enforce it.

Many experts—whether they are realists or liberals—skeptically ask whether international law is really law. Radical theory shares this skepticism, holding that "the form of international law consists of the struggle between states' view of legal right, and the view that prevails will depend on which state happens to be stronger" (Carty 2008, p. 122; Mieville 2006). Yet there are many reasons to have confidence in the rule of law. Although international law is imperfect, actors regularly rely on it to redress grievances (see Joyner 2005). Most global activity falls within the realm of *private international law*—the regulation of the kinds of transnational activities undertaken every day in such areas as commerce, communications, and travel. Although largely invisible to the public, private international law is the location for almost all international legal activities. It is where most transnational disputes are regularly settled and where the record of compliance compares favorably with that achieved in domestic legal systems.

private international law
law pertaining to routine transnational intercourse between or among states as well as nonstate actors.

In contrast, *public international law* covers issues of relations between governments and the interactions of governments with intergovernmental organizations (IGOs) and nongovernmental organizations (NGOs) such as multinational corporations. Some believe that we should use the phrase *world law* to describe the mixture of public and private, domestic and international transactions that public international law seeks to regulate in an increasingly globalized world. However, it is the regulation of government-to-government relations that dominates the headlines in discussion of public international law. This area of activity also receives most of the criticism, for here, failures—when they occur—are conspicuous. As Israeli diplomat Abba Eban cynically quipped, "International law is that law which the wicked do not obey and the righteous do not enforce." This is especially true with respect to the breakdown of peace and security. When states engage in armed conflict, criticism of public international law's shortcomings escalates.

public international law
law pertaining to government-to-government relations as well as countries' relations with other types of transnational actors.

Without a doubt, the inability of public international law to control armed aggression is regarded as its greatest weakness. To cut deeper into the characteristics of contemporary international law, the chapter will next look briefly at some of its other salient characteristics.

Core Principles of International Law Today

No principle of international law is more important than state sovereignty. Ever since the 1648 Treaties of Westphalia, states have tried to reserve the right to perform within their territories in any way the government chooses. That norm is the basis for all other legal rules; the key concepts in international law all speak to the rules by which sovereign states say they wish to abide.

Sovereignty means that no authority is legally above the state, except that which the state voluntarily confers on the international organizations it joins. In fact, as conceived by theoreticians schooled in the realist tradition since the seventeenth century, all the rules of international law express codes of conduct that protect a state's freedom to preserve its sovereign independence.

Nearly every legal doctrine supports and extends the cardinal principle that states are the primary subjects of international law. Although the *Universal Declaration of Human Rights* in 1948 expanded concern about states' treatment of individual people, states remain supreme. Accordingly, the vast majority of rules address the rights and duties of states, not people. As Gidon Gottlieb has observed, "Laws are made to protect the state from the individual and not the individual from the state." For instance, the principle of **sovereign equality** entitles each state to full respect by other states as well as equal protection by the system's legal rules. The right of independence also guarantees states' autonomy in their domestic affairs and external relations, under the logic that the independence of each presumes that of all. Similarly, the doctrine of **neutrality** permits states to avoid involvement in others' conflicts and coalitions.

Furthermore, the noninterference principle forms the basis for the *nonintervention norm*—requiring states to refrain from uninvited activities within in another country's territory. This sometimes-abused classic rule gives governments the right to exercise jurisdiction over practically all things on, under, or above their bounded territory. (There are exceptions, however, such as **diplomatic immunity** for states' ambassadors from the domestic laws of the country where their embassies are located and **extraterritoriality**, which allows control of embassies on other states' terrain.)

In practice, domestic jurisdiction permits a state to enact and enforce whatever laws it wishes for its own citizens. In fact, international law was so permissive toward the state's control of its own domestic affairs that, before 1952, "there was no precedent in international law for a nation-state to assume responsibility for the crimes it committed against a minority within its jurisdiction" (Wise 1993). A citizen was not protected against the state's abuse of human rights or **crimes against humanity**.

Limitations of the International Legal System

Sovereignty and the legal principles derived from it shape and reinforce international anarchy. This means that world politics is reduced to the level of interaction without meaningful regulation or true global governance; international politics is legally dependent on what governments choose to do with

---

sovereign equality
the principle that states are legally equal in protection under international law.

neutrality
the legal doctrine that provides rights for states to remain nonaligned with adversaries waging war against each other.

diplomatic immunity
the legal doctrine that gives a country's officials when abroad (e.g., diplomats and ambassadors) release from the local legal jurisdiction of the state when they are visiting or stationed abroad to represent their own government.

extraterritoriality
the legal doctrine that allows states to maintain jurisdiction over their embassies in other states.

crimes against humanity
a category of activities, made illegal at the Nuremberg war crime trials, condemning states that abuse human rights.

one another and the kinds of rules they voluntarily support. Throughout most of modern history, international law as constructed by realists was designed by states to protect the state, and thereby made sovereignty the core principle to ensure states' freedom to act in terms of their perceived national interests. Moreover, the great powers alone have the capacity to promote wide acceptance and then enforce the *transnational norms* of statecraft they favor.

transnational norms the regular customs widely practiced by countries in their relations with other countries and the kinds of behavior that the international community accepts as what ought to be practiced.

To liberal theoreticians, putting the state ahead of the global community was a serious flaw that undermined international law's potential effectiveness. Many theorists consider the international legal system institutionally defective due to its dependence on states' willingness to participate. Because formal legal institutions (such as those within states) are weak at the global level, critics make the following points.

First, in world politics, no legislative body is capable of making binding laws. Rules are made only when states willingly observe or embrace them in the treaties to which they voluntarily subscribe. There is no systematic method of amending or revoking treaties. Article 38 of the Statute of the International Court of Justice (or World Court) affirms this. Generally accepted as the authoritative definition of the "sources of international law," it declares that international law derives from (1) custom, (2) international treaties and agreements, (3) national and international court decisions, (4) the writings of legal authorities and specialists, and (5) the "general principles" of law recognized since the Roman Empire as part of "natural law" and "right reason."

Second, in world politics, no judicial body exists to authoritatively identify and record the rules accepted by states, interpret when and how the rules apply, and identify violations. Instead, states are responsible for performing these tasks themselves. The World Court does not have the power to perform these functions without states' consent, and the UN cannot speak on judicial matters for the whole global community (even though it has recently defined a new scope for Chapter VII of the UN Charter that claims the right to make quasi-judicial authoritative interpretations of global laws).

Finally, in world politics there is no executive body capable of enforcing the rules. Rule enforcement usually occurs through the unilateral self-help actions of the victims of a transgression or with the assistance of their allies or other interested parties. No centralized enforcement procedures exist, and compliance is voluntary. The whole system rests, therefore, on states' willingness to abide by the rules to which they consent and on the ability of each to enforce through retaliatory measures violations of the norms of behavior they value.

Consequently, states themselves—not a higher authority—determine what the rules are, when they apply, and how they should be enforced. This raises the question of greatest concern to liberal advocates of world law: When all are above the law, are any truly ruled by it? It is precisely this problem that prompts reformers to restrict the sovereign freedom of states and expand their common pursuit of shared legal norms in order to advance collective global interests over the interests of individual states.

Beyond the barriers to legal institutions that sovereignty poses, still other weaknesses reduce confidence in international law:

- **International law lacks universality.** An effective legal system must represent the norms shared by those it governs. According to the precept of Roman law, *ubi societas, ibi jus* (where there is society, there is law), shared community values are a minimal precondition for forming a legal system. Yet the contemporary international order is culturally and ideologically pluralistic and lacks consensus on common values, as evidenced by the "clash of civilizations" (Berger and Huntington 2002) and the rejection by terrorists and others of the Western-based international legal order. The simultaneous operation of often incompatible legal traditions throughout the world undermines the creation of a universal, *cosmopolitan* culture and legal system (Bozeman 1994).

- **Under international law, legality and legitimacy do not always go hand in hand.** As in any legal system, in world politics what is legal is not necessarily legitimate. While legality is important in determining an action's legitimacy, other values play a role—such as the propriety of effectively addressing substantial threats. Moreover, the legality of an action does not always assure its wisdom or utility. "The UN Security Council's decision to deny weapons to victims of ethnic and religious abuse in Yugoslavia in the early 1990s, for example, was legal but arguably illegitimate, whereas NATO's unauthorized use of force to prevent abuses in Kosovo was illegal but arguably legitimate" (Sofaer 2010, p.117).

- **International law is an instrument of the powerful to oppress the weak.** In a voluntary consent system, the rules to which the powerful willingly agree are those that serve their interests. These rules therefore preserve the existing global hierarchy (Goldsmith and Posner 2005). For this reason, some liberal theorists claim that international law has bred the so-called *structural violence* resulting from the hierarchical

structural violence
the condition defined by Norwegian peace researcher Johan Galtung as the harm and injury caused by the global system's unregulated structure, which gives strong states great opportunities to victimize weak states that cannot protect themselves.

global system in which the strong benefit at the expense of the weak (Galtung 1969).

■ **International law is little more than a justification of existing practices.** When a particular behavior pattern becomes widespread, it becomes legally obligatory; rules of behavior become rules *for* behavior (Leopard 2010). Eminent legal scholar Hans Kelsen's (2007, p.369) contention that "states ought to behave as they have customarily behaved" reflects the *positivist legal theory* that when a type of behavior occurs frequently, it becomes legal. In fact, positive legal theory stresses that law is socially constructed. States' customary practices are the most important source from which laws derive in the absence of formal machinery for creating international rules. When the origins of international law are interpreted in this way, the actions of states construct law, not vice versa.

positivist legal theory a theory that stresses states' customs and habitual ways of behaving as the most important source of law.

■ **International law's ambiguity reduces law to a policy tool for propaganda purposes.** The vague, elastic wording of international law makes it easy for states to define and interpret almost any action as legitimate. "The problem here," observes Samuel S. Kim (1991, p. 111), "is the lack of clarity and coherence [that enables] international law [to be] easily stretched, . . . to be a flexible fig leaf or a propaganda instrument." This ambivalence makes it possible for states to exploit international law to get what they can and to justify what they have obtained.

The Abiding Relevance of International Law

Although international law has deficiencies, this should not lead to the conclusion that it is irrelevant or useless. States themselves find international law useful and expend much effort to shape its evolution. States' actual behavior demonstrates that countries interpret international law as real law and obey it most of the time (Joyner 2005).

The major reason that even the most powerful states usually abide by international legal rules is that they recognize that adherence pays benefits that outweigh the costs of expedient rule violation. International reputations are important. They contribute to a state's *soft power.* Those that play the game of international politics by recognized rules receive rewards, whereas states that ignore international law or opportunistically break customary norms pay costs for doing as they please. Other countries will be reluctant to cooperate with them. Violators also must fear retaliation by those victimized, as well as the loss of prestige. For this reason, only the most ambitious or reckless state is apt to flagrantly disregard accepted standards of conduct.

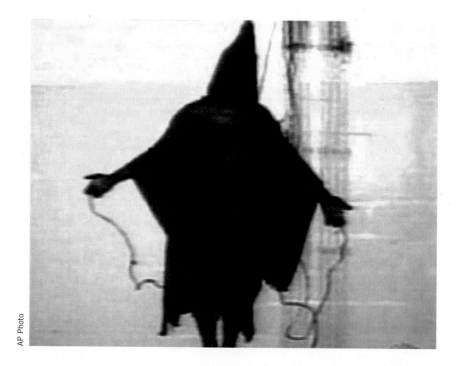

WAR CRIMES AND THE LOSS OF GLOBAL LEGITIMACY In 2004, scandal erupted when over one thousand graphic photos taken at the Abu Ghraib prison in Baghdad were televised worldwide, ostensibly showing U.S. personnel torturing Iraqi prisoners. Similar methods—including electric shocks, prolonged exposure to frigid temperatures, and simulated drowning—were purportedly used to interrogate terror suspects detained at the U.S. Guantanamo Naval Base as well, which has become a negative symbol of U.S. power in the Muslim world. Shortly after taking office, President Obama signed an executive order to ban harsh interrogation tactics and shut down the detention site by January 2010. However, "stymied by political opposition and focused on competing priorities, the Obama administration has sidelined efforts to close the Guantanamo prison, making it unlikely that President Obama will fulfill his promise to close it before his term ends in 2013" (Savage 2010, p.A13).

A primary reason why states value international law and affirm their commitment to it is that they need a common understanding of the "rules of the game." Law helps shape expectations, and rules reduce uncertainty and enhance predictability in international affairs. These communication functions serve every member of the global system. As constructivist theory elucidates, transnational norms historically change in conjunction with each major transformation in world politics—with fundamental changes in prevailing global conditions, such as shifts in the primary foreign policy goals that states are pursuing. According to this constructivist interpretation, throughout history the rules of international statecraft have changed in the aftermath of changes in the customary practices of how states are mostly behaving.

Every breakdown of international law, of course, does not prove the existence of general lawlessness. Conditions of crisis strain *all* legal systems, and few, when tested severely, can contain all violence. Today, with street crime in cities worldwide at epidemic proportions and ethnic and religious warfare *within* countries exacting a deadly toll against hundreds of minority groups, states' domestic legal systems are clearly failing to prevent killing. Powerful organized crime threatens the stability and security of many countries and poses a global threat through transnational activities such as the trafficking of drugs, slaves, weapons, and precious gems. This suggests that even when strong formal institutions for rule enforcement are in place, they do not and cannot guarantee compliance. No legal system can deter all of its members from breaking existing laws. Consequently, it is a mistake to expect a legal system to prevent all criminal behavior or to assert that any violation of the law proves the inadequacy of the legal structure. Law is designed to deter crime, but it is unreasonable to expect it to prevent it. Thus, the allegedly "deficient" international legal system may perform its primary task—inhibiting interstate violence—even more effectively than supposedly more-sophisticated domestic systems. Perhaps, then, the usual criteria by which critics assess legal systems are dubious. Should critics be less concerned with structures and institutions and more concerned with performance?

> *International law is an institutional device for communicating to the policymakers of various states a consensus on the nature of the international system.*
>
> —William D. Coplin, international legal theoretician

THE LEGAL CONTROL OF ARMED AGGRESSION

Liberal reformers often complain that international law is the weakest in controlling armed aggression—the realm of behavior most resistant to legal control. If under international law, as fashioned by realist leaders, states are "legally bound to respect each other's independence and other rights, and yet free to attack each other at will" (Brierly 1944, p. 21), international law may not impede war. The ethical and jurisprudential *just war doctrine* from which the laws of war stem shapes discussions of contemporary public international law (Wills 2004). As constructivists point out, throughout history, changes in international law have followed changes in the moral consensus about the ethics of using armed force in interstate relations. Therefore, it is important to understand the origins of just war theory and the way it is evolving today, before reviewing contemporary changes in the legal rules of warfare that have led to the formation of *security regimes*—sets of rules to contain armed aggression.

just war doctrine
the moral criteria identifying when a just war may be undertaken and how it should be fought once it begins.

Just War Doctrine: The Changing Ethics Regarding the Use of Armed Force

Many people are confused by international law because it both prohibits and justifies the use of force. The confusion derives from the just war tradition in "Christian realism," in which the rules of war are philosophically based on *morals* (principles of behavior) and *ethics* (explanations of why these principles are proper). In the fourth century, St. Augustine questioned the strict view that those who take another's life to defend the state necessarily violate the commandment "Thou shalt not kill." He counseled that "it is the wrong-doing of the opposing party which compels the wise man to wage just wars." The Christian was obligated, he felt, to fight against evil and wickedness. To St. Augustine, the City of Man was inherently sinful, in contrast to the City of God. Thus, in the secular world, it was sometimes permissible to kill—to punish a sin by an aggressive enemy (while still loving the sinner) to achieve a "just peace." This realist logic was extended by Pope Nicholas I, who in 866 proclaimed that any defensive war was just.

> **morals**
> principles clarifying the difference between good and evil and the situations in which they are opposed.

The modern just war doctrine evolved from this perspective, as developed by such humanist reformers as Hugo Grotius. He challenged the warring Catholic and Protestant Christian powers in the Thirty Years' War (1618–1648) to abide by humane standards of conduct and sought to replace the two "cities," or ethical realms of St. Augustine, with a single global society under law. For Grotius, a just war was only one fought in self-defense to punish damages caused by an adversary's blatant act of armed aggression: "No other just cause for undertaking war can there be excepting injury received." For war to be moral it must also be fought by just means without harm to innocent noncombatants. From this distinction evolved the modern version of just war doctrine, consisting of two categories of argument, *jus ad bellum* (the justice of a war) and *jus in bello* (justice in a war). The former sets the legal criteria by which a leader may wage a war. The latter specifies restraints on the range of permissible tactics to be used in fighting a just war.

> **jus ad bellum**
> a component of just war doctrine that establishes criteria under which a just war may be initiated
>
> **jus in bello**
> a component of just war doctrine that sets limits on the acceptable use of force

At the core of the just war tradition is the conviction that the taking of human life may be a "lesser evil" when it is necessary to prevent further life-threatening aggression (Ignatieff 2004b). Christian theologian St. Thomas More (1478–1535) contended that the assassination of an evil leader responsible for starting a war was justified if it would prevent the taking of innocent lives. From this premise, a number of other principles now follow. The criteria today include ten key ideas:

■ All other means to a morally just solution of conflict must be exhausted before a resort to arms can be justified.

- War can be just only if employed to defend a stable political order or a morally preferable cause against a real threat or to restore justice after a real injury has been sustained.

- A just war must have a reasonable chance of succeeding in these limited goals.

- A just war must be proclaimed by a legitimate government authority.

- War must be waged for the purpose of correcting a wrong rather than for malicious revenge.

- Negotiations to end a war must be a continuous process as long as fighting continues.

- Particular people in the population, especially noncombatants, must be immune from intentional attack.

- Only legal and moral means may be employed to conduct a just war.

- The damage likely to be incurred from a war may not be disproportionate to the injury suffered.

- The final goal of the war must be to reestablish peace and justice.

WAR AND THE BIRTH OF MODERN INTERNATIONAL LAW Enraged by inhumane international conditions that he witnessed during his lifetime, Dutch reformer Hugo Grotius (1583–1645) wrote *De Jure Belli et Pacis (On the Law of War and Peace)* in 1625 in the midst of the Thirty Years' War. His treatise called on the great powers to resolve their conflicts by judicial procedures rather than on the battlefield and specified the legal principles he felt could encourage cooperation, peace, and more humane treatment of people.

These ethical criteria continue to color thinking about the rules of warfare and the circumstances under which the use of armed force is legally permissible. However, the advent of nuclear and chemical or biological weapons of mass destruction that would violate many of these principles has created a crisis of relevance in just war doctrine (Hensel 2007), which has been further exacerbated by the trend toward intrastate conflicts involving both state and nonstate actors (Hudson 2009). Fuzzy circumstances have materialized with the innovations of the *revolution in military technology* (RMT). For example, insurgent terrorists and now the armies fighting them are increasingly relying on Improvised Explosive Devices (IEDs) planted on animal carcasses, mobile cell phones, or human cadavers in addition to IEDs left in the open in order to kill without risk of death to the killers. Today's IEDs, first invented by the United States and now on the global black market for purchase by any transnational extremist, are cheap and easy-to-make gadgets such as garage-door openers used to detonate bombs. How can international law control such innovative new ways of carrying out armed aggression, when the aggressors using them can not be treated as criminals? Because containment and prevention of violence have become the chief purposes of arms and armies today, leaders and scholars are struggling to revise just war doctrine to deal with the new strategic realities of contemporary weapons and warfare (J. Johnson 2005).

As Figure 10.2 shows, since World War I the international community has increasingly rejected the traditional legal right of states to use military force to achieve their foreign policy objectives. Just war theory reflects the continuing quest to place legal constraints on the use of armed force in order to create a moral consensus about the conditions under which ends justify means, even though today disagreements continue about the criteria that should be accepted. These differences became especially evident in the heated debate after the U.S. preemptive invasion of Iraq in 2003. Many condemned the U.S. invasion as a breach of international law (Paust 2007), calling the United States a "rogue

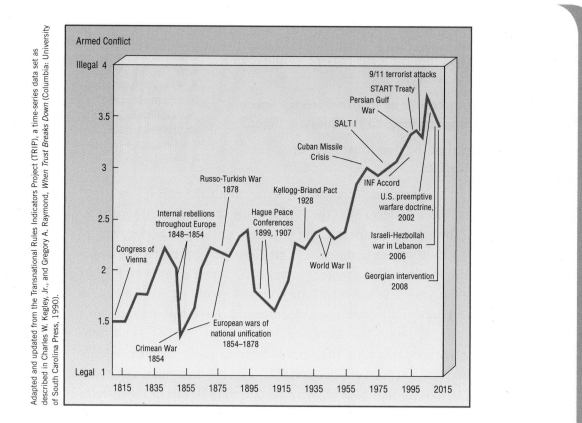

Adapted and updated from the Transnational Rules Indicators Project (TRIP), a time-series data set as described in Charles W. Kegley, Jr., and Gregory A. Raymond, *When Trust Breaks Down* (Columbia: University of South Carolina Press, 1990).

FIGURE 10.2

THE LEGAL PROHIBITION AGAINST INITIATING WARS, 1815–2010 Legal restraints on the historic right of states to start a war have fluctuated over time, but have increased steadily since World War I when that carnage prompted the global community to make wars of conquest illegal. Since 9/11, these legal prohibitions have been questioned in the aftermath of the U.S. efforts to promote *preemption* as a legal right to repel the *potential* aggression of another state or nonstate terrorist network even before its threat of attack is imminent, which blurs the distinction between preemptive war and preventive war.

nation" and an outlaw state (Gareau 2004; Hathaway 2007). Even famous realists (Mearsheimer and Walt 2003) joined liberals in labeling the U.S. invasion of Iraq "an unnecessary war" (see Controversy: Was the War in Iraq a Just War?). However, others disagreed (Elsthain 2003), with some suggesting that U.S. intent in waging war was justifiable as Saddam Hussein intentionally let the United States believe Iraq had weapons of mass destruction.

The U.S. invasion of Iraq made the legality of the use of force a hot topic, and concerns emerged regarding the preemptive and preventive use of force. The Bush administration's support for preventive action that included the

CONTROVERSY:

WAS THE WAR IN IRAQ A JUST WAR?

Before the March 2003 U.S. invasion of Iraq, U.S. President Bush claimed to have solid evidence that Iraqi dictator Saddam Hussein possessed and was concealing "some of the most lethal weapons ever devised." The Bush administration further claimed that Saddam Hussein had close ties with the Al Qaeda terrorist network that orchestrated the 9/11 attack on the United States. Warning that Saddam Hussein would "stop at nothing until something stops him," the United States undertook a massive attack to overthrow the rogue dictatorship. The preemptive strike to attack Iraq before it could attack the United States resulted in a quick and overwhelming intervention that drove the Iraqi leader into hiding (and later, death by hanging).

On May 1, 2003, President Bush, dramatically dressed in an Air Force uniform, spoke from the flight deck of the *USS Abraham Lincoln* behind a flying banner that declared, "Mission Accomplished." However, that was not to be the case; more than six years later, American troops remained locked in deadly fighting with Iraqi insurgents and suicide terrorist bombers seeking to drive the United States from occupied Iraq, Afghanistan, and Islamic holy lands. Though many in the United States expected to be welcomed with rice and rose petals, instead 80 percent of the Iraqi population saw the American troops as an invading army rather than their liberators.

As the body toll of American troops climbed to the thousands, criticism of the war's purposes, conduct, and strategy mounted in American public opinion. Furthermore, after exhaustive searches, even U.S. intelligence agencies could uncover no evidence, as the United States had claimed, that Saddam Hussein had been either hiding weapons of mass destruction or had supported Al Quada's 9/11 terrorist attack. Interrogations with Saddam Hussein after his capture similarly revealed that though he had intentionally misled the world about Iraqi WMD in an effort to present a strong face to its hostile neighbor Iran, Iraq did not in fact possess such weapons nor was it aligned with Osama bin Laden, whom Saddam Hussein dismissed as a "zealot" (Gamel 2009). The initial definition of the Iraq war's mission was then modified, with the United States declaring in 2005 that henceforth it would "seek and

(continued)

WAS THE WAR IN IRAQ A JUST WAR? (Continued)

support the growth of democratic movements and institutions in every nation and culture, with the ultimate goal of ending tyranny in our world."

This "liberal-hawk" (Judt 2007) abrupt shift in the American rationale for the Iraq war raises important questions about the conditions, if any, under which it is just for any country to wage war against an adversary. When is warfare justified (*jus ad bellum*)? What are the just means by which a military might fight a war (*jus in bello*)?

These types of questions are central to the ethical evaluation of international behavior and lie at the intersection of the debate between realists and liberals. Policy makers and analysts are divided about the purposes for which military force might be justifiably used. For instance, former National Security Advisor General Brent Scowcroft, who served the senior Bush presidency and who calls himself an "enlightened realist" as well as a "cynical ideal-ist," criticized the U.S. intervention as a misguided example of putting liberal idealism over national self-interest because "a true realist does not employ the military for selfless humanitarian operations" and does not enter a war without an exit strategy. In contrast, former U.S. diplomat Richard Holbrooke voiced a liberal justification for the use of military force when it is able to "marry idealism and realism. . . . Support for American values is part of [U.S.] national-security interests, and it is realistic to support humanitarian and human-rights interventions." Here a liberal policymaker sided with the neoconservative realist Paul Wolfowitz, the Deputy Secretary of Defense in the Bush administration, who most vigorously advocated the war in Iraq when he argued that "people can look around and see the overwhelming success of representative government."

To illustrate the spectrum of opinion about the war further, many neoliberals complain that the Bush administration abused "liberal democratic peace theory" and applied it inappropriately to justify an illegal preventive war against an enemy that posed no real threat (Russett 2005). To fight a war to overthrow a tyrant and establish by force democratic regimes in the Middle East are "rationales [that] strain the traditional understanding of humanitarian interven-tion" (Nardin 2005, p. 21). In this context, George W. Bush's claim that "the advance of freedom leads to peace" has empirical merit (Rasler and Thompson 2005), but critics can agree with the warning of Jiirgen Habermas that "bad consequences can discredit good intentions." To fight for noble causes and risk waging an unjust war can become a form of "humanitarian imperialism" (Nardin 2005). These viewpoints suggest an ethical principle about the politics of military intervention argued by the famed realist Lutheran theologian Reinhold Niebuhr: "Every nation is caught in the moral paradox of refusing to go to war unless it can be proved that the national interest is imperiled, and of continuing in the war only by proving that something much more than national interest is at stake."

WHAT DO YOU THINK?

- Drawing on the criteria proposed by just war theorists, would you characterize the 2003 U.S. war against Iraq as a just war? Was it initiated for a just cause and with the right intentions? Was it undertaken as a last resort with the appropriate authorization?

- Remembering Chapter 1's lessons, how do perceptions, or possibly misperceptions, play a role in determining military interventions? Can a war be just and unjust at the same time?

- How does the rise of non-state-actor aggression, such as terrorism, affect attempting to wage *jus ad bellum*? How about *jus in bello*?

use of force against states that either supported or failed to oppose terrorism was particularly controversial since such use of force is generally viewed as a violation of international law. "The International Court of Justice (ICJ) and most international legal authorities currently construe the United Nations Charter as prohibiting any use of force not sanctioned by the UN Security Council, with the exception of actions taken in self-defense against an actual or imminent state-sponsored 'armed attack'" (Sofaer 2010, p.110). The doctrine of *military necessity* still accepts the use of military force as legal but only as a last recourse for defense (Raymond 1999).

However, a hegemonic superpower has the capacity to challenge prevailing norms and change international law. As former U.S. diplomat Richard N. Cooper notes, "throughout history dominant states have shaped international law." The Bush Doctrine's endorsement of preemptive military strikes to prevent and counter anticipated threats could pave the way for the legalization of *preventive war* for all countries, as well as the preventive use of force to counter genocide, massive human rights violations, and the spread of criminal activities such as piracy and drug trafficking (Caldwell and Williams 2006; Sofaer 2010).

New Rules for Military Intervention

International law has recently begun to fundamentally revise its traditional prohibition against military intervention in the wake of the recent wave of terrorism by states against their own people. For humanitarian purposes, the belief that governments have a right, even an obligation, to intervene in the affairs of other states under certain conditions has won advocates. Today international law has defined military intervention as a right and duty to alleviate human suffering, stop genocide and ethnic cleansing, and prevent the repression by states of basic human rights and civil liberties (Feinstein and Slaughter 2004; Finnemore 2003). The result has been the collapse of the Westphalian principle that what a state does within its own borders is its own business. International law has relaxed its restrictive definition of when the global community can legally use military intervention to make it increasingly permissive (see Figure 10.3). The world has made a choice on genocide, declaring organized savagery illegal: "The last fifty years have seen the rise of universally endorsed principles of conduct," defining humanitarian intervention as a legal right to protect *human rights*—political rights and civil liberties now recognized by the global community as inalienable and valid for all individuals in all countries. This rule change permits states and international organizations to punish acts of genocide by re-interpreting the

military necessity
the legal principle that violation of the rules of warfare may be excused for defensive purposes during periods of extreme emergency.

preventive war
strictly outlawed by international law, a war undertaken by choice against an enemy to prevent it from suspected intentions to attack sometime in the distant future—if and when the enemy might acquire the necessary military capabilities.

Animated Learning
Module: *The Use of Force*

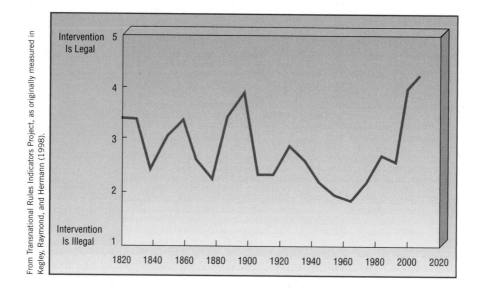

From Transnational Rules Indicators Project, as originally measured in Kegley, Raymond, and Hermann (1998).

FIGURE 10.3

THE CHANGING STATUS OF THE NONINTERVENTION NORM IN INTERNATIONAL LAW SINCE 1820 Over time, the illegality of intervening in sovereign states has changed, as measured by changes in international law about the prevailing consensus regarding rules for international conduct. Since 1960, international law has adopted an increasingly permissive posture toward this form of coercive diplomacy for a variety of purposes, including humanitarian aid, preventing genocide, protecting civil liberties, promoting democracy through "reform interventions," and combating global terrorism.

traditional rule against external interference in the internal affairs of another state and making outside intervention permissible. This includes even the right to military invasion and occupation.

This sea change suggests that international law develops and changes most rapidly when global problems arise that require collective solutions and legal remedies. The spread of genocide and atrocities in failed states and countries ruled by tyrants has spawned new sets of legal rules to arrest these dangers. Likewise, the rising frequency of global terrorism has pushed efforts to rewrite international law to permit interventions within countries that provide terrorists a secure base of operations, in order to contain terrorist acts of violence.

> Attention to terrorism has led to increased cooperation and spawned new branches of international law. Terrorism has prompted states to step up their mutual cooperation on criminal matters based on common interest, both to prevent terrorist groups from attacking innocent civilians or state officials, and, in case such attacks are carried out, to arrest the culprits and bring them to justice. Treaties which demand that states either extradite or prosecute those accused of terrorism committed outside their territory have multiplied and are now copied in fields such as money laundering, corruption, and drug trafficking (Cassese and Clapham 2001, p. 411).

THE JUDICIAL FRAMEWORK OF INTERNATIONAL LAW

Laws regulating the methods that states may use in war (*jus in bello*) have also grown. These restraints include the principles of discrimination and *noncombatant immunity*, which attempt to protect innocent civilians by restricting military targets to soldiers and supplies. The laws of retaliation specify conditions under which certain practices are legitimate. One category of *coercive power*, *reprisals* (hostile and illegal acts permitted only if made in proportionate response to a prior hostile and illegal act), stipulates procedures for military occupations, blockades, shows of force, and bombardments. Another category, *retorsion* (hostile but legal retaliatory acts made in response to similar legal acts initiated by other states), provides rules for embargoes, boycotts, import quotas, tariffs, and travel restrictions to redress grievances.

The advent of a new set of legal justifications for military intervention to protect civilians is explained by the fact that noncombatants have become the primary victims in warfare. "World War I was a mass-conscription, democratic war with a vengeance, but it still was limited in its direct effect on civilians. The ratio of soldiers to civilians killed between 1914 and 1918 was about 90 to 10. In World War II, the ratio was 50-to-50. In recent years, it has been 90 civilian casualties to every 10 military losses—a reversal of the World War I ratio" (Pfaff 1999, p. 8).

To be sure, liberal and constructivist reformers have a long way to travel to fulfill their wish to see international law strengthen so that it can more effectively police international armed aggression. The institutional weaknesses remain. However, reformers take heart from the trends that have recently enabled international law to increase its capacity to manage the threat of war within states, between states, and through global terrorism. They point with confidence to these steps. And they question those cynics who still contend that international law is and should remain irrelevant to states' use of armed force. They argue that:

- International law is not intended to prevent *all* warfare. Aggressive war is illegal, but defensive war is not. It is a mistake, therefore, to claim that international law has broken down whenever war breaks out.

- Instead of doing away with war, international law preserves it as a sanction against breaking rules. Thus, war is a method of last resort to punish aggressors and thereby maintain the global system's legal framework.

noncombatant immunity
the legal principle that military force should not be used against innocent civilians.

coercive power
the use of threats and punishment to force the target to alter its behavior.

reprisals
the international legal practice of resorting to military force short of war in retaliation for losses suffered from prior illegal military actions.

retorsion
retaliatory acts (such as economic sanctions) against a target's behavior that is regarded as objectionable but legal (such as trade restrictions) to punish the target with measures that are legal under international law.

■ International law is an institutional substitute for war. Legal procedures exist to resolve conflicts before they erupt into open hostilities. Although law cannot prevent war, legal procedures often make recourse to violence unnecessary by resolving disputes that might otherwise escalate to war.

International Court of Justice (ICJ)
the primary court established by the United Nations for resolving legal disputes between states and providing advisory opinions to international agencies and the UN General Assembly.

The demonstrable capacity of legal methods to reduce the frequency of war does not mean that international adjudicative machinery is well developed or functionally effective. Nowhere is this more evident than with the *International Court of Justice (ICJ)*, known as the World Court, which was created after World War II as the highest judicial body on Earth—the only international court with universal scope and general jurisdiction. The court is highly regarded in principle: 192 states are party to the statute of the court, and 66 have made declarations that they accept the court's compulsory jurisdiction. In addition, more than three hundred bilateral or multilateral treaties provide for the World Court to have jurisdiction in the resolution of disputes arising from their application for a legal interpretation.

A weakness in the World Court is that it can make rulings only on disputes freely submitted by states exercising their sovereign rights; the court cannot rule on cases that states do not bring to it. State sovereignty is protected, and many states have traditionally been hesitant to use the court because ICJ decisions are final—there is no opportunity to appeal. This is why between 1946 and 2010 states granted the court permission to hear only 148 cases, about one-fourth of which the disputants withdrew before the court could make a ruling.

The trends in the World Court's activity are not encouraging to advocates of world law. Whereas the number of sovereign states since 1950 has tripled, the court's caseload has not increased at the same rate. It is instructive that over half of today's states have never appeared before the ICJ, and the Global North liberal democracies have most actively agreed to litigate disputes before the court (the United States, 22 cases; Britain, 13; France, 13; Germany, 7; and Belgium, 5), with Central America following closely behind (Nicaragua, 7; and Honduras, 6). Once the court has ruled on these cases, the disputants have complied with ICJ judgments only a little more than half of the time. This record suggests that while approval for using the court of law to resolve international conflicts is increasingly voiced, most states remain reluctant to voluntarily use judicial procedures to settle their most important international disputes.

However, adjudication to bring armed aggression under more potent legal controls is now spread across the jurisdiction of several other international judicial bodies. It is encouraging that the global community has radically revised international law to prevent the horror of civilian casualties and contain the mass slaughter that has increasingly taken place, and it now holds leaders of countries accountable for war crimes as war criminals. International law prohibits leaders from allowing their militaries to undertake actions in violation of certain principles accepted by the international community, such as the protection of innocent noncombatants.

Formerly, when violations occurred, little could be done except to condemn those acts because international law then failed to hold government leaders to the same standards it held soldiers and military officers who committed atrocities against enemy civilians and captured soldiers. Previously, international law exempted leaders from legal jurisdiction under the doctrine of "sovereign immunity," even when their commands ignored the laws of war. Although they might behave as criminals, leaders traditionally were treated with respect (perhaps because they were the only people with whom negotiations could be held to settle disputes). This tradition has now been legally rejected, as reflected in the premise of the Nuremberg International Military Tribunal (which tried World War II German Nazi war criminals) that "crimes against international law are committed by men, not by abstract entities, and only by punishing individuals who commit such crimes can the provisions of international law be enforced."

The formation of *international criminal tribunals* in 1993 signaled to would-be perpetrators the global community's intolerance for these atrocities. The International Criminal Tribunal for the former Yugoslavia (ICTY) was established in 1993, followed by the International Criminal Tribunal for Rwanda (ICTR) in 1994. One of the most famous tribunal detainees was Slobodan Milosevic, the former Yugoslav president and architect of four wars in the 1990s that killed more than 250,000 and tore the Balkans apart, who died in March 2006 in his Hague prison cell while facing trial. Both the ICTY and the ICTR were set up by the United Nations on an ad hoc basis for a limited time period and a specific jurisdiction, and underscored the need for a permanent global criminal court.

international criminal tribunals special tribunals established by the United Nations to prosecute those responsible for wartime atrocities and genocide, bring justice to victims, and deter such crimes in the future.

With the ratification of the Rome Statute by 111 countries (there are now 139 signatories, with Bangladesh becoming the newest member in March 2010), the *International Criminal Court (ICC)* was launched in 2002 as an independent court of last resort that investigates and prosecutes terrible mass crimes such as genocide, crimes against humanity, and war crimes that have been committed since the court's inception. The ICC only pursues a case when a state's courts are unwilling or unable to do so, and brings

International Criminal Court (ICC) a court established by international treaty for indicting and administering justice to people committing war crimes.

charges only against individuals as opposed to states. To date, the ICC has opened investigations into atrocities in Uganda, the Democratic Republic of Congo, the Central African Republic, and Darfur. Despite resistance from some members of the African Union, in February 2010 the ICC ruled that Sudanese President Omar al-Bashir could be charged with genocide for his part in the five-year campaign of lethal violence in Sudan's Darfur region that, according to UN estimates, cost 300,000 people their lives and forced another 2.5 million from their homes.

In June 2010, a conference was held in Uganda to review the workings of the ICC. The ICC is gaining authority as the appropriate court of last resort for cases involving crimes against humanity, genocide, and war crimes, but it is still too early to render a verdict on the success of the ICC in protecting human rights and securing global justice. The ICC is criticized for the length of time it takes for cases to be brought to trial, and it lacks the independent ability to enforce its decisions or bring in the accused. Some, such as humanitarian relief worker Conor Foley, fear that it could change "from an instrument of justice to one of diplomacy. . . . The ICC could become a useful mechanism for dealing with mid-level thugs and warlords, or retired dicators, where in-country prosecutions are considered too contentious. But it will not be the instrument of impartial, universal justice that its supporters claim." Among the most prominent legal issues facing the court is the need to refine the currently vague definition of "crimes of aggression," and this could run contrary to the interests of many states, particularly those in the Global North. Even within the Global South, the ICC needs to proactively work to establish and consolidate its legitimacy (Glasius 2009). Nonetheless, the criminalization of rulers' *state-sponsored terrorism* raises the legal restraints on the initiation and conduct of war to an all-time high, widening the scope of acts now classified as *war crimes*.

Law's Contribution to Peace and Justice

World order will depend to a considerable extent on the future uses to which states put international law. Alleged shortcomings of international law do not lie with the laws but with their creators—states and their continuing realpolitik dedication to preserving sovereignty as a legal right in order to protect states' independence and autonomy.

The crucial factor in determining the future role of international law depends on which trend prevails. Will states choose to strengthen international law or, instead, insist on continuing to resist the compulsory jurisdiction to the World Court and other international tribunals?

war crimes
acts performed during war that the international community defines as crimes against humanity, including atrocities committed against an enemy's prisoners of war, civilians, or the state's own minority population.

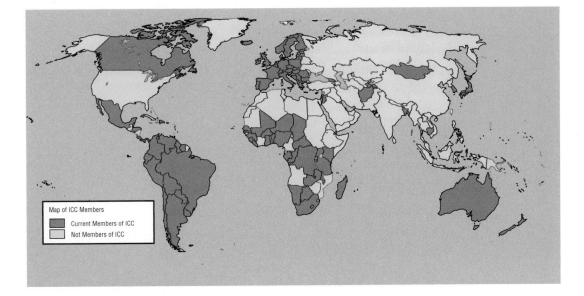

Dorling Kindersley/Getty Images

MAP 10.1

WHICH WORLD COURT? In 1945, the International Court of Justice (ICJ), which is known as the World Court, was established by the UN Charter. It is the primary judicial body of the United Nations, with global jurisdiction to settle legal disputes between states and provide advisory opinions to international agencies and the UN General Assembly. Shown (left) is the Peace Palace, which houses the ICJ in The Hague, Netherlands. Also commonly referred to as a "world court," the International Criminal Court (ICC) is an independent court of last resort that tries those accused of committing the most horrendous of mass crimes, such as war crimes and genocide. Founded through ratification of an international treaty in 2002, it is legally independent of the United Nations. As 2011 began, 111 countries had ratified the treaty and joined the ICC (see map), though the United States, Russia, and China have not.

One path is displayed by the United States, which in 2002 pledged that it would continue to act in accordance with its so-called Connally amendment that reserves the U.S. right to determine which cases it will permit the World Court to hear. The U.S. preference is to try cases in U.S. courts and to let others use U.S. courts as global arbiters of global rights and wrongs. The use of American courts by foreigners to sue for human rights violations stems from the 1789 *Alien Tort Claims Act* (which was written to fight piracy). It now enables victims of torture, genocide, slavery, and war crimes throughout the world to try to get justice in U.S. courts. This trend is accelerating as the United States transforms itself from "global policeman" to "global attorney" (Glaberson 2001; Slaughter 2004a), and in 2004 the U.S. Supreme Court upheld this old law by allowing victims of the Abu Ghraib prison abuses to sue U.S. contractors.

The international climate of opinion is changing and is increasingly receptive to the tenet of liberal theory advanced by U.S. President Eisenhower, who counseled that it "is better to lose a point now and then in an international tribunal and gain a world in which everyone lives at peace under the rule of law." Now at the regional level the EU's twenty-seven members give the European Court of Human Rights the power to exercise authoritative jurisdiction, and in Central and South America the Inter-American Court on Human Rights routinely makes binding decisions. The global community could, in principle, follow Europe's and South America's lead and strengthen international law's capacity. Still, many barriers remain to creating, as John F. Kennedy expressed liberal theory's hope, "a new world of law, where the strong are just and the weak secure and the peace preserved."

In this chapter, you have inspected two of the major liberal paths to peace: procedures for the negotiated settlement of international disputes and the legal control of armed aggression. Both routes have pitfalls but, as the construction of international norms and ideas in world politics evolves to place greater emphasis on global responsibility, humanitarianism, and the importance of justice for all, there are promising prospects for a more just and stable world order. This notion of global "responsibility to protect" is advocated by former Australian foreign minister Gareth Evans, who counsels that our goal should be "to institutionalize the idea that all states have an obligation to shield their own citizens from mass atrocities, and that if a state fails to do so, it falls to other states to take on that obligation" (Malcomson 2008, p. 9; see also Alston and Macdonald 2008). In the next chapter, you will consider other liberal and constructivist avenues to enhance collective security and international peace.

A just war is in the long run far better for a nation's soul than a most prosperous peace obtained by acquiescence in wrong and injustice.

—Theodore Roosevelt, U.S. President

Take an Online Practice Quiz

www.cengagebrain.com/shop/ISBN/0495802204

Suggested Readings

Alston, Philip, and Euan Macdonald, eds. (2008) *Human Rights, Intervention, and the Use of Force.* Oxford, UK: Oxford University Press.

Armstrong, David, and Jutta Brunée. (2009) *Routledge Handbook of International Law.* New York, NY: Taylor & Francis.

Bercovitch, Jacob, and Scott Sigmund Gartner. (2008) *International Conflict Mediation.* New York: Routledge.

Evans, Gareth. (2008) *The Responsibility to Protect: Ending Mass Atrocity Crimes Once and for All.* Washington, DC: Brookings Institution Press.

Foley, Conor. (2008) *The Thin Blue Line: How Humanitarianism Went to War.* New York: Verso Books.

Hudson, Kimberly A. (2009) *Justice, Intervention and Force in International Relations: Reassessing Just War Theory in the 21st Century.* New York, NY: Taylor & Francis.

CHAPTER 11
INSTITUTIONAL AND NORMATIVE APPROACHES TO COLLECTIVE SECURITY

CHAPTER OUTLINE

BEATING SWORDS INTO PLOWSHARES

Disarmament versus Arms Control as Routes to Peace

Bilateral Arms Control and Disarmament

Multilateral Arms Control and Disarmament

The Problematic Future of Arms Control and Disarmament

CONTROVERSY: ARMS RACES AND THE PRISONER'S DILEMMA

MAINTAINING COLLECTIVE SECURITY THROUGH INTERNATIONAL ORGANIZATIONS

The League of Nations and Collective Security

The United Nations and Peacekeeping

Regional Security Organizations and Collective Defense

UNITING ONE WORLD IN A COMMON CULTURE OF SHARED MORAL VALUES

Trade Ties of Common Interest

A Democratic Peace Pact

CONTROVERSY: IS TAIWAN "LIVING PROOF" OF THE LIBERAL PATH TO PEACE AND PROSPERITY?

INSTITUTIONS, NORMS, AND WORLD ORDER

The 21st century must be, if we are to survive it, an age that all nations . . . understand as ill-suited to gladiators and leviathans— an age that will reward countries that share a commitment to transparency, cooperation, and mutual benefit.

—Strobe Talbott, former U.S. Deputy Secretary of State

David Silpa/UPI Photo/Landov Media

A FERVENT CALL FOR PEACE Shown here, mourners gather to remember the eleven victims of a bomb blast at a café in Pune, India, on February 13, 2010. Many Indians blame Pakistan, which has a record of terrorism in India. A previously unheard of Pakistani militant group, Lashkar-e-Taiba Al Alami, claimed responsibility. Liberals, and many constructivists, are dissatisfied with the world and would like to change it. They have mobilized to exert pressure to contain arms races, warfare, global warming, and world poverty, among other causes.

Many global trends are sweeping the world. Most of them appear to be moving at accelerating rates. Major transformations may be in store in your future world. But not all trends are converging, and some are pulling against others in opposite directions. Whatever their collective synergistic impact on one another, it seems certain that your future world will be different from the one that now exists.

Another certainty: Your own values are clashing. Some values can only be achieved at the expense of others. The things you desire cannot all be obtained, and so you will confront making trade-offs among incompatible choices about how to set priorities and best help forge a better world.

Many of your value preferences lie at the vortex of the contest between realist and liberal thought, and they defy easy reconciliation. Sure, you want your country to be militarily powerful for defense, but you do not want other countries to build their military capabilities, and you must dread the prospect of a world darkened by the worldwide proliferation of weapons. Yes, you would like to see your country's economy grow, but what if it can't unless your country accepts free trade, which spells a potential loss of your employment opportunities at home and the rise of other countries' economies at rates that exceed that of your own country? To be sure, you would prefer your country to have the capacity to unilaterally make foreign policy decisions independently without foreign approval, but what if many of the dangers you foresee—global warming, the spread of contagious diseases across borders, the protection of innocents from genocide or starvation or tyranny—cannot be solved without the collective cooperation of other countries? Ouch! Many of the things you value can only be served by some sacrifice of other values.

In this chapter, focus your attention on some of the major ways in which liberal international thought directly challenges the assumptions underlying realist thinking about world politics. Also consider, from constructivist and identity perspectives, the importance of progressive ideas and norms in shaping international behavior and collective conceptions of world politics. This will require you to contemplate the consequences that are likely to result if three major roads to world order are pursued: disarmament, collective security through international organizations, and the building of a single world culture through the promotion of norms supporting free trade and free governments worldwide. All three are questioned and are opposed by the dominant strains of thought in the realist theoretical tradition.

> *The quest for international security involves the unconditional surrender by every nation, in a certain measure, of its liberty of action, its sovereignty that is to say, and it is clear beyond all doubt that no other road can lead to such security.*
>
> —Albert Einstein, scientist

BEATING SWORDS INTO PLOWSHARES

The realist road to national security counsels, "if you want peace prepare for war." On the surface this makes intuitive sense. If your country is militarily stronger than its rivals, it is not very likely to be attacked. With an emphasis on deterrence, this traditional approach to security holds that not only do conventional weapons enhance the strategic capabilities of a state, but that "nuclear weapons on average . . . enhance the security and diplomatic influence of their possessors" (Gartzke and Kroenig 2009, p. 152).

Using *counterfactual* logic by asking yourself what would be the likely consequences if all countries adhered to this advice, you might arrive at another conclusion. Your country may become less secure, not more, as it builds its military might. That is the deduction of liberal thought. In this construction, the *security dilemma* figures prominently—when a country builds armaments, alarmed neighbors mistrust its claims that the weapons are for defensive purposes, and in fearful reaction begin to vigorously arm themselves also. An *arms race* results, with no arming state more secure. All the arming parties are now more vulnerable; wanting peace, war preparations increase the likelihood of war.

arms race
The buildup of weapons and armed forces by two or more states that threaten each other, with the competition driven by the conviction that gaining a lead is necessary for security.

This liberal conviction goes back to antiquity. Jesus Christ warned, "For all those who take up the sword perish by the sword" (Matthew 26:52). Centuries earlier, the Hebrew prophet Isaiah voiced in the same spirit a recommendation that is inscribed on the United Nations headquarters in New York City: "the nations shall beat their swords into plowshares" (Isaiah 2:4).

This liberal axiom and advice has been echoed many times. For example, Sir John Frederick Maurice wrote in his memoirs, "I went into the British Army believing that if you want peace you must prepare for war. I now believe that if you prepare thoroughly for war you will get it." The same liberal conviction was expressed by French political philosopher Charles de Montesquieu when he observed that the quest for a preponderance of power in relation to rivals "inevitably becomes a contagious disease; for, as soon as one state increases what it calls its forces, the others immediately increase theirs, so that nothing is gained except mutual ruination."

The destructiveness of today's weapons has inspired many people to embrace the conclusion that reducing the weapons of war can increase the prospects for global peace. While there is no single constructivist position on armaments or armed aggression, there is a widespread interest in moving beyond a limited traditional conception of security to one that takes into account the consequence of progressive ideas and human creativity. Constructivists "argue that violent political behavior and thereby its resolution and future prevention could be explained and even understood by focusing on the role of norms and ideas as determinants of such behavior" (Conteh-Morgan 2005, p. 72). Thus, while realists, and even liberals, emphasize the material underpinnings of war and peace, constructivists take into account both the material and communicative sources. As ideas "do not float freely (but) are embedded in an elaborate set of rules, norms, regimes and institutions" (Kolodziej 2005, p. 297), the constructivist perspective is often complimentary to the liberal emphasis on institutional and normative paths to peace, and the idea that constraints on the development and spread of weapons of war are critical to global security.

Many feminist scholars share a critical view of the role of weapons of mass destruction in ensuring global security. In particular, the "antiwar feminist" tradition rejects and tries to change the social processes that associate norms of masculinity with militarized violence and war making (see Chapter 2). "It calls for ways of thinking that reveal the complicated effects on possessor societies of developing and deploying these weapons, that portray the terror and potential suffering of target societies, and that grapple with the moral implications of the willingness to risk such massive destruction" (Cohn and Ruddick 2008, p. 459).

There is hope that reduction in armaments will lead to less armed aggression and a safer and more secure world. This program for reform is advanced even while liberal policy makers accept the notion that it is morally defensible to use constrained and proportional armed force to repel an imminent military attack by an adversary (Mapel 2007). But in thinking about the control of the spread of weapons around the world, keep in mind that it is not strictly a tenet of liberal theory alone. While realists are reluctant to view arms control as a path to peace, most policy makers who have negotiated agreements to limit arms have been realists who perceived such treaties as prudent tools to promote security by balancing military power with power to maintain the threat of war.

Disarmament versus Arms Control as Routes to Peace

disarmament
agreements to reduce or destroy weapons or other means of attack.

arms control
multilateral or bilateral agreements to contain arms races by setting limits on the number and types of weapons states are permitted.

Simulation: *Theories of International Relations: Realism versus Liberalism*

bilateral agreements
exchanges between two states, such as arms control agreements negotiated cooperatively to set ceilings on military force levels.

multilateral agreements
cooperative compacts among three or more states to ensure that a concerted policy is implemented toward alleviating a common problem, such as levels of future weapons capabilities.

Several distinctions must be made in any consideration of this approach to international security. The first is between the terms "disarmament" and "arms control." Sometimes the terms are used interchangeably. They are not, however, synonymous. ***Disarmament*** is ambitious. It aims to reduce or eliminate armaments or classes of armaments completely, usually by a negotiated reciprocal agreement between two or more rivals, in efforts to prevent the use of those weapons in warfare. ***Arms control*** is less ambitious. Arms control is designed to regulate arms levels either by limiting their growth or by restricting how they might be used. It results from agreements between potential enemies to cooperate in order to reduce the probability that conflicting interests will erupt in warfare, and to reduce the scope of violence in any armed conflict that may nonetheless occur.

Both liberalism and realism see limitations on weapons as useful. Where they part ways is in their respective posture toward the advantages of disarmament versus arms control. Liberals are more willing to take a heroic leap of faith and consider disarmament as a workable possibility for peace. Because arms control is based on recognition that a true conflict of interest between rivals exists, it is favored by realists who see a positive contribution potentially made when enemies negotiate an agreement to balance their weapons and through that balancing build mutual confidence.

Controlling war by reducing weapons inventories is hardly a novel idea. Yet, until recently, few states have negotiated disarmament agreements. True, some countries in the past did reduce their armaments. For example, in 600 BCE the Chinese states formed a disarmament league that produced a peaceful century for the league's members. Canada and the United States disarmed the Great Lakes region through the 1817 Rush–Bagot Agreement. Nonetheless, these kinds of achievements have been relatively rare in history. Most disarmament has been involuntary, the product of reductions imposed by the victors in the immediate aftermath of a war, as when the Allied powers attempted to disarm a defeated Germany after World War I.

In addition to differentiating between arms control and disarmament, you should also distinguish between ***bilateral agreements*** and ***multilateral agreements***. Because the former involves only two countries, such agreements are often easier to negotiate and to enforce than are the latter, which are agreements among three or more countries. As a result, bilateral arms agreements tend to be more successful than multilateral agreements.

By far the most revealing examples are the superpower agreements to control nuclear weapons. This chapter will look briefly at the record of Soviet–American negotiations before examining the checkered history of multilateral arms control and disarmament.

Bilateral Arms Control and Disarmament

The Cold War between the Soviet Union and the United States never degenerated into a trial of military strength. One of the reasons was the series of more than twenty-five arms control agreements that Moscow and Washington negotiated in the wake of the Cuban Missile Crisis. Beginning with the 1963 Hot Line Agreement, which established a direct radio and telegraph communications system between the two governments, Soviet and American leaders reached a series of modest agreements aimed at stabilizing the military balance and reducing the risk of war. Each of these bilateral treaties lowered tensions and helped build a climate of trust that encouraged efforts to negotiate further agreements.

The most important agreements between the superpowers were the *Strategic Arms Limitation Talks (SALT)* of 1972 and 1979; the *Intermediate-Range Nuclear Forces (INF) Treaty* of 1987; the *Strategic Arms Reduction Treaty (START)* of 1991, 1993, 1997, and 2010; and the *Strategic Offensive Reductions Treaty (SORT)* of 2002. The first two agreements stabilized the nuclear arms race, and the remaining agreements reduced the weapons in each side's inventories. When the Cold War ended in 1991, the United States still had more than ninety-five hundred nuclear warheads and Russia had about eight thousand. Then disarmament began in earnest. Since their 1986 peak, the sizes of the two superpowers' nuclear arsenals have declined by over 90 percent, and they will decline much further by 2020 if the terms of the new Strategic Arms Reduction Treaty signed in April 2010 by Presidents Obama and Medvedev are implemented. According to this agreement, both sides will reduce strategic warheads to fifteen hundred and fifty in just over ten years—which is more than a 30 percent reduction of the maximum twenty-two hundred allowed by 2012 as required under the previous SORT accord.

This disarmament achievement has inspired other nuclear powers to discontinue building and expanding their nuclear arsenal. Most nuclear powers have not increased their stockpile of nuclear weapons, and forty countries that have the technical ability to construct nuclear arsenals have renounced nuclear weapons (Ferguson 2010). That said, threatened states are always tempted to rearm, and therefore fears that disarmament will not continue are rising (Ferguson 2010; Lobal 2010). Provoking concerns was the U.S. decision to continue developing its "Star Wars" missile defense from outer space.

Intermediate-Range Nuclear Forces (INF) Treaty the U.S.–Russian agreement to eliminate an entire class of nuclear weapons by removing all intermediate and short-range ground-based missiles and launchers with ranges between 300 and 3,500 miles from Europe.

Strategic Arms Reduction Treaty (START) the U.S.–Russian series of negotiations that began in 1993 and, with the 1997 START-III agreement ratified by Russia in 2000, pledged to cut the nuclear arsenals of both sides by 80 percent of the Cold War peaks, in order to lower the risk of nuclear war.

Strategic Offensive Reductions Treaty (SORT) the U.S.–Russian agreement to reduce the number of strategic warheads to between 1,700 and 2,200 for each country by 2012.

Animated Learning Module: *Nonproliferation Treaty*

Also dispelling disarmament hopes was Russia's successful test in August 2008 of a new long-range nuclear missile that has a range of 6,125 miles, posing a threat to peace in Europe. The record of successful bilateral arms control and even disarmament between the United States and Russia attests to the possibilities for rival military powers to contain by agreement a dangerous arms race. But the fragility of these agreements underscores the difficulties.

Multilateral Arms Control and Disarmament

History provides many examples of multilateral arms control and disarmament efforts. As early as the eleventh century, the Second Lateran Council prohibited the use of crossbows in fighting. The 1868 St. Petersburg Declaration prohibited the use of explosive bullets. In 1899 and 1907, International Peace Conferences at The Hague restricted the use of some weapons and prohibited others. The leaders of the United States, Britain, Japan, France, and Italy signed treaties at the Washington Naval Conferences (1921–1922) agreeing to adjust the relative tonnage of their fleets.

Nearly thirty major multilateral agreements have been signed since the Second World War (see Table 11.1). Of these, the 1968 Nuclear Nonproliferation Treaty (NPT), which prohibited the transfer of nuclear weapons and production technologies to nonnuclear weapons states, stands out. This twenty-four-hundred-word contract that some say saved the world is historically the most symbolic multilateral arms control agreement. With 189 signatory countries, the NPT has had considerable success in promoting the nonproliferation of nuclear weapons of mass destruction (WMD), and efforts to bolster and extend nonproliferation persist. In April 2010, the United States hosted a nuclear-security summit where 47 countries established a four-year timetable for securing bomb-usable fissile material and agreed that "nuclear terrorism is one of the most challenging threats to international security" (*The Economist,* April 17, 2010, p. 67). The United States and Russia further agreed to eliminate 68 tons of weapons-grade plutonium and reduce deployed strategic warheads to 1550 apiece. The 2010 NPT review conference was also held in June 2010, where the 189 members unanimously reaffirmed their commitment to "getting the nuclear powers to give up their bombs; preventing others from acquiring them; and promoting nuclear power for peaceful uses only" (*The Economist,* June 5, 2010, p. 68).

Nonetheless, there have been several notable setbacks to the aims of the NPT. Though not signatories, in 1998 India and Pakistan broke the NPT's barriers to become nuclear-weapon states. Likewise, despite initially signing the treaty, North Korea violated the NPT with its secret development of nuclear weapons.

Fears of nuclear proliferation have been further inflamed by Iran's pursuit of nuclear capabilities. In September 2009, Iran test-fired missiles capable of striking Israel, Europe, and American bases in the Persian Gulf. A secret underground nuclear plant that purportedly manufactures nuclear fuel was also unveiled, leading to global speculation that Iran is using its civilian nuclear energy program to mask efforts to develop nuclear weapons.

In June 2010, the United Nations adopted new sanctions against Iran, including a prohibition of Iranian investment in uranium mining and activity involving ballistic missiles capable of delivering nuclear weapons. Yet some continue to be skeptical of the UN's ability and willingness to monitor and punish nuclear development. The "most urgent challenge facing this body is to prevent the tyrants of Tehran from acquiring nuclear weapons," argued Israeli Prime Minister Benjamin Netanyahu. "Are the member states of the United Nations up to that challenge?" Former U.S. National Security Adviser Brent Scowcroft reinforced these concerns, testifying that "we're on the cusp of an explosion of proliferation, and Iran is now the poster child. If Iran is allowed to go forward, in self-defense or for a variety of reasons, we could have half a dozen countries in the region and twenty or thirty more around the world doing the same thing just in case."

Control and disarmament of nuclear arms faces three intimidating obstacles—the insecurity of states, the idea that nuclear weapons are the great equalizer, and the proliferation risk that occurs when a nuclear power builds civilian reactors for a non-nuclear state (Ferguson 2010). Furthermore, some states that signed the original agreement wonder whether the deal they were handed by the "nuclear club" in 1968 was a raw one. They observe the failure of the original nuclear powers to honor their pledge to disarm and perceive the NPT as "an instrument for the haves to deny the have-nots" (Allison 2010, p. 80). Nearly seventy-five hundred nuclear war heads remain (SIPRI 2010), and countries in the Global South such as Saudi Arabia, the United Arab Emirates, and Egypt have indicated intent to explore nuclear options, albeit peaceful ones (Coll 2009). Given this trend, it is all the more alarming that "new nuclear states, with a nascent arsenal and lack of experience in nuclearized disputes, play the 'nuclear card' significantly more often than their more experienced nuclear counterparts, making them more likely to reciprocate militarized disputes" (Horowitz 2009, p. 235).

Video: *Shifting Alliances in Iran*

The ability and will to stem further nuclear nonproliferation remains much in doubt, and in recognition of these serious trends, President Obama challenged the world to renew its commitment to confronting the spread of nuclear weapons. He underscored the high stakes of complacency in the face

Table 11.1   Major Multilateral Arms Control Treaties since 1945

Date	Agreement	Number of Parties (signed, 2010)	Principal Objectives
1959	Antarctic Treaty	45	Prevents the military use of the Antarctic, including the testing of nuclear weapons
1963	Partial Test Ban Treaty	136	Prohibits nuclear weapons in the atmosphere, outer space, and underwater
1967	Outer Space Treaty	134	Outlaws the use of outer space for testing or stationing any weapons, as well as for military maneuvers
1967	Treaty of Tlatelolco	33	Creates the Latin American Nuclear Free Zone by prohibiting the testing and possession of nuclear facilities for military purposes
1968	Nuclear Nonproliferation Treaty	189	Prevents the spread of nuclear weapons and nuclear-weapons-production technologies to nonnuclear weapons states
1971	Seabed Treaty	115	Prohibits the development of weapons of mass destruction and nuclear weapons on the seabed beyond a twelve-mile coastal limit
1972	Biological and Toxic Weapons Convention	171	Prohibits the production and storage of biological toxins; calls for the destruction of biological weapons stockpiles
1977	Environmental Modifications Convention (ENMOD Convention)	87	Bans the use of technologies that could alter Earth's weather patterns, ocean currents, ozone layer, or ecology
1980	Protection of Nuclear Material Convention	132	Obligates protection of peaceful nuclear material during transport on ships or aircraft
1981	Inhumane Weapons Convention	108	Prohibits the use of such weapons as fragmentation bombs, incendiary weapons, booby traps, and mines to which civilians could be exposed
1985	South Pacific Nuclear Free Zone (Roratonga) Treaty	19	Prohibits the testing, acquisition, or deployment of nuclear weapons in the South Pacific
1987	Missile Technology Control Regime (MTCR)	34	Restricts export of ballistic missiles and production facilities
1990	Conventional Forces in Europe (CFE)	30	Places limits on five categories of weapons in Europe and lowers force levels
1990	Confidence- and Security-Building Measures Agreement	53	Improves measures for exchanging detailed information on weapons, forces, and military exercises
1991	UN Register of Conventional Arms	101	Calls on all states to submit information on seven categories of major weapons exported or imported during the previous year
1992	Open Skies Treaty	35	Permits flights by unarmed surveillance aircraft over the territory of the signatory states
1993	Chemical Weapons Convention (CWC)	181	Requires all stockpiles of chemical weapons to be destroyed
1995	Protocol to the Inhumane Weapons Convention	135	Bans some types of laser weapons that cause permanent loss of eyesight
1995	Treaty of Bangkok	10	Creates a nuclear-weapon-free zone in Southeast Asia
1995	Wassenaar Export-Control Treaty	40	Regulates transfers of sensitive dual-use technologies to nonparticipating countries

Date	Agreement	Number of Parties (signed, 2010)	Principal Objectives
1996	ASEAN Nuclear Free Zone Treaty	10	Prevents signatories in Southeast Asia from making, possessing, storing, or testing nuclear weapons
1996	Comprehensive Test Ban Treaty (CTBT)	177	Bans all testing of nuclear weapons
1996	Treaty of Pelindaba	21	Creates an African nuclear-weapon-free zone
1997	Antipersonnel Landmines Treaty (APLT)	155	Bans the production and export of landmines and pledges plans to remove them
1999	Inter-American Convention on Transparency in Conventional Weapons Acquisitions	34	Requires all thirty-four members of the Organization of American States (OAS) to annually report all weapons acquisitions, exports, and imports
2005	Nuclear Nonproliferation Treaty Review Conference	123 (delegates)	Final communiqué voices approval to continue support for the NPT treaty
2007	Treaty on Nuclear Free Zone in Central Asia (Treaty of Semipolinsk)	5	Obligates parties not to acquire nuclear weapons
2008	Convention on Cluster Munitions	94	Prohibits the use, production, stockpiling, and transfer of cluster munitions
2010	Nuclear Nonproliferation Treaty Review Conference	189 (delegates)	Reaffirmed support for the NPT accord

SIPRI Yearbook (2010; 2009, p. 11; 2007, pp. 667–689).

of nuclear proliferation, warning that "Some argue that the spread of these weapons cannot be stopped. . . . Such fatalism is a deadly adversary. For if we believe that the spread of nuclear weapons is inevitable, then in some way we are admitting to ourselves that the use of nuclear weapons is inevitable."

The Problematic Future of Arms Control and Disarmament

The obstacles to arms control and disarmament are formidable. Critics complain that these agreements frequently only regulate obsolete armaments or ones that the parties to the agreement have little incentive for developing in the first place. Even when agreements are reached on modern, sophisticated weapons, the parties often set ceilings higher than the number of weapons currently deployed, so they do not have to slash their inventories.

A second pitfall is the propensity of limits on one type of weapon system to prompt developments in another system. Like a balloon that is squeezed at one end but expands at the other, constraints on certain parts of a country's arsenal can lead to enhancements elsewhere. An example can be seen in the

1972 SALT I agreement, which limited the number of intercontinental ballistic missiles possessed by the United States and Soviet Union. Although the number of missiles was restricted, no limits were placed on the number of nuclear warheads that could be placed on each missile. Consequently, both sides developed *multiple independently targeted reentry vehicles* (MIRVs). In short, the quantitative freeze on launchers led to qualitative improvements in their warhead delivery systems.

antipersonnel landmines (APLs) weapons buried below the surface of the soil that explode on contact when any person— soldier or citizen— steps on them.

Also reducing faith in future meaningful arms control is the slow, weak, and ineffective ability of the global community to ban some of the most dangerous and counterproductive weapons. Consider the case of *antipersonnel landmines (APLs)*, which cannot discriminate between soldiers and civilians. More than one hundred to three hundred million landmines are believed to be scattered on the territory of more than seventy countries (with another one hundred million in stockpiles). It is estimated that about one mine exists for every fifty people in the world and that each year they kill or maim more than twenty-six thousand people—almost all of them civilians.

In 1994, not a single state would endorse a prohibition on these deadly weapons. It took peace activist Jody Williams to organize the International Campaign to Ban Landmines, which led to the *Convention on the Prohibition of the Use, Stockpiling, Production and Transfer of Antipersonnel Mines* that opened for signature in December 1997. For her efforts, Williams received the Nobel Peace Prize. But the United States, Russia, and other great powers stubbornly resisted the APL convention until a coalition of NGO peace groups mounted sufficient pressure for them to produce this epic treaty (still without U.S. acceptance). The challenge of enforcing the ban, now signed by 156 states, and the task of removing APLs, remains staggering.

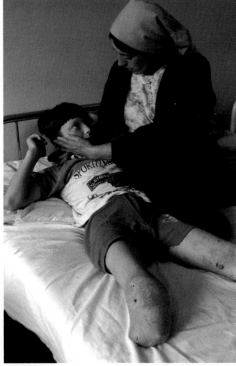

Pier Paolo Cito/AP Photo

Antipersonnel mines are triggered by the contact or presence of a person. Indiscriminate weapons of war that do not recognize a ceasefire or termination of hostilities, they kill or cause injuries such as destroyed limbs, burns and blindness. Pictured here is a 12-year old victim, Burin, in a hospital with his mother where he is being treated for the loss of his right leg and other serious wounds that he received while picking strawberries in a field in southern Kosovo.

A final problem facing those advocating arms control and disarmament is continuous innovation. By the time that limits are negotiated on one type of weapon, a new generation of weapons has emerged. Modern technology is creating an ever-widening range of novel weapons— increasingly smaller, deadlier, and easier to conceal.

Why do states often make decisions to arm that apparently imprison them in the grip of perpetual insecurity? On the surface, the incentives for meaningful arms control seem numerous. Significant controls would save money,

CONTROVERSY:

ARMS RACES AND THE PRISONER'S DILEMMA

Realists and liberal theorists both agree that the world could be a better place if countries would see their self-interests served by international cooperation. But realists and liberals hold differing views about the prospects for cooperation. The two schools of thought have been engaged in a controversial debate about why competition often trumps cooperation.

One way to address this question is to examine the logic underlying the well-known "Prisoner's Dilemma" game. It illuminates the circumstantial barriers to international cooperation among distrustful transnational actors across many arenas of international politics, and is especially relevant to arms control and arms races.

Imagine two suspects following an armed robbery are taken into police custody and placed in separate cells by the district attorney, who is certain that they are guilty but only has sufficient evidence to convict them on an illegal weapons charge. The district attorney tells prisoner **A** and prisoner **B** that there are two choices: confess to the robbery, or remain silent. If one prisoner confesses and the other doesn't, he will be given immunity from prosecution for providing evidence whereas his accomplice will get a sentence of ten years in the state penitentiary. If both confess, they will be given a reduced sentence of five years in the penitentiary. If neither confesses, they will be convicted on the weapons charge and serve only six months in the county jail. Because both prisoners want to spend as little time incarcerated as possible, their preferences are rank ordered from the best to the worst outcomes as follows: (1) immunity from prosecution; (2) six months in the county jail; (3) five years in the state penitentiary; and (4) ten years in the penitentiary. The accompanying matrix depicts the results that will occur depending on whether each prisoner chooses to cooperate with his accomplice by remaining silent or defect by confessing to the district attorney.

Faced with this situation, what should each prisoner do? Remember that they both want as little time behind bars as possible, and they are being interrogated separately so they cannot communicate. Furthermore, neither prisoner is sure that he can trust the other.

Although the optimal strategy for both prisoners would be to tacitly cooperate with each other and keep quiet so each receives only a six-month sentence (the payoff of 2, 2 in the matrix), the structural properties of this situation are such that there are powerful incentives to defect from your partner and provide incriminating evidence to the district attorney. First, there is an offensive incentive to defect based on the prospect of getting immunity by confessing. Second, there is a defensive incentive to defect grounded in the fear of being double-crossed by an accomplice who squeals. If one prisoner refuses to talk but the other confesses, the one who tried to cooperate with his accomplice to get a mutually beneficial result would receive the worst possible payoff (4, or ten years in the penitentiary), whereas the prisoner who defected to the district attorney would receive the best payoff (1, or immunity). Not wanting be a "sucker" who spends a decade incarcerated while his partner in crime goes free, both prisoners conclude that it is in their self-interest to defect and testify against one another; consequently, they both receive a less than optimal result (the payoff 3, 3 in the matrix, or five years in prison) than if they had tacitly cooperated by remaining silent. The dilemma is that seemingly rational calculations by each individual actor can yield collectively worse results for both than had they chosen other strategies.

(continued)

ARMS RACES AND THE PRISONER'S DILEMMA (Continued)

	A cooperate	A defect
B cooperate	2, 2	4, 1
B defect	1, 4	3, 3

FIGURE 11.1

NOTE The first number in each cell of this matrix is A's payoff; the second number is B's payoff. The number 1 represents the most preferred outcome, whereas 4 represents the least preferred outcome.

Many theorists liken arms races to the Prisoner's Dilemma game. Consider two countries (**A** and **B**) that are approximately equal in military capability, uncertain of whether they can trust one another, and currently facing two choices: cooperate in lowering arms spending or defect by increasing arms spending. Suppose that each country prefers to have a military advantage over the other and fears being at a serious disadvantage, which would happen if one increased arms spending while the other reduced expenditures (the payoffs 4, 1 and 1, 4 in the accompanying matrix). By cooperating to lower arms spending they could devote more resources to other national needs such as education and health care (the payoff 2, 2), but given offensive and defensive incentives that are similar to those tempting the two prisoners in our earlier example, they both conclude that it is in their individual self-interest to play it safe and arm. As a result of their joint defection (payoff 3, 3), they end up worse off by locking themselves into an expensive arms race that may destabilize the prevailing balance of power.

Although this version of the Prisoner's Dilemma game is a simplification that does not take into account what might happen in repeated plays over time (see Axelrod 1984), it highlights for you some of the difficulties in reaching mutually beneficial arms control agreements among self-interested actors who distrust their peers.

WHAT DO YOU THINK?

- Do you see any practical methods for escaping this dilemma in regard to arms control agreements?

- As we have learned, there are many important actors beyond the state. Along those lines, how might the addition of international institutions change the nature of this "game?"

- How might the prisoner's decision be altered if he or she abides by realist theory? By liberal theory? By constructivist theory?

reduce tension, decrease environmental hazards, and diminish the potential destructiveness of war. However, most countries are reluctant to limit their armaments because of the self-help system that requires each state to protect itself. Thus, states find themselves caught in a vicious cycle summarized by two basic principles: (1) "Don't negotiate when you are behind. Why accept a permanent position of number two?" and (2) "Don't negotiate when you are ahead. Why accept a freeze in an area of military competition when the other side has not kept up with you?" (Barnet 1977).

Here policy makers read from the realist script, which insists that national security is best protected by developing military capabilities and not by reducing armaments or military spending. Realists regard treaties to be dangerous in an anarchical world in which the promises of self-interested rivals cannot be trusted (see Controversy: Arms Races and the Prisoner's Dilemma). They counsel against putting faith in arms control treaties, because deception and broken promises are to be expected by ruthless leaders in the global jungle. Thus, instead of holding commitments to arms control agreements that cannot be enforced, realists advise reliance on unilateral self-help through military preparedness.

The realist mind-set was very evident in U.S. decisions at the turn of the century to reject an array of international treaties designed to control the threat of nuclear weapons. During 2001 alone, the United States decided to abrogate the 1972 Anti-Ballistic Missile (ABM) Treaty, withdraw from a UN conference to impose limits on illegal trafficking of small arms, and reject proposed enforcement measures for the 1972 Biological Weapons Convention. This disregard for arms control set a standard for other states to follow.

Simulation:
Prisoner's Dilemma

Especially troubling was the U.S. repudiation of the 1972 ABM treaty, which was regarded by many as the cornerstone of nuclear arms control, as that announcement was the first time in modern history that the United States had renounced a major international accord. It ignited fears that a global chain reaction of massive repudiations of arms control agreements by other states would follow. For example, in 2007 Russia threatened to quit the INF missile treaty and to place a moratorium on the CFE treaty. However, while acknowledging a continued commitment to defensive military preparation, U.S. President Barack Obama indicated a renewed interest in controlling the spread of deadly weapons, stating that "we are spending billions of dollars on missile defense. And I actually believe that we need missile defense . . . but I also believe that, when we are only spending a few hundred million dollars on nuclear proliferation, then we're making a mistake." Further signaling a change in policy, in September 2009 the United States announced plans to scrap its missile defense shield program in Poland and the Czech Republic.

The tendency of states to make improving their weapons a priority over controlling them is illustrated by the example of nuclear testing (see Map 11.1). The eight known nuclear states have conducted a total of 2,054 nuclear explosions since 1945—an average of one test every twelve days (SIPRI 2010). Both China and the United States regularly conduct so-called zero-yield nuclear experiments and are suspected of conducting explosive tests so small that they cannot be detected. Moreover, the partial test ban treaty of 1963, which prohibited atmospheric and underwater testing but not underground explosions, did not slow the pace of testing. Over three-fourths of all nuclear tests took place after the ban went into effect.

The past record of arms control and disarmament has dispirited liberal and constructivist reformers whose hopes for negotiated compromises to curtail

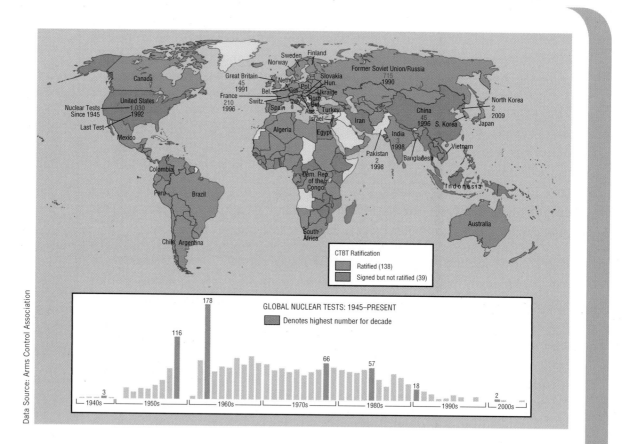

Data Source: Arms Control Association

MAP 11.1

TRICK OR TREATY? CAN ARMS-CONTROL TREATIES ARREST THE PROLIFERATION OF WEAPONS?
Since the dawn of the nuclear age, the eight known nuclear powers have conducted 2,054 documented tests of their weapons. As the timeline at the bottom of the map shows, testing declined since the 1960s, but following North Korea's tests in 2009 and China's proposal in 2010 to sell two nuclear-power reactors to Pakistan, fears of intensified nuclear arms rivalry and a potential wave of new testing have accelerated.

the global arms race have not been fulfilled. It appears that realists, and their abiding emphasis on peace through military preparations, are trumping those liberals who counsel that weapons acquisitions are not a safe road toward world order. Someday, Woodrow Wilson's cause of world disarmament may yet triumph, as he hoped and prayed. As long as the threat of armed aggression haunts the world, leaders are unlikely to think it prudent to disarm. Many liberals and constructivists perceive other paths to peace as more promising. The construction of international organizations for collective security benefits from a more encouraging history, in part because so many military crises require multilateral cooperation to be peacefully managed.

MAINTAINING COLLECTIVE SECURITY THROUGH INTERNATIONAL ORGANIZATIONS

International organizations throughout history have all advanced the preservation of peace as one of the prime rationales for their formation. An institutional pathway to international peace is sculpted in liberal and constructivist thinking, with liberals focusing on interdependence and the possibility of cooperation and constructivists emphasizing the centrality of ideas and norms. Such an approach is voiced as an alternative to the balance of power advocated by realist thinkers to maintain peace by redistributing power through the free-floating mechanism of shifting alliances and alignments. The global community has usually trodden down paths to peace through international organization when each previous balance of power has collapsed in large-scale warfare (as all past balances of power have sooner or later).

Note that reliance on international organization is opposed vigorously by classical realist thinking. *Realism*, it should be recalled, prizes the sovereign independence of states as a core value, and berates international organization as a barrier to states' foreign policy autonomy, freedom, and flexibility of unilateral action. Indeed, prescriptions for the global community to "get organized" by creating institutions *above* states as a route to global stability are rejected by realist thought. The only exception to this realist posture is when great powers have elected to create supranational multilateral institutions for the management of military power in international relations, and this *only* when the great powers forming them were certain that the organizations would be managed authoritatively *by* them for their own self-interests (Claude 1962).

For liberal and constructivist reformers, *collective security* is conceived as an alternative to balance-of-power politics favored by realists. By definition, collective security requires collective decisions for collective purposes to contain international armed aggression, guided by the principle that an act of aggression by any state will be met with a unified response from the rest. International organizations are seen as key to peaceful conflict management as "organizations with interventionist capabilities encourage disputing members to attempt peaceful conflict resolution" (Shannon 2009, p. 145.)

> *Collective security assumes that every nation perceives every challenge to the international order in the same way, and is prepared to run the same risk to preserve it.*
>
> —Henry Kissinger, former U.S. Secretary of State

The League of Nations and Collective Security

Perhaps more than any other event, World War I discredited the realist argument that peace was a by product of a stable balance of power. Citing arms races, secret treaties, and competing alliances as sources of acute tension, many liberals viewed power balancing as a *cause* of war instead of as an instrument for its prevention. U.S. President Woodrow Wilson voiced the strongest opposition to balance-of-power politics; Point XIV of his Fourteen Points proposals for postwar peace called for "a general association of nations for the purpose of preserving the political independence and territorial integrity of great and small states alike." This plea led to the formation of the League of Nations to replace the balance of power with a global governance system for world order in which aggression by any state would be met by a united response.

Yet long before Wilson and other reformers called for the establishment of a League of Nations, the idea of collective security had been expressed in various peace plans. Between the eleventh and thirteenth centuries, for example, French ecclesiastic councils held in Poitiers (1000), Limoges (1031), and Toulouse (1210) discussed rudimentary versions of collective security. Similar proposals surfaced in the writings of Pierre Dubois (1306), King George Podebrad of Bohemia (1462), the Duc de Sully (1560–1641), and the Abbé de Saint-Pierre (1713). Underlying these plans was the belief that an organized "community" of power would be more effective in preserving peace than shifting alliances aimed at balancing power.

Collective security is based on the creed voiced by Alexandre Dumas's d'Artagnan and his fellow Musketeers: "One for all and all for one!" In order for collective security to function in the rough-and-tumble international arena, its advocates usually translate the Musketeer creed into the following rules of statecraft:

■ **All threats to peace must be a common concern to everyone.** Peace, collective security theory assumes, is indivisible. If aggression anywhere is ignored, it eventually will spread to other countries and become more difficult to stop; hence, an attack on any one state must be regarded as an attack on all states.

■ **Every member of the global system should join the collective security organization.** Instead of maneuvering against one another in rival alliances, states should link up in a single "uniting" alliance. Such a universal collectivity, it is assumed, would possess the international legitimacy and strength to keep the peace.

■ **Members of the organization should pledge to settle their disputes through pacific means.** Collective security is not wedded to the status quo. It assumes that peaceful change is possible when institutions are available to resolve conflicts of interest. In addition to providing a mechanism for the mediation of disagreements, the collective security organization would also contain a judicial organ authorized to issue binding judgments on contentious disputes.

■ **If a breach of the peace occurs, the organization should apply timely, robust sanctions to punish the aggressor.** A final assumption underpinning the theory holds that members of the collective security organization would be willing and able to give mutual assistance to any state suffering an attack. Sanctions could range from public condemnation to an economic boycott to military retaliation.

Putting the pieces of these premises together, this approach to international peace through collective security organizations aims to control national self-help warfare by guaranteeing states' defense through collective regulation. Ironically, therefore, liberal reformers accept the use of military might—not to expand state power, but rather to deter potential aggressors by confronting them with armed force organized by the united opposition of the entire global community. Might *can* be used to fight for right.

To the disappointment of its advocates, the League of Nations never became an effective collective system. It was not endorsed by the United States, the very power that had most championed it in the waning months of World War I. Moreover, its members disagreed over how to define "aggression," as well as how to share the costs and risks of mounting an organized response to aggressors. While the League failed to realize the lofty goal of states being as committed to the protection of others as they were to the protection of themselves, the principles of collective security guided the subsequent formation of the United Nations.

The United Nations and Peacekeeping

Like the League, the United Nations was established to promote international peace and security after a gruesome world war. The architects of the United Nations were painfully aware of the League's disappointing experience with collective security. They hoped a new structure would make the United Nations more effective than the defunct League. The goal was to construct, in the words of U.S. President Harry Truman, "a permanent partnership . . . among the peoples of the world for their common peace and common well being." Recall from Chapter 5 that the UN Charter established a Security Council of fifteen members, a General Assembly composed of representatives from all member states, and an administrative apparatus (or Secretariat) under the leadership of a Secretary-General. Although the UN's founders voiced support for collective security, they were heavily influenced by the idea of a *concert* of great powers. The UN Charter permitted any of the Security Council's five permanent members (the United States, the Soviet Union, Great Britain, France, and China) to veto and thereby block proposed military actions. Because the Security Council could approve military actions only when the permanent members fully agreed, the United Nations was hamstrung by great power rivalries, especially between the United States and the Soviet Union. During the Cold War, "it became a formula for political paralysis" (Urquhart 2010, p. 26) with more than 230 Security Council vetoes stopping action of any type on about one-third of the UN's resolutions.

Because the UN's structure limited its ability to function as a true collective security organization, the United Nations fell short during the Cold War of many of the ideals its more ambitious founders envisioned. Nevertheless, like any adaptive institution, the UN found other ways to overcome the compromising legal restrictions and lack of great power cooperation that inhibited its capacity to preserve world order. For example, in contrast to peace enforcement as in the Korean War, the UN undertook a new approach, termed *peacekeeping*, that aimed at separating enemies (Urquhart 2010). The UN Emergency Force (UNEF), authorized in 1956 by the *Uniting for Peace Resolution* in the General Assembly in response to the Suez crisis, was the first of many other peacekeeping operations.

In addition, in 1960, Secretary-General Dag Hammarskjöld sought to manage security through what he termed *preventive diplomacy* by attempting to resolve conflicts before they reached the crisis stage, in contrast to ending wars once they erupted. Likewise, in 1989, Secretary-General Javier Pérez de Cuéllar, frustrated with the superpowers' prevention of the UN to "play as effective and decisive a role as the charter certainly envisaged for it," pursued

peacekeeping
the efforts by third parties such as the UN to intervene in civil wars and/or interstate wars or to prevent hostilities between potential belligerents from escalating, so that by acting as a buffer, a negotiated settlement of the dispute can be reached.

preventive diplomacy
diplomatic actions taken in advance of a predictable crisis to prevent or limit violence.

what was called *peacemaking* initiatives designed to obtain a truce to end the fighting so that the UN Security Council could then establish operations to keep the peace. UN Secretary-General Kofi Annan concentrated the UN's efforts on *peace building* by creating the conditions that make renewed war unlikely, while at the same time working on peacemaking (ending fighting already under way) and managing the UN's *peace operations* to police those conflicts in which the threat of renewed fighting between enemies is high. These endeavors have emphasized *peace enforcement* operations, relying on UN forces that are trained and equipped to use military force if necessary without the prior consent of the disputants.

For more than four decades, the UN was a victim of superpower rivalry. However, the end of the Cold War removed many of the impediments to the UN's ability to lead in preserving peace. For example, in 1999, the Security Council swung into action to authorize military coercion to force Iraq to withdraw from Kuwait, which it had invaded. This successful collective security initiative jump started optimism for use of the UN for peacekeeping leadership. After 1990, the UN launched over three times as many peacekeeping missions as it had in its previous forty years of its existence. On average, since 1990 it has managed just under six operations each year (see Map 11.2).

In 1945, there were virtually no global problems that a single state could not successfully address alone. Today, the world faces intimidating challenges such as nuclear proliferation, international terrorism, global pandemics, environmental deterioration, and resource scarcities—global problems that require cooperative solutions. "As a universal organization, the United Nations should be uniquely suited to provide leadership and coordinate action on such matters, but the capacity of its members to use it as a place for cooperating on dangerous global problems has been limited and disappointing" (Urquhart 2010, p. 26). Although liberals have great hope for the UN as a means of promoting human rights and a global rule of law (Mertus 2009), the constraints that it faces as an organization may be due in part to its continued structural emphasis on sovereignty and power politics. From a realist perspective, the "UN was founded to perpetuate the global dominance of Britain and America while accommodating the unwelcome emergence of the Soviet Union . . . as an institution whereby power politics could be pursued by other means" (Gray 2010, p. 79; Mazower 2009). In order to fundamentally enhance the ability of the UN to function as a truly global authority, its members may need to relinquish their individual prerogatives and grant greater authority to the UN (Weiss et al. 2009). UN analyst Brian Urquhart embraces this view, which he sees as critical to the continued relevance of the UN in this age of globalization:

peacemaking
the process of diplomacy, mediation, negotiation, or other forms of peaceful settlement that arranges an end to a dispute and resolves the issues that led to conflict.

peace building
post-conflict actions, predominantly diplomatic and economic, that strengthen and rebuild governmental infrastructure and institutions in order to avoid renewed recourse to armed conflict.

peace operations
a general category encompassing both peacekeeping and peace enforcement operations, undertaken to establish and maintain peace between disputants.

peace enforcement
the application of military force to warring parties, or the threat of its use, normally pursuant to international authorization, to compel compliance with resolutions or with sanctions designed to maintain or restore peace and order.

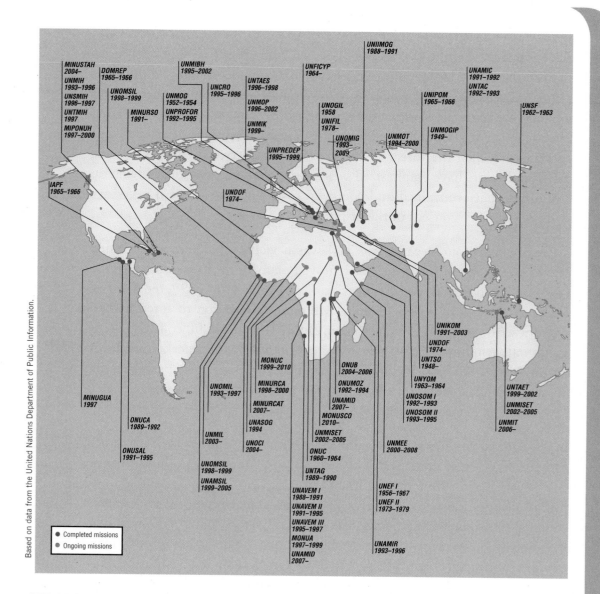

Based on data from the United Nations Department of Public Information.

MAP 11.2

UN PEACE MISSIONS SINCE 1948 In its first forty years, the United Nations undertook a mere eighteen peacekeeping operations. But since 1990, the UN has been much more active, sending Blue Helmet peacekeepers to fifty-six flash points. Since 1990, on average, the UN has had almost six operations under way each year, and as the following figure shows, most of the sixty-four missions between 1948 and 2011 have been in operation for at least a decade.

If governments really considered the effectiveness of the United Nations an urgent priority, this (state sovereignty) would be the first problem they would have to tackle. As it is, one can only wonder which of the great global problems will provide the cosmic disaster that will prove beyond doubt, and probably too late, that our present situation demands a post-Westphalian international order (Urguhart 2010, p. 28).

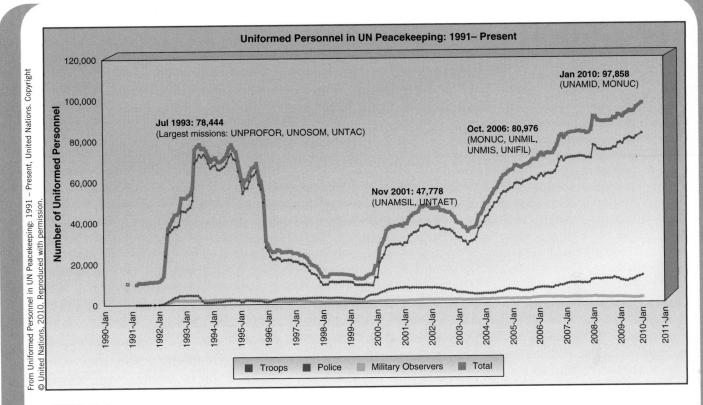

FIGURE 11.2

THE INCREASING DEMAND FOR "PEACE" The above chart shows a clear trend in the demand for peacekeepers over time, as the total number of personnel involved in peacekeeping missions has increased fivefold since 1999. The other trend lines show two of the other key functions increasingly performed by these personnel: military observers (who monitor conditions on the ground and have no mandate to engage militarily) and police. At the start of 2010, uniformed personnel included 82,868 troops, 12,781 police, and 2,209 military observers who were contributed by 115 countries.

It is not only the priorities of the Security Council's great powers that constrain the United Nations but also its limited infrastructure and financial resources. For the UN's sixty-four peacekeeping operations since 1948, expenditures have totaled more than $69 billion, and for the period from July 2009 through June 2010, the budget support to 124,000 UN peacekeeping personnel was $7.9 billion. This represents a nine-fold increase in UN peacekeepers since 1999, on what amounts to only half of one percent of global military spending.

For the UN to succeed, the world community must match the means given to it with the demands made on it. As argued by UN analysts Thorsten Benner, Stephan Mergenthaler, and Philipp Rotmann (2008, p. 6), "UN peacekeeping is the victim of its own success," as the increased demand for peacekeepers, as well as the increasingly diverse nature of their missions, has not been matched by increases in infrastructure and training. Yet UN peacekeeping forces are generally less expensive than the costs of troops deployed by countries in the Global North, NATO, or regional organizations. According to Susan Rice, the U.S. Permanent Representative to the UN, "If the US was to act on its own—unilaterally—and deploy its own forces in many of these countries; for every dollar that the US would spend, the UN can accomplish the Mission for twelve cents."

Despite its imperfections, the United Nations remains the only global institution effective at organizing international collaboration to meet security crises in situations where states are unwilling or unprepared to act alone. However, the use of regional security organizations is rising as regional IGOs are stepping into the breach in those situations where UN Blue Helmets have not been given the support necessary to do the job.

Regional Security Organizations and Collective Defense

If the UN reflects the lack of shared values and common purpose characteristic of a divided global community, perhaps regional organizations, whose members already share some interests and cultural traditions, offer better prospects. The kinds of wars raging today do not lend themselves to control by a worldwide body because these conflicts are now almost entirely civil wars. The UN was designed to manage only international wars *between* states; it was not organized or legally authorized to intervene in internal battles *within* sovereign borders.

Regional IGOs are different. Regional IGOs see their security interests vitally affected by armed conflicts within countries in their area or adjacent to it, and historically they have shown the determination and discipline to police bitter civil conflicts "in their backyards." The "regionalization" of peace operations is a global trend. As 2010 began, no less than fifty-four peace missions served by 219,278 military and civilian personnel were carried out by regional organizations and UN-sanctioned coalitions of states (SIPRI 2010). Hence, regional security organizations can be expected to play an increasingly larger role in the future security affairs of their regions.

The North Atlantic Treaty Organization (NATO) is the best-known regional security organization. Others include the Organization for Security and Cooperation in Europe (OSCE), the ANZUS pact (Australia, New Zealand, and the United States), and the Southeast Asia Treaty Organization (SEATO). Regional organizations with somewhat broader political mandates beyond defense include the Organization of American States (OAS), the League of Arab States,

Mohammad Kheirkhah/UPI/Landov

A LIBERAL MILITARY INTERVENTIONIST ROAD TO PEACE?   For the first time invoking its Article 5, which requires collective defense of a member under attack, NATO joined the war in Afghanistan in a strong show of support for the United States in the aftermath of 9/11. Nonetheless, many European states have imposed restrictions and been reluctant participants in NATO's International Security Assistance Force (ISAF). American fighting forces ruefully quip that the alliance mission's initials equate to "I Saw America Fight," and U.S. Defense Secretary Robert Gates warned that this situation "demonstrates that NATO risks slipping toward a two-tier alliance, divided between those that can and will fight . . . and those that cannot or will not because of public opinon at home" (Shanker and Erlanger 2009, p. 1). Pictured here are NATO soldiers at the scene of a suicide attack in Kabul, Afghanistan.

the Organization of African Unity (OAU), the Nordic Council, the Association of Southeast Asian Nations (ASEAN), and the Gulf Cooperation Council.

Many of today's regional security organizations face the challenge of preserving consensus and solidarity without a clearly identifiable external enemy or common threat. Cohesion is hard to maintain in the absence of a clear sense of the alliance's mission. Consider NATO. The ambiguous European security setting is now marked by numerous ethnic and religious conflicts that NATO was not originally designed to handle. Its original charter envisioned only one purpose—mutual self-protection from external attack. It never defined policing civil wars as a goal. Consequently, until 1995, when NATO took charge of all military operations in Bosnia-Herzegovina from the UN, it was uncertain whether the alliance could adapt to a broadened purpose. Since that intervention, NATO *has* redefined itself. In 1999 it intervened to police the civil violence in Kosovo and in 2001, following the terrorist attacks on the United States, it intervened in the war in Afghanistan.

COURSEMATE

Video: *A Long-Term Decision*

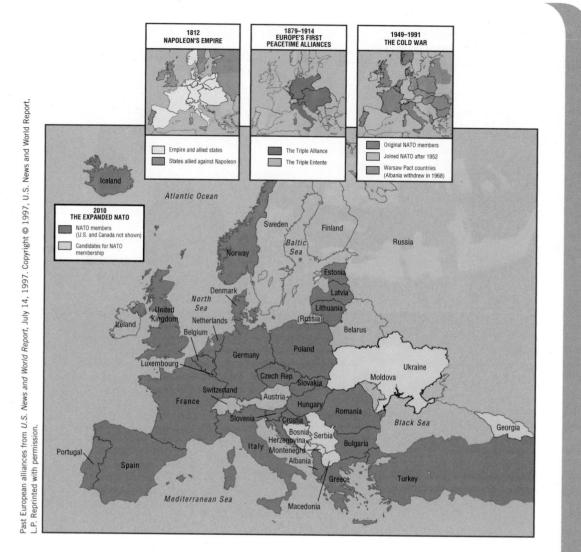

Past European alliances from *U.S. News and World Report*, July 14, 1997. Copyright © 1997, U.S. News and World Report, L.P. Reprinted with permission.

MAP 11.3

THE ENLARGED NATO IN THE NEW GEOSTRATEGIC BALANCE OF POWER

The twenty-first-century geostrategic landscape has been transformed by NATO's expansion to twenty-eight full members, with Albania and Croatia formally joining as the newest members on April 1, 2009. An additional twenty-two countries now work as Partners for Peace in the Euro-Atlantic Partnership Council (EAPC). As shown in this map, NATO now casts its security umbrella across and beyond Europe in its endeavor to create a collective security regime including states that were once its enemies.

Today, NATO is an enlarged alliance, with its membership growing from the twelve founding members in 1949 to the current twenty-eight members through six rounds of enlargement in 1952, 1955, 1982, 1999, 2004, and 2009 (see Map 11.3). There are a number of countries in Eastern Europe that are candidates for future membership, and many feel that it is in NATO's interests and those of Europe to integrate Russia into the membership as well. NATO has transformed itself to become both a *military* alliance for security between states and within them and for containing the spread of global terrorism, as well as a *political* alliance for encouraging the spread of democracy. That said, the primary purpose remains putting NATO's twenty-eight members under a security umbrella, with the promise that an attack on one would be considered an attack on all. Commemorating the sixtieth anniversary of NATO in 2009, NATO Secretary-General Jaap de hoop Scheffer emphasized the continued importance of security through multinational cooperation, proclaiming that "NATO is alive and kicking because it still has a unique job to do: to be the place where Europe and North America stand together, consult together and act together to ensure their common security."

The barriers to collective security faced by regional organizations are similar to those faced by the United Nations. Liberal and constructivist reformers are well aware of these obstacles and are seeking to strengthen global and regional institutions for collective defense to help overcome the weaknesses standing in the way of their peacekeeping performance.

The recent record indicates that there are several key preconditions that must be met for collective security organizations to work both globally and regionally. First, these security organizations are most capable of creating successful peacekeeping operations only when their most powerful members reach agreement about the benefits of any proposed operation. Second, such third-party peacekeeping operations have been most successful in those cases when the target is neither a great power nor has a military alliance with a major power. Third, the success rate of peace missions improves when the operations are aimed at a target country where a great power, the United Nations, or a regional IGO has previously intervened to contain a civil war or a secessionist movement (Mullenbach 2005). Finally, past cases indicate that security organizations' capacity to control controversial conflicts depends on pressure from world public opinion to mobilize international organizations to take action. The absence of some of these preconditions accounts for the frequent failure of IGOs to engineer a timely response to tragic situations where slaughter and genocide occur; the slow and insufficient reaction to stop the bloodshed in the Darfur region of Sudan and Somalia in the Horn of Africa are the most recent examples of inadequate collective global action.

The processes through which transformation toward greater collective security might be engineered require the formation of a global consensus about the core values from which a common or *cosmopolitan* (cosmos = world; polity = governing unit) world culture might emerge, as liberals and many constructivists hope. Are global trends unfolding that increase the prospects for such a transformation in world politics?

UNITING ONE WORLD IN A COMMON CULTURE OF SHARED MORAL VALUES

Liberal and constructivist perspectives on war and peace, armed aggression, and international security are fundamentally shaped by the importance attached to shared ethics and morality in world politics. Liberalism places the power of principle over the principle of power (Kegley 1992) because it is based on the conviction that peace depends on acting by moral motives. Such emphasis is also embedded in the fabric of many world religions, including Christianity, as seen in Jesus Christ's proclamation "Blessed are the peacemakers, for they shall be called sons of God." The liberal road to peace begins with a dedication to doing what is right and not doing what is wrong; and constructivism, though itself conventionally thought of as ethically neutral, serves as a means for explaining systems of ethical beliefs. This differs greatly from much realist theorizing that "holds international politics to be beyond the concern of morality" (Suganami 1983).

Ethics is about the criteria for evaluating right and wrong behavior and motives; *morality* is about the norms for behavior that should govern actors' interactions. Liberals, and many constructivists, understandably focus on humanitarian concerns and human rights when they emphasize the importance of normative values as factors shaping global conditions. One of the greatest moral ethicists who grappled with war and peace in an immoral world was German philosopher Immanuel Kant. In 1798, Kant wrote "the character of the human race . . . is that of a multitude of persons living one after another and one beside another, unable to *do without* peaceful coexistence, yet also unable to *avoid* being constantly hateful to one another . . . ; a coalition always threatened with dissolution, but on the whole progressing towards a worldwide *civil society*." A global civil society is one in which institutions are created to protect civil liberties and use peaceful methods for conflict resolution. The world does not yet benefit from either these institutions or agreement about the **mores** or normative convictions that should guide international decision making. However, liberals believe that these ethical standards can gain acceptance and create a civil society at the global level of analysis.

mores
the customs of a group accepted as morally binding obligations.

In 1795, Kant wrote a famous essay titled *Perpetual Peace.* In it, he asked how enduring peace might be created. He advanced two liberal ideas that were revolutionary at the time. Picturing war as a consequence of illogical reasoning because its practice works against states' long-term interests, Kant proposed using humans' capacity to reason rationally to discover paths that would truly serve their real long-term interests in living in an orderly and just world. He emphasized two pathways that form the bedrock of liberal approaches to world peace: free trade and free governments.

These were both radical ideas in Kant's time. Most powerful states in his era were then (1) great powers practicing narrow *mercantilism* to expand their national economies at others' expense through imperialism and colonialism and (2) monarchies ruled by kings opposed to democratic liberties for the subjects under their absolute reign. Needless to say, Kant was repelled by the acceptance and frequent use of warfare by these realist rulers to increase by military means the power of their states. So Kant advocated a total transformation of the realist values on which world politics was then functioning, replacing that chaotic global environment with a new and more secure one based on liberal free trade and citizens' freedom to choose their leaders through democratic elections.

These radical ideas resonated in the ears of other innovators in liberal thought, such as Adam Smith, Thomas Jefferson, and James Madison; and they later were made pillars of the peace program that Woodrow Wilson proposed in his Fourteen Points Address. Point III advocated free trade through the abolition of protective tariffs: "the removal, so far as possible, of all economic barriers and the establishment of an equality of trade conditions among the nations [seeking] peace and associating themselves for its maintenance." Likewise, Wilson echoed Kant when Wilson opined "making the world safe for democracy" would make "the world fit and safe to live in." These twin highways to peace require the global acceptance of the norms for international conduct that together capture the third major liberal path to international security.

Trade Ties of Common Interest

Commercial liberalism is based on the proposition that when barriers to trade between and among countries are reduced through cooperative agreements, the prosperity of the trading parties will rise (see Chapter 12). However, there exists another expanding side-payoff to free-trade: When it increases, it ties the trading partners together in an expanding web of interdependence from which all the trading parties to the free-trade agreement benefit. It is therefore rational, according to liberal economic theory, to promote free trade. Over the long run, the benefits outweigh the short-term costs. Self-interests are served by trade cooperation, not competition. Additionally, since parties to active free exchanges of goods across borders increasingly need each other for the growth of their wealth, they are therefore less tempted to go to war

commercial liberalism an economic theory advocating free markets and the removal of barriers to the flow of trade and capital as a locomotive for prosperity.

with one another. Armed aggression would end the cooperation that makes their mutual prosperity grow.

In this regard, global economic trade interdependence among nations provides a strong underpinning for peace. *Interdependence* (when the behavior of states greatly affects the others with whom they come into frequent contact, and the parties to such active exchanges become increasingly mutually vulnerable to each others' actions) thus fosters the trade-interdependent countries' mutual need for each other for their own welfare. Accordingly, when free trade increases, the incentives for war decline: Why attack another country on which your own state's economy is dependent for growth? In this construction, therefore, trade interdependence is a financial path to peace.

The global trend for the past six decades has been a profound progression toward the reduction of barriers to free trade such as tariffs and import quotas (see Chapter 12). This expansion of free trade worldwide has witnessed alongside it a drastic reduction in the number of armed conflicts *between* states; interstate wars have almost now vanished from the global scene (recall Chapter 7). Extolling the virtues of free trade for world peace, political economist Richard Cobden exclaimed, "Free trade! What is it? Why, breaking down the barriers that separate nations; those barriers behind which nestle the barriers of pride, revenge, hatred and jealousy, which every now and then burst their bounds and deluge whole countries with blood; those barriers which nourish the poison of war and conquest."

For this nonmilitary path to global security to truly arrive at its preferred pacific destination, constructivists remind us that the global community must accept the norms of behavior on which this approach is predicated. Realists warn that, if and when economic conditions deteriorate, countries are then likely to return to ruthless economic competition and trade protectionism to gain at others' expense. Liberal reformers agree with realist pessimism; they also see a civil society with peace dependent on the preservation of normative values and mores that must retain global acceptance. Should such a free-trade liberal climate of global world opinion decay, so will the prospects for world order. It is with these concerns in mind that some have worried about the impact of the current global economic crisis on peace and stability throughout the world.

That said, the far distance the global community has journeyed down the free-trade avenue toward prosperity and peace has instilled growing faith that this progress will persist, so long as countries continue to recognize that their interests are advanced through peace and economic interdependence.

interdependence
a situation in which the behavior of international actors greatly affects others with whom they have contact, making all parties mutually sensitive and vulnerable to the others' actions.

Case Study: *The Promise and Perils of Interdependence*

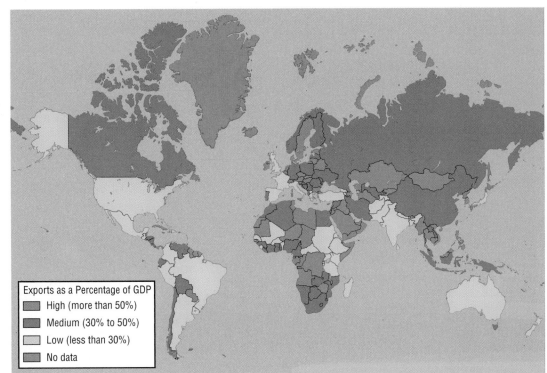

Based on data from the World Development Indicators 2010

Exports as a Percentage of GDP
- High (more than 50%)
- Medium (30% to 50%)
- Low (less than 30%)
- No data

MAP 11.4

COUNTRIES DEPENDENT ON TRADE In the globalized marketplace, the level of states' dependence on exports for economic prosperity is growing. This map shows the great extent to which many countries are today dependent on trade. "Without imports many products that consumers want would be unavailable or more expensive [and] without exports many jobs would be eliminated" (S. Allen 2006).

Will the majority of countries accept this construction? Time will tell. Liberal and constructivist reformers are well aware of the potential fragility of trade interdependence as a condition for fostering international security. However, there may be a better payoff to an alternative route to cement international peace: the construction and proliferation of liberal norms supporting democratic values.

A Democratic Peace Pact

What is now widely known as the *democratic peace* is the theory that because democratic states almost never fight wars with one another, the spread of democratic governance throughout the world will reduce greatly the probability of war. This is not a new theory or approach to international security. In 1792 James Madison, president of the United States, voiced this proposition when he argued that "in the advent of republican governments would be found not only the prospect of a radical decline in the role played by war but the prospect as well of a virtual revolution in the conduct of diplomacy." Three short years later, Immanuel Kant advanced the same liberal speculation in his more famous *Perpetual Peace*, when he, too, hypothesized that giving peace-loving citizens the right to vote could stop violence—that allowing ballots for citizens could become a sturdy barrier against authoritarian rulers' habitual use of bullets and bombs.

History demonstrates that there are sound reasons for accepting this liberal proposition. Many scholarly quantitative studies of modern international history have convincingly shown that "democracies rarely fight one another because they share common norms of live-and-let-live and domestic institutions that constrain the recourse to war" (Rosato 2003, p. 585; see also Lektzian and Souva 2009; Rasler and Thompson 2005).

Case Study: *Democracy and Peace*

This lesson was not lost on leaders of democratic states seeking to find a principle on which to ground their national security policies. "Ultimately the best strategy to insure our security and to build a durable peace is to support the

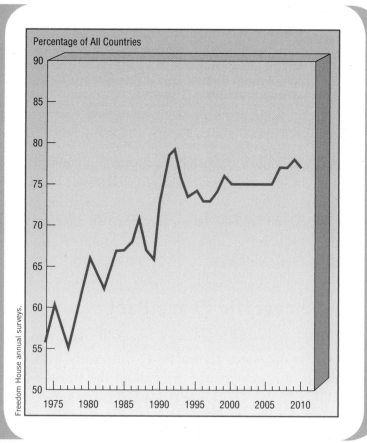

FIGURE 11.3

WILL A FREEDOM FENCE EMERGE FROM THE GLOBAL GROWTH OF DEMOCRATIC GOVERNANCE? This figure shows that as 2010 began, 76 percent of the countries in the world were either fully or partially democratic, according to Freedom House. This is a 2 percent decline from the year prior, with 2.3 billion people living in countries where their fundamental political rights and civil liberties are not respected. Nonetheless, the long-term trend towards greater freedom inspires liberals' hopes that a global peace among democracies will continue to spread and deepen.

advance of democracy elsewhere," the 1994 *U.S. National Security Strategy* concluded. That doctrine was officially endorsed earlier by the other major EU and NATO liberal democracies whose members insisted on states being democratically ruled as a condition for membership. In addition, the major international organizations have also endorsed the promotion of democracy as a policy priority, including the *Group of Eight (G-8),* the World Bank, the International Monetary Fund (IMF), the Organization for Economic Cooperation and Development (OECD), and the Organization of American States (OAS).

Democratic reforms over the past four decades have produced impressive results worldwide. Since the mid-1970s, freedom and civil liberties within countries have expanded through a series of liberalizing governmental reforms in many new countries. Throughout the world, countries that were formerly ruthlessly ruled by autocratic military dictators practicing political repression have collapsed, as the "quiet revolution" in South America's successful deepening of democratic institutions and civil liberties attests (Fukuyama 2007). Today the community of liberal democracies (countries ruled by "free" or "partially free" governments) has now spread to more than three-fourths of the globe's states (see Figure 11.3).

Some realist skeptics question whether democracies should really be counted upon to put their liberal ideals ahead of their narrow national interests by resisting the natural temptation to use armed force when serious disputes surface. And both realists and liberals are very worried about the possibility that a democratic great power will abuse this liberal principle by forcing "democracy at gunpoint" (Pickering and Peceny 2006; O'Reilly and Renfro 2007). What if other liberal powers emulate the United States' 2003 invasion and occupation of Iraq and dispatch soldiers to foreign lands for "regime change" to push countries toward democracy (or accepting their religious preferences)? If the export of democratic institutions for state-building is mismanaged, the basis for resting global security on the growth of democracy is likely to lead to more wars, not fewer (Coyne 2007).

These doubts about a lasting "democratic peace pact" not withstanding, liberal reformers are heartened by past trends. These provide strong evidence to support the liberal tenet that democracy is conducive to the construction of many beneficial moral values, including freedom, human rights, civil liberties, prosperity, and especially an increased capacity to deter wars within and between members of the democratic community of states (See Controversy: Is Taiwan "Living Proof" of the Liberal Path to Peace and Prosperity?). Empirical studies have found, among other things, "that democracies are systematically different from other regime types because of a greater ability to

CONTROVERSY:

IS TAIWAN "LIVING PROOF" OF THE LIBERAL PATH TO PEACE AND PROSPERITY?

In 1949 Chiang Kai-shek and his party the Kuomintang (KMT) lost the Chinese Civil War and retreated from the Mainland to Taiwan with one to two million followers and troops. Taiwan began the 1950s poor and ruled by an immigrant, authoritarian regime.

Policy choices economically transformed Taiwan, including initiating land reform, extending free and universal education, moving from import-substitution to trade-led export growth, and emphasizing heavy and then-high-tech industrial policy. U.S. aid and foreign investments were also crucial.

Combined with favorable international conditions, the development strategies worked, and Taiwan experienced an "economic miracle." By the 1990s Taiwan was one of the "East Asian Tigers" with a trading economy based on small and medium sized businesses, leadership in many high-tech industries, and an extensive, educated middle class. Population grew from 7.5 to 23 million, and GDP per capita grew from $900 in 1949, to $5,300 in 1987, to $30,200 by the start of 2010.

Perhaps even more important was Taiwan's "democratic miracle." In 1987 Chiang's son, Chiang Ching-kuo, lifted martial law; in 1991–1992 parliamentary elections occurred; in 1996 direct presidential elections took place; in 2000 and 2004 the opposition Democratic Progressive Party (DPP) won the presidency; and in 2008 the KMT returned to power in transparent, free elections. Taiwan became the only example of a Chinese society with a multiparty democracy, and stood as a counter to the argument by Malaysia's and Singapore's leaders for the cultural distinctiveness of Asian values and the limits of Asian democracy.

What happened? First, democracy advocates and a Taiwanese ethnic majority that was politically repressed by mainlanders were empowered by economic prosperity and pressured the regime to change. Next, Chiang Ching-kuo and part of the KMT preferred compromise to confrontation. Finally, international circumstances made democracy Taiwan's best hope for support and survival in an ongoing competition with China.

But what about peace? Will Taiwan have to choose between unification into China or war? Since 1949, Taiwan has exercised *de facto,* if not *de jure,* sovereignty in international affairs. China, however, rejects this distinction and views Taiwan as a "breakaway province," taken by Japan as a colony in 1895, occupied by the KMT after World War II, and rightfully a part of China. In 2005 China passed an Anti-Secession Law formalizing its long-standing commitment to use "non-peaceful means" if Taiwan declares formal independence.

In Taiwan, the 2000–2008 DPP government envisioned *de jure* independence. Following the election of KMT President Ma Yin-jeou in 2008, tensions relaxed as the government committed to a diplomatic truce with China. Trade also increasingly links Taiwan to the mainland, with as much as $200 billion invested and as many as one million Taiwanese managers living there. In June 2010, Taiwan and China signed a major trade deal that would further increase the interdependence of the two economies by lowering tariffs and removing barriers to service sectors such as banking.

Linked closely by trade, a democratic China might either allow Taiwan to go its own way peacefully or make unification palatable to the Taiwanese. However, Chinese leadership has been resiliently authoritarian and has used

IS TAIWAN "LIVING PROOF" OF THE LIBERAL PATH TO PEACE AND PROSPERITY? (Continued)

economic development to dampen democratic impulses. The grand bargain between party and people is this: the CCP provides prosperity and receives legitimacy. What are Taiwan's options if authoritarian government in China remains robust and long-lived? In the short-term, the majority of Taiwanese opt for economic linkage, domestic prosperity, the political status, and ambiguity: no unification but no independence and no war.

The possibility of international conflict deepens this ambiguity. The Taiwan Strait remains one of the world's most dangerous places where two nuclear powers could come into conflict. As a result of the Cold War, the United States limited diplomatic dealings with China until President Nixon's 1972 visit. In 1979 the United States diplomatically recognized China, and Taiwanese recognition was withdrawn. The U.S. Congress then passed the Taiwan Relations Act stating that any threat to the peace and security of Taiwan is of grave concern to the United States and committed America to provide Taiwan with defensive weapons. In the face of protest from China, in January 2010, the Obama administration agreed to $6.4 billion in arms sales to Taiwan, including sophisticated weapons such as Black Hawk helicopters and Harpoon anti-ship missiles. Yet America has a deep, multifaceted relationship with China, balanced against nervousness about China's future role and commitments to Taiwan. Other issues, such as anti-terrorism, North Korea, nonproliferation, and global finance, intensify the linkage.

In 1996 before Taiwanese elections, China tested missiles near Taiwan. In response, President Clinton deployed aircraft carrier battle groups toward the Taiwan Strait. American–Chinese tensions similarly escalated in the 1999 NATO bombing of China's Embassy in Belgrade, in the 2001 mid-air collision between a U.S. surveillance plane and a Chinese fighter, and in reactions to the 2008 unrest in Tibet. Chinese nationalism was inflamed by these incidents, and the 2008 Olympics showcased Chinese pride and China's aspirations as a major global power.

China's path to democracy is uncertain, and even if China democratizes without major civil strife, there will be a transitional period. Democracies don't fight each other, but transitional regimes are often belligerent. This is partly because domestic democratic institutions are young, and politicians may use nationalism or demonizing each other to secure their own power. Hence, democratic peace theory may be double edged.

In the long term, a democratic China may offer solutions both to Taiwan's future and to the structuring of peace in East Asia. However, in the next fifty years, are Taiwan's miracles and East Asian peace at risk?

WHAT DO YOU THINK?

- Why was Taiwan able to achieve multiple miracles? Are Taiwan's outcomes unique because of size, policies, enlightened elite, domestic forces, or Taiwan's international environment?

- Are the same liberal "miracles" likely in China, since economic development is well under way and the middle class has grown dramatically? Or, has the elite of the Chinese Communist Party (CCP) learned history's lessons, found ways to limit democratization, and solidified its hold on power?

- Does the case of Taiwan, and the strategic triangle including China and the United States, suggest that trade interdependence and the expansion of democracy reduce the risk of war? What are the prospects for the future?

Note: Prepared with the advice and assistance of William C. Vocke, Ph.D.

more credibly reveal information" (Lektzian and Souva 2009, p. 35). There-fore, providing that democratic states continue to abide by their past record of dealing with conflicts through negotiation, mediation, arbitration, and adjudication, the existing liberal democracies' efforts to enlarge their community could usher in a major transformation of world politics. Pope John Paul II's expressed hopes could make an ancient dream a reality: "No more war, war never again." However, promise dictates neither performance nor destiny. As former Prime Minister Ingvar Caarlsson of Sweden cautioned, "If we fail to nurture democracy—the most fundamental political project—we will never be able to realize our goals and the responsibilities which the future will call for."

> *During the coming decades global challenges will continue and may increase. There is more and more of an overlap between national interests and global responsibilities. The task of multilateral diplomacy is to cope with new issues, new demands and new situations [through] "shared responsibilities" and "strengthened partnerships."*
>
> —J.N. Kinnis, liberal international relations scholar

INSTITUTIONS, NORMS, AND WORLD ORDER

Liberal paths to the control of armed aggression embrace the conviction that war and international instability are primarily caused by deeply rooted global institutional deficiencies that reduce incentives for international cooperation (Barrett 2007). Thus, liberals advocate institutional methods to pool sovereignty in order to collectively manage global problems. With the expansion of global norms that support collective solutions to conflicts in world politics, constructivists envision greater possibilities for the peaceful resolution of situations that might otherwise lead to armed aggression.

Yet we must remain cognizant of the various concerns about the capacity of independent and competing sovereign states to engineer a hopeful future for humanity. On balance, sovereign states have not used their foreign policies to create a safe and secure global environment. Instead, states historically have been constructed to make war with others (Wagner 2007), and, as constructivist international theory instructs, great powers have persistently been primarily "predator and parasite" agents of transnational harm (Löwenheim 2007). Moreover, it is a paradox that despite their continuing power, the governments of sovereign states' governments have proven to be very weak at either preventing armed aggression within their borders or commanding widespread citizen loyalty and respect.

Borders and oceans cannot isolate or insulate states from threats to security; they can only be controlled in the global commons by a collective effort. It is for this reason that many international organizations originally came into being, and it is the persistence of collective threats produced by an increasingly globalized world that makes these institutions durable. As the globe shrinks and borders prove to be increasingly ineffective as barriers, we can predict that liberal and constructivist paths to peace and prosperity will continue to find favor and policy makers will take seriously the call to help create what former Swedish Foreign Minister Anna Lindh described as "a global culture of conflict prevention."

Whether disarmament agreements, multilateral international organizations, and the liberal community of economically interdependent and peace-loving states can organize a collective response through multilateral action to the multitude of global needs will likely be judged by future generations. What is clear is that countries *are* making bold *efforts* to unite in a common civic culture behind common values to construct global institutions to jointly protect themselves against the many problems they face in common. They appear to increasingly accept the once radical liberal view that, as Kofi Annan argues, "a new, broader definition of national interest is needed" that would unify states to work on common goals that transcend national interests.

If the paths you have explored in this and the previous chapter are pursued, will acceptance of the belief that peace is best preserved through ethical policies break the violent historical pattern? The world awaits an answer. But what is clear at this time is that the global agenda facing the world is huge. The biggest problems facing humanity are transnational, and none can be solved effectively with a unilateral national response. A multilateral approach is required to address the staggering number of global problems that require peaceful management through collective solutions.

Simulation: *Collective Security Problem*

In Part 4, you will have an opportunity to look at trends in the economic, human, and environmental conditions that prevail as the cascading globalization of world politics accelerates. This survey can aid understanding of the world as it presently exists and allow you to contemplate, as caring and responsible global citizens, the prospects for transformations that could create a better world.

Take an Online Practice Quiz

www.cengagebrain.com/shop/ISBN/0495802204

Suggested Readings

Cohn, Carol, and Sara Ruddick. (2008) "A Feminist Ethical Perspective on Weapons of Mass Destruction." In *Essential Readings in World Politics,* 3rd ed. Karen A. Mingst, Jack L. Snyder, Editors, 458–77. New York: W.W. Norton & Company.

Jolly, Richard, Louis Emmerij, and Thomas G. Weiss (2009) *UN Ideas That Changed the World.* Bloomington, IN: Indiana University Press.

Kegley, Charles W., Jr., and Gregory A. Raymond. (2002) *Exorcising the Ghost of Westphalia: Building World Order in the New Millennium.* Upper Saddle River, NJ: Prentice Hall.

Lektzian, David, and Mark Souva. (2009) "A Comparative Theory Test of Democratic Peace Arguments, 1946–2000," *Journal of Peace Research* 46 (1): 17–37.

Puchala, Donald, Katie Verlin Laatikainen, and Roger A. Coate. (2007) *United Nations Politics.* Upper Saddle River, NJ: Prentice Hall.

Shannon, Megan (2009) "Preventing War and Providing the Peace? International Organizations and the Management of Territorial Disputes," *Conflict Management and Peace Science* 26 (2): 144–163.

Part 4
HUMAN SECURITY, PROSPERITY, AND RESPONSIBILITY

"The rich and poor worlds are linked as never before—by economics and trade, migration, climate change, disease, drugs, conflict and yes, terrorism. We know that elections are won and lost on local issues— that is true for every country. But it is global issues . . . that will shape the world our children live in."

—James Wolfenshohn, former World Bank President

MUTUAL UNDERSTANDING IN A GLOBALIZED WORLD The growing web of globalization enhances the prospect and need for mutual toleration and cooperation. Shown here are the Vancouver 2010 Winter Olympics, which opened with a celebration of Canadian cultural diversity and international goodwill. Originally founded to promote peace and bridge cultural divides, the renaissance spirit of the Olympic Games was reflected in Organizing Committee CEO John Furlong's welcoming comments: "The Olympic flame has touched many millions and prompted spontaneous, peaceful celebration. Reminding us all that those values that unite and inspire the best in us—we must never abandon. As the Olympic Cauldron is lit, the unique magic of the Olympic Games will be released upon us. Magic so rare that it cannot be controlled by borders—the kind of magic that invades the human heart touching people of all cultures and beliefs. Magic that calls for the best that human beings have to offer. Magic that causes the athletes of the world to soar—and the rest of us to dream."

A S MONEY, GOODS, AND PEOPLE TRAVEL ACROSS NATIONAL BORDERS WITH BLINDING SPEED, GLOBALIZATION IS TRANSFORMING WORLD POLITICS. The chapters in Part 4 explore the global condition and the ways in which the erosion of national borders is transforming international relations and affecting global welfare throughout the world. Each explores some facet of the challenges to prosperity and human security that we face in our globalized world and the extent to which we have the ability, and responsibility, to respond and seek solutions to them.

Chapter 12 inspects how the globalization of finance is altering the international economic landscape, and Chapter 13 considers how the globalization of international trade is transforming the world. Chapter 14 then examines the demographic dimensions of globalization as well as how the rise of the global information age is shaping culture and perceptions of identity. Chapter 15 looks at the human condition, and how global actors and their activities affect the welfare and basic rights of all humanity. Finally, Chapter 16 considers threats to the global environment that many people now see as a serious danger to the well-being of the planet and humanity's continued survival.

CHAPTER 12
THE GLOBALIZATION OF INTERNATIONAL FINANCE

CHAPTER OUTLINE

INTERPRETING CONTEMPORARY ECONOMIC CHANGE

International Political Economy

What Is Globalization?

MONEY MATTERS: THE TRANSNATIONAL EXCHANGE OF MONEY

The Globalization of Finance

Monetary Policies: Key Concepts and Issues

The Bretton Woods System

Financial and Monetary Aspects of the Bretton Woods System

The End of Bretton Woods

Floating Exchange Rates and Financial Crises

CONTROVERSY: The IMF, World Bank, and Structural Adjustment Policies: Is the "Cure" Worse than the "Disease"?

The Crisis of 2008

REFORMING THE INTERNATIONAL FINANCIAL ARCHITECTURE?

Globalization is no longer a buzzword: it has arrived. There is substantial evidence for an increasingly globalized marketplace. World trade is expanding much faster than world production and cross-border investments are growing at a more rapid rate than trade. People in one country are more likely to be affected by economic actions in other nations in many capabilities: as customers, entrepreneurs and investors, managers and taxpayers, and citizens.

—Murray Weidenbaum, political economist

Peter Macdiarmid/Getty Images News/Getty Images

SEEKING GLOBAL FINANCIAL RECOVERY In continued response to the recent financial crisis, the leaders of the G-20—an informal group of the twenty largest economies that meets periodically to discuss the coordination of financial policy—met in Toronto in June 2010 to discuss recovery strategies. Recognizing that too much austerity could undermine global recovery, yet shaken by the European debt crisis, world leaders generally supported plans to cut spending and raise taxes with a goal of reducing government debt of the wealthier countries by 50 percent by 2013.

M oney makes the world go "round." "Money is the root of all evil." "All that glitters is not gold." "Money can't buy you happiness." "There's hell in not making money."

You have all heard these old sayings at one time or another. They all contain elements of truth, even though such aphorisms and clichés are somewhat contradictory. Your challenge is to separate fact from fantasy by sorting out the place of money in your life and in the world in which you live. This task will heavily depend on your personal values and preferences. However, the wisdom or folly of your conclusions will depend on your analytic skills in evaluating how money is a factor affecting many dimensions of world politics—and your own personal future financial fate.

Increasingly, this age-old intellectual task is more difficult than in the past. Today, more than ever, money truly *is* moving around the world, and at ever-quickening speed. And the rapidity of the movement of finance capital across borders directly affects your quality of life every day. When you make a purchase, the odds are now very high that the goods have been produced overseas. What is more, when you buy a sandwich, a sweater, a car, or gasoline to make it run, the cost of your payment is very likely to be affected by the rate at which your own country's currency is valued and exchanged for the currency of the producer abroad. Should you have the opportunity to travel overseas for work or for tourism, you will instantly discover how powerfully the global exchange of national currencies will determine whether you can afford to attend a rock concert or buy an extra bottle of wine.

This chapter is about how money markets in the global financial system operate. It looks at the processes governing currency exchanges, concentrating on how the transfer of money across borders affects levels of national prosperity and human security. Note that this topic is part of the larger one of international economics in general, and serves as an introduction to the coverage in Chapter 13 on international trade in the global political economy. Neither dimension of international economics—money and marketplaces for trade—can be considered without the other; the two are tied intimately, and only by looking at both together can you gain an understanding of how money and markets drive the rise and fall of wealth for individuals and for countries. You therefore will be looking at a phenomenon as old as recorded history and inspecting how it is influencing life in the twenty-first century.

Financial markets are like the mirror of mankind, revealing every hour of each working day the way we value ourselves and the resources of the world around us.

—Niall Ferguson, British Historian

INTERPRETING CONTEMPORARY ECONOMIC CHANGE

When changes occur in the world, they force people to think about and interpret world politics in fresh ways. Of all the many recent changes, perhaps none has been more continually invasive and far-reaching than those occurring in the economic world. This is one of the main fields on which the game of world politics is played. In fact, to some analysts, *geo-economics* (the geographic distribution of wealth) will replace *geopolitics* (the distribution of strategic military and political power) as the most important axis around which international competition will revolve and will determine the globe's future destiny (see Chapter 3). To interpret the dynamics underlying the rules of this geo-economic game, it is helpful to gain perspective by turning to economic *theory* (a set of propositions that explain why observable repetitions and regularities are evident in some phenomena).

geo-economics
the relationship between geography and the economic conditions and behavior of states that define their levels of production, trade, and consumption of goods and services.

geopolitics
the relationship between geography and politics and their consequences for states' national interests and relative power.

International Political Economy

Fortunately, a large body of theory has been constructed that speaks to questions about how changes in one country's economics and politics influence trends in world politics and the global economy. As an area of scholarly study, *international political economy (IPE)* emerged in the early 1970s as economic events such as the fall of the Bretton Woods order (covered later in this chapter) and the Oil Crisis of 1973, which led to a fourfold increase in the price of oil as a result of an embargo by the Organization of Petroleum Exporting Countries (OPEC), sent shock waves throughout the world. The political fallout of these economic events called into question the traditional partitions between the study of international economics and international politics, and IPE began to investigate many key issues that lay at the intersection of the two.

international political economy (IPE)
the study of the intersection of politics and economics that illuminates why changes occur in the distribution of states' wealth and power.

As Stephen Krasner (2001) elaborates, "International political economy tries to answer such questions as: How have changes in the international distribution of power among states affected the degree of openness in the international trading system? Do the domestic political economies of some states allow them to compete more effectively in international markets? Is the relative poverty of the [Global South] better explained by indigenous conditions in individual countries or by some attribute of the international economic system? When can economic ties among states be used for political leverage?"

globalization
the integration of states through increasing contact, communication, and trade, as well as increased global awareness of such integration.

IPE remains relevant because it focuses on the vortex of politics and economics that has become so controversial in today's age of *globalization* of world finance and trade. The growth of the interdependence of states' economies can be viewed as the recent culmination of a trend that began more than a century ago, but its current level is without precedent. As states' economies have become more closely linked, traditional ideas about states, currency exchange mechanisms, trade, and markets have been reexamined in a new light. The contest between the rich states in the Global North and the poor states in the Global South has risen to the top of the international agenda in policy and theoretical debates.

The economic game of world politics has assumed increasing importance because the undercurrents in economics are shaping the foundation of international politics. Today, high interest rates in one country lead to high interest rates in others. A stock market free fall starting in Asia will spread like wildfire to New York and London. Depression abroad means recession at home. Inflation is shared everywhere, and it now seems beyond the control of any single actor. The balance of fiscal power is now as important to a country's national security as is the global balance of military power. These are some of the consequences of globalization, seen by the International Monetary Fund as "the increasingly close international integration of markets both for goods and services, and for capital."

COURSEMATE

Case Study:
International Political Economy: Globalization

What Is Globalization?

Globalization has become a very common term—"the most ubiquitous in the language of international relations" (Ostry 2001)—and hundreds of attempts have been made to define it. Though some regard globalization as little more than a euphemism for capitalism (Petras and Veltmeyer 2004), it is important to keep in mind that globalization is a multifaceted phenomena, which encompasses the development of interconnected material relations (such as the economic ties cited in the definition in the previous paragraph), the increasing rapidity through which they take place, and a "cognitive shift" (Held and McGrew 2003) as such changes enter into public perception. Globalization is thus a shorthand for a cluster of interconnected phenomena, and you will find the term used to describe a process, a policy, a predicament, or the product of vast invisible international forces producing massive changes worldwide. Moreover, most analysts would probably agree that globalization is a permanent trend leading to the probable *transformation* of world politics—the end of one historic pattern and the beginning of a new one in history.

As a leading analyst of globalization, political journalist Thomas L. Friedman, thinks, this prophecy is accurate: "This new era of globalization will prove to be such a difference of degree that it will be seen, in time, as a difference in kind. . . . The world has gone from round to flat. If I am right about the flattening of the world, it will be remembered as one of those fundamental changes—like the rise of the nation-state or the Industrial Revolution—each of which, in its day, produced changes in the role of individuals, the role and form of governments, the way we innovated [and] the way we conducted business." Given the broad and multifaceted scope of globalization, this chapter, as well as the remaining chapters in *World Politics*, will deal with different dimensions of globalization and their implications.

Friedman raises the rhetorical question for you to consider in the context of evaluating the financial dimensions of globalization:

> What is globalization? The short answer is that globalization is the integration of everything with everything else. A more complete definition is that globalization is the integration of markets, finance, and technology in a way

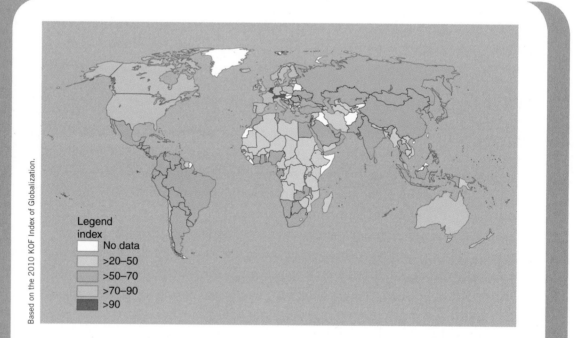

Based on the 2010 KOF Index of Globalization.

Legend
index

No data
>20–50
>50–70
>70–90
>90

MAP 12.1

GLOBALIZATION AROUND THE WORLD This map depicts the extent of globalization in 2010 and is rendered from the 2010 Index of Globalization released by the KOF Swiss Economic Institute. The index is based on twenty-four different measures of economic, social, and political aspects of globalization, such as trade flows, personal contacts across borders, and participation in international organizations. As shown here, globalization varies across countries and regions. European countries are among the most global (fourteen of the fifteen most globalized countries are from that region). The United States ranked 27th in 2010, with a globalization index score of 78.80. There are also some trends among the least globalized, as they tend to be underdeveloped and largely autocratic regimes such as Myanmar, Sudan, and Rwanda.

that shrinks the world from a size medium to a size small. Globalization enables each of us, wherever we live, to reach around the world farther, faster, deeper, and cheaper than ever before and at the same time allows the world to reach into each of us farther, faster, deeper, and cheaper than ever before (Friedman and Kaplan 2002, p. 64).

Nowhere is this integration more apparent than in the world of international finance and capital. So we will next focus our attention on the dynamics of the *international monetary system* through which currencies and credits are calculated as capital freely moves across national boundaries through investments, trade, foreign aid, and loans.

MONEY MATTERS: THE TRANSNATIONAL EXCHANGE OF MONEY

Part of the equation on which global economic destiny depends is the character of *laissez-faire* capitalism, in which there is no regulation above the level of states. State governments have taken some tentative steps to create rules for adjusting their currencies with one another and stabilizing wide fluctuations in their exchange rates. However, the process through which money between and among countries is exchanged after financial transactions have been conducted does not have strong supranational regulatory institutions. Moreover, states often have very limited ability in controlling either those transactions or the relative value of their currencies on the world market. At the same time, these transactions, as noted, are escalating with feverish pitch. What does this trend mean?

The Globalization of Finance

Global finance encompasses a broad variety of portfolio-type transactions, including international loans, foreign aid, and currency trading, as well as cross-border investments such as the purchases of stocks, bonds, or derivatives. It also includes financial services that are conducted across borders. Another major facet of global finance is *foreign direct investment* (FDI)—transactions "involving significant control of producing enterprises" (Cohen 2005) ranging from the purchase of a substantial share of a foreign company's stock to setting up production facilities in another country (see Chapter 4).

The *globalization of finance* refers to the increasing transnationalization or centralization of these markets through the worldwide integration of capital flows. The central characteristic of the emerging consolidated system of

international monetary system
the financial procedures used to calculate the value of currencies and credits when capital is transferred across borders through trade, investment, foreign aid, and loans.

laissez-faire
from a French phrase (meaning literally "let do") that Adam Smith and other commercial liberals in the eighteenth century used to describe the advantages of freewheeling capitalism without government interference in economic affairs.

globalization of finance
the increasing transnationalization of national markets through the worldwide integration of capital flows.

financial arrangements is that it is not centered on a single state. Thus, globalization implies the growth of a single, unified *global* market. Whereas telecommunications specialists talk about the "death of distance," financial specialists talk about the "end of geography" because geographic location is no longer important to finance.

Evidence of financial globalization abounds. Although trade has grown dramatically, since World War II the volume of cross-border capital flows has increased even more. For example, in 2007, there was over $1.8 trillion in FDI throughout the globe, a 30 percent increase from 2003 (UNCTAD 2008) and twelve-fold increase since 1980 (Oatley 2010, p.167). Yet the growth in the *arbitrage* market—in which currencies are bought and sold for profit based off differences in their relative values—has been truly staggering. Since 1973 this market has grown sixty times faster than the value of world trade (McGrew 2008), and routinely handles over $2 trillion worth of currency on a daily basis.

arbitrage
the selling of one currency (or product) and purchase of another to make a profit on changing exchange rates.

Another indicator of the expansion of the global capital market is captured by the fact that its rise has far exceeded the actual rise in global GDP, as newer, more speculative, financial instruments have exponentially increased the size and scope of these capital flows. As noted by Niall Ferguson (2008), for 2006 the total value of all the stock markets in the world ($51 trillion) was about 10 percent larger than actual global GDP ($47 million). The total value of all bonds, domestic and international, was even higher at $68 trillion. The value of the derivatives market—newer financial instruments that are essentially "side bets" placed on the prospective future value of assets such as stocks and bonds—are much greater. During that same year, $473 trillion of derivatives were bought and sold. In other words, the market for these purely speculative financial instruments was ten times larger than the actual amount of goods and services produced in the world! As Ferguson (2008, p. 4) put it, "Planet Finance is beginning to dwarf Planet Earth."

Global flows of capital are not entirely new. In an early form of globalization, a network of financial centers flourished along the Baltic and North Seas, and city-states such as Lübeck, Hamburg, and Bergen dominated finance and trading. At the turn of the nineteenth century, London supplanted Amsterdam as the world's leading financial center, and New York began to rival London in the early twentieth century—antecedents of today's shifting of financial hubs to Tokyo, Singapore, and Dubai. Moreover, international financial crises are certainly nothing new; economist Charles Kindlberger (2000) notes the "manics, panics, and crashes" of global finance began in the early seventeenth century, with twenty-seven major financial crises occurring before the beginning of the twentieth century.

What is different now is the speed and spread of the movement of finance capital throughout the entire globe. Financial centers are proliferating, and big transactions are made by many participants "sitting in front of computer screens, moving zillions of dollars, pounds, euros and yen around the globe at the flick of a key. Technology, the mobility of capital and the spread of deregulation around the globe have created a vibrant and growing network . . . between financial centers as investors have diversified across regions. Yet interconnectedness has a cost. In an era of greater volatility, the latest market news spreads from one continent to another in an instant" (*Economist* 2007). Today's globalized finance creates linkages across the world at unprecedented levels, connecting capital, people, and exchanges as these trends expand cross-border consolidation.

These developments, combined with the trends toward market deregulation that began to take hold across much of the world during the 1980s and 1990s, represented a marked policy shift toward *commercial liberalism*. This economic variant of liberal theory views the spread of free markets, and limited government intervention in the market, as forces for global prosperity (see Chapter 11). Indeed, commercial liberals heralded this policy shift as a means to bring economic growth into the Global South and ensure continued success in the Global North. Encouraged by the rise of global finance, and further emboldened by the "victory" of free-market liberalism in the Cold War, commercial liberalism was a dominant economic ideology during this period (Caryl 2009). However, the recent financial crisis has caused many to reexamine the merits of this approach.

The globalization of finance has had broader political and economic influences upon the international system. As the global financial market has become increasingly interconnected, capital has become extremely mobile. As a result, the system has proven increasingly volatile. Such ties have made imperative the need for a reliable system of money exchange to cope with the broadening array of fluctuating national currencies.

Politically, the global capital market reveals limitations in the power of the state. Specifically, as the volume of currencies traded far exceeds the actual amount of reserve currencies held by governments, the ability of governments to influence exchange rates is limited. In 2010, exchange rate tensions increased, with the U.S. government urgently seeking to raise the price of the Chinese currency against the U.S. dollar and modify the rates at which currencies are exchanged. While acknowledging that China "needs a market-based exchanged rate regime," the governor of the People's Bank of China Zhou Xiaochuan countered that the process would have to occur "in a gradual way . . . rather than shock therapy." With globalization undermining states' regulatory capabilities, the assumption of realist theory that states are autonomous, unitary actors in control of their own international economic affairs is being undermined: "'realist orthodoxy' . . . has trouble integrating change, especially globalization" (Hoffmann 2005).

Though commercial liberals argue that such a system benefits all countries, the globalization of finance does not affect all countries equally. A vast majority of global capital goes to the Global North and Global East, and all countries are mutually vulnerable to rapid transfers of capital in this globalized system. Indeed, in the 2008 economic crisis, the problems with banks centered primarily in the Global North (Laeven and Valencia 2010). However, the Global South is typically the most dependent and vulnerable to shifts in the financial marketplace. Of the 361 systemic banking, currency, or debt crises that occurred since 1970, 335 have been in the developing world (Laeven and Valencia 2008). This circumstance suggests why bankers and economists have called for the creation of more reliable multilateral mechanisms for policy coordination to better manage the massive movement of cross-border capital. For instance, in 2004 Director-General Juan Somavia of the International Labour Organization called for a new compact of different institutions to steer globalization, which is "changing the policy landscape and distribution of power and gains" in order to better defend "social justice for all seekers of sustainable growth."

The globalization of finance also has implications for international trade (see Chapter 13), and concern and debate has understandably increased about the monetary factors underlying trade transactions. Controversies have risen over whether the international monetary system in place is causing inequalities or, worse still, reducing growth in international commerce. States' exports and imports depend on many factors, such as changes in global demand for the goods and services countries produce, and the prices they charge in the global marketplace. Among these, the mechanisms that set the currency exchange rate by which goods are priced heavily influence changes in the flow of international trade across borders. Indeed, the **monetary system** is the most critical factor allowing for international trade. Without a stable and predictable method for calculating the value of sales and foreign investments, those transactions would become too risky, and trade and investment activities would fall.

monetary system
the processes for determining the rate at which each state's currency is valued against the currency of every other state, so that purchasers and sellers can calculate the costs of financial transactions across borders, such as foreign investments, trade, and cross-border travel.

In assessing the implications of capital mobility for the global system, as well as the global economy as a whole, it is thus necessary to understand the international monetary system, the processes through which the relative value of each state's currencies are set. With that in mind, we will next examine the core concepts of the global monetary system, some of the key issues and dilemmas surrounding monetary policy, and the some of its historical context.

Monetary Policy: Key Concepts and Issues

Monetary and financial policies are woven into a complex set of relationships between states and the global system, and involve some esoteric terminology. To help you to better understand these issues, Table 12.1 lays out some of the key concepts related to monetary policy and the role of currency. As you read through these explanations, keep in mind that these are not separate phenomena but a related set of factors through which the global financial system operates.

To begin to put together how these factors are related, and the importance of a state's *monetary policy* as a determinant of its well-being, we will consider why a country's *exchange rate* fluctuates daily and the challenges states face in dealing with these fluctuations. As you will see, states face a variety of "trade-offs" in navigating monetary policies, and must seek a difficult balance between sometimes competing values, goals, and priorities. Moreover, states are ultimately limited in their ability to control monetary outcomes.

Money works in several ways and serves different purposes. First, money must be widely accepted, so that people earning it can use it to buy goods and services from others. Second, money must serve to store value, so that people will be willing to keep some of their wealth in the form of money. Third, money must act as a standard of deferred payment, so that people will be willing to lend money knowing that when the money is repaid in the future, it will still have purchasing power.

Movements in a state's exchange rate occur in part when changes develop in peoples' assessment of the national currency's underlying economic strength or the ability of its government to maintain the value of its money. A deficit in a country's balance of payments, for example, would likely cause a decline in the value of its currency relative to that of other countries. This happens when the supply of the currency is greater than the demand for it. Similarly, when those engaged in international economic transactions change their expectations about a currency's future value, they might reschedule their lending and borrowing. Fluctuations in the exchange rate could follow.

Arbitrage speculators who buy and sell money also affect the international stability of a country's currency. Speculators make money by guessing the future value of currencies. If, for instance, they believe that the Japanese yen will be worth more in three months than it is now, they can buy yen today and sell them for a profit three months later. Conversely, if they believe that the yen

monetary policy
The decisions made by states' central banks to change the country's money supply in an effort to manage the national economy and control inflation, using fiscal policies such as changing the money supply and interest rates.

exchange rate
the rate at which one state's currency is exchanged for another state's currency in the global marketplace.

Table 12.1   Understanding Currency: Basic Terms and Concepts

Term	Concept
Balance of Payments	A calculation summarizing a country's financial transactions with the external world, determined by the level of credits (export earnings, profits from foreign investment, receipts of foreign aid) minus the country's total international debits (imports, interest payments on international debts, foreign direct investments, and the like).
Balance of Trade	The difference in the value of the goods a country sells (exports) minus the goods it purchases (imports). If a country imports more than it exports, it is said to have a balance-of-trade deficit. For example, in 2009 the United States exported approximately $1.8 trillion in goods and services and imported $2.5 trillion, for a balance of trade deficit of more than $7 billion (WDI 2010).
Central Bank	The primary monetary authority within a state. It is responsible for issuing currency, setting monetary policy, acting as a bank for the government, and helping to administer the state's banking industry.
Monetary Policy	Central bank policy tools for managing their economies. Policies fall into two basic categories—altering the money supply (the amount of money in circulation) and adjusting interest rates (the relative "price" for using money). An expansionary monetary policy would entail such things as selling additional bonds and lowering interest rates. Such policies would make money relatively more plentiful and less expensive to borrow.
Fiscal Policy	Governmental policy tools for managing economies. Basic policy options are taxation and spending. An expansionary fiscal policy would consist of lowering taxes and/or increasing spending, while a "tight" or contractionary policy would involve raising taxes and/or decreasing spending.
Devaluation	The lowering of the official exchange rate of one country's currency relative to other currencies. This is generally done to increase exports, as devaluation lowers the relative prices of a country's exports. However, it can also reduce the spending power of citizens within that country.
Exchange Rate	The rate at which one state's currency is exchanged for another state's currency in the global marketplace. For example, on July 17, 2010, for one U.S. dollar you would have received 0.77 euro or 12.9 Mexican pesos. Exchange rates are subject to constant fluctuations. Daily changes are generally quite small, though they can vary greatly over the long run. For example, on June 28, 2001, the U.S. dollar was worth 1.17 euros and 9.08 Mexican pesos.
Fixed Exchange Rate	A system in which a government sets the value of its currency at a fixed rate for exchange in relation to another country's currency (usually the U.S. dollar) or another measure of value (such as a group of different currencies or a precious metal such as gold) so that the exchange value is not free to fluctuate in the global money market.
Floating Exchange Rate	System in which the relative value of a country's currency is set by market forces. In principle, the value of a country's currency is indicative of the underlying strengths and weaknesses of its economy.
Fixed-but-Adjustable Exchange Rate System	A system in which a government fixes its currency in relation to that of another country's currency, but may still change the fixed price to reflect changes in the underlying strengths and weaknesses of their economies. The general expectation is that such changes are rare and only occur under specially defined circumstances.

Term	Concept
Inflation	An increase in the prices of goods and services within an economy. It is generally expressed in percentages and calculated on a yearly basis. Inflation reduces the buying power of citizens, as it decreases the value of their currency. Very high levels of inflation (hyperinflation) can cause severe disruptions within a society, as the currency becomes largely worthless. For example, the inflation rate of Zimbabwe reached well over 12,563 percent by the start of 2010.
Capital Controls	Government attempts to limit or prevent global capital transactions. Examples range from placing taxes on foreign exchanges to outright bans on the movement of capital out of a country. These policies are generally intended as a means to "insulate" an economy from the global capital market.

will be worth less in three months, they can sell yen today for a certain number of dollars and then buy back the same yen in three months for fewer dollars, making a profit. The globalization of finance now also encourages managers of investment portfolios to rapidly move funds from one currency to another in order to realize gains from differences in states' interest rates and the declining value of other currencies in the global network of exchange rates. Short-term financial flows are now the norm: the International Monetary Fund estimates that more than 80 percent of futures (speculative markets based on the future values of assets) and arbitrage transactions are completed in one week or less, providing significant profit opportunities in a short time period.

In the same way that governments try to protect the value of their currencies at home, they often try to protect them internationally by intervening in currency markets. Their willingness to do so is important to importers and exporters, who depend on predictability in the value of the currencies in which they deal to carry out transnational exchanges. Governments intervene when countries' central banks buy or sell currencies to change the value of their own currencies in relation to those of others. Unlike speculators, however, governments are pledged not to manipulate exchange rates so as to gain unfair advantages, for states' reputations as custodians of monetary stability are valuable. In any event, the extent to which governments can ultimately affect their currencies' value in the face of large transnational movements of capital is increasingly questionable (see Figure 12.1).

Within this system, governments are faced with the difficult task of balancing the demands of the global currency market with the need to manage their own economies. There are many difficulties in navigating these channels, and

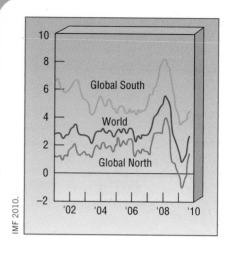

FIGURE 12.1

CALCULATING THE CHANGING COSTS OF GOODS IN THE GLOBAL ECONOMY **People from the United States who travel abroad must use currency exchange rates to convert the price of their purchases abroad to the value of U.S. dollars, and sometimes are alarmed at the higher price (the U.S. dollar has dropped 40 percent against the euro since 2001). Economists usually calculate currency exchange rates in terms of purchasing power of parity (PPP) because that index of the value of exchange rates measures the cost of identical goods or services in any two countries. Shown on the right, this index uses a McDonald's Big Mac, which is available for sale in more than 130 countries. The least expensive burger could be purchased in Hong Kong for $1.90 versus an average price of $3.58 in the United States. Inflation also affects the cost of goods and services as a general increase in the level of prices means that each unit of currency purchases less. Shown on the left, the figure indicates a decline in inflation in 2009 for both the Global South and the Global North, with inflation edging back up in 2010.**

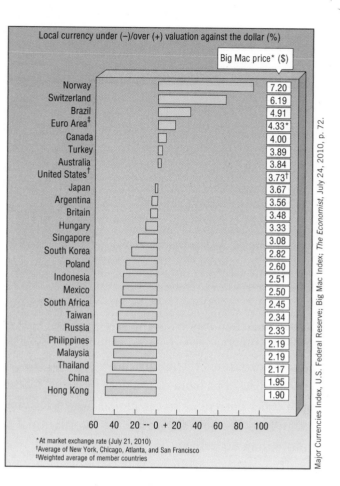

Local currency under (−)/over (+) valuation against the dollar (%)

Big Mac price* ($)

Country	Big Mac price* ($)
Norway	7.20
Switzerland	6.19
Brazil	4.91
Euro Area‡	4.33*
Canada	4.00
Turkey	3.89
Australia	3.84
United States†	3.73†
Japan	3.67
Argentina	3.56
Britain	3.48
Hungary	3.33
Singapore	3.08
South Korea	2.82
Poland	2.60
Indonesia	2.51
Mexico	2.50
South Africa	2.45
Taiwan	2.34
Russia	2.33
Philippines	2.19
Malaysia	2.19
Thailand	2.17
China	1.95
Hong Kong	1.90

60 40 20 -- 0 + 20 40 60 80 100

*At market exchange rate (July 21, 2010)
†Average of New York, Chicago, Atlanta, and San Francisco
‡Weighted average of member countries

IMF 2010.

Major Currencies Index, U.S. Federal Reserve; Big Mac Index; *The Economist*, July 24, 2010, p. 72.

states face three main sets of competing values, or "trade-offs"—inflation versus unemployment, strong versus weak currency valuation strategies, and the competing values of stability versus autonomy.

Governments attempt to manage their currencies to prevent inflation. Inflation occurs when the government creates too much money in relation to the goods and services produced in the economy. As explained in Table 12.1, high degrees of inflation can undercut the ability of a currency to serve effectively as a store of value or medium of exchange. However, the creation of money—whether through increasing the *money supply* or lowering interest rates—does serve to stimulate the economy, at least in the short term. Alternatively, restrictive monetary policy is very useful in curbing inflation

money supply
the total amount of currency in circulation in a state, calculated to include demand deposits, such as checking accounts in commercial banks, and time deposits, such as savings accounts and bonds, in savings banks.

or helping the government to reduce debt. Yet such actions slow an economy down, which is generally associated with increased unemployment and even recession. This is one of the most commonly noted trade-offs associated with monetary policy—inflation versus unemployment.

A related dilemma regards currency values, specifically whether states should seek to maintain "strong" or relatively "weak" currencies. Ostensibly, in a flexible exchange rate regime, the exchange rate for a given currency should reflect the health of its economy (or lack thereof). As mentioned, states are generally encouraged to refrain from manipulating the value of their currencies, or the currencies of other countries, in order to maintain predictability and stability. However, there are benefits to maintaining a weak currency, through such means as capital controls, fixing exchange rates, or even currency devaluations. Though a weaker currency has a negative effect on the spending power of the domestic consumers, it makes exporting industries more competitive in that their goods are relatively less expensive in the global marketplace. This has been a major source of controversy regarding the Chinese currency, as critics contend that the unduly low exchange rate represents unfair competition in the global trade arena. Alternatively, currencies that are relatively strong face the opposite dilemma—though their consumers have relatively more spending power, both at home and abroad, their exporting industries suffer, and they are more likely to run a balance-of-trade deficit.

This taps into a trade-off that is at the core of global monetary policy, namely the choice between currency stability and policy autonomy. The basic problem is that in a system where capital flows freely (that is, there are no substantial capital controls), it is impossible to have both stability and autonomy. In principle, both are desirable in their own right. Stable exchange rates ensure that a country's currency can perform the primary functions of a currency cited earlier, and the lack of volatility provides both policy makers and potential investors with a stable set of expectations for the future. Autonomy gives states the flexibility to pursue monetary policies that best suit their particular economic situation, such as the use of expansionary policies to stimulate growth.

A flexible exchange rate regime gives states autonomy to conduct their own monetary policies. For example, all else being equal, the market would respond to expansionary monetary policy by lowering the exchange rate of a currency (as the currency would be relatively more plentiful and/or offer lower interest rates). In this case, autonomy is gained, though there is no guarantee of stability, as the currency is subject to the vicissitudes of the global currency markets.

A fixed exchange rate regime provides currency stability, yet it gives states practically no freedom to conduct monetary policy. For example, if a country with a fixed exchange rate was to lower interest rates, the exchange rate could not move to take the decreased demand for the currency into account. As a result the country would have a balance-of-payments deficit. To fill this deficit, the country would need to intervene into the foreign exchange market to reduce the oversupply of currency—a "tight" monetary policy that would essentially undo the initial policy—or get rid of the fixed exchange rate altogether. Such dilemmas were faced by the United States near the end of the Bretton Woods era, France in the early 1980s, and Argentina in the late 1990s.

In conducting monetary policy, states thus have to balance competing interests—the desire to help their economy grow with the necessity to maintain their currencies, the relative utility of strong versus weak currency valuation, and the incompatibility between the ideals of stability and policy autonomy. Moreover, states face all of these dilemmas within the context of a global monetary system over which they have very little actual control. It is important to keep these trade-offs and limitations on state power in mind as you consider the monetary policies of the Bretton Woods era, as well as some of the current issues in international finance.

The Bretton Woods System

In July 1944, forty-four states allied in war against the Axis powers met in the New Hampshire resort of Bretton Woods to devise new rules and institutions to govern international trade and monetary relations after World War II. As the world's pre-eminent economic and military power, the United States played the leading role.

Its proposals were shaped by the perceived causes of the 1930s economic catastrophe and its beliefs about the need for active U.S. leadership. The United States sought free trade, open markets, and monetary stability—all central tenets of what would become the "Bretton Woods system"—based on the theoretical premises of *commercial liberalism,* which advocates free markets with few barriers to trade and capital flows.

Britain also played an important role at the conference. Led by John Maynard Keynes—whose theories about the state's role in managing inflation, unemployment, and growth still influence economic thinking throughout the world—the British delegation won support for the principle of strong government action by states facing economic problems. That ideology conforms

Greg Baker/AP Photo

GROWING FROM ECONOMIC INTEGRATION   New skyscrapers—a symbol of *Global East* economic growth—dot the skyline of Shanghai, which held a WTO Honor Day on July 22, 2010. Recognizing Shanghai as one of the globe's leading financial centers, WTO Director-General Pascal Lamy marked the occasion noting that "the wealth of the great Merchant Cities extends far beyond money. As cities open to trade and traders, these communities have served as centers for the exchange of ideas and culture as well as goods and services."

less closely with liberalism than with the principles of *mercantilism*, which assigns states a greater role than markets in managing economic interactions as a strategy for acquiring national wealth (see Chapter 4 and Chapter 13).

Despite these differences, the rules established at Bretton Woods reflected a remarkable level of agreement. They rested on three political bases. First, power was concentrated in the rich Western European and North American countries, which reduced the number of states whose agreement was necessary for effective management by restricting the potential challenges from Japan, the Global South, and the then-communist Soviet Union and its sphere of influence in Eastern Europe. Indeed, the onset of the Cold War helped to cement Western unity along these lines. Second, a compromise was reached between the contrasting ideologies of the United States and Britain. In particular, the emergent order honored both commercial liberal preferences for an open international economy and the more mercantilist desires for active state involvement in their domestic economies. This mix of ideologies that underpinned the Bretton Woods order was eventually termed *embedded liberalism* (Ruggie 1982). Third, Bretton Woods worked because the United States assumed the burdens of hegemonic leadership, and others willingly accepted that leadership.

embedded liberalism dominant economic approach during the Bretton Woods system, which combined open international markets with domestic state intervention to attain such goals as full employment and social welfare.

Commercial liberalism's preference for open markets spread worldwide during this time and remains dominant today. Thus, it is still useful to characterize the contemporary international economic system as a *Liberal International Economic Order (LIEO)*—one based on such free-market principles as openness and free trade. Three institutions were formed to maintain the LIEO. The General Agreement on Tariffs and Trade (GATT), which later became the World Trade Organization (WTO), was formed to encourage trade liberalization. The International Bank for Reconstruction and Development, which later became the World Bank, and the International Monetary Fund (IMF) were created to bolster financial and monetary relations (see Chapter 5).

Liberal International Economic Order (LIEO)
the set of regimes created after World War II, designed to promote monetary stability and reduce barriers to the free flow of trade and capital.

Financial and Monetary Aspects of the Bretton Woods System

The global economic collapse of the 1930s provided specific lessons for monetary relations. In particular, as the major economies contracted in the late 1920s, they found themselves unable to maintain their fixed exchange rate regime. The resultant flexible regime was highly unstable, replete with *speculative attacks* on currencies and currency devaluations. Eventually states began to close off their monetary and trade regimes from the global market, and the global economy collapsed into "closed imperial blocks" (Ravenhill 2008, p. 12).

speculative attacks
massive sales of a country's currency, caused by the anticipation of a future decline in its value.

To avoid repeating these financial disasters, the leaders sought to construct a common set of concepts to define monetary and currency policy for conducting international trade and finance. The negotiating parties agreed that the postwar monetary regime should be based on *fixed exchange rates*,

fixed exchange rate
a system in which a government sets the value of its currency at a fixed rate for exchange in relation to another country's currency so that the exchange value is not free to fluctuate in the global money market.

MONEY MATTERS Currency now moves effortlessly across borders, and the globalization of international finance is wreaking havoc on the efforts of state governments to control rapid fluctuations in economic conditions. Shown here is an example of how monetary policies sometimes unleash hostile feelings: Pictured left, activists protest during the G-20's 2010 summit in Canada. Pictured right, Greek demonstrators march in Athens on May 4, 2010 to speak out against austerity spending cuts.

and governments were assigned the primary responsibility for enforcing the rules of the new order. To provide a stabilization fund to help countries offset short-term balance-of-payments problems, they set up what eventually became the International Monetary Fund (IMF). The IMF was to function somewhat like a global "credit union"—countries contributed to the fund and were able to draw capital from it to help them maintain balance-of-payments equilibrium, and hence exchange rate stability. Along somewhat similar lines, they established the International Bank for Reconstruction and Development, later known as the World Bank, to provide capital for longer-term development and recovery projects.

Today the IMF and World Bank are important, if controversial, players in the global monetary and financial systems. Eighty-five percent of their state members belong to both IGOs that serve as "lenders of last resort" to members facing financial crises, providing those seeking assistance meet the often painful conditions requiring domestic adjustments to strengthen their economies (see Controversy: The IMF, World Bank, and Structural Adjustment Policies). In the period immediately after World War II, these institutions commanded too little authority and too few resources to cope with the enormous devastation of the war. The United States stepped into the breach.

The U.S. dollar became the key to the hegemonic role that the United States eagerly assumed as manager of the international monetary system. Backed by a vigorous and healthy economy, a fixed relationship between gold and the dollar (pegged at $35 per ounce of gold), and the U.S. commitment to exchange gold for dollars at any time (known as "dollar convertibility"), the dollar became a universally accepted "parallel currency." It was accepted in exchange markets as the reserve used by monetary authorities in most countries and by private banks, corporations, and individuals for international trade and capital transactions.

To maintain the value of their currencies, central banks in other countries used the dollar to raise or depress their value. Thus, the Bretton Woods monetary regime was based on fixed-but-adjustable exchange rates based on the dollar and gold, which ultimately required a measure of government intervention for its operation.

To get U.S. dollars into the hands of those who needed them most, the Marshall Plan provided Western European states billions of dollars in aid to buy the U.S. goods necessary for rebuilding their war-torn economies. The United States also encouraged deficits in its own balance of payments as a way of

international liquidity
reserve assets used
to settle international
accounts.

providing *international liquidity*. Such liquidity was intended to enable these countries to pursue expansionary monetary and fiscal policies, as well as to facilitate their participation in the global economy.

In addition to providing liquidity, the United States assumed a disproportionate share of the burden of rejuvenating Western Europe and Japan. It supported European and Japanese trade competitiveness, permitted certain forms of protectionism (such as Japanese restrictions on importing U.S. products), and accepted discrimination against the dollar (as the European Payments Union did by promoting trade within Europe at the expense of trade with the United States). The United States willingly agreed to pay these costs of leadership because subsidizing economic growth in Europe and Japan increased the U.S. export markets and strengthened the West against communism's possible popular appeal.

The End of Bretton Woods

Though this system initially worked well, its costs began to grow. By the 1960s it became apparent that the system was ultimately unsustainable. As use of the dollar—as well as the amount of dollars in circulation—continued to expand, the resultant U.S. balance-of-payments deficit became increasingly problematic. Unlike other countries, the United States was not able to adjust the value of its currency, as it was pegged to gold. Though strict adherence to a fixed exchange regime supposedly limits the policy autonomy of a state, the United States nonetheless began to pursue expansionary macroeconomic tactics during the 1960s to finance policies such as the Vietnam War and increased social spending. Such spending further exacerbated the balance-of-payments deficit. By 1970, the total amount of foreign claims for dollars, $47 billion, was over four times the value of the $11 billion in gold holdings in the United States (Oatley 2010, p. 230). This gap between the amount of dollars in circulation and the amount of dollars actually supported by gold holdings was known as *dollar overhang*. Simply put, though the dollar was officially "as good as gold," the monetary reality was far different.

dollar overhang
condition that pre-
cipitated the end of the
Bretton Woods era, in
which total holdings
of dollars outside of
the U.S. central bank
exceeded the amount
of dollars actually
backed by gold.

This left the Bretton Woods system in a tenuous position, and the United States very constrained in its options. Tight monetary policies on behalf of the United States would have reduced the balance-of-payments deficit. However, given the scope of the deficit, such cuts would have dealt a major shock to the U.S. economy. Such policies would have international ramifications as well, as reducing the supply of dollars would damage countries that relied on the dollar for liquidity purposes. Another potential option, currency devaluation, could conceivably have reduced the balance-of-payments problem. This option was also problematic, as its effect could be undone if other states devalued their currencies in kind (so as not to give the United States any advantage in selling goods on the world marketplace). Though some of the other major economies were willing to intervene to support the dollar, there were limits to what these countries would do, and it was widely known that the status quo was not sustainable.

The architecture of the international finance system must be reformed to reduce the susceptibility to crises. The ultimate key is not economics or finance, but politics—the art of developing support for strong policy.

—Robert Rubin, former U.S. Secretary of the Treasury

Floating Exchange Rates and Financial Crises

In 1971, U.S. President Richard Nixon cut this "Gordian knot" by abruptly announcing—without consulting with allies—that the United States would no longer exchange dollars for gold. With the price of gold no longer fixed and dollar convertibility no longer guaranteed, the Bretton Woods system gave way to a substitute system based on *floating exchange rates*. Market forces, rather than government intervention, now determine currency values. A country experiencing adverse economic conditions now sees the value of its currency fall in response to the choices of traders, bankers, and businesspeople. This was expected to make exports cheaper and imports more expensive, which in turn would pull the currency's value back toward equilibrium—all without the need for central bankers to support the value of its currency. In this way, it was hoped that the politically humiliating devaluations of the past could be avoided.

floating exchange rates an unmanaged process in which governments neither establish an official rate for their currencies nor intervene to affect the value of their currencies, and instead allow market forces and private investors to influence the relative rate of exchange for currencies between countries.

Moreover, though flexible exchange rates give governments the autonomy to conduct their own fiscal and monetary policies, these same market forces hold governments accountable for their policies and actions. In short, exposure to the market exerts a "disciplinary effect on the conduct of policies, because international capital flows adversely respond to imprudent macroeconomic policies" (IMF 2005). As a result, states should be forced to closely monitor their fiscal and monetary policies to avoid balance-of-payments deficits and inflation.

Those expectations were not met. Beginning in the late 1970s, escalating in the 1980s, and persisting through the present, a rising wave of financial crises, both in currency and banking, occurred. These crises were (and remain) compounded by massive defaults by countries unable to make interest payments on their debts. This chronic problem in the crushing sea of circulating capital flows throughout the globe has strained the international monetary process to the brink of collapse. Almost a quarter of the world's countries have foreign debts in excess of $10 billion, and altogether emerging and developing economies are facing over $3.7 trillion in external debt owed to foreigners (WDI 2010).

Worse still, the average total external debt of these emerging and developing economies was equivalent to 22.1 percent of their GNI (WDI 2010, pp. 390–392). Needless to say, this staggering debt load greatly reduces these countries' capability to chart their future by themselves—as sovereign states are supposed to do. In 2010, Greece suffered from a debilitating debt crisis and turned to the European Union and the IMF for assistance. Yet even the most powerful countries are vulnerable. The United States may be the reigning hegemon with the globe's largest economy, but it is borrowing from foreign creditors about $4 billion every day to sustain its enormous current account deficit (Bergsten 2009). By March of 2010 the U.S. government's external debt to foreigners amounted to $13.9 trillion, continuing to rival its $14.26 trillion economy and representing an almost $3 trillion increase since 2007 (U.S. Department of Treasury 2010; CIA World Fact Book 2010).

Rather than increasing stability through the free exchange of currencies, the post–Bretton Woods era has been plagued by financial crises. Such crises have become increasingly frequent throughout the world as a result of the inability of states to manage their debt, inflation, and interest rates, and the global monetary system is experiencing wild currency-exchange-rate gyrations. In the past forty-five years, more than one hundred major episodes of banking insolvency occurred in nine of ten rapidly growing Global East countries. This financial disease is also spreading to the Global North countries and their banking institutions. The financial cost of these currency crises, in terms of the percentage of GDP lost, has been huge and threatens to increase. The disastrous debts generated by banking and currency disruptions forced governments to suffer, on average, costs amounting to as much as 55 percent of GDP, an amount that does not even include costs of interest rates and other indirect costs of recovery (World Bank 2009b, p. 9).

In reaction to growing awareness of the extent to which the global prosperity of each country depends on a stable international currency system, the call has risen with increasing voice about the need for the great powers and all others to collectively coordinate, through multilateral agreements, the stabilization of international exchange rates.

CONTROVERSY:

THE IMF, WORLD BANK, AND STRUCTURAL ADJUSTMENT POLICIES: IS THE "CURE" WORSE THAN THE "DISEASE"?

Protests and riots against the IMF and the World Bank have become relatively commonplace. In some instances, such as the 2003 "Black Friday" protests in Bolivia in which thirty-three people were killed, the violence can turn deadly. In the case of Indonesia in 1998, such protests and riots can sometimes help to overturn a government.

Why is there so much controversy surrounding organizations whose primary purpose is to spur development within the Global South, and whose mission statements include such laudable goals as "global poverty reduction and the improvement of living standards" and fostering "economic growth and high levels of employment"?

Of great contention are Structural Adjustment Policies (SAPs), the package of policy reforms that accompany IMF and World Bank financial assistance. The basic goal of SAPs is to help countries repay their foreign debts through a combination of fiscal and monetary policy reforms, as well as increased participation in the global economy. SAPs were first introduced in the early 1980s as a way of helping countries in Latin America recover from the debt crisis. Since then, over one hundred countries have undertaken some type of SAP (Abouharb and Cingranelli 2007). SAPs utilize a common policy "playbook":

• Fiscal "austerity" (reductions in state spending)

• A decreased role of the state in the economy, including a reduction in the overall size of the public sector as well as the privatization of state-run industries (most commonly utilities)

• Monetary policy changes, including increased interest rates and currency devaluation

• Trade liberalization measures, such as the cessation of tariffs and nontariff barriers to foreign trade

The overall goal of SAPs is to help a state resolve its balance-of-payments problems by reducing spending and increasing the flow of capital. Though this "playbook" is in line with basic macroeconomic principles for reducing deficits, the political and economic results of these measures have been subject to a great deal of criticism.

SAPs—which are often enacted very rapidly—are very recessionary, particularly in the short run. Decreases in government spending often translate into decreases in government jobs (thus increased unemployment), as well as decreased levels of support for education, healthcare, and economic welfare. Interest rate increases make it more expensive for citizens to acquire loans, while currency devaluation lowers individual spending power. In many instances, the reduction of state subsidies may result in drastic increases in the prices that citizens pay for basic services, such as electricity and water, or goods that were formerly subsidized, including fuel and food. For example, in 2001 Ghana was forced to increase its water prices by 95 percent, while Nicaragua was forced to increase its water prices by 30 percent (Grusky 2001). These difficulties can be further exacerbated by trade liberalization, as inefficient domestic industries may be incapable of competing with their foreign counterparts. As a result, these industries may be forced to cut jobs or close down entirely.

Politically, participation in SAPs is also problematic. The IMF and World Bank are largely controlled by the states of the Global North—indeed the policy mix represented by the IMF is often referred to as the "Washington

(continued)

THE IMF, WORLD BANK, AND STRUCTURAL ADJUSTMENT POLICIES: IS THE "CURE" WORSE THAN THE "DISEASE"?
(Continued)

Consensus." Countries in the Global South may view these institutions as another manifestation of "neocolonialism," which serves more to meet the interests of global investors and corporations rather than citizens of the Global South. Indeed, in many instances "privatization" results in many large state-run industries being sold off to multinational corporations from the Global North. For example, when Bolivia was forced to privatize its water industry, the contract was awarded to a company controlled by Bechtel (Forero 2005), while water privatization contracts in Argentina were picked up by Enron (Nichols 2002).

Many of the criticisms against the IMF were primarily from more populist and Marxist sources and focused on individual cases. However, recent studies have begun to systematically examine the impact of SAPs upon their recipient states. The empirical results paint an overwhelmingly negative picture—SAPs have been linked to reductions in social spending, greater income inequality, and lower levels of economic growth (Vreeland 2003). Moreover, the social unrest that can occur due to SAPs is often met with state repression (Abouharb and Cingranelli 2007).

Though acknowledging an imperfect record, the World Bank and the IMF defend their role in the international financial system. Pointing to successes such as Poland, officials note that the IMF has played a key role in helping countries recover. Moreover, countries only apply for help when they are in financial trouble, and thus it is hard to blame these organizations for problems that the country was facing anyway. Finally, political leaders may find it expedient to "scapegoat" the IMF and the World Bank, which can provide them "cover" for enacting necessary, though unpopular, economic policies. Ultimately, as argued by IMF economist Kenneth Rogoff, countries would be much worse off if they isolated themselves from the global economy. "Perhaps poor nations won't need the IMF's specific macroeconomic expertise—but they will need something awfully similar" (Rogoff 2003).

WHAT DO YOU THINK?

- What do the controversies surrounding SAPs reveal about the "trade-off" between stability and policy autonomy? Inflation versus unemployment?

- What steps, if any, could be taken to improve the developing worlds' perception of the IMF?

- How would the various theories of development, particularly the modernization and dependency approaches, view the IMF?

THE CRISIS OF 2008

The current global financial system is still recovering from the massive crisis that came to a head in 2008. A myriad of economic and political factors have been cited as causing this crash, and the particulars of the crisis, especially the investment instruments themselves, are bafflingly complex. Indeed, former Chair of the U.S. Federal Reserve Alan Greenspan noted that a key cause of the crisis was the inability of the world's "most sophisticated investors" and regulators—the people who actually created and worked with these instruments—to understand them (Comisky and Madhogarhia 2009).

Video: *Economic Dominoes Fall*

Yet the broad dynamics of the crisis are hardly unprecedented, as they fall in line with the basic cycle described in Kindleberger's sweeping history of financial crises (Kindleberger, Aliber, and Solow 2005). The first phase of a crisis cycle is "displacement," which refers to a change in the system that alters profit opportunities and creates new opportunities for financial gain. There were several developments that brought increased attention to the mortgage and securities markets during the beginning of the century, including massive cash holdings by states such as China and the OPEC members, the real estate boom in the United States, extremely low interest rates in the United States, and the new investment instruments that banks and investment firms created. These factors were inextricably linked—the initial dilemma that led to this crisis was how to put the "giant pool of money" (Glass and Davidson 2008) that these states were holding into use. U.S. interest rates were extremely low, which meant that investing in dollars—traditionally considered the safest move for investors with large amounts of money—was not sufficiently profitable (U.S. Treasury Bills at the time were only yielding 1%). At the same time, the low interest rates in the United States meant that mortgages were less expensive for homeowners. As housing prices were increasing, buying new or larger homes (financed by mortgages) was a good "investment" for homeowners. Sensing opportunity, banks created instruments to link the "pool" of money to the housing market, by selling securities based off of these mortgages to large investors. As a result, the investors made a higher rate of return from the mortgages, homeowners reaped the benefits of lower interest rates, and banks made billions of dollars as intermediaries.

The second phase of the crisis—the so-called "boom" period in which money pours into these new opportunities—thus began. As the investors and bankers continued to reap profits, the "pool of money" became ever larger, and trillions of dollars continued to flow into this market. Banks began to invent more investment instruments based off of this market (essentially different ways to "bundle" these mortgages together), and huge speculative markets based off of the performance of these instruments began to emerge.

This led to the "overtrading" stage, which traditionally involves such things as "pure speculation for a price rise, an overestimate of prospective returns," and excessive leveraging or "gearing," where additional debt is taken on purely for the purposes of making investments (Kindleberger 2000). At some point in this process, the market for traditional mortgages became saturated; basically everyone who was willing and able to purchase and/or refinance a home had already done so. Yet the "pool" continued to grow, and demand for these securities continued. To keep the market going, banks began to sell mortgages to "subprime" buyers who would have never qualified for mortgages under normal circumstances. The rationalization for doing this was that even if some loans were not repaid, there would still be a sufficient flow of capital to keep the overall securities serviced. Even if the loans defaulted, the banks would get the real estate, which was considered to be an appreciating asset.

However, around 2007 the "revulsion" or "panic" stage began due to several directly related factors: increasing loan defaults by homeowners, plummeting real estate values, and severe liquidity problems of the banks that were overleveraged in this entire process. As homeowners failed to repay the mortgages, banks quickly found themselves without a stream of income from mortgage holders, holding properties whose value was declining and that they were unable to sell, and facing debt loads that were sometimes over thirty times greater than their own net worth. As the mortgage market began to fall, the speculative markets and instruments built around it—whose total cash value was many times more than the value of the mortgages themselves—also collapsed. As a result, banks and investors literally ran out of money, and the credit market in the United States and much of the world collapsed.

Though financial crises are not new to the global financial system, the current crisis has had a particularly profound impact upon the global financial order, as well as the international system as a whole. First, the sheer amount of money involved is staggering—according to recent estimates, the U.S. government alone has devoted $13 trillion dollars thus far to help bail out its own financial sector, including direct financial assistance to the banks as well as the selling of bonds to help increase the supply of money (French 2009). As a result of the crisis, global FDI and trade both experienced unprecedented declines in 2009—FDI outflows fell approximately 42 percent, and world trade slid over 12 percent. In all, total global output, as measured by GDP, contracted by 2.3 percent in 2009, the worst worldwide decrease since World War II (UNCTAD 2010; WTO 2010; IMF Survey 2009).

Second, this crisis originated in the United States, and "much of the world . . . blames U.S. financial excesses for the global recession" (Altman 2009, p. 2). Given the leading role of the United States in maintaining the liberal financial order, as well as the prevalence of the dollar as the currency of choice in international finance, this crisis has thus brought into question the leadership of the United States, as well as some of the fundamental ideals of the global financial system.

Though the dominance of the dollar has decreased since the end of the Bretton Woods order, it is still the leading currency in the global financial system. According to the IMF, in 2009, 61 percent of all foreign exchange reserves (money that states hold to help them maintain their balance of payments) were in dollars. Also, seventeen countries use the dollar as their currency, and another forty-nine anchor or "peg" the value of their currency to the dollar in some way (IMF 2010). Though the value of the dollar on the world market has recovered somewhat since the onset of the crisis, some of the leading economies in the world—most notably China—have suggested that the dollar be replaced as the major currency of the global marketplace. Though the general need for a dominant currency is broadly noted among economists, and there is "no obvious replacement" (Samuelson 2009) for the dollar as the dominant currency, such suggestions do indicate damage to the reputation of the dollar and the future possibility of a less dollar-centered global economy.

The crisis has brought increasing criticism to the ideological underpinnings of the global financial system: the free-market-oriented "Washington Consensus." Though the free exchanges of currencies, and the free movement of capital, are viewed as foundational to liberal economics, the financial crisis has served to undercut basic contentions regarding the efficacy of the marketplace. Among the larger economies of the world, the ones that fared the best in the crisis were India and China, arguably the two major countries most insulated from the global financial order. Indeed, Moldova, a very small country with a "cash-only system" (Tayler 2009) of finance—that is, a system in which banks and credit cards are largely nonexistent and savings are generally stored under mattresses or in drawers—was recently ranked by a leading financial journal as the fifth most stable economy in the world. As concluded by Roger Altman, a former U.S. Treasury Department official and a leading adviser to President Clinton, "the long movement towards market liberalization has stopped," and "globalization itself is reversing. The long-standing wisdom that everyone wins in a single world market has been undermined" (2009, p. 2).

To critics of liberalism, the crisis has revealed strengths in alternative perspectives on the global economy. Marxists have long noted the inherent instability of capitalism, its susceptibility to speculative panics, and the need for strong state intervention into the financial system. Cuban President Raul

AP Photo/Susan Walsh

WOMEN CLEANING UP WALL STREET Only 3 percent of Fortune 500 companies have a woman as CEO, and each of the large banks—from Citigroup to Goldman Sachs—employ just a few women in senior positions. In efforts to identify underlying reasons for the recent global financial crisis, many have critically pointed to "a testosterone-filled trading culture" (Scherer 2010) and wondered if things would have been different if more women held positions of power on Wall Street. Pictured here is Elizabeth Warren, one of the women who has helped lead economic recovery in the United States. Warren is chair of the panel overseeing the Troubled Asset Relief Program (TARP) bank bailout and the chief advocate for new consumer-finance regulations.

Castro, for example, forcefully argued that "neoliberalism has failed as an economy policy" and that "any objective analysis raises serious questions about the myth of the goodness of the market and its deregulation. . . . and the credibility of the financial institutions." As one analyst concludes, global capitalism is "in an ideological tailspin" and the crisis "has spawned a resurgence of interest in Karl Marx" (Panitch 2009, p. 140).

For their part, feminist scholars note that males are both primarily responsible for the crisis and suffering the most from its effects. Many point out the traditionally "male" traits—risk-taking, aggression, and hyper-competitiveness—were driving forces behind the speculative surges that helped to create the financial crisis, and that "the presence of more women on Wall Street might have averted the downturn" (Kay and Shipman 2009). Just as the crisis was driven by male dominance, the current financial crisis will have a disproportionate impact upon males. In the United States, for example, over

80 percent of the job losses since November 2008 fell upon men, as traditionally male sectors (e.g., construction and manufacturing) were hardest hit. Indeed, some have termed the current crisis a "he-cession." As one scholar concludes, the financial crisis "will be not only a blow to the macho men's club called finance capitalism that got the world into the current economic catastrophe; it will be a collective crisis for millions and millions of working men around the globe" (Salam 2009, p. 66).

There may also be geopolitical ramifications. To the extent that the crisis weakens the economic and ideological power of the United States and its Western allies, the United States is less able to assert itself in international negotiations. The crisis has also served to improve the relative global position of China, whose share of world markets increased during the global recession to almost 10 percent in 2010 and an anticipated 12 percent by 2014, making it the world's largest exporter. The economic crisis and U.S. recession drastically increased China's prominence as the largest holder of U.S. debt securities, as its share of the total U.S. debt increased from roughly one third to almost 50 percent from 2008 to 2010—with China holding almost $900 billion in U.S. debt securities. (*The Economist* 2010, p.73; U.S. Department of Treasury 2010). As the crisis spilled over into many developing countries, including fragile states such as Pakistan and the Democratic Republic of Congo as well as resource-driven states such as Iran and Venezuela, the potential for political instability in various regions of the world that could eventually "tilt the scales even further in the direction of a fragmented and dysfunctional international system with a heightened risk of conflict" (Burrows and Harris 2009, p. 38) increased. Yet overall the Global South weathered the global economic crisis better than expected, with the largest developing country stockmarkets rebounding and private capital flows resuming. By 2014, government debt of G20 countries in the Global North is expected to be 114 percent of GDP, while the forecast for those in the Global South is drastically lower at 35 percent (Beddoes 2010).

REFORMING THE INTERNATIONAL FINANCIAL ARCHITECTURE?

Financial crises have traditionally been followed by a multitude of suggestions for reform. "After the East Asian crisis, such debates filled library shelves with myriad proposals for a new global financial architecture" (Pauly 2005, p. 199). In dealing with the crisis of 2008, efforts were made improving the rather informal system of financial cooperation between states.

Video: *Trickle Down Prosperity*

In particular, whereas such matters were traditionally discussed among the seven or eight largest economies (the so-called "G-7" or "G-8"), a much larger group consisting of the twenty largest economies (the "G-20") met to discuss ways to deal with the financial crisis. The rationale behind the larger group was that the larger economies of the developing world, such as Argentina, Brazil, Indonesia, and Saudi Arabia, should have input into forging a common response to the crisis.

> *For the great difference between an ordinary casino where you can go into or stay away from, and the global casino of high finance, is that in the latter all of us are involuntarily engaged in the days' play.*
>
> —Susan Strange, economist and international relations scholar

What these and other proposals seek is a mechanism for creating the currency stability and flexibility on which prosperity depends. However, there is little agreement about how to bring about reforms. With the spread of democracy throughout the globe, most governments now face increasing domestic pressures to sacrifice such goals as exchange rate stability for unemployment reduction. So it seems likely that the reality of a new financial system will remain elusive, and floating exchange rates, with all their costs and uncertainties, are here to stay. As one observer notes,

> The . . . leading powers in the world economy have too much of a stake in existing arrangements to show much appetite for reinventing the IMF or for charting a new Bretton Woods. For these actors, the IMF remains a preferred instrument for coping with financial crises. Hence, while the schemes for alternatives proliferate, the prospects are for incremental tinkering rather than wholesale restructuring. (Babai 2001, p. 418)

The mixed results of the G-20 summits illustrate the difficulty in bringing about any fundamental change. Despite their common interest in recovering from the current crisis and averting future crises, the members could not agree on a common set of policies to help their own economies recover and did not want to establish a supranational regulatory body to deal with global financial exchanges. Countries valued their own domestic policy autonomy over their common interest in monetary stability. However, in 2009 the group did agree to increase financial support to the IMF to help developing countries recover from the crisis, pledging $250 billion in additional support to the institution (*The Economist* 2009, p. 69), though no real efforts were made toward reforming the IMF itself (Bowring 2009; see Controversy: The IMF, World Bank, and Structural Adjustment Policies). In 2010, the emphasis at the G-20 summit shifted to one of debt reduction.

While some members, such as the United States, favored continued fiscal stimulus and expressed concern that pushing austerity measures too far might undermine economic recovery, others focused on the debt crises in Europe and pressed for reductions in government spending with national deficits to be halved by 2013.

We are thus left with a troubling situation: Global investment flows continue to proliferate, and there is every reason to expect that the currency dilemmas facing the world will continue to intensify. Yet a fundamental reform of the present international financial system is unlikely.

regional currency union
the pooling of sovereignty to create a common currency (such as the EU's euro) and single monetary system for members in a region, regulated by a regional central bank within the currency bloc.

Such a conclusion was highlighted by the "solution" to the currency problem the European countries adopted in 2002, which severed dependence on the U.S. dollar in preference for a *regional currency union* to try to stabilize erratic exchange rate fluctuations. To this end, the EU created the euro in the hopes that a single currency would make the EU a single market for business, and that the euro would promote economic growth, cross-border investment, corporate innovation and efficiency, and political integration.

Muchtar Zakaria/AP Photo

SURRENDERING TO THE IMF? A controversy surrounding multilateral institutions, such as the IMF, is that their policies are seen as another way in which powerful states of the Global North seek domination over those in the Global South. In this picture, taken on January 15, 1998, Indonesian President Suharto signs an agreement for a $43 billion assistance and reform package, while IMF Managing Director Michel Camdessus looks on. This picture proved damaging for both Suharto and the IMF. Indonesians, who place a great value on symbolism and body language, viewed the picture as a humiliating loss of face for the president, who was forced out of office four months later. It was also an economic and public relations disaster for the IMF. In addition to helping to solidify negative opinions of the IMF within the developing world (Camdessus later apologized for his arm-crossing and his stance), Suharto subsequently reneged on many aspects of the deal, particularly those that called for the dismantling of business monopolies owned by his family members.

As innovative as the creation of the euro appears, it may not serve as a model for other countries and regions. The EU's common currency represents much more than an economic policy, but the end result of a decades-long process of economic integration. In any event, the euro remains controversial even in Europe, especially among important EU states (Britain, Denmark, and Sweden so far have rejected it). To critics it is also an overly ambitious *political* change designed to create a European superstate and thereby erase the individuality and economic and political sovereignty of European states. This solution through currency integration in Europe is best seen as a response to U.S. domination of the global economy. Indeed, the euro has quickly become the second most popular reserve currency in existence, accounting for just over 15 percent of the world's total currency reserves (IMF 2010).

However, the U.S. dollar remains the primary global currency for settling international accounts, and it is doubtful that countries with smaller economies could successfully create their own regional currency blocs. Indeed, some scholars have began to question the very efficacy of having more than a few major currencies in existence, and that "monetary nationalism"—the belief that countries can produce and control their own currencies—is fundamentally incompatible with economic globalization (Steil and Hinds 2009). Along those lines, economic globalization would largely mean the "dollarization" of the international political economy. Thus as long as U.S. economic and military supremacy continues, it is unlikely that the present free-floating exchange mechanism for currency exchanges valued in terms of the U.S. dollar will be overturned by creation of new global institutions accepting supranational management.

This means that the debate over currency and monetary policies will remain as intense as ever, particularly in the turbulent arena of international trade. It is that twin dimension of economic globalization that we will next consider in Chapter 13.

Take an Online Practice Quiz

www.cengagebrain.com/shop/ISBN/0495802204

Suggested Readings

Ferguson, Niall. (2008) *The Ascent of Money: A Financial History of the World*. New York: Penguin Press.

Friedman, Jeffrey. (2007) *Global Capitalism: Its Rise and Fall in the Twentieth Century*. New York: Norton.

Kindleberger, Charles, Robert Ailber, and Robert Solow. (2005) *Manics, Panics, and Crashes: A History of Financial Crises*, 5th edition. Hoboken, NJ: Wiley.

Lechner, Frank, and John Boli. (2007) *The Globalization Reader*, 3rd edition. Hoboken, NJ: Wiley-Blackwell.

Oatley, Thomas. (2010) *International Political Economy*, 4th edition. New York: Pearson.

World Bank. (2010) *Global Economic Prospects 2010: Crisis, Finance, and Growth*. Washington, D.C.: The International Bank for Reconstruction and Development/The World Bank.

CHAPTER 13
INTERNATIONAL TRADE IN THE GLOBAL MARKETPLACE

CHAPTER OUTLINE

GLOBALIZATION AND TRADE

Trade, Multinational Corporations, and the Globalization of Production

The Globalization of Labor

CONTENDING TRADE STRATEGIES FOR AN INTERDEPENDENT WORLD

The Shadow of the Great Depression

The Clash between Liberal and Mercantilist Values

TRADE AND GLOBAL POLITICS

THE FATE OF FREE TRADE

Trade Tricks

The Uneasy Coexistence of Liberalism and Mercantilism

TRIUMPH OR TROUBLE FOR THE GLOBAL ECONOMY

The Development of the WTO

CONTROVERSY: Globalization's Growing Pains: Is The World Trade Organization a Friend or Foe?

An Emerging Regional Tug-of-War in Trade?

World Trade and the Financial Crisis

Globalization has changed us into a company that searches the world, not just to sell or to source, but to find intellectual capital — the world's best talents and greatest ideas.

—Jack Welch, former CEO of General Electric

Imaginechina/AP Photo

GLOBALIZATION AND CARBONATION The Coca-Cola logo is one of the most recognizable images in the world, and the global reach of this product is massive. According to company reports, the average global per capita consumption of its products over the course of a year is eighty-five cans—in other words over 1.5 billion servings of Coca-Cola are consumed daily. Shown here are some of its products in China. Coca-Cola has been active there for over eighty years, and controls over half of China's carbonated beverage market. The bottle in the middle is from the Huiyuan Company, which Coca-Cola attempted to buy in 2009. The Chinese government rejected the deal, which some analysts argued was driven by retaliation for alleged U.S. discrimination against Chinese firms and goods in other sectors (*The Economist* 2009).

As you struggle to make payments toward your college tuition, your father calls with some bad news: His employer has decided to move its production to India in order to save money by hiring lower-paid foreign workers without trade unions. Now your father will face unemployment. The downside of globalized international trade has come home to roost, and the quality of your life is declining. Or so it would appear as you contemplate your future clad in Levi jeans no longer produced in the United States and Calvin Klein shirts made in China. Trying to find meaning in the whirlwind of international trade going on around you, you race off to your international economics course, where you hope you can derive some insight. And you are in luck. Your professor hones in on her theme for today's lesson: "The Impact of International Trade on Global and National Circumstances." She introduces her topic by telling you that trade across national borders is the biggest part of the globalization of world politics. She begins by quoting former World Bank President Paul Wolfowitz: "I like globalization; I want to say it works, but it's hard to say that when 6,000,000 people are slipping backwards."

As you next learn, scholars also hold competing views about the consequences of the globalization of international trade. To construct an objective evaluation of these rival interpretations, consider leading ideas about states' trade policies, which are rooted in past thinking. In this chapter, you will focus on the contest between liberalism and mercantilism, two dominant sets of values that underlie the different trade strategies states pursue in their quest for power and wealth. However, to provide a broader context, the place to start is with data that describes trends in the globalization of international trade.

We must ensure that the global market is embedded in broadly shared values and practices that reflect global social needs, and that all the world's people share the benefits of globalization.

—Kofi Annan, former Secretary-General of the United Nations

GLOBALIZATION AND TRADE

Evidence of global trade is as close to you as the clothes you wear and the coffee you drink in the morning. Yet how can we gauge the true extent that commerce has indeed become more global? Is the increasing prevalence of imports and exports really significant, or is it just an artifact of the increased amount of total goods—both foreign and domestic—now available to us?

Fortunately, there is a relatively straightforward index that provides insights into the degree of *trade integration* in the world economy. The commonly used measure of trade integration is simply the extent to which the growth rate in world trade increases faster than the growth rate of world gross domestic product (GDP). As trade integration grows, so does globalization, because states' interdependence increases when countries' exports account for an increasing percentage of their GDP (the goods and services produced within a given country). As Michael Mazarr (1999, p. 161) explains, "Measuring global trade as a percentage of GDP is perhaps the simplest and most straightforward measure of globalization. If trade in goods and merchandise is growing faster than the world economy as a whole, then it is becoming more integrated."

trade integration
the difference between gross rates in trade and gross domestic product (GDP).

The index of trade integration reveals that international trade has become increasingly global over the past decades. For example, since World War II, the world economy (as measured by GDP) has expanded by a factor of six while global trade has increased twenty times (Samuelson 2006, p. 89). As shown in Figure 13.1, these trends still continue as the growth in world trade

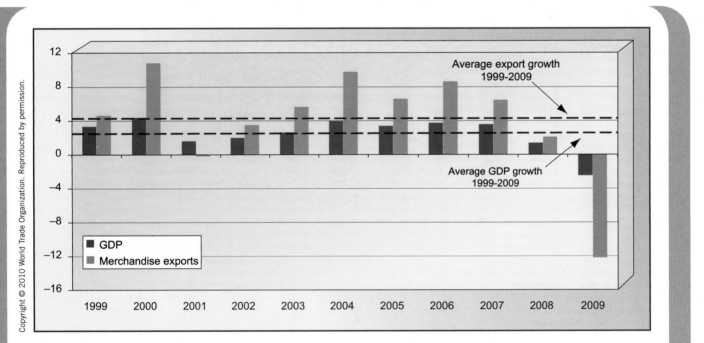

FIGURE 13.1

THE GROWTH OF GLOBAL TRADE INTEGRATION 1999–2009 When the percentage change each year in the volume of world trade grows faster than the annual rate of growth of the combined world economy, "trade integration" increases. As shown in this figure, world trade generally grows faster than GDP, with an average 4.1 percent increase since 1999. However, in 2009 world trade experienced a dramatic decline of 12.2 percent, a casualty of the recent global economic crisis. Some regions, such as North America and Europe, saw exports drop by 14.4 percent while the decline was less severe in the *newly industrialized countries,* where the decline was 5.9 percent.

consistently exceeds the growth in global GDP. Though the general trend is toward greater integration, countries differ in the degree to which their economies participate in global commerce. Global trade integration has become most rapid as a result of the mounting contribution of the Global East and Global South to world trade, which is also important to continued economic growth in the Global North. The Global South's share of global exports in manufactured products has grown from 10 percent in 1980 to 59 percent in 2010 (WDI 2010), fueled predominantly by the Global East's growth in the share of new export products.

Trade in services (intangible products such as tourism and banking financial assistance) and telecommunications are increasing as well. Such commercial ties have expanded more than threefold since 1980, with the Global North reaping most of the benefits. However, the spread of information technology, the ease with which new business software can be used, and the comparatively lower wage costs in developing economies are among reasons why the World Bank predicts that developing countries will capture an increasing share of world trade in services. Global East countries such as India, with significant numbers of educated, English-speaking citizens, are already operating call centers and consumer assistance hotlines for Global North companies.

Trade is one of the most prevalent and visible aspects of the globalized world economy. However, globalization is a multifaceted phenomenon (see Chapter 9), encompassing a variety of often interrelated actions. There is a close relationship between trade and the global financial markets, as exchange rates set the values for the goods traded, and capital flows are often necessary to finance these commercial activities. Trade is also inextricably linked to two other aspects of globalization, the globalization of production and the globalization of labor. Understanding these components of globalization, as well as their relationship with trade, is important to understanding the complexities of the world economy.

> *The idea of economic competition among nations is flawed. Companies compete. But economically, countries depend on each other.*
>
> —Robert J. Samuelson, political economist

Trade, Multinational Corporations, and the Globalization of Production

Selling products to consumers in another country often requires companies to establish a presence abroad, where they can produce goods and offer services. Traditionally, the overseas operations of *multinational corporations* (see Chapters 4 and 5) were "appendages" of a centralized hub. The pattern today is to dismantle the hub by dispersing production facilities worldwide, which was made economically feasible by the revolutions in communication and transportation. As a result, the production of goods is commonly dispersed as different components are made in different countries. Consider the global nature of the production of Dell computers, whose supply chain involves eight countries outside of the United States (see Map 13.1). Every Dell computer that is sold is, in effect, generating trade between nine different countries.

globalization of production
transnationalization of the productive process, in which finished goods rely on inputs from multiple countries outside of their final market.

This *globalization of production* is transforming the international political economy. It once made sense to count trade in terms of flows between countries, and that practice continues because national account statistics are still gathered with states as the unit of analysis. But that picture increasingly fails to portray current realities. Countries do not really trade with each other; corporations do. Together MNCs are now responsible for about one-fourth of the world's production and two-thirds of global exports. As much

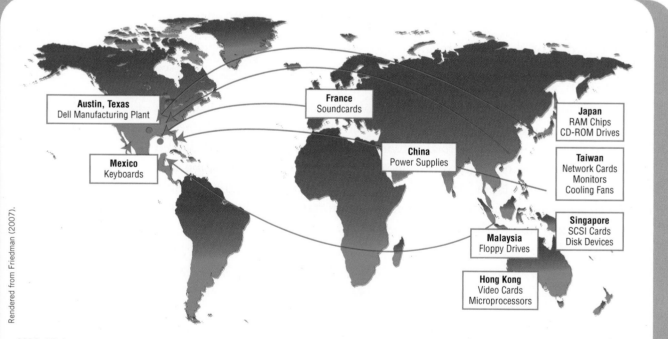

Rendered from Friedman (2007).

Austin, Texas
Dell Manufacturing Plant

France
Soundcards

Japan
RAM Chips
CD-ROM Drives

Mexico
Keyboards

China
Power Supplies

Taiwan
Network Cards
Monitors
Cooling Fans

Singapore
SCSI Cards
Disk Devices

Malaysia
Floppy Drives

Hong Kong
Video Cards
Microprocessors

MAP 13.1

THE GLOBAL SUPPLY CHAIN The globalization of production means that it is often hard to discern exactly where a good is "from." This map shows the supply chain for the production of Dell computers. Supply chains such as this have a significant influence on the world economy, reflecting increasing levels of cross-border integration and the "networked" nature of interdependence. Thomas Friedman even goes so far as to offer a "Dell Theory" of conflict prevention, which posits that states that are part of common major supply chains are less likely to go to war.

as 40 percent of global trade is *intra-firm trade*, that is, commerce *between* MNCs' cross-border affiliates (Oatley 2010, p. 167).

MNCs are the primary agents in the globalization of production. By increasingly forming strategic corporate alliances with companies in the same industry, and by merging with one another, MNCs have become massive NGOs rivaling states in financial resources (see Table 5.3). These global actors have grown in influence also because many MNC parent companies are now linked with one another in *virtual corporations* and alliances of co-ownership and coproduction. These MNC networks pursue truly global strategies for financial gain, often through long-term supplier agreements and licensing and franchising contracts. As they funnel large financial flows across national borders, these global corporate conglomerates are integrating national economies into a worldwide market. In the process, this huge movement of investments across borders is leading to economic convergence by causing "countries to adopt similar institutions and practices to organize economic life. . . . It is important to know not only how much FDI a country receives but from where. The effect of inward FDI needs to be appreciated beyond its usual role of alleviating resource scarcities and creating jobs in host countries. FDI is a conveyor of norms, technologies, and corporate practices" (Prakash and Potoski 2007, p. 738). In addition to changing the way that we view world trade, the globalization of production has implications for the economic norms and practices of societies throughout the world. In short, it affects global identities as well as global trade.

Though the ultimate effects of FDI are controversial (see Chapter 4), there is agreement that the globalization of production will only increase. FDI flows throughout the world since 1970 increased one-hundred-fold by 2000 to $1.4 trillion, and peaked at over $1.9 trillion in 2007. They declined by 15 percent in 2008 and fell an additional 39 percent in 2009 to just over $1 trillion (UNCTAD 2010). The direction of FDI flows is constantly changing, but a trend is apparent in the rise of the Global East and the Global South as fully engaged participants in this enormous transnational investment activity. Developing countries are increasingly the recipients of investments from abroad. From an initial level of $98 billion in 1995, net inflows of FDI to developing countries increased to over $598 billion in 2009. The Global South countries are also investing outside of their own borders. In 2009, net outflows of FDI from developing countries reached $225 billion, about 11 percent of total FDI outflows (WDI 2010). The recent financial crisis has heightened this pattern. Though the developed countries experienced a 25 percent drop in FDI inflows, investment into

intra-firm trade
cross-national trade of intermediate goods and services within the same firm.

virtual corporations
agreements between otherwise competitive MNCs, often temporary, to join forces and skills to coproduce and export particular products in the borderless global marketplace.

the Global South continued to grow (WIPS 2009). However, large differences exist among the companies investing overseas to expand their global financial presence and trade, as well as among the targets of FDI inflows (see Figure 13.2).

The Globalization of Labor

Goods cannot be produced without labor. The globalization of production is thus inextricably linked to the globalization of labor as well as trade. Labor is a particularly contentious aspect of globalization in that it directly links individuals with the global economy, as exemplified by issues such as undocumented immigration (see Chapter 14), the use of child labor, and "outsourcing."

The globalization of labor has emerged as a result of interrelated changes in the world economy and global demographics. As evidenced by the large volume of global FDI, an increasing amount of productive capital is mobile, and can readily change locations according to the specific needs of the firm as well as perceived advantages of prospective host countries. Businesses are increasingly able to use labor from multiple countries and to switch locations when conditions change.

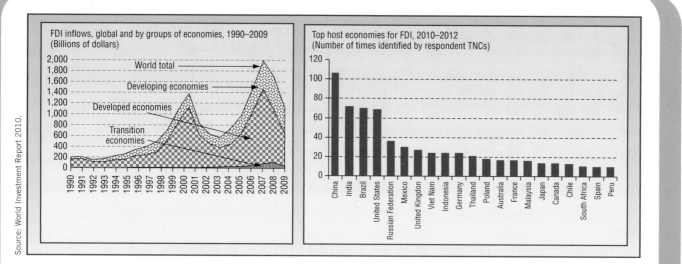

Source: World Investment Report 2010.

FIGURE 13.2

THE SHIFTING DISTRIBUTION OF FOREIGN DIRECT INVESTMENTS As the figure (left) demonstrates, there has been dramatic growth in FDI since 1990. Between 1990 and 2007, global foreign direct investment increased roughly ten-fold, from about $200 billion to a record $1.98 trillion. This was followed by a sharp decline in global FDI in 2008 and 2009, due to the worldwide financial crisis. However, FDI is expected to rebound, with optimistic predictions foreseeing a recovery to pre-crisis levels in 2012. Shown right are the most popular FDI destinations, based on a survey of transnational corporations. The BRIC members (Brazil, Russia, India, and China) comprise four of the five top recipients of FDI and reflect a growing interest for investing in developing and transition economies.

At the same time, there is mobility in the workforce as individuals move from one country to another. Though completely accurate estimates of migrant flows are virtually impossible to obtain, the UN estimates that around 200 million people work outside of their home countries. Moreover, the overall size of the global workforce has increased greatly over the past few decades. By 2010, the total size of the global labor force was over 3 billion people, having increased more than fourfold since 1980 with much of the growth coming from China, India, and the former Eastern bloc countries (World Bank 2010).

Taken at face value, these trends do not bode well for global labor. In terms of economic laws of supply and demand, the increased supply of labor would act to lower the "price" of labor (wages). Outsourcing has commonly occurred in the manufacturing sector; but in part a reaction to the global economic slow-down, outsourcing in higher-skill industry areas—from human resources to legal research—is on the rise as well. In Gurgaon, India, for example, lawyer Ritu Solanki earns $50 an hour working for a legal-outsourcing company to draft contracts and legal memos. A London law firm would likely charge up to $400 an hour for that type of work, and law firms and corporate legal departments are beginning to look at outsourcing as a way to cut costs. According to Indian estimates, legal-process outsourcing has grown from $146 million in 2006 to $440 million in 2010, with an anticipated $1.1 billion in 2014 (*The Economist* 2010, p. 69).

globalization of labor integration of labor markets, predicated by the global nature of production as well as the increased size and mobility of the global labor force.

The basic issue is the extent that globalization undermines the bargaining power of labor to obtain two main goals: sufficient wages and worker rights. Though the logic of supply and demand does bode poorly for the wage levels of workers, it oversimplifies the situation by treating labor as a relatively homogeneous, and thus interchangeable, good. Such a view ignores a key factor in business decisions—the productivity of labor. For example, it would not make sense for a corporation to move to a place where labor is 50 percent less expensive if the productivity of that labor was 75 percent less than the current location, as such a move would result in a net increase in operating expenses. Wages are thus not the only factor that determines where global capital will locate.

That said, empirical studies of this issue do indicate that globalization is problematic to lower-skilled labor, which is more readily interchangeable across countries (Blanton and Blanton 2009). Moreover, even though some workers may face lower wages, globalization acts to increase the purchasing power of these workers. Along the lines of liberal economic theory, global commerce enables consumers to purchase greater selections of goods at lower prices than would be the case without globalization. Indeed, a recent

IMF study found that though globalization had lowered the wage levels in some states, the losses were offset by increases in their purchasing power. In short, though globalization "reduced labor's share of the pie, it has made the whole pie bigger" (*The Economist*, 2007, p. 84).

A similar dynamic is apparent between the globalization of labor and labor rights. In this case the concern is that competition for capital and the increased supply of labor could prove harmful to the protection of labor rights, including the right to form unions (collective bargaining) and to legal protections from morally questionable labor practices such as the use of child labor and slave labor. Anecdotal evidence about "sweatshops" and the repression of union rights in the name of foreign investment abound; companies as varied as Unocal, Walt Disney, and Nike have suffered embarrassment and financial costs for their associations with poor labor practices.

Pavel Rahman/AP Photo

CHILD LABOR IN A GLOBAL SYSTEM **Globalization is sped not only by the rapid expansion of technology but by the availability of cheap labor in some countries that take advantage of their peoples' low wages to make products highly competitive in the globalized marketplace. Here, a child labors under hazardous conditions and at near slave wages in Bangladesh, producing goods that cost less than those made where labor unions protect workers.**

Yet comprehensive studies reveal a more complex reality. MNCs, for example, often bring in better technology and labor policies than domestic corporations (Graham 2000). To the extent that they are drawn to skilled labor pools, they can also encourage countries to increase the skill and productivity of their labor force via education and health care (Blanton and Blanton 2007; Mosley 2008). Moreover, increased FDI has been found to be related to decreased incidents of the use of child labor (Neumayer and de Soysa 2005).

Though most studies have found the globalization of production and the globalization of labor to be—on balance—positive developments for societies, the gains have not been spread equally across or within societies. As noted by economist Dani Rodrik (2008), "Globalization has exposed a deep fault line between groups who have the skills and mobility to flourish in global markets and those who either do not have these advantages or perceive the expansion of unregulated markets as inimical to social stability." Moreover, whatever the overall relationship between globalization and societal well-being, fears about it persist. Though globalization creates winners and losers, the negative consequences of globalization—companies "outsourcing" their work or using child labor—are quite visible and strike deeply into people's lives. A statement by an American whose software-testing job was outsourced to India is telling: "The fact that they not only outsourced my job, but my entire industry, makes me feel powerless and paralyzed. . . . Frankly, this situation has created problems that are way too big for one person like me to solve" (Cook and Nyhan 2004). Alternatively, the gains from globalization, such as less expensive products and the gradual diffusion of technologies, are often unnoticed. Similar dynamics are apparent in many of the controversies surrounding trade policy.

CONTENDING TRADE STRATEGIES FOR AN INTERDEPENDENT WORLD

As you have learned, international trade is a far-reaching dimension of globalization and is one of the most hotly debated. Disputes have intensified because the major participants in international trade are taking opposed foreign economic policy approaches. To understand the trade strategies different states are pursuing, it is important to understand the economic philosophies of liberalism and mercantilism that guide their international economic decisions.

The Shadow of the Great Depression

The institutional basis for the post–World War II economic order was begun at the 1944 meeting at Bretton Woods (see Chapter 12). Over the course of the next three years, the leaders founded the liberal economic order based around convertible currencies and the free flows of goods and capital. While the International Monetary Fund and the World Bank emerged as the leading financial institutions, the task of liberalizing world trade later fell to the General Agreement of Tariffs and Trade (GATT).

The basic mission of the GATT was to encourage free trade among countries by reducing barriers to trade and serving as a common forum for resolving trade disputes. The GATT had three primary principles: reciprocity, nondiscrimination, and transparency. First, the basic *reciprocity* premise of the GATT was for the mutual lowering of trade barriers, thus countries that lowered their tariffs could expect their trading partners to do the same. Second,

reciprocity
GATT principle calling for mutual or reciprocal lowering of trade barriers.

nondiscrimination
GATT principle that goods produced by all member states should receive equal treatment, as embodied in the ideas of most-favored nation (MFN) and national treatment.

transparency
with regard to the GATT, the principle that barriers to trade must be visible and thus easy to target.

according to the principle of *nondiscrimination*, all members have the same level of access to the markets of other member states. In particular, nondiscrimination was put into practice in two specific forms, most-favored nation (MFN) principle and national treatment. The MFN principle holds that the tariff preferences granted to one state must be granted to all others—in other words, there could be no "favored nation" among members. National treatment means that foreign goods are treated equally with domestic goods, and that countries are not able to enact policies, such as taxes or capricious regulations, to give their domestic products any advantage over foreign products. Third, the GATT called for *transparency* in trade policy, meaning that trade regulations and barriers need to be clearly known among all states.

Overall, the GATT has been successful in liberalizing trade. When the institution was formed, the primary barrier to trade was tariffs (taxes on imported goods). In a series of successive meetings or "rounds" held from 1947 to 1994, average tariff levels were lowered from 40 percent to just under 5 percent. When the Uruguay Round was concluded in 1994 the GATT became the World Trade Organization (WTO), which further strengthened the organization by giving it the power to settle disputes between members. This dispute settlement mechanism gave the WTO the ability to enforce its rules, and the WTO has settled hundreds of disputes among its members since 1994. In addition to gaining additional power as an institution, the organization has grown stronger in terms of members—since 1947 its membership has grown from 23 countries to 153.

Though liberalization has spread worldwide as a policy principle (Simmons and Elkins 2004), not all states consistently support the liberal tenet that governments should not interfere by managing trade flows. Indeed, *commercial liberalism* (see Chapter 12)

Iain Masterton/Alamy

CASCADING GLOBALIZATION: COMMUNIST CHINA CHOOSES TO CONVERT TO CAPITALISM AND CONSUMERISM Shown here is one example of China's growing consumerism: a view of the huge South China Mall in Donggum, the world's biggest shopping center. Opened in 2005, the mall has 7.1 million feet of leasable shopping area, and includes windmills and theme parks. In all, China has four of the world's ten largest malls (Van Riper 2009). China now has utterly embraced America's "shop-'til-you-drop" ethos and is in the midst of a buy-at-the-mall frenzy (Barboza 2005, pp. 1, 4).

is under attack in many states, including some of liberalism's supposed proponents, which are pressured domestically to protect industries and employment at home.

We will next review the basic philosophical stances underlying trade policy and the role of trade within the global political system, and assess some of the specific policy tools that states use in international trade.

The Clash Between Liberal and Mercantilist Values

How should states rationally cope in the globalized political economy to best manage economic change? The choices inspire different philosophies and policies. They force governments to attempt to reconcile the overriding need for states to cooperate in trade liberalization if they are to maximize their wealth with each state's natural competitive desire to put its own welfare first.

Most controversies in international political economy are ultimately reducible to differences between liberalism and mercantilism. A comparison of their divergent theoretical positions on five central questions illuminates the issues of debate that divide these schools today (see Table 13.1).

Let's look deeper at these contending economic perspectives:

Commercial Liberalism Commercial liberalism proceeds from the premise that humankind's natural inclination is to cooperate. Thus, progress through mutually beneficial exchanges is possible, both to increase prosperity and to enlarge individual liberty under law. In commercial liberalism, economic activity can lead to global welfare, and the major problems of capitalism (boom-and-bust cycles, trade wars, poverty, and income inequalities) can be managed. One of the globe's "great causes" (Bhagwati 2004) is to promote

Table 13.1 Key Differences Between Liberalism and Mercantilism

	Liberalism	Mercantilism
Economic Relations	Harmonious	Conflictual
Major Actors	Households, Firms	States
Goal of Economic Activity	Maximize global welfare	Serve the national interest
Priority of Economics vs. Politics	Economics determines politics	Politics determines economics
Explanation for Global Change	A dynamic ever-adjusting equilibrium	The product of shifts in the distribution of states' relative power

free international trade to lift the poor from poverty and to expand political liberties.

Adam Smith laid the foundations for commercial liberalism. In 1776, he wrote the now-classic *The Wealth of Nations*. In it, he argued how the "invisible hand" in an unregulated market fueled by humans' natural tendency to "truck, barter, and exchange" in pursuit of private interest could serve the globe's collective or public interest by permitting efficiency and gains. According to Smith, if individuals rationally pursue their own self-interest, they will maximize societal interests as well.

absolute advantage
the liberal economic concept that a state should specialize only in the production of goods in which the costs of production are lowest compared with those of other countries.

Regarding trade between states, the key concept that Smith fostered was the idea of *absolute advantage*, the idea that countries should produce goods in which their costs of production are lowest in comparison with other countries. As Smith reasoned, "If a foreign country can supply us with a commodity cheaper than we ourselves can make it, better buy it off them with some part of the produce of our own industry, employed in a way in which we have some advantage." Though the idea was revolutionary, it raises an obvious dilemma—what if a country does not have an absolute advantage in anything?

comparative advantage
the concept in liberal economics that, even if a state does not have an absolute advantage in the production of any good, a state will still benefit if it specializes in the production of those goods that it can produce at a lower opportunity cost.

This issue was addressed by another eighteenth-century political economist, David Ricardo, and his concept of *comparative advantage*. Ricardo argued that all parties, even those with no absolute advantage in anything, can benefit from trade. How? According to the principle of comparative advantage, countries should specialize in whichever good has a lower *opportunity cost* (the value of whatever the country forgoes producing). In other words, a country should focus on the production of goods that it produces comparatively cheaply, rather than other goods that it could conceivably produce but at a higher cost.

opportunity cost
the sacrifice that sometimes results when the decision to select one option means that the opportunity to realize gains from other options is lost.

This was a very profound concept with important implications for liberal theory as well as the discipline of economics. As it shows that trade benefits all parties that partake in it, this principle is the basis for commercial liberalism's advocacy of free trade as a means for all countries to mutually achieve economic progress.

Consider a brief hypothetical situation to help clarify the logic behind comparative advantage. Assume an "economy" of two people, basketball superstar LeBron James and yourself, and two "goods," playing basketball and grass-cutting. As a successful professional basketball player, LeBron James makes $10,000 per hour. However, given his athleticism, he is also good at cutting grass, and could earn $50 per hour in this line of work. Let us also assume that you, as a poor and overworked student, do not have adequate time to practice basketball and rarely cut grass. As such your basketball skills only command $10 per hour and your grass-cutting is only worth $20 per hour. You do not have an absolute advantage in anything. LeBron James, who has a large yard, needs his grass cut. What should he do? According to the logic of comparative advantage, he should hire you to cut his grass, as the opportunity cost for playing basketball ($50 per hour) is much smaller than that for cutting grass ($10,000 per hour). If he thus hires you, you will be able to specialize in what you do relatively best (grass-cutting) while allowing LeBron James more time to devote to basketball. Thus both parties benefit from the exchange. Though this is a very simplified example, it does reveal the basic dynamic—both parties can benefit from the exchange of goods (or services in this case).

The implicit assumption is that markets succeed according to their own logic. This provides a fairly straightforward set of policy recommendations. For liberals, state regulation of the national economy should be minimal to maximize growth and prosperity. The best government is one that stays out of business, and politics should be divorced from the economic market. A free market is the foundation for broad-based, steady economic growth that allows democratic institutions to flourish (Naím 2007). As Benjamin Franklin once quipped, "No nation was ever ruined by trade."

There is a fly in this liberal ointment, however. Although commercial liberal theory promises that the "invisible hand" will maximize efficiency so that everyone will gain, it does not promise that everyone will gain equally. Instead, "everyone will gain in accordance with his or her contribution to the whole, but . . . not everyone will gain equally because individual productivities differ. Under free exchange, society as a whole will be more wealthy, but individuals will be rewarded in terms of their marginal productivity and relative contribution to the overall social product" (Gilpin 2001).

This applies at the global level as well. The gains from international trade are distributed quite unequally, even if the principle of comparative advantage governs. Globalization has not benefited middle-income countries as much as richer and poorer states (Garrett 2004). Commercial liberal theory ignores these differences, as it is most concerned with *absolute gains* for all rather than *relative gains*. Mercantilist theory, in contrast, is more concerned with the political competition among states that determines how economic rewards are distributed.

Mercantilism *Mercantilism* is largely an economic extension of realist thinking. Unlike liberals, who focus on the rationality of the marketplace, mutual gains, and a minimal role for the state, mercantilists see power politics (see Chapter 2) as determining economics and posit that the government has an affirmative role to play in the economic well-being of a state.

Classic mercantilism emerged in the late fifteenth century during the first wave of colonialism (Wallerstein 2005). Classic mercantilists viewed the acquisition of gold and silver as the route to state power and wealth, and imperialistically acquiring overseas colonies was seen as a means to that end. In the early nineteenth century, what we now call mercantilism (also called economic nationalism) emerged largely as a response to the rise of liberalism—indeed, one of the leading mercantilist works, Friedrich List's *National System of Political Economy*, is to a large extent a direct critique of *The Wealth of Nations*. Though economic nationalists draw from some of the core ideas of liberalism, such as the importance of productivity, the benefits of specialization, and the efficiency of the marketplace, they draw a different set of political conclusions.

In particular, mercantilists diverge from liberal thought in three main ways. First, whereas liberals view wealth and economic growth as ends in themselves, mercantilists view them as instruments toward increasing national power. This is very much in line with the realist focus on national interest (see Chapter 2), which posits that "economic activities are and should be subordinate to the goal of state building and the interests of the state" (Gilpin 2001).

Second, while liberal thought expounds upon the gains of specialization, it implicitly treats all specializations as equal in value. Mercantilists question this assumption, positing that "the power of producing wealth is therefore infinitely more important than wealth itself" (List 1841). For example, during the early years of the United States, Treasury Secretary Alexander Hamilton recommended that the United States specialize in manufacturing instead of agriculture, as it would better serve U.S. national interests. As opposed to agriculture, manufacturing required higher levels of technological advancement. Such industrialization would thus increase the "diversity of talents" in the country, and industrial capabilities would be more readily convertible to military might.

Finally, mercantilists view the state as having an active and vital role in their economies. Specifically, as some specializations are superior to others, states can encourage the development of certain industries by subsidizing them and "protecting" them from foreign competition. As Hamilton (1791) noted, in key instances of national interest, the "public purse must supply the deficiency of private resources."

This perspective yields a different set of recommendations for economic policy. Whereas commercial liberals emphasize the mutual benefits of cooperative economic agreements, mercantilists focus on the likelihood of *zero-sum* competition and are therefore more concerned that the gains realized by one party in a trade exchange will come at the expense of the other trade partner. For mercantilists, *relative gains* are more important than both parties' absolute gains. Though mercantilists recognize the superior efficiency of free trade, they have a more guarded view of its political benefits. They view free trade as an acceptable practice for a powerful country, in that it often serves to solidify power. For growing countries, trade ties can sometimes be manipulated to the economic advantage of the perhaps more powerful, more developed state (Hirschman 1945).

However, in many instances adherence to liberal trade can undermine the pursuit of national security and long-term economic development. Indeed, as mercantilists point out, powerful countries who profess to liberal practices, most notably the United States and the U.K., were quite protectionist when their industries were developing: "While American industry was developing, the country had no time for laissez-faire. After it had grown strong, the United States began preaching laissez-faire to the rest of the world" (Fallows 1993).

TRADE AND GLOBAL POLITICS

Trade plays a central role in the global system. In addition to being a key facet of economic globalization, it has many implications for the global political system. Indeed, a good part of *IPE* scholarship deals with some aspect of the relationship between trade and world politics. With that in mind, let us briefly touch upon some of the key concepts and issues at the systemic and state levels of analysis (see Chapter 1).

At the systemic level, one of the most influential theories involving global trade is *hegemonic stability theory*. Hegemonic stability theory is based on the proposition that free trade and international peace depend on a single predominant great power, or *hegemon*, that is willing and able to use its economic and military strength to protect rules for international interaction. A hegemon is much more than a powerful state; rather it refers to an instance where a single state has a preponderance of economic and military power, a dominant ideology shared throughout the world, and the willingness to be the leading state in the international system and to establish a set of common rules.

The underlying assumption to hegemonic stability theory is that a stable and prosperous global economy approximates a public or **collective good**, in

collective good
public good, such as drinking water, from which everyone benefits.

collective action dilemma
paradox regarding the provision of collective goods, in which though everyone can enjoy the benefits of the good, no one is accountable for paying the costs of maintaining or providing the good.

that it provides benefits that are shared by all and from which no one can be selectively excluded. If a public good is shared by all, why does it require a hegemon to provide it? This is due to the problematic nature of providing public goods, the *collective action dilemma.* In this dilemma, the provision of public goods is problematic due to two basic problems, accountability and rationality. First, though a public good generates benefits, there are certain costs associated with providing or maintaining the good. If the benefit has a large group of potential recipients, it is not possible to hold any single party accountable for paying the costs to provide this good. The recipients are thus faced with a dilemma: why should they have to pay for the good when they can enjoy it without paying for it? If we assume that the actors are rational, then they would enjoy the good for free as "free-riders." However, if everyone is "rational," then no one will pay to maintain the good and it will eventually disappear.

The analogy of a public park helps to clarify this principle. If there were no central government to provide for the maintenance of the park, individuals themselves would have to cooperate to keep the park in order (the trees trimmed, the lawn mowed, litter removed, and so on). But some may try to come and enjoy the benefits of the park without pitching in. If enough people realize that they can get away with this—that they can enjoy a beautiful park without helping with its upkeep—it will not be long before the once beautiful park looks shabby. Cooperation to provide a public good is thus hard to sustain.

free-riders
those who obtain benefits at others' expense without the usual costs and effort.

This is also the case with the collective good of a liberal international economy, because many states that enjoy the collective good of an orderly, open, free market economy pay little or nothing for it. These are known as *free-riders.* A hegemon typically tolerates free-riders, partly because the benefits that the hegemon provides, such as a stable global currency, encourage other states to accept the leader's dictates. Thus, both gain—much as liberalism sees the benefits of cooperation as an absolute gain outcome because all parties to a bargain stand to benefit from their exchanges. If the costs of leadership begin to multiply, however, a hegemon will tend to become less tolerant of others' free riding. In such a situation, cooperation will increasingly be seen as one-sided or zero-sum because most of the benefits come at the expense of the hegemon. Then the open global economy will crumble amid a competitive race for individual gain at others' expense.

The theory is thus quite parsimonious in that it explains very broad political and economic trends in terms of the presence of one condition—hegemonic leadership. Though theorists may disagree about how many instances of hegemony have existed throughout history, there is widespread agreement about the most recent case, the United States during the post–World War II period.

Studies within this area have considered the issue of a U.S. decline from hegemony, and its implication for the world economic order (i.e., Keohane 1984; Wallerstein 2002; Zakaria 2009).

At the state level of analysis, studies have assessed the relationship between trade and military conflict, with a preponderance of the studies supporting the *commercial liberal* argument that trade ties tend to discourage military conflict (Gartzke 2007; Oneal and Russett 1999). On a broader scale, Russett and Oneal (2001) posit that trade, alongside democracy and international organizations, is a key part of the "Kantian triad" that encourages lasting peace between states. Similarly, openness to trade is beneficial to societies, as it is positively related to economic growth, levels of democratization, life expectancy, education, human rights, and food security, and negatively related to child labor, poverty, and environmental degradation (i.e., Bhagwati 2008b, Wolf 2005). "Despite all the misgivings about international trade, the fact remains that countries in which the share of economic activity related to exports is rising grow one and a half times faster than those with more stagnant exports" (Naím 2007, p. 95). That fact accounts for the continuing popularity of the liberal belief that the exponential growth of trade contributes enormously to economic prosperity, as the last sixty years suggest.

Trade is also used as both a "carrot" and a "stick" in interstate relations. Trade ties, and the granting of preferential access to markets, are commonly established with developing countries as a way to help them compete in the global market and thus achieve economic growth. Leading examples include the WTO's Generalized System of Preferences, which exempts developing countries from some of the nondiscrimination and reciprocity roles of the organization, the Lomé Convention, which gives seventy-one developing countries preferential access to the EU markets, and the African Growth and Opportunities Act, which gives sub-Saharan African countries duty-free access to the U.S. market.

Economic sanctions—deliberate actions against a target country to deprive it of the benefits of continuing economic relations—are common ways that trade ties are used as a tool for coercive diplomacy. Indeed, sanctions have been used with increasing frequency since WWII, and particularly since the end of the Cold War. A considerable body of work has examined the utility of sanctions, and most question their usefulness as a strategic tool. Sanctions "are seldom effective in impairing the military potential" of their targets (Hufbauer, Schott, and Elliot 1990, p. 94), and are rarely successful as a substitute to warfare. Indeed, military conflict actually became "as much as six times more likely to occur between two countries than if sanctions had not been imposed" (*Foreign Policy* 2007, p. 19). Moreover, as revealed by such notable failures

economic sanctions punitive economic actions, such as the cessation of trade or financial ties, by one global actor against another to retaliate for objectionable behavior.

Miguel Alvarez/AFP/Getty Images

STICKS AND STONES OF ECONOMIC STATECRAFT In 1962, the United States extended sanctions on Cuba to a near-total commercial, economic, and financial embargo. Pictured here are protestors in front of the United Nations headquarters in Nicaragua demanding the end of the blockade of Cuba. Their banner reads "Cuba is America—End the Blockade!" In March 2010, the United States loosened sanctions against Cuba, Iran, and Sudan to permit U.S. companies to export services and software used for personal communications over the Internet. According to Adam Szubin, director of the U.S. Treasury's Office of Foreign Assets Control, such smart sanctions facilitate the U.S. foreign policy goal of promoting democratic change through greater Internet freedom (Fletcher 2010).

as U.S. sanctions against the Castro regime in Cuba, sanctions often have little effect on autocratic regimes and often hurt the country's citizenry rather than its leaders. Autocratic leaders can simply "shunt the costs of sanctions off into the general public, who have little influence over policy outcomes or leadership retention" (Allen 2008, p. 255). As concluded by journalist Fareed Zakaria, "Sanctions are like the Energizer Bunny of foreign policy. Despite a dismal record, they just keep on ticking."

Despite these problems, the use of sanctions continues to proliferate. Why is this the case? Pragmatically, sanctions are very easy to implement, as they require little in the way of preparation or mobilization (unlike, say, military conflict). Though sanctions do impose economic costs to the sender, as it forgoes a potential trading partner, they are still perceived as a "cheap" tool that allows governments to symbolically demonstrate to their citizens and other countries that they are punishing unacceptable behavior. Moreover, as Baldwin (1999/2000, p. 84) argues, examining whether or not sanctions are "effective" in meeting a given end may not be the correct way to view the situation. Policymakers have a

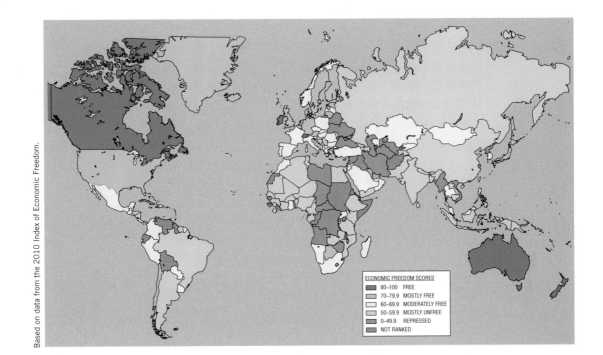

MAP 13.2

ECONOMIC FREEDOM IN THE WORLD Economic liberals and mercantilists portray two different visions of international economics, one in which the market has virtually free reign and the other in which the state actively intervenes to regulate and manipulate market forces. Yet the reality is more nuanced, as there are differences in the degree to which free markets operate within each state. This map depicts economic freedom as measured by the 2010 Index of Economic Freedom. By using measures across ten economic areas, including government policies on trade, labor, investment, and property rights, the Economic Freedom Index assesses the extent to which "individuals are free to work, produce, consume, and invest in any way they please, with that freedom both protected by the state and unconstrained by the state" (Heritage Foundation, 2010). Though there are differences in the degree to which economic freedom is enjoyed across countries, there appears to be a strong relationship between economic freedom and prosperity.

variety of "tools" at their disposal, all of which have various costs and benefits. Thus "it is not enough to show the disadvantages of sanctions, one must show that some other policy option is better" for a given situation.

Given the benefits of trade, it is not surprising that many states today welcome an open trading system. "Commercial common sense supported by evidence shows a statistical link between freer trade and economic growth," the WTO summarizes. "Liberal trade policies—policies that allow the unrestricted flow of goods and services—produce the best results."

These payoffs notwithstanding, there persist many reasons why so many states still attempt to increase their own domestic standard of living through trade protectionism. Some of these feel that free trade is neither free nor fair because it does not benefit everyone equally. Moreover, even though the percentage of countries practicing "domestic economic liberty" has increased throughout the globe for twelve straight years, many states remain unwilling to open their domestic markets to foreign imports because they are also unwilling to undertake reforms at home to create a free domestic economy. According to the Heritage Foundation's *Index of Economic Freedom,* at the start of 2010 only seven countries, or 4 percent, of the world's states were "free." Twenty-two (15 percent) were "mostly free," and the remaining countries (81 percent) were "moderately free," "mostly unfree," or "repressed" (see Map 13.2 on the previous page).

Economic freedom at home may produce the highest economic growth rates, provide the safest environments with the least risk for investments, and lead to foreign trade, but many governments are unwilling to realize these benefits through the liberalization of their local economies. This is largely to their detriment, as it is not an accident that economically closed governments rule countries that also tend to be the poorest and the most corrupt. Indeed, many countries in the lowest tier of the economic freedom ranking, which includes such countries as Myanmar, Chad, and Uzbekistan, are also some of the most corrupt countries in the world (Transparency International 2010).

This evidence underscores the influence of internal conditions on states' international economic practices. It suggests that the future preservation of the free-trade regime is unlikely in the absence of increases in the globe's percentage of free governments and free economies.

THE FATE OF FREE TRADE

Although many countries have reduced tariff barriers restricting imports from the rest of the world, there is much room for additional reductions. Fifty-six countries still impose tariffs of 10 percent or more, and the Global South average tariff wall (8.8 percent) remains high in comparison to the wealthy Global North's low average (4.2 percent) (WDI 2010). Unfortunately for the fate of the existing liberal rules supporting freer trade, the threats to global prosperity are multiplying at the same time that countries' growing dependency on volatile export and import markets is creating a precariously unstable situation. If the entire global economy begins to decline, scores of countries are likely to turn away from the free-trade regime that has engineered their previous period of unprecedented growth. In hard times, people are tempted to build barriers against foreign competitors. Even in many economically open countries, protectionist pressures inevitably increase when jobs are lost. Such was reflected in U.S. Congresswoman Maxine Waters' (D-CA) call to "bring jobs back home" as a way to reduce the unemployment rate in the United States.

The age-old debate between free traders and mercantilists is likely to persist as a global issue, and the World Trade Organization stands center stage as the major target about which debate centers (see Controversy: Globalization's Growing Pains: Is the World Trade Organization a Friend or Foe?). As is the case with international finance (see Chapter 12), there is an esoteric vocabulary attached to trade policy issues. Thus before assessing current issues facing the world trading order, it is helpful to develop an understanding of the "trade tricks" that countries can use.

Trade Tricks

Trade liberalization has played a key role in the growth of the global economy since World War II, and there is virtual unanimity among economists regarding the potential benefits of free trade. As Nobel Prize-winning economist Paul Krugman noted, "If there were an Economist's Creed, it would surely contain the affirmations 'I Understand the Principle of Comparative Advantage' and 'I Advocate Free Trade'" (1987, p. 131).

However, free trade is at a *political* disadvantage to mercantilism. This is due to the nature of the costs and benefits that accompany free trade. In the aggregate, the societal benefits of free trade greatly outweigh the costs. Yet these benefits, particularly the consumer gains that result from imports, are spread throughout an entire society, and are often not noticed. For example, though foreign trade may enable you to save ten dollars on a sweatshirt, you are probably unaware that imports are the reason behind your savings. There is thus little incentive to politically organize in the interests of imports—if you discovered that the price of sweatshirts had risen by ten dollars, you would probably not take the time to organize "pro-import" protest marches. However, the "costs" of free trade are quite concentrated and visible. It is quite common, for example, to hear of plants being closed and jobs being lost due to the presence of cheaper imports. There are thus greater political incentives to organize against free trade and for these forces to influence the political process. In short, "bad economics is often the cornerstone of good politics" (Drezner 2000, p. 70).

Given this dilemma, trade squabbles are likely to continue, as states have political incentives to enact mercantilist policies. This section will explain some of these policy tools, all which fall under the broad rubric of *protectionism*—policies designed to "protect" domestic industries from foreign competition.

■ *Tariffs*—a tax placed on imported goods—are the most well-known protectionist policy tools. Though average tariff levels have greatly decreased due to the WTO, they are still occasionally employed. For

protectionism
barriers of foreign trade, such as tariffs and quotas, that protect local industries from competition for the purchase of products local manufacturers produce.

tariffs
tax assessed on goods as they are imported into a country.

example, in 2002 President Bush imposed tariffs ranging from 8 percent to 30 percent on steel imports.

import quotas
numerical limit on the quantity of particular products that can be imported.

export quotas
barriers to free trade agreed to by two trading states to protect their domestic producers.

orderly market arrangements (OMAs) voluntary export restrictions through government-to-government agreements to follow specific trading rules.

voluntary export restrictions (VERs)
a protectionist measure popular in the 1980s and early 1990s, in which exporting countries agree to restrict shipments of a particular product to a country to deter it from imposing an even more burdensome import quota.

nontariff barriers (NTBs)
measures other than tariffs that discriminate against imports without direct tax levies and are beyond the scope of international regulation.

infant industry
newly established industries ("infants") that are not yet strong enough to compete against mature foreign producers in the global marketplace until in time they develop and can then compete.

- *Import quotas* unilaterally specify the quantity of a particular product that can be imported from abroad. In the late 1950s, for example, the United States established import quotas on oil, arguing that they were necessary to protect U.S. national security. Hence the government, rather than the marketplace, determined the amount and source of imports.

- *Export quotas* result from negotiated agreements between producers and consumers and restrict the flow of products (e.g., shoes or sugar) from the former to the latter. *Orderly market arrangements (OMAs)* are formal agreements through which a country accepts limiting the export of products that might impair workers in the importing country, often under specific rules designed to monitor and manage trade flows. Exporting countries are willing to accept such restrictions in exchange for concessions from the importing countries. The Multi-Fiber Arrangement (MFA) was an example of an elaborate OMA that restricted exports of textiles and apparel. It originated in the early 1960s, when the United States formalized earlier, informal *voluntary export restrictions (VERs)* with Japan and Hong Kong to protect domestic producers from cheap cotton imports. The quota system was later extended to other importing and exporting countries and then, in the 1970s, to other fibers, when it became the MFA. The MFA expired in 1995.

- As quotas and tariffs have been reduced, a broader category of trade restrictions known as *nontariff barriers (NTBs)* has been created to impede imports without direct tax levies. These cover a wide range of creative government regulations designed to shelter particular domestic industries from foreign competition, including health and safety regulations, government purchasing procedures, subsidies, and antidumping regulations (to prevent foreign producers from selling their goods for less than they cost domestically). Unlike tariffs and quotas, NTBs are more difficult to detect and dismantle.

- Among developing countries whose domestic industrialization goals may be hindered by the absence of protection from the Global North's more efficient firms, the *infant industry* argument is often used to justify mercantilist trade policies. According to this argument, tariffs or other forms of protection are necessary to nurture young industries until they eventually mature and lower production costs to successfully compete in the global marketplace. Import-substitution industrialization policies, which were once popular in Latin America and elsewhere, often depended on protection of infant industries (see Chapter 4).

- In the Global North and Global East, creating comparative advantages now motivates the use of what is known as *strategic trade policy* as a mercantilist method to ensure that a country's industries will remain competitive. Strategic trade policies focus government subsidies toward particular industries so they gain comparative advantages over foreign producers.

- Increasingly popular protectionist strategies include duties leveled against foreign subsidies. *Countervailing duties* impose tariffs to offset alleged subsidies, and their use is fairly common to offset agricultural subsidies. *Antidumping duties* counter competitors' sale of products below the cost of production. In 2008, WTO members launched 208 new investigations of alleged dumping, a 17 percent increase from 2007 (WTO Press Briefing, 2009).

Though much of liberalism is founded upon the virtues of free trade, realist theory helps to account for states' impulse to pursue mercantilist policies. Recall that realism argues that states often compete rather than cooperate because international anarchy without global governance feeds states' distrust of each other. Moreover, states seek self-advantage and economic primacy. In this sense, mercantilist strategic trade is a prime example of this realist explanation of states' concern for self-interest and relative gains. "It focuses on economic development as a matter of strategic significance. It explicitly aims to achieve trade surpluses and large dollar reserves. It's aimed at fostering production and a high savings rate but suppressing consumption" (Holstein 2005).

The Uneasy Coexistence of Liberalism and Mercantilism

Given the political advantages of mercantilism, states often have a hard time resisting the constant demands of domestic industries and interest groups for protection. They do so even if, according to liberalism, their relations with their trade partners will deteriorate and all will suffer in the long run, as trade partners retaliate with clever and innovative new counter-protectionist actions, of which there are many.

The result is that states simultaneously pursue liberalism and mercantilism. Such a paradoxical approach to trade policy shows states' determination to reap the benefits of interdependence while minimizing its costs. It also reveals the tension between states and markets, between the promise that everyone will benefit and the fear that the benefits will not be equally distributed. The absence of world government encourages each state to be more concerned with how it fares competitively in relation to other states—its relative gains—than collectively with its absolute gains. U.S. trade policy reflects twin

strategic trade policy government subsidies for particular domestic industries to help them gain competitive advantages over foreign producers.

countervailing duties government tariffs to offset suspected subsidies provided by foreign governments to their producers.

antidumping duties taxes placed on another exporting state's alleged selling of a product at a price below the cost to produce it.

rents higher-than-normal financial returns on investments that are realized from governmental restrictive interference or monopolistic markets.

instincts: to push for trade liberalization in foreign markets while cushioning the short-term costs of imports to the U.S. economy and employment rate.

How U.S. trade partners and rivals view the American commitment to free trade will heavily shape their own trade policies and whether they will choose free trade over protectionism. America's trade competitors have long noted that the United States, the principal advocate of free trade in the post–World War II era, has often failed to live up to its own rhetoric and has increasingly engaged in protectionism.

Indeed, some of the ways in which the United States uses its foreign economic tools are illustrative in this regard. First, a major portion of U.S. foreign aid is "tied" to the purchase of U.S. goods and services. Certain types of aid—particularly food—are legally required to be used to purchase goods made in the United States. A quote from a 2003 report by the USAID (US Agency for International Development) is telling: "The principal beneficiary of America's foreign assistance programs has always been the United States. Close to 80 percent of USAID's contracts and grants go directly to American firms" (e.g., Easterly and Pfutze 2008; Terlinden and Hilditch 2003). This turns foreign aid into a de facto subsidy for domestic corporations.

Security aims can also figure into U.S. trade liberalization efforts. The implementation of the African Growth and Opportunities Act (AGOA) has been particularly contentious in this regard. The original mandate of the AGOA was to encourage democratic governance and respect for human rights (Blanton and Blanton 2001), though this emphasis has reportedly been supplanted by strategic interests. For example, when the United States was seeking UN Security Council approval for military operations in Iraq, the AGOA was reportedly used to "ransom" the support of African members of the Security Council—"The message was clear: either you vote with us or you lose your trade privileges" (Deen 2009).

Additionally, though overall tariff levels in the United States are lower than those in the developing world, the United States, like the rest of the developed countries, still protects several key sectors, most notably agriculture. In 2009 the United States spent $15.4 billion on agricultural subsidies, and the total amount of all these subsidies across all the rich OECD countries was $252.5 billion (Bjerga 2010; OECD 2010). Such mercantilist moves are particularly damaging to the liberal trade regime, given the U.S. stature as the globe's leading economic superpower and its liberal rhetoric. This is particularly troublesome for developing countries, as they often have very powerful agricultural sectors as well. The gap between the ideals and the actions of the developed world also brings back vestiges of colonialism and past hypocrisy on the part of the rich countries. "Perhaps the greatest hypocrisy," writes Ian Campbell (2004, p. 112), "is that the United States, which preaches the merits of free trade more strongly than almost any other country, spends tens of billions of dollars to prevent its own markets from being free."

To free-trade liberals, as well as Marxists, the trade game is rigged by the routine and lucrative corruption known as "rent-seeking" (economic actors getting governments to impose handicaps on competitors). Rents that create obstacles to participants in the global marketplace harm everyone, but especially the poor (Klein 2007). Even by 2020, however, an intelligence team of forecasting experts (NIC 2004) predicts, "the benefits of globalization won't be global. . . . Gaps will widen between those countries benefiting from globalization economically . . . and those underdeveloped nations or products within nations left behind [despite the likelihood that] the world economy is projected to be about 80 percent larger in 2020 than it was in 2000."

TRIUMPH OR TROUBLE FOR THE GLOBAL ECONOMY?

The pressures on free trade notwithstanding, "rapid globalization has done nothing to undermine the confidence liberals have always placed in trade. No serious economist questions the case for international integration through flows of goods and services, though there is a lively argument over how integration through trade can be brought about" (Crook 2003, p. 3). Will that confidence prevail? To better assess this key issue, let us next examine the progression of the liberal trade order, as well as the current issues it faces.

The Development of the WTO

Though it is difficult to maintain a liberal trade regime, and there are problems with the global trading system, it has a better-developed "architecture" than the global financial system. As discussed in Chapter 12, the financial arrangement established by the Bretton Woods order broke down in 1971, and the current system is prone to "manics, panics, and crashes" (Kindleberger 2000)—currencies fluctuate according to the dictates of the markets, there are only discussion forums to address issues of financial and monetary cooperation, and the IMF merely provides for the monitoring of financial systems and "crisis management" for countries that are in dire financial straits.

By contrast, the WTO provides a well-developed institutional structure for the world trading system. The GATT/WTO has had a rather tumultuous and uneven history and has been criticized for its lack of progress throughout its existence. The 1950s were declared a "lost decade" (Stiles 2005), and "post mortems" have been written during the Uruguay Round negotiations (Schott 1983) as well as the Doha Round (Narlikar and Wilkinson 2004). In the aftermath of the financial crisis, legal scholar Richard Steinberg recently declared that "As a location for trade negotiation, the WTO is dead" (Steinberg 2009).

Yet to paraphrase Mark Twain, rumors of the institution's death have been "greatly exaggerated," and the GATT and WTO made progress in liberalizing global trade. During the Bretton Woods era, successive meetings or "rounds" of the GATT were very successful in cutting tariffs. The initial Geneva Round of negotiations in 1947 reduced tariffs by 35 percent, while successive rounds of negotiations in the 1950s, 1960s (the Kennedy Round), 1970s (Tokyo Round), and the 1980s and 1990s (Uruguay Round) virtually eliminated tariffs on manufactured goods. The Doha Round, which officially began in 2002, has a very ambitious agenda for trade liberalization that addresses many of the remaining nontariff barriers as well as other trade-related items that are high on the global agenda, including intellectual property rights, environmental issues, trade in services, and trade-related investment measures. Another sign of success is its expanding membership. The WTO currently has 153 members, while another thirty states have "observer" status and have taken significant measures toward gaining WTO membership (see Map 13.3).

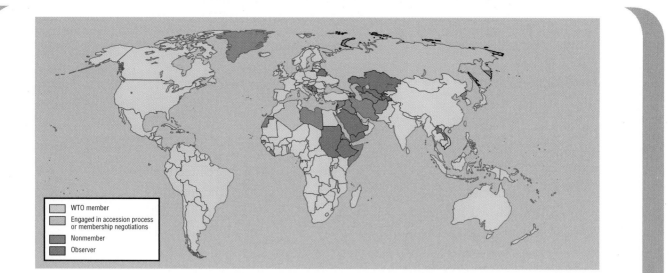

WTO member

Engaged in accession process or membership negotiations

Nonmember

Observer

MAP 13.3

THE WORLD TRADE ORGANIZATION GOES GLOBAL When the GATT began in 1949, it had twenty-three members. At the start of 2011, 153 countries, over seventy percent of the world's 212 states, were members of the World Trade Organization. In addition, 30 "observers" are in the process of negotiating to become formal members (such as Russia). Thus whatever the controversies surrounding the WTO, its near universal membership attests to the appeal of the institution among political leaders.

The Uruguay Round transformed the GATT into the WTO, a rules-based regime with a powerful dispute-resolution mechanism that arbitrates trade-related conflicts among members and holds them accountable for mercantilist measures. The WTO has handled over 300 disputes since 1995 (WTO 2010) and can hold even its most powerful members accountable for their trade practices. For example, the WTO played a pivotal role in forcing the United States to rescind its 2002 steel tariffs—according to a WTO ruling, had the United States not ended the protection of its steel markets, the EU would have been able to impose some $4 billion worth of trade sanctions against the United States (Becker 2003). Currently, the WTO is trying to get the U.S. to terminate its cotton subsidies and to force China to open up its markets for foreign music and films (Bradsher 2009).

In addition to having policy "sticks" to bring member states in line, the "carrot" of WTO membership, which brings with it access to the markets of the 153 member states, can serve to open up societies and improve the quality of state governance. Recent additions to the WTO—Cambodia, China, and Saudi Arabia—were all forced to undergo sweeping reforms of their trading regimes, including increases in the accountability and transparency of their trade policies, in order to make it through the "accession process" and join the WTO. According to Peter Sutherland, a Founding Director of the WTO, "Cambodia, China, and Saudi Arabia have changed dramatically— and mostly for the better—in the context of acceding to the WTO" (2008, p. 127). Moreover, Aaronson and Zimmerman (2007) note that the WTO accession process, as well as the periodic trade policy reviews required of WTO members, may have positive effects for the overall quality of governance within states, including increases in state transparency and levels of political participation.

Yet ironically the WTO is, to a large extent, a "victim" of its successes. When the GATT was formed it contained twenty-three members and was charged with one central goal—the reduction of tariffs. As tariffs have declined as a policy tool, the WTO has begun to confront a broad variety of issues related to international trade, including agricultural policy, intellectual property rights, trade in services, environmental protection measures, labor standards, and government procurement policies. As demonstrated by the wave of protests in South Korea over U.S. beef imports (Sang-Hun 2008), these new issues are much more difficult to resolve than the reduction of tariff levels, in that they may contradict the laws of individual countries. This taps into key concerns about state sovereignty (see Controversy: Globalization's Growing Pains: Is the World Trade Organization a Friend or Foe?).

CONTROVERSY:

GLOBALIZATION'S GROWING PAINS: IS THE WORLD TRADE ORGANIZATION A FRIEND OR FOE?

In late November 1999, the then-135 member countries of the World Trade Organization (WTO) and thirty additional observer states made final preparations to stage in Seattle what was billed as the *Millennium Round* on trade negotiations—the follow-up to the Uruguay Round of trade talks completed in 1993. The mood was optimistic. The meeting promised to celebrate the free-trade regime for the global marketplace and the contributions that lower trade barriers arguably had made to the growth of international exports and, for many members (particularly the United States), their longest and largest peacetime economic expansion in the twentieth century. There appeared to be widespread recognition that a half-century of generally rising prosperity had generated a climate of enthusiasm for the power of free trade. Fears of imports tend to recede in good economic times, and, with the best decade ever, most leaders in the twilight of the twentieth century emphasized the sunnier side of free trade. The goal of this meeting was to attain some consensus on how to build upon the success of the Uruguay Round.

That mood and the seeming consensus on which it was based were shattered when the Seattle trade talks opened. An estimated fifty to one hundred thousand protesters and grassroots anti-WTO activists, who differed widely in their special interests (poverty, environment, labor, women, indigenous people) joined hands to shout their common opposition to the general idea of globalization and free trade. A plane trailed a banner proclaiming "People Over Profits: Stop WTO" as part of what became known as "The Battle in Seattle" or, alternatively, the "Carnival against Capitalism." A tirade against open trade ensued, fueled by citizen backlash (Aaronson 2002; Weir 2007).

The immediate target of the demonstrations was the WTO; however, the organization itself was simply a convenient symbol of a much larger sea of discontent. The WTO protests (and the failure of the WTO conference attendees to compromise on tightly held positions and agree on even a minimal accord) exposed the deep divisions about the best ways to open global commerce and adopt new rules at a time of rapid change.

Controversies about globalization, free trade, and global governance are multiple. At the core is the question of whether globalization is an antidote to suffering or an enemy of human welfare. The debates are explosive, because everyone is affected, but in quite different ways. Many enjoyed the 1990s boom years under liberalized trade engineered by the WTO's trade agreements. But the celebration is confined largely to the top—the privileged, powerful, and prosperous. Many others see themselves as clear victims of an open global economy, as when a factory closes and workers lose their jobs. Those discontented with globalized free trade include a diverse coalition of protestors, many of whom harbor specific concerns about wages, the environment, and human rights issues. Labor leaders contend that the WTO is sacrificing worker rights; environmental groups complain that when green values collide with world commerce, environmental standards are left out of trade negotiations; and human rights activists accuse the WTO of undercutting human rights in the pursuit of free markets. In addition, some Global South trade ministers view efforts by the Global North to address labor and environmental standards as thinly guised efforts at "murky protectionism," arguing that the Global North's high-sounding rules are an excuse to impose high tariffs on their products and take away the comparative advantages Global South nations enjoy with lower wage scales and weaker environmental regulations.

These and other issues continue; and "for more than a decade trade talks have been described as 'acrimonious', 'grid locked' and 'stagnant,'" as exemplified in June 2007, when the trade ministers meeting in Doha, Qatar, denounced each other as "uncooperative" and departed without agreement (Naím 2007, p. 96). Though the G-20 nations pledged to complete the Doha Round by the end of the decade, multilateral negations remain largely at an impasse (Bluestein 2010).

WHAT DO YOU THINK?

- Former WTO Director-General Mike Moore posited that "Trade is the ally of working people, not their enemy. As living standards improve, so does education, health, the environment and labor standards." Do you agree with this assessment?

- How do you think Marxist and dependency theorists would view the WTO, and what solutions do you think they would suggest?

- What do these struggles reveal about broader issues regarding the strength and legitimacy of international law?

These issues are particularly difficult in that they raise concerns beyond free trade and protectionism. In particular, areas such as labor and environmental standards take the discussions into deeper controversies about core human rights and the policies a state should enact to protect its environment. As trade policy specialist I. M. Destler posits, a "new politics" of international trade is emerging, and these new issues involve "not the balance to be struck among economic interests and goals, but rather the proper balance between economic concerns and other societal values." Given the breadth of these matters, they are far more difficult to reconcile, and pose "a challenge that longstanding trade policy institutions were ill-equipped to meet or even to understand" (Destler 2005, p. 253).

The increase in membership has also brought additional challenges to WTO negotiations. Traditionally GATT/WTO negotiations followed a "club model" (Esty 2002) in which a small group of trade officials ironed out policy largely out of the public eye. For example, the conclusion of the Tokyo Round, which was widely heralded by experts as a sweeping victory for trade liberalization, was reported on page 18 of the Business Section (Section D) of the *Washington Post*—hardly prime placement for news items. Also, rounds were largely led by a small group of states, namely the United States, EU, and Japan, with other countries basically falling in line behind them.

Daniel Aguilar/Reuters/Landov

IS THE WTO "KILLING" AGRICULTURE?   The liberalization of agriculture has long been one of the most intractable items on the WTO agenda. Many countries view agriculture as a vital part of their culture and security, and thus often have visceral responses to any potential "threat" to the status quo. South Korea is certainly no exception to this, particularly with regard to its rice market. This picture, taken at the 2003 WTO Ministerial Conference in Cancun, Mexico, shows South Korean rice farmer Lee Kyung Hae (at left, with sign) protesting rice liberalization. Shortly after this picture was taken, Lee, a longtime advocate for rice farmers, publicly stabbed himself in the heart as a dramatic display of his opposition to trade liberalization and died shortly thereafter.

This "club model" is no longer applicable. As evidenced by the massive protests that have become ubiquitous at every meeting, WTO rounds now generate vigorous public attention. The power structure in the organization has also become much more multipolar, as some of the larger markets within the Global South, particularly the "G5" emerging economies—China, India, Brazil, Mexico, and South Africa—have become very assertive in trade negotiations (Parker, Dinmore, and Beattie 2009).

The WTO thus faces an interesting dilemma—having largely succeeded in its goal of lowering tariffs, and having attracted almost every state into the organization, it is now tasked with getting an increasing number of states to agree on an increasing number of very difficult and contentious issues. Indeed, the most recent round of WTO negotiations, the Doha Round, has been ongoing since 2002 and still faces a variety of major obstacles (Blustein 2010; WTO 2010). The current economic context has hardly served to make these matters easier.

An Emerging Regional Tug-of-War in Trade?

Another recent trade trend has been the proliferation of regional and bilateral trade agreements. The EU was the earliest and most successful example of regional integration, and similar, albeit less successful, initiatives occurred elsewhere in the Global North during the 1960s and 1970s. However, the rapid proliferation of *regional trade agreements (RTAs)* and bilateral trade agreements began in earnest in the early 1990s—according to the WTO the number of trade agreements in force increased over tenfold since 1990. As of July 31, 2010, the WTO had been notified of 474 RTAs, and 283 agreements were in force (WTO 2010).

regional trade agreements (RTAs) treaties that integrate the economies of members through the reduction of trade barriers.

"Most countries are members of a regional trade bloc, and more than a third of world trade takes place within such arrangements. While trade blocs vary in structure, they have the same objective: to reduce trade barriers between members" (WTO 2010, p. 377) and increase trade. For example, trade among the full members of Mercosur—Argentina, Brazil, Paraguay, Uruguay (there are also six associate members)—increased to $43 billion in 2008 from only $8 billion in 1990. During that same time period, trade among the ten-member Association of Southeast Asian Nations (ASEAN) climbed from $55 billion to $251 billion (WDI 2010).

Many feel that NAFTA and other regional free-trade zones are consistent with WTO principles. They see regional trade agreements as catalysts to trade because they encourage trade liberalization, albeit among smaller groups of states. Political leaders assume that there is no natural conflict between

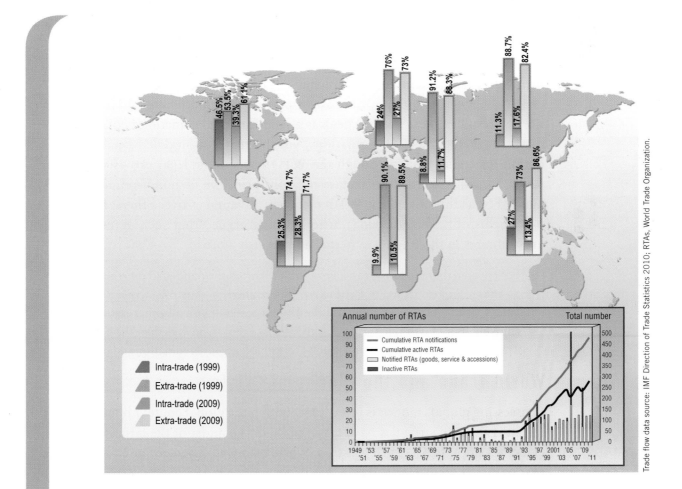

MAP 13.4

TRADE FLOWS WITHIN AND BETWEEN MAJOR REGIONS This map shows trade volumes both within and between regions. While the majority of global trade is between regions, there are notable differences in the patterns across the world and how they changed over the past decade. Intraregional trade volumes remain quite small in Africa and the Middle East, while trade within Latin America, Asia, and Europe increased. Trade patterns in North America and the former Soviet Republic states reveal increased trade with partners outside of their respective regions. A factor that has encouraged intraregional trade is the growth of regional trade associations (RTAs). According to the WTO, it had received notification of more than 460 RTAs as of the start of 2011.

bilateralism, regionalism, and multilateralism. For example, Robert Zoellick, former U.S. trade representative and current president of the World Bank, argued that through a process of "competitive liberalization," the formation of bilateral and regional trade deals could pressure countries into strengthening multilateral institutions. Moreover, the political struggles over these trade deals, such as NAFTA bilateral trade agreements between the United States and South Korea, are framed largely as a struggle between free trade and protectionism, with the trade agreements representing the former (Destler 2005). Along the lines of liberal theory, the development of bilateral and regional trade agreements is also politically effective—whatever its economic effects, the economic integration serves to strengthen foreign policy ties among member states (Krugman 1995).

Yet others who support a liberal trading order are less sanguine about these agreements. Politically, they argue that such agreements represent a "chimera" in which "attention and lobbying has been diverted to inconsequential deals" (Bhagwati 2008a) at the cost of pushing for multilateralism. Legally, the end result of these various deals is a confusing and sometimes contradictory "spaghetti bowl" of regulations, which creates a muddled legal foundation for trade. Finally, though the WTO has specific legal provisions for RTAs, in principle they do violate the core principle of nondiscrimination and MFN, as they give some WTO members advantages over others. Economist Jagdish Bhagwati (2008a), who has long argued that such agreements are "termites in the trading system," humorously noted:

> I discovered that the European Union, which started the pandemic (of regionalism) . . . applied its MFN tariff to only six countries—Australia, New Zealand, Canada, Japan, Taiwan, and the United States—with all other nations enjoying more favorable tariffs. I asked Pascal Lamy, who was then the E.U. Trade Commissioner, 'Why not call it the LFN (least favored nation) tariff?'

World Trade and the Financial Crisis

Video: *The Contagious Economy*

In assessing global trade, it is important to keep the global context in mind, as recent issues and struggles have taken place in the midst of the largest financial crisis since the Great Depression. World trade fell 9 percent in 2008—the first time that annual world trade has decreased since 1982—and declined an additional 12.2 percent in 2009. This decrease in trade was steeper and more sudden than the drop that accompanied the Great Depression (Eichengreen and O'Rourke 2009). In 2010, however, as the global economy showed signs of recovering, global trade was expected to grow by about 10 percent according to WTO Director-General Pascal Lamy.

The global market is interdependent, and events in one area quickly affect other areas. The linkages between the financial crisis and changes in the level of world trade reveal much about how the facets of economic globalization impact each other.

There are three main ways that the financial crisis precipitated a drop in world trade. First, the crisis led to a downturn in the overall world economy, which created a huge fall in consumer demand. There was less of a market for foreign goods, as well as products in general. The globalization of production, in particular the nature of supply chains, further magnified this effect. For example, for each unit decrease in sales of Dell computers in the United States, trade between nine countries is reduced. Global supply chains thus mean that trade reduction has a "multiplier effect," and that the pain of trade contractions is shared among a larger group of companies. Additionally, with the collapse in credit markets, trade finance dried up. International trade often requires short- to medium-term credit. Exporters, for example, may need short-term loans during the time period between when their goods are produced and when the revenue from their sales makes it back. In some instances, if neither seller nor buyer can obtain credit to facilitate the transactions, trade will not occur (Auboin 2009). The end result was a contraction in trade that was "sudden, severe, and synchronized" (Baldwin and Evenett 2009) across the major trading states.

Economic downturns tend to encourage protectionism, and the recent financial crisis is no exception. Yet it is unlikely that the world's economies will repeat the mistakes of the Great Depression, during which protectionist measures of individual states (the most notable was the ill-fated Smoot Hawley Act of 1932, which increased all U.S. tariffs by 50 percent) triggered a series of retaliatory measures and eventually the collapse of world trade. Nevertheless, though the G-20 countries pledged from the onset of the crisis not to revert to protectionism, seventeen of the G-20 countries put in place a total of forty-seven trade-restricting measures since the crisis (Gamberoni and Newfarmer 2009), including subsidies to automobile industries, European subsidies to various dairy products, and a variety of smaller measures such as India's banning of Chinese toys.

Though none of these measures (with the partial exception of automobiles) were particularly sweeping, they do not bode well for trade liberalization. The automobile subsidies are particularly problematic, as they may be indicative of broader shifts toward what Baldwin and Evenett (2009; see also Drezner 2009) call *murky protectionism*. This refers to more subtle NTBs that may

murky protectionism
nontariff barriers to trade that may be "hidden" in government policies not directly related to trade, such as environmental initiatives and government spending.

not be direct violations of WTO laws, but rather "abuses of legitimate discretion" on behalf of policy makers that serve to reduce trade.

Examples of such protectionism include abuses of safety and environmental initiatives, as well as policies related to government spending and procurement. Several countries are considering imposing additional tariffs on "carbon intensive" goods from other countries, as well as "green" laws that subsidize domestic industries that produce environmentally beneficial goods, such as advanced battery cells (Evenett and Whalley 2009). The stimulus packages that countries enacted, which called for increases in public works and other government spending, may also discriminate against foreign trade. In the UK, banks receiving government assistance were encouraged to make loans exclusively to domestic borrowers. There were also contentious "buy American" clauses in the U.S. stimulus package that gave steel and manufactured goods preferential access to government contracts.

One of the more controversial examples is the U.S. "bailout" of its domestic automobile industries with $30 billion in subsidies. This was quickly pounced upon by foreign governments as unfair to international trade, whose economies were also suffering and whose industries were also requesting assistance. As French President Sarkozy argued, "you cannot accuse any country of being protectionist when the Americans put up $30 billion to support their automotive industry" (e.g., Baldwin and Evenett 2009). Along these lines, the governments of other automobile-producing states have passed almost $13 billion in subsidies to their own industries, and additional subsidies are under consideration (Gamberoni and Newfarmer 2009).

Despite these threats to the global trade order, the rampant protectionism that characterized the 1930s did not resurface (Naim, 2010). Not only was the level of market integration higher, but, unlike the 1930s, there is an institutional structure to safeguard free trade. Yet the financial crisis, and the resultant contraction of international trade, certainly did not help the WTO to reach agreement on the Doha Round. As trade law expert Gregory Shaffer (2009) noted, the Doha Round "looks pallid in light of the staggering financial crisis that confronts us." As countries scramble to pull their own economies out of recessions, it is hard to take on the nuanced and complex tasks necessary for completing the Doha Round.

Yet while negotiations are currently at an impasse, "dispute settlement is very much alive and empowered," and these mechanisms "may be crucial to fighting protectionism during the current downturn" (Steinberg 2009). These struggles do, however, reveal that there are still many challenges facing the global trading system. As political scientist Daniel Drezner (2009) concludes, "Too many people benefit too much from cross-border trade for the world to revisit the nineteen thirties. Still, the possibility of a vicious cycle is not zero."

The world trading system is thus in a precarious position, as countries look at mercantilist measures to help their individual economies recover, while the WTO encounters continued difficulties in expanding its power and legitimacy in a more multipolar system. Such problems in the trading system do provide some corroboration to the realist viewpoint that there are definite limits to the strength of international organizations, as countries will focus on their domestic interests when threats arise, be they economic or political. Yet at the same time, a liberal case can be made—for the WTO to maintain legitimacy during such tumultuous times does attest to its underlying strength and utility within the global economy. Whatever the current "balance" between the two, the perennial struggle between mercantilism and liberalism will continue into the future.

> *Trade is not the cause of the current economic crisis, but is likely to be one of its most important casualties.*
>
> —Stephen Leo, CEO, Center for Economic Policy Research

This chapter, as well as the previous one, has shown that globalization is a "double-edged sword"—the same processes and ties that help our economies grow also ensure that crises are shared by all. Moreover, you have seen the interdependent nature of the various facets of economic globalization, such as the linkages between global finance, production, labor, and trade. Yet globalization is more than just economics; it involves individuals and cultures. To understand that part of the broader puzzle of globalization, the next chapter will take you beyond the economics of globalization, by addressing the cultural and demographic dimensions of our global society.

Case Study:
The Promise and Perils of Interdependence

Take an Online Practice Quiz

www.cengagebrain.com/shop/ISBN/0495802204

Suggested Readings

Bhagwati, Jadish. (2008b) *In Defense of Globalization.* New York: Oxford University Press.

Friedman, Thomas. (2007) *The World Is Flat 3.0: A Brief History of the 21st Century.* New York: Farrar, Straus and Giroux.

Irwin, Douglas. (2009) *Free Trade under Fire,* 3rd edition. Princeton, NJ: Princeton University Press.

Rodrik, Dani. (2008) *One Economics, Many Recipes: Globalization, Institutions, and Economic Growth.* Princeton, NJ: Princeton University Press.

Stiglitz, Joseph, and Andrew Charlton. (2006) *Fair Trade for All: How Trade Can Promote Development.* New York: Oxford University Press.

World Trade Organization. (2010) World Trade Report 2010: Trade in Natural Resources. www.wto.org.

CHAPTER 14
THE DEMOGRAPHIC AND CULTURAL DIMENSIONS OF GLOBALIZATION

In the globalized world that is ours, maybe we are moving towards a global village, but that global village brings in a lot of different people, a lot of different ideas, lots of different backgrounds, lots of different aspirations.
—Lakhdar Brahimi, UN envoy and advisor

CHAPTER OUTLINE

POPULATION CHANGE AS A GLOBAL CHALLENGE

World Population Growth Rates

Global Migration Trends

NEW PLAGUES? THE GLOBAL IMPACT OF DISEASE

THE GLOBAL INFORMATION AGE

The Evolution of Global Communications

The Politics and Business of Global Communication

GLOBALIZATION AND THE GLOBAL FUTURE

CONTROVERSY: IS GLOBALIZATION HELPFUL OR HARMFUL?

Jan Bauer/AP Photo

THE EXPORT OF MASS CULTURE THROUGHOUT THE GLOBE As a primary information highway, the Internet fuels globalization and allows individuals to become part of a "digital public" that transcends national borders and identities (Tiessen 2010). Over 69 percent of citizens in the Global North are Internet users, as are over 15 percent of people in the Global South (WDI 2010), and Internet usage continues to grow. This photo of a Huli tribal chief from Papua New Guinea presenting his new website illustrates how the spread of information technology facilitates the global flow of ideas and information.

Everyone in the world is becoming more alike each and every day. It really is a small world, after all. As you probably already have at one time or another imagined, beneath the skin every human being is essentially similar. We all share the same planet. And we all tend to respond to the same experiences that almost everyone everywhere feels at one time or another—love, fear, alienation, or a sense of a common community and destiny. And everyone also certainly shares a similar aspiration for a better world, as expressed by world futurist Rafael M. Salas: "The final binding thought is to shape a more satisfying future for the coming generations, a global society in which individuals can develop their full potential, free of capricious inequalities and threats of environmental degradation."

There is rising expectation that this universal hope will be fulfilled. Why? One explanation is that growing numbers of people throughout the world are pursuing these human goals, because globalization is bringing all of humanity together as never before in bonds of interdependence. Do you, like them, think that breaking down barriers and boundaries can bring people together in a human family that recognizes no East, West, North, or South, but every individual as part of the same human race? Should you therefore practice not cutthroat politics, but morals? And if that goal is your passion, should you, like many others joining together in nongovernmental organizations (NGOs) across the globe, promote not partisanship, but the recognition of true merit wherever found?

Is this rising consciousness and global activism warranted? Is the vision on which people are increasingly defining themselves as global citizens reasonable? Will a truly global society come into being in your lifetime, propelled by the pressure of cascading globalization that is tearing down visions of separate states, nations, and races that throughout past history have so divided humanity? This chapter opens a door to evaluating the prospect for such a jaw-dropping development. You will be asked to consider if global trends might transform the world, and the world politics that condition it.

Once you have glimpsed the world as it might be, as it ought to be, as it's going to be (however that vision appears to you), it is impossible to live compliant and complacent anymore in the world as it is.

—Victoria Safford, Unitarian minister

POPULATION CHANGE AS A GLOBAL CHALLENGE

To formulate your interpretation of this human dimension of globalization and world politics, it is instructive to first look at how changes in world population are a part of the globalization of world politics.

"Chances are," notes an expert in *demography*, Jeffrey Kluger (2006), "that you will never meet any of the estimated 247 human beings who were born in the past minute. In a population of (over) 6.7 billion, 247 is a demographic hiccup. In the minute before last, however, there were another 247. In the minutes to come, there will be another, then another, then another. By next year at this time, all those minutes will have produced millions of newcomers in the great human mosh pit. That kind of crowd is very hard to miss."

demography
the study of population changes, their sources, and their impact.

As the population on this planet increases, globalization is bringing us closer together in a crowded *global village* where transnational challenges characterize our borderless world. Evidence strongly suggests that unrestrained population growth will result in strife and environmental degradation (see Chapters 7 and 16). Population change also forces consideration of standards for ethics (the criteria by which right and wrong behavior and motives should be distinguished). Some people regard the freedom to parent as a human right. Others claim that controls on family size are necessary because unregulated population will "parent" a crowded and unlivable future world without the resources necessary to sustain life for all people. For this reason, politics—the exercise of influence in an attempt to resolve controversial issues in one's favor—surrounds debate about population policies. To understand why the globalization of population has become such a controversial issue, it is helpful to trace the global trends in population growth that have made this topic so problematic.

global village
a popular cosmopolitan perspective describing the growth of awareness that all people share a common fate because the world is becoming an integrated and interdependent whole.

World Population Growth Rates

The rapid growth of world population is described by a simple mathematical principle that Reverend Thomas Malthus noticed in 1798: unchecked, population increases in a geometric or exponential ratio (e.g., 1 to 2, 2 to 4, 4 to 8), whereas subsistence increases in only an arithmetic ratio (1 to 2, 2 to 3, 3 to 4). When population increases at such a geometric rate, the acceleration can be staggering. Carl Sagan illustrated this principle governing growth rates with a parable he termed "The Secret of the Persian Chessboard":

> The way I first heard the story, it happened in ancient Persia. But it may have been India, or even China. Anyway, it happened a long time ago. The Grand

Vizier, the principal adviser to the King, had invented a new game. It was played with moving pieces on a board of 64 squares. The most important piece was the King. The next most important piece was the Grand Vizier—just what we might expect of a game invented by a Grand Vizier. The object of the game was to capture the enemy King, and so the game was called, in Persian, shahmat—shah for king, mat for dead. Death to the King. In Russia it is still called shakhmaty, which perhaps conveys a lingering revolutionary ardor. Even in English there is an echo of the name—the final move is called "checkmate." The game, of course, is chess.

As time passed, the pieces, their moves and the rules evolved. There is, for example, no longer a piece called the Grand Vizier—it has become transmogrified into a Queen, with much more formidable powers.

Why a king should delight in the creation of a game called "Death to the King" is a mystery. But, the story goes, he was so pleased that he asked the Grand Vizier to name his own reward for such a splendid invention. The Grand Vizier had his answer ready: He was a humble man, he told the King. He wished only for a humble reward. Gesturing to the eight columns and eight rows of squares on the board he devised, he asked that he be given a single grain of wheat on the first square, twice that on the second square, twice that on the third, and so on, until each square had its complement of wheat.

No, the King remonstrated. This is too modest a prize for so important an invention. He offered jewels, dancing girls, palaces. But the Grand Vizier, his eyes becomingly lowered, refused them all. It was little piles of wheat he wanted. So, secretly marveling at the unselfishness of his counselor, the King graciously consented.

When the Master of the Royal Granary began to count out the grains, however, the King was in for a rude surprise. The number of grains starts small enough: 1, 2, 4, 8, 16, 32, 64, 128, 256, 512, 1,024. . . . But by the time the 64th square is approached, the number becomes colossal, staggering. In fact the number is nearly 18.5 quintillion grains of wheat. Maybe the Grand Vizier was on a high fiber diet.

How much does 18.5 quintillion grains of wheat weigh? If each grain were 2 millimeters in size, then all the grains together would weigh around 75 billion metric tons, which far exceeds what could have been stored in the King's granaries. In fact, this is the equivalent of about 150 years of the world's present wheat production (Sagan 1989, p. 14).

The story of population growth is told in its statistics. The annual rate of population growth in the twentieth century increased from less than 1 percent in 1900 to a peak of 2.2 percent in 1964. It has since dropped to about 1.3 percent and is expected to drop slightly more to 1.1 percent between now and 2015, where seventy-four million new people (the equivalent to the population of Turkey) will be added each year. In terms of absolute numbers, the world population has grown dramatically in the twentieth century. Even in the past twenty years the population has grown from 5.3 billion in 1990 to 6.7 billion in 2008 and is expected to reach 7.2 billion by 2015 (WDI 2010, p. 64). Robert S. McNamara, as World Bank President, noted that "If one postulates that the human race began with a single pair of parents, the population has had to double only thirty-one times to reach its huge total." Plainly, the planet is certain to have many people by the mid-twenty-first century, well beyond the over 6.8 billion in 2011 (see Figure 14.1).

The Demographic Divide Between Global North and Global South   Population is growing much more rapidly in the developing Global South countries (which are least able to support their existing populations) than in the wealthy Global North, where population is declining gradually despite increasingly longer life spans. Of the population growth the world has experienced since 1900, most—80 percent

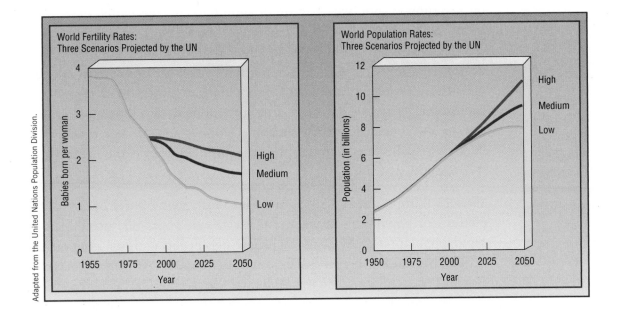

Adapted from the United Nations Population Division.

FIGURE 14.1

WORLD POPULATION GROWTH PROJECTIONS TO THE YEAR 2050 **By 2050 an additional 2.4 billion people are forecast to be living on the Earth, the UN predicts, raising the total to over 9.1 billion. Such predictions are uncertain because growth rates depend on a variety of factors, but increased longevity in the Global North and a burgeoning youth bulge in the Global South are contributing to this trend. The UN figure on the left depicts the decreasing fertility rates in high, medium, and low income countries. The figure on the right displays the range of world population forecasts by the year 2050.**

replacement-level fertility
one couple replacing themselves on average with two children so that a country's population will remain stable if this rate prevails.

fertility rate
the average number of children born to a woman (or group of women) during her lifetime.

since 1950—has been in the Global South. "The uneven regional growth reduced the developed countries' share of world population from one-third to one-fifth over the century. Europe's relative share of world population fell most—from one-quarter in 1900 to merely one-eighth in 2000" (World Bank 2009, p. 24). This portends fulfillment of the "demographic divide" predicted in Map 14.1, which is based on the probability that the population of the Global North will fall (from 23 percent of total world population in 1950 and 16 percent in 2008) to only 10 percent by 2050 (WDI 2010).

Global population cannot stabilize until it falls below *replacement-level fertility*. That will not happen until the total *fertility rate*, the worldwide average number of children born to a woman, falls from the rate of 2.5 today to 2.1. World population is projected to continue to surge because of "population momentum" resulting from the large number of women now entering their childbearing years. But "by about 2020, the global fertility rate will dip below the global replacement rate for the first time" (*The Economist*, 2010, p. 29). World population will reach over 9.1 billion in 2050, at which point it will stabilize.

However, like the inertia of a descending airliner when it first touches down on the runway, population growth simply cannot be halted even with an immediate, full application of the brakes. Not until the size of the generation giving birth to children is no larger than the generation among which deaths are occurring will the population "airplane" come to a halt. In the meantime, regional differences in population growth will become more prominent. "Virtually all of this growth will be in developing countries. . . . one in six countries—all of them developing and all but three of them in Africa—will more than double their population over the next 40 years" (HDR 2009, p. 43).

Western Europe and sub-Saharan Africa illustrate the force of two different pictures of population momentum. Africa's demographic profile is one of rapid population growth, as each new age group (cohort) contains more people than the one before it. Thus, even if individual African couples choose to have fewer children than their parents, Africa's population will continue to grow because there are now more men and women of childbearing age than ever before. In contrast, Europe's population profile is one of slow growth, as recent cohorts have been smaller than preceding ones. In fact, Europe has moved beyond replacement-level fertility to become a stagnant population with low birthrates and a growing number of people who survive middle age. A product of an extended period of low birthrates, low death rates, and increased longevity, Europe is best described as an aging society, where the

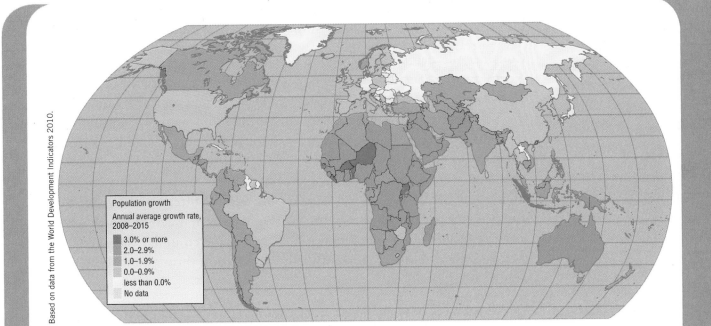

Based on data from the World Development Indicators 2010.

Population growth

Annual average growth rate, 2008–2015

- 3.0% or more
- 2.0–2.9%
- 1.0–1.9%
- 0.0–0.9%
- less than 0.0%
- No data

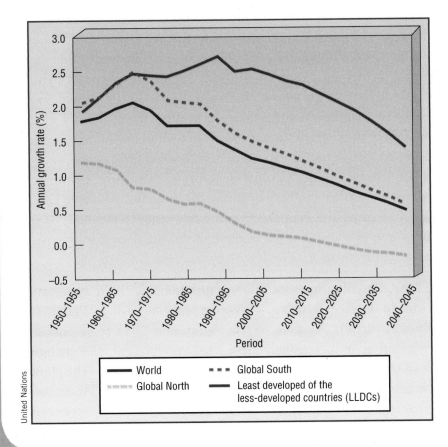

United Nations

MAP 14.1

THE GEOGRAPHIC POPULATION DIVIDE **It took until the early 1800s for world population to reach 1 billion people, and today another billion people are added every twelve to fourteen years. World population is expected to exceed 9.1 billion by 2050, with almost all of the population growth occurring in the Global South. By the year 2015, 85 percent of the globe's population will be living in the Global South, with China projected to be home to over 1.3 billion people, India over 1.2 billion, and the United States at a distant third with 323.5 million (WDI 2010).**

low birthrates and aging populations have caused alarm that the number of European newborns will not be sufficient to renew populations.

Consider the demographic divide between the Global South and Global North further. Fertility rates in the Global South are roughly twice as high as the Global North. Because each cohort is typically larger than the one before it, the number of young men and women entering their reproductive years continues to grow. Though the pace of aging is actually faster in the Global South than in the Global North—in the less-developed countries the population of people over the age of sixty-five will rise to 35 percent by 2050—people between the ages of fifteen and twenty-nine comprise more than 25 percent of the population in much of North Africa and the Middle East (Slackman 2008), and children under the age of fifteen comprise about 30 percent of the population throughout the Global South (WDI 2010).

youth bulge
a burgeoning youth population, thought to make countries more prone to civil conflicts.

High birthrates pose challenges for economic growth and political stability, and a low birthrate is seen by some as a prerequisite for successful development. It is difficult for public policy to meet the needs of citizens and generate national wealth as "soaring unemployment, endemic poverty, and flailing schools are quite simply impossible to combat when every year adds more and more people" (Potts and Campbell 2009, p. 30). Furthermore, as a *youth bulge* develops wherein a burgeoning youth population in the Global South faces poor economic conditions and a lack of resources to provide for a family, many are turning to religious fundamentalism to counter their frustration and despair and are propelling an Islamic revival. Particularly in conjunction with economic stagnation, youth bulges have been linked to a greater propensity for domestic armed conflict (Urdal 2006). Explains Michelle Gavin, an international affairs fellow with the Council on Foreign Relations, "If you have no other options and not much else going on, the opportunity cost of joining an armed movement may be low."

At the same time, a revolution in longevity is unfolding, with life expectancy at birth worldwide at a record-high of sixty-nine years and rising (WDI 2010). Life expectancy at birth is expected to rise by the year 2015 to seventy-five years. This is creating an increasingly aged world population, and changing the contours of the global community. By 2015, over 9 percent of the globe's expected 7.3 billion people are likely to be sixty-five or older (HDR 2008, p. 243). Global aging is occurring at rates never seen before, in part because of improvements in medicine and health care, with some physicians now beginning to make a distinction between chronological and biological aging. Even the number of people who reach age eighty and older is on the rise.

In 1950, 14.5 million people had seen their eightieth birthday. By 2009, the number had risen to 101.9 million and by 2050 the number is expected to be almost 395 million (*Time*, February 22, 2010).

While the "aging and graying" of the human population is a global population trend that poses its own set of public policy dilemmas, it is more pronounced in the Global North than the Global South. There are concerns that due to rapidly aging populations, the Global North will be especially burdened by rising old-age dependency and face an array of economic, budgetary, and social challenges. While the effects are expected to vary among developed countries, these could include a decreasing labor supply; a decline in economic growth and per capita income; increased demand for public expenditures on healthcare, long-term care, and pensions; and an increased need to invest in the human capital development of future generations in order to boost overall productivity.

Resolving this dilemma in the Global North will require, in part, the promotion of demographic renewal by creating better conditions for families. As advocated by the European Commission's 2009 Aging Report:

> Demographic renewal requires action to develop an overall societal climate receptive of the needs of families, a shift towards a children-friendly society and creating conditions allowing a better work-life balance. In countries where it is difficult to reconcile work and private life, employment rates of women tend to be low, as mothers often drop out of the labour market, and birth rates are low because many people feel that they cannot afford to have children. Policies to promote reconciliation and gender equality, entailing in particular better conditions for parental leave and incentives for fathers to take such leave, and increased provision of high-quality childcare, should remain a priority (Commission of the European Communities 2009, p. 8).

Additionally, over the past few years, there has been growing debate within the Global North, particularly Europe, as to whether policy makers should adopt "pro-natal" policies designed to stimulate a rise in birthrates and combat norms for small families. Russia, for one, has begun a protracted effort to encourage marriage and child bearing, offering financial incentives to women who have multiple children.

The resulting differences in demographic momentums are producing quite different population profiles in the developed and the developing worlds, and "twenty-first century international security will depend less on how many people inhabit the world than on how the global population is composed and distributed: where populations are declining and where they are growing, which countries are relatively older and which are more youthful, and how demographics will influence population movements across regions" (Goldstone 2010, p. 31). The poor Global South is home to a surplus of youth, with rising birthrates and growing populations; the rich Global North is aging, with falling birthrates and declining populations. In the Global South, the working-age population will shoulder the burden of dependent children for years to come, while in the Global North it is the growing proportion of elderly adults that will pose a dependency burden. It is not difficult to see how this facet of globalization is *not* making people in the world more alike. Differentials in the geographical distribution of population are increasing differences in the quality of life experienced on the planet.

population density
the number of people within each country, region, or city, measuring the geographical concentration of the population as a ratio of the average space available for each resident.

Urbanization When interpreting projections in demographics, consider also the geographic concentration of people within each country. Known as *population density*, this measures how close together people are living. Some

Alexei Filippov/ITAR-TASS

FROM RUSSIA WITH LOVE In response to Russia's demographic crisis, policy makers are offering married couples incentives to procreate. With September 12th declared Family Contact Day throughout Russia in an effort to encourage marital intimacy, the governor of the Ulyanovsk region coined it the "Day of Conception" and offered prizes to couples that give birth nine months later on June 12, Russia's Independence Day. Shown here is a couple on the Bench of Reconciliation in a Moscow park, which is curved to promote physical contact and help couples to work out their differences.

countries and regions are very crowded and others are not. For example, Singapore is the most congested country in the world, with 6,943 people for each square kilometer, and people in Mongolia are the least likely to bump into one another, with only two people for each square kilometer (WDI 2010).

Today, the majority of people worldwide live in cities, and the urbanization of the world is accelerating and spreading. In 2010, 3.3 billion people, almost half of the total world population, lived in urban areas with a projected urban population growth rate of 2.2 percent (WDI 2010). "By 2030, [the world urban population] is expected to swell to almost 5 billion" (UNFPA 2007). What is more, already three-fourths of the populations in the Global North live in these big cities that are getting bigger, but cities are growing fastest in the developing Global South countries. "This will be particularly notable in Africa and Asia where the urban population will double between 2000 and 2030 . . . By 2030, the towns and cities of the developing world will make up 81 percent of urban humanity" (UNFPA 2007).

This urbanizing trend is producing a related kind of demographic divide: the increasing concentration of population in giant megacities (see Map 14.2). As the percentage of world population residing in urban agglomerations increases worldwide, the "*dualism*" between city dwellers and those living in the rural and poor periphery will make the urbanized core cities more similar to each other in outlooks, values, and lifestyles, with people in megacities communicating and computing with one another at greater rates than they do with people living in the countryside within their own states (Dogan 2004). "The process of urbanization, through which populations are increasingly concentrated in towns and cities, is an apparently inexorable transition and associated with rising living standards. No highly developed society is primarily rural" (Skeldon 2010, p. 25).

However, the impact of global urbanization is likely to aggravate health and environmental problems, straining supplies of clean water, shelter, and sanitation. If the urbanization throughout the global community continues at its current pace, which is almost certain, this trend will lead to still another kind of *transformation* in the world. We will consider another example next—the movement of people across borders through migration.

Global Migration Trends

The movement of populations across frontiers has reached unprecedented proportions, producing a *global migration crisis*. By some estimates, the number of legal and illegal migrants is 200 million (Roberts 2008). As floods

global migration crisis a severe problem stemming from the growing number of people moving from their home country to another country, straining the ability of the host countries to absorb the foreign emigrants.

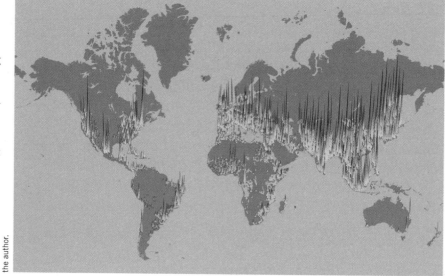

Atlantic Monthly, October 2005: pp. 48–49. Reproduced by permission from the author.

MAP 14.2

A WORLD THAT IS "SPIKY," NOT FLAT As this map shows, "more and more people are clustering in urban areas—the world's demographic mountain ranges, so to speak. The share of the world's population living in urban areas, just 3 percent in 1800, was nearly 30 percent by 1950" (Atlantic Monthly 2005, p. 48). At the start of 2011, nearly half of the world's population lives in urban areas (WDI 2010). "Rapid urban growth . . . can pose major challenges. While people may be attracted by the better opportunities available in cities, it is nonetheless true that local services and amenities may come under severe strain. This can be seen in large cities, such as Calcutta and Lagos, as well as the myriad medium-sized cities, from Colombo to Guayaquil to Nairobi" (HDR 2009, p. 86).

of people leave their homeland for another country each year, cross-national migration has become a norm—so common in some places that leaving one's native country has almost become an expectation.

The mass movement by people living abroad has raised a host of moral issues, such as the ethnic balance inside host countries, the meaning of citizenship and sovereignty, the distribution of income, labor supply, *xenophobia*, the impact of multiculturalism, protection of basic human rights and prevention of exploitation, and the potential for large flows of migrants and refugees from *failed states*—countries whose governments no longer enjoy support from their rebelling citizens and from displaced peoples who either flee the country or organize revolts to divide the state into smaller independent units—to undermine democratic governance and state stability (see Chapters 5 and 7). Particularly troubling is the moral inconsistency between liberal democracies that simultaneously defend the fundamental right of refugees to emigrate and the absolute right of sovereign states to control their borders.

The governments of sovereign states are losing their grip on regulating the movement of foreigners inside their borders, and no multilateral IGOs for meaningful global governance exist to deal with the consequences of the escalating migration of people (and labor) around the globe. Porous borders create ambiguous ethics about mass migration movements, but one consequence is clear: there are both winners and losers through the globalization of migration.

People most commonly migrate in search of better jobs. For host countries, this can contribute to economic growth. For example, the Hellenic Migration Policy Initiative in Greece attributes 1.5 to 2.0 percent of the growth in GDP each year to immigration (Roberts 2008). For the home countries, many of which are poor Global South countries, the growing flow of *remittances* or money that migrants earn while working abroad and then send to their families in their home countries provides one of the biggest sources of foreign currency (Singer 2010; Lopez et al. 2010). In 2009, migrants from the Global South sent home $316 billion (*The Economist* 2010, p. 97).

Yet there are worries that migration may reduce the job opportunities for natives and place a strain on public services. These fears are all the more exacerbated by the weak global economy, and many countries have adopted measures intended to stem the flow of peoples across borders (Koser 2010). In the United States, construction continues to extend the line of fences along the border with Mexico. In 2009, the European Parliament implemented controversial immigration rules that provide for illegal immigrants to be detained up to eighteen months and then expelled. Even countries in the Global South, such as Nigeria, took steps to counter what is seen as a security threat posed by large flows of illegal immigrants (Ekhoragbon 2008).

The Global Refugee Crisis   Another trend in our "age of migration" is the flight of people not in search of economic opportunity but out of fear of persecution. *Refugees* are individuals whose race, religion, nationality, membership in a particular social group, or political opinions make them targets of persecution in their homelands and who, therefore, migrate from their country of origin, unable to return. According to the UN High Commissioner for Refugees (UNHCR), at the start of 2010, the world's refugee population was a staggering 15.2 million, of whom 10.4 million fell under UNHCR's mandate and 4.8 million Palestinian refugees fell under the responsibility of the United Nations Relief and Works Agency for Palestinian Refugees in the Near East (UNRWA). Also included as "persons of concern" are internally displaced persons (IDPs), which the UNHCR estimated at 27.1 million worldwide (see Figure 14.2). These may be conservative estimates, however; they only account for individuals who fell under the

refugees
people who flee for safety to another country because of a well-founded fear of political persecution, environmental degradation, or famine.

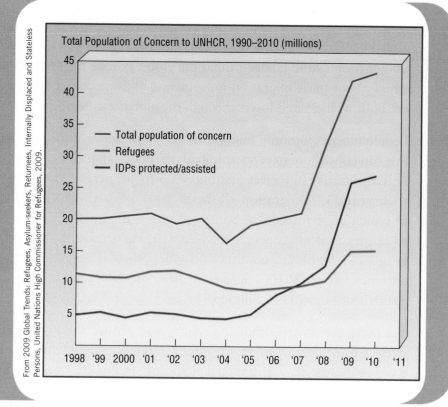

From 2009 Global Trends: Refugees, Asylum-seekers, Returnees, Internally Displaced and Stateless Persons, United Nations High Commissioner for Refugees, 2009.

FIGURE 14.2

THE CHRONIC GLOBAL REFUGEE CRISIS **The UN Refugee Agency (UNHCR) defines "persons of concern" as refugees and internally displaced persons (IDPs). The problem is huge and has become steadily worse since 2004, climbing to over 43 million forcibly displaced people at the start of 2010 (UNHCR 2010). Forty-one percent of refugees are children under eighteen years of age.**

genocide
the attempt to eliminate, in whole or in part, an ethnic, racial, religious, or national minority group.

ethnic cleansing
the extermination of an ethnic minority group by a state.

Simulation: *Forces of Globalization vs. Nationalism and Religion*

UNHCR's mandate. Additionally, though not considered displaced *per se*, there are about 12 million stateless people worldwide and 983,000 asylum seekers (UNHCR 2010). This does not include the additional millions of children and women kidnapped by crime rings in the huge sex-trafficking trade and smuggled across borders as captives for prostitution.

Refugees and displaced persons alike are often the victims of war and political violence. For example, *genocide* in Rwanda in 1994 drove more than 1.7 million refugees from their homeland; the persecution, *ethnic cleansing*, and armed conflict that accompanied the breakup of the former Yugoslavia uprooted nearly 3 million victims, moving Europe to the list of continents with large numbers of refugees—over 6 million—for the first time since World War II. More recently, the UNHCR estimates that Afghan and Iraqi refugees comprise almost half of all refugees. At the start of 2010, one out of four refugees in the world was from Afghanistan while 1.8 million Iraqis sought refuge in other countries (UNHCR 2010).

A large proportion of the world's refugees and displaced people flee their own homelands when ethnic and religious conflicts erupt in failed states where governments fail to preserve domestic law and order. In addition, millions of refugees flee their homelands because when disaster strikes they are denied basic human rights such as police protection, access to fair trials in courts, and public assistance. A combination of push-and-pull forces now propels migration trends. Human rights violations, environmental degradation, unemployment, overpopulation, famine, war, and ethnic conflict and *atrocities* within states—all push millions beyond their homelands (see Map 14.3).

atrocities
brutal and savage acts against targeted citizen groups or prisoners of war, defined as illegal under international law.

Migrants also are pulled abroad by the promise of political freedom elsewhere, particularly in the democratically ruled Global North countries. "We are now faced with a complex mix of global challenges that could threaten even more forced displacement in the future," explains António Guterres, the UN high commissioner. "They range from multiple new conflict-related emergencies in world hot spots to bad governance, climate-induced environmental degradation that increases competition for scarce resources and extreme price hikes that have hit the poor the hardest and are generating instability in many places" (*International Herald Tribune*, 2008, p. 3).

Video: *A Ticking Bomb*

From UNHCR 2010, p. 8. Reproduced with permission

Major refugee origin
- > 500,000
- 250,000 to 500,000
- 100,000 to 250,000
- 10,000 to 100,000
- < 10,000

MAP 14.3

FROM WHENCE DO THEY FLEE? Oppressive and violent conditions cause many people to leave their homes in the interest of security and survival. While it is commonly assumed that Western states admit the most refugees from conflict, evidence indicates instead that most refugees flee to neighboring countries in the Global South. Indeed, the UNHCR estimates that between 83 and 90 percent of refugees remain within their region of origin. As the leading country of origin of the world's refugees, at the start of 2010, 2.9 million refugees were from Afghanistan and were located in 71 asylum countries. Iraq was the second largest country of origin, responsible for 1.8 million refugees. Somali and Congolese refugees followed as third and fourth, respectively, with over 678,000 and 455,000 refugees.

xenophobia
the suspicious dislike, disrespect, and disregard for members of a foreign nationality, ethnic, or linguistic group.

Yet today's refugees are not finding safe havens; shutting the door is increasingly viewed as a solution (Koser 2010) and *xenophobia* is on the rise. Among both developed and developing countries, there is a growing unwillingness to provide refuge for those seeking a better life. With a weakening global economy, people are ever more resistant to foreigners competing for domestic jobs or resources. Moreover, as security concerns since 9/11 have escalated worldwide, the linkage drawn between refugees and the probability of terrorism has tightened immigration controls.

Not only have countries in the Global North restricted the flow of people across borders, but those in the Global South are increasingly unwilling to bear the burden of hosting refugees. This places blame for insecurity on the victims—refugees seeking refuge—because "as a general rule, individuals and communities do not abandon their homes unless they are confronted with serious threats to their lives and liberty. Flight from one's country is the ultimate survival strategy. . . . Refugees serve both as an index of internal disorder and the violation of human rights and humanitarian standards" (Loescher 2005, p. 47).

sanctuary
a place of refuge and protection.

asylum
the provision of sanctuary to safeguard refugees escaping from the threat of persecution in the country where they hold citizenship.

That said, efforts to stem the tide of migrants have not reversed the trend of people seeking *sanctuary*. By the start of 2010, a total of 922,500 applications for *asylum* or refugee status were submitted to governments and UNHCR offices in 159 countries (UNHCR 2010). This represented the third consecutive annual increase and constituted a 5 percent increase over the prior year. The increase can be explained by the more than 222,000 asylum applications to South Africa, making it the globe's largest recipient of individual applications, followed by the United States and France. Over 18,700 asylum applications, the highest number in four years, were submitted by unaccompanied children in seventy-one countries, with most from Afghan and Somali children (UNHCR 2010).

human security
a measure popular in liberal theory of the degree to which the welfare of individuals is protected and promoted, in contrast to realist theory's emphasis on putting the state's interests in military and national security ahead of all other goals.

The ethical issue is whether in the future the wealthy countries will respond to the plight of the needy with indifference or with compassion. How will *human security* be reconciled with *national security*? The welfare and survival of everyday people are endangered, and the need for their protection is increasing.

national security
a country's psychological freedom from fears that the state will be unable to resist threats to its survival and national values emanating from abroad or at home.

The globe on the horizon is, by these accounts, rife with challenge. Globalization portends many prospects on which people are basing their hopes. But globalization is breeding many demographic countertrends spelling doom and gloom that are provoking peoples' fears about their future. Threats, such as the outbreak of a widespread and deadly disease, could produce a *population implosion*. Next we will look at examples of life-threatening diseases that are sweeping a globe without borders.

population implosion
a rapid reduction of population that reverses a previous trend toward progressively larger populations; a severe reduction in the world's population.

NEW PLAGUES? THE GLOBAL IMPACT OF DISEASE

Although infant and child mortality rates remain discouragingly high in much of the developing countries, at least they are decreasing. On a global level, life expectancy at birth each year since 1950 has increased, climbing by UN estimates to sixty-nine years (WDI 2010, p. 146). However, this trend in

John Moore/Getty Images

UNICEF/AP Photo

DESPERATE REFUGEES ON THE RUN On average, over the last decade about 15 million refugees *each year* have become homeless people in search of sanctuary. Shown here (left) is one example: immigrants from Zimbabwe who are trying to get into a refugee center in Johannesburg, South Africa. Political violence surrounded the illegitimate reelection of President Robert Mugabe in 2008, with some saying "they had been coerced, fearing punishment or even death unless they could produce a finger colored with red ink as evidence of having cast a ballot" (*International Herald Tribune*, 2008, p. 3). Shown right is actress Angelina Jolie, pictured with refugee children in northeastern Congo. As a Goodwill Ambassador for the United Nations High Commissioner for Refugees (UNHCR), an agency that currently assists over 20 million refugees in roughly 120 countries, Jolie explains that "I just had to do something to help."

rising longevity could reverse if globally transmittable diseases cut into the extension of life spans made possible by improvements in healthcare, nutrition, water quality, and public sanitation.

Throughout history, the spread of bacteria, parasites, viruses, plagues, and diseases to various ecospheres, regardless of state borders, has suspended development or brought down once mighty states and empires (Kolbert 2005). In our age of globalization, a disease such as drug-resistant strains of tuberculosis (TB), which affects more than nine million people worldwide each year (WDI 2010, p. 34, 42), knows no borders. It can spread with a sneeze or a cough on an international flight. Likewise, there are about 250 million cases of malaria each year, leading to more than 1 million deaths (WHO Malaria Report 2008, p. 9). Because communicable diseases cause one-third of deaths worldwide (UC Atlas of Global Inequality 2009), global health is a concern and a threat to human security (see Figure 14.3).

The grim possibility that virulent disease will decimate the world's population because we all share a common global environment is made nowhere more evident than in the spread of the *human immunodeficiency virus (HIV)* that causes *acquired immune deficiency syndrome (AIDS)*. Since the 1970s onset of the AIDS pandemic, the UN estimates that "every day

human immunodeficiency virus (HIV)
a virus that can lead to the lethal acquired immune deficiency syndrome (AIDS).

acquired immune deficiency syndrome (AIDS)
an often fatal condition that can result from infection with the human immunodeficiency virus (HIV).

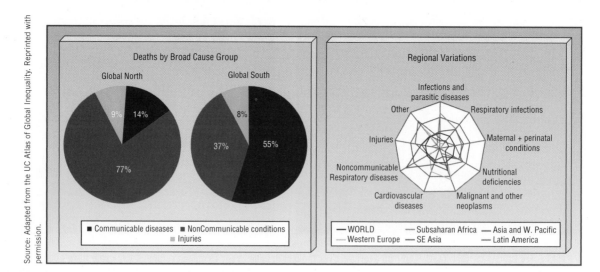

Source: Adapted from the UC Atlas of Global Inequality. Reprinted with permission.

FIGURE 14.3

THE BURDEN OF DISEASE Globally, one out of three people die from infectious disease. Yet a death divide is apparent between the Global North and the Global South. Shown on the left, over half of deaths in the Global South are caused by communicable disease, with HIV/AIDS as the most common culprit. In the Global North, people tend to live longer and die from noncommunicable conditions such as cardiovascular disease and cancer. On the right, the radar graph shows regional differences in the cause of death.

more than 8,000 people die of AIDS. Every hour almost 600 people become infected. Every minute a child dies of the virus." Today, 5.4 billion people worldwide between the ages of fifteen and forty-nine have HIV (WDI 2010), though some regions of the world suffer more from the disease than others. Sub-Saharan Africa, which is home to just over 10 percent of the global population, holds 67 percent of the people living with HIV/AIDS (Iqbal and Zorn 2010).

The circumstances are tragic, and stopping the tragedy is "a moral duty" even though the UN estimates that the AIDS pandemic is beginning to lose momentum. At the start of 2009, more than 33 million people worldwide were infected with HIV; the number of new infections peaked in 1998 at 3.4 million and the number of deaths peaked in 2005 (UNAIDS 2009). This does not mean that the epidemic is vanishing: in many of the most seriously AIDS-affected countries, deaths are projected to overtake births and cause population decreases in the next few years. Thus, as world public health expert Laurie Garrett notes, "Tackling the world's diseases has become a key feature of many nations' foreign policies."

DOES GLOBALIZATION MAKE THE WHOLE WORLD SICK? The dangerous threat of a global flu pandemic "ranks higher than a major terrorist attack, even one involving weapons of mass destruction" (*Newsweek* 2005). Shown here is a cause for global alarm: at a market in Shanghai, workers sleep with their chickens, and close contact with infected birds is the primary source of deadly hybrids of human and animal viruses.

Sadly, there are many diseases that pose significant threats to human well-being and remind us of just how permeable are our national borders. Malaria is a major threat to global health, with the Center for Disease Control reporting 300 to 500 million cases of malaria annually, of which over one million result in death (Lyons 2010). This is tragic because the disease, which is transmitted by mosquitoes to humans, is largely preventable and treatable. Efforts to combat the spread of the disease include the distribution of millions of insecticide-treated bed nets.

Avian flu, the so-called bird flu, is also of global concern as, according to the WHO, the most recent outbreak "has been the most deadly of all the influenza viruses that have spread from birds to humans, killing more than half of the people infected" (Vital Signs 2007–2008, p. 90), with fatal cases continuing to be reported in 2010. Since the outbreak in 2003, at least 298 people have died from the disease (World Health Organization 2010) and hundreds of millions of chickens, ducks, and other birds have been killed in an effort to curb its spread. Experts believe the disease can be spread through the direct handling of chickens and the processing of meat and are extremely concerned that the disease "will mutate into a virus that can easily spread from person-to-person, sparking a pandemic."

Video: *Treating Swine Flu*

What makes influenza different from other global diseases is the frightening ease with which it spreads. Another deadly strain of influenza, one that crossed the species barrier between pigs and people and is known as H1N1 or swine flu, captured global attention as it reached pandemic proportions and policy makers and healthcare officials raced to combat the infectious disease through public health measures. First appearing in Mexico in March 2009 and then spreading quickly to the United States, by July 2010 it had appeared in at least 214 countries and overseas territories (see Map 14.4).

Though the pandemic was of only moderate severity, diseases with a risk of widespread population vulnerability to infection pose a particular challenge for public officials as they seek to identify and enact protective measures for the population. A number of countries, particularly China and Russia, took vigorous quarantine measures against people who had traveled to countries suffering from a high number of infected people.

The spread and control of infectious diseases such as AIDS, tuberculosis, malaria, Lassa fever, Ebola, lymphatic filariasis, Avian flu, mad cow disease, and swine flu have established themselves on the radar screen

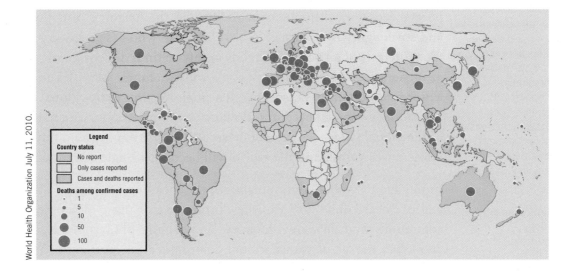

World Health Organization July 11, 2010.

MAP 14.4

PANDEMIC (H1N1) 2009... AND COUNTING **This map shows the severity of the swine flu global health crisis. First detected in Mexico, on June 11, 2009 the outbreak of swine flu was declared a global pandemic. This was the first designation by the World Health Organization of a worldwide influenza pandemic in forty-one years, though it was criticized by some as overstating the threat of the disease. As of August 2010 the disease had claimed the lives of 18,449 people from 214 countries, though the number of incidents in 2010 had declined dramatically from the year prior.**

of policy makers throughout the world. They will not vanish from sight anytime soon, and are a stark reminder of the transnational threats that are present in our borderless world and necessitate global cooperation and coordination.

> *A relationship exists between the health of individuals within a state and that state's national security. A population's health is of utmost importance to the state's ability to survive.*
>
> —Jeremy Youde, global health expert

THE GLOBAL INFORMATION AGE

Pessimists predict that one result of globalization is competition between states as they seek to preserve their sovereign independence, retain the allegiance of their citizens, resist the homogenizing forces now sweeping the world, and ensure their own national security. In contrast, in a more optimistic scenario,

cosmopolitan
an outlook that values viewing the cosmos or entire world as the best polity or unit for political governance and personal identity, as opposed to other polities such as one's local metropolis or city of residence (e.g., Indianapolis or Minneapolis).

communications technology
the technological means through which information and communications are transferred.

liberal theory anticipates a globalization of cultures that transcends contemporary geopolitical boundaries and erodes the meaning of national identity and sovereignty by creating "global citizens" who assign loyalty to the common interests of all peoples. Trends in this cultural dimension of globalization are generating changes in how people construct their identities and encourage a more *cosmopolitan* perspective. The major source of this global transformation is the growing speed and flow of communications, which is a hallmark of the *global village*—a metaphor used by many to portray a future in which borders will vanish and the world will become a single community.

In the age of global communication, the meaning of "home" and "abroad" and of "near" and "far" vanishes, promoting changes in people's images of community and their own identity. Will cellular phones, the Internet, blogs, and other means of transnational communication portend consensus, and, perhaps, an integrated global village? Or is this vision of such a global village, in which shared information breeds understanding and peace, pure mythology? Worse, will the virus of interconnectiveness within globalization do away with private life, erasing what remains of identity, individualism, and independence?

Visions of America LLC/Alamy Limited

THE WORLD AT ONE'S FINGER TIPS   The revolution in telecommunications has contributed to "the death of distance," as virtually instantaneous communications are possible nearly everywhere. Here, in a remote and desolate region of northern Kenya, a Masai warrior makes a call on his cellular telephone.

The Evolution of Global Communications

The increased ease and volume of international communications is causing "the death of distance" and radically altering people's decisions about where to work and to live, as well as their images of "us" and "them." No area of the world and no arena of politics, economics, society, or culture is immune from the pervasive influence of *communications technology*. Communication between areas as diverse as rural communities in the Global South and "wired" Global North countries is facilitated by personal computers and the "wireless world" of mobile or cellular phones. In addition to the abundance of more than one billion personal computers (PCs) and one billion fixed-line telephones, the "four billion cellphones in use around the world carry personal information and provide access to the Web and are being used more and more to navigate the real world" (Markoff 2009, p. 1).

The result of the expanding worldwide use of the Internet is the creation of a *cyberspace*, a global information superhighway allowing people everywhere to communicate freely without constraints as they surf the Web, exchange e-mails, and join social networking sites. The increasing number of Internet users (by about a million *weekly*) is promoting a cultural revolution by giving most of the world access to information for the first time. This creates a single globe, united in shared information. This face of globalization submerges borders and breaks barriers. It lays the foundation for a smaller, shrinking, and flatter world and propels "an exciting new era of global interconnectedness that will spread ideas and innovations around the world faster than ever before" (Giles 2010, p. 4).

The growth of Internet *blogs*, or active diarists known as "bloggers" who share their opinions with a global audience, adds to the influence of what has become known as "the information age." Drawing on the content of the international media and the Internet, bloggers weave together an elaborate network with agenda-setting power on issues ranging from human rights in China to the U.S. occupation of Iraq to electoral fraud in Iran. "What began as a hobby is evolving into a new medium that is changing the landscape for journalists and policymakers alike" (Drezner and Farrell 2006).

That trend is accelerating by leaps and bounds with the rapid diffusion of iPods, text messaging, and the microblogging service known as Twitter that "restricts each entry, or tweet, to 140 characters (and) has managed to transcend basic instant messaging and social networking" (Kutcher 2009, p. 60). Added to this is the enormous popularity of *podcasts,* which allow people to create their own website channels and share audio and visual versions of new uploads with anyone throughout the world who signs on, and social networking sites such as Facebook, which enable people to share information with their friends.

If one constant stands out, it is continuous change in technological innovation. The rapid pace of *information technology (IT)* development drives globalization. It can make today's methods of communicating look ancient in a few years, and in the process is transforming how people communicate as well as which countries lead (and prosper) and which follow.

To enthusiasts, the advantages of the global communications revolution are a blessing for humanity. When people are connected worldwide through the revolution in digital communications, the shared information propels human development and productivity. Proponents also see the globalized digital revolution as producing many side payoffs: reducing oppressive dictators' authority, allowing small business to successfully compete globally,

cyberspace
a metaphor used to describe the global electronic web of people, ideas, and interactions on the Internet, which is unencumbered by the borders of the geopolitical world.

blogs
online diaries, which spread information and ideas worldwide in the manner of journalists.

podcasts
technology that enables individuals to create audio and visual programs and make them available as digital downloads.

information technology (IT)
the techniques for storing, retrieving, and disseminating through computerization and the Internet recorded data and research knowledge.

empowering transnational activists to exercise more influence, and providing opportunities for a diversity of voices and cultures.

For example, in 2009, through the use of information technology such as Twitter and the online video-sharing site YouTube, Iranians were able "to document and disseminate to the world images of and information on repression in the wake of the recent election. Through these online outlets, photographs and short films showing police forces beating and bloodying protesters" circumvented the Iranian government's attempts to control Internet access (Quirk 2009). They were seen around the world, and served to sustain Iranian dissatisfaction with the ruling regime, particularly among those two-thirds of Iranians that are thirty years of age and younger. As famous actor and Twitter enthusiast Ashton Kutcher hopefully noted, "Right now the word *revolution* is spelled with 140 characters."

On the other hand, there is a "dark side" to the global communications revolution. Critics complain that the growing electronic network has created a new global condition known as ***virtuality***. In such a world, one can conceal one's true identity, which threatens to make the activities of international organized crime and terrorist groups easier, as illustrated by the global terrorist network Al Qaeda's use of computers to coordinate the destruction of the World Trade Center towers in New York on September 11, 2001.

virtuality
imagery created by computer technology of objects and phenomena that produces an imaginary picture of actual things, people, and experiences.

The specter is also raised that "privateness will become passé [through] the spread of surveillance technology and the rise of Websites like YouTube, which receives more than 65,000 video uploads daily and is driving a trend toward cyber-exhibitionism" (*Futurist* 2007, p. 6). New privacy issues are likely to arise as researchers and corporations figure out how to use all of the information about a user's location that can be determined through information technology services, such as that by Internet providers and cell phone companies. "You may use your phone to find friends and restaurants, but somebody else may be using your phone to find you and find out about you" (Markoff 2009, p. 1). Similarly, online social networks, like Facebook which has a global membership that would place it as the world's third most populous country, encourage users to share information. Then, the networks mine the data on members' personal preferences (Fletcher 2010).

In the name of national security, governments are also developing extensive surveillance systems that discreetly monitor activities, many in public spaces. One example is the high-tech surveillance program in China, known as "Golden Shield," that will identify dissent and allow the government to address it before it turns into a mass movement. Using people-tracking technology supplied by American corporations like General Electric, IBM, and Honeywell, the goal is to create "a single, nationwide network, an all-seeing system that will be capable of tracking and identifying anyone who comes within its range" (Klein 2008, p. 60).

Venezuelan President Hugo Chavez also uses the power of the Web to interact with his country's people. "But far from embracing the democratic spirit of the Web, the Venezuelan strongman is harnessing it as a tool of repression" (Margolis and Marin 2010, p. 6). He launched his Twitter account in an effort to encourage people to report on the activities of others—particularly the wealthy—announcing that "my Twitter account is open for you to denounce them."

Critics also warn that even as Internet use and commerce grow, the communications revolution is widening the gap between the rich and the poor, leading to the globalization of poverty and the destruction of local culture. Noting that access to and use of the Internet is heavily concentrated in the Global North (see Map 14.5), the critics fear that the advantages of the digital communication for small entrepreneurs in the Global South will not be shared and that the *digital divide* in access to *communications technology* is not closing as rapidly as expected. At present, the Global North (and particularly the United States, where the Internet was developed) remains predominant and the primary beneficiary of the IT revolution. However, the growing capacity of many U.S. rivals to excel in IT innovation is rapidly closing the gap.

digital divide
the division between the Internet-technology-rich Global North and the Global South in the proportion of Internet users and hosts.

The Politics and Business of Global Communication

The more than $1 trillion global telecommunications industry is without question the major vehicle for the rapid spread of ideas, information, and images worldwide. That impact accelerated after the World Trade Organization (WTO) created the World Telecom Pact in 1997. This *regime* ended government and private telecommunications monopolies in many states and the resulting cuts in phone costs were widely seen as a catalyst to the world economy's expansion.

This development has been augmented by advances in information technology, and the expansive scope of global media. Yet, contrary to conventional wisdom that the media has the ability to drive a country's foreign policy, the type of power the media wield over international affairs is arguably specific and limited. Scholarship shows that the media influence what people *think about* more than what they *think*. In this way, the media primarily function to set the agenda of public discussion about public affairs instead of determining public opinion.

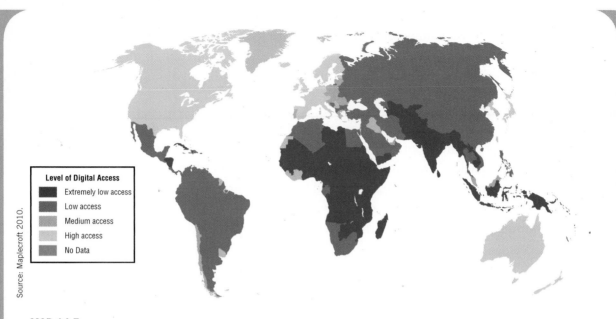

Level of Digital Access

- Extremely low access
- Low access
- Medium access
- High access
- No Data

MAP 14.5

THE DIGITAL DIVIDE IN INFORMATION AND COMMUNICATION TECHNOLOGIES **Information and communication technology (ICT) has spread rapidly in recent years. However, the level of penetration varies both among and within countries; a digital divide has emerged where some countries have high levels of access and others have limited access. Based on the Digital Inclusion Risk Index 2010, which takes into account access to personal computers, internet and broadband, mobile telephones and fixed-line telephones, the map above depicts relative levels of access to ICT across the globe. Countries are grouped into four categories that range from high to low ICT access. As shown, the United States enjoys high access while countries in Sub-Saharan Africa have limited access.**

agenda setting
the thesis that by their ability to identify and publicize issues, the communications media determine the problems that receive attention from governments and international organizations.

In the process of *agenda setting,* the media demonstrably shape international public policy (see Gilboa 2002). For example, global broadcasts of the ruthless repression and illegitimate tactics associated with Mugabe's bid for reelection in Zimbabwe in 2008 ignited a worldwide chain reaction to aid that country's refugees and pressure the government to reform. Similarly, reports by professional journalists and individual activists helped to fan Iranian resistance and protest over the declared electoral victory of incumbent president Mahmoud Ahmadinejad in 2009.

These examples of the power of information technology in international politics aside, some people caution that this kind of "virtual diplomacy" has real limitations. Not only can it constrain the policy options available to global decision makers, but it can provide biased or incomplete information that may contribute to an inaccurate or limited understanding of global problems.

Moreover, though ours is often described as the information age, a remarkably large portion of the available information is controlled by a *cartel* of a handful of huge multinational media corporations. Headquartered mostly in the rich Global North, these industry leaders are merging to combine their resources and, in the process, expanding their global reach. They keep "us fully entertained and perhaps half-informed, always growing here and shriveling there, with certain of its members bulking up, while others slowly fall apart or get digested whole. But while the players tend to come and go—always with a few exceptions—the overall leviathan itself keeps getting bigger, louder, mightier, forever taking up more time and space, in every street, in countless homes, in every other head" (Miller 2006). The world's population is a captive audience, and the information presented by these corporate giants shapes our values and our images of what the world is like.

Not surprisingly, the message of international events and ideas projected by the media is highly reflective of Western culture. The handful of news and information agencies operate like a giant circulatory system, pumping ideas, information, and ideals from the wealthy center to the remote periphery in the Global South. The Internet, CNN, and MTV are media channels with global reach centered in the Global North.

What Global South opponents of globalization complain about is not so much modernization and trade; rather, they oppose "corporate globalization" dictated by mass media multinational corporations (MNCs) that, they contend, ignore the values and needs of the vast majority in the developing world. Nonetheless, most of the growth in the media industries is expected to occur in the Global South over the next five years. "The fastest growth is expected in Latin America, with spending set to jump at a 10.6 percent annual rate," followed by the Asia-Pacific region at 8.8 percent, and the Middle East, Africa, and Europe at 6.8 percent (Pfanner 2008, p. 13).

Whatever its true character, advocates see global telecommunications as a vehicle for progress, liberating minds, expanding choices, penetrating societies closed to diplomatic communication, and creating a single, more united, homogenized global culture. Others disagree, however. They note that the airwaves can broadcast divisive messages as well as unifying ones, and that what is said is more important than how much is said.

A counterpoint, therefore, to the "McWorld" of transnational media consumerism is "Jihad"—a world driven by "parochial hatreds," not "universalizing markets" (Barber 1995). Because globalized communications and information may be used as tools for terrorism and revolution as well as

cartel
a convergence of independent commercial enterprises or political groups that combine for collective action, such as limiting competition, setting prices for their services, or forming a coalition to advance their group's interests.

for community and peace, the creation of a world without boundaries, where everybody will know everything about anybody's activities, will not necessarily be a better world. You should ask: Would the world be better or worse if it were to become an increasingly impersonal place, with rootless individuals with declining connections to their own country's culture and history?

> *People from all over the world will draw knowledge and inspiration from the same technology platform, but different cultures will flourish on it. It is the same soil, but different trees will grow. The next phase of globalization is going to be more glocalization—more and more local content made global.*
>
> —Thomas L. Friedman, *international journalist*

GLOBALIZATION AND THE GLOBAL FUTURE

Rapid globalization, propelled in large measure by revolutions in technology, is almost certain to continue. Is globalization desirable, or despicable?

Expect the controversies about globalization's alleged virtues and vices to heighten as finance, trade, population, labor, communications, and cultures continue to converge globally. Whereas globalization has narrowed the distance between the world's people, some have gained and others have lost ground. The *global village* is not proving to be an equally hospitable home for everyone. Indeed, levels of satisfaction with cascading globalization vary widely, as do the levels to which countries and people are linked to globalization's multiple forces (see Figure 14.4). Winners in the game downplay the cost of global integration, and critics deny globalization's benefits. And the debate about globalization's problematic impact is intensifying, but without resolution, as the debaters are hardening their positions without listening to the counter arguments.

You have now taken into account a number of dimensions of the trend toward globalization—in international economics, demography, global communication, and the potential spread of universal values for the entire world. If the trends you have surveyed actually do culminate for the first time in a global consensus uniting all of humanity, these values and understandings might unify all people on Earth into a common global culture. This could conceivably prepare the way for the advent of a global *civil society*, even with the eventual emergence of supranational institutions to govern all of humanity.

Yet this worldview and set of predictions strikes fear into the hearts of many people who experience *cognitive dissonance* when they confront a frightening vision that challenges their customary way of thinking about world affairs. These people (and there are multitudes) strenuously reject the idea that the traditional system of independent sovereign states can or should be replaced by a global community with strong supranational regulatory institutions for global governance.

So conclude your inspection of globalization's influence on world politics by evaluating the available evidence and sorting out the balance sheet of globalization's costs and benefits (see Controversy: Is Globalization Helpful or Harmful?). What do prevailing trends tell you? Is Thomas Friedman's "flat world" concept that globalization has emasculated the state as an "electronic herd" tramples down borders valid? Or is Daniel Drezner (2007) more accurate in arguing that "states make the rules" and that powerful governments are still in control of shaping global destiny because "great powers cajole and coerce those who disagree with them into accepting the same rulebook"?

THE MAKING OF A GLOBAL CULTURE? Some people regard globalization as little more than the spread of values and beliefs of the globe's reigning hegemon, the United States. Shown here is one image that fuels that point of view—an enormous inflated Santa Claus in front of a hotel in downtown Hanoi, Vietnam—a predominantly Buddhist city still subscribing to the communist principles emphasizing the greed of market capitalism and the class divisions it is believed to create. The sale of Christmas trees is rising there, too.

Globalization is real, for better or for worse. Many people recommend globalization for international public policy, because they believe that its consequences are basically good for humankind. However, critics argue that globalization's costs far outweigh its benefits. As the pace of globalization has become a recognized force in world politics, it also has become a heated topic of debate. Globalization has hit a political speed bump, provoking intense critical evaluation of globalization's causes, characteristics, and consequences and inspiring fresh ethical examination of the elevated interdependence of countries and humans. The uncertain wisdom and morality of globalization may be the most discussed issue on today's global agenda, receiving even more attention than poverty, disease, urbanization, or the preservation of identity.

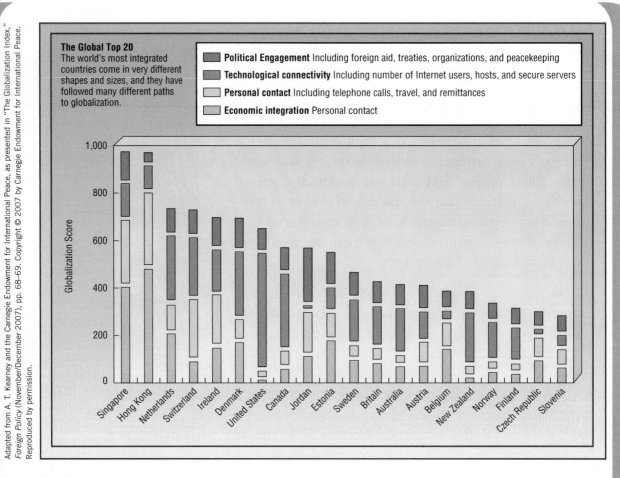

The Global Top 20
The world's most integrated countries come in very different shapes and sizes, and they have followed many different paths to globalization.

■ **Political Engagement** Including foreign aid, treaties, organizations, and peacekeeping
■ **Technological connectivity** Including number of Internet users, hosts, and secure servers
□ **Personal contact** Including telephone calls, travel, and remittances
□ **Economic integration** Personal contact

FIGURE 14.4

LEVELS OF GLOBALIZATION In an effort to take stock of globalization's progress, this index examines multiple indicators spanning trade, business, politics, and information technology to determine the rankings of the seventy-two countries that together account for 97 percent of the world's gross domestic product and 88 percent of the world's population to gauge which countries are globalizing and which are not (*Foreign Policy* 2007, pp. 68–69).

COURSEMATE

Case Study:
*Interdependence and
Future International
Politics*

The age of globalization has far-reaching implications for humanity. In the next chapter of *World Politics,* you will consider the circumstances of the 6.8 billion human beings striving throughout the world to sustain themselves, improve the human condition, and obtain the human rights promised in the U.S. Declaration of Independence: life, liberty, and happiness for all humanity.

CONTROVERSY:

IS GLOBALIZATION HELPFUL OR HARMFUL?

To many students of international relations, globalization displays two faces, one positive and the other negative. To those whose perceptions focus on globalization's benefits, globalization is a blessing that should be promoted to deepen and widen its helpful effects. They believe that globalization helps to break down traditional divisions of humanity—between races, nations, and cultures—that are barriers to peace, prosperity, and justice. To others, globalization is a harmful phenomenon, breeding such things as global disease and threats to local job security, and therefore a force to be resisted.

Imagine yourself writing a report such as the evaluation that the International Labour Organization undertook when it challenged itself to provide "new thinking to break the deadlock and bridge the divide about the globalization debate." To frame your analysis, see if your evaluation would support or question the World Commission's conclusion (Somavia 2004, p. 6):

> Globalization can and must change. [We acknowledge] globalization's potential for good—promoting open societies, open economies, and freer exchange of goods, knowledge, and ideas. But the Commission also found deep-seated and persistent imbalances in the current workings of the global economy that are ethically unacceptable and politically unsustainable.

> The gap between people's income in the richest and poorest countries has never been wider . . . Global unemployment is at its highest level ever. More than one billion people are either unemployed, underemployed, or working poor. Clearly, globalization's benefits are out of reach for far too many people.

An alternative exercise would be to make an ethical assessment of the morality or immorality of globalization. This is what the philosopher Peter Singer did in *One World: The Ethics of Globalization* (2004). In it, he applies as a criterion the utilitarian principle that it is a moral duty to maximize the happiness and welfare of all human beings and even animal welfare. Singer sees great benefits to the retreat of the doctrine of state sovereignty and to the advance of the view that the entire world should be the unit of ethical analysis. Global interdependence encourages global thinking and a moral outlook because it promotes one's ethical responsibilities to act from awareness that there is only "one community," "one law," "one economy," and "one atmosphere." This is beneficial, to Singer, because globalization gives all of us great incentives to perform our utilitarian duty toward others. His conclusion springs from a UN report that observed, "In the global village, someone else's poverty very soon becomes one's own problem: illegal immigration, pollution, contagious disease, insecurity, fanaticism, terrorism." Under globalization, altruism and concern for others pay dividends, whereas narrow selfish behavior causes the selfish competitor counterproductive harm. To this logic, globalization is beneficial.

Or try one last thought experiment. Think like an economist. This is what the famous Harvard social scientist Jagdish Bhagwati did in writing *In Defense of Globalization* (2004). Would your similar economic analysis of globalization agree with his conclusions? Richard N. Cooper (2004, pp. 152–53) summarizes Bhagwati's liberal theoretical position and propositions:

(continued)

CONTROVERSY:

IS GLOBALIZATION HELPFUL OR HARMFUL? (Continued)

The book addresses a slate of charges against globalization: that it increases poverty, encourages child labor, harms women, threatens democracy, imperils culture, lowers wages, erodes labor standards, worsens the environment, and gives full reign to predatory corporations. Bhagwati also discusses capital market liberalization and international migration before turning to fixes for globalization's downsides: improving governance, accelerating social agendas, and managing the speed of transitions. He concedes a few points to globalization's critics but, wielding logic and fact, demolishes most of the allegations made against it. His conclusion: that the world, particularly its poorest regions, needs more globalization, not less. . . . To the claim that globalization increases poverty, Bhagwati's response is, rubbish.

WHAT DO YOU THINK?

- On balance, do you think that the benefits of globalization outweigh the costs?

- As globalization creates both winners and losers, what policies do you think should be enacted to better protect the "losers" of globalization?

- How do you think realists would view the debate over globalization? To what extent would they part company with liberal and constructivist interpretations of globalization?

Take an Online Practice Quiz

www.cengagebrain.com/shop/ISBN/0495802204

| Suggested Readings |

Drache, Daniel. (2008) *Defiant Publics: The Unprecedented Reach of the Global Citizen.* Cambridge, UK: Polity.

Friedman, Thomas L. (2007) *The World Is Flat: A Brief History of the 21st Century.* New York: Farrar, Straus, and Giroux.

Trask, Bahira Sherif. (2010) *Globalization and Families: Accelerated Systemic Social Change.* New York: Springer.

UNDP. (2010) *Human Development Report 2010.* New York: United Nations.

UNHCR. (2008) *2007 Global Trends: Refugees, Asylum-Seekers, Returnees, Internally Displaced and Stateless Persons.* Geneva: UN High Commissioner for Refugees.

World Bank. (2009) *Atlas of Global Development*, 2nd edition. Washington, D.C.: World Bank.

CHAPTER 15
THE PROMOTION OF HUMAN DEVELOPMENT AND HUMAN RIGHTS

CHAPTER OUTLINE

PUTTING PEOPLE INTO THE PICTURE

How Does Humanity Fare?: The Human Condition Today

Measuring Human Development and Human Security

Globalization, Democratization, and Economic Prosperity

HUMAN RIGHTS AND THE PROTECTION OF PEOPLE

Internationally Recognized Human Rights

The Precarious Life of Indigenous Peoples

CONTROVERSY: What Is Security?

Gender Inequality and Its Consequences

Slavery and Human Trafficking

Children and Human Rights

RESPONDING TO HUMAN RIGHTS ABUSES

The Human Rights Legal Framework

The Challenge of Enforcement

CONTROVERSY: Should Tyranny and Human Rights Violations Justify Humanitarian Intervention?

*The only society that works today is also one founded on mutual respect,
on a recognition that we have a responsibility collectively and individually,
to help each other on the basis of each other's equal worth. A selfish society
is a contradiction in terms.*

—Tony Blair, former British Prime Minister

Omar Sobhani/Reuters/Landov

LIFE WITHOUT LIBERTY "The cost of liberty is less than the price of repression," African-American sociologist W.E.B. Dubois argued. Shown here are women protesting in Kabul, Afghanistan, to demand the repeal of a law that authorizes a range of extreme restrictions on human rights, including marital rape. Marching for rights and equality, Fatima Husseini said, "It means a woman is a kind of property, to be used by the man in any way that he wants."

Surfing the web last night, you came across a number of news stories that depicted the horrors that some people face in their daily lives. From living in conditions of squalor and poverty to being victimized by raping and pillaging by paramilitary forces, you are stunned and sickened at the trials and tribulations that many of those less fortunate than you must endure. Like most people with a heart and interest in making the world a better place, you hope for a better future for all of humanity. So what can be done to promote your values and bring about the needed transformations in world politics?

For many people the future is bleak, resembling how in 1651 the English political philosopher Thomas Hobbes described life as "solitary, poor, nasty, brutish, and short." The opportunities and choices that are most basic to freedom from fear and poverty are unavailable for most people in the Global South's poorest countries. They experience much slower rates of development and less *human security* than in the Global North, and the prospects of the "have-nots" are not improving.

human security
a measure popular in liberal theory of the degree to which the welfare of individuals is protected and promoted, in contrast to realist theory's emphasis on putting the state's interests in military and national security ahead of all other goals.

Given the serious deprivations facing so many people, there are many reasons for humanitarian concern. The denial to most humans of the inalienable rights to which all humans are presumably entitled—the "life, liberty, and the pursuit of happiness" of which the U.S. Declaration of Independence speaks—attests to the extent to which fundamental human security is not being met. This problem prompted Mary Robinson, the former UN High Commissioner for Human Rights, to "call on global actors—corporations, governments and the international financial organizations—to join with globalized civil society and share responsibility for humanizing globalization."

PUTTING PEOPLE INTO THE PICTURE

Until relatively recently in the unfolding evolution of the theoretical study of world politics, the needs of the faceless billions of everyday people were neglected. That past theoretical legacy, in this tradition, pictured the mass of humanity as marginalized victims or left them invisible by painting their fates as controlled by forces over which hapless people have little influence. French world-systems historian Fernand Braudel (1973, p. 1244) wrote that "when I think of the individual, I am always inclined to see him imprisoned within a destiny in which he himself has little hand, fixed in a landscape in which the infinite perspectives of the long-term stretch into the distance both behind and before."

When thinking about world affairs, the average person has long been relegated to a mere "subject" whom rulers were traditionally permitted to manipulate to advance their states' interests. That vision has been rejected throughout the world. A consensus now supports the view that people are important, that they have worth, and, therefore, that *ethics* and *morality* belong in the study of international relations. As defined by ethicist Ronald Dworkin (2001, p. 485), "Ethics includes convictions about what kinds of lives are good or bad for a person to lead, and morality includes principles about how a person should treat other people." These principles apply to interstate relations, and they are at the heart of analyses of human security in world politics.

That consensus notwithstanding, many observers embrace the traditional assumption of realism that vast global forces make people powerless. Realists recognize that people participate politically but claim they have no real power because an invisible set of powerful forces described as the "system" gives most human beings only superficial involvement without real influence.

agency
the capacity of actors to harness power to achieve objectives.

This denial of the importance and influence of individual human *agency* seems increasingly strange, because classic thinking about the world has long concentrated on people and on the essential character of human nature. As anthropologist Robert Redfield (1962) argued, "Human nature is itself a part of the method [of all analysis]. One must use one's own humanity as a means to understanding. The physicist need not sympathize with his atoms, nor the biologist with his fruit flies, but the student of people and institutions must employ [one's] natural sympathies in order to discover what people think or feel." A humanistic interpretation is needed that gives people status and value. Moreover, in the global community there is emerging a *civil society*. A normative consensus has grown about the inherent moral worth and status of humans and the concomitant obligation of states to recognize and protect that status (Fields and Lord 2004).

How can we progress to a world that is free of poverty and persecution? If you, as a student of international affairs, are to develop a more complete comprehension of the forces behind the prevailing trends in world politics, it is important to consider the conditions faced by humanity. This chapter introduces information about the human condition to enable you to evaluate the unfolding debate about the role of humans as actors on the global stage, the prospect for human development, and the ethics of *human rights*. Will humanity be valued, and will human welfare and rights be protected?

human rights
the political rights and civil liberties recognized by the international community as inalienable and valid for individuals in all countries by virtue of their humanity.

These are critical questions. Where does humanity fit into the prevailing and most popular *paradigms* or theoretical orientations that policy makers and scholars construct about what matters in world politics? For the most part, classical realism worships the state and its ruler's sovereign freedom, and, except for building its image of international reality from a pessimistic

AFP/Getty Images

HUMAN RIGHTS VERSUS STATES' RIGHTS "More than two-thirds of the countries of the world have abolished the death penalty in law or in practice. While fifty-eight countries retained the death penalty in 2009, most did not use it. Eighteen countries were known to have carried out executions, killing a total of at least 714 people" (Amnesty International 2010). The five countries with the greatest number of executions in 2009 were China—which refused to divulge official figures, though it is known that thousands of executions took place—Iran (at least 388), Iraq (at least 120), Saudi Arabia (at least 69), and the United States (52).

conception of human nature, it ignores the role of leaders and the *nongovernmental organizations* (NGOs) that people form. Liberals attach more importance to humans, following the ethical precept of German philosopher Immanuel Kant that people should be treated as ends and not means, and that therefore human rights and human dignity should be safeguarded. *Constructivism* goes further; it makes humanity the primary level of analysis and emphasizes how human ideas define identities that in turn impart meaning to material capabilities and the behavior of actors (see Chapter 2).

HOW DOES HUMANITY FARE? THE HUMAN CONDITION TODAY

"Man is born free, and everywhere he is in chains," political philosopher Jean Jacques Rousseau bemoaned in his famous 1762 book, *Social Contract*. Times have since changed. But in many respects Rousseau's characterization of the human condition remains accurate. How should we evaluate the depth of human deprivation and despair against this fact? Can the poorest proportion of humanity sever the chains of their disadvantages to realize their human potential and obtain the high ideals of human security, freedom, and dignity?

The inequalities and disparities evident in people's standards of living cannot help but to evoke sympathy for the difficult conditions faced by many people, especially for those in the less developed Global South countries. One American graduate student, when working on his Ph.D., painfully learned about the plight of people in the Global South during his field research in South America. Brian Wallace found a reality far different from his own experience of growing up in the southern United States. In 1978 he was moved to write:

> I spent the first 24 years of my life in South Carolina. When I left . . . for Colombia [South America], I fully expected Bogotá to be like any large U.S. city, only with citizens who spoke Spanish. When I arrived there I found my expectations were wrong. I was not in the U.S., I was on Mars! I was a victim of culture shock. As a personal experience this shock was occasionally funny and sometimes sad. But after all the laughing and the crying were over, it forced me to reevaluate both my life and the society in which I live.
>
> Colombia is a poor country by American standards. It has a per capita GNP of $550 and a very unequal distribution of income. These were the facts that I knew before I left.
>
> But to "know" these things intellectually is much different from experiencing firsthand how they affect people's lives. It is one thing to lecture in air conditioned classrooms about the problems of world poverty. It is quite another to see four-year-old children begging or sleeping in the streets.
>
> It tore me apart emotionally to see the reality of what I had studied for so long: "low per capita GNP and maldistribution of income." What this means in human terms is children with dirty faces who beg for bread money or turn into pickpockets because the principle of private property gets blurred by empty stomachs.
>
> It means other children whose minds and bodies will never develop fully because they were malnourished as infants. It means street vendors who sell candy and cigarettes 14 hours a day in order to feed their families.
>
> It also means well-dressed businessmen and petty bureaucrats who indifferently pass this poverty every day as they seek asylum in their fortified houses to the north of the city.
>
> It means rich people who prefer not to see the poor, except for maids and security guards.
>
> It means foreigners like me who come to Colombia and spend more in one month than the average Colombian earns in a year.

It means politicians across the ideological spectrum who are so full of abstract solutions or personal greed that they forget that it is real people they are dealing with.

Somewhere within the polemics of the politicians and the "objectivity" of the social scientists, the human being has been lost.

Despite wide differences that enable a proportion of humanity to enjoy unprecedented standards of living, a daunting scale of poverty and misery is evident throughout the world, from which only a small fraction of people in many countries have begun to escape (see Map 15.1). One indicator is money. According to the World Bank's definition of extreme poverty as income of one dollar and twenty-five cents or less a day, about 1.4 billion people (about 25 percent of the world) live in extreme poverty and another 2.6 billion (about 40 percent of world population) seek to survive on two dollars or less a day (WDI 2010, p. 92).

Income inequality is a serious global problem from which many other difficulties and disputes result. And that problem is entrenched: Consumption patterns show that the division between the rich and the poor is growing. Only about one-fifth of the globe's wealthiest people consume anywhere from two-thirds to nine-tenths of its resources. These proportions reflect the World Bank's estimates that only 15 percent of the population in low-income and middle-income countries has access to and uses the Internet as compared to 70 percent of the population in high-income countries (WDI 2010, p. 338). In addition, only 13 percent of the population in the Global South has access to and uses phone lines as compared to 47 percent of the population in the Global North (WDI 2010, p. 334). High-income countries also account for 70 percent of all export markets (WDI 2010, p. 284).

A select few are prospering in comparison with the many who are barely surviving, and "there is some evidence that the forces of globalization in trade, investment and the labor forces are working to increase" the gap between rich and poor people, much as it appears to widen the gap between the wealthy Global North and poor Global South countries (Babones and Turner 2004, p. 117; see Chapter 4). "One-fifth of humanity live in countries where many people think nothing of spending $2 a day on a cappuccino. Another fifth of humanity survive on less than $1 a day and live in countries where children die for want of a simple anti-mosquito bed net," according to the United Nations Development Programme. This trend has produced a world in which the poorest fifth of the global population produce and consume only 2 percent of the world's goods and services, creating huge inequalities: "A homeless person panhandling for two U.S. dollars a day on the streets of Boston would sit in the top half of the world in income distribution" (Dollar 2005, p. 80).

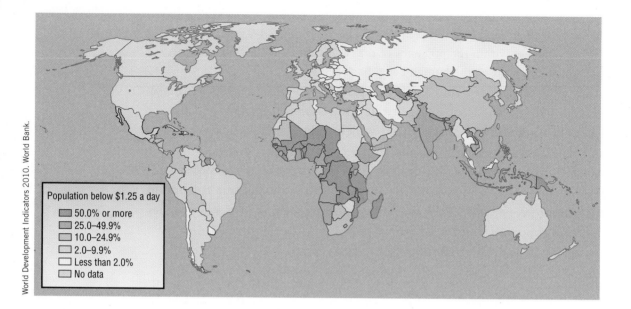

World Development Indicators 2010. World Bank.

Population below $1.25 a day

- 50.0% or more
- 25.0–49.9%
- 10.0–24.9%
- 2.0–9.9%
- Less than 2.0%
- No data

MAP 15.1

WHERE POVERTY PREVAILS IN THE WORLD: THE SHARE OF PEOPLE LIVING ON LESS THAN $1.25 A DAY
As this map shows, billions of people in a wide range of countries are struggling to exist under conditions of extreme poverty. The most people living in extreme poverty are in Asia, but Africa has the largest number of high-poverty countries. The World Bank warns that many Global South countries are not on track to achieve the UN goal of cutting poverty in half by the year 2015.

Against this grim picture are trends that inspire some hope. For some segments of humanity things have improved: "On average, people in developing countries are healthier, better educated, and less impoverished—and they are more likely to live in a multiparty democracy. Since 1990 life expectancy in developing countries has increased by 4 years. There are 3.3 million fewer children out of school. More than 400 million people have escaped extreme poverty" (WDI 2009). These human development gains should not be underestimated. Nor should they be exaggerated.

Much evidence captures the extreme suffering of people in many parts of the world, but especially in the low-income countries of the Global South where life has changed little from that of their ancestors. For example, life expectancy in the Global South averages sixty-seven years, whereas in the Global North it is eighty years. In the Global South, infant mortality rates are among the highest in the world; agriculture remains the dominant form of productive activity; and 55 percent of people live in rural areas even as the world is undergoing rapid urbanization (WDI 2010). Former World Bank President

James Wolfensohn (2004) acknowledged the growing threat of global poverty, noting that "2 billion people have no access to clear water; 120 million children never get a chance to go to school; over 40 million people in the developing countries are HIV-positive with little hope of receiving treatment for this dreadful disease. . . . So the world is at a tipping point: either we recommit to deliver on the goals, or the targets will be missed, the world's poor will be left even further behind—and our children will be left to face the consequences."

To make the promotion of human development a global priority, a precise measure of human welfare is needed. How can human welfare—its level and the prospects for humanity's escape from poverty—best be gauged?

> *The great feature of poverty is the fact that it annihilates the future.*
>
> —George Orwell, British author

Measuring Human Development and Human Security

The human dimension of development first gained attention in the 1970s, partly in response to the growing popularity of *dependency theory* (see Chapter 4). This theory, advanced by Global South leaders, attributed persistent poverty to exploitation caused by dependent relationships of the less developed countries with the wealthy Global North. It also reflected the realization that more is not necessarily better. Advocates of a basic *human needs* perspective sought new ways to measure development beyond those focusing exclusively on economic indicators such as the average income for each person in each country.

human needs
those basic physical, social, and political needs, such as food and freedom, that are required for survival and security.

In 1990, Mahbud ul Haq, a famous social scientist, constructed for the United Nations Development Programme (UNDP) a *Human Development Index (HDI)* to measure states' comparative ability to provide for their citizens' well-being. Successive *Human Development Reports* have provoked fresh debate about the meaning of human development in international forums such as the World Summit for Social Development.

Human Development Index (HDI)
an index that uses life expectancy, literacy, average number of years of schooling, and income to assess a country's performance in providing for its people's welfare and security.

The HDI, as the UNDP most recently defines it, seeks to capture as many aspects of human development as possible in one simple, composite index and to rank human-development achievements. Although no multiple-indicator index (a detailed set of statistical measures) can perfectly monitor progress in human development, the HDI comes close as an estimating procedure. It measures three dimensions of human welfare—living a long and healthy life, being educated, and having a decent standard of living.

The HDI is a more comprehensive measure than per capita income and has the advantage of directing attention from material possessions toward human needs. Income is only a means to human development, not an end. Nor is it the sum total of human lives. Thus, by focusing on aspects of human welfare beyond average income for each person—by treating income as a proxy for a decent standard of living—the HDI provides a more complete picture of human life than income does. By this measure, the evidence provides a basic profile of the extent to which humanitarian aspirations are succeeding and failing.

The HDI ranges from 0 to 1. The HDI value for a country shows the distance that it has already traveled toward the maximum possible value of 1 and allows for comparison with other countries. The difference between the value achieved by a country and the maximum possible value shows how far it has to go, and the challenge for every country is to find ways to reduce that discrepancy.

COURSEMATE

Simulation:
*Measuring
Development*

When we look at the ability of countries to contribute to the human development of the people living within their borders, as measured by the HDI, we derive a revealing picture of the way personal welfare is provided (see Figure 15.1). These indicators show that consumption is not the same as human welfare and that economic growth does not automatically produce human development. In fact, if not managed, high consumption can produce inequalities and poverty that erode the capacity of people "to participate in the decisions that affect one's life and to enjoy the respect of others in the community. . . . The HDI can give a more complete picture of the state of a country's development than can income alone [since many countries] highlight the importance of policies that translate wealth into human development. In particular, well designed public policy and provision of services by governments, local communities and civil society can advance human development even without high levels of income or economic growth" (UNDP 2004, p. 128).

However, a problem with the HDI is that "it does not include measures of the other aspects of human development such as leisure, security, justice, freedom, human rights, and self respect. It would be possible to register a high HDI in a zoo or even in a well-run prison. And, although at low incomes illness often leads to death, the HDI has no independent indicator of morbidity, the absence of which is surely one of the most basic needs. Life can be nasty, brutish, and long" (Streeten 2001). Thus, despite its strengths as an indicator

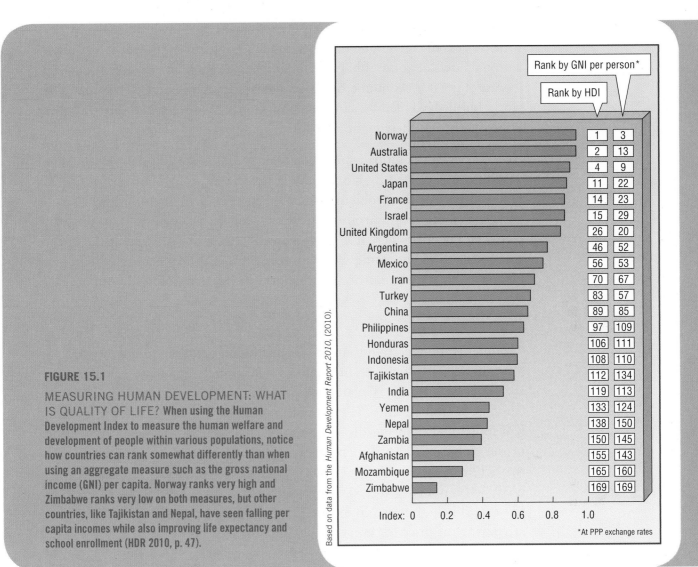

FIGURE 15.1

MEASURING HUMAN DEVELOPMENT: WHAT IS QUALITY OF LIFE? When using the Human Development Index to measure the human welfare and development of people within various populations, notice how countries can rank somewhat differently than when using an aggregate measure such as the gross national income (GNI) per capita. Norway ranks very high and Zimbabwe ranks very low on both measures, but other countries, like Tajikistan and Nepal, have seen falling per capita incomes while also improving life expectancy and school enrollment (HDR 2010, p. 47).

of human well-being across the globe, there are many important aspects of human security and human rights that it does not assess.

So, what factors affect people's ability to live a good life? And why does human development vary greatly in the countries of the world? Let us consider several explanations.

Globalization, Democratization, and Economic Prosperity

The rapid transfer of global capital and investment across borders is integrating the world's economies and has led to widespread speculation that globalization will provide a cure for the chronic poverty facing the majority of humanity. There exists "a widely shared image of globalization—a world-wide process of converging incomes and lifestyles driven by ever-larger international flows of goods, images, capital, and people as formidable equalizers [because] greater economic openness has made small parts of the changing world full-fledged members of the global village . . . so that globalized islands of prosperity are thriving in many developing nations" (Heredia 1999).

However, critics of globalization complain that it is the culprit—that relative deprivation is caused by globalization, not cured by it. They see globalization as a part of the problem of human suffering, not the solution. Capital may flow more freely around the world, but it flows most slowly to the places and people where it is most scarce. To their constructed image of the consequences of cascading globalization, a more global economy increases inequality in some countries, particularly in the marginalized periphery of the Global South.

Critics decry the "human harms" wrought by globalization, arguing that "nothing is more certain than the inequality and exploitation generated by a totally free market. The inequalities that global capitalism generates are inequities because they violate the principles of egalitarian individualism. . . . This sin of globalization is thus both collective (an assault on the nation) and individual (injuring the nation's citizens), making it a severe violation of the global moral order" by creating "risks of injury and incapacitation that strike at the very being of human beings" (Boli, Elliott, and Bieri 2004, p. 395). It is not only argued that globalization fails to benefit the people that most need help, but as economist Rombert Weakland lamented, "The poor are paying the price for everyone else's prosperity."

Although progress in human development has occurred and will likely persist, so will trends toward declining human welfare, making the twenty-first century appear to be both the best of times and the worst of times. Thus, the future of world politics will be not only a struggle between the Global North and the Global South but also a contest between those who hopelessly expect continuing human poverty and those who envision possible further progress in human development.

Yet, where human development has expanded, one factor stands out—the degree to which countries rule themselves democratically and protect citizens' civil liberties. Where democracy thrives, human development and human rights also tend to thrive. Recall the states where democracy and political liberties exist (see Map 6.2, "How Free Is Your Country?"). That geographical profile supports the conclusion that at the start of 2010, eighty-nine

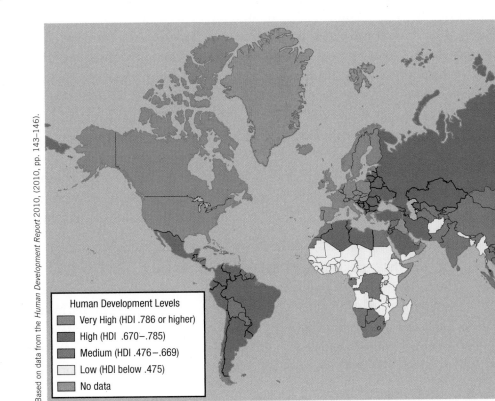

Based on data from the *Human Development Report 2010*, (2010, pp. 143–146).

MAP 15.2

THE MAP OF HUMAN DEVELOPMENT This map measures the level of human development in the countries of the world, using the HDI scale. Note the wide variation. Although the Global East and some Global South countries have made big gains in the past quarter-century (following political reforms leading to greater democracy and economic reforms leading to free markets), a gap in people's quality of life and in their levels of human development is apparent and parallels to some degree the gap between the Global North and the Global South.

countries, or less than half of the countries in the world (46 percent), were "free," providing their citizens with a broad range of civil liberties in their political, civic, educational, cultural, ethnic, economic, and religious rights (Freedom House 2010).

Now compare the location where people benefit from such freedom with Map 15.2, which shows the various levels of human development in countries across the globe. The two go hand in hand: Where democracy flourishes, human development flourishes. But in autocratic governments not ruled by the will of the people, human development fails to occur and human rights are denied.

Along with democratization, rising economic prosperity within a country clearly helps the pace of human development, as previously shown in Figure 15.1, which indicates the wealth of each person for countries based on *purchasing power parity (PPP)* exchange-rate comparisons. This is why levels of human development are generally highest in the Global North, where economic prosperity on average is also highest (as opposed to the low-income Global South and some countries in the Global East). Evidence also supports the conclusion that those countries that respect human rights encourage trade that reduces poverty (Blanton and Blanton 2007). But the exceptions demonstrate the general rule that how countries organize themselves for governance, and their protection of the civil rights and political liberties of their populations, makes a crucial difference in achieving levels of human development.

Some question the "trickle-down" hypothesis (that if the rich first get richer eventually the benefits will trickle down to help the poor) while accepting the evidence that meeting basic human needs promotes long-term economic growth. Others maintain that redistributive policies to enhance human welfare and growth-oriented policies focusing on "trickle-down" benefits function at cross-purposes because the latter can only be attained at the expense of the former.

Many now recommend fostering human development through a *"Third Way"* strategy that combines the efficiency of a free-enterprise capitalistic market with the compassion of governmental economic planning and regulation in an effort, through a fused administrative system, to cooperatively produce the greatest good for the greatest number. Proponents agree that this mixed approach would enable a free market to generate rapid growth while providing a safety net for those most in need of assistance, and this formula is the best solution for engineering economic growth with a moral human purpose.

HUMAN RIGHTS AND THE PROTECTION OF PEOPLE

Most states have publicly embraced "the universalist claim that all human beings have the same moral status; to accept universal human rights [is to make on states] the moral demand to respect the life, integrity, well-being and flourishing of . . . *all* human beings" (Vandersluis and Yeros 2000a). This claim was expressed in the ringing words of the 1948 Universal Declaration of Human Rights: "Recognition of the inherent dignity and of the equal and inalienable rights of all members of the human family is the foundation of freedom, justice, and peace in the world." This treaty expressed the hope that people should be empowered and therefore no longer reduced to "simply hapless victims of fate, devoid of any historical agency" (Saurin 2000).

In the idea that those who suffer "no grievance or injury" have the obligation to speak up for those who have suffered them lies the birth of the vision that human rights are universal.

—Adam Hoschschild, humanitarian historian

Internationally Recognized Human Rights

The body of legal rules and norms designed to protect individual human beings is anchored in the ethical requirement that every person should be treated with equal concern and respect. As the most authoritative statement of these norms, the 1948 *Universal Declaration of Human Rights* "establishes a broad range of civil and political rights, including freedom of assembly, freedom of thought and expression, and the right to participate in government. The declaration also proclaims that social and economic rights are indispensable, including the right to education, the right to work, and the right to participate in the cultural life of the community. In addition, the preamble boldly asserts that 'it is essential, if man is not to be compelled to have recourse, as a last resort, to rebellion against tyranny and oppression, that human rights should be protected by the rule of law'" (Clapham 2001).

These rights have since been codified and extended in a series of treaties, most notably in the *International Covenant on Civil and Political Rights* and the *International Covenant on Economic, Social, and Cultural Rights*. There are many ways to classify the rights listed in these treaties. International ethicist Charles Beitz (2001, p. 271) groups them into five categories:

- ■ **Rights of the person:** "Life, liberty, and security of the person; privacy and freedom of movement; ownership of property; freedom of thought, conscience, and religion, including freedom of religious teaching and practice 'in public and private'; and prohibition of slavery, torture, and cruel or degrading punishment."

- ■ **Rights associated with the rule of law:** "Equal recognition before the law and equal protection of the law; effective legal remedy for violation of legal rights; impartial hearing and trial; presumption of innocence; and prohibition of arbitrary arrest."

- ■ **Political rights:** "Freedom of expression, assembly, and association; the right to take part in government; and periodic and genuine elections by universal and equal suffrage."

- **Economic and social rights:** "An adequate standard of living; free choice of employment; protection against unemployment; 'just and favorable remuneration'; the right to join trade unions; 'reasonable limitation of working hours'; free elementary education; social security; and the 'highest attainable standard of physical and mental health.'"

- **Rights of communities:** "Self-determination and protection of minority cultures."

Although the multilateral treaties enumerating these rights are legally binding on the states ratifying them, many have either not ratified them or done so with significant reservations. When states specify reservations, they are expressing agreement with the broad declarations of principle contained in these treaties while indicating that they object to certain specific provisions and elect not to be bound by them. The United States, for example, ratified the *International Covenant on Civil and Political Rights* with reservations in 1992, but it has not ratified the *International Covenant on Economic, Social, and Cultural Rights*. As this example illustrates, countries who agree with the general principle that all human beings possess certain rights that cannot be withheld may still disagree on the scope of these rights. Thus, some emphasize rights associated with the rule of law and political rights, whereas others stress the importance of economic and social rights.

Unfortunately, not everyone enjoys the human rights recognized by international law. Three groups for whom respect for human rights remains particularly problematic are indigenous peoples, women, and children.

The Precarious Life of Indigenous Peoples

As you learned in the Chapter 5 introduction to *nonstate actors*, *indigenous peoples* are representative of one type of ethnic and cultural group that were once native to a geographic location. According to the World Health Organization, the globe is populated by an estimated 370 million indigenous peoples living in more than seventy countries worldwide, each of which has a unique language and culture and strong, often spiritual, ties to an ancestral homeland. In most cases indigenous peoples were at one time politically sovereign and economically self-sufficient. Today, as many as 350 million indigenous peoples are without a

Binsar Bakkara/AP Photo

CRUEL AND UNUSUAL, OR SIMPLY USUAL? The UN Human Rights Commission holds annual sessions that deal with accusations that some UN members are violating human rights treaties. This photo shows the kind of human rights abuse that some countries practice: a woman being punished by Shariah law authorities in Banda Aceh, Indonesia. Stipulated in Islam's holy book, the Quran, caning is practiced in some Islamic countries.

ETHNIC CLEANSING In 1994, ethnic conflict escalated to genocide in Rwanda as the Hutu militia attacked the Tutsi, and later as the Tutsi-dominated Rwandan Patriotic Front retaliated against the Hutus. This photo depicts the results of one such bloodbath, where as many as 800,000 Tutsis died.

homeland or self-rule and live within the borders of about seventy of the globe's independent countries (World Health Organization 2007).

Many indigenous peoples feel persecuted because their livelihoods, lands, and cultures are threatened. In part, these fears are inspired by the 130 million indigenous peoples who were slaughtered between 1900 and 1987 by state-sponsored violence in their own countries (Rummel 1994). The mass killing of Armenians by Turks, of Jews (and other groups) by Hitler, of Cambodians by the Khmer Rouge, and of the Tutsi of Rwanda by the Hutu exemplify the atrocities committed during the twentieth century.

Case Study: *International Law and Organization: Indigenous Peoples*

Responding to the tragedy of the Nazi holocaust, Polish jurist Raphael Lemkin coined the word *genocide* from the Greek word *genos* (race, people) and the Latin *caedere* (to kill), and called for it to be singled out as the gravest violation of human rights, a heinous crime the international community would be morally responsible for punishing. In his view, genocide has several dimensions, including physical (the annihilation of members of a group), biological (measures taken to reduce the reproductive capacity of a group), and cultural (efforts to eliminate a group's language, literature, art, and other institutions). *Ethnocentrism* often underlies genocidal policies. "Brute force realpolitik," concludes Manus Midlarski (2005), "often provides a rationale rooted in ethnocentrism for the physical extermination of victim minorities by leaders claiming genocide is a necessary 'altruistic punishment' for the good of the dominant nationality."

ethnocentrism
a propensity to see one's nationality or state as the center of the world and therefore special, with the result that the values and perspectives of other groups are misunderstood and ridiculed.

Various native peoples are now fighting back across the globe against the injustice they perceive states to have perpetrated against them. The members of many such nonstate nations are divided about objectives, and militants who are prepared to fight for independence are usually in a minority. In fact, most indigenous movements only seek a greater voice in redirecting the policies and allocation of resources within existing states and are eliciting the support of NGOs and IGOs to pressure states to recognize their claims and protect their rights.

A substantial number of indigenous movements in the last decade have successfully negotiated settlements resulting in *devolution*—the granting of regional political power to increase local self-governance. Examples include the Miskitos in Nicaragua, the Gagauz in Moldova, and most regional separatists in Ethiopia and in India's Assam region. Yet, as suggested by the continuing hostilities between the Chechens and the Russian Federation, resolving clashes between aspiring peoples and established states can be extremely difficult.

The goal expressed in the UN Charter of promoting "universal respect for, and observance of, human rights and fundamental freedoms" for everyone is a challenge for many nationally diverse countries. The division of these states along ethnic and cultural lines makes them inherently fragile. Consider the degree to which minority groups compose many states: for example, the share of indigenous populations in Bolivia is 62 percent and Peru, 48 percent (The Hunger Project 2009). Or consider the number of distinct languages spoken in some countries, with Indonesia's 722 languages, Nigeria's 521, India's 445, Australia's 207, and Brazil's 193 being conspicuous examples (Lewis 2009).

Racism and intolerance are hothouses for fanaticism and violence. The belief that one's nationality is superior to all others undermines the concept of human rights (Clapham 2000). Although interethnic competition is a phenomenon that dates back to biblical times, it remains a contemporary plague. According to The Minorities at Risk Project (2009), since 1998, more than 283 politically motivated minority groups throughout the globe suffered in their home countries from organized discriminatory treatment and mobilized in collective action to defend themselves and promote their self-defined interests. Some analysts predict that conflict within and between ethnically divided states will become a major axis on which twenty-first-century world politics revolves.

Efforts to toughen domestic refugee legislation and criteria for granting asylum raise important ethical issues. Where will the homeless, the desperate, the weak, and the poor find *sanctuary*—a safe place to live where human rights are safeguarded? Will the rich countries act with compassion or respond with indifference? And more broadly, what is the best way to view human security and reconcile it with national security (see Controversy: What Is Security?)? The policy proposals crafted to address these questions may involve controversial trade-offs, and point to the difficulties in responding to the global refugee crisis in particular (see Chapter 14), and human rights abuse in general.

Simulation: *Rwanda*

CONTROVERSY:

WHAT IS SECURITY?

How should security be defined? Policy makers disagree. Some see it primarily in military terms, others in human welfare terms. Underlying the disagreement is a different conception of what is most important on the global agenda. One tradition gives states first priority and assumes that protecting their territorial integrity must be foremost in the minds of national leaders. Others challenge this conception and give primacy to the security of individual people, arguing that social and environmental protection must therefore be seen as a global priority.

In considering this question, take into consideration the traditional realist view that national security is essentially the freedom from fear of attack by another country or nonstate terrorists. Realists maintain that armed aggression is a paramount security priority and that preparing for war to prevent war is each state's supreme imperative overriding any other security concerns. Safeguarding the state by military force matters most. Therefore "security" must be defined primarily in terms of each country's capacity to resist armed threats to survival and national values by either foreign enemies or insurgents at home. This definition puts the protection of entire states' interests above those of individual people.

In contrast, "human security" has risen as a recent concept that focuses on protecting individuals from *any* threat. The Human Security Centre (2006, p. 35) elaborates this new conception that derives from liberal thought, explaining that "secure states do not automatically mean secure peoples. Protecting citizens from foreign attack may be a necessary condition for the security of individuals, but it is not a sufficient one. Indeed, during the last one hundred years far more people have been killed by their own governments than by foreign armies. All proponents of human security agree that its primary goal is a protection of individuals. But consensus breaks down over what threats individuals should be protected from . . . The UN's *Commission on Human Security* argues that the threat agenda should be broadened to include hunger, disease, and natural disasters because these kill far more people than war, genocide and terrorism combined."

Extending this perspective, note that so-called "environmental security" is one of the many points of departure in the "human security" approach to national security that stresses the threat of global environmental degradation to human well-being and welfare throughout the planet (see Chapter 16). That liberal position "rests primarily on evidence that there has been serious degradation of natural resources (fresh water, soils, forests, fishery resources, and biological diversity) and vital life-support systems (the ozone layer, climate system, oceans, and atmosphere) [and that] these global physical changes . . . are comparable to those associated with most military threats that national security establishments prepare for" (Porter 1995, p. 216).

WHAT IS SECURITY? (Continued)

WHAT DO YOU THINK?

- To what extent is the "national security" approach emphasized by realists and the "human security" approach favored by liberals a contradiction and in competition with one another? Might they instead be complementary and mutually reinforcing?

- Can either type of security be achieved in the absence of the other? If so, as a policy maker, which type of security would you choose as the most likely guarantor of your country's overall well-being? Why?

- What are some considerations that a feminist theorist would include in this debate? How might this affect your perception of security?

Gender Inequality and Its Consequences

For more than three decades, global conferences have highlighted the critical role of women and how it can be a human rights concern (see Table 15.1). A global consensus emerged about the need to improve the status of women if human rights and development were to progress. These conferences are signposts that increasingly depict gender equality and empowerment across political, social, and economic arenas as a fundamental right. They have educated the world to the incontrovertible evidence that women's status in society, and especially their education, has an important influence on human development, and that women's treatment is a global rights issue that affects everyone.

Gender Empowerment Measure (GEM)
the UN Development Programme's attempt to measure the extent of gender equality across the globe's countries, based on estimates of women's relative economic income, high-paying positions, and access to professional and parliamentary positions.

As measured by the UN's *Gender Empowerment Measure (GEM)*, women throughout the world continue to be disadvantaged relative to men across a broad spectrum (HDR 2010). Disparities between men and women persist, for example, in literacy rates, school and college enrollments, and targeted educational resources. Moreover, women enjoy less access to advanced study and training in professional fields, such as science, engineering, law, and business. In addition, within occupational groups, they are almost always in less-prestigious jobs, they face formidable barriers to political involvement, and they typically receive less pay than men.

gender inequalities
differences between men and women in opportunity and reward that are determined by the values that guide states' foreign and domestic policies.

Indeed, in most countries, *gender inequalities*—differences in living standards between men and women—remain widespread both within and across states, despite the measurable improvement in the daily lot and future prospects of millions of women during the past several decades. Although many facets of human development are improving, the prevalent worldwide gender gap remains

Table 15.1   Important Steps on the Path toward Human Rights and Women's Rights

Year	Conference	Key Passage
1975	World Conference on International Women's Year (Mexico City)	Launched a global dialogue on gender equality and led to the establishment of the United Nations Development Fund for Women (UNIFEM)
1979	Convention on the Elimination of All Forms of Discrimination against Women (Women's Convention, New York)	Article 12 calls on countries to "take all appropriate measures to eliminate discrimination against women in the field of health care in order to ensure, on a basis of equality of men and women, access to health care services, including those related to family planning"
1980	Second World Conference on Women (Copenhagen)	Calls for governments to enact stronger measures that will ensure women's ownership and control of property, and will improve women's rights to inheritance, child custody, and recognition of nationality
1985	Third World Conference on Women (Nairobi)	Recognized the need for governments to bring gender concerns into the mainstream and develop institutional mechanisms to promote broad-based gender equality and empowerment of women
1993	United Nations World Conference on Human Rights (Vienna)	The Vienna Declaration includes nine paragraphs on "The Equal Status and Human Rights of Women," and for the first time recognizes that "violence against women is a human-rights abuse"
1995	United Nations Fourth World Conference on Women (Beijing)	Sets a wide-ranging, ambitious agenda for promoting human development by addressing gender inequality and women's rights
2004	NATO Conference on Trafficking in Humans (Brussels)	Seeks a convention to contain the growing problem of human trafficking and export of people across borders—particularly women and children
2004	United Nations Conference on Sexual and Reproductive Rights (New York)	Launches action plan to uphold women's "fundamental human rights including sexual and reproductive rights"
2005	United Nations World Conference on Women (Beijing)	*110 Platform for Action* charts strategies for empowerment of women and girls
2010	Commission on the Status of Women (New York)	Conducts a 15-year review of the implementation of the Beijing Declaration, and assesses the Platform for Action

especially wide in three Global South regions: Southern Asia, the Middle East, and sub-Saharan Africa. "Women's wage work is important for economic growth and the well-being of families. But restricted access to education and vocational training, heavy workloads at home and in nonpaid domestic and market activities, and labor market discrimination often limit women's participation in paid economic activities, lower their productivity, and reduce their wages . . . In many developing countries women are a large part of agricultural employment, often as unpaid family workers. Among people who are unsalaried, women are more likely than men to be unpaid family workers, while men are more likely than women to be self-employed or employers" (WDI 2010, p. 49).

The need to extend women equal human rights for economic growth is clear-cut. "When women are educated and can earn and control income, a number of good results follow: infant mortality declines, child health and nutrition improve, agricultural productivity rises, population growth slows, economies expand, and cycles of poverty are broken" (Coleman 2010b, p. 13). Yet despite the fact that "since the eighteenth century feminists, scholars, and activists have taken up the task of revealing just how much political life has been built on presumptions about femininity and masculinity . . . there is abundant evidence now that regimes and the states beneath them in fact have taken deliberate steps to sustain a sort of hierarchical gendered division of labor that provides them with cheapened, often completely unpaid, women's productive labor" (Enloe 2001, p. 311).

Johan Spanner/The New York Times/Redux Pictures

Franka Bruns/AP Photo

HOW TO TRANSCEND THE GENDER GAP? Shown here are examples of how the empowerment of women is changing. Following a traditional medieval ritual that is slowly vanishing, a woman in a clan of Northern Albania could claim the right to live and rule her family as a man only if she forsook her womanhood (left). As the first female Chancellor of Germany (right), Angela Merkel is one of the most powerful women in the world.

Much the same holds true in politics: Since 1900 only 15 percent of the world's countries have had one or more female heads of state (*Harper's* 2008, p. 15). Today, women continue to be vastly underrepresented in decision-making positions in government, even in democracies and developed countries. "Gender parity in parliamentary representation is still far from being realized. In 2009, women accounted

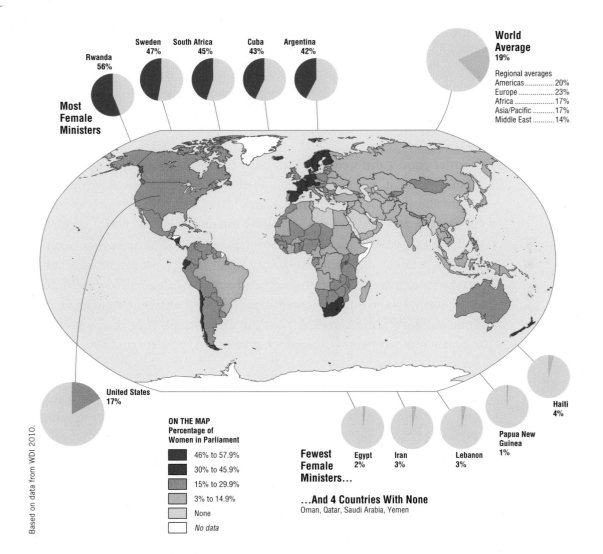

Based on data from WDI 2010.

Most Female Ministers

Rwanda 56%
Sweden 47%
South Africa 45%
Cuba 43%
Argentina 42%

World Average 19%

Regional averages
Americas...............20%
Europe 23%
Africa 17%
Asia/Pacific 17%
Middle East 14%

United States 17%

ON THE MAP
Percentage of Women in Parliament

- 46% to 57.9%
- 30% to 45.9%
- 15% to 29.9%
- 3% to 14.9%
- None
- *No data*

Fewest Female Ministers...

Egypt 2%
Iran 3%
Lebanon 3%
Papua New Guinea 1%
Haiti 4%

...And 4 Countries With None
Oman, Qatar, Saudi Arabia, Yemen

FIGURE 15.2

GENDER POLITICS There are now more women in government than ever before. The proportion of women in national parliaments grew by only 1 percent between 1975 and 1995, compared to 8 percent between 1998 and 2008. Nonetheless, gender parity remains lacking in democratic governance. There is only one woman to every four males in legislatures around the world, and by the start of 2010 only seventeen heads of state were female. "Even if the present accelerated rate of increase in women's representation continues as compared to previous decades, we . . . will not reach the 40 percent threshold of women in public office until near to the end of this century" (UNIFEM 2010).

for 19 percent of parliamentarians worldwide" (WDI 2010, p. 39; see also Figure 15.2). It is also clear is that "societies with greater equality are more likely to be prosperous and sustain stable democratic institutions" (Htun and Weldon 2010, p. 207). As U.S. Secretary of State Hillary Clinton pronounced, "There cannot be true democracy unless women's voices are heard. There cannot be true democracy unless women are given the opportunity to take responsibility for their own lives."

Yet there are signs that a transformation is under way, and that an encouraging trend of greater female participation in politics is spreading across many countries. "Women are running for public office in growing numbers . . . exceeding 30 percent of representatives in national assemblies in 22 countries . . . Women are using their votes to strengthen their leverage as members of interest groups, including groups with an interest in gender equality" (UNIFEM 2009 p. 17).

Further gender differences continue at the most basic levels of human development, and it is easy to conclude that women remain victims of human rights abuse and discrimination nearly everywhere. More girls than boys die at a young age, and females' access to adequate healthcare is more restricted (WDI 2010, p. 49). Nearly half (47 percent) of all refugees are women and their dependent children (UNHCR 2010), and women continue to be the primary victims of sex trafficking and sexual violence. "In the Middle East and South Asia, women deemed insufficiently conservative in their dress are attacked with acid. Across Africa, the use of mass rape as an instrument of war has jumped from one conflict to another" (Coleman 2010, p. 128).

gendercide
systematic killing of members of a specific gender.

A growing number of countries in Asia are also experiencing the effects of a generation of *gendercide,* where Indian economist Amartya Sen estimates that well over 100 million females are "missing" due to abortion, murder, and death through neglect. More than 120 boys continue to be born for every 100 girls in northern India and China, due to a cultural partiality for sons, a modern preference for small families, and the availability of technology that enables couples to determine the sex of their unborn child.

Gender myopia, denying the existence of the many barriers that prevent women equal freedoms and privileges enjoyed by men, is pervasive. Though the "river of thought on human rights and development runs inexorably toward the emancipation of women everywhere, and the equality of men and women . . . eddies and rivulets carry the water backwards every day—as when pregnant girls are expelled from school, or when the genitals of young women are cut in a ritual destruction of their capacity for sexual pleasure" (State of the World 2002). Indeed, it was not until 2001 that "sexual enslavement" was established at The Hague as a war crime, a fact that feminists point out as an example of the traditional disregard for women's human rights.

Video: *No Rights, No Dreams*

And blatant disregard for the individual sexual and reproductive rights of women continues today, as reflected in current-day Afghanistan. Though the language of the law supported by Afghan President Hamid Karzai in April 2009 was toned down in the face of international opposition, in August later that year a similar law was quietly passed that permitted men to deny their wives food and sustenance if they did not obey their husbands' sexual demands, gave guardianship of children to the fathers and grandfathers, required permission from the husband for a woman to work, and allowed a rapist to avoid prosecution by paying "blood money" to the victim.

Protecting women's rights is difficult because the issues touch deeply entrenched, as well as widely divergent, religious and cultural beliefs. In many Islamic countries, for example, women must hide their faces with veils in public, and women and men are often completely separated in social and religious activities. As American sociologist Herbert Spencer says, "A people's condition may be judged by the treatment which women receive under it." For many in liberal Western countries focused on social, political, and economic equality of the sexes, these traditions are difficult to understand.

"Gender empowerment" is based on the conviction that only the realization of the full potential of all human beings can enable true human development, and that this entails the realization of women's human rights. Once this concept gained acceptance as a lens through which to construct a view of the core issues on the global agenda, gender issues became a central concern. Feminist theory, a departure from classical realist theory, seeks to rectify the ways conventional but distorted images of world politics are, as *constructivism* informs us, socially constructed (see Chapter 2). The objective is to sensitize the world to the neglect of gender and the place of women in global society and to offer an alternative theoretical vision that empowers women, secures their basic human rights, and challenges realist theories that honor the state and military power (Enloe 2007; Tickner 2010).

Slavery and Human Trafficking

A human rights horror to which women, as well as children, are particularly vulnerable is human trafficking. While many people assume that slavery is an obsolescent practice, the reality is that trade in humans bought, sold, or forced into a miserable life of subjugation and servitude is huge. The growing slave trade crisscrosses the entire globe and, "despite more than a dozen international conventions banning slavery in the past 150 years, there are more slaves today than at any point in human history" (Skinner 2010, p. 56). Roughly 80,000 Africans were brought to the New World each year during the peak of the slave trade in the 1780s. By way of comparison, today, according to the U.S. State Department, between 600,000 and 800,000 people are trafficked across borders each year to suffer the fate of being bought and sold as sex slaves or bonded laborers (Coleman 2010). As Ethan Kapstein explains:

> Slavery and the global slave trade continue to thrive to this day; in fact, it is likely that more people are being trafficked across borders against their will now than at any point in the past. This human stain is not just a minor blot on the rich tapestry of international commerce. It is a product of the same political, technological, and economic forces that have fueled globalization. Just as the brutal facts of the Atlantic slave trade ultimately led to a reexamination of U.S. history—U.S. historiography until the 1960s had been largely celebratory—so must growing awareness of the modern slave trade spark a recognition of the flaws in our contemporary economic and governmental arrangements. The current system offers too many incentives to criminals and outlaw states to market humans and promises too little in the way of sanctions. Contemporary slavery typically involves women and children being forced into servitude through violence and deprivation (2006, p. 103).

The UN has found that the leading form of human trafficking, at 79 percent, is sexual exploitation. Most of the victims are women and girls. The second leading form of human trafficking is forced labor (18 percent), and about one in five victims are children. Over one million children are sold into labor every year and are faced with brutality and horrific work conditions (Vital Signs 2007–2008, p. 113). "Children's nimble fingers are exploited to untangle fishing nets, sew luxury goods or pick cocoa," reports the UN. "Their innocence

Shiho Fukada/WpN/Photoshot

Jemal Countess/Getty Images

MODERN-DAY SLAVERY "More must be done to reduce the vulnerability of victims, increase the risks to traffickers, and lower demand for the goods and services of modern-day slaves" says Antonio Maria Costa, Executive Director of the UN Office on Drugs and Crime. Shown on the left is a seventeen year old sex worker in Bangladesh after her service with a customer. She ran away from home to escape marriage at the age of fifteen, and sought work at a factory where she was deceived and sold to a brothel. Pictured on the right is actress Mira Sorvino who, in an effort to increase public awareness of human trafficking and generate greater commitment to combating the problem, was appointed by the United Nations as a Goodwill Ambassador to Combat Human Trafficking.

is abused for begging, or exploited for sex as prostitutes, pedophilia or child pornography. Others are sold as child brides or camel jockeys."

While many victims of human trafficking are moved across continents, intraregional and domestic trafficking is far more common. Human trafficking is a lucrative criminal activity. According to Luis CdeBaca, who directs the U.S. State Department's Office to Monitor and Combat Trafficking in Persons, this shadow economy "turns a $32 billion annual profit for traffickers" (Ireland 2010). It is the third largest illicit global business after trafficking in drugs and the arms trade (Obuah 2006, p. 241). And according to the U.S. State Department, slave labor in developing countries such as Brazil, China, and India has fueled in part their huge economic growth.

Children and Human Rights

Children are one of the most dependent and vulnerable groups in society, and their human rights are frequently violated. They face horrific neglect and abuse, as evident in their suffering from unmitigated hunger and illness, being forced into slavery for labor or sexual exploitation, and conscription as child soldiers. Amnesty International, a human rights NGO, describes conditions that many children throughout the world face:

> Children are tortured and mistreated by state officials; they are arbitrarily or lawfully detained, often in appalling conditions; in some countries they are subjected to the death penalty. Countless thousands are killed or maimed in armed conflicts, many more have fled their homes to become refugees. Children forced by poverty or abuse to live on the streets are sometimes detained, attacked and even killed in the name of social cleansing. Many millions of children work at exploitative or hazardous jobs, or are the victims of child trafficking and forced prostitution. Because children are "easy targets", they are sometimes threatened, beaten or raped in order to punish family members who are not so accessible (Amnesty International 2009).

Human rights abuse of children takes place all across the globe. However, "weak states typically have worse human rights records than strong ones" as they lack the capacity to effectively protect human rights (Englehart 2009, p. 163). They are often plagued by corruption, ineffectively police their territory, and are unable to provide basic services.

To bring about a transformation in the human condition, UNICEF contends that "improvements in public health services are essential, including safe water and better sanitation. Education, especially for girls and mothers, will also save children's lives. Raising income can help, but little will be achieved unless a greater effort is made to ensure that services reach those who need them most." Though child mortality has declined in every region of the world since 1960, almost 10 million children every year still do not live to see their fifth birthday. "Of these, the vast majority dies from causes that are preventable through a combination of good care, nutrition, and simple medical treatment" (World Bank 2009, p. 44).

Most of the children that die every year live in the Global South, where death claims 7 in 100 children under the age of five, as compared to the Global North where less than 1 in 100 children die (WDI 2010, p. 146). Malnutrition lies at the root of more than half of the deaths of children worldwide; it weakens children's immune systems and leaves them vulnerable to illness and disease, such as malaria, pneumonia, diarrhea, measles, and AIDS (see Chapter 14). Yet "rapid declines in under-five mortality (more than 50 percent) have been seen in Latin America and the Caribbean, Central and Eastern Europe and the Commonwealth of Independent States (CEE/CIS), and East Asia and the Pacific. There remain, however, many countries with high levels of child mortality, particularly in sub-Saharan Africa and South Asia" (UNICEF 2009).

Poor human rights conditions are exacerbated in countries where there is armed conflict. Not only are children often orphaned or separated from their family and left without food or care, but many are direct participants in war.

Khaled Fazaa/AFP/Getty Images

Piers Benetar/Panos Pictures

HUMAN RIGHTS VIOLATIONS "Women between the ages of fifteen and forty-four are more likely to be maimed or killed by male violence than by war, cancer, malaria, and traffic incidents combined. More women have been killed by neglect and violence in the last 50 years than men have by all the wars of the twentieth century" (Coleman 2010, p. 127). Pictured (left) is Bibi Aisha, an Afghan woman whose husband cut off her nose and ears as punishment for running away from her abusive in-laws. Children are also victims of human rights violations. On the right, a starving farmer in Afghanistan, Akhtar Mohammed, watches his ten-year-old son, Sher, whom he traded to a wealthy farmer in exchange for a monthly supply of wheat. "What else could I do?" he asked. "I will miss my son, but there was nothing to eat."

In 2010, the United Nations estimated that 300,000 boys and girls under the age of eighteen were recruited and used as child soldiers in violation of international law. The prior year, the UN had identified fourteen countries where the use of child soldiers was commonplace.

Because children are smaller than adults and more easily intimidated, they typically make obedient soldiers. Some are abducted from their homes, others fight under threat of death, and others join out of desperation or a desire to avenge the death of family members. A special report to the United Nations, *Impact of Armed Conflict on Children*, concluded:

> In the past decade alone, an estimated 2 million children have been killed in armed conflict. Three times as many have been seriously injured or permanently disabled. Countless others have been forced to witness or even to take part in horrifying acts of violence. These statistics are shocking enough, but more chilling is the conclusion to be drawn from them: more and more of the world is being sucked into a desolate moral vacuum, a space devoid of the most basic human values, a space in which children are slaughtered, raped and maimed, where children are exploited as soldiers, starved and exposed to extreme brutality.

In order to confront the problem of child soldiers, "their legal protection is essential. But it is only possible to reduce the involvement of children in war if the political leaders are more interested in the welfare of the child than in military strategies" (Druba 2002, p. 271).

On August 4, 2009, the UN Security Council unanimously adopted a resolution that expands the Secretary-General's annual report on grave violations of children by groups involved in armed conflict to include the names of groups that kill or maim children contrary to international law, or perpetrate grave sexual violence against children in wartime. "This is a major step forward in the fight against impunity for crimes against children and a recognition of the reality of conflict today, where girls and boys are increasingly targeted and victimized, killed and raped, as well as recruited into armed groups" said Radhika Coomaraswamy, Special Representative of the UN Secretary-General for Children and Armed Conflict.

The treatment of children has traditionally been seen as a "private" issue of family life that is firmly rooted in cultural values and traditions. Nonetheless, as innocents in our global society, many believe that security and sustenance are basic human rights to which children are entitled, and that the international community must assist in the protection of these human rights. These sentiments were embraced by the Convention on the Rights of the Child (CRC), which the United Nations adopted on November 20, 1989. The basic human rights that the CRC establishes for children everywhere, spelled out in fifty-four articles and two optional protocols, include:

- the right to survival;
- to develop to the fullest;
- to protection from harmful influences, abuse, and exploitation;
- to participate fully in family, cultural, and social life.

Emphasizing an entitlement to human dignity and harmonious development, and ratified by all of the UN member states except the United States and Somalia, this treaty is widely seen as a landmark victory for human rights. As the human rights NGO Amnesty International enthusiastically proclaimed, "Here for the first time was a treaty that sought to address the particular human rights of children and to set minimum standards for the protection of their rights. It is the only international treaty to guarantee civil and political rights as well as economic, social, and cultural rights."

RESPONDING TO HUMAN RIGHTS ABUSES

There are at least three arguments that oppose the promotion and enforcement of human rights by the global community. Realists reject human rights promotion because, as Executive Director of Amnesty International William Shulz explains, they "regard the pursuit of rights as an unnecessary, sometimes even a dangerous extravagance, often at odds with the national interest." Statists or legalists reject human rights promotion in target states because it represents an unwarranted intrusion into the domestic affairs of others and an infringement upon the principle of state sovereignty. Relativists or pluralists view human rights promotion as a form of moral imperialism (Blanton and Cingranelli 2010; Donnelly 2003).

Nonetheless, there is an "increasing willingness to regard concern for human rights violations as acceptable justification for various kinds of international intervention in the domestic affairs of states ranging from diplomatic and economic sanctions to military action" (Beitz 2001, p. 269). As constructivists tell us, the evolution of global values can have a powerful impact on international behavior. "Virtually any explanation of the rise of human rights must take into account the political power of norms and ideas and the increasingly transnational way in which those ideas are carried and diffused" (Sikkink 2008, p. 172).

The most common manifestation of this trend is the expansion in recent years of laws that regulate the practices that sovereign states may use. The human rights revolution has advanced moral progress by breaking states' monopoly on international affairs and over citizens (Ignatieff 2004b). In this sense, liberalism triumphed and *realism* was repudiated, for the human rights movement has rejected the harsh realist vision expressed by Thomas Hobbes, who argued in the seventeenth century that because world politics is "a war of all against all, the notions of right and wrong, justice and injustice have there no place."

Moreover, international law has fundamentally revised the traditional realist protection of the state by redefining the relationship of states to humans. As former UN Secretary-General Kofi Annan often notes, "States are now widely understood to be instruments at the service of their people, and not *vice versa*. When we read the Charter today, we are more than ever conscious that its aim is to protect individual human beings, not to protect those who abuse them."

If you are neutral in a situation of injustice, you have chosen the side of the oppressor.

—Archbishop Desmund Tutu, Nobel Prize winner

The Human Rights Legal Framework

The global community has expanded its legal protection of human rights significantly over the past sixty years. Multilateral treaties have proliferated as part of a global effort to construct consensus on the rights of humanity and to put an end to human rights abuse. A large number of conventions have been enacted that have steadily endowed individuals with rights—asserting that people must be treated as worthy of the freedom and dignity traditionally granted by international law to states and rulers. Moreover, from the perspective of international law, a state is obligated to respect the human rights of its own citizens as well as those of another country, and the international community has the prerogative to challenge any state that does not do so. Table 15.2 highlights eight international agreements, in addition to the Universal Declaration of Human Rights, that provide a fundamental foundation for the international human rights legal framework.

Among these treaties and instruments of international law, the Universal Declaration of Human Rights, the International Covenant on Economic, Social and Cultural Rights, and the International Covenant on Civil and Political Rights together form the "International Bill of Human Rights." Additionally, there are hundreds of legal instruments and political declarations across

Table 15.2   Core Conventions of the International Human Rights Legal Framework

1948	Universal Declaration of Human Rights
1965	International Convention on the Elimination of All Forms of Racial Discrimination (ICERD)
1966	International Covenant on Civil and Political Rights (ICCPR)
1966	International Covenant on Economic, Social, and Cultural Rights (ICESCR)
1979	Convention on the Elimination of All Forms of Discrimination against Women (CEDAW)
1984	Convention against Torture and Other Cruel, Inhumane or Degrading Treatment or Punishment (CAT)
1989	Convention on the Rights of the Child (CRC)
1990	International Convention on the Protection of the Rights of All Migrant Workers and Members of Their Families (ICRMW)
2006	Convention on the Rights of Persons with Disabilities (CRPD)

a wide array of human rights issues, many of which have been accepted by most states. They provide specific standards for human rights protection for vulnerable groups such as women, children, migrant workers, and disabled persons and for collective rights for minorities and indigenous groups. The United Nations and its members have been a driving force behind the development of a global human rights legal system. The International Labor Organization (ILO) and regional organizations such as the African Union, the Inter-American Commission on Human Rights, and the European Court of Human Rights have established human rights protections as well.

The Challenge of Enforcement

Once the content of human rights obligations was enumerated in multilateral treaties, international attention shifted to monitoring their implementation and addressing violations. Unfortunately, "the deepening international human rights regime creates opportunities for rights-violating governments to display low-cost legitimating commitments to world norms, leading them to ratify human rights treaties without the capacity or willingness to comply with the provisions" (Hafner-Burton et al. 2008, p. 115; see also Powell and Staton 2009). There are some countries that endorse human rights treaties as merely a superficial symbolic commitment and continue to repress human rights.

Moreover, full agreement has yet to be reached on the extent to which the international community has a responsibility to intervene in order to enforce human rights. As the International Commission on Intervention and State

Sovereignty noted in its report, *The Responsibility to Protect*, "If intervention for human protection purposes is to be accepted, including the possibility of military action, it remains imperative that the international community develop consistent, credible, and enforceable standards to guide state and intergovernmental practice." While expanding global norms that elevate human security do much to advance the cause of human rights, critical policy questions remain about what steps can and should be taken to safeguard these rights and prevent violations (Ramcharan 2010).

CONTROVERSY:

SHOULD TYRANNY AND HUMAN RIGHTS VIOLATIONS JUSTIFY HUMANITARIAN INTERVENTION?

Imagine yourself an American on a vacation in a foreign country. You find yourself unjustly imprisoned on accusations that you were transporting illegal drugs, spying for your government, trafficking in the practice and sale of children for prostitution, you name it. You are innocent and you are angry! Your human right to basic civil liberties has been violated. To make matters incredibly worse, you discover that the jail in which you are incarcerated is full of thousands of political prisoners held, and abused, by their guards, who are employed by a military dictatorship that claims the sovereign right to treat all accused lawbreakers any way they want. Never in the authorities' explanation is mention made of human rights, such as trial by a jury of peers and prohibition against the cruel punishment of prisoners.

What can you do? You are an innocent victim. Do you, and for that matter the hundreds of other possibly innocent victims in prison with you, have any hope?

For centuries, the answer was that your fate was hopeless. You had no power. Power was monopolized by state governments, which could do anything and everything to protect and promote their self-interests by preempting potential threats to their self-preservation. That code of conduct, enshrined in the 1648 Westphalian treaties drafted by realists, proclaimed that state authority was sacrosanct and that people and their human rights were subservient. For the state and its rulers, anything goes toward subjects within a sovereign country's territory.

However, there is protection: recently, international law has radically changed. "For nearly 60 years after the creation of the Universal Declaration of Human Rights in 1948, there [was] still no international consensus about when [human] rights violations in one state justify other states to interfere" (Ignatieff 2004a). But no longer. Now protecting human rights in foreign states has become legal for the first time under international law. The law has been "updated 'to close the gap between legality and legitimacy' [so that] rules and international law [now have been changed] to permit armed intervention for humanitarian protection" (Slaughter 2004b). There is hope for justice!

Or is there? An ideology that helps to protect your human rights also undermines the national interests of sovereign states. What may be beneficial for you may be harmful to your country. Consider the globe's reigning

(continued)

SHOULD TYRANNY AND HUMAN RIGHTS VIOLATIONS JUSTIFY HUMANITARIAN INTERVENTION? (Continued)

hegemon, the United States, which, even as a liberal democracy that places high value on human rights, has repeatedly placed national security ahead of humanitarian protection. For instance, the United States cited the sovereign right to imprison suspected culprits of the 9/11 terrorist attacks without the right to legal defense or jury in its military prison in Guantánamo, Cuba, and to the imprisonment and (it was later discovered) inhumane treatment of captives in Iraq—to the outrage of the global community. The United States initially claimed a right to indefinitely detain "enemy combatants" on the grounds of "necessity" in times of warfare—this time against faceless terrorists—though the U.S. Supreme Court later ruled in 2008 that detainees had a constitutional right to challenge their detention in federal court.

As you contemplate this hypothetical controversy, keep in mind many countries' entrenched defense of the traditional right of their state to be protected against foreign intervention—even for humanitarian purposes. This is a major issue on the global agenda. Many states, especially the weak and relatively defenseless governments in the Global South, vigorously resist humanitarian interference within their borders and maintain that their resistance to a norm of humanitarian intervention is legal. Even China and the United States oppose the idea that other actors in the global community might claim the right to intervene to protect human rights within their sovereign territory.

WHAT DO YOU THINK?

- How can you reconcile your understandable love of country and its claimed sovereign national interests with your personal need to be shielded by a global code of state conduct that protects the human rights of all?

- In contemplating the priority that you personally give to human rights, with what construction of "security" in our globalized world does it most closely align?

- What role might IGOs and NGOs play in reconciling the potential contradiction between state security and human security as they pertain to human rights?

humanitarian intervention

the use of peacekeeping troops by foreign states or international organizations to protect endangered people from gross violations of their human rights and from mass murder.

Humanitarian intervention encompasses the international community's actions to assist the population of a state experiencing severe human suffering caused by political collapse, deliberate government policy, or natural disaster. The principles that guide humanitarian intervention continue to be a matter of heated debate (see Controversy: Should Tyranny and Human Rights Violations Justify Humanitarian Intervention?). The issue is not whether there exists a compelling need and moral obligation to express concerns about populations at risk of slaughter, starvation, or persecution; the issue is about how to craft a just response, when any response will comprise interference in the domestic affairs of a sovereign state. Humanitarian intervention is controversial because it pits the legal principle of territorial sovereignty against what some see as a moral duty to protect vulnerable populations from egregious violations of human rights.

While the construction of global human rights norms has made great strides over the past sixty years, the enforcement of human rights laws has lagged. Within the United Nations, the Office of the High Commissioner for Human Rights (OHCHR) is responsible for implementing international human rights agreements, overseeing major human rights programs, and providing global leadership on the promotion and protection of human rights. It also supervises the Human Rights Council (HRC).

The HRC is a relatively new *intergovernmental organization*, having been created by the UN General Assembly on March 15, 2006, for the purpose of evaluating situations of human rights abuse and making recommendations about them. At that time, the United States, the Marshall Islands, and Palau voted against the resolution; Iran, Venezuela, and Belarus did not vote. There were concerns that the UNHCR did not have the ability to prevent states with poor human rights records from membership on the Council, and that the agency's mission undermined the principle of nonintervention. In June 2008, the United States relinquished its observer status and disengaged from the HRC, much to the disappointment and concern of human rights advocates who felt that this greatly diminished the role of the IGO and sent a negative message about the importance of human rights around the world. In May 2009, however, the United States sought and was elected to a three-year term on the HRC. "While we recognize that the Human Rights Council has been a flawed body that has not lived up to its potential," explained U.S. ambassador to the United Nations Susan Rice, "we believe that working from within, we can make the council a more effective forum to promote and protect human rights."

Studies have shown that international organizations such as the United Nations "play an important role" in punishing human rights violators and "that seemingly symbolic resolutions of a politically motivated IO can carry tangible consequences" (Lebovic and Voeten 2009, p. 79; see also Greenhill 2010; Mertus 2009). Nonetheless, despite the significant efforts to monitor human rights and enforce norms and agreements, the effectiveness of the United Nations and other intergovernmental organizations is constrained, as they can exercise only the authority that member states delegate to them.

In response to these limitations, nongovernmental organizations (NGOs) have assumed an important role in promoting human rights. They have developed an array of transnational advocacy networks and strategies designed to pressure governments to modify their behavior to conform to prevailing human rights norms and laws (Keck and Sikkink 2008). As Ellen Lutz, Executive Director of *Cultural Survival* (an NGO that protects the human rights of indigenous peoples) explains:

> These organizations investigate human rights abuses wherever they occur, including in places enduring armed conflict. Because of their reputation for accuracy, their findings are relied on by the news media, many governments, and most intergovernmental institutions. While these NGOs hope their reports will bring about a change in the behavior of the government or other entity whose abuses they spotlight, their main targets are the policymakers who are in a more powerful position to put pressure on human rights violators. They lobby other governments to take human rights into account in their foreign aid and press the United Nations and other intergovernmental organizations to put pressure on rights abusers (Lutz 2006, p. 25).

With greater openness to institutional activism in the post–Cold War era, human rights activists have pressed to strengthen enforcement mechanisms. Their efforts account in part for the establishment of UN tribunals to review gross human rights abuse, as in the cases of the former Yugoslavia and Rwanda, and the creation of the International Criminal Court. Activists are also credited with monitoring human rights situations and targeting a "spotlight" of publicity and public scrutiny on abusive practices to shame those that violate human rights into changing their behavior (Blanton and Blanton 2007; Ottaway 2001).

Jerome Delay/AP Photo

PRINCIPLED SECURITY Shown here are inmates in Iraq's Abu Ghraib prison crying for freedom when dictator Saddam Hussein still ruled. After the 2003 U.S. invasion of Iraq, American occupation forces used the same prison to torture suspected insurgents, and Amnesty International condemned this method for fighting terrorism as "atrocious human rights violations." Proclaiming that the United States does not torture, U.S. President Obama signaled a shift in policy, saying, "We must adhere to our values as diligently as we protect our safety, with no exceptions."

While some individuals remain skeptical of claims that we all have transcendent moral obligations to humanity as a whole, others believe that everyone, by virtue of being human, has certain inherent and inalienable rights that warrant international protection. Challenging the realist premise that human rights are at odds with national interest, Executive Director of Amnesty International William Schulz laments that "What they seem rarely to garner is that in far more cases than they will allow, defending human rights is a prerequisite to protecting that interest." Human rights buttress political and economic freedom, "which in turn tends to bring international trade and prosperity. And governments that treat their own people with tolerance and respect tend to treat their neighbors in the same way."

Promoting the rights and dignity of ordinary people around the world is a formidable challenge. Yet, as global security analyst David Rieff notes, "The old assumption that national sovereignty trumps all other principles in international relations is under attack as never before." Because concerns for human rights have gained stature under international law and are being monitored more closely by IGOs and NGOs than ever before, we can expect human rights to receive continuing attention, as long as people are caught in emergency situations such as genocide or the threat of famine. Eleanor Roosevelt championed the *cosmopolitan* ideal, and her energetic leadership was largely responsible for global acceptance in 1948 of the *Universal Declaration of Human Rights*. When thinking about the human condition in the early twenty-first century, we can profit by the inspiration of her nightly prayer: "Save us from ourselves and show us a vision of a world made new."

> *For most of the world's people, the glittering opportunities of the new century are beyond reach . . . The problems may seem insurmountable, but they are not. We have the tools; we have brilliant dedicated people to find answers. All we need is a sense of sharing and the will to change. The will can grow from understanding. Once we care, we can change.*
>
> —Jimmy Carter, U.S. President

John D. Rockefeller, Jr. once said, "I believe that every right implies a responsibility; every opportunity, an obligation; every possession, a duty." In the next chapter of *World Politics*, you will have an opportunity to look at another major issue that entails rights and responsibility to humanity. As the cascading globalization of our world accelerates, the human choices about our natural environment have consequences for the entire planet and affect the Earth's capability to sustain human life and security.

Take an Online Practice Quiz

www.cengagebrain.com/shop/ISBN/0495802204

| *Suggested Readings* |

Blanton, Shannon Lindsey, and David L. Cingranelli. (2010) "Human Rights and Foreign Policy Analysis," in Robert Denemark et al. (eds.), *The International Studies Compendium Project*. Oxford: Wiley-Blackwell.

Landman, Todd. (2006) *Studying Human Rights*. New York: Routledge.

Mertus, Julie. (2009) *Human Rights Matters: Local Politics and National Human Rights Institutions*. Stanford, CA: Stanford University Press.

Ramcharan, Bertrand. (2010) *Preventive Human Rights Strategies*. New York: Routledge.

Skinner, E. Benjamin. (2008) "A World Enslaved," *Foreign Policy* (March/April): 62–67.

UNDP. (2010) *Human Development Report 2010*. New York: United Nations.

CHAPTER 16
GLOBAL RESPONSIBILITY FOR THE PRESERVATION OF THE ENVIRONMENT

*To waste, to destroy our natural resources, to skin and exhaust the
land instead of using it so as to increase its usefulness, will result in
undermining in the days of our children the very prosperity which we
ought by right to hand down to them amplified and developed.*

—Theodore Roosevelt, U.S. President

CHAPTER OUTLINE

THE GLOBALIZATION OF
ENVIRONMENTAL DANGERS

CONTROVERSY: Why Is There
a Global Food Crisis?

Framing the Ecological Debate

The Ecopolitics of the
Atmosphere

The Ecopolitics of Biodiversity,
Deforestation, and Water
Shortages

The Ecopolitics of Energy Supply
and Demand

TOWARD SUSTAINABILITY
AND HUMAN SECURITY

The Tragedy of the Commons

Global Solutions

National and Local Solutions

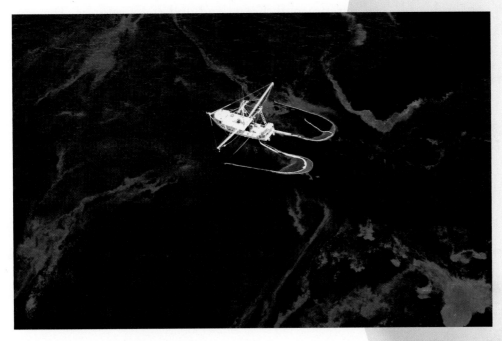

OIL AND WATER DON'T MIX On April 20, 2010, an explosion and fire on BP's Deep Horizon drilling rig killed 11 workers
and led to a massive oil spill that coated the Gulf Coast. The Flow Rate Technical Group, supervised by the U.S.
Geological Survey and the U.S. Department of Energy, estimated that at least 4.9 million barrels—or 205.8 million
gallons—had been dumped into the Gulf of Mexico by the time the well was capped and sealed on July 15. With oil
slicks causing devastation on the surface and dispersants pushing the compounds to deep water areas, the damage
could take decades, or longer, to repair. "It's going to cause very substantial and noticeable damage—marsh loss
and coastal erosion and impact on fisheries, dead birds, dead turtles—but we'll know what that is. It's the things
we don't see that worry me most," worries chemist Ed Overton of Louisiana State University (Begley 2010, p. 26).
Pictured here, a shrimp boat collects oil with booms off the coast of Louisiana.

"Where you stand depends on where you sit" is an aphorism used to describe the determinants of people's positions when they make decisions (recall Chapter 6). Where do you stand on one of the most "hotly" debated issues created by a warming globe and deteriorating environment? You may already have strong feelings about this controversy. Many others do. On whichever side of the environmental debate you fall, there is at least one scholar and several politicians who share your opinion.

Some scientists and politicians reject the view that the planet is really in danger; they claim that there is not a real problem because technological innovation can reverse the trends in global warming (which they argue may not even be "real" because the long-term cyclical pattern of the Earth's evolution suggests that our present period of rising temperatures is temporary). These people claim that environmental deterioration and resource depletion have many people needlessly alarmed.

Other scientists are pessimistic and are now certain that the threats are real. They are themselves alarmed by optimists who fail to face the "clear and present danger" of environmental threats and undertake reforms. The ecological threats that rivet the worried scientific community were documented in Al Gore's famous movie and book on global warming, *An Inconvenient Truth,* for which he won a 2007 Nobel Peace Prize. Those frightened climate experts are advocating big changes by governments, and *now*—before it becomes too late to save the human race from certain doom.

In this chapter, you have the opportunity to sharpen your own thinking by weighing the available evidence about prevailing global trends conditioning the environment shared by all on Earth. So take a look at various dimensions of the planet's ecology now in transformation. Then base your stand on this global issue on information that can better ground your existing opinions, and consider what responsibility humanity has to preserve our global environment.

"Future prosperity and stability means rethinking how we exploit the planet's natural assets."

—UN Secretary-General, Ban Ki-moon

THE GLOBALIZATION OF ENVIRONMENTAL DANGERS

Global environmental issues engage the competing perspectives of optimistic *cornucopians* and pessimistic *neo-Malthusians.* Cornucopians adhere to the belief that if free markets and free trade are practiced, ecological imbalances

cornucopians
optimists who question limits-to-growth perspectives and contend that markets effectively maintain a balance between population, resources, and the environment.

neo-Malthusians
pessimists who warn of the global ecopolitical dangers of uncontrolled population growth.

that threaten humanity will eventually be corrected. For them, prices are the key adjustment mechanism that in time produces the greatest good for the greatest number of people.

Neo-Malthusians, on the other hand, share more in common with economic *mercantilism*, which argues that free markets fail to prevent excessive exploitation of both renewable and nonrenewable resources and that, accordingly, intervention by governing institutions is necessary. This latter perspective rejects the belief that the free market will always maximize social welfare.

Cornucopians and neo-Malthusians paint very different pictures of our future, and how we frame our understanding of environmental challenges will affect our policy prescriptions. Whether the world community has the political will and capacity to cope with ecological problems and expand the possibilities for humanity will be critical for *human security*. A paradigm, or popular way of organizing thought, about international problems is rising among scholars and policy makers who are now convinced that threats to the preservation of the global commons likewise threaten our basic welfare and security.

Framing the Ecological Debate

Environmental concerns are linked to other values that states prize, notably, security, economic prosperity, and social well-being. "Security" means freedom from fear, risk, and danger. Because fears of a nuclear holocaust and other forms of violence have long haunted the world, security has been conventionally equated with *national security*, the struggle for state power central to *realist theory* and its emphasis on armed aggression.

Environmental security broadens the definition of national security by pushing visions beyond borders and their protection. It focuses on the transborder character of challenges to preserving the global environment by recognizing that threats such as global warming, ozone depletion, and the loss of tropical forests and marine habitats can threaten the future of humanity as much as the threat of warfare using weapons of mass destruction. Because environmental degradation undercuts states' economic well-being and the quality of life of their citizens, *liberalism* informs current thinking about how states can cooperate with international organizations (IGOs) and nongovernmental organizations (NGOs) to preserve the global environment. The liberal *epistemic community* has redefined "security" in order to move beyond realism's conventional state-centric and militaristic portrayal of international politics.

environmental security a concept recognizing that environmental threats to global life systems are as dangerous as the threat of armed conflicts.

epistemic community scientific experts on a subject of inquiry such as global warming that are organized internationally as NGOs to communicate with one another and use their constructed understanding of "knowledge" to lobby for global transformations.

Today, many experts urge people and governments to construct a broader definition of what really constitutes security (as the U.S. Department of Defense did in April 2007 when it warned that global warming should be regarded as a threat to American national security). This reconstruction is compatible with liberal theory, which emphasizes that security should be defined as the capacity to protect quality of life. Out of conditions of global poverty and want emerge the so-called *politics of scarcity,* which anticipates that future international conflict will likely be caused by resource scarcities—restricted access to food, oil, and water, for example—rather than by overt military challenges. Moreover, insufficient or polluted resources will depress the living conditions of all of the people on the Earth, but particularly those in the Global South where the ability and political will to address environmental challenges are limited (see Controversy: Why Is There a Global Food Crisis?).

Ecologists—those who study the interrelationships of living organisms and the Earth's physical environment—use the term *the global commons* to highlight our growing interdependence, because they see the Earth as a common environment made up of the totality of organisms. In a world where everything affects everything else, the fate of the global commons is the fate of humanity. The planet's *carrying capacity*—the Earth's ability to support and sustain life—is at the center of discussion about the future of the global commons. One concerned view about this declining capacity is voiced by Lester R. Brown, the president of the Earth Policy Institute, who argued:

> Throughout history, humans have lived on the Earth's sustainable yield— the interest from its natural endowment. Now, however, we are consuming the endowment itself. In ecology, as in economics, we can consume principal along with interest in the short run, but, for the long term, that practice leads to bankruptcy.

The pessimists sounding the alarm about the signs of ecological deterioration, and the optimists confidently extolling the virtues of free markets and technological innovation in saving the planet, portray very different visions of the global future.

Sustainable development is now popularly perceived as an alternative to the quest for unrestrained growth. The movement began in earnest in 1972, when the UN General Assembly convened the first UN Conference of the Human Environment in Stockholm. Since then, conferences on a wide range of environmental topics have produced scores of treaties and new international agencies to promote cooperation and monitor environmental developments.

politics of scarcity
the view that the unavailability of resources required to sustain life, such as food, energy, or water, can undermine security in degrees similar to military aggression.

the global commons
the physical and organic characteristics and resources of the entire planet—the air in the atmosphere and conditions on land and sea—on which human life depends and which is the common heritage of all humanity.

carrying capacity
the maximum number of humans and living species that can be supported by a given territory.

sustainable development
economic growth that does not deplete the resources needed to maintain life and prosperity.

CONTROVERSY:

WHY IS THERE A GLOBAL FOOD CRISIS?

You do not have to go far to learn about the impact of the global food crisis. Indeed, a quick trip to the grocery store is revealing—since 2003, bread prices have gone up almost 75 percent, pork prices have more than doubled, and the price of bananas has gone up over 40 percent (Dykman 2008, p. 35). Globally, increased food prices have created a good deal of civil unrest as well as a wave of humanitarian crises in the developing world. Between 2007 and the start of 2009, nearly forty countries had food riots—such as the "tortilla riots" in Mexico and the "pasta riots" in Italy (Landeau 2010). "Oddly enough, almost none of the food riots had emerged from a lack of food . . . . The riots had been generated by the lack of money to buy food" (Kaufman 2009, p. 51). As World Bank President Robert Zoellick concluded, "we are entering a danger zone" that threatens to drive over 100 million additional people into extreme poverty (World Bank 2008).

Examining some of the major factors that are pushing us into this "danger zone" provides insight into the interconnected nature of global threats, the trade-offs inherent in trying to provide for human needs, as well as the ways in which the policies of individual governments and international organizations can influence the international system as a whole. With that in mind, let us briefly touch upon some of the major root causes of the food crisis:

- Environmental Stress. Changing demographics and climates contribute to the crisis. For example, increases in urbanization have resulted in increased stress upon the agricultural sectors—not only is key agricultural land often incorporated into rapidly growing urban areas, but government support formerly targeted at agricultural sectors (such as assistance with irrigation and farm equipment) may be diverted to urban development (Teslik 2008). One of the primary effects of climate change is an increase in "extreme weather" events, and such events have had a key role in damaging agricultural production. For example, droughts in Australia cut its wheat production in half, while flooding in Ecuador played a key role in the recent rise of banana prices.

- Government Policies. As noted in Chapter 13, governments have traditionally protected their agricultural markets through subsidies and tariffs, which have served to increase the price of many agricultural goods. Moreover, recent food shortages have resulted in a proliferation of another form of government intervention—limits on the export of agricultural products such as wheat and rice. Indeed, the UN World Food Programme found that forty countries were currently engaging in such export bans (Teslik 2008). These bans serve to decrease the world supply of these goods, which thus increases prices. Along these lines, government encouragement of biofuel production has had an impact upon food prices. "About 30 percent of the projected increases in global food prices over the next several decades can be attributed to increased biofuel production worldwide" (Runge and Runge 2010, p. 14).

- Prices. The cost of agricultural inputs has risen greatly. Agriculture relies heavily on petroleum for many aspects of production as well as transport, and the sector has thus been hit hard by increases in energy prices (Mendelsohn 2009). Moreover, fertilizer prices have also risen dramatically. For example, the price of nitrogen fertilizer has increased over 350 percent since 1999 (*Financial Times* 2007).

(continued)

WHY IS THERE A GLOBAL FOOD CRISIS? (Continued)

- Food Consumption Patterns. In emerging markets, such as China, India, Russia, and Brazil, people have changed their eating habits as their countries have developed. In particular, these countries have greatly increased their consumption of meat and dairy products. For example, meat consumption in China, traditionally a vegetarian society, has more than doubled since 1980, and dairy consumption has tripled (Dymkan 2008). Dairy consumption in Brazil doubled from 2005 to 2007 (*Financial Times* 2007). This has contributed to increased demand for these products, as well as the inputs necessary for their production (such as cattle feed).

According to the UN's Food and Agricultural Organization, in order to meet the growing demands of a global population that is expected to surpass 9 billion by 2050, food production must increase by 70 percent. But there are concerns that the food crisis is intensifying due to three ominous trends: the rate of increase in crop yields appears to be slowing, agricultural research expenditures have diminished (especially in Africa), and global food supplies have begun to decline relative to demand as food prices have begun to increase (Runge and Runge 2010). Unfortunately, many of the causes of the food crisis are the result of structural changes that are quite averse to change in the short term. As Josette Sheeran, Executive Director of the United Nations World Food Programme, lamented, "If we do not act quickly, the bottom billion will become the bottom two billion virtually overnight as their purchasing power is cut in half due to a doubling in food and fuel prices."

This raises a related issue—how should we respond to this crisis? Most every international organization has begun to articulate some type of response, though maintaining the political will to enact fundamental changes is always difficult. Developed countries, for example, are very resistant to reducing agricultural subsidies. Moreover, some of the suggested solutions, such as the increased use of *genetic engineering* and *transgenetic crops* and livestock, are quite controversial and not supported by a variety of countries and NGOs. The dominant cornucopian social paradigm stressing the right to conspicuous consumption is under global attack, but many challenges remain to achieving sustainable development worldwide.

WHAT DO YOU THINK?

- Of the causes of the food crisis mentioned here—environmental stress, government policies, prices of agricultural inputs, and food consumption patterns—which do you think is most important to address in overcoming the crisis? Why?

- As a policy maker, how would you balance the need for addressing domestic poverty with the need to contribute to assisting with the international humanitarian food crisis?

- The food crisis raises a question fundamental to our existence: is our world capable of supporting itself? What insights do realist, liberal, and constructivist theories provide as to our future prospects?

The concept of sustainable development is even more directly traceable to *Our Common Future,* the 1987 report of the World Commission on Environment and Development, popularly known as the "Brundtland Commission," after the Norwegian prime minister who chaired it. The commission concluded that the world cannot sustain the growth required to meet the needs and aspirations of the world's growing population unless it adopts radically different approaches to basic issues of economic expansion, equity, resource management, energy efficiency, and the like. Rejecting the "limits to growth" maxim popular among neo-Malthusians, it emphasized instead "the growth of limits." The commission defined a "sustainable society" as one that "meets the needs of the present without compromising the ability of future generations to meet their own needs."

Another milestone in the challenge to the then-dominant cornucopian social paradigm occurred at the 1992 Earth Summit in Rio de Janeiro, Brazil, on the twentieth anniversary of the Stockholm conference. The meeting brought together more than 150 states, 1,400 nongovernmental organizations, and 8,000 journalists. Before the Earth Summit, the environment and economic

genetic engineering research geared to discover seeds for new types of plant and human life for sale and use as substitutes for those produced naturally.

transgenetic crops new crops with improved characteristics created artificially through genetic engineering that combine genes from species that would not naturally interbreed.

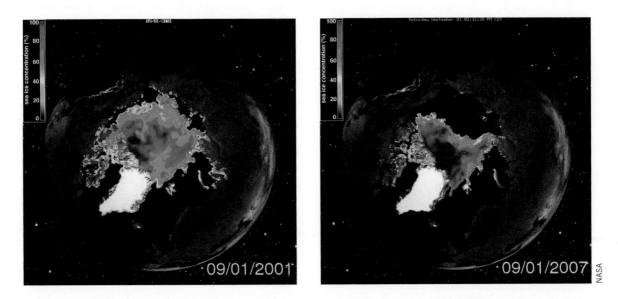

ENVIRONMENTAL THREATS ON A PLANETARY SCALE   When U.S. astronauts first viewed Earth from the Apollo spacecraft, they told millions of listeners about the "big blue marble" planet they saw and how the clouds and continents flowed into one another without regard to the political boundaries imposed by humans on a pristine planet. Today, improvement in space technology allows the world to see uncomfortable images—of atmospheric poisons that encircle the globe, violent winter and summer storms pounding islands and continental shores, vanishing forests, widening deserts, and expansion of the massive hole in the ozone layer. Pictured are NASA satellite images of the Arctic icecap in September 2001 and September 2007. As you can see, the Arctic icecap is rapidly melting and is "only half the size that it was fifty years ago" (Borgerson 2008, p.63).

development had been treated separately—and often regarded as being in conflict with each other because economic growth frequently imperils and degrades the environment. In Rio, the concept of sustainability galvanized a simultaneous treatment of environmental and development issues.

Other international conferences have since punctuated the strong consensus behind the proposition that all politics—even global politics—are local, that what happens any place ultimately affects conditions every place, and accordingly that the protection of Earth's environment is a primary international security issue. In anticipation of the climate conference in Copenhagen in December 2009, UN Secretary-General Ban Ki-moon urgently called on members to concretely address climate change and greenhouse gas emissions, stating, "We must harness the political will to seal the deal on an ambitious new climate agreement. . . . If we get it wrong we face catastrophic damage to people, to the planet." Others recognized that the challenges to reaching a global agreement were great and anticipated that a comprehensive treaty would not be reached at the Copenhagen meeting (Levi 2009; Bueno de Mesquita 2009).

Sustainability cannot be realized without substantial changes. Is that possible? Are individuals willing to sacrifice personal consumption for the common good? Will they sacrifice now to enrich their heirs? To make a prediction, the next step is for you to characterize and estimate the nature and magnitude of environmental threats and challenges. Consider next three interrelated clusters of problems on the global ecopolitical agenda: (1) climate change and ozone depletion, (2) biodiversity and deforestation, and (3) energy supply and demand. The clusters illustrate some of the obstacles to the sustainable development of common properties and renewable resources.

The Ecopolitics of the Atmosphere

The scores of government negotiators and nongovernmental representatives who converged on Rio de Janeiro in 1992 came in the wake of the hottest decade on record. For years, scientists had warned that global warming—the gradual rise in world temperature—would cause destructive changes in world climatological patterns and that rising sea levels, melting glaciers, and freak storms would provoke widespread changes in the globe's political and economic systems and relationships. Perhaps because they had been burned by the chronic heat wave throughout the 1980s, negotiators agreed at Rio to a *Framework Convention on Climate Change*. Since then, fears have increased in conjunction with the continuing rise of planetary temperatures. In response to the series of record-setting global temperatures in the twenty-first century, attention to the pollutants blamed for global warming has risen.

Climate Change and Global Warming   Major gaps in knowledge about climate change remain, but most climate scientists are now convinced that the gradual rise in the Earth's temperature, especially evident since the late eighteenth century when the invention of power-driven machinery produced the Industrial Revolution, is caused by an increase in human-made gases that alter the atmosphere's insulating effects. The gas molecules, primarily carbon dioxide (CO_2) and chlorofluorocarbons (CFCs), form the equivalent of a greenhouse roof by trapping heat remitted from Earth that would otherwise escape into outer space. Since 1950, the emissions of carbon dioxide from the burning of fossil fuels have climbed steadily and risen fourfold. Additionally, deforestation has contributed to global warming, as it "accounts for 17 to 25 percent of global greenhouse gas emissions . . . second only after energy use" (Jenkins 2009, p. 87).

As these gases are released into the atmosphere, they have created a *greenhouse effect,* which has caused global temperatures to rise. As shown in Figure 16.1, the average global temperature on the Earth's surface since the late 1800s has increased between 0.7 and 1.4 degrees Fahrenheit (0.4 to 0.8 degree Celsius). "Many experts estimate that the average global temperature will rise an additional 2.5 to 10.4 degrees F (1.4 to 5.8 degrees Celsius) by 2100. That rate of increase would be much larger than most past rates of increase," meaning that the warming trend is accelerating (NASA 2007).

greenhouse effect
the phenomenon producing planetary warming when gases released by burning fossil fuels act as a blanket in the atmosphere, thereby increasing temperatures.

FIGURE 16.1

RISING AVERAGE GLOBAL TEMPERATURES AT THE EARTH'S SURFACE SINCE 1867   **The World Meteorological Organization (WMO) monitors average global surface temperatures at thousands of sites around the world. Its records show that so-called global warming is not a myth. For 150 years, the globe's temperature has seesawed up and down, usually by tiny fractions of degrees. However, since the mid-1970s the mercury has been rising, and the 1996–2010 period has been the warmest since reliable measurements began. The UN's Intergovernmental Panel on Climate Change (IPCC) predicts that, depending on greenhouse-gas emissions, global temperature will probably rise about 2 to 12 degrees Fahrenheit by 2100, with longer and more intense heat waves. NASA makes a similar forecast, anticipating that temperature may increase by 2.5 to 10.4 degrees Fahrenheit within that time span.**

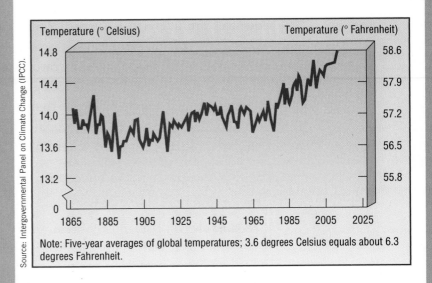

Source: Intergovernmental Panel on Climate Change (IPCC).

Note: Five-year averages of global temperatures; 3.6 degrees Celsius equals about 6.3 degrees Fahrenheit.

The globe's temperature is now projected to further increase dramatically by 2100 if aggressive preventive action is not taken. Although CO_2 is the principal greenhouse gas, concentrations of methane in the atmosphere are growing more rapidly. Methane gas emissions arise from livestock populations, rice cultivation, and the production and transportation of natural gas. To the alarm of many scientists, the largest concentrations of methane are not in the atmosphere but locked in ice, permafrost, and coastal marine sediments. This raises the probability that warming will cause more methane to be released into the atmosphere, which would then increase global temperatures because of methane's strong warming potential.

Some scientists insist that the rise in global temperature is only part of a cyclical change the world has experienced for thousands of years. They are able to cite evidence of "sudden and dramatic temperature swings over the past 400,000 years, from warm climates to ice ages. [These] global warming skeptics say the climate changes we're seeing today reflect these natural variations" (Knickerbocker 2007), and that cold water needs to be poured on all the "hot air" because global warming is a climate myth.

But "most climate scientists say human-induced greenhouse gases are at work—and note that these temperature changes correlate with levels of carbon dioxide" (Knickerbocker 2007). The UN team of hundreds of atmospheric scientists from around the world known as the Intergovernmental Panel on Climate Change (IPCC) first conclusively stated in 1995 its belief that global climate trends are "unlikely to be entirely due to natural causes," that humans are to blame for at least part of the problem, and that the consequences are likely to be very harmful and costly. The implications were self-evident: without significant efforts to reduce the emission of greenhouse gases, the increase in global temperatures by the year 2100 could be equivalent to that which ended the last ice age. Even at the lower end of the panel's estimates, the rise would be faster than any experienced in recorded human history. According to the IPCC, global warming is not coming, it's here, and it has led to a rising number of natural disasters.

The IPCC warns that the effects of continued rising temperatures will be both dramatic and devastating:

- Sea levels will rise, mostly because of melting glaciers and the expansion of water as it warms up. This will produce massive floods of vast areas of low-lying coastal lands, especially in Asia and the U.S. Atlantic coast. New York City could be submerged. Millions of people are likely to be displaced by major floods each year.

GLOBAL WARMING, CLIMATIC CATASTROPHES, AND MASS SUFFERING   As the globe heats up, so have the numbers of natural disasters. A devastating outbreak of wildfires was set loose by drought and the most intense heat wave seen in Russia in 130 years. Shown (left) are people wearing face masks in Moscow's Red Square in August 2010 to protect themselves from forest-fire smog that contains harmful toxins. Over fifty lives were lost and 3,000 left homeless from more than 800 individual forest fires. Also shown (right) is the damage caused in January 2010 by a massive 7.0 earthquake in Haiti that left roughly 300,000 people dead, 1.5 million homeless, and destroyed 280,000 homes and businesses. Months after the devastation occurred, Haiti still struggled to recover.

- Winters will get warmer and heat waves will become increasingly frequent and severe, producing avalanches from melting glaciers in high altitudes.

- Rainfall will increase worldwide, and deadly storms such as the devastating Asian cyclone in 2008 will become more common. As ocean temperatures continue to rise, hurricanes, which draw their energy from warm oceans, will become increasingly stronger and more frequent.

- Because water evaporates more easily in a warmer climate, drought-prone regions will become even drier.

- Up to 30 percent of living species will face an increasing risk of extinction as entire ecosystems vanish from the planet. A hotter Earth will drive some plant life to higher latitudes and altitudes, requiring farmers to change their crops and agricultural practices.

- The combination of flooding and droughts will cause tropical diseases such as malaria and dengue fever to flourish in previously temperate regions that were formerly too cold for their insect carriers; "a warmer CO_2-rich world will be very, very good for plants, insects, and microbes that make us sick" (Begley 2007).

- The world will face increased hunger and water shortages, especially in the poorest countries. Africa will be the hardest hit, with up to 250 million people likely to suffer water shortages by 2020 (Bates et al. 2008).

Not all countries are contributing to global warming at the same rate. The high-income Global North states contribute more than half of global carbon emissions, in large measure because of their big buildings, millions of cars, and relatively inefficient industries. However, the Global East dynamos China and India have rapidly increased their emissions as their economies have grown and generated increasing demands for fossil fuel energy. In 2010, China surpassed the United States as the world's top emitter of greenhouse gases, with responsibility for over 20 percent of all emissions (WDI 2010, p. 184). The International Energy Agency forecasts that the increase of greenhouse-gas emissions from 2000 to 2030 from China alone will nearly equal the increase from the entire industrialized world. India, though behind its Global East rival, could see greenhouse-gas emissions that rise 70 percent by 2025 (Walsh 2006, p. 61).

Compare the existing and new industrial giants' consumption of energy and production of greenhouse gases with the low-income Global South countries. They, too, are growing rapidly (see Chapter 4), and their appetite for fossil fuel energy sources is growing along with their economic development. The Global South produces over 60 percent of global energy and is responsible for just over half of the world's energy use (WDI 2010, p. 180). Thus, countries in all regions are contributing, at different rates, to the global trend in the growing level of carbon added to the atmosphere.

Yet, rather than comparing rich and poor countries, the *Proceedings of the National Academy of Sciences* has suggested that "it is rich people, rather than rich countries, who need to change the most. The authors suggest setting a cap on total emissions, and then converting that cap into a global per-person limit…. So the high-living, carbon guzzling rich minority in India and China would not be able to hide behind their poor and carbon-thrifty compatriots" (*The Economist* 2009, p. 62). While far too difficult to implement, the proposal highlights how the lower level of carbon emissions in the Global South masks the variation within states where the wealthy contribute at a far higher rate to environmental degradation than the poor.

These trends in greenhouse-gas emissions, as well as the changing percentage of world greenhouse-gas emissions by sector, suggests that the energy picture will change but that global warming and the environmental damage it causes are problems that are not likely to change (see Figure 16.2).

The politics of global warming is dramatically illustrated by the tensions between countries over carving up the Arctic in order to reap economic payoffs from exploitation of the resources that lie beneath the polar icecap.

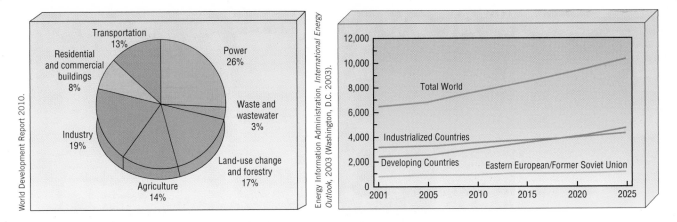

FIGURE 16.2

TRENDS IN GREENHOUSE GASES   Despite the global economic recession, concentrations of CO_2 in the atmosphere rose 2.1 parts per million in 2008 (Begley 2009b). The figure on the left charts the sources of greenhouse-gas emissions by each major sector. The figure on the right identifies the distribution of carbon-equivalent greenhouse-gas emissions by region from 2001 and projected through the year 2025.

Climate change affects the Arctic intensely, because the average temperature there has risen at a rate about twice as fast as the rest of the planet (*Futurist* 2007, p. 33), with the melting of Arctic sea ice occurring more rapidly than projected by the IPCC "largely because emissions of carbon dioxide have topped what the panel" expected (Begley 2009, p. 30). This trend is paving the way for a geopolitical struggle over ecopolitics among the five countries already laying claim to the resource-rich central zone (Russia, Norway, Canada, the United States, and Denmark).

The primary motive: possession of as much as one-fourth of the world's remaining oil and gas reserves buried beneath the seabed under Arctic ice. A "cold rush" is under way in the battle for the melting north (Funk 2007). The disappearing ice also offers the possibility of new sea routes, at least for part of the year, which would significantly reduce the time it takes for ships to travel from Europe to Asia. "As global warming melts the Arctic ice, dreams of a short sea passage to Asia—and riches beneath the surface—have been revived. With Russia planting a flag on the ocean floor at the North Pole, Canada talking tough and Washington wanting to be a player, who will win the world's new Great Game?" (Graff 2007). None of this international friction would have materialized had global warming not made competition for control of this geostrategic arena possible.

Joel Sartore/National Geographic/Getty Images

FEELING THE HEAT The UN's intergovernmental Panel on Climate Change (IPCC), composed of 600 scientists from forty countries, concluded that evidence of the Earth's rising temperatures was "unequivocal" and that global warming was more than 90 percent likely to be the product of human activity. Shown here is one consequence: dramatic melting of Arctic ice. As demographic environmentalist Bill McKibbin warns, "We are heating up the planet, substantially. This is not a problem for the distant future, or even the near future. The planet has already heated up a degree or more. We are perhaps a quarter of the way into the greenhouse era, and the effects are already being felt."

ozone layer
the protective layer of the upper atmosphere over the Earth's surface that shields the planet from the sun's harmful impact on living organisms.

Ozone Depletion and Protection The story of climate change is similar to states' efforts to cope with the depletion of the atmosphere's protective *ozone layer* In this case, however, an international regime has emerged, progressively strengthened by mounting scientific evidence that environmental damage is directly caused by human activity.

Ozone is a pollutant in the lower atmosphere, but in the upper atmosphere it provides the Earth with a critical layer of protection against the sun's harmful ultraviolet radiation. Scientists have discovered a marked depletion of the ozone layer—most notably an "ozone hole" over Antarctica that has grown larger than the continental United States. They have conclusively linked the thinning of the layer to CFCs—a related family of compounds known as halons, hydrochlorofluorocarbons (HCFCs), methyl bromide, and other chemicals. Depletion of the ozone layer exposes humans to health hazards of various sorts, particularly skin cancer, and threatens other forms of marine and terrestrial life.

Scientists began to link halons and CFCs to ozone depletion in the early 1970s. The 1987 landmark *Montreal Protocol on Substances That Deplete the Ozone Layer* treaty, which as of June 2010 had been ratified by

196 parties, has led to a huge 90 percent reduction since the late 1980s in global atmospheric concentrations of chlorofluorocarbons (UNEP 2010; WDI 2007). The expansion of the ozone regime was made possible by growing scientific evidence and by having an active NGO epistemic community to actively promote the treaty. However, in spite of reductions in CFCs over the past twenty years, the ozone hole over Antarctica continues to expand, and depletion of the protective ozone shield is expected to continue before it begins to regenerate itself.

Production of CFCs in the Global North declined sharply in the 1990s as the largest producers (and consumers) of these ozone-damaging products prepared for their complete phase-out. However, production in the Global South surged, and increased demand for refrigerators, air conditioners, and other products using CFCs offset the gains realized by stopping production in the Global North. Developed countries agreed to provide aid to help the developing countries adopt CFC alternatives, but they have failed to provide all of the resources promised. Without this support, many in the Global South may not be able to keep their end of the global bargain. Meanwhile, a significant illegal trade in both virgin and recycled CFCs has emerged, threatening to further undermine the positive effects of the ozone regime.

The Ecopolitics of Biodiversity, Deforestation, and Water Shortages

Success at containing ozone depletion has raised hopes that other environmental threats also can be given higher priority than vested financial interests. Forests are critical in preserving the Earth's *biodiversity* and protecting the atmosphere and land resources. For these reasons, they have been a rising ecological issue on the global agenda. Some rules have emerged to guide international behavior in the preservation of biodiversity, but issues concerning forests have proven much more difficult to address.

biodiversity
the variety of plant and animal species living in the Earth's diverse ecosystems.

Threats to Global Biodiversity Biodiversity, or biological diversity, is an umbrella term that refers to the Earth's variety of life. Technically, it encompasses three basic levels of organization in living systems: genetic diversity, species diversity, and ecosystem diversity. Until recently, public attention has been focused almost exclusively on preserving species diversity, including old forests, tall grass prairies, wetlands, coastal habitats, and coral reefs.

Forests, especially tropical forests, are important to preserving biodiversity because they are home to countless species of animals and plants, many of them still unknown. Scientists believe that the global habitat contains between eight and ten million species. Of these, only about 1.5 million have been named, and most of them are in the temperate regions of North America, Europe, Russia, and Australia. Destruction of tropical forests, where two-thirds to three-fourths of all species are believed to live, threatens the destruction of much of the world's undiscovered biological diversity and genetic heritage.

Many experts worry that the globe is relentlessly heading toward major species extinction. Of the nearly 300,000 plant species surveyed by the World Conservation Union, more than 8,000 are threatened with extinction, mainly as a result of clearing land for housing, roads, and industries. The Intergovernmental Panel on Climate Change predicts that global warming increases the risk of extinction for almost 70 percent of species, with Arctic animals such as the polar bear most likely to die out first. Others doubt the imminence of a massive die-out, estimating that only a small fraction of the Earth's species have actually disappeared over the past several centuries. Indeed, optimistic cornucopians argue that species extinction may not be bad news, as new species may evolve that will prove even more beneficial to humanity (McKibben 2006).

enclosure movement
the claiming of common properties by states or private interests.

Because so much of the Earth's biological heritage is concentrated in the tropics, the Global South also has a growing concern about protecting its interests in the face of MNCs' efforts to reap profits from the sale of biologically based products. MNCs in the Global North are major players in the so-called *enclosure movement* geared to privatize and merchandize the products derived from plant and animal genes that are the genetic bases for sustained life. Pharmaceutical companies in particular have laid claim to Global South resources. They actively explore plants, microbes, and other living organisms in tropical forests for possible use in prescription drugs. Concern in the Global South is centered on the claim that the genetic character of the many species of plants and animals should be considered a part of the global commons and therefore available for commercial use by all, for their medical benefit.

Biogenetic engineering threatens to escalate the loss of global diversity. Biological resources—animal and plant species—are distributed unevenly in the world. Map 16.1 shows the major "biodiversity bastions" where more than half the Earth's species are found in primarily tropical wilderness territories laden with plant and animal species yet covering only 2 percent of the land. It also shows the location of "biodiversity hot spots," where human activity threatens to disturb and potentially destroy many species that international law defines as collective goods, a resource for all humanity from which everyone benefits. According to the UN, about fifty thousand plant and animal species become extinct each year as the global community wrestles with the ethics of biodiversity preservation and management policies.

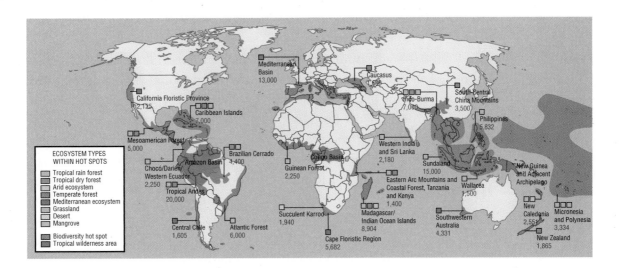

MAP 16.1

LOCATING BIODIVERSITY BASTIONS AND ENDANGERED BIODIVERSITY HOT SPOTS   This map provides a picture of global "danger zones" in identifying the estimated number of plant and animal species that are endangered in these biodiversity "hot spots." German Environment Minister Sigmar Gabriel estimated that "up to 150 species become extinct every day."

Shrinking Forests, Dust Bowls, and Water Shortages Trends since the 1980s point toward considerable *deforestation* throughout much of the world. Over the past eight thousand years, the World Resources Institute estimates that almost half of the forests once covering the Earth have been converted for ranching, farmland, pastures, and other uses, and that "one-fifth of the Earth's original forest remains in large, relatively natural ecosystems—what are known as 'frontier forests.'" Three-fourths of the world's forests are located in the Global South (WDI 2010, p. 156). "Deforestation is occurring most rapidly in the remaining tropical moist forests of the Amazon, West Africa, and parts of Southeast Asia (WDR 2008, p. 191). Destruction of tropical rain forests in such places as Brazil, Indonesia, and Malaysia is a matter of special concern because much of the world's genetic heritage is found there.

Nonetheless, the Global South objects vigorously to the socially constructed view that the world's forests are a common property resource, the "common heritage of mankind." The developing countries feared that legally accepting this view would enable the Global North to interfere with the local management of their tropical forest resources. As Ogar Assam Effa, a tree plantation director in Nigeria, observes, "The developed countries want us to keep the forests, since the air we breathe is for all of us, rich countries and poor countries. But we breathe the air, and our bellies are empty." He asks "Can air give you

deforestation
the process of clearing and destroying forests.

protein? Can air give you carbohydrates? It would be easy to convince people to stop clearing the forest if there was an alternative" (Harris 2008, p. A2).

Meanwhile, high population growth rates, industrialization, and urbanization increase pressure to farm forests and marginal land poorly suited to cultivation. This has led to deforestation and **desertification,** which turn an increasing portion of the Earth's landmass into deserts useless for agricultural productivity or wildlife habitats. "The world is running out of freshwater. There's water everywhere, of course, but less than three percent of it is fresh, and most of that is locked up in polar ice caps and glaciers, unrecoverable for practical purposes. Lakes, rivers, marshes, aquifers, and atmospheric vapor make up less than one percent of the Earth's total water, and people are already using more than half of the accessible runoff. Water demand and water use in many areas already exceed nature's ability to recharge supplies, and demand seems destined to exceed supplies since ground water overdraft and aquifer depletion are expected to increase 18 percent between 1995 and 2025" (*Vital Signs* 2005–2006, p. 104).

"The proportion of people living in countries chronically short of water, which stood at 8 percent (500 million) at the turn of the 21st century, is set to rise to 45 percent (four billion) by 2050" (Grimond 2010, p. 3). Local water shortages are increasingly common, and as a recent report by the UN World Water Assessment Programme concluded, "It is clear that urgent action is needed if we are to avoid a global water crisis." Part of the problem is demographic, for as the world's population has risen, the demand for water has likewise increased. Furthermore, as countries across the world become more prosperous, their populations tend to shift from vegetarian diets to meaty ones that require more water to produce. Additionally, "there is growing evidence that global warming is speeding up the hydrologic cycle—that is, the rate at which water evaporates and falls again as rain or snow. . . . It brings longer droughts between more intense periods of rain" (*The Economist*, 2009, p. 60). With rising population and consumption, in the absence of serious water-conservation measures and cooperation among mutual water users for watershed preservation, water availability will become an ever-growing resource issue.

Additionally, soil degradation has stripped billions of acres of the Earth's surface from productive farming. Soil erosion and pollution are problems both in densely populated developing countries and in the more highly developed regions of mechanized industrial agriculture. "Global demand for food is projected to double in the next fifty years as urbanization proceeds and income

desertification

the creation of deserts due to soil erosion, overfarming, and deforestation, which converts cropland to nonproductive, arid sand.

rises. But arable land per capita is shrinking" (WDI 2007, p. 124; see also WDI 2010). The threat will surely increase because land degradation is increasing and deforestation continues at about 79,000 square kilometers a year (WDI 2010). Map 16.2 shows the trends across regions where desertification is occurring most rapidly.

Arko Datta/AFP/Getty Images

FROM FARMLAND TO DUST BOWL   Desertification has hit many areas hard and "man-made climate change is also causing more droughts on top of those that occur naturally" (Begley 2008, p. 53). Since 1970, the amount of the Earth stricken by severe drought has increased 100 percent (*Harpers*, December 2005, p. 13).

In the Global North, reforestation has alleviated some of the danger. This is not the case, however, in many cash-starved Global South countries where the reasons for rapid destruction vary. South American forests, most notably the Amazon, are generally burned for industrial-scale soybean farming or cattle grazing. In Southeast Asia, forests are burned or cut for large-scale planting of palm to obtain the oil that is used in a wide array of products, including cosmetics and food processing. In Africa, individuals hack out small plots for farming (Harris 2008).

And most recently, deforestation is being spurred by the global demand for biofuels. In Brazil, deforestation roughly doubled in 2008 alone due in part to the dramatic expansion in agriculture aimed at producing farm-grown fuels. As John Carter, founder of a nonprofit that promotes sustainable ranching in the Amazonian region, lamented "You can't protect it. There's too much money to be made tearing it down." However, in March 2010 in an encouraging step to address the problem of deforestation, the United States and Brazil signed a memorandum of understanding aimed at reducing emissions through incentive payment programs, capacity-building in climate change sectors, and joint efforts on research and sharing of technologies to combat climate change.

While biofuels such as ethanol are often touted as being eco-friendly, critics point out that ethanol destroys forests, contributes to global warming, and inflates food prices. Moreover, the clearing and burning of tropical rain forests to make room for farms and ranches are doubly destructive because agriculture uses 70 percent of freshwater globally (WDI 2010). From the viewpoint of climate change, green plants remove CO_2 from the atmosphere during photosynthesis. So the natural processes that remove greenhouse gases are destroyed when forests are cut down, and, as the forests decay or are burned, the amount of CO_2 released into the atmosphere increases. The Amazon rain forest is "an incomparable storehouse of carbon, the very carbon that heats up the planet when it's released into the atmosphere" (Grunwald 2008, p. 40).

The Ecopolitics of Energy Supply and Demand According to naturalist Loren Eiseley, human history can be thought of as our ascent up "the heat ladder" where "coal bested firewood as an amplifier of productivity, and oil and natural gas bested coal" (Owen 2009, p. 21). Throughout the twentieth century, demand for and consumption of oil—the primary fossil fuel supplying energy—spiraled upward. An abundant supply of oil at low prices facilitated the recovery of Western Europe and Japan from World War II and encouraged consumers to use energy-intensive technologies, such as the private automobile.

An enormous growth in the worldwide demand for and consumption of energy followed. The International Energy Agency predicts that, even taking into account gains in efficiency (the United States has doubled its energy efficiency since the 1970s), the world will be using 50 percent more oil by 2030. While the Global North remains a major consumer of oil, this

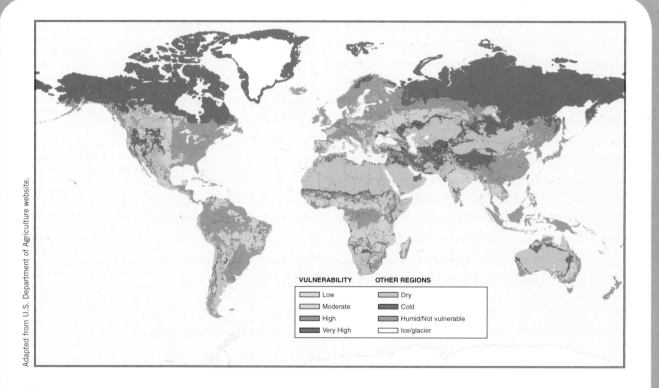

Adapted from U.S. Department of Agriculture website.

MAP 16.2

LOSS OF FOREST AND GROUND TO DESERTS   Desertification affects roughly 25 percent of the world's landmass, and in an effort to raise awareness and promote action, in August 2010 the United Nations launched the "Decade for Deserts and the Fight against Desertification (2010–2020)." This map displays the extent to which certain regions are experiencing desertification or degraded dry lands. "Continued land degradation—whether from climate change, unsustainable agriculture or poor management of water resources—is a threat to food security, leading to starvation among the most acutely affected communities and robbing the world of productive land," said UN Secretary General Ban Ki-moon.

century has witnessed a globalization of demand, with 85 percent of the surge in oil demand occurring in emerging markets such as China, India, and the Middle East (Yergin 2009).

The suppliers of oil have also changed over the past decade. Oil companies such as Chevron and ExxonMobil continue to be "supermajors" within the oil industry, though others such as Amoco have disappeared. But traditional MNCs no longer maintain overriding control of the oil industry. Rather, "much larger state-owned companies, which, along with governments, today control more than 80 percent of the world's oil reserves. Fifteen of the world's 20 largest oil companies are state-owned" (Yergin 2009, p. 92). Moreover, oil has moved from being just a physical commodity to now also being a financial asset, where there has been a massive growth in the number of oil investors and traders.

Old players such as the Organization of Petroleum Exporting Countries (OPEC) remain, of course. To maximize profits, OPEC emerged as an important intergovernmental organization. Because the resources OPEC controls cannot be easily replaced, it has monopoly power. In March 1999, OPEC began to flex its economic muscles by cutting production to limit supplies. Oil prices tripled within a year, showing that OPEC could still make oil a critical global political issue—as it has again since 2004 in an effort to use oil prices as an instrument of *coercive diplomacy* to influence, by the use of threats, the course of the unfolding war on terrorism.

Oil supplies assume great importance in world politics because oil is not being discovered at the same rate it is being used. For every two barrels pumped out of the ground, the giant oil companies discover only one new barrel. Production in the United States peaked thirty years ago, and that Russia peaked in 1987. About 70 percent of the oil consumed today was found twenty-five years ago or longer. Meanwhile demand for oil keeps escalating, and the era of cheap and abundant oil is ending (Klare 2008).

Or at least, that is what analysts thought when, on July 11, 2008, the price of a barrel of oil hit a high of $147.27. It was believed that the days of affordable oil were over. This may still be the case, but what we have now witnessed is that the price of oil as a commodity is extremely volatile. In December 2008, the price of oil had fallen to $32.40 per barrel; on July 11, 2009, exactly a year after the peak oil price, the price of oil was as low as $59.87 per barrel. In July 2010, the cost of a barrel of crude oil had risen to about $78. These dramatic price swings may be even more threatening than an end to cheap prices, as it introduces a great deal of instability into our global economic and political systems, affects an array of industries and the individual consumer, and makes it very difficult to plan future energy investments (see Figure 16.3). Despite our quest for stability, "the changing balance of supply and demand—shaped by economics, politics, technologies, consumer tastes, and accidents of all sorts—will continue to move prices" (Yergin 2009, p. 95).

What strikes fear in the minds of those who study oil supplies against rising demand is the widespread "illusion" of petroleum plenty. Future petroleum scarcities are certain to come, sooner or later. As Michael Klare, an expert on peace and world security, contends, "We are nearing the end of the Petroleum Age and have entered the Age of Insufficiency." Even if there are no major supply disruptions caused by wars in the Middle East or bullying tactics by oil exporters, "the world may have arrived at Peak Oil: that condition when dwindling oil reserves no longer permit much, if any, annual increase in production" (Samuelson 2008, p. 39).

This alarming predicament suggests that a "new geopolitics of oil" has arisen over how the oil producers will use their supplies in international bargaining with those oil-importing countries that are dependent and vulnerable to supply disruptions. The world today does not face the immediate threat of running out of oil; it faces instead the problem that over half of the proven oil reserves are now concentrated in a small number of OPEC countries that are drawing down their reserves at half the average global rate. It seems almost inevitable that OPEC's share of the world oil market will grow. This means that OPEC is critical to global oil supply, the Middle East is critical to OPEC, and countries that depend on oil imports from this volatile, unstable source are highly vulnerable to disruptions. "As the center of gravity of world oil production shifts decisively to OPEC suppliers and state-centric energy producers like Russia, geopolitical rather than market factors will come to dominate the marketplace" (Klare 2008, p. 19). Indeed, the war between Russia and Georgia was seen by many "as an intense geopolitical contest over the flow of Caspian Sea energy to markets in the West."

Another challenge facing the world, starkly illustrated by the massive oil spill in the Gulf of Mexico in 2010, is how to balance the demand for oil against the environmental, economic, and health risks posed by drilling. "A combination of industry recklessness and regulatory failure led to the Gulf of Mexico catastrophe" (Walsh 2010, p. 51), yet the public also played a role by demonstrating at the ballot box their preference for cheap oil underwritten by risky drilling instead of a government committed to industry regulation. As political historian Sarah Elkind said, "This failure of government is government acting the way American people have said they want it to act."

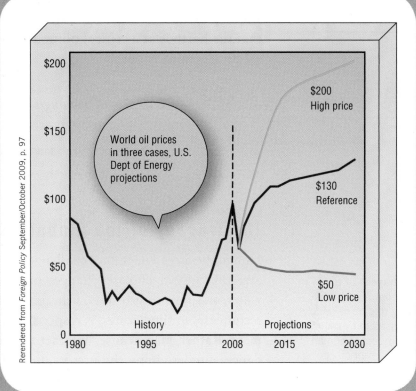

FIGURE 16.3

THE UPS AND DOWNS OF THE PRICE FOR OIL   As seen above, there are three very different projections regarding world oil prices between now and 2030. Most analysts, however, expect that oil demand will grow quickly as the world economy recovers and that we will see another oil spike, perhaps as soon as 2012. Price hikes could result from a number of factors: the restriction of oil supply by OPEC as it imposes strict production quotas and takes spare capacity offline, the anticipation of future oil scarcity by traders, and the eagerness of the Global South for energy—which will likely account for 90 percent of the surge in demand over the next decade.

Rerendered from *Foreign Policy* September/October 2009, p. 97

Do we have the capacity and will to make changes in our energy production and consumption? In response to the threat of future shortages and the risk of heavy dependence on oil, the Global North may be on the verge of a potentially historic juncture that would overturn the pivotal place of oil in the global political economy. In 2008, China and Japan ended a long-time dispute by agreeing to jointly develop two natural gas fields in the East China Sea; in August 2009, Russia reached an agreement with Turkey to build a gas pipeline from the Black Sea to the Mediterranean via the Anatolian Peninsula. There is also an array of efforts under way to develop alternative clean-energy fuel sources, such as wind and solar power, to break our dependence on fossil fuels.

TOWARD SUSTAINABILITY AND HUMAN SECURITY

Across the globe, people desire to live in a clean and green environment and seek to avoid ones that are polluted, dangerous to health, and prone to floods, hurricanes, tornadoes, and typhoons. Why, then, have human threats to the global ecology increased despite their conflictual relationship with global human interests and values? Environmental activists argue that the Earth is at a critical point and even more attention to environmental preservation is needed.

> *Earth provides enough to satisfy every man's need,*
> *but not every man's greed.*
>
> —Mohandas Gandhi, Indian peace activist

The Tragedy of the Global Commons

tragedy of the commons
a metaphor, widely used to explain the impact of human behavior on ecological systems, that explains how rational self-interested behavior by individuals may have a destructive and irrational collective impact.

Humanity faces enormous challenges of unprecedented scope and danger: arresting global climate change, preserving biodiversity, providing clean water, and restoring forests, fisheries, and other overly exploited renewable resources. No single cause is responsible for the trends in the global environment. Rather, many causes interact with each other to produce the dreaded dangers undermining the preservation of the world's life systems on which human existence depends. But among the ecologists who scientifically study the origins of planetary predicaments and problems, one explanation has become very popular—environmental degradation is seen, in part, as a product of the individual pursuit of private gain.

GAS GUZZLING IN SHANGHAI   Shown here is routine traffic congestion on one of the many superhighways in Shanghai: an example of what happens when a country's economy rapidly grows and demand for oil skyrockets. "China has emerged from being a net oil exporter in the early 1990s to become the world's third-largest net importer of oil" (Energy Information Administration 2009).

At least that is the consensus of many experts who study the environment and are so worried about the potentially dismal prospects for preserving the planet's ecology. The *tragedy of the commons* is a popular term constructed to capture the human roots of the growing threats to the planet's resources and its delicately balanced ecological system. First articulated in 1833 by English political economist William Foster Lloyd, the concept was later popularized and extended to contemporary global environmental problems by human ecologist Garrett Hardin, in a famous article published in 1968 in the journal *Science*, "The commons" emphasizes the impact of human behavior driven by the search for personal self-advantage, and although it stresses the importance of individual action and personal motivations, it also ascribes those motives to collectivities or groups such as corporations and entire countries. The central question asked through the "commons" analogy is, what is the probable approach to resources held in common in an unregulated environment? If individuals (and corporations and countries) are interested primarily in advancing their own personal welfare, what consequences should be anticipated for the finite resources held in common and hence for all?

Lloyd, and later Hardin, asked observers to consider what happened in medieval English villages, where the village green was typically common property on which all villagers could graze their cattle. Freedom of access to the commons was a cherished village value. Sharing the common grazing area worked well as long as usage by individuals (and their cattle) didn't reduce the land's usefulness to everyone else. Assuming that the villagers were driven by the profit motive and that no laws existed to restrain their greed, herders had maximum incentive to increase their stock for gain as much as possible. If pushed, individual herders might concede that the collective interest of all would be served if each contained the size of their herd rather than increasing it, so that the commons could be preserved. But self-restraint—voluntary reduction of the number of one's own cattle to relieve the pressure on the common village green—was not popular. Indeed, there was no guarantee that others would do the same. By contrast, the addition of one more animal to the village green would produce a personal gain whose costs would be borne by everyone. Therefore, economic *rational choice* to pursue wealth encouraged all to increase indiscriminately the size of the herds, and it discouraged self-sacrifice for the common welfare. Ultimately, the collective impact of each effort to maximize individual gain was to place more cattle on the village green than it could sustain. In the long run, the overgrazed green was destroyed. The lesson? "Ruin is the destination toward which all men rush," Hardin (1968) concluded, "each pursuing his own best interest."

The tragedy of the commons has become a standard concept in ecological analysis because it illuminates so well the sources of environmental degradation and many other global problems and predicaments. It is particularly applicable to the debate today about pressures on the global environment because the English common green is comparable to planetary "common property," such as the oceans and the atmosphere from which individual profit is maximized on the basis of a first-come, first-served principle. Overuse of common property is also highlighted, as when the oceans and atmosphere are used by a few as sinks for environmental pollutants whose costs are borne by many.

Are the dynamics underlying the tragedy of the commons responsible for global ecological dangers? Many people think so. However, you have probably already guessed that experts disagree about the moral and ethical implications of Hardin's interpretation. Note that the logical conclusion is that reforms are required to save planet Earth. The needed changes will require both some self-restraint on people's freedom of choice as well as a modicum of regulation in order to control the ruinous consequence of the tragedy of an unmanaged global commons.

Theorists adhering to *realism* and free-market *mercantilism* go very far in defending freedom of economic choice without regulation as the best and safest path to realizing the greatest good for the greatest number. Theorists from these traditions believe that the pursuit of self-interest and personal profit will in the long run benefit all, producing more income and technological innovation than would occur by supervisory regulation of corporations, entrepreneurs, and investors given free reign to seek profits. They also feel that minimal interference in the pursuit of personal gain is helpful to the preservation of the Earth's ecological health. To their way of reasoning, the pursuit of private gain with little restraint is a virtue, not a vice. Greed is good.

Almost all religious moral traditions highly question this realist and mercantilist conclusion. Christianity, for example, follows ancient Hebrew ethics in defining greed as one of the seven deadly sins. In Timothy 6:10, the Bible warns, "For the love of money is the root of all evil." The predictable outcome of selfishness and blind dedication to personal financial gain over other values such as altruistic love and compassion for the community of humankind is a certain path to ruin and to sin. In this sense, religious traditions join some of the thinking underlying radical Marxist theorizing (see Chapter 2). These streams of thoughts argue that concern for the welfare of all provides happiness and benefits because only if community interests are protected can individuals realize their most precious personal interest in advancing such common values as the opportunity for maintaining a clean and sustainable environment.

Ecopolitics forces you to weigh rival perspectives and to evaluate competing values. Do you want income and prosperity? Of course, but at what intended and unintended costs? Countries and companies all seek wealth. Does this mean that their quest for profits justifies allowing them to dump toxic wastes into lakes, rivers, and oceans, and let others bear the burden of their actions for personal profit?

Joana Coutinho, McRCP/AP Photo

ON THE PRECIPICE OF EXTINCTION? A 2009 report by the International Union for Conservation of Nature (IUCN) found that 21 percent of mammal species are at risk for extinction, and that overfishing and acidification of the oceans are threatening marine life. "We may have entered what will be the planet's sixth great extinction wave. And this time the cause isn't an errant asteroid or megavolcanoes. It's us" (Walsh 2009, p. 46). Shown here is a "dead forest" in Madagascar, which has lost over 80 percent of its forest due mostly to slash-and-burn rice farming that also exhausts the soil and destroys the habitats of countless species.

These and other ethical questions are directly in the crossfire of the debate about what is causing the threats to the planetary commons and what, if anything, should be undertaken to contain them, and at what costs. Environmental decay seems to recognize few borders; it is a worldwide problem, for both poor and rich countries. "Overall, there are considerable signs that the capacity of ecosystems to continue to produce many of the goods we depend on is declining," cautions the World Resources Institute (2009). That transformation makes protection of the planetary environment a necessity, but the solutions are hard to find when many people put their personal advantage ahead of those of all humanity. Recommended changes to protect and preserve the planet Earth's ecology may be expensive. But it is prudent to try.

What approaches are under way? A number stand out. While the goal of sustainable development remains distant and frustrations about lost opportunities high, government and nonstate actors' acceptance of the concept continues to inspire creative, environmentally sensitive responses. In the first category are solutions at the *global level of analysis*. Taking their point of departure from the adage "think globally, act locally," there are also under way movements to save planet Earth at the *state level of analysis* and *individual level of analysis*.

Global Solutions

In a political world in which growing population means growing demand for energy, food, and other resources, the politics of scarcity becomes central. This is the vulnerability created by interdependent globalization. Moreover, how countries meet their growing demand for energy directly influences the evolution and preservation of the global commons.

Left unchecked, threats to environmental security will compromise human security. "Though governments have an enormous role to play… nongovernmental organizations, philanthropists, the private sector, social entrepreneurs, and technologists can help" to overcome the adverse effects of environmental degradation (Brainard et al. 2009, p. 1). Some of the initiatives to counter environmental degradation are carried out at a global level.

Converting to Renewable Sources of Energy A new and less destructive source of energy could emerge because of the advent of revolutionary new technologies that derive energy from the sun, wind, and other abundant and renewable sources of energy such as hydrogen. The impact of such a global transformation would be huge, overturning the past 125-year pattern in world energy development and consumption. Could the era of "big oil" really be ending? That could be the case. Together, widely fluctuating but rising oil prices and public alarm about global warming are pushing the world, however haltingly, toward cleaner and cheaper energy systems.

The supply of fossil fuels will not run out anytime soon, but the *externalities* or consequences of environmental and health threats make the burning of fossil fuels excessively dangerous. The combustion of oil and coal are traced to lung cancer and many other health hazards. And what is more, it leads to air pollution, urban smog, and *acid rain* that damage forests, water quality, and soil. There are powerful incentives to harness technology to shift to renewable sources of energy. Solar, tidal, and wind power, as well as geothermal energy and bioconversion, are among the alternatives to oil most likely to become technologically and economically viable, as Figure 16.4 shows.

acid rain
precipitation that has been made acidic through contact with sulfur dioxide and nitrogen oxides.

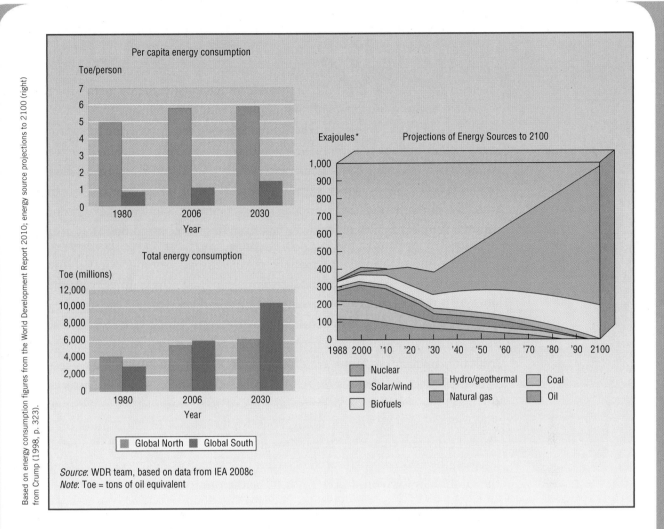

FIGURE 16.4

SUPPLYING THE WORLD'S GROWING ENERGY NEEDS BY THE YEAR 2100   The demand for energy continues to rise, requiring more energy than is ultimately available from nonrenewable resources. The Global North consumes, on average, five times more energy per capita than the Global South (top left). However, the energy consumption of developing countries is on the rise—and is expected to account for 90 percent of the projected increase in global energy consumption over the next twenty years (bottom left). As a fossil-free energy supply becomes increasingly probable (top right), it might become possible to tap renewable sources to meet the world's entire energy needs by the end of the twenty-first century.

Among known technologies, nuclear energy has often been championed as the leading alternative to fossil fuel dependence. Currently, existing nuclear plants provide only 20 percent of America's electricity (WDI 2010). However, the United States is now spending billions of dollars to enhance nuclear plants to ease its dependence on the foreign suppliers that provide five billion of the 7.3 barrels of oil (68 percent) the United States consumes each year (Nelson

2009). In 2010, the United States approved its first new nuclear project since the 1980s and provided $8.3 billion in federal loan guarantees to construct two nuclear reactors. When the reactors become active in 2017, they will generate power for 1.5 million people. However, safety and financial costs may limit the surge toward nuclear power; these problems have led some countries to reduce (or, like Germany, Sweden, and Spain, phase out) their nuclear programs. Well-publicized nuclear accidents in the United States at the Three Mile Island nuclear power plant in Pennsylvania in 1979 and at Chernobyl in Ukraine in 1986 and no less than five major accidents between 1995 and 1999 at Japan's fifty-two nuclear power plants (which supply about a third of Japan's electricity) dramatized the potential dangers of nuclear power. Since then, fears have decreased, and the demand for nuclear power has risen despite continuing safety fears.

Concerns about the risks of nuclear power extend beyond safety. How and where to dispose of highly radioactive nuclear waste that comes from the 438 nuclear power plants in thirty countries around the world (and the 61 additional reactors under construction in fifteen countries in 2010) is an unresolved issue virtually everywhere (European Nuclear Society 2010). For example, at least fifty nuclear weapons are on the ocean's floor out of reach as a result of U.S. and Soviet accidents (*Harper's* March 2004). There are no safe procedures for handling the fifty-two thousand tons of toxic radioactive nuclear waste, some of which will remain dangerous for hundreds of thousands of years. "Not in my back yard" (NIMBY) is a divisive cry on the global ecopolitical agenda; the Global North prefers to dump waste outside its own territory, and the Global South would prefer not to be the dump—but often is.

A related fear is that countries that currently do not possess nuclear know-how might develop nuclear weapons. Most nuclear-energy–generating facilities continue to produce weapons-grade material, specifically highly enriched uranium and plutonium, which is a national security concern because "with the underlying technical infrastructure able to support both weapons and electrons, there is no clear way to ensure nuclear energy can be developed without also building capabilities for weapons" (*Vital Signs* 2006–2007, p. 34). This dilemma was highlighted as a significant concern with regard to North Korea's nuclear development program.

Other efforts to develop alternative potential fuel sources have also begun in hopes of breaking our dependence on fossil fuels. Recognizing the importance of such efforts, U.S. President Obama declared that "to truly transform our economy, protect our security and save our planet from the ravages of climage change, we need to ultimately make clean, renewable energy the profitable kind of energy." Thomas L. Friedman (2008) echoed this sentiment, arguing that countries that cling to fossil fuels will see their security and prosperity decline as compared to those that pioneer renewable-energy technologies. This emphasis reflects a shift over the past decade or two from a focus on conventional pollution issues to one on clean-energy opportunities.

Reflective white roofs that reduce air-conditioning costs by 20 percent, and hence produce far fewer carbon dioxide emissions, are becoming more popular as a way to save energy and fight global warming (Barringer 2009). Seaweed fields of algae are touted as a potential wave of the future, as "algal oil can be processed into biodiesel or nonpetroleum gasoline, the carbohydrates into ethanol, and the protein into animal feed or human nutritional supplements. The whole biomass can generate methane, which can be combusted to produce electricity" (Gies 2008, p. 3). Indonesia and the Philippines, located within the "Pacific Ring of Fire," are looking to harness volcanic power in developing geothermal power. Indonesia has at least 130 active volcanoes, and according to Lester Brown, president of the Earth Policy Institute, "Indonesia could run its economy entirely on geothermal energy and has not come close to tapping the full potential" (Davies and Lema 2008, p. 13).

And while presently too expensive for most people, Honda Motor has begun production of the world's first hydrogen-powered fuel-cell car. Says Takeo Fukui, president of Honda, "This is a must-have technology for the future of the earth" (Fackler 2008, p. 16). Technological, economic, cultural, and environmental changes suggest that the early stage of a major energy transformation is under way, forced by supply scarcities and demand increases.

Conversion to renewable sources of energy represents a possible avenue away from global environmental degradation. Many believe this will not happen soon enough. They propose another path to reduce the dangers: forging international treaties among countries that provide for the protection of the environment and establish compliance mechanisms.

International Treaties for Environmental Protection The 1992 Earth Summit in Stockholm was precedent-setting. From it, a separate treaty set forth a comprehensive agreement for the preservation of biodiversity throughout the world. It committed state governments to devise national strategies for conserving habitats, protecting endangered species, expanding protected areas, and repairing damaged ones. Since then, the world has attempted to cooperate through increasingly concerted efforts to reach agreements and to back them with ratified treaties to protect the sustained global commons.

Success breeds success. The *Biodiversity Treaty* was followed by other international efforts to deal with environmental problems by agreements globally.

A big example was the Kyoto protocol of 2005 in which 156 countries accounting for at least 55 percent of global greenhouse emissions pledged to cut emissions of gases linked to global warming below 1990 levels by the year 2012. Only the United States refused to cooperate. But that resistance may change. U.S. President Obama has pledged to work with the international community to "roll back the spector of a warming planet," and one of his first presidential policy pronouncements was to call for a federal "cap-and-trade" system to greatly reduce U.S. greenhouse emissions.

In anticipation of the impending 2012 deadline for negotiating a successor to the 1997 Kyoto Protocol, the UN climate-change summit convened in Copenhagen in December 2009. There were hopes that leadership from the United States could propel greater concensus and commitment to international efforts to address environmental degradation and the threats that it poses to human security. However, while the Global North committed to providing the Global South $30 billion in financing by 2012 and a total of $100 billion by 2020 to combat problems caused by climate change, the countries participating in the meeting failed to reach a long-term binding agreement on global climate change. Negotiations at the 2010 UN Climate Change Conference in Mexico were similarly hindered by the reluctance of many countries to commit to any binding international formula.

Simulation: *The Kyoto Treaty*

International environmental treaties have grown exponentially in the last 130 years. However, many skeptics fear that these efforts are too little, too late, and that not enough is being done to save the global commons for future generations. Many question the ability of today's existing treaties to manage the environmental dangers they are meant to address. Some are weak and introduce expressions of concern without commanding necessary policy changes to remedy the various problems they identify. Of particular concern is the reluctant backing of the globe's superpower, the United States. Of the UN's thirty-one major global environmental agreements, the United States has only ratified ten. Environmental protection activists worry that if the American hegemon refuses to lead, the prospects for strengthening the rules of the environmental preservation regime are dim.

Trade, the Environment, and Sustainable Development Multinational corporations are key players in the ecopolitics game that has the potential to determine the Earth's fate. Corporations rule globally, and they are strong advocates with powerful lobbyists of free trade. Is their power and quest supportive, or detrimental, to sustainable development? The question is especially pertinent in a rapidly globalizing world in which trade increasingly links politics, economics, ecology, and societies and cultures in webs of ever-tightening interdependencies.

Yanin Arthus Bertrand/Terra/CORBIS

THE UNFORGIVING COST OF NUCLEAR POWER FAILURE   Shown here is the town of Pripyat, Ukraine, which was abandoned after the Chernobyl nuclear accident. Rather than learning from this lesson, and despite strong opposition from the public, Russia opened its borders to become the largest international repository for radioactive nuclear wastes, in the hope of earning billions of dollars over the next two decades.

Beyond the issue of the gains from and the costs of trade, environmentalists and liberal economists differ in their assessments of the wisdom of using trade to promote environmental standards. Liberal economists see such efforts as market distortions, whereas environmentalists view them as useful instruments for correcting market failures, such as markets' inability to compensate for the externalities of environmental exploitation (for example, atmospheric pollution by chemical companies). Some countries, however, particularly in the Global South, view the use of trade mechanisms to protect the environment as yet another way the rich states block entry into lucrative Global North markets and keep the Global South permanently disadvantaged.

Trade-offs must sometimes be made between goals that, in principle, all seem designed to increase human well-being and security. However, another interpretation maintains that trade encourages states to live beyond their means. According to some ecologists, trade magnifies the damaging ecological effects of production and consumption by expanding the market for commodities beyond

Ruth Fremson/The New York Times/Redux Pictures

PLAYING IN THE "POISON POND"   Children play in the shadow of the former Union Carbide factory in Bhopal, India, the site of one of the worst industrial accidents in history. The "pond" in which they are playing was originally a sludge pit containing chemical by products from the former pesticide plant, and the actual color of the "water" was closer to black. Though the chemical leakage at Bhopal, which resulted in over three thousand deaths, occurred in 1984, the area—which still contains over four hundred tons of toxic waste—has yet to be cleaned up. The picture is a stark reminder of how environmental crises can long outlive the political will necessary to resolve them.

state borders. Countries that have depleted their resource bases or passed strict laws to protect them can easily look overseas for desired products, in ways that shift the environmental stress of high consumption to other states' backyards.

The tragedy of the commons suggests a bleak future. Is ruin the destination toward which humanity must rush? Or is a more optimistic scenario possible? A trend is under way in the culture of corporate global finance that bodes well for the potential for global corporations to begin to recognize that their profits will improve if they invest in and develop products for which there is rising consumer demand worldwide because they are environmentally green and popular among consumers.

Consider Wal-Mart. This mega-corporation recently shifted its marketing strategy by seeking to attract still new customers, promising to cut its energy consumption and to sell products that are environmentally friendly. This was a response to global demand. What these and other changes suggest is that newly "green" corporations are beginning to realize financial payoffs. Producing products that global consumers value may make profits. In the context of "green" industries seeking to sell environmentally protective products, a new "code of corporate responsibility" is gaining acceptance that

Table 16.1 Green Performance Ranking of Selected Major Corporations

Rank	Company	Environmental Impact Score	Green Policies Score	Reputation Survey Score	GREEN SCORE	Principal Actions
1	Dell	81.49	100	84.33	100	Implementing an aggressive sustainability strategy, which includes an extensive recycling program and a commitment to cut emissions by 40 percent before 2015
2	Hewlett-Packard	90.60	94.09	95.35	99.32	Extensive reporting of production line's environmental footprint as well as engaged in reducing products' energy requirements; if customers replaced all their old HP equipment, they would save $10.4 billion
3	IBM	98.71	89.52	98.42	99.20	Successful history of improving operational efficiency, cutting its own power-use by 5.1 billion kilowatt hours in the 1990s, and producing computer systems to help other business do the same
4	Johnson & Johnson	74.95	98.86	80.34	99.02	Decreased its CO_2 pollution by 16 percent in 2010, more than double its stated commitment, as well as continued efforts to diminish energy and packaging waste
5	Intel	95.74	88.79	92.71	97.57	Awards yearly bonuses based on meeting range of environmental benchmarks, such as finding alternatives to toxic chemicals used in its products; renewable energy fulfills about 50 percent of company's energy needs
6	Sprint Nextel	99.70	94.58	44.72	94.98	Wireless leader in pushing emission reductions, promising to slim emissions by 15 percent before 2017; also supports a comprehensive, postage-paid recycling initiative
7	Adobe Systems	89.61	88.08	72.57	94.15	Invested heavily in four LEED-certified platinum buildings to reduce waste and energy-consumption; also boasts a recycling and composting program that reuses 97 percent of solid waste
8	Applied Materials	91.98	87.33	60.06	92.67	Among largest supplier to solar power industry and invests heavily in new fossil fuel replacement technology; cut both its own emissions and water-use by about 20 percent last year while also reducing use of dangerous chemicals in production
9	Yahoo	68.62	89.07	59.74	92.67	Hosts web site with hints for sustainable-living; uses renewable energy, while also reducing waste and improving efficiency

(continued)

Table 16.1   Green Performance Ranking of Selected
Major Corporations (Continued)

Rank	Company	Environmental Impact Score	Green Policies Score	Reputation Survey Score	GREEN SCORE	Principal Actions
10	Nike	67.63	77.53	97.39	92.66	Plans on making all company-owned buildings carbon neutral by 2015 and cutting energy costs with more efficient lights, cooling, and communication systems

Source: Based on *Newsweek* Green Rankings 2010 of U.S. MNCs (Deveny 2010, pp.50–57). The Green Score is a weighted average of the Environmental Impact Score (45 percent), which is based on over seven hundred metrics; the Green Policies Score (45 percent), which assesses corporate initiatives and policies; and the Reputation Survey Score (10 percent), which is based on a survey of CEOs, academics, and environmental officers.

could spawn a new era of changes in the development of new products for sale that are designed to protect the environment, rather than seeking to realize short-term financial gains by selling products that contaminate the planetary condition (see Table 16.1).

The possibility that the international political economy will provide economic incentives for producing products that can contribute to global environment sustainability has inspired hope that the dangers to environmental preservation may be contained. That hope is rising because some governments and individuals are seeking local solutions to environmental sustainability.

National and Local Solutions

A huge concern is that some very powerful states, advantageously positioned in the global hierarchy, are selfishly resisting making painful and costly adjustments now. They are resisting reforms of their own existing environmental protection policies. Yet there are exceptions to this response to environmental degradation. A number of countries have managed to balance the risk of short-term economic loss against the expectation of long-term economic growth by investing in renewable and costly programs that can enable them to experience sustainable growth with development. Consider Figure 16.5. It charts the rankings of countries according to the Environmental Performance Index. The score measures their investments in efforts to protect their future environments. Clearly, some countries see environmental sustainability as a priority that protects their interest more so than others, which fail to do so.

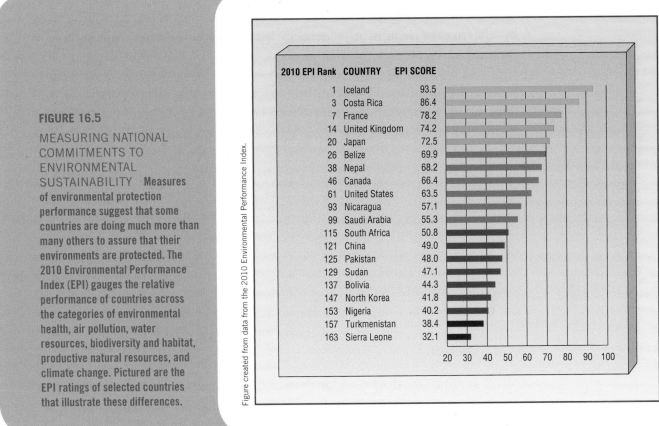

Figure created from data from the 2010 Environmental Performance Index.

2010 EPI Rank	COUNTRY	EPI SCORE
1	Iceland	93.5
3	Costa Rica	86.4
7	France	78.2
14	United Kingdom	74.2
20	Japan	72.5
26	Belize	69.9
38	Nepal	68.2
46	Canada	66.4
61	United States	63.5
93	Nicaragua	57.1
99	Saudi Arabia	55.3
115	South Africa	50.8
121	China	49.0
125	Pakistan	48.0
129	Sudan	47.1
137	Bolivia	44.3
147	North Korea	41.8
153	Nigeria	40.2
157	Turkmenistan	38.4
163	Sierra Leone	32.1

FIGURE 16.5

MEASURING NATIONAL COMMITMENTS TO ENVIRONMENTAL SUSTAINABILITY **Measures of environmental protection performance suggest that some countries are doing much more than many others to assure that their environments are protected. The 2010 Environmental Performance Index (EPI) gauges the relative performance of countries across the categories of environmental health, air pollution, water resources, biodiversity and habitat, productive natural resources, and climate change. Pictured are the EPI ratings of selected countries that illustrate these differences.**

Many people worldwide are dissatisfied with the tardy reaction of national governments to the appalling dangers to the global ecology. Another solution is rapidly materializing. In the United States, many of the fifty states have joined the lead pushed by Governor Arnold Schwarzenegger of California. He proclaimed in his inaugural address, "We all breathe the same air. Let's get our act together, fix this problem, and fight global warming." In September 2006, the respected "Governator" signed the *Global Warming Solutions Act* requiring California to reduce its greenhouse-gas emissions 25 percent by 2020, and in 2008 he stood firm in his support for the moratorium against new off-shore drilling. "Everybody recognized that it was so important that we should not argue over philosophy. I am a business-friendly guy. I'm all about economic growth. I am not here to harm businesses. I am here to make businesses boom, but let's also protect our environment. Let's make our air clear. Let's make our water clean. And let's fight global warming because we know now that this is a major danger, that this is not a debate anymore," Governor Schwarzenegger explained. Since then, three-fifths of American states have taken initiatives to also make rules in their home states to protect their local environments. What is more, since 2007 more than 150 American cities followed these initiatives by enacting environment-protection legislation to combat the threats in their urban locales.

It is hard to determine whether this reaction was a result of pressure from huge numbers of private citizens who believe that it is crucial to set limits on climate-changing greenhouse emissions because they feel that this is the right thing to do. Whatever the incentives, the pressure from citizens and even corporations for better laws to protect the global environment is growing. They are voicing their preferences in numbers too large to ignore. Within the United States, in March 2007, thirteen corporations joined with fifty-two institutional investors ($4 trillion under management) to lobby the U.S. government for limits on carbon emissions that come from burning fossil fuels. They were joined at the same time by fifteen other state governors who ordered limits of their own, encouraged by the decision of the U.S. Supreme Court that affirmed the right of the Environmental Protection Agency to regulate auto emissions and emissions from power plants (*Newsweek* 2007).

What should you do as a global citizen? Should you join the thousands on thousands of people worldwide who are demanding changes in existing practices and policies to curtail the threats to planet Earth that they perceive certain to destroy their future if protective measures are not taken soon? If so, ecologists will tell you quickly that you can make a difference, all by yourself, or more powerfully, by joining an NGO that shares your concerns and is pressuring governments to take the perceived needed urgent steps for change. The opportunities for participation in this debate are many. Environmentalists recommend many alternative steps that you might take. In *An Inconvenient Truth*, former U.S. presidential candidate Al Gore recommended five simple things you can do to help stop global warming:

- ■ Change a light. Replacing one regular light bulb with a compact fluorescent light bulb will save 150 pounds of carbon dioxide a year.

- ■ Recycle more. You can save 2,400 pounds of carbon dioxide per year by recycling just half of your household waste.

- Use less hot water. It takes a lot of energy to heat water. Use less hot water by installing a low-flow showerhead and washing your clothes in cold or warm water.

- Drive less. Walk, bike, carpool, or take mass transit more often. You'll save one pound of carbon dioxide for every mile you don't drive.

- Conserve electricity. Simply turning off your TV, DVD player, stereo, and computer when you're not using them will save you thousands of pounds of carbon dioxide a year.

There are, of course, many other actions that individuals can undertake that might affect the future of the planet. There is such a long list of things that could be done and that should be done that the options are about as unlimited as are the multiple threats to the planetary ecological predicament. Efforts to develop alternative fuels, reduce greenhouse gases, and resurrect the auto industry by producing environmentally friendly, energy-efficient vehicles are high on everybody's list. The entire world stands at a critical juncture. The path humanity takes will affect human security far into the future. Evidence of serious ecological problems is getting harder and harder to ignore. Because the stakes are so high, all the pieces in the puzzle—population growth, natural resources, technology, and changing preferences in lifestyles—must be addressed simultaneously.

If necessity really is the mother of invention, there is hope. The planet *must* be saved, or all other opportunities will be closed, the global environment will face certain doom, and human history will end. Therefore, the stakes are so high that perhaps solutions will be found. As the world struggles, the debate about solutions is likely to continue on two tracks: between those who think humankind's concentration should be geared to trying to reverse environmental deterioration, and those who prefer to concentrate on creating new technologies to contain environmental damage. Both strategies appear to be urgently needed.

Our entire planet, its land and water areas, the Earth's surface and its subsoil provide today the arena for a worldwide economy, the dependence of whose various parts upon each other has become indissoluble.

—Leon Trotsky, Russian radical communist theoretician

Take an Online Practice Quiz

www.cengagebrain.com/shop/ISBN/0495802204

| Suggested Readings |

Brainard, Lael, Abigail Jones, and Nigel Purvis, eds. (2009) *Climate change and global poverty*. Washington: Brookings Institution Press.

Brown, Lester B. (2009) *Plan B 4.0: Mobilizing to save civilization*. Washington: Earth Policy Institute.

Friedman, Thomas L. (2008) *Hot, flat, and crowded: Why we need a green revolution, and how it can renew America*. New York: Farrar, Straus and Giroux.

Levi, Michael A. (2009) Copenhagen's inconvenient truth: How to salvage the climate conference. *Foreign Affairs* 88 (5): 92–104.

World Bank. (2010) *World Development Report 2010: Development and Climate Change*. Washington: The International Bank for Reconstruction and Development/The World Bank.

Yergin, Daniel. (2009) It's Still the One. *Foreign Policy* September/October, 88–95.

Part 5
THINKING ABOUT THE FUTURE
OF WORLD POLITICS

"Trend is not destiny."
—Rene Dubos, French futurist

Jay Directo/AFP/Getty Images

GLOBAL DESTINY: DELIGHT OR DESPAIR? This photo captures the dramatic inequalities that exist in many, if not all, cities across the globe—some enjoying rising prosperity, some living in desperate squalor. Both conditions are products of prevailing trends in world politics. In which world are most people in the future likely to live?

Most conjectures about the global future are based on some extrapolation from earlier events and experiences. People usually speculate about future prospects based on their understanding of prevailing trends. What makes prediction so difficult is the sheer complexity of uncertainties surrounding world politics—some trends move forward seemingly in the same direction, while others change direction; some trends intersect, whereas others diverge over time; and some trends increase the speed of other trends, while still different global trends reduce the impact of the others. Your challenge in deciphering the meaning of prevailing but diverse trends is twofold: (1) to distinguish between those that are transient and those that are likely to have a significant and lasting impact on world politics, and (2) to project the configuration of the most important trends, rather than become preoccupied with any single trend in isolation.

How will the combination of major trends unfolding in world politics today influence your global future? Will the twenty-first century find previous efforts to construct world order useful, or will it reject past approaches as new issues arise on the global agenda?

Part 5 of *World Politics* poses in a concluding chapter *not* answers or predictions, but instead some important, thought-provoking questions for you to contemplate about the prospects for the twenty-first century. When thinking about the issues raised by these questions, ask yourself how they might be addressed to create a more peaceful and just global future.

CHAPTER 17
LOOKING AHEAD AT GLOBAL TRENDS AND TRANSFORMATIONS

CHAPTER OUTLINE

GLOBAL TRENDS AND
FORECASTS

HOW TO THINK ABOUT HOW
PEOPLE THINK ABOUT
THE WORLD

THE GLOBAL PREDICAMENT:
KEY QUESTIONS ABOUT A
TURBULENT WORLD

Is Globalization a Cure
or a Curse?

Will Technological Innovation
Solve Pressing Global
Problems?

What Types of Armed Aggression
Will Become the Major Fault
Line in the Geostrategic
Landscape?

Will the Great Powers Intervene
to Protect Human Rights?

Is the World Preparing for the
Wrong Kind of War?

Is This the "End of History" or
the End of Happy Endings?

NEW WORLD ORDER OR NEW
WORLD DISORDER?

The challenges of change are always hard. It is important that we begin to unpack those challenges . . . and realize that we each have a role that requires us to change and become more responsible for shaping our own future.

—Hillary Rodham Clinton, U.S. Secretary of State

Markus Schreiber/AP Photo

A TIME FOR CHANGE? In front of a crowd of an estimated two hundred thousand Germans at the Victory Column at Tiergarten Park in Berlin, Barack Obama called for global cooperation and purpose. "Now is the time to build new bridges across the globe as strong as the one that bound us across the Atlantic. Now is the time to join together, through constant cooperation, strong institutions, shared sacrifice, and a global commitment to progress, to meet the challenges of the 21st century."

Opposing global trends are unfolding. Some point toward integration, and others to fragmentation; the world looks like it is coming together and at the same time it is coming apart. A new global system is on the horizon, but it is one whose characteristics have yet to develop definition. Understandably, uncertainty and unpredictability are today's prevailing mood. But one thing is certain: seismic shifts under way are challenging the wisdom of old beliefs and orthodox visions. Because both turmoil and turbulence describe contemporary international affairs, they require asking unconventional questions about conventional ideas. They push us to think five-dimensionally in order to understand the political, military, market, demographic, and environmental pressures that are increasingly being brought to bear on the countries of the world, the people who reside in them, and their interactions.

Facing the future, you confront an awesome investigative challenge: anticipating and interpreting the probable future contours of world affairs and constructing compelling theoretical explanations of their causes. To do so, you must consider a number of unusual and controversial questions that are rising to the top of the global agenda for public debate throughout the world. Experts whose profession it is to help you may be somewhat informative. However, the rival conclusions boldly advanced by would-be prophets are not likely to be very definitive, and they diverge wildly.

Those caught up in revolutionary change rarely understand its ultimate significance.

—Boutros Boutros-Ghali, former UN Secretary-General

GLOBAL TRENDS AND FORECASTS

A bewildering array of problems and challenges are expected to confront humanity in the future. As recognized by former UN Secretary-General Kofi Annan (2006, p. 205), "We face a world of extraordinary challenges—and of extraordinary interconnectedness. We are all vulnerable to new security threats, and to old threats that are evolving in complex and unpredictable ways." The UN's report, *A More Secure World* (2004, p. 2), further outlines the following six clusters of threats with which the world must be concerned now and in the decades ahead:

■ Economic and social threats—including poverty, infectious disease, and environmental degradation

■ Interstate conflict

■ Internal conflict—including civil war, genocide, and other large-scale atrocities

■ Nuclear, radiological, chemical, and biological weapons

■ Terrorism

■ Transnational organized crime

This inventory suggests what the world will be like in the years to come. To construct your own images of the future of world affairs, begin by thinking about what key questions are likely to dominate international relations in the coming decades. The questions you identify will determine which scenarios and theories better inform your understanding of your global future. To assist you, *World Politics* concludes this chapter (and this book) with some additional questions to consider, and those questions will require you to weigh plausible contending interpretations to further prepare you intellectually to interpret the problematic future of world politics.

HOW TO THINK ABOUT HOW PEOPLE THINK ABOUT THE WORLD

As you construct scenarios about what kinds of global futures are possible, probable, and preferable, begin by keeping in mind that your images, like those of everyone, are shaped heavily by your prior perceptions of reality and the inherited values and expectations that underlie them (see Chapter 1). So proceed cautiously and with an open mind to views that may be different from those you now hold. Take the insight and received wisdom about how people think, as expressed in the following observations:

■ "Any frontal attack on ignorance is bound to fail because the masses are always ready to defend their most precious possession—their ignorance."

—Hendrik Willem van Loon, Dutch-American journalist

■ "The most fatal illusion is the settled point of view. Since life is growth and motion, a fixed point of view kills anybody who has one."

—Brooks Atkinson, American drama critic

■ "Fanaticism consists in redoubling your effort when you have forgotten your aim."

—George Santayana, Spanish philosopher

■ "Men are more apt to be mistaken in their generalizations than in their particular observations."

—Niccoló Machiavelli, seventeenth-century Italian realist theoretician

■ "One of the sources of pride in being a human being is the ability to bear present frustrations in the interests of longer purposes."

—Helen Merrel Lynd, American sociologist

■ "The philosophies of one age have become the absurdities of the next, and the foolishness of yesterday has become the wisdom of tomorrow."

—Sir William Osler, Canadian physician and educator

■ "It is better to know some of the questions than all of the answers."

—James Thurber, American writer

Armed with an understanding about how ideas about international relations form and are retained, rejected, or replaced, imagine yourself at the end of a semester preparing to take a final exam in your course about international relations. Your entire grade, your instructor tells you, will be determined by an essay exam with only one question. Sitting nervously, you open your blue book and are astonished at the instructions: "(1) define the question which you wish had been asked in this exam for this course, and (2) then answer it; you will be graded on both the understanding you display in the kind of question you ask and the answers you provide." How would you respond?

Believe it or not, this kind of question is not altogether fictional. It has been used to sort out candidates on exams for entry into the foreign service of several countries. There really are no right or wrong questions about international relations. Indeed, there is little agreement about the trends and issues that are the most important in international affairs, and no scholarly consensus among experts and policy makers exists about the questions most deserving of attention today.

To stimulate your thinking, make a preliminary list, based on what you now know after reading *World Politics*, of what you believe will be the crucial questions to ask when you make predictions about the future of the world. How would you go about interpreting your own questions? What rival theories (see Chapter 2) would you rely on to frame your analyses? This mental exercise will sharpen your evaluative skills and will tell you as much about yourself and your reasoned perspective as it does about your capacity to describe the present global condition, predict its future course, and explain *why* world politics is changing and also displaying continuities with the past.

Rather than leave you in the lurch, *World Politics* puts itself to the same test. It concludes now by identifying a series of questions about the global future that are high on the agenda for debate. As a further catalyst to framing your own thinking, look critically at them, for how they are answered is widely expected to give shape to world politics throughout the remainder of the twenty-first century.

THE GLOBAL PREDICAMENT: KEY QUESTIONS ABOUT A TURBULENT WORLD

World Politics has argued that international relations are subject to recurring patterns and regularities. Despite changes and chaos, behavior by transnational actors is not random. It is governed by patterned propensities, and this makes it possible to uncover "laws" or generalized action-and-reaction patterns. As realist theoretician Hans J. Morganthau argued in his classic text *Politics Among Nations*, the past historical record speaks with sufficient continuity to make the scientific study of international politics a meaningful intellectual endeavor. There are some lessons about how countries interact that are constant across time and place. It is the purpose of scholarship to uncover these patterns and make sound policy decisions based on the lessons history provides.

Under certain conditions, it can be assumed that certain types of transnational actors respond the same way to the same kinds of stimuli. Yet, there are exceptions. Sometimes similar actors in similar situations make different decisions. Thus despite the existence of regularities in world politics, social scientists cannot draw on a body of uniform, deterministic laws to predict the global future precisely. Instead, they make contingent forecasts about what is likely to happen, other things being equal (Singer 2000).

Another factor that makes it difficult to predict what will come to pass is the role of happenstance in world politics. History is replete with what Greek philosopher Aristotle called accidental conjunctions—situations in which things come together by chance. Consider, for example, the outbreak of World War I. Recall from Chapter 3 that one of the proximate causes of the war was Austrian Archduke Franz Ferdinand's assassination in Sarajevo on June 28, 1914. Earlier that day, several would-be assassins had failed to find an opportunity to kill the archduke and apparently gave up in frustration. When Ferdinand's motorcade made a wrong turn en route to visit patients in a city hospital, it stopped briefly in front of a café where Gavrilo Princip, one of the frustrated assassins, coincidentally had gone to get something to eat. Astonished to find the archduke's open-air car just five feet away, Princip fired two shots, killing the archduke and his wife. Given the political climate in Europe at the time, if Franz Ferdinand had not been assassinated, something else might have precipitated the war. But as political scientist Stuart Bremer (2000, p. 35) asks, "Who can say whether a different triggering event, a day, a month, or a year later, would have led to the same chain of events that produced World War I?"

Myriad possible futures lie ahead. Some are desirable; others, frightening. Although we cannot predict with certainty which one will materialize, we can narrow the range of possibilities by forecasting how current trends will probably develop and how steps might be taken to channel the course of events toward a global future we prefer.

What follows are six questions designed to help you think about the future of world politics. Each question is based on information presented in previous chapters. When pondering the long-term implications of these questions, you are encouraged to (1) imagine what conceivable global futures are possible, (2) estimate which are the most probable, and (3) consider what policies would be of the most help to bring about the global future you prefer.

> *The glorious thing about the human race is that it does change the world—constantly. It is the human being's capacity for struggling against being overwhelmed which is remarkable and exhilarating.*
>
> —Lorraine Hansberry, American author

Is Globalization a Cure or a Curse?

Why does it now appear that the world and the states within it are spinning out of control? One answer is ascribed to "globalization," a widely accepted socially constructed code word understood as a transforming force that is creating sweeping governance crises in a new age of increasing interdependent complexity. *Globalization* captures the idea that everything on the planet is now more closely connected than ever before, but on an institutional foundation that is shaky and unprepared for managing the massive adjustments brought on by accelerating worldwide changes.

The integration of the globe in this transformed, interconnected, borderless world and common *cosmopolitan culture* (Appiah 2006) has reduced old feelings of independence, identity, and autonomy, and driven many states to surrender some of their sovereignty in order to benefit from collaborative participation in a competitive global marketplace. The message has been heard everywhere: borders and barriers cannot be revived in a nationalistic effort to close off a country in solitary isolation. "Join the world or become irrelevant" is the way that Edouard Balladur, former French prime minister, described "the end of nationalism."

From an optimistic perspective, an awareness of the common destiny of all, alongside the declining ability of many sovereign states to cope with global problems through unilateral *self-help* approaches, will energize efforts to put aside interstate competition. According to this reasoning, conflict will recede as humanity begins to better recognize that national borders and oceans provide little protection against the multiple challenges arising from the global revolution in travel, communications, and trade. These shared problems can only be managed through collective, multilateral cooperation (Barrett 2007). Globalization is creating a strong web of constraints on the foreign policy behavior of those who are plugged into the network of global transactions. Consequently, because globalization makes it imperative that states cooperate, this continued tightening of interstate linkages should be welcomed.

What is especially favorable about globalization is that when everyone depends on everyone else, all *must* work together. Global interdependence makes it imperative for states to renounce their competition because they increasingly have a shared interest in cooperation and fewer and fewer incentives to fight. Globalization, optimists argue, is an irreversible motor for unity and progress, and ought to be promoted because ultimately it will increase the wealth of everyone everywhere (Norberg 2006).

From a more pessimistic perspective, the current era of globalization that now seems unstoppable could be passing its peak (Abdelal and Segal 2007). Even if the present period of globalization continues to create ever-increasing interconnectedness rather than ending, as the previous 1870–1914 era of globalization disastrously did, pessimists fret, as well they should, about how to cope with our "flat, hot, and crowded" planet Earth (Friedman 2008). Globalization may not lead to greater transnational cooperation, but instead to cut-throat competition. Regardless of how compelling the need or how rewarding the benefits, increased contact and the trend toward an integrated single society of states may breed enmity, not amity.

According to this view, globalization empowers advantaged states but constrains the prospects of weak states, producing new inequalities as the gap between the wealthy and the poor widens. "The problem," writes James Surowiecki (2007), "is that the number of countries that have dramatically improved their standard of living in the era of globalization is surprisingly small. It is not surprising that people are made unhappy by the sight of others getting richer while they stay the same or actually get poorer."

Because its benefits will not be distributed equally, globalization will likely generate conflict between winners and losers. As neorealist theorist Kenneth Waltz observed, "interdependence promotes war as well as peace." Intertwined economies will sour relations more than sweeten them. Under conditions of fierce competition, scarcity, and resurgent nationalism, the temptation to seek isolation from the assault of globalization on national autonomy by creating barriers to trade and other transactions may be irresistible. The temptation to achieve political benefits by military force will also continue. Thus, the tightening web of globalization could lead to either danger or to opportunity.

Case Study:
Interdependence and Future International Politics

GOING GLOBAL Former UN Secretary-General Kofi Annan once noted that "it has been said that arguing against globalization is like arguing against the laws of gravity." In your reading of *World Politics*, you have considered many facets of globalization and the positive and negative implications of the increasing interconnectedness of the globe's states and peoples. Shown here in Egypt are horse drawn carriages parked in front of a McDonalds, reflecting a blending of cultures and economies, traditionalism and modernity. While globalization certainly presents many challenges, it also provides opportunities to learn, prosper, and enjoy a world of great diversity and possibility.

Will Technological Innovation Solve Pressing Global Problems?

The surge in globalization that followed on the heels of late-twentieth-century discoveries in microelectronics and information processing has unleashed revolutionary changes. "Biotechnology will dominate our lives during the next fifty years," predicts physicist philosopher Freeman Dyson (2007), "at least as much as computers have dominated our lives during the previous fifty years." The consequences of the technological revolution, however, are not certain. Technological innovations solve some problems but cause others. "Like any irrepressible force," observes Nobel laureate economist Wassily Leontief, "technology can bestow on us undreamed benefits but also inflict irreparable damage." It can increase productivity and economic output, but it can also displace workers and trigger social unrest and environmental damage.

Although acknowledging that there is often a significant time lag between the diffusion of new technology and the adjustment of society to the changes it fosters, some people assert that technological innovation promises humanity a more secure and bountiful future (Fidler and Gostin 2008). Indeed, the most optimistic members of this group believe that because of promising developments in such fields as biotechnology and digital software, humanity is entering the most innovative period in history. From their perspective, sufficient resources exist to fuel continued progress. With patience, technological solutions eventually will be found to ease the most serious problems facing the world today. Malnutrition and disease, they note as an example, may still exist, but, as a result of technological advances in agriculture and medicine, many people are alive today who might have perished in previous centuries. Others are hopeful about the potential role of technology in futuristic geoengineering initiatives to curb global warming, such as "directly scrubbing the air with devices that resemble big cooling towers" (Victor et al. 2009, p. 68).

In contrast to those who envision technological innovation as a way to increase economic growth and alleviate social welfare problems, others remain concerned that some proposed technological solutions will compound current problems. Whereas genetically modified crops are seen by members of the former group as a way to reduce famine, members of the latter group worry about the public health consequences. Even the so-called green revolution had its drawbacks, they argue. Although fertilizers, pesticides, and herbicides initially increased crop yields in various Global South countries, they eventually spawned new problems such as contaminated water supplies. Without wise management, technological advances can have detrimental side effects. Consider the case of the world's fisheries. At first, larger ships and improvements in maritime technology resulted in increases in the amount of fish harvested from the world's oceans. Over time, however, many fisheries were depleted. Applying more technology could not increase catches once the ecosystem had collapsed. As one member of this school of thought has put it: "[M]any of our new technologies confer upon us new power without automatically giving us new wisdom" (Gore 2006, p. 247).

What do you think? Is the customary way of seeing technological discoveries as the engines of progress really valid? Or is the tendency to overrate the positive impact of new technology based on wishful thinking (Edgerton 2007)? "Learning how to make new technology is one thing; learning how to use it is another" (Shapin 2007, p. 146). So, when you look at new technologies (stem cells, nanotechnology, human genomes, etc.), think counterfactually and imagine how things might turn out if new technologies had not been previously invented or how new ones might influence life on planet Earth for better or for worse.

What Types of Armed Aggression Will Become the Major Fault Line in the Geostrategic Landscape?

Prevalent practices tend to wither away when they cease to serve their intended purpose, as the examples of slavery, dueling, and colonialism illustrate. Trends point toward the possibility that this may happen as well for wars between states, which have declined nearly to the vanishing point. Even more impressively, the period since 1945 has been the longest span of great power peace since the sixteenth century. This achievement is raising expectations that large-scale warfare between countries will disappear and armed aggression between countries will become obsolete. Part of the confidence in that prediction is based on the assumption that no sane national leader would dare to wage war against another state because any conceivable rewards would be greatly exceeded by the cost of mass destruction.

To be sure, most leaders are still preparing for traditional kinds of warfare against other states and are convinced by the abiding wisdom of ancient Greek philosopher Aristotle: "A people without walls is a people without choice." That said, the use of traditional weapons of warfare against the emergent threats that now haunt the globe is of questionable usefulness. How can countries combat effectively with the weapons in their arsenals the dangers presented by faceless and invisible nonstate terrorists willing to die in suicide bombings for their cause? Can these attacks be deterred when the adversary lacks territory to target? How does a state destroy an enemy with preemptive strikes when those adversaries have neither a location nor things of value to attack?

The old forms of military power still used by states today may be becoming impotent, and no level of military might can guarantee a state's invulnerability. When countries' primary security problem is no longer an attack by another country but instead the threat of internal aggression (a civil war) or an attack by a transnational terrorist network such as Al Qaeda, the question is how to fight wars against the major military threats in today's globe.

The conduct of war has undergone several "generational" changes since the Thirty Years' War drew to a close and gave birth to the modern state system. Whereas "third-generation" military thinking has influenced most countries since World War II, today the threat of being attacked by the military forces of another country has receded, particularly in the Global North. Instead, a "fourth generation" of warfare has emerged in which states are pitted against nonstate actors in hostilities that lack front lines and clear distinctions between soldiers and civilians (Hammes 2004). Unable to defeat conventional armies on the field of battle, irregular forces using unconventional tactics focus on their adversary's will, using patience, ingenuity, and gruesome acts of violence to compel their opponent to weigh the mounting costs of continuing a long, drawn-out struggle. Some political and military leaders, however, continue to think of warfare in third-generational terms, dismissing this new face of war as an annoyance that detracts from preparations for decisive, large-scale engagements (Woodward 2006). Do the current wars in Afghanistan and Iraq provide a glimpse into the future? Will most military clashes in the early twenty-first century follow their pattern?

Will the Great Powers Intervene to Protect Human Rights?

Conflicts within countries are raging throughout the world. Many civilians are targets of overt oppression and violence by governments presumably created to preserve law and order in courts and through ballots. Of great concern is whether the moral outrage of the globe's major powers will be sufficient for them to make concerted peacekeeping and peacemaking interventions to end human rights abuses in those countries where standards of conduct accepted in international law have been blatantly disregarded. Atrocities in many failed states each year force a mass exodus of tens of millions of refugees and displaced people from their homes to seek safety. The global community is being put to a test of its true ideals and its capacity to defend them, at potentially high costs. Will a humanitarian concern for the victims targeted for extermination crystallize into a response? Or will the victims perish in a sea of indifference?

Human rights law in principle now provides unprecedented protection for people everywhere to live in freedom without fear. The traditional legal rule of state sovereignty and its corollary—the *nonintervention norm* prohibiting external interference in the internal affairs of states—has been revised. Former UN Secretary-General Kofi Annan described well the redefinition when he noted that "states are now widely understood to be instruments at the service of their people, and not vice versa."

Principle is one thing; the reality of human suffering is another. Will the great powers in the globalized community back their expressed convictions with action to free humanity from the oppression of mass murder? Can the great powers agree on rules for humanitarian intervention that define when it is legitimate to militarily respond to gross violations of "human rights, wherever they take place, and also on ways of deciding what action is necessary, and when, and by whom"?

The challenge is to transcend traditional notions of sovereignty and to construct a global consensus for intervention that, in the words of civil rights activist Dr. Martin Luther King, Jr., is based on the belief that "Injustice anywhere is a threat to justice everywhere." If the global community truly recognizes that all people have rights that transcend state borders and defines

Karel Prinsloo/AP Photo

IGNORING SYSTEMATIC SLAUGHTER IN SUDAN? Shown here is a Sudanese refugee after she and her family reached sanctuary on the Chad border after hiding for a year in a cave in Sudan's Darfur region. Called the worst genocide since the World War II Holocaust, this slaughter (like the simmering conflicts in Congo and Somalia that have killed millions) raises deep concerns that the world's great powers will intervene only when vital security interests or needed resources such as oil are threatened.

those human rights as the core of the community's "common global interests," then it will have to answer and act on essential unresolved questions: What is the common interest? Who shall define it? Who shall defend it? Under whose authority? And by what means of intervention?

Is the World Preparing for the Wrong War?

To preserve peace, one must prepare for war. That remains the classical realist formula for national security. But would states not be wiser to prepare to conquer the conditions that undermine prosperity, freedom, and welfare?

Leaders have long been loath to fall prey to the single-mindedness of preparing to compete with other states. As France's former President Francois Mitterand once urged, "together we must urgently find the solutions to the real problems at hand—especially unemployment and underdevelopment. This is the battlefield where the outlines of the [future] will be drawn." India's former Prime Minister Indira Gandhi warned that "either nuclear war will annihilate the human race and destroy the Earth, thus disposing of any future, or men and women all over must raise their voices for peace and for an urgent attempt to combine the insights of different civilizations with contemporary knowledge. We can survive in peace and goodwill only by viewing the human race as one, and by looking at global problems in their totality." These prescriptions adhere to a fundamental premise, as expressed by Martti Ahtisaari, then president of Finland: "To deal with the great security challenges of our time, including population growth, the spread of weapons of mass destruction, crime, environmental degradation, and ethnic conflicts, we must resolutely adopt new methods of managing change and building global security."

These rhetorical positions reflect the problems and self-interests these leaders faced at home and abroad. Nonetheless, they reveal a minority view. The war of people against people goes on. Human security remains precarious.

A large percentage of humanity faces famine, poverty, and a denial of basic human rights. Millions are threatened by genocide and terrorism sponsored by their own governments. "As human activities disrupt a growing number of ecological systems, it will become increasingly clear that the biggest threats to national security," argues Erik Assadourian (2010, p. 117) of the WorldWatch Institute, is "the weakened state of the planet." Humankind may consequently self-destruct, not because it lacks opportunities, but because of its collective inability to see and to seize them. "Perhaps we will destroy ourselves. Perhaps the common enemy within us will be too strong for us to recognize and overcome," eminent astronomer Carl Sagan (1988) lamented.

"But," he continued, "I have hope. . . . Is it possible that we humans are at last coming to our senses and beginning to work together on behalf of the species and the planet?"

Is This the "End of History" or the End of Happy Endings?

To many observers, the history of world affairs is the struggle between tyranny and liberty. The contest has taken various forms since antiquity: between kings and mass publics, despotism and democracy, ideological principle and pragmatic politics. Labels are misleading and sometimes dangerous. However, they provide the vocabulary of diplomacy and inform theoretical discussion of governance and statecraft (Rousseau 2006). History, in this image, is a battle for hearts and minds. It is an ideological contest for the allegiance of humanity to a particular form of political, social, and economic organization.

With the defeat of fascism in World War II and the collapse of the international communist movement a generation later, it has become fashionable to argue that the world had witnessed the end of a historic contest of epic proportions—and thus the triumph of liberalism and what Francis Fukuyama called the *end of history:*

> The twentieth century saw the developed world descend into a paroxysm of ideological violence, as liberalism contended first with the remnants of absolutism, then bolshevism and fascism, and finally an updated Marxism that threatened to lead to the ultimate apocalypse of nuclear war. But the [twentieth] century that began full of self-confidence in the ultimate triumph of Western liberal democracy [seemed] at its close to be returning full circle to where it started: . . . to the unabashed victory of economic and political liberalism (Fukuyama 1989, p. 3).

The abrupt repudiation of communism raised expectations that history had indeed "ended," in the sense that liberal democratic capitalism had triumphed throughout most of the world. Liberals, inspired by the belief that "liberal democracy and a market-oriented economic order are the only viable options for modern societies" (Fukuyama 1999b; see also Fukuyama 2004), are heartened by the doubling since the mid-1980s of the number of countries practicing multi-party elections and capitalism at home and in foreign trade. World order, they believe, can best be created by free governments practicing free trade. As Woodrow Wilson argued, making the world "safe for democracy" would make the world itself safe. From this liberal perspective, the diffusion of democratic capitalism bodes well for the future of world politics.

A less reassuring possibility is that history has not "ended" and that the battle between totalitarian and democratic governance is not truly over. "The continued spread of democracy in the twenty-first century is no more inevitable than it is impossible" (Mandelbaum 2007). There are signals that the march of democracy's spread is stalling, and many democracies remain ruled by one-party despots who, although elected, disregard constitutional limits on their power and deny their citizens basic political freedoms and religious and economic human rights. What is more, *new* democracies often lack the rule of law, political parties, or a free news media and as a consequence are unstable and warlike (Mansfield and Snyder 2005). This persistence of leaders unaccountable to the electorate suggests that we may *not* be witnessing history's end.

The global economic crisis has also led to renewed speculation about the merits and shortcomings of global capitalism. "If he were observing the current downturn, Marx would certainly relish pointing out how flaws inherent in capitalism led to the current crisis. He would see how modern developments in finance, such as securitization and derivatives, have allowed markets to spread the risks of global economic integration" (Panitch 2009, 141). Though many countries are starting to regain their financial footing, the consensus on the virtues of commercial liberalism has been shattered. The free market economies most exposed to the global economy bore the brunt of the financial damage, while countries that were relatively less open—ranging from India and China to Moldova—were less affected by the downturn.

> *Global, overarching forces such as modernization and widespread interconnectivity are converging to reshape our lives. These "metatrends" are transformational or transcendent phenomena, not simply big, pervasive ones. . . . But human adaptability—itself a meta-trend—will help keep our future from spinning out of control.*
>
> —David Pearce Snyder, futurologist

A NEW WORLD ORDER OR NEW WORLD DISORDER?

The paradox of contemporary world politics is that a world no longer haunted by the paralyzing fear of a looming all-out war between great powers now faces a series of challenges every bit as threatening and as potentially unmanageable. Globalization has simultaneously enlarged the responsibilities and expanded the issues to be confronted. In a prosperous and stable period of history, when confidence in peace and economic growth was high, and his administration was still in office, former U.S. President Bill Clinton found it necessary to warn that "profound and powerful forces are shaking and remaking our world. And the urgent question of our time is whether we can make change our friend and not our enemy."

The changes in recent years have spawned transnational threats to world order, in addition to the resurgence of nationalism, ethnic conflict, failed states, and separatist revolts. These include acid rain, AIDS, H1N1, other contagious diseases, drug trafficking, international organized crime, ozone depletion, climate change, obstacles to gender equality, energy and food scarcities, desertification and deforestation, financial crises and collapsing economies, and neomercantile trade protectionism.

The potential impact of these additional threats is formidable, as emerging trends suggest that nonmilitary dangers will multiply alongside the continuing threat of arms and armed aggression in civil wars, as well as interstate wars in particular regions and terrorism almost any place and at any time in the world. The distinction between geostrategic issues of security that pertain to matters of war and peace and global issues related to economic, social, demographic, and environmental aspects of relations between governments and people may disappear. How will humanity set priorities for action on a planet crowded with so many interrelated issues and problems, all of which require attention if peace and prosperity with justice is to prevail?

Previously established patterns and relationships have been obliterated. Something revolutionary, not simply new, appears to be unfolding. This book has focused on global change. It has identified the most important changes underway that are potentially leading to transformations in world politics.

Change, as we have seen, can be abrupt or slow. It moves constantly, but at its own pace; and history reminds us that the evolutionary direction of global change is uncertain. Many trends are unfolding at the same time, and their impact in combination can move the world along an unexpected trajectory. In addition, trends can reverse themselves, and each trend that moves forward advances at its own rate. Some trends move incredibly slowly in an evolutionary process that can only result in dramatic transformations over many centuries, whereas others exhibit short bursts of rapid change, interrupted by long periods without much change. Many examples of reversible, interrupted, and constant trends exist, as you have learned in this book. It is in their mix that the future will be shaped.

PICTURING GLOBAL DESTINY This view of a globe without borders is captured by the photo taken of the eastern Mediterranean from the Earth-orbiting space shuttle *Columbia*. It pictures an integrated world community, in which humanity shares a common destiny. It also captures the kinds of environmental threats confronting humanity in a globalized world, where problems do not stop at borders. Note the difference in visibility in this panorama, which scientists believe is the result of pollution contaminating the atmosphere over the Black Sea.

To appreciate the diverse ways trends may combine to affect each other, it is helpful for you to construct your images by both using memories of the past and by being inspired by visions of the future. In 1775, American revolutionary Patrick Henry underscored the importance of history, observing that he had "but one lamp by which my feet are guided, and that is the lamp of experience. I know of no way of judging the future but by the past." Decades later, in 1848, another patriot, Italian political leader Guiseppe Mazzini, stressed the importance of futurist thinking when he observed, "great things are achieved by guessing the direction of one's century." All of us need both perspectives, constructed with keen awareness that our images of history and of the future must avoid the temptation to see ourselves and our own country as we wish to be seen without taking into account how differently others might view us and our state.

It now appears that the collective impact of the divergent trends underway is signaling a major transformation in world politics. Yet, juxtaposed against the revolutionary is the persistent—the durability of enduring rituals, existing rules, established institutions, and entrenched customs that resist the pull of the momentous recent changes in world politics. Persistence and change coexist uneasily, and it is this mixture that makes the future so uncertain.

The outcomes of two races will determine the difference between the world that is and the world that will be. The first is the race between knowledge and oblivion. Ignorance stands in the way of global progress and justice. Advances in science and technology far outpace the resolution of the social and political problems they generate. Building the knowledge to confront these problems may therefore present the ultimate challenge. "The splitting of the atom," Albert Einstein warned, has "changed everything save our modes of thinking, and thus we drift toward unparalleled catastrophe. Unless there is a fundamental change in [our] attitudes toward one another as well as [our] concept of the future, the world will face unprecedented disaster."

"Knowledge is our destiny," philosopher Jacob Bronowski declared. If the world is to forge a promising future, it must develop more sophisticated knowledge. Sophistication demands that we see the world as a whole, as well as in terms of its individual parts; it does not permit picturing others according to our self-images or projecting onto others our own aims and values. We must discard belief in a simple formula for a better tomorrow and resist single issue approaches to reform. Toleration of ambiguity, even the pursuit of it, is essential.

The future of world politics also rests on the outcome of a race between states' ability to cooperatively act together and their historic tendency to compete and fight. Only concerted international cooperation stands in the way of slipping back into military conflicts and ruthless competition. To meet the global challenges of the future, and to make wise decisions to implement needed changes for bringing about a world that is more secure and just, vision is required.

> *If our image of the future were different, the decisions of today would be different. [An inspiring vision] will impel us to action. But if there is no commonly held image of what is worth striving for, [global] society will lack both motivation and direction.*
>
> —Willis Harman, policy analyst

The future is not fixed, and headlines are not trend lines. So we can overcome threatening present dangers by making wise and ethical choices. How, then, should we proceed?

"In times like these," futurologist David Pearce Snyder (2006, p. 17) counsels, "the best advice comes from ancient ideas that have withstood the test of time." Greek philosopher Heraclitus observed twenty-five thousand years ago that "nothing about the future is inevitable except change." Two hundred years later, mythic Chinese general Sun Tzu advised that "the wise leader exploits the inevitable." Their combined message is clear: "The wise leader exploits change."

Therefore, rather than fear the global future, we should welcome its opportunities as we strive to build a more peaceful and just world. The moving words of former U.S. President John F. Kennedy thus describe a posture we might well assume: "However close we sometimes seem to that dark and final abyss, let no man of peace and freedom despair. For he does not stand alone. . . . Together we shall save our planet or together we shall perish in its flames. Save it we can, and save it we must, and then shall we earn the eternal thanks of mankind."

Take an Online Practice Quiz

www.cengagebrain.com/shop/ISBN/0495802204

| *Suggested Readings* |

Bueno de Mesquita, Bruce. (2009) *The Predictioneer's Game: Using the Logic of Brazen Self-Interest to See & Shape the Future*. New York: Random House.

Carland, Maria Pinto and Candace Faber, eds. (2008) *Careers in International Affairs*. Washington, D.C., Georgetown University Press.

Denemark, Robert A., ed. (2010) *The International Studies Encyclopedia*. Boston, MA: Blackwell Publishing.

Glenn, Jerome C., Theodore J. Gordon, and Elizabeth Florescu. (2010) *2010 State of the Future*. Washington, D.C.: The Millennium Project.

The World Bank. (2010) *World Development Report 2010: Development and Climate Change*. Washington, D.C.: The World Bank.

Worldwatch Institute. (2010) *State of the World 2010: Transforming Cultures: From Consumerism to Sustainability*. New York: Norton.

glossary

A

absolute advantage The liberal economic concept that a state should specialize in the production of goods in which the costs of production are lowest compared with those of other countries.

absolute gains Conditions in which all participants in exchanges become better off.

acid rain Precipitation that has been made acidic through contact with sulfur dioxide and nitrogen oxides.

acquired immune deficiency syndrome (AIDS) An often fatal condition that can result from infection with the human immunodeficiency virus (HIV).

actor An individual, group, state, or organization that plays a major role in world politics.

adjudication A conflict-resolution procedure in which a third party makes a binding decision about a dispute in an institutional tribunal.

agency The capacity of actors to harness power to achieve objectives.

agenda setting The thesis that by their ability to identify and publicize issues, the communications media determine the problems that receive attention from governments and international organizations.

agent-oriented constructivism A variant of constructivism that sees ideas and identities as influenced in part by independent actors.

alignments The acceptance by a neutral state threatened by foreign enemies of a special relationship short of formal alliance with a stronger power able to protect it from attack.

alliances Coalitions that form when two or more states combine their military capabilities and promise to coordinate their policies to increase mutual security.

anarchy A condition in which the units in the global system are subjected to few if any overarching institutions to regulate their conduct.

antidumping duties Taxes placed on another exporting state's alleged selling of a product at a price below the cost to produce it.

antipersonnel landmines (APLs) Weapons buried below the surface of the soil that explode on contact with any person—soldier or citizen—stepping on them.

appeasement A strategy of making concessions to another state in the hope that, satisfied, it will not make additional claims.

arbitrage The selling of one currency (or product) and purchase of another to make a profit on changing exchange rates.

arbitration A conflict-resolution procedure in which a third party makes a binding decision between disputants through a temporary ruling board created for that ruling.

armed aggression Combat between the military forces of two or more states or groups.

arms control Multilateral or bilateral agreements to contain arms races by setting limits on the number and types of weapons states are permitted.

arms race The buildup of weapons and armed forces by two or more states that threaten each other, with the competition driven by the conviction that gaining a lead is necessary for security.

Asian Tigers The four Asian NICs that experienced far greater rates of economic growth during the 1980s than the more advanced industrial societies of the Global North.

asylum The provision of sanctuary to safeguard refugees escaping from the threat of persecution in the country where they hold citizenship.

asymmetric warfare Armed conflict between belligerents of vastly unequal military strength, in which the weaker side is often a nonstate actor that relies on unconventional tactics.

atrocities Brutal and savage acts against targeted citizen groups or prisoners of war, defined as illegal under international law.

autocratic rule A system of authoritarian or totalitarian government in which unlimited power is concentrated in a single leader.

B

balance of power The theory that peace and stability are most likely to be maintained when military power is distributed to prevent a single superpower hegemon or bloc from controlling the world.

balancer Under a balance-of-power system, an influential global or regional great power that throws its support in decisive fashion to a defensive coalition.

bandwagoning The tendency for weak states to seek alliance with the strongest power, irrespective of that power's ideology or type of government, in order to increase their security.

bargaining model of war An interpretation of war's onset as a choice by the initiator to bargain through aggression with an enemy in order to win on an issue or to obtain things of value, such as territory or oil.

barter The exchange of one good for another rather than the use of currency to buy and sell items.

behavioralism The methodological research movement to incorporate rigorous scientific analysis into the study of world politics so that conclusions about patterns are based on measurement, data, and evidence rather than on speculation and subjective belief.

bilateral Interactions between two transnational actors, such as treaties they have accepted to govern their future relationship.

bilateral agreements Exchanges between two states, such as arms control agreements, negotiated cooperatively to set ceilings on military force levels.

biodiversity The variety of plant and animal species living in the Earth's diverse ecosystems.

bipolarity A condition in which power is concentrated in two competing centers so that the rest of the states define their allegiances in terms of their relationships with both rival great-power superstates, or "poles."

blogs Online diaries, which spread information and ideas worldwide in the manner of journalists.

blowback The propensity for actions undertaken for national security to have the unintended consequence of provoking retaliatory attacks by the target when relations later sour.

bounded rationality The concept that decision maker's capacity to choose the best option is often constrained by many human and organizational obstacles.

boycotts Concerted efforts, often organized internationally, to prevent transactions such as trade with a targeted country in order to express disapproval or to coerce acceptance of certain conditions.

brinkmanship The intentional, reckless taking of huge risks in bargaining with an enemy, such as threatening a nuclear attack, to compel its submission.

bureaucracies The agencies and departments that conduct the functions of a central government or of a nonstate transnational actor.

bureaucratic politics model A description of decision making that sees foreign policy choices as based on bargaining and compromises among competing government agencies.

Bush Doctrine The unilateral policies of the George W. Bush administration proclaiming that the United States will make decisions only to meet America's perceived national interests, not to concede to other countries' complaints or to gain their acceptance.

C

carrying capacity The maximum number of humans and living species that can be supported by a given territory.

cartel A convergence of independent commercial enterprises or political groups that combine for collective action, such as limiting competition, setting prices for their services, or forming a coalition to advance their groups interests.

caucuses Informal groups that individuals in governments and other groups join to promote their common interests.

civil society A community that embraces shared norms and ethical standards to collectively manage problems without coercion and through peaceful and democratic procedures for decision making aimed at improving human welfare.

civil wars Wars between opposing groups within the same country or by rebels against the government.

clash of civilizations Political scientist Samuel Huntington's controversial thesis that in the twenty-first century the globe's major civilizations will conflict with one another, leading to anarchy and warfare similar to that resulting from conflicts between states over the past five hundred years.

classical liberal economic theory A body of thought based on Adam Smith's ideas about the forces of supply and demand in the marketplace, emphasizing the benefits of minimal government regulation of the economy and trade.

coercive diplomacy The use of threats or limited armed force to persuade an adversary to alter its foreign and/or domestic policies.

coercive power The use of threats and punishment to force the target to alter its behavior.

cognitive dissonance The general psychological tendency to deny discrepancies between one's preexisting beliefs (cognitions) and new information.

Cold War The 42-year (1949–1991) rivalry between the United States and the Soviet Union, as well as their competing coalitions, which sought to contain each other's expansion and win worldwide predominance.

collective action dilemma Paradox regarding the provision of collective goods in which, though everyone can enjoy the benefits of the good, no one is accountable for paying the cost.

collective good A public good, such as safe drinking water, from which everyone benefits.

collective security A security regime agreed to by the great powers that set rules for keeping peace, guided by the principle that an act of aggression by any state will be met by a collective response from the rest.

colonialism The rule of a region by an external sovereign power.

commercial liberalism An economic theory advocating free markets and the removal of barriers to the flow of trade and capital as a locomotive for prosperity.

communications technology The technological means through which information and communications are transferred.

communism The radical ideology maintaining that if society is organized so that every person produces according to his or her ability and consumes according to his or her needs, a community without class distinctions will emerge, sovereign states will no longer be needed, and imperial wars of colonial conquest will vanish from history.

communist theory of imperialism The Marxist-Leninist economic interpretation of imperialist wars of conquest as driven by capitalism's need for foreign markets to generate capital.

comparative advantage The concept in liberal economics that a state will benefit if it specializes in the production of those goods which it can produce at a lower opportunity cost.

compellence A method of coercive diplomacy usually involving an act of war or threat to force an adversary to make concessions against its will.

complex interdependence A model of world politics based on the assumptions that states are not the only important actors, security is not the dominant national goal, and military force is not the only significant instrument of foreign policy. This theory stresses cross-cutting ways in which the growing ties among transnational actors make them vulnerable to each other's actions and sensitive to each other's needs.

concert A cooperative agreement in design and plan among great powers to manage jointly the global system.

conciliation A conflict-resolution procedure in which a third party assists both parties to a dispute but does not propose a solution.

conflict Discord, often arising in international relations over perceived incompatibilities of interest.

consequentialism An approach to evaluating moral choices on the basis of the results of the action taken.

constitutional democracy Government processes that allow people, through their elected representatives, to exercise power and influence the state's policies.

constructivism A paradigm based on the premise that world politics is a function of the ways that states construct and then accept images of reality and later respond to the meanings given to power politics; as consensual definitions change, it is possible for either conflictual or cooperative practices to evolve.

containment A strategy to prevent a great power rival from using force to alter the balance of power and increase its sphere of influence.

cornucopians Optimists who question limits-to-growth analyses and contend that markets effectively maintain a balance between population, resources, and the environment.

cosmopolitan An outlook that values viewing the cosmos or entire world as the best polity or unit for political governance and personal identity, as opposed to other polities such as one's local metropolis or city of residence (e.g., Indianapolis or Minneapolis).

counterforce targeting strategy Targeting strategic nuclear weapons on particular military capabilities of an enemy's armed forces and arsenals.

countervailing duties Government tariffs to offset suspected subsidies provided by foreign governments to their producers.

countervalue targeting strategy A bargaining doctrine that declares the intention to use weapons of mass destruction against an enemy's most valued nonmilitary resources, such as the civilians and industries located in its cities.

coup d'etat A sudden, forcible takeover of government by a small group within that country, typically carried out by violent or illegal means with the goal of installing their own leadership in power.

covert operations Secret activities undertaken by a state outside its borders through clandestine means to achieve specific political or military goals with respect to another state.

crimes against humanity A category of activities, made illegal at the Nuremberg war crime trials, condemning states that abuse human rights.

crisis A situation in which the threat of escalation to warfare is high and the time available for making decisions and reaching compromised solutions in negotiations is compressed.

cultural conditioning The impact of national traditions and societal values on the behavior of states, under the assumption that culture affects national decision making about issues such as the acceptability of aggression.

cyberspace A metaphor used to describe the global electronic web of people, ideas, and interactions on the Internet, which is unencumbered by the borders of the geopolitical world.

cycles The periodic reemergence of conditions similar to those that existed previously.

D

decolonization The achievement of sovereign independence by countries that were once colonies of the great powers.

deconstructivism The postmodern theory that the complexity of the world system renders precise description impossible and that the purpose of scholarship is to understand actors' hidden motives by deconstructing their textual statements.

deforestation The process of clearing and destroying forests.

democratic peace The theory that although democratic states sometimes wage wars against nondemocratic states, they do not fight one another.

demography The study of population changes, their sources, and their impact.

dependency theory A theory hypothesizing that less developed countries are exploited because global capitalism makes them dependent on the rich countries that create exploitative rules for trade and production.

dependent development The industrialization of peripheral areas within the confines of the dominance-dependence relationship between the Global North and the Global South, which enables the poor to become wealthier without ever catching up to the core Global North countries.

desertification The creation of deserts due to soil erosion, overfarming, and deforestation, which converts cropland to nonproductive, arid sand.

détente In general, a strategy of seeking to relax tensions between adversaries to reduce the possibility of war.

deterrence Preventive strategies designed to dissuade an adversary from doing what it would otherwise do.

developed countries A category used by the World Bank (WDI 2009) to identify Global North countries, with a GNI per capita of $11,456 or more annually.

developing countries A category used by the World Bank to identify low income Global South countries with a 2009 GNI per capita below $935 and middle income countries with a GNI per capita of more than $935 but less than $11,456.

development The processes, economic and political, through which a country develops to increase its capacity to meet its citizens' basic human needs and raise their standard of living.

devolution States' granting of political power to minority ethnic groups and indigenous people in particular national regions under the expectation that greater autonomy will curtail the groups' quest for independence as a new state.

diasporas The migration of religious or ethnic groups to foreign lands despite their continuation of affiliation with the land and customs of their origin.

digital divide The division between the Internet technology–rich Global North and the Global South in the proportion of Internet users and hosts.

diplomacy Communication and negotiation between global actors that is not dependent upon the use of force and seeks a cooperative solution.

diplomatic immunity The legal doctrine that gives a country's officials (e.g., diplomats and ambassadors) release from the local legal jurisdiction of the state when they are visiting or stationed abroad to represent their own government.

disarmament Agreements to reduce or destroy weapons or other means of attack.

diversionary theory of war The hypothesis that leaders sometimes initiate conflict abroad as a way of increasing national cohesion at home by diverting national public attention away from controversial domestic issues and internal problems.

doctrines The guidelines that a great power or an alliance embraces as a strategy to specify the conditions under which it will use military power and armed force for political purposes abroad.

dollar overhang Condition that precipitated the end of the Bretton Woods era, in which total holdings of dollars outside of the U.S. central bank exceeded the amount of dollars actually backed by gold.

domino theory A metaphor popular during the Cold War that predicted that if one state fell to communism, its neighbors would also fall in a chain reaction, like a row of falling dominoes.

dualism The separation of a country into two sectors, the first modern and prosperous centered in major cities, and the second at the margin, neglected and poor.

E

ecological fallacy The error of assuming that the attributes of an entire population—a culture, a country, or a civilization—are the same attributes and attitudes of each person within it.

economic sanctions Punitive economic actions, such as the cessation of trade or financial ties, by one global actor against another to retaliate for objectionable behavior.

ecopolitics How political actors influence perceptions of, and policy responses to,

changing environmental conditions, such as the impact of carbon dioxide emissions on the temperature of the Earth.

embedded liberalism Dominant economic approach during the Bretton Woods system, which combined open international markets with domestic state intervention to attain such goals as full employment and social welfare.

enclosure movement The claiming of common properties by states or private interests.

end of history Francis Fukuyama's thesis that an end-point in the ideological debate about the best form of government and economy had been reached, with liberal capitalism and democracy prevailing throughout the world without serious competition from advocates of either communism or autocracy.

enduring internal rivalries Protracted violent conflicts between governments and insurgent groups within a state.

enduring rivalries Prolonged competition fueled by deep-seated mutual hatred that leads opposed actors to feud and fight over a long period of time without resolution of their conflict.

entente An agreement between states to consult one another and take a common course of action if one is attacked by another state.

environmental security A concept recognizing that environmental threats to global life systems are as dangerous as the threat of armed conflicts.

epistemic communities Scientific experts on a subject of inquiry such as global warming that are organized internationally as NGOs to communicate with one another and use their constructed understanding of "knowledge" to lobby for global transformations.

epistemology The philosophical examination of the ways in which knowledge is acquired and the analytic principles governing the study of phenomena.

ethics Criteria for evaluating right and wrong behavior and the motives of individuals and groups.

ethnic cleansing The extermination of an ethnic minority group by a state.

ethnic groups People whose identity is primarily defined by their sense of sharing a common ancestral nationality, language, cultural heritage, and kinship.

ethnic nationalism Devotion to a cultural, ethnic, or linguistic community.

ethnicity Perceptions of likeness among members of a particular racial grouping leading them to prejudicially view other nationality groups as outsiders.

ethnocentrism A propensity to see one's nationality or state as the center of the world and therefore special, with the result that the values and perspectives of other groups are misunderstood and ridiculed.

European Commission The executive organ administratively responsible for the European Union.

European Union (EU) A regional organization created by the merger of the European Coal and Steel Community, the European Atomic Energy Community, and the European Economic Community (called the European Community until 1993) that has since expanded geographically and in its authority.

exchange rate The rate at which one state's currency is exchanged for another state's currency in the global marketplace.

export quotas Barriers to free trade agreed to by two trading states to protect their domestic producers.

export-led industrialization A growth strategy that concentrates on developing domestic export industries capable of competing in overseas markets.

extended deterrence The protection received by a weak ally when a heavily militarized great power pledges to "extend" its capabilities to it in a defense treaty.

externalities The unintended side effects of choices that reduce the true value of the original decision, such as trade protectionism against foreign imports increasing the costs of goods to consumers and stimulating inflation.

extraterritoriality The legal doctrine that allows states to maintain jurisdiction over their embassies in other states.

F

failed states Countries whose governments have so mismanaged policy that their citizens, in rebellion, threaten revolution to divide the country into separate independent states.

fascism A far-right ideology that promotes extreme nationalism and the establishment of an authoritarian society built around a single party with dictatorial leadership.

feminist theory Body of scholarship that emphasizes gender in the study of world politics.

fertility rate The average number of children born to a woman (or group of women) during her lifetime.

firebreak The psychological barrier between conventional wars and wars fought with nuclear weapons as well as weapons of mass destruction.

First World The relatively wealthy industrialized countries that share a commitment to varying forms of democratic political institutions and developed market economies, including the United States, Japan, the European Union, Canada, Australia, and New Zealand.

fixed exchange rates A system in which a government sets the value of its currency at a fixed rate for exchange in relation to another country's currency so that the exchange value is not free to fluctuate in the global money market.

floating exchange rates An unmanaged process in which governments neither establish an official rate for their currencies nor intervene to affect the value of their currencies, and instead allow market forces and private investors to influence the relative rate of exchange for currencies between countries.

foreign aid Economic assistance in the form of loans and grants provided by a donor country to a recipient country for a variety of purposes.

foreign direct investment (FDI) A cross-border investment through which a person or corporation based in one country purchases or constructs an asset such as a factory or bank in another country so that a long-term relationship and control of an enterprise by nonresidents results.

foreign policy The decisions governing authorities make to realize international goals.

free-riders Those who obtain benefits at others' expense without the usual costs and effort.

functionalism The theory advanced by David Mitrany and others explaining how people can come to value transnational institutions (IGOs, integrated or merged states) and the steps to giving those institutions authority to provide the public goods (for example, security) previously, but inadequately, supplied by their own state.

G

game theory Mathematical model of strategic interaction where outcomes are determined not only by a single actor's preferences, but also by the choices of all actors involved.

gendercide Systematic killing of members of a specific gender.

Gender Empowerment Measure (GEM) The UN Development Programme's attempt to measure the extent of gender equality across the globe's countries, based on estimates of women's relative economic income, high-paying positions, and access to professional and parliamentary positions.

gender inequalities Differences between men and women in opportunity and reward that are determined by the values that guide states' foreign and domestic policies.

General Agreement on Tariffs and Trade (GATT) An UN-affiliated IGO designed to promote international trade and tariff reductions, replaced by the World Trade Organization.

genetic engineering Research geared to discover seeds for new types of plant and human life for sale and use as substitutes for those produced naturally.

genocide The attempt to eliminate, in whole or in part, an ethnic, racial, religious, or national minority group.

geo-economics The relationship between geography and the economic conditions and behavior of states that define their levels of production, trade, and consumption of goods and services.

geopolitics The relationship between geography and politics and their consequences for states' national interests and relative power.

Global commons The physical and organic characteristics and resources of the entire planet—the air in the atmosphere and conditions on land and sea—on which human life depends and which is the common heritage of all humanity.

Global East The rapidly growing economies of East and South Asia that have made those countries competitors with the traditionally dominant countries of the Global North.

global level of analysis Analyses that emphasize the impact of worldwide conditions on foreign policy behavior and human welfare.

global migration crisis A severe problem stemming from the growing number of people moving from their home country to another country, straining the ability of the host countries to absorb the foreign emigrants.

Global North A term used to refer to the world's wealthy, industrialized countries located primarily in the Northern Hemisphere.

Global South A term now often used instead of "Third World" to designate the less-developed countries located primarily in the Southern Hemisphere.

global structure The defining characteristics of the global system—such as the distribution of military capabilities—that exist independently of all actors but powerfully shape the actions of every actor.

global system The predominant patterns of behaviors and beliefs that prevail internationally to define the major worldwide conditions that heavily influence human and national activities.

global village A popular cosmopolitan perspective describing the growth of awareness that all people share a common fate because the world is becoming an integrated and interdependent whole.

globalization The integration of states through increasing contact, communication, and trade, as well as increased global awareness of such integration.

globalization of finance The increasing transnationalization of national markets through the world-wide integration of capital flows.

globalization of labor Integration of labor markets, predicated by the global nature of production as well as the increased size and mobility of the global labor force.

globalization of production
Transnationalization of the productive process, in which finished goods rely on inputs from multiple countries outside of their final market.

globally integrated enterprises MNCs organized horizontally with management and production located in plants in numerous states for the same products they market.

good offices Provision by a third party to offer a place for negotiation among disputants but does not serve as a mediator in the actual negotiations.

great powers The most powerful countries, militarily and economically, in the global system.

greenhouse effect The phenomenon producing planetary warming when gases released by burning fossil fuels act as a blanket in the atmosphere, thereby increasing temperatures.

gross national income (GNI) A measure of the production of goods and services within a given time period, which is used to delimit the geographic scope of production. GNI measures production by a state's citizens or companies, regardless of where the production occurs.

Group of 77 (G-77) The coalition of Third World countries that sponsored the 1963 *Joint Declaration of Developing Countries* calling for reform to allow greater equality in North–South trade.

groupthink The propensity for members of a group to accept and agree with the group's prevailing attitudes, rather than speaking out for what they believe.

gunboat diplomacy A show of military force, historically naval force, to intimidate an adversary.

H

hard power The ability to exercise international influence by means of a country's military capabilities.

heavily indebted poor countries (HIPCs) The subset of countries identified by the World Bank's Debtor Reporting System whose ratios of debt to gross national product are so substantial they cannot meet their payment obligations without experiencing political instability and economic collapse.

hegemon A preponderant state capable of dominating the conduct of international political and economic relations.

hegemonic stability theory A body of theory that maintains that the establishment of hegemony for global dominance by a single great power is a necessary condition for global order in commercial transactions and international military security.

hegemony The ability of one state to lead in world politics by promoting its worldview and ruling over arrangements governing international economics and politics.

high politics Geostrategic issues of national and international security that pertain to matters of war and peace.

history-making individuals model An interpretation that sees foreign policy decisions that affect the course of history as products of strong-willed leaders acting on their personal convictions.

horizontal nuclear proliferation An increase in the number of states that possess nuclear weapons.

Human Development Index (HDI) An index that uses life expectancy, literacy, average number of years of schooling, and income to assess a country's performance in providing for its peoples' welfare and security.

human immunodeficiency virus (HIV) A virus that can lead to the lethal acquired immune deficiency syndrome (AIDS).

human needs Those basic physical, social, and political needs, such as food and freedom, that are required for survival and security.

human rights The political rights and civil liberties recognized by the international community as inalienable and valid for individuals in all countries by virtue of their humanity.

human security A measure popular in liberal theory of the degree to which the welfare of individuals is protected and promoted, in contrast to realist theory's emphasis on putting the state's interests in military and national security ahead of all other goals.

humanitarian intervention The use of peacekeeping troops by foreign states or international organizations to protect endangered people from gross violations of their human rights and from mass murder.

hypotheses Speculative statements about the probable relationship between independent variables (the presumed causes) and a dependent variable (the effect).

I

ideology A set of core philosophical principles that leaders and citizens collectively construct about politics, the interests of political actors, and the ways people ought to behave.

imperial overstretch The historic tendency for past hegemons to sap their own strength through costly imperial pursuits and military spending that weaken their economies in relation to the economies of their rivals.

imperialism The policy of expanding state power through the conquest and/or military domination of foreign territory.

import quotas Numerical limit on the quantity of particular products that can be imported.

import-substitution industrialization A strategy for economic development that centers on providing investors at home incentives to produce goods so that previously imported products from abroad will decline.

indigenous peoples The native ethnic and cultural inhabitant populations within countries ruled by a government controlled by others.

individual level of analysis An analytical approach that emphasizes the psychological and perceptual variables motivating people, such as those who make foreign policy decisions on behalf of states and other global actors.

individualistic fallacy The logical error of assuming that an individual leader, who has legal authority to govern, represents the people and opinions of the population governed, so that all citizens are necessarily accountable for the vices and virtues (to be given blame or credit) of the leaders authorized to speak for them.

infant industry Newly established industries ("infants") that are not yet strong enough to compete against mature foreign producers in the global marketplace until in time they develop and can then compete.

information age The era in which the rapid creation and global transfer of information through mass communication contributes to the globalization of knowledge.

information technology (IT) The techniques for storing, retrieving, and disseminating through computerization and the Internet recorded data and research knowledge.

information warfare Attacks on an adversary's telecommunications and computer networks to degrade the technological systems vital to its defense and economic well-being.

infowar tactics Attacks on an adversary's telecommunications and computer networks to penetrate and degrade an enemy whose defense capabilities depend heavily on these technological systems.

instrumental rationality A conceptualization of rationality that emphasizes the tendency of decision makers to compare options with those previously considered and then select the one that has the best chance of success.

intellectual property Inventions created by the use of human intelligence in publications, art, and design by individuals that are often illegally used for commercial purposes without credits or royalties to their creators in violation of GATT's agreement.

interdependence A situation in which the behavior of international actors greatly affects others with whom they have contact, making all parties mutually sensitive and vulnerable to the others' actions.

intergovernmental organizations (IGOs) Institutions created and joined by states' governments, which give them authority to make collective decisions to manage particular problems on the global agenda.

Intermediate-Range Nuclear Forces (INF) Treaty   The U.S.-Russian agreement to eliminate an entire class of nuclear weapons by removing all intermediate and short-range ground-based missiles and launchers with ranges between 300 and 3,500 miles from Europe.

International Court of Justice (ICJ)   The primary court established by the United Nations for resolving legal disputes between states and providing advisory opinions to international agencies and the UN General Assembly.

International Criminal Court (ICC)   A court established by the UN for indicting and administering justice to people committing war crimes.

international criminal tribunals   Special tribunals established by the UN prosecute those responsible for war time atrocities and genocide, bring justice to victims, and deter such crimes in the future.

international liquidity   Reserve assets used to settle international accounts.

International Monetary Fund (IMF)   A financial agency now affiliated with the UN, established in 1944 to promote international monetary cooperation, free trade, exchange rate stability, and democratic rule by providing financial assistance and loans to countries facing financial crises.

international monetary system   The financial procedures used to calculate the value of currencies and credits when capital is transferred across borders through trade, investment, foreign aid, and loans.

international political economy (IPE)   The study of the intersection of politics and economics that illuminates why changes occur in the distribution of states' wealth and power.

international regime   Embodies the norms, principles, rules, and institutions around which global expectations unite regarding a specific international problem.

international relations   Relationships that exist between pairs or among groups of global actors.

international terrorism . The threat or use of violence as a tactic of terrorism against targets in other countries.

interspecific aggression   Killing others that are not members of one's own species.

intra-firm trade   Cross-national trade of intermediate goods and services within the same firm.

intraspecific aggression   Killing members of one's own species.

irredentism   A movement by an ethnic national group to recover control of lost territory by force so that the new state boundaries will no longer divide the group.

isolationism   A policy of withdrawing from active participation with other actors in world affairs and instead concentrating state efforts on managing internal affairs.

J

jus ad bellum   A component of just war doctrine that establishes criteria under which a just war may be initiated.

jus in bello   A component of just war doctrine that sets limits on the acceptable use of force.

just war doctrine   The moral criteria identifying when a just war may be undertaken and how it should be fought once it begins.

just war theory   The theoretical criteria under which it is morally permissible, or "just," for a state to go to war and the methods by which a just war might be fought.

K

Kellogg-Briand Pact   A multilateral treaty negotiated in 1928 that outlawed war as a method for settling interstate conflicts.

L

laissez-faire   From a French phrase (meaning literally "let do") that Adam Smith and other commercial liberals in the eighteenth century used to describe the advantages of free-wheeling capitalism without government interference in economic affairs.

laissez-faire economics   The philosophical principle of free markets and free trade to give people free choices with little governmental regulation.

least developed of the less developed countries (LLDCs)   The most impoverished countries in the Global South.

levels of analysis   The different aspects of and agents in international affairs that may be stressed in interpreting and explaining global phenomena, depending on whether the analyst chooses to focus on "wholes" (the complete global system and large collectivities) or on "parts" (individual states or people).

Liberal International Economic Order (LIEO)   The set of regimes created after World War II, designed to promote monetary stability and reduce barriers to the free flow of trade and capital.

liberalism   A paradigm predicated on the hope that the application of reason and universal ethics to international relations can lead to a more orderly, just, and cooperative world; liberalism assumes that anarchy and war can be policed by institutional reforms that empower international organization and law.

"linkage" strategy   A set of assertions claiming that leaders should take into account another country's overall behavior when deciding whether to reach agreement on any one specific issue so as to link cooperation to rewards.

long peace   Long-lasting periods of peace between any of the militarily strongest great powers.

long-cycle theory   A theory that focuses on the rise and fall of the leading global power as the central political process of the modern world system.

low politics   The category of global issues related to the economic, social, demographic, and environmental aspects of relations between governments and people.

M

macroeconomics   The study of aggregate economic indicators such as GDP, the money supply, and the balance of trade that governments monitor to measure changes in national and global economies such as the rates of economic growth and inflation or the level of unemployment.

Marxist-Leninism   Communist theory as derived from the writings of Karl Marx, Vladimir Lenin, and their successors, which criticizes capitalism as a cause of class struggle, the exploitation of workers, colonialism, and war.

massive retaliation   The Eisenhower administration's policy doctrine for containing Soviet communism by pledging to respond to any act of aggression with the most destructive capabilities available, including nuclear weapons.

matchpolitik   The German realist philosophy in statecraft that sees the expansion of state power and territory by use of armed force as a legitimate goal.

mediation   A conflict-resolution procedure in which a third party proposes a nonbinding solution to the disputants.

mercantilism   Political economic perspective that views international trade in zero-sum terms and calls for active state intervention into domestic economies.

militant religious movements   Politically active organizations based on strong religious convictions, whose members are fanatically devoted to the global promotion of their religious beliefs.

military intervention   Overt or covert use of force by one or more countries that cross the borders of another country in order to affect the target country's government and policies.

military necessity   The legal principle that violation of the rules of warfare may be excused for defensive purposes during periods of extreme emergency.

military-industrial complex   A combination of defense establishments, contractors who supply arms for them, and government agencies that benefit from high military spending, which act as a lobbying coalition to pressure governments to appropriate large expenditures for military preparedness.

mirror images   The tendency of states and people in competitive interaction to perceive each other similarly—to see others the same hostile way others see them.

modernization   A view of development popular in the Global North's liberal democracies that wealth is created through efficient production, free enterprise, and free trade, and that countries' relative wealth depends on technological innovation and education more than on natural endowments such as climate and resources.

monetary policy   The decisions made by states' central banks to change the country's money supply in an effort to manage the national economy and control inflation, using fiscal policies such as changing the money supply and interest rates.

monetary system   The processes for determining the rate at which each state's currency is valued against the currency of every other state, so that purchasers and sellers can calculate the costs of financial transactions across borders such as foreign investments, trade, and cross-border travel.

money supply   The total amount of currency in circulation in a state, calculated to include demand deposits, such as checking accounts in commercial banks, and time deposits, such as savings accounts and bonds, in savings banks.

morality   Principles about the norms for behavior that should govern actors' interactions.

morals   Principles clarifying the difference between good and evil and the situations in which they are opposed.

mores   The customs of a group accepted as morally binding obligations.

most-favored-nation principle (MFN)   The central GATT principle of unconditional nondiscriminatory treatment in trade between contracting parties underscoring the WTO's rule requiring any advantage given by one WTO member to also extend it to all other WTO members.

multilateral agreements   Cooperative compacts among many states to ensure that a concerted policy is implemented toward alleviating a common problem, such as levels of future weapons capabilities.

multilateralism   Cooperative approaches to managing shared problems through collective and coordinated action.

multinational corporations (MNCs)   Business enterprises headquartered in one state that invest and operate extensively in many other states.

multiple advocacy   The concept that better and more rational choices are made when decisions are reached in a group context, which allows advocates of differing alternatives to be heard so that the feasibility of rival options receives critical evaluation.

multiple independently targetable reentry vehicles (MIRVs)   A technological innovation permitting many weapons to be delivered from a single missile.

multipolarity   The distribution of global power into three or more great-power centers, with most other states allied with one of the rivals.

murky protectionism   Nontariff barriers to trade that may be "hidden" in government policies not directly related to trade, such as environmental initiatives and government spending.

mutual assured destruction (MAD)   A condition of mutual deterrence in which both sides possess the ability to survive a first strike with weapons of mass destruction and launch a devastating retaliatory attack.

N

nation   A collectivity whose people see themselves as members of the same group because they share the same ethnicity, culture, or language.

national character   The collective characteristics ascribed to the people within a state.

national interest   The goals that states pursue to maximize what they perceive to be selfishly best for their country.

national security   A country's psychological freedom from fears that the state will be unable to resist threats to its survival and national values emanating from abroad or at home.

nationalism   A mind-set glorifying a particular state and the nationality group living in it, which sees the state's interest as a supreme value.

nature versus nurture   The controversy over whether human behavior is determined more by the biological basis of "human nature" than it is nurtured by the environmental conditions that humans experience.

negotiation   Diplomatic dialogue and discussion between two or more parties with the goal of resolving through give-and-take bargaining perceived differences of interests and the conflicts they cause.

neo-Malthusians   Pessimists who warn of the global ecopolitical dangers of uncontrolled population growth.

neocolonialism (neoimperialism)   The economic rather than military domination of foreign countries.

neoliberalism   The "new" liberal theoretical perspective that accounts for the way international institutions promote global change, cooperation, peace, and prosperity through collective programs for reforms.

neomercantilism   A contemporary version of classical mercantilism that advocates promoting domestic production and a balance-of-payment surplus by subsidizing exports and using tariffs and nontariff barriers to reduce imports.

neorealism   A theoretical account of states' behavior that explains it as determined by differences in their relative power within the global hierarchy, defined primarily by the distribution of military power, instead of by other factors such as their values, types of government, or domestic circumstances.

neutrality   The legal doctrine that provides rights for states to remain nonaligned with adversaries waging war against each other.

New International Economic Order (NIEO)   The 1974 policy resolution in the UN that called for a North–South dialogue to open the way for the less-developed countries of the Global South to participate more fully in the making of international economic policy.

newly industrialized countries (NICs)   The most prosperous members of the Global South, which have become important exporters of manufactured goods as well as important markets for the major industrialized countries that export capital goods.

Nonaligned Movement (NAM)   A group of more than one hundred newly independent, mostly less-developed, states that joined together as a group of neutrals to avoid entanglement with the superpowers' competing alliances in the Cold War and to advance the Global South's primary interests in economic cooperation and growth.

nonaligned states   Countries that do not form alliances with opposed great-powers and practice neutrality on issues that divide great powers.

nonalignment   A foreign policy posture that rejects participating in military alliances with rival blocs for fear that formal alignment will entangle the state in an unnecessary involvement in war.

noncombatant immunity   The legal principle that military force should not be used against innocent civilians.

nondiscrimination   GATT principle that goods produced by all member states should receive equal treatment, as embodied in the ideas of most-favored nation (MFN) and national treatment.

nongovernmental organizations (NGOs)   Transnational organizations of private citizens maintaining consultative status with the UN; they include professional associations, foundations, multinational corporations, or simply internationally active groups in different states joined together to work toward common interests.

nonintervention norm   A fundamental international legal principle, now being challenged, that traditionally has defined interference by one state in the domestic affairs of another as illegal.

nonlethal weapons (NLWs)   The wide array of "soft kill," low-intensity methods of incapacitating an enemy's people, vehicles, communications systems, or entire cities without killing either combatants or noncombatants.

nonproliferation regime   Rules to contain arms races so that weapons or technology do not spread to states that do not have them.

nonstate nations   National or ethnic groups struggling to obtain power and/or statehood.

nontariff barriers (NTBs)   Measures other than tariffs that discriminate against imports without direct tax levies and are beyond the scope of international regulation.

norms   Generalized standards of behavior that, once accepted, shape collective expectations about appropriate conduct.

North American Free Trade Agreement (NAFTA)   An agreement that brings Mexico into the free-trade zone linking Canada and the United States.

North Atlantic Treaty Organization (NATO)   A military alliance created in 1949 to deter a Soviet attack on Western Europe that since has expanded and redefined its mission to emphasize not only the maintenance of peace but also the promotion of democracy.

Nth country problem   The expansion of additional new nuclear weapon states.

nuclear deterrence   Dissuading an adversary from attacking by threatening retaliation with nuclear weapons.

Nuclear Nonproliferation Treaty (NPT)   An international agreement that seeks to prevent horizontal proliferation by prohibiting further nuclear weapons sales, acquisitions, or production.

nuclear winter   The expected freeze that would occur in the Earth's climate from the fallout of smoke and dust in the event nuclear weapons were used, blocking out sunlight and destroying the plant and animal life that survived the original blast.

O

official development assistance (ODA)   Grants or loans to countries from donor countries, now usually channeled through multilateral aid institutions such as the World Bank for the primary purpose of promoting economic development and welfare.

opportunity cost   The sacrifices that sometimes results when the decision to select one option means that the opportunity to realize gains from other options is lost.

orderly market arrangements (OMAs)   Voluntary export restrictions through government-to-government agreements to follow specific trading rules.

outsourcing   The transfer of jobs by a corporation usually headquartered in a Global North country to a Global South country able to supply trained workers at lower wages.

ozone layer   The protective layer of the upper atmosphere over the Earth's surface that shields the planet from the sun's harmful impact on living organisms.

P

pacifism   The liberal idealist school of ethical thought that recognizes no conditions that justify the taking of another human's life, even when authorized by a head of state.

paradigm   Derived from the Greek, *paradeigma*, meaning an example, a model, or an essential pattern; a paradigm structures thought about an area of inquiry.

peace building   Postconflict actions, predominantly diplomatic and economic, that strengthen and rebuild governmental infrastructure and institutions in order to avoid renewed recourse to armed conflict.

peace enforcement   The application of military force to warring parties, or the threat of its use, normally pursuant to international authorization, to compel compliance with resolutions or with sanctions designed to maintain or restore peace and order.

peace operations   A general category encompassing both peacekeeping and peace enforcement operations undertaken to establish and maintain peace between disputants.

peaceful coexistence   Soviet leader Nikita Khrushchev's 1956 doctrine that war between capitalist and communist states is not inevitable and that inter-bloc competition could be peaceful.

peacekeeping   The efforts by third parties such as the UN to intervene in civil wars and/or interstate wars or to prevent hostilities between potential belligerents from escalating, so that by acting as a buffer a negotiated settlement of the dispute can be reached.

peacemaking   The process of diplomacy, mediation, negotiation or other forms of peaceful settlement that arranges an end to a dispute and resolves the issues that led to conflict.

podcasts   Technology that enables individuals to create audio and visual programs and make them available as digital downloads.

polarity   The degree to which military and economic capabilities are concentrated in the global system that determines the number of centers of power, or "poles."

polarization   The formation of competing coalitions or blocs composed of allies that align with one of the major competing poles, or centers, of power.

policy agenda   The changing list of problems or issues to which governments pay special attention at any given moment.

policy networks   Leaders and organized interests (such as lobbies) that form temporary alliances to influence a particular foreign policy decision.

political economy   A field of study that focuses on the intersection of politics and economics in international relations.

political efficacy   The extent to which policy makers' self-confidence instills in them the belief that they can effectively make rational choices.

political integration   The processes and activities by which the populations of many or all states transfer their loyalties to a merged political and economic unit.

politics   To Harold Lasswell, the study of "who gets what, when, how, and why."

politics of scarcity   The view that the unavailability of resources required to sustain life, such as food, energy, or water, can undermine security in degrees similar to military aggression.

pooled sovereignty   Legal authority granted to an IGO by its members to make collective decisions regarding specified aspects of public policy heretofore made exclusively by each sovereign government.

population density   The number of people within each country, region, or city, measuring the geographical concentration of the population as a ratio of the average space available for each resident.

population implosion   A rapid reduction of population that reverses a previous trend toward progressively larger populations; a severe reduction in the world's population.

positivist legal theory   A theory that stresses states' customs and habitual ways of behaving as the most important source of law.

postmodern terrorism   To Walter Laqueur, the terrorism practiced by an expanding set of diverse actors with new weapons "to sow panic in a society to weaken or even overthrow the incumbents and to bring about political change."

power   The factors that enable one actor to manipulate another actor's behavior against its preferences.

power balance   A division of global military and economic capabilities among more than one center or dominant superpower.

power potential   The capabilities or resources held by a state that are considered necessary to its asserting influence over others.

power transition   A narrowing of the ratio of military capabilities between great-power rivals that is thought to increase the probability of war between them.

power transition theory   The theory that war is likely when a dominant great power is threatened by the rapid growth of a rival's capabilities, which reduces the difference in their relative power.

preemption   A quick, first-strike military attack in self defense to prevent an aggressor from launching a war of aggression, for which there is overwhelming evidence that the aggressor's threat is real and imminent or about to be undertaken.

preemptive war   A quick first-strike attack that seeks to defeat an adversary before it can organize an initial attack or a retaliatory response.

preventive diplomacy   Diplomatic actions taken in advance of a predictable crisis to prevent or limit violence.

preventive war   Strictly outlawed by international law, a war undertaken by choice against an enemy to prevent it from suspected intentions to attack sometime in the distant future—if and when the enemy might acquire the necessary military capabilities.

Prisoner's Dilemma   From game theory, a non-zero-sum situation in which two prisoners have incentives to cooperate and if they do they will both benefit, so that is the rational decision to make; however, if one defects to maximize personal gain at the expense of the other prisoner, both will suffer—a dilemma that raises questions about what is the prudent or rational course of action in circumstances of distrust.

private military services   The outsourcing of activities of a military-specific nature to private companies, such as armed security, equipment maintenance, IT services, logistics, and intelligence services.

private international law   Law pertaining to routine transnational intercourse between or among states as well as nonstate actors.

proliferation   The spread of weapon capabilities from a few to many states in a chain reaction, so that an increasing number of states gain the ability to launch an attack on other states with devastating (e.g., nuclear) weapons.

prospect theory   A social psychological theory explaining decision making under conditions of uncertainty and risk that looks at the relationship between individual risk propensity and the perceived prospects for avoiding losses and realizing big gains.

protectionism   Barriers of foreign trade, such as tariffs and quotas, that protect local industries from competition for the purchase of products local manufacturers produce.

public international law   Law pertaining to government-to-government relations as well as countries' relations with other types of transnational actors.

purchasing power parity (PPP)   An index that calculates the true rate of exchange among currencies when parity—when what can be purchased is the same—is achieved; the index determines what can be bought with a unit of each currency.

R

rapprochement   In diplomacy, a policy seeking to reestablish normal cordial relations between enemies.

rational choice   Decision-making procedures guided by careful definition of situations, weighing of goals, consideration of all alternatives, and selection of the options most likely to achieve the highest goals.

realism   A paradigm based on the premise that world politics is essentially and unchangeably a struggle among self-interested states for power and position under anarchy, with each competing state pursuing its own national interests.

realpolitik   The theoretical outlook prescribing that countries should increase their power and wealth in order to compete with and dominate other countries.

reciprocity   GATT principle calling for mutual or reciprocal lowering of trade barriers.

refugees   People who flee for safety to another country because of a well-founded fear of political persecution, environmental degradation, or famine.

regional currency union   The pooling of sovereignty to create a common currency (such as the EU's euro) and single monetary system for members in a region, regulated by a regional central bank within the currency bloc.

regional trade agreements (RTAs)   Treaties that integrate the economies of members through the reduction of trade barriers.

relative burden of military spending   Measure of the economic burden of military activities calculated by the share of each state's gross domestic product allocated to military expenditures.

relative deprivation   Inequality between the wealth and status of individuals and groups, and the outrage of those at the bottom about their perceived exploitation by those at the top.

relative gains   Conditions in which some participants in cooperative interactions benefit more than others.

remittances   The money earned by immigrants working in rich countries (which almost always exceeds the income they could earn working in their home country) that they send to their families in their country.

rents   Higher-than-normal financial returns on investments that are realized from governmental restrictive interference or monopolistic markets.

replacement-level fertility   One couple replacing themselves on average with two children so that a country's population will remain stable if this rate prevails.

reprisals   The international legal practice of resorting to military force short of war in retaliation for losses suffered from prior illegal military actions.

responsible sovereignty   A principle that requires states to protect not only their own people but to cooperate across borders to protect global resources and address transnational threats.

retorsion   Retaliatory acts (such as economic sanctions) against a target's behavior that is regarded as objectionable but legal (such as trade restrictions) to punish the target with measures that are legal under international law.

revolution in military technology (RMT)   The sophisticated new weapons technologies that make fighting war without mass armies possible.

roles   The constraints written into law or custom that predispose decision makers in a particular governmental position to act in a manner and style that is consistent with expectations about how the role is normally performed.

S

sanctions   Punitive actions (short of military force) by one global actor against another to retaliate for its previous objectionable behavior.

sanctuary   A place of refuge and protection.

satisficing   The tendency for decision makers to choose the first satisfactory option rather than searching further for a better alternative.

schematic reasoning   The process of reasoning by which new information is interpreted according to a memory structure, a schema, which contains a network of generic scripts, metaphors, and simplified characterizations of observed objects and phenomena.

secession, or separative revolts   A religious or ethnic minority's efforts, often by violent means, to gain independent statehood by separating territory from an established sovereign state.

Second World   During the Cold War, the group of countries, including the Soviet Union, its (then) Eastern European allies, and China, that embraced communism and central planning to propel economic growth.

second-strike capability   A state's capacity to retaliate after absorbing an adversary's first-strike attack with weapons of mass destruction.

security community   A group of states whose high level of institutionalized or customary collaboration results in the settlement of disputes by compromise rather than by military force.

security dilemma   The tendency of states to view the defensive arming of adversaries as threatening, causing them to arm in response, so that all states' security declines.

security regime   Norms and rules for interaction agreed to by a set of states to increase security.

selective engagement   A great power grand strategy using economic and military power to influence only important particular situations, countries, or global issues by striking a balance between a highly interventionist "global policeman" and an uninvolved isolationist.

self-determination The liberal doctrine that people should be able to determine the government that will rule them.

self-help The principle that because in international anarchy all global actors are independent, they must rely on themselves to provide for their security and well-being.

semiperiphery To world-system theorists, countries midway between the rich "core" or center, and the poor "periphery" in the global hierarchy, at which foreign investments are targeted when labor wages and production costs become too high in the prosperous core regions.

small powers Countries with limited political, military, or economic capabilities and influence.

smart bombs Precision-guided military technology that enables a bomb to search for its target and detonate at the precise time it can do the most damage.

social constructivism A variant of constructivism that emphasizes the role of social discourse in the development of ideas and identities.

socialization The processes by which people learn to accept the beliefs, values, and behaviors that prevail in a given society's culture.

soft power The capacity to co-opt through such intangible factors as the popularity of a state's values and institutions, as opposed to the "hard power" to coerce through military might.

sovereign equality The principle that states are legally equal in protection under international law.

sovereignty The legal doctrine that states have supreme authority to govern their internal affairs and manage their foreign relations with other states and nonstate actors.

speculative attacks Massive sales of a country's currency, caused by the anticipation of a future decline in its value.

sphere of influence A region of the globe dominated by a great power.

spiral model A metaphor used to describe the tendency of efforts to enhance defense to result in escalating arms races.

standard operating procedures (SOPS) Rules for reaching decisions about particular types of situations.

state An independent legal entity with a government exercising exclusive control over the territory and population it governs.

states' attributes State characteristics that shape foreign policy behavior, such as its size, wealth, and the extent to which its leaders are accountable to its citizens in comparison with other states.

state level of analysis An analytical approach that emphasizes how the internal attributes of states influence their foreign policy behaviors.

state sovereignty A state's supreme authority to manage internal affairs and foreign relations.

state-sponsored terrorism Formal assistance, training, and arming of foreign terrorists by a state in order to achieve foreign policy and/or domestic goals.

statehood The legal criteria by which a country and its government become a state in the global community.

statelessness The growing band of people who have no citizenship rights in any country and are forced out of one country and not accepted in any other.

Strategic Arms Limitation Talks (SALT) Two sets of agreements reached during the 1970s between the United States and the Soviet Union that established limits on strategic nuclear delivery systems.

Strategic Arms Reduction Treaty (START) The U.S.–Russian series of negotiations that began in 1993 and, with the 1997 START-III agreement ratified by Russia in 2000, pledged to cut the nuclear arsenals of both sides by 80 percent of the Cold War peaks, in order to lower the risk of nuclear war.

Strategic Defense Initiative (SDI) The so-called Star Wars plan conceived by the Reagan administration to seek to deploy an antiballistic missile system using space-based lasers that would destroy enemy nuclear missiles before they could reenter the Earth's atmosphere.

Strategic Offensive Reductions Treaty (SORT) The U.S.–Russian agreement to reduce the number of strategic warheads to between 1,700 and 2,200 for each country by 2012.

strategic trade policy Government subsidies for particular domestic industries to help them gain competitive advantages over foreign producers.

strategic weapons Weapons of mass destruction that are carried on intercontinental ballistic missiles (ICBMs), submarine-launched ballistic missiles (SLBMs), or long-range bombers and are capable of annihilating an enemy state.

structural realism The neorealist theory postulating that the structure of the global system determines the behavior of transnational actors within it.

structural violence The condition defined by the Norwegian peace researcher Johan Galtung as the harm and injury caused by the global system's unregulated structure, which gives strong states great opportunities to victimize weak states that cannot protect themselves.

structuralism The neorealist proposition that states' behavior is shaped primarily by changes in the properties of the global system, such as shifts in the balance of power, instead by individual heads of states or by changes in states' internal characteristics.

survival of the fittest A realist concept derived from Charles Darwin's theory of evolution that advises that ruthless competition is ethically acceptable to survive, even if the actions violate moral commands not to kill.

sustainable development Economic growth that does not deplete the resources needed to maintain life and prosperity.

T

tariffs Tax assessed on goods as they are imported into a country.

terrorism Premeditated violence perpetrated against noncombatant targets by subnational or transnational groups or clandestine agents, usually intended to influence an audience.

theocracy A country whose government is organized around a religious dogma.

theory A set of hypotheses postulating the relationship between variables or conditions advanced to describe, explain, or predict phenomena and make prescriptions about how positive changes ought to be engineered to realize particular goals and ethical principles.

Third Way An approach to governance advocated primarily by many European leaders who, while recognizing few alternatives to liberal capitalism, seek to soften the cruel social impact of free-market individualism by progressively allowing government intervention to preserve social justice and the rights of individuals to freedom from fear of the deprivations caused by disruptions in the global economy.

Third World A Cold War term to describe the less-developed countries of Africa, Asia, the Caribbean, and Latin America.

tit-for-tat strategy A bargaining approach that consistently reciprocates in kind the offers or threats made by the other party in a negotiation, with equivalent rewards returned and equivalent punishing communications returned in retaliation.

trade integration The difference between gross rates in trade and gross domestic product.

tragedy of the commons A metaphor, widely used to explain the impact of human behavior on ecological systems, that explains how rational self-interested behavior by individuals may have a destructive and irrational collective impact.

transformation A change in the characteristic pattern of interaction among the most active participants in world politics of such magnitude that it appears that one "global system" has replaced another.

transgenetic crops New crops with improved characteristics created artificially through genetic engineering that combine genes from species that would not naturally interbreed.

transnational banks (TNBs) The globe's top banking firms, whose financial activities are concentrated in transactions that cross state borders.

transnational norms The regular customs widely practiced by countries in their relations with other countries and the kinds of behavior that the international community accepts as what is to be practiced.

transnational relations Interactions across state boundaries that involves at least one actor that is not the agent of a government or intergovernmental organization.

transnational religious movements A set of beliefs, practices, and ideas administered politically by religious organizations to promote the worship of their conception of a transcendent deity and its principles for conduct.

transparency With regard to the GATT, the principle that barriers to trade must be visible and thus easy to target.

Truman Doctrine The declaration by President Harry S. Truman that U.S. foreign policy would use intervention to support peoples who allied with the United States against communist external subjugation.

two-level games A concept referring to the growing need for national policy makers to make decisions that will meet both domestic and foreign goals.

U

unilateralism An approach that relies on self-help, independent strategies in foreign policy.

uni-multipolar A global system where there is a single dominant power, but the settlement of key international issues always requires action by the dominant power in combination with that of other great powers.

unipolarity A condition in which the global system has a single dominant power or hegemon capable of prevailing over all other states.

unitary actor A transnational actor (usually a sovereign state) assumed to be internally united, so that changes in its domestic opinion do not influence its foreign policy as much as do the decisions that actor's leaders make to cope with changes in its global environment.

V

vertical nuclear proliferation The expansion of the capabilities of existing nuclear powers to inflict increasing destruction with their nuclear weapons.

virtual corporations Agreements between otherwise competitive MNCs, often temporary, to join forces and skills to coproduce and export particular products in the borderless global marketplace.

virtual nuclear arsenals The next generation of "near nuclear" military capabilities produced by the revolution in military technology that would put strategic nuclear weapons of mass destruction at the margins of national security strategies by removing dependence on them for deterrence.

virtuality Imagery created by computer technology of objects and phenomena that produces an imaginary picture of actual things, people, and experiences.

voluntary export restrictions (VERs) A protectionist measure popular in the 1980s and early 1990s, in which exporting countries agree to restrict shipments of a particular product to a country to deter it from imposing an even more burdensome import quota.

W

war A condition arising within states (civil war) or between states (interstate war) when actors use violent means to destroy their opponents or coerce them into submission.

war crimes Acts performed during war that the international community defines as crimes against humanity, including atrocities committed against an enemy's prisoners of war, civilians, or the state's own minority population.

war weariness hypothesis The proposition that fighting a major war is costly in terms of lost lives and income, and these costs greatly reduce a country's tolerance for undertaking another war until enough time passes to lose memory of those costs.

Washington consensus The view that Global South countries can best achieve sustained economic growth through democratic governance, fiscal discipline, free markets, a reliance on private enterprise, and trade liberalization.

World Bank Also known as the International Bank for Reconstruction and Development (IBRD), the World Bank is the globe's major IGO for financing economic growth and reducing poverty through long-term loans.

world politics The study of how global actors' activities entail the exercise of influence to achieve and defend their goals and ideals, and how it affects the world at large.

World Trade Organization (WTO) A multilateral agency that monitors the implementation of trade agreements and settles disputes among trade partners.

world-system theory A body of theory that treats the capitalistic world economy originating in the sixteenth century as an interconnected unit of analysis encompassing the entire globe, with an international division of labor and multiple political centers and cultures whose rules constrain and share the behavior of all transnational actors.

X

xenophobia The suspicious dislike, disrespect, and disregard for members of a foreign nationality, ethnic, or linguistic group.

Y

Yalta Conference The 1945 summit meeting of the Allied victors to resolve postwar territorial issues and to establish voting procedures in the United Nations to collectively manage world order.

Yoshida Doctrine Japan's traditional security policy of avoiding disputes with rivals, preventing foreign wars by low military spending, and promoting economic growth through foreign trade.

youth bulge A burgeoning youth population, thought to make countries more prone to civil conflicts.

Z

zeitgeist The "spirit of the times," or the dominant cultural norms assumed to influence the behavior of people living in particular periods.

zero-sum An exchange in a purely conflictual relationship in which what is gained by one competitor is lost by the other.

references

Aaronson, Susan Ariel. (2002) *Taking Trade to the Streets: The Lost History of Public Efforts to Shape Globalization.* Ann Arbor: University of Michigan Press.

Aaronson, Susan, and Jamie Zimmerman. (2007) *Trade Imbalance: The Struggle to Weigh Human Rights Concerns in Trade Policymaking.* Cambridge: Cambridge University Press.

Abdelal, Rawi, and Adam Segal. (2007) "Has Globalization Passed Its Peak?" *Foreign Affairs* 86 (January/February): 103–114.

Abouharb, Rodwan, and David Cingranelli. (2007) Human Rights and Structural Adjustment. New York: Cambridge University Press.

Abrahms, Max. (2008) "Why Terrorism Does Not Work." pp. 418–440 in Karen Mingst and Jack Snyder (eds), *Essential readings in World Politics*, 3rd edition. New York: W.W. Norton.

Abramowitz, Morton. (2002) "The Bush Team Isn't Coping," *International Herald Tribune* (August 20): 6.

Ackerly, Brooke and Jacqui True. (2008) "Reflexivity in Practice: Power and Ethics in Feminist Research on International Relations," *International Studies Review* (10): 693–707.

Addo, Michael K. (ed.). (2005) *International Human Rights Law.* Burlington, Ver.: Ashgate.

Adelman, Kenneth L., and Norman R. Augustine. (1992) "Defense Conversion," *Foreign Affairs* 71 (Spring): 26–47.

Adler, Emanuel. (2002) "Constructivism and International Relations," pp. 95–118 in Walter Carlsnaes, Thomas Risse, and Beth Simmons (eds.), *Handbook of International Relations.* London: Sage.

Adler, Jerry. (2005) "How Big a Threat is the Avian Flu to the U.S.?" *Newsweek* (October 31): 38–45.

Agnew, John. (2007) "Know-Where: Geographies of Knowledge of World Politics," *International Political Sociology* 1 (June): 138–148.

Albert, Mathias. (2007) "'Globalization Theory': Yesterday's Fad or More Lively Than Ever?" *International Political Sociology* 1 (June): 165–182.

Albright, David. (1993) "A Proliferation Primer," *Bulletin of the Atomic Scientists* 49 (June): 14–23.

Albright, Madeleine K. (2005) "United Nations," pp. 219–23 in Helen E. Purkitt (ed.), *World Politics 04/05.* Dubuque, Iowa: McGraw-Hill/Dushkin.

——— (2000) "Time to Renew Faith in the Nonproliferation Treaty," *International Herald Tribune* (March 7): 8.

Alesina, Alberto, and Enrique Spolaore. (2003) *The Size of Nations.* Cambridge, Mass.: MIT Press.

Allen John L. (2006) *Student Atlas of World Politics*, 7th ed. Dubuque, Iowa: McGraw-Hill.

——— (2002) *Student Atlas of World Politics*, 5th ed. New York: Dushkin/McGraw-Hill.

——— (2001) *Student Atlas World Geography*, 2nd ed. New York: McGraw-Hill.

——— (2000) *Student Atlas of World Politics*, 4th ed. New York: Dushkin/McGraw-Hill.

Allen, John L., and Elizabeth J. Leppman. (2004) *Student Atlas of World Politics*, 6th ed. Guilford, Conn.: Dushkin/McGraw-Hill.

Allen, Susan Hannah. (2008) "Political Institutions and Constrained Response to Economic Sanctions," Foreign Policy Analysis (July): 255–274.

——— (2005) "The Determinants of Economic Sanctions Success and Failure," *International Interactions* 31 (April-June): 117–38.

Alley, Roderic. (2004) *Internal Conflict and the International Community: Wars Without End?* Burlington, Ver.: Ashgate.

Allison, Graham T. (2010) "Nuclear Disorder: Surveying Atomic Threats." *Foreign Affairs* 89, No. 1 (January/February): 74–85.

——— (2004) *Nuclear Terrorism: The Ultimate Preventable Catastrophe.* New York: Henry Holt.

Allison, Graham T, and Philip Zelikow. (1999) *Essence of Decision: Explaining the Cuban Missile Crisis*, 2nd ed. New York: Longman.

Al-Samarrai, Bashir. (1995) "Economic Sanctions against Iraq," pp. 133–39 in David Cortwright and George A. Lopez (eds.), *Economic Sanctions.* Boulder, Colo.: Westview.

Alston, Philip, and Euan Macdonald, eds. (2008) *Human Rights, Intervention, and the Use of Force.* Oxford, UK: Oxford University Press.

Altman, Daniel. (2005) "China: Both a Powerhouse and a Pauper," *International Herald Tribune* (October 8–9): 16.

Altman, Lawrence K. (2002) "AIDS Is Called a Security Threat," *International Herald Tribune* (October 2): 1, 10.

Altman, Roger. (2009) "Globalization in Retreat: Further Geopolitical Consequences of the Financial Crisis." *Foreign Affairs* 88(4): 2–16.

Altman, Roger C, and C. Bowman Cutter. (1999) "Global Economy Needs Better Shock Absorbers," *International Herald Tribune* (June 16): 7.

Amnesty International. (2009). *Death Sentences and Executions in 2008.* London: Amnesty International Publications.

(2009). "Children's Rights: The Future Starts Here" Available at: http://www.amnestyusa.org/document.php?lang=e&id=B0275B42F3B4C25380256900006933EF.

Amoore, Louise (ed.). (2005) *The Global Resistance Reader: Concepts and Issues.* New York: Routledge.

Anderlini, Sanam N. (2007) *Women Building Peace: What They Do, Why it Matters.* Boulder, CO: Lynne Rienner.

Andreas, Peter. (2005) "The Criminalizing Consequences of Sanctions," *International Studies Quarterly* 49 (June): 335–60.

Angell, Norman. (1910) *The Grand Illusion: A Study of the Relationship of Military Power in Nations to Their Economic and Social Advantage.* London: Weidenfeld & Nicholson.

Annan, Kofi. (2006) "Courage to Fulfill Our Responsibilities," pp. 205–09 in Helen E. Purkitt (ed.), *World Politics 05/06.* Dubuque, Iowa: McGraw-Hill/Dushkin.

——— (1999) "Two Concepts of Sovereignty," *Economist* (September 18): 49–50.

Appiah, Kwame Anthony. (2006) *Cosopolitanism: Ethics in a World of Strangers.* New York: Norton.

Ariely, Dan. (2008) *Predictably Irrational: The Hidden Forces that Shape our Decisions.* New York: Harper.

Armstrong, David, and Jutta Brunée. (2009) *Routledge Handbook of International Law.* Taylor & Francis.

Arquilla, John. (2010) "The War Issue." *Foreign Policy* (March/April): 61–62.

Arreguín-Toft, Ivan. (2006) *How the Weak Wins Wars: A Theory of Asymmetric Conflict.* New York: Cambridge University Press.

Art, Robert J. (2005) "Coercive Diplomacy," pp. 163–77 in Robert J. Art and Robert Jervis (eds.), *International Politics*, 7th ed. New York: Pearson Longman.

Ash, Timothy Garton. (2004) *Free World: America, Europe, and the Surprising Future of the West*. New York: Random House.

Assadourian, Erik. (2010) "Government's Role in Design." *State of the World: Transforming Cultures, From Consumerism to Sustainability*. New York: W. W. Norton & Company.

Auboin, Marc. (2009) "Restoring Trade Finance: What the G-20 Can Do." In *The Collapse of global trade, murky protectionism, and the crisis: Recommendations for the G20*, Baldwin, Richard and Simon Evenett, eds. London: VoxEU.org. Available at: http://voxeu.org/reports/Murky_Protectionism.pdf.

Auguste, Byron G. (1999) "What's So New about Globalization?" pp. 45–47 in Helen E. Purkitt (ed.), *World Politics 99/00*, 20th ed. Guilford, Conn.: Dushkin/ McGraw-Hill.

Axelrod, Robert M. (1984) *The Evolution of Cooperation*. New York: Basic Books.

Ayoob, Mohammed. (2004) "Third World Perspectives on Humanitarian Intervention," *Global Governance* 10 (January-March): 99–18.

——— (1995) *The Third World Security Predicament*. Boulder, Colo.: Lynne Rienner.

Azios, Tony. (2007) "What Is It That Drives Terrorism?" *Christian Science Monitor* (August 28): 1, 17.

Babai, Don. (2001) "International Monetary Fund," pp. 412–18 in Joel Krieger (ed.), *The Oxford Companion to Politics of the World*, 2nd ed. Oxford: Oxford University Press.

Babcock, Linda and Sara Laschever. (2003) *Women Don't Ask: Negotiation and the Gender Divide*. Princeton: Princeton University Press.

Babones, Jonathan, and Jonathan H. Turner. (2004) "Global Inequality," pp. 101–20 in George Ritzer (ed.), *Handbook of Social Problems*. London: Sage.

Bacevich, Andrew J. (2005). *The New American Militarism: How Americans Are Seduced by War*. New York: Oxford University Press.

——— (ed.). (2003) *The Imperial Tense*. Chicago: Ivan R. Dee/Rowman & Littlefield.

——— (2002) *American Empire*. Cambridge, Mass.: Harvard University Press.

Badey, Thomas J. (ed.). (2005) *Violence and Terrorism 05/06*, 8th ed. Guilford, Conn.: Dushkin/McGraw-Hill.

Baines, Erin K. (2004) *Vulnerable Bodies: Gender, the UN, and the Global Refugee Crisis*. Burlington, Ver.: Ashgate.

Bakke, Kristen M. (2005) "Clash of Civilizations or Clash of Religions?" *International Studies Review* 7 (March): 87–89.

Baker, Aryn, and Kajaki Olya. (2008) "A War That's Still Not Won," *Time* (July 7): 37–43.

Baker, Aryn and Loi Kolay. (2009) "The Longest War," *Time* (April 20): 25–29.

Baker, Peter and Dan Bilefsky. (2010) "Russia and U.S. Sign Nuclear Arms Reduction Act." *The New York Times* (April 8): A8.

Baldwin, David A. (1999/2000) "The Sanctions Debate and the Logic of Choice," *International Security* 24 (Winter): 80–107.

——— (ed.). (1993) *Neorealism and Neoliberalism: The Contemporary Debate*. New York: Columbia University Press.

——— (1989) *Paradoxes of Power*. New York: Basic Blackwell.

Baldwin, Richard and Simon Evenett. (2009) "Introduction and Recommendations for the G-20." In *The collapse of global trade, murky protectionism, and the crisis: Recommendations for the G20*, Baldwin, Richard and Simon Evenett, eds. London: VoxEU.org. Available at: http://voxeu.org/reports/Murky_Protectionism.pdf.

Bamford, James. (2005) *A Pretext for War: 9/11, Iraq, and the Abuse of America's Intelligence Agencies*. New York: Anchor Vintage.

Bradsher, Keith. (2009) "China Gearing Up in Crisis to Emerge even Stronger," *International Herald Tribune* (March 17): 1, 12.

Bandy, Joe, and Jackie Smith. (2004). *Coalitions Across Borders: Transnational Protest and the Neoliberal Order*. Lanham, Md: Rowman & Littlefield.

Baratta, Joseph Preston. (2005) *The Politics of World Federation*. New York: Praeger.

Barber, Benjamin R. (2003) *Fear's Empire*. New York: Norton.

——— (1995) *Jihad vs. McWorld*. New York: Random House.

Barbieri, Katherine. (2003) *The Liberal Illusion: Does Trade Promote Peace?* Ann Arbor: University of Michigan Press.

Barbieri, Katherine, and Gerald Schneider. (1999) "Globalization and Peace," *Journal of Peace Research* 36 (July): 387–404.

Barboza, David. (2005) "For China, New Malls Jaw-Dropping in Size," *International Herald Tribune* (May 25): 1, 4.

Bardhan, Pranab. (2005) "Giants Unchained? Not So Fast," *International Herald Tribune* (November 3): 6.

Barkin, Samuel. (2003) "Realist Constructivism," *International Studies Review* 5 (September): 328–42.

——— (2001) "Resilience of the State," *Harvard International Review* 22 (Winter): 40–46.

Barnes, Joe, Amy Jaffe, and Edward L. Morse. (2004) "The New Geopolitics of Oil," *National Interest* (Winter/Energy Supplement): 3–6.

Barnet, Michael. (2005) "Social Constructivism," pp. 251–270 in John Baylis and Steve Smith (eds.), The Globalization of World Politics, 3rd ed. New York: Oxford University Press.

Barnet, Richard J. (1980) *The Lean Years*. New York: Simon & Schuster.

——— (1977) *The Giants: Russia and America*. New York: Simon & Schuster.

Barnet, Richard J., and John Cavanagh. (1994) *Global Dreams: Imperial Corporations and the New World Order*. New York: Simon & Schuster.

Barnet, Richard J., and Ronald E. Müller. (1974) *Global Reach: The Power of the Multinational Corporations*. New York: Simon & Schuster.

Barnett, Michael. (2005) "Social Constructivism," pp. 251–70 in John Baylis and Steve Smith (eds.), *The Globalization of World Politics*, 3rd ed. New York: Oxford University Press.

Barnett, Michael, and Martha Finnemore. (2004) *Rules for the World: International Organizations in Global Politics*. Ithaca, N.Y: Cornell University Press.

Barnett, Thomas P. M. (2004) *The Pentagon's New Map*. New York: G. P. Putnam's Sons.

Bar-On, Tamir, and Howard Goldstein. (2005) "Fighting Violence: A Critique of the War on Terrorism," *International Politics* 42 (June): 225–45.

Baron, Samuel H., and Carl Pletsch (eds.). (1985) *Introspection in Biography*. Hillsdale, N.J.: Analytic Press.

Barratt, Bethany. (2007) *Human Rights and Foreign Aid: For Love or Money?* New York: Routledge.

Barringer, Felicity. (2009) "Cool roofs offer a tool in fight against global heat," *International Herald Tribune* (July 29): 1.

Barrett, Scott. (2007) *Why Cooperate? The Incentive to Supply Global Public Goods*. New York: Oxford University Press.

Bates, B.C., Z.W. Kundzewicz, S. Wu, and J.P. Palutikof, eds. (2008) *Climate Change and Water*, Technical Paper of the Intergovernmental Panel on Climate Change, IPCC Secretariat, Geneva, 210 pp.

Battelle and R&D Magazine. (2008) "2009 Global R&D Funding Forecast," Battelle and *R&D Magazine*. Available at: http://www.battelle.org/news/pdfs/2009RDFundingfinalreport.pdf.

Baylis, John, and Steve Smith (eds.). (2005) *The Globalization of World Politics*, 3rd ed. New York: Oxford University Press.

Bayne, Nicholas, and Stephen Woolcock (eds.). (2004) *The New Economic Diplomacy*. Burlington, Ver.: Ashgate.

Beattie, Alan and Jean Eaglesham. (2009) "Still No Deadline for Doha Accord," *Financial Times* April 2.

Becker, Elizabeth. (2003) "WTO. Rules Against U.S. On Steel Tariff," *The New York Times* (March 27).

Beckman, Peter R., and Francine D'Amico (eds.). (1994) *Women, Gender, and World Politics*. Westport, Conn.: Bergin & Garvey.

Beddoes, Zanny Minton. (2009) "Looking for a way out: Ending the fiscal and monetary stimulus will be much harder than starting it." *The Economist* (November 22): 137–138.

——— (2005) "The Great Thrift Shift," *Economist* (September 24): 3.

Begley, Sharon. (2010) "What the spill will kill." *Newsweek* (June 14): 25–30.

——— (2009) "Climate-Change Calculus: Why its even sores than we feared.," *Newsweek* (August 3): 30.

——— (2009b) "Good Cop/Bad Cop Goes Green," *Newsweek* (May 4): 49.

——— (2008) "Global Warming is a Cause of This Year's Extreme Weather," *Newsweek* (July 7/14): 53.

——— (2007) "Get Out Your Handkerchiefs," *Newsweek* (June 4): 62.

Behe, Michael J. (2005) "Rationalism and Reform," *First Things* (August-September): 75–79.

Beitz, Charles R. (2001) "Human Rights as a Common Concern," *American Political Science Review* 95 (June): 269–82.

Bell, James John. (2006) "Exploring the 'Singularity'," pp. 207–10 in Robert M. Jackson (ed.), *Global Issues 05/06*. Dubuque, Iowa: McGraw-Hill/Dushkin.

Bellamy, Alex J., and Paul D. Williams. (2005) "Who's Keeping the Peace?" *International Security* 29 (Spring): 157–97.

Benhabib, Seyla. (2005) "On the Alleged Conflict Between Democracy and International Law," *Ethics and International Affairs* 19 (No. 1): 85–100.

Benner, Thorsten, Stephan Mergenthaler, and Philipp Rotman. (2008) "Rescuing the Blue Helmets," *International Herald Tribune* (July 23): 6.

Bennett, Scott, and Allan C. Stam. (2004) *The Behavioral Origins of War*. Ann Arbor: University of Michigan Press.

Benson, Michelle. (2007) "Extending the Bounds of Power Transition Theory," *International Interactions* 33 (July/September): 211–215.

Ben-Yehuda, Hemda, and Meirav Mishali-Ran. (2006) "Ethnic Actors and International Crises," *International Interactions* 32 (January/March): 49–78.

Bercovitch, Jacob, and Scott Sigmund Gartner. (2008) *International Conflict Mediation*. New York: Routledge.

Berdal, Mats, and Mónica Serrano (eds.). (2002) *Transnational Organized Crime and International Security*. Boulder, Colo.: Lynne Rienner.

Bergen, Peter L. (2006) *The Osama bin Laden I Know*. New York: Free Press.

Berger, Peter L., and Samuel P. Huntington (eds.). (2002) *Many Globalizations: Cultural Diversity in the Contemporary World*. Oxford: Oxford University Press.

Berger, Peter, and Thomas Luckmann. (1967) *The Social Construction of Reality*. New York: Anchor.

Bergesen, Albert, and Ronald Schoenberg. (1980) "Long Waves of Colonial Expansion and Contraction, 1415–1969," pp. 231–77 in Albert Bergesen (ed.), *Studies of the Modern World-System*. New York: Academic Press.

Bergsten, C. Fred. (2009) "The Global Crisis and the International Economic Position of the United States," pp. 1–10 of *The Long-Term International Economic Position of the United States,* edited by Fred Bergsten. Washington, DC: Petersen Institute for International Economics.

——— (2005) *The United States and the World Economy*. Washington, D.C.: Institute of International Economics.

——— (2004) "The Risks Ahead for the World Economy," *Economist* (September 11): 63–65.

Bernstein, Jeremy. (2010) "Nukes for Sale." *The New York Review* (May 13): 44–46.

Bernstein, Richard. (2003) "Aging Europe Finds its Pension is Running Out," *New York Times International* (June 29): 3.

Berthelot, Yves. (2001) "The International Financial Architecture—Plans for Reform," *International Social Science Journal* 170 (December): 586–96.

Bhagwati, Jagdish. (2008a) *Termites in the Trading System: How Preferential Agreements Undermine Free Trade*. New York: Oxford University Press.

——— (2008b) *In Defense of Globalization*. New York: Oxford University Press.

——— (2005) "A Chance to Lift the 'Aid Curse,'" *Wall Street Journal* (March 22): A14.

——— (2004) *In Defense of Globalization*. New York: Oxford University Press.

Bigelow, Gordon. (2005) "Let there be markets: The evangelical roots of economics," *Harper's* 310 (May): 33–38.

Bijian, Zheng. (2005) "China's 'Peaceful Rise' to Great-Power Status," *Foreign Affairs* 84 (October): 18–24.

Bishop, William. (1962) *International Law*. Boston Little, Brown.

Blainey, Geoffrey. (1988) *The Causes of War*, 3rd ed. New York: Free Press.

Blanton, Robert G., and Shannon Lindsey Blanton. (2008) "Virtuous or Vicious Cycle? Human Rights, Trade, and Development," pp. 91–103 in Rafael Reuveny and William R. Thompson (eds.), *North and South in the World Political Economy*. Malden, MA: Blackwell.

——— (2007) "Human Rights and Trade," *International Interactions* 33 (April/June): 97–117.

——— (2001) "Democracy, Human Rights, and U.S.-Africa Trade," *International Interactions* 27 (2): 275–295.

Blanton, Shannon Lindsey. (2005) "Foreign Policy in Transition? Human Rights, Democracy, and U.S. Arms Exports," *International Studies Quarterly* 49 (December): 647–67.

——— (1999) "Instruments of Security or Tools of Repression? Arms Imports and Human Rights Conditions in Developing Countries," *Journal of Peace Research* 36 (March): 233–244.

Blanton, Shannon Lindsey and Robert G. Blanton. (2009) "A Sectoral Analysis of Human Rights and FDI: Does Industry Type Matter?" *International Studies Quarterly* 53 (2): 469–493.

——— (2007) "What Attracts Foreign Investors? An Examination of Human Rights and Foreign Direct Investment," *Journal of Politics* 69 (1): 143–155.

Blanton, Shannon Lindsey, and Charles W. Kegley, Jr. (1997) "Reconciling U.S. Arms Sales with America's Interests and Ideals," *Futures Research Quarterly* 13 (Spring): 85–101.

Bloom, Mia. (2005) *Dying to Kill: The Allure of Suicide Terror*. New York: Columbia University Press.

Blum, Andrew, Victor Asal, and Jonathan Wilkenfeld (eds.). (2005) "Nonstate Actors, Terrorism, and Weapons of Mass Destruction," *International Studies Review* 7 (March): 133–70.

Blumenthal, W. Michael. (1988) "The World Economy and Technological Change," *Foreign Affairs* 66 (No 3): 529–50.

Blustein, Paul. (2010) "R.I.P., WTO." *Foreign Policy* (January/February): 66.

Boehmer, Charles and Timothy Nordstrom. (2008) "Intergovernmental Organization Memberships: Examining Political Community and the Attributes of International Organizations," *International Interactions* 34: 282–309.

Boehmer, Charles, Erik Gartzke, and Timothy Norstrom. (2005) "Do International Organizations Promote Peace?" *World Politics* 57 (October): 1–38.

Boin, Arjen, Paul 't Hart, Eric Stern, and Bengt Sunderlius. (2007) *The Politics of Crisis Management.* Cambridge, U.K.: Cambridge University Press.

Boli, John, Michael A. Elliott and Franziska Bieri. (2004) "Globalization," pp. 389–415 in George Ritzer (ed.), *Handbook of Social Problems.* London: Sage.

Boli, John, and Frank L. Lechner. (2004) *World Culture.* London: Blackwell.

Bolton, M. Kent. (2005) *U.S. Foreign Policy and International Politics: George W. Bush, 9/11, and the Global-Terrorist Hydra.* Upper Saddle River, N.J.: Prentice Hall.

Bolzendahl, Catherine. (2009) "Making the Implicit Explicit: Gender Influences on Social Spending in Twelve Industrialized Democracies, 1980–1999," *Social Politics* (16): 40–81.

Boot, Max. (2006) *War Made New.* New York: Gotham.

Borenstein, Seth. (2006) "Pentagon Accused of Wasteful Spending," *The Idaho Statesman* (January 24): Main 3.

———— (2005) "Mankind is Using Up the Earth, Scientists Say," Columbia, S.C., *The State* (March 30): A8.

———— (2003) "U.S. to Revive Dormant Nuclear-Power Industry," Columbia, S.C., *The State* (June 16): A5.

Borer, Douglas A., and James D. Bowen. (2007) "Rethinking the Cuban Embargo," *Foreign Policy Analysis* 3 (April): 127–143.

Borgerson, Scott G. (2008) "Arctic Meltdown: The Economic and Security Implications of Global Warming," *Foreign Affairs* 87 (2): 63–77.

Borrows, Mathew and Jennifer Harris. (2009) "Revisiting the Future: Geopolitical Effects of the Financial Crisis" *Washington Quarterly* 32 (2): 37–48.

Bostdorff, Denise M. (1993) *The Presidency and the Rhetoric of Foreign Crisis.* Columbia: University of South Carolina Press.

Boswell, Terry. (1989) "Colonial Empires and the Capitalist World-Economy," *American Sociological Review* 54 (April): 180–96.

Bowring, Philip. (2009) "Shortchanging the IMF." *International Herald Tribune.* (January 16).

———— (2005) "Russian-Chinese Maneuvers Send a Message," *International Herald Tribune* (August 21–22): 5.

———— (2004) "Echoes of Panic over Global Disease," *International Herald Tribune* (February 18): 7.

———— (2001) "Thinking at Cross-Purposes about Globalization," *International Herald Tribune* (February 1): 8.

Boyer, Mark A., Brian Urlacher, Natalie Florea Hudson, Anat Niv-Solomon, Laura L. Janik, Michael Butler, and Andri Ioannou. (2009) "Gender and Negotiation: Some Experimental Findings from an International Negotiation Simulation." *International Studies Quarterly* 53(1): 23–47.

Boyle, Francis A. (2004) *Destroying World Order.* London: Clarity/Zed.

Bozeman, Adda B. (1994) *Politics and Culture in International History.* New Brunswick, N.J.: Transaction.

Bradsher, Keith. (2009) "WTO Rules Against China's Limits on Imports" *New York Times* August 12.

Brainard, Lael, Abigail Jones, and Nigel Purvis, eds. (2009) *Climate Change and Global Poverty.* Washington, D.C.: Brookings Institution Press.

Brams, Steven J. (1985) *Rational Politics: Decisions, Games, and Strategy.* Washington, D.C.: CQ Press.

Braudel, Fernand. (1973) *The Mediterranean and the Mediterranean World at the Age of Philip II.* New York: Harper.

Braveboy-Wagner, Jacqueline Anne (ed.). (2003) *The Foreign Policies of the Global South.* Boulder, Colo.: Lynne Rienner.

Brecke, Peter. (1999) "The Characteristics of Violent Conflict since 1400 A.D.," paper presented at the annual meeting of the International Studies Association, Washington, D.C., February 17–20.

Breitmeier, Helmut. (2005) *The Legitimacy of International Regimes.* Burlington, Ver.: Ashgate.

Bremer, Ian. (2007) *The J Curve: A New Way to Understand Why Nations Rise and Fall.* New York: Simon and Schuster.

Bremer, Stuart A. (2000) "Who Fights Whom, When, Where, and Why?" pp. 23–36 in John A. Vasquez (ed.), *What Do We Know About War?* Lanham, Md.: Rowman & Littlefield.

Brierly, J.L. (1944) *The Outlook for International Law.* Oxford: The Clarendon Press.

Brinkley, Joel. (2005) "As Nations Lobby to Join Security Council, U.S. Resists Giving Them Veto Power," *New York Times International* (May 15): 12.

Broad, Robin (ed.). (2002) *Global Backlash: Citizen Initiatives for a Just World Economy.* Lanham, Md.: Rowman & Littlefield.

Broad, William J. (2005) "U.S. Has Plans to Again Make Own Plutonium," *New York Times* (June 27): A1, A13.

Broder, David. (2002) "Senator Brings Vietnam Experiences to Bear on Iraq," Columbia, S.C., *The State* (September 18): A15.

———— (1999) "Global Forces May Change Balance between States and Federal Government," Columbia, S.C., *The State* (August 11): A9.

Brody, William R. (2007) "College Goes Global," *Foreign Affairs* 56 (March/April): 122–133.

Bronfenbrenner, Urie. (1961) "The Mirror Image in Soviet-American Relations," *Journal of Social Issues* 17 (No. 3): 45–56.

Brooks, David. (2007) "The Entitlements People," Columbia, S.C., *The State* (October 2): A7.

———— (2005a) "Hunch Power," *New York Times Book Review* (January 16): 1, 12–13.

———— (2005b) "Our Better Understanding of Who the Terrorists Are," Columbia, S.C., *The State* (August 6): A11.

Brooks, Doug, and Gaurav Laroia. (2005) "Privatized Peacekeeping," *The National Interest* 80 (Summer): 121–25.

Brown, John. (2006) "Beyond Kyoto," pp. 209–13 in Helen E. Purkitt (ed.), *World Politics 05/06.* Dubuque, Iowa: McGraw-Hill/Dushkin.

Brown, Justin. (1999) "Arms Sales: Exporting U.S. Military Edge?" *Christian Science Monitor* (December 2): 2.

Brown, Lester B. (2009) *Plan B 4.0: Mobilizing to Save Civilization.* Washington, D. C.: Earth Policy Institute.

———— (2006) "Deflating the World's Bubble Economy," pp. 35–38 in Robert M. Jackson (ed.), *Global Issues 05/06.* Dubuque, Iowa: McGraw-Hill/Dushkin.

———— (2002) "Planning for the Eco-economy," *USA Today* (March): 31–35.

Brown, Lester R., and Brian Halweil. (1999) "How Can the World Create Enough Jobs for Everyone?" *International Herald Journal* (September 9): 9.

Brown, Stuart S. (2006) "Can Remittances Spur Development?" *International Studies Review* 8 (March): 55–75.

Brundtland, Gro Harlem. (2003) "The Globalization of Health," *Seton Hall Journal of Diplomacy and International Relations* (Summer-Fall): 7–12.

Brunk, Darren C. (2008) "Curing the Somalia Syndrome: Analogy, Foreign Policy Decision Making, and the Rwandan Genocide," *Foreign Policy Analysis* 4 (July): 301–320.

Brzezinski, Zbigniew. (2010) "From Hope to Audacity: Appraising Obama's Foreign Policy." *Foreign Affairs* 89(1) (January/February): 16–30.

———— (2005) "George W Bush's Suicidal Statecraft," *International Herald Tribune* (October 14): 6.

———— (2004) *The Choice: Global Domination or Global Leadership.* New York: Basic Books/Perseus.

Bueno de Mesquita, Bruce. (1975) "Measuring Systemic Polarity," *Journal of Conflict Resolution* 22 (June): 187–216.

Bueno de Mesquita, Bruce, and George W Downs. (2005) "Development and Democracy," *Foreign Affairs* 84 (September/October): 77–86.

Bueno de Mesquita, Bruce, George W Downs, and Alastair Smith. (2005) "Thinking Inside the Box: A Closer Look at Democracy and Human Rights," *International Studies Quarterly* 49 (September): 439–57.

Bueno de Mesquita, Bruce, James D. Morrow, Randolph M. Siverson, and Alastair Smith. (2004) "Testing Novel Implications from the Selectorate Theory of War," *World Politics* 56 (April): 363–88.

Bull, Hedley. (2002) *The Anarchical Society: A Study of Order in World Politics,* 3rd ed. New York: Columbia University Press.

Burke, Anthony. (2005) "Against the New Internationalism," *Ethics and International Affairs* 19 (No. 2, Special Issue): 73–89.

Burrows, Mathew J., and Jennifer Harris. (2009) "Revisiting the Future: Geopolitical Effects of the Financial Crisis," *The Washington Quarterly* 32: 27–38.

Buruma, Ian. (2005) "The Indiscreet Charm of Tyranny," *New York Review of Books* 52 (May 12): 35–37.

Bussmann, Margit, and Gerald Schneider. (2007) "When Globalization Discontent Turns Violent: Foreign Economic Liberalization and Internal War," *International Studies Quarterly* 51 (March): 79–97.

Buzan, Barry. (2005) "The Dangerous Complacency of Democratic Peace," *International Studies Review* 7 (June): 292–93.

Buzan, Barry, and Gerald Segal. (1998) *Anticipating the Future.* London: Simon & Schuster.

Buzan, Barry, and Ole Weaver. (2003) *Regimes of Power.* Cambridge: Cambridge University Press.

Byers, Michael, and George Nolte (eds.). (2003) *United States Hegemony and the Foundations of International Law.* New York: Columbia University Press.

Byman, Daniel. (2005) *Deadly Connections: States That Sponsor Terrorism.* Cambridge: Cambridge University Press.

Caldwell, Christopher. (2004) "Select All: Can You Have Too Many Choices?" *New Yorker* (March): 91–93.

Caldwell, Dan, and Robert E. Williams, Jr. (2006) *Seeking Security in an Insecure World.* Lanham, Md.: Rowman & Littlefield.

Calvocoressi, Peter, Guy Wint, and John Pritchard. (1989) *Total War: The Causes and Courses of the Second World War,* 2nd ed. New York: Pantheon.

Campbell, Ian. (2004) "Retreat from Globalization," *National Interest* 75 (Spring): 111–17.

Canetti-Nisim, Daphna, Eran Halperin, Keren Sharvit, and Stevan E. Hobfoll. (2009) "A New Stress-Based Model of Political Extremism: Personal Exposure to Terrorism, Psychological Distress, and Exclusionist Political Attitudes." *Journal of Conflict Resolution* 53 (3): 363–389.

Canton, James. (2007) *The Extreme Future.* New York Penguin.

Caporaso, James A. (1993) "Global Political Economy," pp. 451–481 in Ada W. Finifter (ed.), *Political Science: The State of the Discipline II.* Washington, D.C.: American Political Science Association.

Caporaso, James A., and David P. Levine. (1992) *Theories of Political Economy.* New York: University Press.

Caprioli, Mary. (2005) "Primed for Violence: The Role of Gender Inequality in Predicting International Conflict," *International Studies Quarterly* 49 (June): 161–78.

——— (2004) "Feminist IR Theory and Quantitative Methodology," *International Studies Review* 6 (June): 253–69.

Carment, David. (1993) "The International Dimensions of Ethnic Conflict," *Journal of Peace Research* 30 (May): 137–50.

Carpenter, R. Charli. (2005) "Women, Children and Other Vulnerable Groups: Genders, Strategic Frames, and the Protection of Civilians as a Transnational Issue," *International Studies Quarterly* 49 (June): 295–334.

Carpenter, Ted Galen. (1991) "The New World Disorder," *Foreign Policy* 84 (Fall): 24–39.

Carpenter, Ted Galen, and Charles V. Peña. (2005) "Re-Thinking Non-Proliferation," *The National Interest* 80 (Summer): 81–92.

Carr, E. H. (1939) *The Twenty-Years' Crisis, 1919–1939.* London: Macmillan.

Carter, Jimmy. (2005) *Our Endangered Values: America's Moral Crisis.* New York: Simon and Schuster.

Carty, Anthony. (2008) "Marxist International Law Theory as Hegelianism," *International Studies Review* 10 (March): 122–125.

Caryl, Christian. (2009) "1979: The Great Backlash." *Foreign Policy* (July/August): 50–64.

——— (2005) "Why They Do It," *New York Review of Books* 52 (September 22): 28–32.

Casetti, Emilio. (2003) "Power Shifts and Economic Development: When Will China Overtake the USA?" *Journal of Peace Research* 40 (November): 661–75.

Cashman, Greg, and Leonard C. Robinson. (2007) *An Introduction to the Causes of War.* Lanham, Md.: Rowman & Littlefield.

Caspary, William R. (1993) "New Psychoanalytic Perspectives on the Causes of War," *Political Psychology* 14 (September): 417–46.

Cassese, Antonio, and Andrew Clapham. (2001) "International Law," pp. 408–11 in Joel Krieger (ed.), *The Oxford Companion to Politics of the World,* 2nd ed. Oxford: Oxford University Press.

Cassidy, John. (2005) "Always with US?" *New Yorker* (April 11): 72–77.

Cassis, Youssef. (2007) *Capitals of Capital.* New York: Cambridge University Press.

Castles, Stephen, Mark J. Miller; Guiseppe Ammendola. (2003) *The Age of Migration: International Population Movements in the Modern World.* New York: The Guilford Press.

Castles, Stephen, and Mark Miller. (2004) *The Age of Migration,* 3rd ed. London: Palgrave Macmillan.

Cavallo, Alfred. (2004) "Oil: The Illusion of Plenty," *Bulletin of the Atomic Scientists* (January-February): 20–22, 70.

CCEIA (Carnegie Council for Ethics in International Affairs). (2005) *Human Rights Dialogue.* Carnegie Council for Ethics in International Affairs, Series 2 (Spring) 1–34.

Cederman, Lars-Erik, and Kristian Skrede Gleditsch. (2004) "Conquest and Regime Change," *International Studies Quarterly* 48 (September): 603–29.

Center for World Indigenous Studies. (2005) *The State of Indigenous People.* Olympia, Wash.: Center for World Indigenous Studies.

Central Intelligence Agency. (2010) *The World Factbook.* Available at https://www.cia.gov/library/publications/the-world-factbook/geos/us.html.

——— (2002) *Global Trends 2015.* Washington, D.C.: Central Intelligence Agency.

——— (2001) *Handbook of International Economic Statistics 2000.* Langley, Va.: Central Intelligence Agency.

Cetron, Marvin J. (2007) "Defeating Terrorism," *The Futurist* (May/June): 17–25.

Cetron, Martin J., and Owen Davies. (2005) *53 Trends Now Shaping the Future.* Bethesda, Md.: World Future Society.

CGD/FP (Center for Global Development/Foreign Policy). (2005) "Ranking the Rich," *Foreign Policy* (September-October): 76–83.

Chaliand, Gérald, and Jean-Pierre Rageau. (1993) *Strategic Atlas,* 3rd ed. New York: Harper Perennial.

Chant, Sylvia and Cathy McIlwaine. (2009) *Geographies of Development in the 21st Century: An Introduction to the Global South.* Edward Elgar Publishing.

Chapman, Dennis. (2005) "US Hegemony in Latin America and Beyond," *International Studies Review* 7 (June): 317–19.

Chapman, Terrence, and Scott Wolford. (2010) "International Organizations, Strategy, and Crisis Bargaining." *The Journal of Politics* 72(1) (January): 227–242.

Charette, Robert N. (2008) "What's Wrong with Weapons Acquisitions?" IEEE Spectrum Special Report. Available at: http://www.spectrum.ieee.org/aerospace/military/whats-wrong-with-weapons-acquisitions/0

Chase-Dunn, Christopher, and E. N. Anderson (eds.). (2005) *The Historical Evolution of World-Systems.* London: Palgrave.

Checkel, Jeffrey T. (1998) "The Constructivist Turn in International Relations Theory," *World Politics* 50 (January 1998): 324–48.

Chen, Lincoln, Jennifer Leaning, and Vasant Narasimhan (eds.). (2003). *Global Health Challenges for Human Security.* Cambridge, Mass.: Harvard University Press.

Chernoff, Fred. (2008) *Theory and Metatheory in International Relations.* London: Palgrave Macmillan.

——— (2004) "The Study of Democratic Peace and Progress in International Relations," *International Studies Review* 6: 49–77.

Chesterman, Simon, ed. (2007) *Secretary or General?: The UN Secretary-General in World Politics.* New York: Cambridge University Press.

Chesterman, Simon, Michael Ignatieff, and Ramesh Thakur (eds.). (2005) *Making States Work: State Failure and the Crisis of Governance.* Tokyo: United Nations University Press.

Choi, Ajin. (2004) "Democratic Synergy and Victory in Wars, 1816–1992," *International Studies Quarterly* 48 (September): 663–82.

Choi, Seung-Whan, and Patrick James. (2005) *Civil–Military Dynamics, Democracy, and International Conflict.* New York: Palgrave Macmillan.

Chomsky, Noam. (2004) *Hegemony or Survival: America's Quest for Global Dominance.* New York: Metropolitan Books/Henry Holt.

Christensen, Eben J. and Steven B. Redd. (2004) "Bureaucrats versus the Ballot Box in Foreign Policy Decision Making: An Experimental Analysis of the Bureaucratic Politics Model and the Poliheuristic Theory," *Journal of Conflict Resolution* 48 (1): 69–90.

Chua, Amy. (2008) *Day of Empire: How Hyperpowers Rise to Global Dominance—and Why They Fail.* New York: Doubleday.

Chuluv, Martin. (2010) "Iraq violence set to delay US troop withdrawl." *guardian.co.uk* (May 12). Available at http://www.guardian.co.uk/world/2010/may/12/iraq-us-troop-withdrawal-delay.

Cincotta, Richard P., and Robert Engelman. (2004) "Conflict Thrives Where Young Men Are Many," *International Herald Tribune* (March): 18.

Cirincione, Joseph. (2008) "The Incredible Shrinking Missile Threat," *Foreign Policy* (May/June): 68–70.

Clapham, Andrew. (2001) "Human Rights," pp. 368–70 in Joel Krieger (ed.), *The Oxford Companion to Politics of the World,* 2nd ed. New York: Oxford University Press.

Clark, Gregory. (2008) *A Farewell to Alms: A Brief Economic History of the World.* Princeton, N.J.: Princeton University Press.

Clark, Ian, and Christian Reus-Smit. (2007) "Preface," *International Politics* 44 (March/May): 153–156.

Clarke, Richard A. (2004) *Against All Enemies.* New York: Simon & Schuster.

Claude, Inis L., Jr. (1989) "The Balance of Power Revisited," *Review of International Studies* 15 (January): 77–85.

——— (1971) *Swords into Plowshares,* 4th ed. New York: Random House.

——— (1967) *The Changing United Nations.* New York: Random House.

Clemens, Michael A. (2007) "Smart Samaritans," *Foreign Affairs* (September/October): 132–140.

Cline, William. (2004) *Trade Policy and Global Poverty.* Washington D.C.: Institute for International Economics.

Cobb, Roger, and Charles Elder. (1970) *International Community.* New York: Harcourt, Brace & World.

Cohen, Benjamin J. (ed.). (2005) *International Political Economy.* Burlington, Ver.: Ashgate.

——— (2000) *The Geography of Money.* Ithaca, N.Y: Cornell University Press.

——— (1996) "Phoenix Risen: The Resurrection of Global Finance," *World Politics* 48 (January): 268–96.

——— (1973) *The Question of Imperialism.* New York: Basic Books.

Cohen, Daniel. (2006) *Globalization and its Enemies.* Cambridge, Mass.: MIT Press.

Cohen, Eliot A. (1998) "A Revolution in Warfare," pp. 34–46 in Charles W Kegley, Jr., and Eugene R. Wittkopf (eds.), *The Global Agenda,* 4th ed. New York: McGraw-Hill.

Cohen, Joel E. (1998) "How Many People Can the Earth Support?" *New York Review of Books* 45 (October 8): 29–31.

Cohen, Roger. (2005) "Next Step: Putting Europe Back Together," *New York Times International* (June 5): Section 4, 3.

——— (2000) "A European Identity," *New York Times* (January 14): A3.

Cohen, Saul Bernard. (2003) *Geopolitics of the World System.* Lanham, Md.: Rowman & Littlefield.

Cohn, Carol and Sara Ruddick. (2008) "A Feminist Ethical Perspective on Weapons of Mass Destruction," pp. 458–477 in Karen A. Mingst and Jack L. Snyder (eds.), *Essential Readings in World Politics,* 3rd edition, New York: W.W. Norton & Company.

Cole, Juan. (2006) "9/11," *Foreign Policy* 156 (September/October): 26–32.

Coleman, Isobel. (2010) "The Better Half: Helping Woman Help the World." *Foreign Affairs* 89(1) (January/February): 126–130.

——— (2010) "The Global Glass Ceiling: Why Empowering Women Is Good for Business." *Foreign Affairs* 89(3) (May/June): 13–20.

Coll, Steve. (2009) "Comment: No Nukes," *The New Yorker* (April 20): 31–32.

Collier, Paul. (2009). "The Dictator's Handbook," Foreign Policy (May/June): 146–149.

——— (2007) *The Bottom Billion.* New York: Oxford University Press.

——— (2005) "The Market for Civil War," pp. 28–32 in Helen E. Punkitt (ed.), *World Politics 04/05.* Dubuque, Iowa: McGraw-Hill/Dushkin.

——— (2003) "The Market for Civil War", *Foreign Policy* 136 (May/June): 38–45.

Comisky, Mike and Pawan Madhogarhia. (2009) "Unraveling the Financial Crisis of 2008." *PS: Political Science & Politics* 42: 270–275.

Conteh-Morgan, Earl. (2005) "Peacebuilding and Human Security: A Constructivist Perspective," *International Journal of Peace Studies* 10 (Spring/Summer): 69–86.

CRS (Congressional Research Service). (2008) *Conventional Arms Transfers to Developing Nations, 2000–2007.* Washington, D.C. Congressional Research Service (October 23; prepared by Richard F. Grimmett).

——— (2007). *Conventional Arms Transfers to Developing Nations, 1999–2006.* Washington, D.C. Congressional Research Service (September 26; prepared by Richard F. Grimmett).

Cook, John and Paul Nyhan. (2004) "Outsourcing's Long-Term Effects on U.S. Jobs an Issue," *Seattle Post-Intelligencer.* March 10.

Cooper, Richard N. (2004) "A False Alarm: Overcoming Globalization's Discontents," *Foreign Affairs* 83 (January-February): 152–55.

Coplin, William D. (1971) *Introduction to International Politics.* Chicago: Markham.

——— (1965) "International Law and Assumptions about the State System," *World Politics* 17 (July): 615–34.

Copeland, Dale C. (2006) "The Constructivist Challenge to Structural Realism: A Review Essay," pp. 1–20 in Stefano Guzzini and Anna Leander (eds.), *Constructivism and International Relations.* New York: Rutledge.

Cornish, Edward. (2004) *Futuring: Re-Exploration of the Future.* Bethesda, Md.: World Future Society.

Cortright, David, and George A. Lopez (eds.). (2008) *Uniting Against Terror.* Cambridge, Mass.: MIT Press.

—— (2002) *Smart Sanctions: Targeting Economic Statecraft.* Lanham, Md.: Rowman & Littlefield.

—— (1995) "The Sanctions Era: An Alternative to Military Intervention," *Fletcher Forum of World Affairs* 19 (May): 65–85.

Coser, Lewis. (1956) *The Functions of Social Conflict.* London: Routledge & Kegan Paul.

Cox, Robert J., with Timothy J. Sinclair. (1996) *Approaches to World Order.* Cambridge: Cambridge University Press.

Coyne, Christopher J. (2007) *After War: The Political Economy of Exporting Democracy.* Palo Alto, Calif.: Stanford University Press.

Craig, Gordon A., and Alexander L. George. (1990) *Force and Statecraft,* 2nd ed. New York: Oxford University Press.

Crawford, Neta C. (2003) "Just War Theory and the U.S. Counterterror War," *Perspectives on Politics* 1 (March): 5–25.

Crenshaw, Martha. (2003) "The Causes of Terrorism," pp. 92–105 in Charles W. Kegley, Jr. (ed.), *The New Global Terrorism.* Upper Saddle River, N.J.: Prentice Hall.

Crook, Clive. (2003) "A Cruel Sea of Capital," *Economist* (May 3): 3–5.

—— (1997) "The Future of the State," *Economist* (September 20): 5–20.

Crump, Andy. (1998) *The A to Z of World Development.* Oxford: New Internationalist.

Daadler, Ivo H., and James M. Lindsay. (2005) "Bush's Revolution," pp. 83–90 in Helen E. Purkitt (ed.), *World Politics 04/05.* Dubuque, Iowa: McGraw-Hill/Dushkin.

—— (2004) "An Alliance of Democracies," *Washington Post* (May 24): B.07.

—— (2003) *America Unbound: The Bush Revolution in Foreign Policy.* Washington, D.C.: Brookings Institution Press.

Dahl, Robert Alan, Ian Shapiro, and Jose Antonio Cheibub. (2003) The Democracy Sourcebook. Cambridge: MIT Press.

D'Amico, Francine, and Peter R. Beckman (eds.). (1995) *Women in World Politics.* Westport, Conn.: Bergin and Garvey.

Danner, Mark. (2005) "What Are You Going to Do with That?" *New York Review of Books* 52 (June 23): 52–57.

Davies, Ed, and Karen Lema. (2008) "Pricey Oil Making Geothermal Projects More Attractive," *International Herald Tribune* (June 30): 13.

Davis, Wade. (1999) "Vanishing Cultures," *National Geographic* (August): 62–89.

de las Casas, Gustavo. (2008) "Is Nationalism Good for You?" *Foreign Policy* (March/April): 51–57.

Deen, Thalif. (2009) "Tied Aid Strangling Nations, Says U.N." *Inter Press Service,* July 6. Available at: http://ipsnews.net/interna.asp?idnews=24509.

Deets, Stephen. (2009) "Constituting Interests and Identities in a Two-Level Game: Understanding the Gabcikovo-Nagymaros Dam Conflict" *Foreign Policy Analysis* 5 (January): 37–56.

Deffeyes, Kenneth. (2005) "It's the End of Oil," *Time* (October 31): 66.

Dehio, Ludwig. (1962) *The Precarious Balance.* New York: Knopf.

Dempsey, Judy. (2008) "War Scrambles Strategic Map of Europe," *International Herald Tribune* (August): 1, 3.

Denemark, Robert A., Jonathan Friedman, Barry K. Gills, and George Modelski (eds.). (2002) *World System History: The Social Science of Long-Term Change.* London: Routledge.

Deng, Yong, and Thomas G. Moore. (2006) "China Views Globalization: Toward a New Great-Power Politics," pp. 147–56 in Helen E. Purkitt (ed.), *World Politics 05/06.* Dubuque, Iowa: McGraw-Hill/Dushkin.

DeParle, Jason. (2007) "Migrant Money Flow," *New York Times* (November 18): Week in Review, 3.

DeRivera, Joseph H. (1968) *The Psychological Dimension of Foreign Policy.* Columbus, Ohio: Merrill.

DeRouen, Karl R. Jr., and Jacob Bercovitch. (2008) "Enduring Internal Rivalries: A New Framework for the Study of Civil War." *Journal of Peace Research* 45 (January): 55–74.

DeRouen, Karl R. Jr, and Christopher Sprecher. (2006) "Arab Behaviour Towards Israel: Strategic Avoidance or Exploiting Opportunities?" *British Journal of Political Science* 36 (3): 549–560.

De Soysa, Indra, Thomas Jackson, and Christin Ormhaug. (2009) "Does Globalization Profit the Small Arms Bazaar?" *International Interactions* 35: 86–105.

Destler, I. M. (2005) *American Trade Politics,* 4th ed. Washington, D.C.: Institute of International Economics.

Deutsch, Karl W. (1974) *Politics and Government.* Boston: Houghton Mifflin.

—— (1957) *Political Community and the North Atlantic Area.* Princeton, N.J.: Princeton University Press.

—— (1953) "The Growth of Nations: Some Recurrent Patterns in Political and Social Integration," *World Politics* 5 (October): 168–95.

Deutsch, Karl W., and J. David Singer. (1964) "Multipolar Power Systems and International Stability," *World Politics* 16 (April): 390–406.

Deutsch, Morton. (1986) "Folie à deux: A Psychological Perspective on Soviet-American Relations," pp. 185–196 in Margaret P. Kearns (ed.), *Persistent Patterns and Emerging Structures in a Waning Century.* New York: Praeger.

Diamond, Jared. (2005) *Collapse: How Societies Choose to Fail or Succeed.* New York: Viking.

—— (2003) "Environmental Collapse and the End of Civilization," *Harper's* (June): 43–51.

Diamond, Larry (2005) *Squandered Victory: The American Occupation and the Bungled Effort to Bring Democracy to Iraq.* New York: Henry Holt.

Dickinson, G. Lowes. (1926) *The International Anarchy, 1904–1914.* New York: Century.

Diehl, Paul F. (ed.). (2005) *The Politics of Global Governance,* 3rd ed. Boulder, Colo.: Lynne Rienner.

Dillon, Dana. (2005) "Maritime Piracy: Defining the Problem," *SAIS Review* 25 (Winter-Spring): 155–65.

Dimerel-Pegg, Tijen and James Moskowitz. (2009) "US Aid Allocation: The Nexus of Human Rights, Democracy, and Development" *Journal of Peace Research* 46 (2): 181–198.

DiRenzo, Gordon J. (ed.). (1974) *Personality and Politics.* Garden City, N.Y: Doubleday-Anchor.

Dobson, William J. (2006) "The Day Nothing Much Changed," *Foreign Policy* 156 (September/October): 22–25.

Dogan, Mattei. (2004) "Four Hundred Giant Cities Atop the World," *International Social Science Journal* 181 (September): 347–60.

Dolan, Chris. (2005) *In War We Trust: The Ethical Dimensions and Moral Consequences of the Bush Doctrine.* Burlington, Ver.: Ashgate.

Dollar, David. (2005) "Eyes Wide Open: On the Targeted Use of Foreign Aid," pp. 80–83 in Robert J. Griffiths (ed.), *Developing World 05/06.* Dubuque, Iowa: McGraw-Hill/Dushkin.

Dollar, David, and Aart Kraay. (2004) "Spreading the Wealth," pp. 43–49 in Robert Griffiths (ed.), *Developing World 04/05.* Guilford, Conn.: Dushkin/McGraw Hill.

Dombrowski, Peter, and Eugene Gholz. (2007) *Buying Military Transformation.* New York: Columbia University Press.

Donadio, Rachel and Elisabetta Povoledo. (2009) "Earthquake kills scores in Italy," *International Herald Tribune* (April 7): 1.

Donnelly, Sally B. (2005) "Foreign Policy," *Time Inside Business* (June): A17–A18.

Dos Santos, Theotonio. (1971) "The Structure of Dependence," in K.T. Fann and Donald C. Hodges, eds., *Readings in U.S. Imperialism.* Boston: Porter Sargent.

——— (1970) "The Structure of Dependence," *American Economic Review* 60 (May): 231–36.

Dougherty, James E., and Robert L. Pfaltzgraff, Jr. (2001) *Contending Theories of International Relations,* 5th ed. New York: Longman.

Dowd, Maureen. (2004) *Bushworld: Enter at Your Own Risk.* New York: G. P. Putnam's Sons.

Downs, George W. (ed.). (1994) *Collective Security Beyond the Cold War.* Ann Arbor: University of Michigan Press.

Doyle, Michael W. (1997) *Ways of War and Peace.* New York: Norton.

Doyle, Michael W., and G. John Ikenberry (eds.). (1997) *New Thinking in International Relations Theory.* Boulder, Colo.: Westview.

Doyle, Michael W., and Nicholas Sambanis. (2006) *Making War and Building Peace: The United Nations since the 1990s.* Princeton, NJ: Princeton University Press.

Draper, Robert. (2008) *Dead Certain: The Presidency of George W. Bush.* New York: Free Press.

Dreher, Axel, Noel Gaston and Pim Martens. (2008) *Measuring Globalisation – Gauging its Consequences.* New York: Springer.

Drew, Jill. (2008) "Dalai Lama's Envoys in Beijing for Tibet Talks," *Washington Post* (July 1): A07.

Drezner, Daniel W. (2010) *Theories of International Politics and Zombies.* Princeton, NJ: Princeton University Press.

——— (2010) "Night of the Living Wonks," *Foreign Policy* (July/August): 34–38.

——— (2009) "Backdoor Protectionism" *The National Interest Online.* Available at: http://www.nationalinterest.org/Article.aspx?id=21192.

——— (2007) *All Politics is Global.* Princeton, N.J.: Princeton University Press.

——— (2000) "Bottom Feeders," *Foreign Policy* (Nov/Dec): 64–70.

Drezner, Daniel W., and Henry Farrell. (2006) "Web of Influence," pp. 12–19 in Helen E. Purkitt (ed.), *World Politics 05/06.* Dubuque, Iowa: McGraw-Hill/Dushkin.

Drost, Nadja. (2009) "Postcard: Medellin," *Time* (May 4): 8.

Druba, Volker. (2002). "The Problem of Child Soliders," *International Review of Education* 48 (3/4): 271–277.

Drucker, Peter F. (2005) "Trading Places," *The National Interest* 79 (Spring): 101–07.

Dunne, Tim. (2005) "Liberalism," pp. 185–203 in John Baylis and Steve Smith (eds.), *The Globalization of World Politics,* 3rd ed. New York: Oxford University Press.

Dupont, Alan. (2002) "Sept. 11 Aftermath: The World Does Seem to Have Changed," *International Herald Tribune* (August 6): 6.

Durch, William J. (2005) "Securing the Future of the United Nations," *SAIS Review* 25 (Winter-Spring): 187–91.

Durning, Alan (1993) "Supporting Indigenous Peoples," pp. 80–100 in Lester A. Brown, et al. (eds.) *State of the World 1993.* New York: Norton.

Dworkin, Ronald. (2001) *Sovereign Virtue.* Cambridge, Mass.: Harvard University Press.

Dykman, Jackson. (2008) "Why the World Can't Afford Food," *Time* (May 19): 34–35.

Dyson, Freeman. (2007) "Our Biotech Future," *The New York Review of Books* 54 (July 19): 4–8.

Easterbrook, Gregg. (2002) "Safe Deposit: The Case for Foreign Aid," *New Republic* (July 29): 16–20.

Easterly, William. (2007) "The Ideology of Development," *Foreign Policy* (July/August): 31–35.

——— (2006) *The White Man's Burden: Why the West's Efforts to Aid the Rest Have Done So Much Ill and So Little Good.* New York: Penguin.

Easterly, William and Laura Freschi. (2009) "Unsung Hero Resurrects US Tied Aid Reporting," accessed August 13, 2009 at http://blogs.nyu.edu/fas/dri/aidwatch/2009/02/unsung_hero_resurrects_us_tied.html.

Easterly, William, and Tobias Pfutze. (2008) "Where Does the Money Go? Best and Worst Practices in Foreign Aid," *Journal of Economic Perspectives* 22(2): 29–52.

Easton, Stewart C. (1964) *The Rise and Fall of Western Colonialism.* New York: Praeger.

Eberstadt, Nicholas. (2004) "The Population Implosion," pp. 168–77 in Robert J. Griffiths (ed.), *Developing World 04/05,* Guilford, Conn: McGraw-Hill/Dushkin.

Economist. (2010) "the power of nightmares." *The Economist* (June 26): 61–62.

——— (2010) "It takes two." *The Economist* (April 3): 61–62.

——— (2010) "Marching through Red Square." *The Economist* (May 22): 53–54.

——— (2010) "An awkward guest-list." *The Economist* (May 1): 60–61.

——— (2010) "Loaned goals." *The Economist* (June 5): 67–68.

——— (2010) "Old worry, new ideas." *The Economist* (April 17): 67.

——— (2010) "Fear of the dragon." *The Economist* (January 9): 73–75.

——— (2010) "Counting their blessings." *The Economist* (January 2): 25–28.

——— (2010) "By fits and starts." *The Economist* (February 6): 25–27.

——— (2010) "Passage to India." *The Economist* (June 26): 69.

——— (2010) "Economic and financial indicators." *The Economist* (May 1): 97–98.

——— (2009) "Go forth and multiply a lot less." *The Economist* (October 31): 29–32.

——— (2009b) "Agricultural Subsidies," *The Economist* (July 23): 93.

——— (2009) "Cheesed Off," *The Economist* (July 18): 74.

——— (2009) "Not just straw men," *The Economist* (June 20): 63:65.

——— (2009) "Cuba and the United States: It takes Two to Rumba," *The Economist* (April 18): 39–40.

——— (2009) "Taking the Summit by Strategy," *The Economist* (April 11): 42.

——— (2009) "Mission: Possible," *The Economist* (April 11): 69.

——— (2009) "Sin aqua non," *The Economist* (April 11): 59–61.

——— (2009a) "Coca-Cola and China: Hard to Swallow," *The Economist* (March 21): 68–69.

——— (2009) "Not so nano; Emerging-market multinationals," *The Economist* (March 28): 20.

——— (2009) "Trickle-down Economics," *The Economist* (February 21): 76.

——— (2009) "Wanted: fresh air," *The Economist* (July 11): 60–62.

——— (2008) "Winning or Losing? A Special Report on al-Qaeda," *The Economist* (July 19): 1–12.

——— (2008) "Ireland's voters speak; The European Union," *The Economist* (June 21): 61.

——— (2007) "Magnets for Money," *The Economist* (September 15): 3–4.

Economist, April 21, 2007, 109.

——— (2007) "Finance and Economics: Smaller shares, bigger slices," *The Economist* (April 7): 84.

——— (2007) *Pocket World in Figures,* 2007 Edition. London: The Economist.

Economy, Elizabeth C. (2007) "The Great Leap Backward?" *Foreign Affairs* 86 (September/October): 38–59.

Edgerton, David. (2007) *The Shock of the Old: Technology and Global History Since 1900.* New York: Oxford University Press.

Edwards, Stephen R. (1995) "Conserving Biodiversity," pp. 212–65 in Ronald Bailey (ed.), *The True State of the Planet.* New York: Free Press.

Eggen, Dan, and Scott Wilson. (2005) "Suicide Bombs Potent Tools of Terrorists," *Washington Post* (July 17): A1, A20.

Eichengreen, Barry. (2000) "Hegemonic Stability Theories of the International Monetary System," pp. 220–44 in Jeffrey A. Frieden and David A. Lake (eds.), *International Political Economy.* Boston: Bedford/St. Martin's.

Eichengreen, Barry and Kevin O'Rourke. (2009) "A Tale of Two Depressions," *VoxEU.org*, June 4. Available at: http://www.voxeu.org/index.php?q=node/3421.

Eisler, Riane. (2007) "Dark Underbelly of the World's 'Most Peaceful' Countries," *Christian Science Monitor* (July 26): 9.

Eizenstat, Stuart. (1999) "Learning to Steer the Forces of Globalization," *International Herald Tribune* (January 22): 6.

Ekhoragbon, Vincent. (2008) "Nigeria: Influx of Illegal Immigrants Worries Immigration Service," Available at: http://allafrica.com/stories/200808080481.html.

Eland, Ivan. (2004) *The Empire Has No Clothes: U.S. Foreign Policy Exposed.* New York: Independent Institute.

Elliott, Kimberly Ann. (1998) "The Sanctions Glass: Half Full or Completely Empty?" *International Security* 23 (Summer): 50–65.

——— (1993) "Sanctions: A Look at the Record," *Bulletin of the Atomic Scientists* 49 (November): 32–35.

Elliott, Michael. (1998) "A Second Federal Democratic Superpower Soon," *International Herald Tribune* (November 24): 8.

Ellis, David C. (2009) "On the Possibility of "International Community","" *The International Studies Review* 11 (March): 1–26.

Elms, Deborah Kay. (2008) "New Directions for IPE: Drawing From Behavioral Economics," *International Studies Review* 10 (June): 239–265.

Elrod, Richard. (1976) "The Concert of Europe," *World Politics* 28 (January): 159–74.

Elshtain, Jean Bethke. (2003) *Just War against Terror: The Burden of American Power in a Violent World.* New York: Basic Books.

Engelhardt, Henriette, and Alexia Prskawetz. (2004) "On the Changing Correlation between Fertility and Female Employment over Space and Time," *European Journal of Population* 20 (No. 1): 1–21.

Englehart, Neil A. (2009). "State Capacity, State Failure, and Human Rights," Journal of Peace Research 46 (2): 163–180.

Enloe, Cynthia H. (2007) "The Personal is International" pp. 202–206 in Karen A. Mingst and Jack L. Synder (eds.) *Essential Readings in World Politics*, 3rd ed. New York: W.W. Norton & Company.

——— (2004) *The Curious Feminist.* Berkeley: University of California Press.

——— (2001) "Gender and Politics," pp. 311–15 in Joel Krieger (ed.), *The Oxford Companion to Politics of the World*, 2nd ed. New York: Oxford University Press.

——— (2000) *Maneuvers: The International Politics of Militarizing Women's Lives.* Berkeley: University of California Press.

Enriquez, Juan. (1999) "Too Many Flags?" *Foreign Policy* 116 (Fall): 30–50.

Esty, Daniel C., M.A. Levy, C.H. Kim, A. de Sherbinin, T. Srebotniak, and V. Mara. (2008) *2008 Environmental Performance Index.* New Haven, CT: Yale Center for Environmental Law and Policy.

Esty, Daniel. (2002) "The World Trade Organization's Legitimacy Crisis," *World Trade Review* 1(1): 7–22.

Etzioni, Amitai. (2005) *From Empire to Community: A New Approach to International Relations.* London: Palgrave Macmillan.

European Nuclear Society. (2009) "Nuclear Power Plants, Worldwide." Available at: http://www.euronuclear.org/info/encyclopedia/n/nuclear-power-plant-world-wide.htm.

European Union: Commission of the European Communities, *Communication from the Commission to the European Parliament, the Council, The European Economic and Social Committee and the Committee of the Regions. Dealing with the impact of an ageing population in the EU*, 14 April 2009, COM (2009) 180 final. Available at: http://eur-lex.europa.eu/LexUriServ/LexUriServ.do?uri=COM:2009:0180:FIN:EN:PDF.

Evans, Gareth. (2008) *The Responsibility to Protect: Ending Mass Atrocity Crimes Once and for All.* Washington, DC: Brookings Institution Press.

Evans, Peter B. (2001) "Dependency," pp. 212–14 in Joel Krieger (ed.), *The Oxford Companion to Politics of the World*, 2nd ed. New York: Oxford University Press.

Evenett, Simon and John Whalley. (2009) "Resist green protectionism—or pay the price at Copenhagen," In *The collapse of global trade, murky protectionism, and the crisis: Recommendations for the G20*, Baldwin, Richard and Simon Evenett, eds. London: VoxEU.org. Available at: http://voxeu.org/reports/Murky_Protectionism.pdf.

Fackler, Martin. (2009) North Korea Vows to Produce Nuclear Weapons *The New York Times* (June 14): A12.

——— (2008) "Honda Rolls Out Hydrogen-Powered Car," *International Herald Tribune* (June 18): 16.

Falk, Richard A. (2001a) "The New Interventionism and the Third World," pp. 189–98 in Charles W. Kegley, Jr., and Eugene R. Wittkopf (eds.), *The Global Agenda*, 6th ed. Boston: McGraw-Hill.

——— (2001b) "Sovereignty," pp. 789–91 in Joel Krieger (ed.), *The Oxford Companion to Politics of the World*, 2nd ed. Oxford: Oxford University Press.

——— (1970) *The Status of Law in International Society.* Princeton, N.J.: Princeton University Press.

Falk, Richard, and Andrew Strauss. (2001) "Toward Global Parliament," *Foreign Affairs* 80 (January-February): 212–18.

Fallows, James. (2005) "Countdown to a Meltdown," *The Atlantic Monthly* 51 (July-August): 51–63.

——— (2002) "The Military Industrial Complex," *Foreign Policy* 22 (November-December): 46–48.

——— (1993) "How the World Works," *The Atlantic* (December).

Farber, David (ed.). (2007) *What They Think of Us: International Perceptions of the United States Since 9/11.* Princeton, N.J.: Princeton University Press.

Fathi, Nazila. (2009) "In Tehran, A Mood of Melancholy Descends," *The New York Times* (June 28): A6.

Feingold, David A. (2005) "Human Trafficking," *Foreign Policy* (September-October): 26–31.

Feinstein, Lee, and Anne-Marie Slaughter (2004) "A Duty to Prevent," *Foreign Affairs* 83 (No. 1): 136–50.

Ferencz, Benjamin B., and Ken Keyes, Jr. (1991) *Planet-Hood.* Coos Bay, Ore.: Love Line.

Ferguson, Charles. (2010) "The Long Road to Zero: Overcoming the Obstacle to a Nuclear-Free World." *Foreign Affairs* 89(1) (January/February): 86–94.

Ferguson, Niall. (2010) "Complexity and Collapse: Empires on the Edge of Chaos." *Foreign Affairs* 89(2) (March/April): 18–32.

——— (2009) "The Axis of Upheaval," *Foreign Policy* (March-April): 56–58.

——— (2008) *The Ascent of Money.* New York: Penguin Press.

——— (2006) "A World Without Power," pp. 62–68 in John T. Rourke (ed.), *Taking Sides.* Dubuque, Iowa: McGrawHill/Dushkin.

——— (2005) "Our Currency, Your Problem," *New York Times Magazine* (March 13): 19–21.

——— (2004) *Colossus: The Price of America's Empire.* New York: Penguin.

——— (2001) *The Cash Nexus.* New York: Basic Books.

——— (1999) *The Pity of War.* New York: Basic Books.

Festinger, Leon. (1957) *A Theory of Cognitive Dissonance.* Evanston, Ill.: Row, Peterson.

Fidler, David P., and Lawrence O. Gostin. (2008) *Biosecurity in the Global Age.* Palo Alto, Calif.: Stanford University Press.

Fieldhouse, D. K. (1973) *Economics and Empire, 1830–1914.* Ithaca, N.Y: Cornell University Press.

Fields, A. Belden, and Kriston M. Lord (eds.). (2004) *Rethinking Human Rights for the New Millennium.* London: Palgrave.

Filkins, Dexter. (2009) "Afghan women protest restrictive law," *International Herald Tribune* (April 6): 1.

Filson, Darren, and Suzanne Werner. (2002) "A Bargaining Model of War and Peace," *American Journal of Political Science* 46 (No. 4): 819–38.

Financial Times. (2007) "Why are Food Prices Rising," Available at: http://media.ft.com/cms/s/2/f5bd920c-975b-11dc-9e08-0000779fd2ac.html?from=textlinkindepth.

Finnegan, William. (2007) "The Countdown," *New Yorker* (October 15): 70–79.

——— (2002) "Leasing the Rain," *New Yorker* (April 18): 43–53.

Finnemore, Martha. (2009) "Legitimacy, Hypocrisy, and the Social Structure of Unipolarity: Why Being a Unipole Isn't All It's Cracked Up to Be," *World Politics* 61: 58–85.

——— (2003) *The Purpose of Intervention: Changing Beliefs about the Use of Force.* Ithaca, N.Y: Cornell University Press.

Fishman, Ted C. (2005) *China, Inc.* New York: Scribner.

Flanagan, Stephen J., Ellen L. Frost, and Richard Kugler. (2001) *Challenges of the Global Century.* Washington, D.C.: Institute for National Strategic Studies, National Defense University.

Flavin, Christopher, and Seth Dunn. (1999) "Reinventing the Energy System," pp. 23–40 in Lester R. Brown et al., *State of the World 1999.* New York: Norton.

Fletcher, Dan. (2010) "Friends without borders." *Time* (May 31): 32–38.

Flint, Colin (ed.). (2004) *The Geography of War and Peace.* New York: Oxford University Press.

Florida, Richard. (2007) "America's Looming Creativity Crisis," pp. 183–190 in Robert M. Jackson, ed., *Global Issues 06/07.* Dubuque, Iowa: McGraw-Hill Contemporary Learning Series.

——— (2005a) *The Flight of the Creative Class: The New Global Competition for Talent.* New York: HarperBusiness.

——— (2005b) "The World Is Spiky," *Atlantic Monthly* 296 (October): 48–52.

Flynn, Stephen. (2004) *America the Vulnerable.* New York: HarperCollins.

Fogel, Robert. (2010) "$123,000,000,000,000." *Foreign Policy* (January/February): 70–75.

Foley, Conor. (2008) *The Thin Blue Line: How Humanitarianism Went to War.* New York: Verso Books.

Foreign Policy/A.T. Kerney Inc. (2008) "The Terrorism Index," *Foreign Policy* 168 (September/October): 79–85.

——— (2007) "Sanctioning Force," *Foreign Policy (July/August):* 19.

——— (2005) "Measuring Globalization," *Foreign Policy* (May-June): 52–60.

Forero, Juan. (2005) "Bolivia Regrets IMF Experiment," *International Herald Tribune,* (December 14).

Frank, Andre Gunder. (1969) *Latin America: Underdevelopment or Revolution.* New York: Monthly Review Press.

Frankel, Max. (2004) *High Noon in the Cold War: Kennedy, Khrushchev, and the Cuban Missile Crisis.* New York: Random House.

Frazier, Derrick V., and William J. Dixon. (2006) "Third-Party Intermediaries and Negotiated Settlements, 1946–2000," *International Interactions* 32 (December): 385–408.

Frederking, Brian, Michael Artine and Max Sanchez Pagano. (2005) "Interpreting September 11," *International Politics* 42 (March): 135–51.

Freedland, Jonathan. (2007) "Bush's Amazing Achievement," *The New York Review of Books* 54 (June 14): 16–20.

Freedman, Lawrence. (2005) "War," pp. 8–11 in Helen E. Purkitt (ed.), *World Politics 04/05.* Dubuque, Iowa: McGrawHill/Dushkin.

——— (2004) *Deterrence.* Cambridge, Mass: Polity Press.

French, George. (2009) "A Year in Bank Supervision: 2008 and a Few of Its Lessons." *Supervisory Insights* 6(1): 3–18.

French, Howard W. (2002) "Japan Considering Nuclear Weapons," *New York Times* (June 9): A12.

Freud, Sigmund. (1968) "Why War," pp. 71–80 in Leon Bramson and George W Goethals (eds.), *War.* New York: Basic Books.

Fried, John H. E. (1971) "International Law—Neither Orphan nor Harlot, Neither Jailer nor Never-Never Land," pp. 124–76 in Karl W Deutsch and Stanley Hoffmann (eds.), *The Relevance of International Law.* Garden City, N.Y: Doubleday-Anchor.

Friedheim, Robert L. (1965) "The 'Satisfied' and 'Dissatisfied' States Negotiate International Law," *World Politics* 18 (October): 20–41.

Friedman, Benjamin M. (2005a) *The Moral Consequences of Economic Growth.* New York: Knopf.

——— (2005b) "Homeland Security," *Foreign Policy* (July-August): 22–28.

Friedman, Jeffrey. (2007) *Global Capitalism: Its Rise and Fall in the Twentieth Century.* New York: Norton.

Friedman, Thomas L. (2008) *Hot, Flat, and Crowded: Why We Need a Green Revolution, and How It Can Renew America.* New York: Farrar, Straus and Giroux.

——— (2007) "It's a Flat World, After All," pp. 7–12 in Robert M. Jackson, ed., *Global Issues 06/07.* Dubuque, Iowa: McGraw-Hill Contemporary Learning Series.

——— (2007) "Eating Up Energy," Columbia, S.C. *The State* (September 22): A9.

——— (2007) *The World is Flat 3.0: A Brief History of the 21st Century.* New York: Farrar, Straus, and Giroux.

——— (2006) "Looking Ahead from China," Columbia, S.C, *The State* (November 12): A9.

——— (2005a) "Arms Sales Begin at Home," Columbia, S.C, *The State* (March 6): A13.

——— (2005b) "Disarmed in the Science Race," Columbia, S.C, *The State* (April 17): D3.

——— (2005c) "The Revolution Will Be Podcast," Columbia, S.C, *The State* (October 24): A11.

——— (2005d) *The World Is Flat: A Brief History of the Twenty-First Century.* New York: Farrar, Straus, and Giroux.

——— (2004a) "Dreadful Irresponsibility after 9/11," Columbia, S.C, *The State* (December 5): D3.

——— (2004b) "The Third Great Era of Globalization," *International Herald Tribune* (March 5): 9.

——— (2001) "Love It or Hate It, But the World Needs America," *International Herald Tribune* (June 16–17): 6.

——— (1999) *The Lexus and the Olive Tree: Understanding Globalization.* New York: Farrar, Straus, Giroux.

Friedman, Thomas and Robert Kaplan. (2002) "States of Discord," *Foreign Policy* 129 (Mar/Apr): 64–70.

Friedmann, S. Julio, and Thomas Homer-Dixon. (2004) "Out of the Energy Box," *Foreign Affairs* 83 (November-December): 72–83.

Frum, David, and Richard Perle. (2004) *An End to Evil: How to Win the War on Terror.* New York: Random House.

Fukuyama, Francis (ed.). (2008) *Blindside: How to Anticipate Future Events and Wild Cards in Global Politics.* Washington, D.C.: Brookings Institution.

———— (2007) "A Quiet Revolution: Latin America's Unheralded Progress," *Foreign Affairs* 86 (November/ December): 177–182.

———— (2004) *State-Building: Governance and World Order in the 21st Century.* Ithaca, N.Y: Cornell University Press.

———— (2002) "The West May Be Cracking," *International Herald Tribune* (August 9): 4.

———— (1999a) *The Great Disruption: Human Nature and the Reconstitution of Social Order.* New York: Free Press.

———— (1999b) "Second Thoughts: The Last Man in a Bottle," *National Interest* 56 (Summer): 16–33.

———— (1992a) "The Beginning of Foreign Policy," *New Republic* (August 17 and 24): 24–32.

———— (1992b) *The End of History and the Last Man.* New York: Free Press.

———— (1989) "The End of History?" *National Interest* 16 (Summer): 3–16.

Fuller, Graham E. (1995) "The Next Ideology," *Foreign Policy* 98 (Spring): 145–58.

The Fund for Peace and the Carnegie Endowment for International Peace. (2008) "The Failed States Index 2008," *Foreign Policy* (July/August): 64–73.

Funk, McKenzie. (2007) "Cold Rush: The Coming Fight for the Melting North," *Harper's* (September): 45–55.

Gaddis, John Lewis. (2004) *Surprise, Security, and the American Experience.* Cambridge, Mass.: Harvard University Press.

———— (1997) *We Now Know: Rethinking Cold War History.* Oxford: Oxford University Press.

———— (1990) "Coping with Victory," *Atlantic Monthly* (May): 49–60.

———— (1983) "Containment: Its Past and Future," pp. 16–31 in Charles W Kegley, Jr., and Eugene R. Wittkopf (eds.), *Perspectives on American Foreign Policy.* New York: St. Martin's.

Galeota, Julia. (2006) "Cultural Imperialism: An American Tradition," pp. 18–23 in John T. Rourke (ed.), *Taking Sides.* Dubuque, Iowa: McGraw-Hill/Dushkin.

Gall, Carlotta. (2008) "Afghan Highway Drenched in Blood," *The Commercial Appeal* (August 17): A18.

Galtung, Johan. (1969) "Violence, Peace, and Peace Research," *Journal of Peace Research* 6 (No. 3): 167–91.

Gamberoni, Elisa and Richard Newfarmer. (2009) "Trade Protection: Incipient but Worrisome Trends" *World Bank Trade Note* 37. Available at: http://siteresources.worldbank.org/NEWS/Resources/Trade_Note_37.pdf.

Gambetta, Diego (ed.). (2005) *Making Sense of Suicide Missions.* New York: Oxford University Press.

Gamel, Kim. (2009) "FBI notes: Saddam Hussein sought familiar refuge," *Associated Press* (July 3). Available at: http://hosted.ap.org/dynamic/stories/U/US_SADDAM_FBI_INTERVIEWS?SITE=AP&SECTION=HOME&TEMPLATE=DEFAULT&CTIME=2009-07-03-01-59-01.

Gardels, Nathan. (1991) "Two Concepts of Nationalism," *New York Review of Books* 38 (November 21): 19–23.

Gardner, Richard N. (2003) "The Future Implications of the Iraq Conflict," *American Journal of International Law* 1997 (July): 585–90.

Gareau, Frederick H. (2004) *State Terrorism and the United States.* London: Clarity/Zed.

Garrett, Geoffrey. (2004) "Globalization's Missing Middle," *Foreign Affairs* 83 (November-December): 84–96.

Garrett, Laurie. (2007) "The Challenge of Global Health," *Foreign Affairs* 86 (January/February): 14–38.

Garrett, Laurie. (2000) *The Coming Plague: Newly Emerging Diseases in a World Out of Balance,* rev. ed. London: Virago.

———— (2005) "The Scourge of AIDS," *International Herald Tribune* (July 29): 6.

Garrison, Jean. (2006) "From Stop to Go in Foreign Policy," *International Studies Review* 8 (June): 291–293.

Gartzke, Erik. (2007) "The Capitalist Peace," *American Journal of Political Science* 51(1): 166–191.

Gartzke, Erik and Matthew Kroenig. (2009) "A Strategic Approach to Nuclear Proliferation," *Journal of Conflict Resolution* 53: 151–160.

Gazzaniga, Michael S. (2005) *The Ethical Brain.* New York: Dana Press.

Gelb, Leslie H. (2009) *Power Rules: How Common Sense can Rescue American Foreign Policy.* New York: HarperCollins.

Gelb, Leslie H., and Morton H. Halperin. (1973) "The Ten Commandments of the Foreign Affairs Bureaucracy," pp. 250–59 in Steven L. Spiegel (ed.), *At Issue.* New York: St. Martin's.

Gelber, Harry. (1998) *Sovereignty through Interdependence.* Cambridge, Mass.: Kluwer Law International.

Geller, Daniel S., and J. David Singer. (1998) *Nations at War: A Scientific Study of International Conflict.* Cambridge: Cambridge University Press.

George, Alexander L. (2000) "Strategies for Preventive Diplomacy and Conflict Resolution," *PS: Political Science and Politics* 33 (March): 15–19.

———— (1992) *Forceful Persuasion: Coercive Diplomacy as an Alternative to War.* Washington, D.C: United States Institute of Peace.

———— (1986) "U.S.-Soviet Global Rivalry: Norms of Competition," *Journal of Peace Research* 23 (September): 247–62.

———— (1972) "The Case for Multiple Advocacy in Making Foreign Policy," *American Political Science Review* 66 (September): 751–85.

German, F. Clifford. (1960) "A Tentative Evaluation of World Power," *Journal of Conflict Resolution* 4 (March): 138–44.

Gershman, Carl. (2005) "Democracy as Policy Goal and Universal Value," *The Whitehead Journal of Diplomacy and International Affairs* (Winter-Spring): 19–38.

Gerson, Michael. (2006) "The View From the Top," *Newsweek* (August 21): 58–60.

Ghosh, Bobby. (2009) "Obama in Moscow," *Time* (July 13): 14.

Gibler, Douglas M. (2007) "Bordering On Peace," *International Studies Quarterly* 51 (September): 509–532.

Giddens, Anthony. (1984) *The Constitution of Society: Outline of the Theory of Structuration.* Cambridge: Polity.

Gies, Erica. (2008) "New Wave in Energy: Turning Algae to Oil," *International Herald Tribune* (June 30): 3.

Gilbert, Alan. (2000) *Must Global Politics Constrain Democracy?* Princeton, N.J.: Princeton University Press.

Gilboa, Eytan. (2005) "Global Television News and Foreign Policy," *International Studies Perspectives* 6 (August): 325–41.

———— (2003) "Foreign Policymaking in the Age of Global Television," *Georgetown Journal of International Affairs* 4 (Winter): 119–26.

———— (2002) "Global Communication and Foreign Policy," *Journal of Communication* 52 (December): 731–48.

Giles, Martin. (2010) "A world of connections." *The Economist* (January 30): 3–4.

Gill, Stephen. (2001a) "Group of 7," pp. 340–41 in Joel Krieger (ed.), *The Oxford Companion to Politics of the World,* 2nd ed. Oxford: Oxford University Press.

———— (2001b) "Hegemony," pp. 354–86 in Joel Krieger (ed.), *The Oxford Companion to Politics of the World,* 2nd ed. Oxford: Oxford University Press.

Gilligan, Michael, and Stephen John Stedman. (2003) "Where Do the Peacekeepers Go?" *International Studies Review* 5 (No. 4): 37–54.

Gilpin, Robert. (2004) "The Nature of Political Economy," pp. 403–10 in Karen A. Mingst and Jack L. Snyder (eds.), *Essential Readings in World Politics,* 2nd ed. New York: Norton.

—— (2002) *Global Political Economy: Understanding the International Economic Order.* Princeton, NJ: Princeton University Press.

—— (2001) "Three Ideologies of Political Economy," pp. 269–86 in Charles W. Kegley, Jr., and Eugene R. Wittkopf (eds.), *The Global Agenda,* 6th ed. Boston: McGraw-Hill.

—— (1981) *War and Change in World Politics.* Cambridge: Cambridge University Press.

Glaberson, William. (2001) "U.S. Courts Become Arbiters of Global Rights and Wrongs," *New York Times* (June 21): A1, A20.

Gladwell, Malcolm. (2005) *Blink.* New York: Little, Brown.

Glasius, Marlies. (2009) "What is Global Justice and Who Decides?: Civil Society and Victim Responses to the International Criminal Court's First Investigations," *Human Rights Quarterly* 31: 496–520.

Glass, Ira and Adam Davidson. (2008) *This American Life: The Giant Pool of Money.* Radio episode aired on National Public Radio, May 9, 2008. Available at: http://www.thisamericanlife.org/extras/radio/355_transcript.pdf.

Gleditsch, Kristian Skrede. (2004) "A Revised List of Wars Between and Within Independent States, 1816–2002," *International Interactions* 30 (July-September): 231–62.

Glenn, Jerome C, and Theodore J. Gordon. (2008) *2008 State of the Future.* New York: United Nations.

Global Policy Forum. (2009) *UN Finance,* http://www.globalpolicy.org/un-finance.html.

—— (2006) *UN Finance,* http://www.globalpolicy.org/finance/index.htm.

Goertz, Gary. (2003) *International Norms and Decision Making: A Punctuated Equilibrium Analysis.* Lanham, Md.: Rowman & Littlefield.

Goldberg, Jeffrey. (2005) "Breaking Ranks: What Turned Brent Scowcraft Against the Bush Administration?" *New Yorker* (October 31): 52–65.

Goldsmith, Jack. (2008) *The Terror Presidency: Law and Judgment Inside the Bush Administration.* New York: Norton.

Goldsmith, Jack I., and Eric A. Posner. (2005) *The Limits of International Law.* New York: Oxford University Press.

Goldstein, Joshua S. (2005). *The Real Price of War.* New York: New York University Press.

—— (2002) *War and Gender.* Cambridge: Cambridge University Press.

Goldstone, Jack. (2010) "The New Population Bomb: The Four Megatrends That Will Change the World." *Foreign Affairs* 89(1) (January/February): 31–43.

Thompson, ed., *Moral Dimensions of American Foreign Policy.* New Brunswick, N.J.: Transaction Books.

Gordon, John Steele. (2004) *An Empire of Wealth.* New York: HarperCollins.

Gore, Al. (2006) *An Inconvenient Truth: The Planetary Emergency and What We Can Do About It.* Emmaus, Penn.: Rodale.

Gottlieb, Gidon. (1982) "Global Bargaining," pp. 109–30 in Nicholas Greenwood Onuf (ed.), *Law-Making in the Global Community.* Durham, N.C.: Carolina Academic Press.

Graff, James. (2007) "Fight For the Top of The World," *Time* (October 1): 28–36.

Graham, Edward. (2000) *Fighting the Wrong Enemy: Antiglobal Activists and Multinational Enterprises.* Washington, DC: Institute for International Economics.

Grant, Ruth W., and Robert O. Keohane. (2005) "Accountability and Abuses of Power in World Politics," *American Political Science Review* 99 (February): 29–43.

Gray, John. (2010) "World Wide Web: The myth and reality of the United Nations." *Harper's Magazine* (June): 78–82.

Greenhill, Brian. (2010) "The Company you Keep: International Socialization and the Diffusion of Human Rights Norms." *International Studies Quarterly* 54: 127–145.

Greenstein, Fred I. (1987) *Personality and Politics.* Princeton, N.J.: Princeton University Press.

Grey, Edward. (1925) *Twenty-Five Years, 1892–1916.* New York: Frederick Stokes.

Grieco, Joseph M. (1995) "Anarchy and the Limits of Cooperation: A Realist Critique of the Newest Liberal Institutionalism," pp. 151–71 in Charles W. Kegley, Jr. (ed.), *Controversies in International Relations Theory.* New York: St. Martin's.

Griggs, Richard. (1995) "The Meaning of 'Nation' and 'State' in the Fourth World," Occasional Paper No. 18. Capetown, South Africa: Center for World Indigenous Studies.

Grimmett, Richard F. (2008) *Conventional Arms Transfers to Developing Nations, 1999–2006.* Nova Science Publishers.

—— (2007) *Conventional Arms Transfers to Developing Nations, 1999–2006.* Washington, D.C.: Congressional Research Service.

—— (2006) *Conventional Arms Transfers to Developing Nations, 1998–2005.* Washington, D.C.: Congressional Research Service.

Grosby, Steven. (2006) *Nationalism.* New York: Oxford University Press.

Grunwald, Michael. (2009) "How Obama is Using the Science of Change," *Time* (April 13): 28–32.

—— (2008) "The Clean Energy Scam," *Time* (April 7): 40–45.

Grusky, Sara. (2001) "Privatization Tidal Wave: IMF/World Bank Water Policies and the Price Paid by the Poor," *The Multinational Monitor* 22 (September): Available at: http://www.multinationalmonitor.org/mm2001/01september/sep01corp2.htm.

Grussendorf, Jeannie. (2006) "When the Stick Works: Power in International Mediation," *International Studies Review* 8 (June): 318–320.

Gugliotta, Guy. (2004) "Scientists Say Warming to Increase Extinctions," Columbia, S.C., *The State* (January 8): A6.

Gulick, Edward V. (1999) *The Time Is Now: Strategy and Structure for World Governance.* Lanham, Md.: Lexington.

—— (1967 [1955]) *Europe's Classical Balance of Power.* Ithaca, N.Y.: Cornell University Press.

Gurr, Ted Robert. (2001) "Managing Conflict in Ethnically Divided Societies," pp. 173–86 in Charles W Kegley, Jr., and Eugene R. Wittkopf (eds.), *The Global Agenda,* 6th ed. Boston: McGraw-Hill.

—— (2000) *Peoples versus States.* Washington, D.C.: United States Institute of Peace Press.

—— (1993) *Minorities at Risk.* Washington, D.C.: United States Institute of Peace Press.

—— (1970) *Why Men Rebel.* Princeton, N.J.: Princeton University Press.

Gvosdev, Nikolas K. (2005) "The Value(s) of Realism," *The SAIS Review of International Affairs* 25 (Winter-Spring) 17–25.

Haass, Richard N. (2005) *The Opportunity: America's Moment to Alter History's Course.* New York: Public Affairs.

—— (1997) "Sanctioning Madness," *Foreign Affairs* 76 (December): 74–85.

Habermas, Jürgen. (1984) *The Theory of Communicative Action,* 2 vols. Boston: Beacon Press.

Hacking, Ian. (1999) *The Social Construction of What?* Cambridge, Mass.: Harvard University Press.

Haffa, Robert P., Jr. (1992) "The Future of Conventional Deterrence," pp. 5–30 in Gary L. Guertner, Robert Haffa, Jr., and George Quester (eds.), *Conventional Forces and the Future of Deterrence.* Carlisle Barracks, Pa.: U.S. Army War College.

Hafner-Burton, Emilie M., Kiyoteru Tsutsui, and John W Meyer. (2008) "International Human Rights Law and the Politics of Legitimation: Repressive States and Human Rights Treaties," *International Sociology* 23 (January): 115–141.

Haggard, Stephan, and Beth A. Simmons. (1987) "Theories of International Regimes," *International Organization* 41 (Summer): 491–517.

Hall, Anthony J. (2004) *The America Empire and the Fourth World.* Montreal: McGill-Queen's University Press.

Hall, John A. (2001) "Liberalism," pp. 499–502 in Joel Krieger (ed.), *The Oxford Companion to Politics of the World*, 2nd ed. Oxford: Oxford University Press.

Hall, Thomas D. (2004) "Ethnic Conflicts as a Global Social Problem," pp. 139–55 in George Ritzer (ed.), *Handbook of Social Problems.* London: Sage.

Hamilton, Alexander. (1913 [1791]) *Report on Manufactures.* Washington, DC: U.S. Government. Accessed August 1, 2009 at books.google.com.

Hammes, Thomas X. (2004) *The Sling and the Stone: On War in the 21st Century.* St. Paul, Minn.: Zenith Press.

Hannah, Mark. (2009) "Issue Advocacy on the Internet, Part 1," *PBS Online: Mediashift.* (May 7). Available at: http://www.pbs.org/mediashift/2009/05/issue-advocacy-on-the-internet-part-1127.html.

Hansenclever, Andreas, Peter Mayer, and Volker Rittberger (1996) "Interests, Power, and Knowledge," *Mershon International Studies Review* 40 (October): 177–228.

Hanson, Victor Davis. (2003) *Ripples of Battle.* New York: Doubleday.

Harbom, Lotta, and Peter Wallensteen. (2010) "Armed Conflicts, 1946–2009" Journal of Peace Research 47 (No. 4): 501–509.

——— (2009) "Armed Conflicts, 1946–2008," *Journal of Peace Research* 46 (4): 577–587.

——— (2007) "Armed Conflict, 1989–2006," *Journal of Peace Research* 44 (No. 5): 623–634.

Harbom, Lotta, Erik Melander and Peter Wallensteen, (2008), "Dyadic Dimensions of Armed Conflict, 1946–2007", *Journal of Peace Research*, 45(5): 697–710.

Hardin, Garrett. (1993) *Living within Limits.* Oxford: Oxford University Press.

——— (1968) "The Tragedy of the Commons," *Science* 162 (December): 1243–48.

Harknett, Richard J. (1994) "The Logic of Conventional Deterrence and the End of the Cold War," *Security Studies* 4 (Autumn): 86–114.

Hartung, William, and Michelle Ciarrocca. (2005) "The Military Industrial-Think Tank Complex," pp. 103–7, in Glenn P. Hastedt (ed.), *American Foreign Policy 04/05*, 10th ed., Guiford, Conn: Dushkin/McGraw-Hill.

Harries, Owen. (1995) "Realism in a New Era," *Quadrant* 39 (April): 11–18.

Harris, Edward. (2008) "World Chopping Down Trees at Pace That Affects Climate," *The Cincinnati Enquirer* (February 3): A2.

Harvey, David. (2004) *The New Imperialism.* Oxford: Oxford University Press.

Hathaway, Oona A. (2007) "Why We Need International Law," *The Nation* (November 19): 35–39.

Hayden, Patrick. (2005) *Cosmopolitan Global Politics.* Burlington, Ver.: Ashgate.

Haynes, Jeffrey. (2005) *Comparative Politics in a Globalizing World.* Cambridge, U.K.: Polity.

——— (2004) "Religion and International Relations," *International Politics* 41 (September): 451–62.

HDI (2007). *Human Development Indicators.* New York: United Nations Development Programme.

——— (2006) *Human Development Indicators.* New York: United Nations Development Programme.

HDR. (2009) Human *Development Report 2009.* New York: United Nations Development Programme.

——— (2008). *Human Development Report.* New York: United Nations Development Programme.

——— (2007). *Human Development Report.* New York: United Nations Development Programme.

——— (2005) *Human Development Report.* United Nations Development Programme. New York: Oxford University Press.

Hecht, Jeff. (2007). "Military wings Ig-Nobel peace price for 'gay bomb'." *New Scientist.* Available at: http:// www.newscientist.com/article/dn12721.

Hedges, Chris. (2003) "What Every Person Should Know about War," *New York Times* (July 6): www.nytimes.com.

Hegre, Haåvard. (2004) "The Duration and Termination of Civil War," *Journal of Peace Research* 41 (May): 243–52.

Hehir, J. Bryan. (2002) "The Limits of Loyalty," *Foreign Policy* (September-October): 38–39.

Heins, Volker. (2008) *Nongovernmental Organizations in International Society: Struggles over Recognition.* New York: Palgrave Macmillan.

Held, David, and Anthony McGrew. (2003) "The Great Globalization Debate," pp. 1–50 in *The Global Transformations Reader, 2nd ed.*, edited by David Held and Anthony McGrew. Cambridge: Polity Press.

——— (2001) "Globalization," pp. 324–27 in Joel Krieger (ed.), *The Oxford Companion to Politics of the World*, 2nd ed. Oxford: Oxford University Press.

Held, David, and Anthony McGrew, with David Goldblatt, and Jonathan Perraton. (2001) "Managing the Challenge of Globalization and Institutionalizing Cooperation through Global Governance," pp. 136–48 in Charles W. Kegley, Jr., and Eugene R. Wittkopf (eds.), *The Global Agenda*, 6th ed. Boston: McGraw-Hill.

——— (1999) *Global Transformations.* Stanford, Calif.: Stanford University Press.

Hellman, Christopher. (2009) "Analysis of the Fiscal Year 2010 Pentagon Spending Request," Center For Arms Control and Non-Proliferation. (May 8). Available at: http://www.armscontrolcenter.org/policy/missiledefense/articles/050809_analysis_fy2010_pentagon_request/. Accessed June 27, 2009.

Hensel, Howard M. (ed.). (2007) *The Law of Armed Conflict.* Burlington, Ver.: Ashgate.

Heredia, Blanca. (1999) "Prosper or Perish? Development in the Age of Global Capital," pp. 93–97 in Robert M. Jackson (ed.), *Global Issues 1999/00*, 15th ed. Guilford, Conn.: Dushkin/McGraw-Hill.

Hermann, Charles F. (1988) "New Foreign Policy Problems and Old Bureaucratic Organizations," pp. 248–65 in Charles W. Kegley, Jr., and Eugene R. Wittkopf (eds.), *The Domestic Sources of American Foreign Policy.* New York: St. Martin's.

Hermann, Margaret G. (ed.). (2008) *Comparative Foreign Policy Analysis.* Upper Saddle River, N.J.: Prentice Hall.

——— (2007) *Comparative Foreign Policy Analysis: Theories and Methods.* Upper Saddle River, N. J.: Prentice Hall.

——— (1988) "The Role of Leaders and Leadership in the Making of American Foreign Policy," pp. 266–84 in Charles W. Kegley, Jr., and Eugene R. Wittkopf (eds.), *The Domestic Sources of American Foreign Policy.* New York: St. Martin's.

——— (1976) "When Leader Personality Will Affect Foreign Policy," pp. 326–33 in James N. Rosenau (ed.), *In Search of Global Patterns.* New York: Free Press.

Hermann, Margaret G., and Joe D. Hagan. (2004) "International Decision Making: Leadership Matters," pp. 182–88 in Karen A. Mingst and Jack L. Snyder (eds.), *Essential Readings in World Politics*, 2nd ed. New York: Norton.

Hermann, Margaret G., and Charles W. Kegley, Jr. (2001) "Democracies and Intervention," *Journal of Peace Research* 38 (March): 237–45.

Herrmann, Richard K., and Richard Ned Lebow (eds.). (2004) *Ending the Cold War: Interpretations, Causation, and the Study of International Relations.* London: Palgrave Macmillan.

Hersh, Seymour M. (2005) "The Coming Wars: What the Pentagon Can Now Do in Secret," *New Yorker* (January 24 and 31): 40–47.

Hertsgaard, Mark. (2003) *The Eagle's Shadow: Why America Fascinates and Infuriates the World.* New York: Picador/Farrar, Straus & Giroux.

Herz, John H. (1951) *Political Realism and Political Idealism.* Chicago: University of Chicago Press.

Hiatt, Fred. (1997) "Globalization," *International Herald Tribune* (June 12): 8.

Hilsman, Roger. (1967) *To Move a Nation.* New York: Doubleday.

Hindle, Tim. (2004) "The Third Age of Globalization," pp. 97–98 in *The Economist, The World in 2004.* London: Economist.

Hironaka, Ann. (2005) *Neverending Wars.* Cambridge, Mass.: Harvard University Press.

Hirsh, Michael. (2003) *At War with Ourselves: Why America Is Squandering Its Chance to Build a Better World.* Oxford: Oxford University Press.

Hirschman, Albert. (1945) *National Power and the Structure of Foreign Trade.* Berkeley: University of California Press.

Hobson, John A. (1965 [1902]) *Imperialism.* Ann Arbor: University of Michigan Press.

Hodge, Carl Cavanagh. (2005) *Atlanticism for a New Century.* Upper Saddle River, N.J.: Prentice Hall.

Hoebel, E. Adamson. (1961) *The Law of Primitive Man.* Cambridge, Mass.: Harvard University Press.

Hoffman, Eva. (2000) "Wanderers by Choice," *Utne Reader* (July-August): 46–48.

Hoffmann, Stanley. (2005) "Clash of Globalizations," pp. 3–7 in Helen E. Purkitt (ed.), *World Politics 04/05.* Dubuque, Iowa: McGraw-Hill/Dushkin.

——— (1998) *World Disorders.* Lanham, Md.: Rowman & Littlefield.

——— (1992) "To the Editors," *New York Review of Books* (June 24): 59.

——— (1971) "International Law and the Control of Force," pp. 34–66 in Karl W. Deutsch and Stanley Hoffmann (eds.), *The Relevance of International Law.* Garden City, N.Y: Doubleday-Anchor.

——— (1961) "International Systems and International Law," pp. 205–37 in Klaus Knorr and Sidney Verba (eds.), *The International System.* Princeton, N.J.: Princeton University Press.

Hoffmann, Stanley, with Frédéric Bozo. (2004) *Gulliver Unbound: America's Imperial Temptation and the War in Iraq.* Lanham, Md.: Rowman & Littlefield.

Hoge, James F., Jr. (2006) "A Global Power Shift in the Making," pp. 3–6 in Helen E. Purkitt (ed.), *World Politics 05/06.* Dubuque, Iowa: McGraw-Hill/Dushkin.

Hollander, Jack M. (2003) *The Real Crisis: Why Poverty, Not Affluence, Is the Environment's Number One Enemy.* Berkeley: University of California Press.

Holstein, William J. (2005) "One Global Game, Two Sets of Rules," *The New York Times* (August 14): BU9.

Holsti, Kalevi J. (2004) *Taming the Sovereigns: Institutional Changes in International Politics.* Cambridge: Cambridge University Press.

——— (1996) *The State, War, and the State of War.* Cambridge: Cambridge University Press.

——— (1995) "War, Peace, and the State of the State," *International Political Science Review* 16 (October): 319–39.

——— (1992) *International Politics,* 6th ed. Englewood Cliffs, N.J.: Prentice Hall.

——— (1991) *Peace and War.* Cambridge: Cambridge University Press.

——— (1988) *International Politics,* 5th ed. Englewood Cliffs, N.J.: Prentice Hall.

Holsti, Ole R. (2001) "Models of International Relations: Realist and Neoliberal Perspectives on Conflict and Cooperation," pp. 121–35 in Charles W. Kegley, Jr., and Eugene R. Wittkopf (eds.), *The Global Agenda,* 6th ed. Boston: McGraw-Hill.

Holt, Jim. (2005) "Time-Bandits," *New Yorker* (February 28): 80–85.

Homer-Dixon, Thomas. (2006) "The Rise of Complex Terrorism," pp. 214–220 in Thomas J. Badey (ed.), *Violence and Terrorism 06/07.* Dubuque, Iowa: McGraw-Hill.

Hopf, Ted. (1998) "The Promise of Constructivism in International Relations Theory," *International Security* 23 (Summer): 171–200.

Hopkins, Terence K., and Immanuel Wallerstein (eds.). (1996) *The Age of Transitions: Trajectory of World Systems 1945–2025.* London: Zed.

Horkheimer, Max. (1947) *Eclipse of Reason.* New York: Oxford University Press.

Horowitz, Michael. (2009) "The Spread of Nuclear Weapons and International Conflict: Does Experience Matter?" *Journal of Conflict Resolution* 53 (2): 234–257.

Hosenball, Mark. (2009) "The Danger of Escalation," *Newsweek* (April 27): 6.0): 43.

Hough, Peter. (2004) *Understanding Global Security.* New York: Routledge.

Houghton, David Patrick (2007) "Reinvigorating the Study of Foreign Policy Decision Making: Toward a Constructivist Approach," *Foreign Policy Analysis* 3 (January): 24–45.

House, Karen Elliot. (1989) "As Power is Dispersed Among Nations, Need for Leadership Grows," *Wall Street Journal* (February 21): A1, A10.

Howard, Michael E. (1978) *War and the Liberal Conscience.* New York: Oxford University Press.

Howell, Llewellyn D. (2003) "Is the New Global Terrorism a Clash of Civilizations?" pp. 173–84 in Charles W. Kegley, Jr. (ed.), *The New Global Terrorism.* Upper Saddle River, N.J.: Prentice Hall.

——— (1998) "The Age of Sovereignty Has Come to an End," *USA Today* 127 (September): 23.

Htun, Mala, and S. Laurel Weldon. (2010) "When Do Governments Promote Women's Rights? A Framework for the Comparative Analysis of Sex Equality Policy." *Perspectives on Politics* 8(1) (March): 207–216.

Hudson, Kimberly A. (2009) *Justice, Intervention, and Force in International Relations: Reassessing Just War Theory in the 21st Century.* New York: Routledge.

Hudson, Natalie F. (2005) "En-gendering UN Peacekeeping Operations," *International Journal* 60 (3): 785–807.

Hudson, Valerie M. (2007) *Foreign Policy Analysis: Classic and Contemporary Theory.* New York: Rowman & Littlefield Publishers.

Hufbauer, Gary Clyde, Jeffrey J. Schott, and Kimberly Ann Elliott. (1990) *Economic Sanctions Reconsidered,* 2nd ed. Washington, D.C.: Institute for International Economics.

Hughes, Emmet John. (1972) *The Living Presidency.* New York: Coward, McCann and Geoghegan.

Hulsman, John C, and Anatol Lievan. (2005) "The Ethics of Realism," *The National Interest* 80 (Summer): 37–43.

Human Rights Dialogue (2005). Series 2 (Spring): 1–34. New York: Carnegie Council for Ethics in International Affairs.

Human Security Centre. (2006) *Human Security Brief 2006.* Vancouver: The University of British Columbia, Canada.

Hume, David. (1817) *Philosophical Essays on Morals, Literature, and Politics,* Vol. 1. Washington, D.C.: Duffy.

Hunt, Swanee, and Cristina Posa. (2005) "Women Making Peace," pp. 212–17 in Robert J. Griffiths (ed.), *Developing World 05/06.* Dubuque, Iowa: McGraw-Hill/Dushkin.

Huntington, Samuel P. (2005) "The Lonely Superpower" pp. 540–550 in G John Ikenberry (ed.), *American Foreign Policy: Theoretical Essays*. New York: Pearson/Longman.

—— (2004) "The Hispanic Challenge," *Foreign Policy* (March-April): 30–45.

—— (2001a) "The Coming Clash of Civilizations, or the West against the Rest," pp. 199–202 in Charles W Kegley, Jr., and Eugene R. Wittkopf (eds.), *The Global Agenda*, 6th ed. Boston: McGraw-Hill.

—— (2001b) "Migration Flows Are the Central Issue of Our Time," *International Herald Tribune* (February 2): 6.

—— (1996) *The Clash of Civilizations and the Remaking of World Order*. New York: Simon & Schuster.

—— (1991) *The Third Wave: Democratization in the Late Twentieth Century*. Norman: University of Oklahoma Press.

—— (1991b) "America's Changing Strategic Interests," *Survival* (January/February): 5–6.

Hurwitz, Jon, and Mark Peffley. (1987) "How Are Foreign Policy Attitudes Structured?" *American Political Science Review* 81 (December): 1099–1120.

Huth, Paul K., and Todd L. Allee. (2003) *The Democratic Peace and Territorial Conflict in the Twentieth Century*. Cambridge: Cambridge University Press.

Ignatieff, Michael. (2005a) "Human Rights, Power, and the State," pp. 59–75 in Simon Chesterman, Michael Ignatieff, and Ramesh Thakur (eds.), *Making States Work: State Failure and the Crisis of Governance*. Tokyo: United Nations University Press.

—— (2005b) "Who Are the Americans to Think That Freedom is Theirs to Spread?" *New York Times Magazine* (June 28): 40–47.

—— (2004a) "Hard Choices on Human Rights," pp. 54–55 in the *Economist, The World in 2004*. London: Economist.

—— (2004b) *The Lesser Evil: Political Ethics in an Age of Terror*. Princeton, N.J.: Princeton University Press.

—— (2001a) "The Danger of a World Without Enemies," *New Republic* 234 (February 26): 25–28.

—— (2001b) *Human Rights as Politics and Ideology*. Princeton, N.J.: Princeton University Press.

Ikenberry, G. John. (2008) "The Rise of China and the Future of the West," *Foreign Affairs* 87 (January/February): 23–37.

—— (2004) "Is American Multilateralism in Decline?" pp. 262–82 in Karen A. Mingst and Jack L. Snyder (eds.), *Essential Readings in World Politics*, 2nd ed. New York: Norton.

Iklé, Fred Charles. (2007) *Annihilation from Within*. New York: Columbia University Press.

International Labour Office. (2004) *Working Out of Poverty*. Geneva: International Labour Office.

IMF (International Monetary Fund). (2010) "Currency Composition of Official Foreign Exchange Reserves." Available at http://www.imf.org/external/np/sta/cofer/eng/cofer/pdf.

—— (2009) "Global Economy Contracts." *IMF Survey Online*. Available at: http://www.imf.org/external/pubs/ft/survey/so/2009/RES042209A.htm.

—— (2009) "De Facto Classification of Exchange Rate Regimes and Monetary Policy Frameworks". Available at: http://www.imf.org/external/np/mfd/er/2008/eng/0408.htm.

—— (2007) *World Economic Outlook: Spillovers and Cycles in the Global Economy*. New York: International Monetary Fund.

Inglehart, Ronald and Christian Welzel. (2009) "How Development Leads to Democracy," Foreign Affairs 88 (March/April): 33–48.

International Herald Tribune. (2009) "Pakistan Hits Taliban Sites in Key Area Near Capital," *International Herald Tribune* (April 29): 1.

Iqbal, Zaryab, and Christopher Zorn. (2010) "Violent Conflict and the Spread of HIV/AIDS in Africa." *The Journal of Politics* 72(1) (January): 149–162.

Irwin, Douglas. (2009) *Free Trade Under Fire*, 3rd edition. Princeton, NJ: Princeton University Press.

Jackson, Derrick Z. (2007) "Spreading Fear, Selling Weapons," Columbia, S.C., *The State* (August 6): A9.

Jacobson, Harold K. (1984) *Networks of Interdependence*. New York: Knopf.

Jaeger, Hans-Martin. (2007) "Global Civil Society and the Political Depoliticization of Global Governance," *International Political Sociology* 1 (September): 257–277.

Jaffe, Greg, and Jonathan Karp. (2005) "Pentagon Girds for Big Spending Cuts," *Wall Street Journal* (November 5): A7.

James, Barry. (2002a) "Summit Aims, Again, for a Better World," *International Herald Tribune* (August 8): 1, 8.

—— (2002b). "Talks to Tackle Threat to Biodiversity," *International Herald Tribune* (August 23): 1, 9.

James, Patrick. (1993) "Neorealism as a Research Enterprise," *International Political Science Review* 14 (No. 2): 123–48.

Janis, Irving. (1982) *Groupthink: Psychological Studies of Policy Decisions and Fiascoes*, 2nd ed. Boston: Houghton Mifflin.

Janowski, Louis. (2006) "Neo-Imperialism and U.S. Foreign Policy," pp. 54–61 in John T. Rourke (ed.), *Taking Sides*. Dubuque, Iowa: McGraw-Hill/Dushkin.

Jensen, Lloyd. (1982) *Explaining Foreign Policy*. Englewood Cliffs, N.J.: Prentice Hall.

Jervis, Robert. (2005) *American Foreign Policy in a New Era*. New York: Routledge.

—— (1992) "A Usable Past for the Future," pp. 257–68 in Michael J. Hogan (ed.), *The End of the Cold War*. New York: Cambridge University Press.

—— (1985) c *World Politics* 38 (October): 58–79.

—— (1976) *Perception and Misperception in World Politics*. Princeton, N.J.: Princeton University Press.

—— (2008) "Unipolarity: A Structural Perspective," *World Politics* 61:188–213.

Johansen, Robert C. (1991) "Do Preparations for War Increase or Decrease International Security?" pp. 224–44 in Charles W. Kegley, Jr. (ed.), *The Long Postwar Peace*. New York: HarperCollins.

Johnson, Chalmers. (2007) *Nemesis: The Last Days of the American Republic*. New York: Metropolitan.

—— (2004a) *Blowback: The Costs and Consequences of American Empire*. New York: Henry Holt.

—— (2004b) *The Sorrows of Empire*. New York: Metropolitan Books/Henry Holt.

Johnson, James Turner. (2005) "Just War, As It Was and Is," *First Things* 149 (January): 14–24.

—— (2003) "Just War Theory: Responding Morally to Global Terrorism," pp. 223–38 in Charles W. Kegley, Jr. (ed.), *The New Global Terrorism*. Upper Saddle River, N.J.: Prentice Hall.

Johnston, Michael. (2006) *Syndromes of Corruption*. Cambridge: Cambridge University Press.

Jones, Bruce, Carlos Pascual, and Stephen John Stedman. (2009) *Power & Responsibility: Building International Order in an Era of Transnational Threats*. Brookings: Washington D.C.

Jones, Dorothy V. (2002) *Toward a Just World*. Chicago: University of Chicago Press.

—— (1991) *Code of Peace: Ethics and Security in the World of the Warlord States*. Chicago: University of Chicago Press.

Joyce, Mark. (2005) "From Kosovo to Katrina," *International Herald Tribune* (August 8): 6.

Joyner, Christopher C. (2005) *International Law in the 21st Century*. Lanham, Md.: Rowman & Littlefield.

Judis, John B. (2005) *The Folly of Empire*. New York: Scribner.

——— (2004) "Imperial Amnesia," *Foreign Policy* (July-August): 50–59.

Judt, Tony. (2007) "From Military Disaster to Moral High Ground," *New York Times* (October 7): Week in Review, 15.

——— (2005) "The New World Order," *New York Review of Books* 52 (July 14): 14–18.

Judt, Tony, and Denis Lacurne (eds.). (2005) *With US or Against US: Studies in Global Anti-Americanism*. London: Palgrave Macmillan.

Juergensmeyer, Mark. (2003) "The Religious Roots of Contemporary Terrorism," pp. 185–93 in Charles W. Kegley, Jr. (ed.), *The New Global Terrorism*. Upper Saddle River, N.J.: Prentice Hall.

Justino, Patricia. (2009) "Poverty and Violent Conflict: A Micro-Level Perspective on the Causes and Duration of Warfare," *Journal of Peace Research* 46 (3): 315–333.

Kaarbo, Juliet. (2008). "Coalition Cabinet Decision Making: Institutional and Psychological Factors," *International Studies Review* 10: 57–86.

Kadera, Kelly. M. (2001) *The Power-Conflict Story: A Dynamic Model of Interstate Rivalry*. Ann Arbor: University of Michigan Press.

Kadera, Kelly M., and Gerald L. Sorokin. (2004) "Measuring National Power," *International Interactions* 30 (July-September): 211–30.

Kagan, Robert. (2007) *Dangerous Nation*. New York: Knopf.

Kahneman, Daniel. (2003) "Maps of Bounded Nationality," *American Economic Review* 93 (December):1449–1475.

Kaiser, David. (1990) *Politics and War*. Cambridge, Mass.: Harvard University Press.

Kaminski, Matthew. (2002) "Anti-Terrorism Requires Nation Building," *Wall Street Journal* (March 15): A10.

Kane, Hal. (1995) *The Hour of Departure: Forces That Create Refugees and Migrants*. Washington, D.C.: Worldwatch Institute.

Kanet, Roger. (2010) "Foreign Policy Making in a Democratic Society." *International Studies Review* 12: 123–127.

Kant, Immanuel. (1964; 1798). *Anthropologie in Pragmatischer Hinsicht*. Darmstadt, Germany: Werke.

Kaplan, Morton A. (1957) *System and Process in International Politics*. New York: Wiley.

Kaplan, Robert D. (2009a) "The Revenge of Geography" *Foreign Policy* (May/June): 96–105.

——— (2009b) "Center Stage for the Twenty-first Century," *Foreign Affairs* 88 (2): 16–32.

——— (2005a) "How We Would Fight China," *Atlantic Monthly* 295 (May): 49–64.

——— (2005b) "Supremacy by Stealth," pp. 91–100 in Helen E. Purkitt (ed.), *World Politics 04/05*. Dubuque, Iowa: McGraw-Hill/Dushkin.

Kapstein, Ethan B. (2006) "The New Global Slave Trade," *Foreign Affairs* 85 (November/December): 103–115.

——— (2004) "Models of International Economic Justice," *Ethics & International Affairs* 18 (No. 2): 79–92.

——— (1991–92) "We Are Us: The Myth of the Multinational," *National Interest* 26 (Winter): 55–62.

Kapur, Devesh, and John McHale. (2003) "Migration's New Payoff," *Foreign Policy* (November-December): 49–57.

Karns, Margaret P., and Karen A. Mingst. (2004) *International Organizations*. Boulder, Colo: Lynne Rienner.

Kasher, Asa, and Amos Yadlin. (2005) "Assassination and Preventive Killing," *SAIS Review* 25 (Winter-Spring): 41–57.

Kassimeris, Christos. (2009) "The Foreign Policy of Small Powers" *International Politics* 46 (1):84–101.

Katznelson, Ira and Helen V. Milner, eds. (2002) *Political Science: State of the Discipline*. Centennial edition. W.W. Norton & Company.

Kaufman, Frederick. (2009) "Let Them Eat Cash," *Harper's* (June): 51–59.

Kay, Kattie and Claire Shipman. (2009) "Fixing the Economy? It's Women's Work." *Washington Post* (July 12).

Kearney, A. T. (2004) "Measuring Globalization" *Foreign Policy* (March-April): 54–69.

——— (2002) "Globalization's Last Hurrah?" *Foreign Policy* (January-February): 38–71.

Keating, Joshua. (2009) "The Longest Shadow" *Foreign Policy* (May-June): 28.

——— (2009b) "The New Coups" *Foreign Policy* (May-June): 28.

Keck, Margaret E., and Kathryn Sikkink. (2008) "Transnational Advocacy Networks in International Politics," pp. 279–90 in Karen A. Mingst and Jack L. Snyder (eds.), *Essential Readings in World Politics*, 3rd ed. New York: Norton.

Keegan, John. (1999) *The First World War*. New York: Knopf.

——— (1993). A History of Warfare. New York : Alfred A. Knopf.

Kegley, Charles W., Jr. (ed.). (1995) *Controversies in International Relations Theory: Realism and the Neoliberal Challenge*. New York: St. Martin's.

Kegley, Charles W., Jr. (ed.). (1994) "How Did the Cold War Die? Principles for an Autopsy," *Mershon International Studies Review* 38 (March): 11–41.

——— (1993) "The Neoidealist Moment in International Studies? Realist Myths and the New International Realities," *International Studies Quarterly* 37 (June): 131–46.

——— (1992) "The New Global Order: The Power of Principle in a Pluralistic World," *Ethics & International Affairs* 6: 21–42.

Kegley, Charles W., Jr., and Margaret G. Hermann. (2002) "In Pursuit of a Peaceful International System," pp. 15–29 in Peter J. Schraeder (ed.), *Exporting Democracy*. Boulder, Colo.: Lynne Rienner.

——— (1997) "Putting Military Intervention into the Democratic Peace," *Comparative Political Studies* 30 (February): 78–107.

Kegley, Charles W., Jr., and Gregory A. Raymond. (2007a) *After Iraq: The Imperiled American Imperium*. New York: Oxford University Press.

——— (2007b) *The Global Future*, 2nd ed. Belmont, Calif.: Wadsworth/Thomson Learning.

——— (2004) "Global Terrorism and Military Preemption: Policy Problems and Normative Perils," *International Politics* 41 (January): 37–49.

——— (2002a) *Exorcising the Ghost of Westphalia: Building World Order in the New Millennium*. Upper Saddle River, N.J.: Prentice Hall.

——— (2002b) *From War to Peace: Fateful Decisions in World Politics*. Belmont, Calif.: Wadsworth.

——— (1999) *How Nations Make Peace*. Boston: Bedford/St. Martin's.

——— (1994) *A Multipolar Peace? Great-Power Politics in the Twenty-First Century*. New York: St. Martin's.

——— (1990) *When Trust Breaks Down: Alliance Norms and World Politics*. Columbia: University of South Carolina Press.

Kegley, Charles W., Jr., Gregory A. Raymond, and Margaret G. Hermann. (1998) "The Rise and Fall of the Nonintervention Norm: Some Correlates and Potential Consequences," *Fletcher Forum of World Affairs* 22 (Winter-Spring): 81–101.

Kegley, Charles W., Jr., with Eugene R. Wittkopf. (2006) *World Politics*, 10th ed. Belmont, Calif.: Wadsworth/Thomson Learning.

——— (1982) *American Foreign Policy*, 2nd ed. New York: St. Martin's.

Keller, Jonathan W. (2005) "Leadership Style, Regime Type, and Foreign Policy Crisis Behavior," *International Studies Quarterly* 49 (June): 205–31.

Kellman, Barry. (2007) *Bioviolence*. Cambridge: Cambridge University Press.

Kelsen, Hans. (2009) *General Theory of Law and State*. Cambridge, Mass.: Harvard University Press.

Kennan, George F. (1985) "Morality and Foreign Policy," *Foreign Affairs* 64 (Winter): 205–218.

—— (1984a) *The Fateful Alliance.* New York: Pantheon.

—— (1984b) "Soviet-American Relations," pp. 107–20 in Charles W. Kegley, Jr., and Eugene R. Wittkopf (eds.), *The Global Agenda.* New York: Random House.

—— (1967) *Memoirs.* Boston: Little, Brown.

—— (1954) *Realities of American Foreign Policy.* Princeton, N.J.: Princeton University Press.

—— (1951) *American Diplomacy, 1900–1950.* New York: New American Library.

—— ["X"]. (1947) "The Sources of Soviet Conduct," *Foreign Affairs* 25 (July): 566–82.

Kennedy, Paul. (2006) "The Perils of Empire," pp. 69–71 in Helen E. Purkitt (ed.), *World Politics 05/06.* Dubuque, Iowa: McGraw-Hill/Dushkin.

—— (1987) *The Rise and Fall of the Great Powers.* New York: Random House.

Keohane, Robert O. (2002) "Governance in a Partially Globalized World," *American Political Science Review* 94 (March): 1–13.

—— (1989) "International Relations Theory: Contributions from a Feminist Standpoint," *Millennium* 18 (Summer): 245–53.

—— (ed.). (1986a) *Neorealism and Its Critics.* New York: Columbia University Press.

—— (1986b) "Realism, Neorealism and the Study of World Politics," pp. 1–26 in Robert O. Keohane (ed.), *Neorealism and Its Critics.* New York: Columbia University Press.

—— (1984) *After Hegemony: Cooperation and Discord in the World Political Economy.* Princeton: Princeton University Press.

Keohane, Robert O., and Joseph S. Nye. (2001a) *Power and Interdependence,* 3rd ed. New York: Addison WesleyLongman.

—— (2001b) "Power and Interdependence in the Information Age," pp. 26–36 in Charles W. Kegley, Jr., and Eugene R. Wittkopf (eds.), *The Global Agenda,* 6th ed. Boston: McGraw-Hill.

—— (2000) "Globalization: What's New? What's Not? (And So What?)," *Foreign Policy* 118 (Spring): 104–19.

—— (1998) "Power and Interdependence in the Information Age," *Foreign Affairs* 77 (September-October): 81–95.

—— (1977) *Power and Interdependence.* Boston: Little, Brown.

—— (eds.). (1971) *Transnational Relations and World Politics.* Cambridge: Harvard University Press.

Khanna, Parag. (2006) "United They Fall," *Harper's* (January): 31–40.

Kher, Unmesh. (2006) "Oceans of Nothing," *Time* (November 13): 56–57.

Kibbe, Jennifer D. (2004) "The Rise of Shadow Warriors." *Foreign Affairs* 83 (March-April): 102–15.

Kifner, John. (2005) "A Tide of Islamic Fury, and How It Rose," *New York Times* (January 30): Section 4, 4–5.

Kim, Dae Jung, and James D. Wolfensohn. (1999) "Economic Growth Requires Good Governance," *International Herald Tribune* (February 26): 6.

Kim, Samuel S. (1991) "The United Nations, Lawmaking and World Order," pp. 109–24 in Richard A. Falk, Samuel S. Kim, and Saul H. Mendlovitz (eds.), *The United Nations and a Just World Order.* Boulder, Colo.: Westview.

Kindleberger, Charles. (2001) *Manics, Panics, and Crashes: A History of Financial Crises,* 4th ed. Hoboken, NJ: John Wiley and Sons.

—— (2000) Manics, Panics, and Crashes: A History of Financial Crises, 4th ed. New York: John Wiley and Sons.

—— (1973) *The World in Depression, 1929–1939.* Berkeley: University of California Press.

Kindleberger, Charles, Robert Ailber and Robert Solow. (2005) *Manics, Panics, and Crashes: A History of Financial Crises, 5th edition.* Hoboken, NJ: Wiley.

Kingsbury, Kathleen. (2007) "The Changing Face of Breast Cancer," *Time* (October 15): 36–43.

Kinnas, J. N. (1997) "Global Challenges and Multilateral Diplomacy," pp. 23–48 in Ludwik Dembinski (ed.), *International Geneva Yearbook.* Berne, Switzerland: Peter Lang.

King, Gary, and Langche Zeng. (2007) "When Can History Be Our Guide?" *International Studies Quarterly* 51 (March): 183–210.

Kirkpatrick, David D. (2007) "This War is Not Like the Others—Or is It?" *New York Times* (August 26): The Week in Review, 1, 4.

—— (2005) "Battle Splits Conservative Magazine," *New York Times* (13 March): 12.

Kissinger, Henry A. (2004) "America's Assignment," *Newsweek* (November 8): 32–38.

—— (2001) *Does America Need a Foreign Policy?* New York: Simon & Schuster.

—— (1999) *Years of Renewal.* New York: Simon & Schuster.

—— (1994) *Diplomacy.* New York: Simon & Schuster.

—— (1992) "Balance of Power Sustained," pp. 238–48 in Graham Allison and Gregory F. Treverton (eds.), *Rethinking America's Security.* New York: Norton.

—— (1979) *White House Years.* Boston: Little, Brown.

—— (1969) "Domestic Structure and Foreign Policy," pp. 261–75 in James N. Rosenau (ed.), *International Politics and Foreign Policy.* New York: Free Press.

Klare, Michael. (2008) *Rising Powers, Shrinking Planet.* New York: Metropolitan Books.

—— (2007) "Beyond the Age of Petroleum," *The Nation* 285 (November 12): 17–22.

—— (2004) *Blood and Oil.* New York: Henry Holt.

—— (2002) *Resource Wars: The New Landscape of Global Conflict.* New York: Holtzbrinck Academic.

Klein, Naomi. (2008) "China's All-Seeing Eye," *Rolling Stone* (May 29): 59–66.

—— (2007) *The Shock Doctrine: The Rise of Disaster Capitalism.* New York: Metropolitan Books/Henry Holt.

Klimová-Alexander, Ilona. (2005) *The Romani Voice in World Politics: The United Nations and Non-State Actors.* Burlington, Ver.: Ashgate.

Kluger, Jeffrey. (2007) "What Makes Us Moral," *Time* (December 3): 54–60.

—— (2006) "The Big Crunch," pp. 24–25 in Robert M. Jackson (ed.), *Global Issues 05/06.* Dubuque, Iowa: McGraw-Hill/Dushkin.

—— (2001) "A Climate of Despair," *Time* (April 9): 30–35.

Knetch, Thomas and M. Stephen Weatherford. (2006) "Public Opinion and Foreign Policy: The Stages of Presidential Decision Making," *International Studies Quarterly* 50: 705–727.

Knickerbocker, Brad. (2007) "Might Warming Be 'Normal'," *Christian Science Monitor* (September 20): 14, 16.

Knight, W. Andy. (2000) *A Changing United Nations.* London: Palgrave.

Knorr, Klaus, and James N. Rosenau (eds.). (1969) *Contending Approaches to International Politics.* Princeton, N.J.: Princeton University Press.

Knorr, Klaus, and Sidney Verba (eds.). (1961) *The International System.* Princeton, N.J.: Princeton University Press.

Knox, MacGregor, and Williamson Murray. (2001) *The Dynamics of Military Revolution: 1300–2050.* Cambridge: Cambridge University Press.

Kober, Stanley. (1990) "Idealpolitik," *Foreign Policy* 79 (Summer): 3–24.

Kohli, Atul. (2004) *State-Directed Development.* Cambridge: Cambridge University Press.

Kolbert, Elizabeth. (2008) "What Was I Thinking? The Latest Reasoning about Our Irrational Ways," *The New Yorker* (February 25): 77–79.

——— (2005) "The Climate of Man-II," *New Yorker* (May 2): 64–73.

Kolb, Deborah M. (1996) "Her Place at the Table: Gender and Negotiation," pp. 138–144 in Mary Roth Walsh (ed.), *Women, Men, and Gender: Ongoing Debates.* New York: Hamilton.

Kolodziej Edward. (2005). *Security and International Relations.* Cambridge: Cambridge University Press.

Korten, David. (1995) *When Corporations Rule the World.* West Hartford, Conn.: Berrett-Koehler.

Koser, Khalid. (2010) "The Impact of the Global Financial Crisis on International Migration." *The Whitehead Journal of Diplomacy and International Relations* 11(1) (Winter/Spring): 13–20.

Krasner, Stephen P. (2004) "Sharing Sovereignty: New Institutions for Collapsed and Failing States," *International Security* 29 (Fall): 85–120.

——— (2001) "International Political Economy," pp. 420–22 in Joel Krieger (ed.), *The Oxford Companion to Politics of the World,* 2nd ed. New York: Oxford University Press.

Krauthammer, Charles. (2005a) "As Liberty Advances, Opposition Begins to Unite," Columbia, S.C., *The State* (January 21): A9.

——— (2005b) "Door to Power Open to China," Columbia, S.C., *The State* (September 25): D3.

——— (2004) "Democratic Realism: An American Foreign Policy for a Unipolar World." Speech delivered at the American Enterprise Institute (February 10).

——— (2003) "The Unipolar Moment Revisited," *National Interest* 70 (Winter): 5–17.

——— (2002) "NATO Is Dead; We Should Not Work to Revive It," Columbia, S.C., *The State* (May 26): D3.

——— (2001) "The Bush Doctrine," *Time* (March 5): 42.

——— (1993) "How Doves Become Hawks," *Time* (May 17): 74.

Kristof, Nicholas D. (2005) "The Fire Bell in the Night on Climate Change," Columbia, S.C., *The State* (September 28): A11.

——— (2004) "A New Ethnic Cleaning," Columbia, S.C., *The State* (March 25): A9.

——— (1993) "The Rise of China," *Foreign Affairs* 72 (November-December): 59–74.

Kroenig, Matthew. (2009) "Exporting the Bomb: Why States Provide Sensitive Nuclear Assistance," *American Political Science Review* 103: 113–133.

Krueger, Alan B. (2007) *What Makes a Terrorist.* Princeton, N.J.: Princeton University Press.

Krueger, Anne O. (2006) "Expanding Trade and Unleashing Growth," pp. 4–19 in John T. Rourke (ed.), *Taking Sides.* Dubuque, Iowa: McGraw-Hill/Dushkin.

Krugman, Paul. (2005) "America Held Hostage," Columbia, S.C., *The State* (July 1): A19.

——— (2004) "An Oil-Driven Recession Is Possible," *International Herald Tribune* (May 15–16): 9.

——— (2003) *The Great Unraveling: Losing Our Way in the New Century.* New York: Norton.

——— (1993) "The Uncomfortable Truth about NAFTA: It's Foreign Policy, Stupid," *Foreign Affairs* 74 (4): 13–20.

——— (1987) "Is Free Trade Passé?" *Journal of Economic Perspectives* 1 (Autumn): 131–144.

Kugler, Jacek. (2006) "China: Satisfied or Dissatisfied, the Strategic Equation," paper presented at the Annual Meeting of the International Studies Association, March 22–25, San Diego.

——— (2001) "War," pp. 894–96 in Joel Krieger (ed.), *The Oxford Companion to Politics of the World.* 2nd ed. New York: Oxford University Press.

Kugler, Jacek, Ronald L. Tammen, and Brian Efird. (2004) "Integrating Theory and Policy," *International Studies Review* 6 (December): 163–79.

Kuhnhenn, Jim. (2009) "Trillions Devoted to Bank Bailout," *The Commercial Appeal* (July 21): A1.

Kunzig, Robert. (2003) "Against the Current," *U.S. News & World Report* (June 2): 34–35.

Kupchan, Charles A. (2003) *The End of the American Era: U.S. Foreign Policy and the Geopolitics of the Twenty-First Century.* New York: Knopf.

Kupchan, Charles A., and Clifford A. Kupchan. (2000) "Concerts, Collective Security, and the Future of Europe," pp. 218–265 in Michael Brown, et. al. (eds.), *America's Strategic Choices.* Cambridge, MA: The MIT Press.

——— (1992) "A New Concert for Europe," pp. 249–66 in Graham Allison and Gregory F. Treverton (eds.), *Rethinking America's Security.* New York: Norton.

Kurzweil, Ray. (2005) *The Singularity is Near: When Humans Transcend Biology.* New York: Penguin Group (USA).

Kutcher, Ashton. (2009) "Builders and Titans," *Time* (May 11): 60.

Lacayo, Richard. (2009) "A Brief History of : Photographing Fallen Troops," *Time* (March 16): 19.

Laeven, Luc and Fabian Valencia. (2010) "Resolution of Banking Crises: The Good, the Bad, and the Ugly." *IMF Working Paper* 10/146. Washington, D.C.: The International Monetary Fund.

——— (2008) "Systemic Banking Crises: A New Database." *IMF Working Paper.* Available at: http://www.imf.org/external/pubs/ft/wp/2008/wp08224.pdf.

Lai, Brian, and Dan Reiter. (2005) "Rally Round the Union Jack?" *International Studies Quarterly* 49 (June): 255–72.

Landau, Julia. (2010) "Food Riots or Food Rebellions?: Eric Holt-Giménez Looks at the World Food Crisis." *CommonDreams.org* (March 25). Available at http://www.commondreams.org/view/2010/03/25–11.

Landes, David S. (1998) *The Wealth and Poverty of Nations: Why Are Some So Rich and Some So Poor?* New York: Norton.

Landler, Mark and David E. Sanger. (2009) "Leaders Reach $1 Trillion Deal," *International Herald Tribune* (April 3): 1,4.

Landman, Todd. (2006) *Studying Human Rights.* New York: Routledge.

Laqueur, Walter. (2006) "The Terrorism to Come," pp. 229–36 in Thomas J. Badey (ed.), *Violence and Terrorism 06/07.* Dubuque, Iowa: McGraw Hill/Dushkin.

——— (2003) "Postmodern Terrorism," pp. 151–59 in Charles W. Kegley, Jr. (ed.), *The New Global Terrorism.* Upper Saddle River, N.J.: Prentice Hall.

——— (2001) "Terror's New Face," pp. 82–89 in Charles W. Kegley, Jr., and Eugene R. Wittkopf (eds.), *The Global Agenda,* 6th ed. Boston: McGraw-Hill.

Larkin, John. (2005) "India Bets on Nuclear Future," *Wall Street Journal International* (November 4): A12.

Lebovic, James H. (2004) "Uniting for Peace?" *Journal of Conflict Resolution* 48 (December): 910–36.

Lebovic, James H. and Erik Voeten. (2009) "The Cost of Shame: International Organizations and Foreign Aid in the Punishing of Human Rights Violators" *Journal of Peace Research* 46 (1): 79–97.

Lebow, Richard Ned. (2003) *The Tragic Vision of Politics: Ethics, Interests, and Orders.* Cambridge: Cambridge University Press.

——— (1981) *Between Peace and War.* Baltimore: Johns Hopkins University Press.

Lechner, Frank and John Boli. (2007) *The Globalization Reader,* 3rd edition. Hoboken, NJ: Wiley-Blackwell.

Legrain, Philippe. (2003) "Cultural Globalization Is Not Americanization," *Chronicle of Higher Education* (May 9): B7–B70.

Legro, Jeffrey W. (2007) *Rethinking the World: Great Power Strategies and International Order.* Ithaca, N.Y: Cornell University Press.

Legro, Jeffrey W., and Andrew Moravcsik. (1999) "Is Anybody Still a Realist?" *International Security* 24 (Fall): 5–55.

Lektzian, David and Mark Souva. (2009) "A Comparative Theory Test of Democratic Peace Arguments, 1946–2000." *Journal of Peace Research* 46 (1): 17–37.

Lemann, Nicholas. (2001) "What Terrorists Want," *The New Yorker* (October 29): 36.

Lemke, Douglas. (2003) "Development and War," *International Studies Review* 5 (December): 55–63.

Lentner, Howard H. (2004) *Power and Politics in Globalization: The Indispensable State.* New York: Routledge.

Leonard, Mark. (2005) *Why Europe Will Run the 21st Century.* New York: Fourth Estate.

Leopard, Brian D. (2010) *Customary International Law: A New Theory with Practical Applications.* New York: Cambridge University Press.

Leow, Rachel. (2002) "How Can Globalization Become 'O.K.' for All?" *International Herald Tribune* (February 15): 9.

Levi, Michael. (2009) "Copenhagen's Inconvenient Truth: How to Salvage the Climate Conference" *Foreign Affairs* 88 (September/October): 92–104.

———— (2008) "Stopping Nuclear Terrorism," *Foreign Affairs* 87 (January/February): 131–140.

Levingston, Steven. (1999) "Does Territoriality Drive Human Aggression?" *International Herald Tribune* (April 14): 9.

Levitt, Peggy. (2007) *God Needs No Passport.* New York: New Press.

Levy, Jack S. (2003) "Applications of Prospect Theory to Political Science," *Syntheses* 135 (May): 215–41.

———— (2001) "War and Its Causes," pp. 47–56 in Charles W. Kegley, Jr., and Eugene Wittkopf (eds.), *The Global Agenda,* 6th ed. Boston: McGraw-Hill.

———— (1998a) "The Causes of War and the Conditions of Peace," *Annual Review of Political Science* 1 (June): 139–65.

———— (1998b) "Towards a New Millennium," pp. 47–57 in Charles W. Kegley, Jr., and Eugene R. Wittkopf (eds.), *The Global Agenda,* 5th ed. New York: McGraw-Hill.

———— (1997) "Prospect Theory, Rational Choice, and International Relations," *International Studies Quarterly* 41 (March): 87–112.

———— (1990–91) "Preferences, Constraints, and Choices in July 1914," *International Security* 15 (Winter): 151–86.

———— (1989a) "The Causes of War: A Review of Theories and Evidence," pp. 209–333 in Philip E. Tetlock, Jo L. Husbands, Robert Jervis, Paul C. Stern, and Charles Tilly (eds.), *Behavior, Society, and Nuclear War.* New York: Oxford University Press.

———— (1989b) "The Diversionary Theory of War," pp. 259–88 in Manus I. Midlarsky (ed.), *Handbook of War Studies.* Boston: Unwin Hyman.

Levy, Jack S., and Katherine Barbieri. (2004) "Trading with the Enemy During Wartime," *Security Studies* 13 (Spring): 1–47.

Lewis, M. Paul ed. (2009). *Ethnologue: Languages of the World 16ᵗʰ Edition.* Dallas, Tex.: SIL International. {On-line} Available at: version: http://www.ethnologue.com.

Lieber, Robert J. (2005) *The American Era.* New York: Cambridge University Press.

Lind, Michael. (1993) "Of Arms and the Woman," *New Republic* (November 15): 36–38.

Lindberg, Todd, (ed.). (2005) *Beyond Paradise and Power: Europe, America, and the Future of a Troubled Relationship.* New York: Routledge.

Lindblom, Charles E. (1979) "Still Muddling, Not Yet Through," *Public Administration Review* 39 (November-December): 517–26.

Lindsay, James M. (1986) "Trade Sanctions as Policy Instruments," *International Studies Quarterly* 30 (June): 153–73.

Lipson, Charles. (1984) "International Cooperation in Economic and Security Affairs," *World Politics* 37 (October): 1–23.

Lissitzyn, Oliver J. (1963) "International Law in a Divided World," *International Conciliation* 542 (March): 3–69.

List, Friedrich. (1841) *National System of Political Economy.* Available at: http://socserv2.socsci.mcmaster.ca/~econ/ugcm/3ll3/list/list.

Little, David. (1993) "The Recovery of Liberalism," *Ethics & International Affairs* 7: 171–201.

Lodal, Jan, et al. (2010) "Second Strike: Is the U.S. Nuclear Arsenal Outmoded?" *Foreign Affairs* 89(2) (March/April): 145–152.

Loescher, Gil. (2005) "Blaming the Victim: Refugees and Global Security," pp. 126–29 in Robert J. Griffiths (ed.), *Developing World 05/06.* Dubuque, Iowa: McGraw-Hill/Dushkin.

Lomborg, Bjørn. (2007) *Solutions for the World's Biggest Problems.* New York: Cambridge University Press.

———— (ed.). (2004) *Global Crisis, Global Solutions.* Cambridge: Cambridge University Press.

Longman, Phillip. (2005) "The Global Baby Bust," pp. 173–179 in Robert J. Griffiths (ed.), *Developing World 05/06.* Dubuque, Iowa: McGraw-Hill/Dushkin.

Lopez, George A., and David Cortright. (1995) "Economic Sanctions in Contemporary Global Relations," pp. 3–16 in David Cortright and George A. Lopez (eds.), *Economic Sanctions.* Boulder, Colo.: Westview.

Lopez, J. Humberto, et al. (2010) "Big Senders." *Foreign Policy* (January/February): 35.

Lorenz, Konrad. (1963) *On Aggression.* New York: Harcourt, Brace & World.

Löwenheim, Oded. (2007) *Predators and Parasites.* Ann Arbor: Pluto Books, University of Michigan Press.

Lumpe, Lora. (1999) "The Lender of the Pack," *Bulletin of the Atomic Scientists* 58 (January-February): 27–33.

Lupovici, Amir. (2009) "Constructivist Methods: A Plea and Manifesto for Pluralism," *Review of International Studies* 35: 195–218.

Lutz, Ellen L. (2006) "Understanding Human Rights Violations in Armed Conflict," pp.23–38 in Julie Mertus and Jeffrey W. Helsing (eds.), *Human Rights and Conflict: Exploring the Links Between Rights, Law, and Peacebuilding.* Washington DC: United States Institute of Peace Press.

Lutz, Wolfgang. (1994) "The Future of World Population," *Population Bulletin* 49 (June): 1–47.

Lynch, Colum. (2008) "U.N. Chief to Prod Nations on Food Crisis," *Washington Post* (June 2): A07.

Lynn, Jonathan. (2008) "Diplomats See Reason for Hope in WTO Talks," *International Herald Tribune* (May 29).

Lyons, Daniel. (2010) "Short-circuiting malaria." *Newsweek* (April 19): 36–41.

Mackinder, Sir Halford. (1919) *Democratic Ideals and Reality.* New York: Holt.

Mahan, Alfred Thayer. (1890) *The Influence of Sea Power in History.* Boston: Little, Brown.

Mahbulbani, Kishore. (2009) *The New Asian Hemisphere: The Irresistible Shift of Global Power to the East.* Basic Civitas Books.

———— (2005) "Understanding China," *Foreign Affairs* 84 (October): 49–60.

Majeed, Akhtar. (1991) "Has the War System Really Become Obsolete?" *Bulletin of Peace Proposals* 22 (December): 419–25.

Malaquias, Assis V. (2001) "Humanitarian Intervention," pp. 370–74 in Joel Krieger (ed.), *The Oxford Companion to Politics of the World,* 2nd ed. New York: Oxford University Press.

———— (2008) "The Benefits of Goliath," pp. 55–64 in Eugene R. Wittkopf and James M. McCormick, eds., *The Domestic Sources of American Foreign Policy.* Lanham, Md.: Rowman and Littlefield.

Malcomson, Scott. (2008) "Humanitarianism and its Politicization," *International Herald* Tribune (December 13–14): 9.

Mandelbaum, Michael. (2007) "Democracy Without America," *Foreign Affairs* 86 (September/October): 119–130.

——— (2006a) "David's Friend Goliath," *Foreign Policy* (January-February): 49–56.

——— (2006b) *The Case for Goliath: How America Acts as the World's Government in the 21st Century.* New York: Public Affairs.

——— (2002) *The Ideas That Conquered the World: Peace, Democracy, and Free Markets in the Twenty-First Century.* New York: Public Affairs/Perseus.

Mann, Charles C. (2005) "The Coming Death Shortage," *Atlantic Monthly* 295 (May): 92–102.

Mann, James. (2004) *Rise of the Vulcans: The History of Bush's War Cabinet.* New York: Viking.

Mankoff, Jeffrey. (2009) *Russian Foreign Policy: The Return of Great Power Politics.* New York: Rowman and Littlefield.

Mansfield, Edward D., Helen V. Milner, and B. Peter Rosendorff. (2002) "Replication, Realism, and Robustness: Analyzing Political Regimes and International Trade," *American Political Science Review* 96 (March): 167–69.

Mansfield, Edward D., and Brian M. Pollins (eds.). (2003) *Economic Interdependence and International Conflict.* Ann Arbor: University of Michigan Press.

Mansfield, Edward D., and Jack Snyder. (2005a) *Electing to Fight.* Cambridge, Mass.: MIT Press.

——— (2005b) "When Ballots Bring Bullets," *International Herald Tribune* (November 29–30): 6.

Mapel, David R. (2007) "The Right of National Defense," *International Studies Perspectives* 8 (February): 1–15.

Margolis, Max, and Alex Marin. (2010) "Venezuela and the Tyranny of Twitter." *Newsweek* (June 14): 6.

Markoe, Lauren, and Seth Borenstein. (2005) "We Overpay by 20% for Military Goods," Columbia, S.C., *The State* (October 23): A1, A8.

Markoff, John. (2009) "A Map of the World, in 4 Billion Pockets," *International Herald Tribune* (February 188): 1, 11.

Marshall, Monty G., and Ted Robert Gurr. (2003) *Peace and Conflict 2003.* College Park, Md.: Center for International Development and Conflict Management.

Martel, William C. (2008) *Victory in War.* New York: Cambridge University Press.

Martell, Luke. (2007) "The Third Wave in Globalization Theory," *International Studies Review* 9 (Summer): 173–196.

Marx, Anthony W (2003) *Faith in Nation: Exclusionary Origins of Nationalism.* New York: Oxford University Press.

Mathews, Jessica T. (2000) "National Security for the Twenty-First Century," pp. 9–11 in Gary Bertsch and Scott James (eds.), *Russell Symposium Proceedings.* Athens: University of Georgia.

Matlock, Jack F. (2004) *Reagan and Gorbachev: How the Cold War Ended.* New York: Random House.

May, Ernest R. (2000) *Strange Victory.* New York: Hill and Wang.

Mayall, James. (2001) "Mercantilism," pp. 535 and 540 in Joel Krieger (ed.), *The Oxford Companion to Politics of the World,* 2nd ed. New York: Oxford University Press.

Mazarr, Michael J. (1999) *Global Trends 2005.* London: Palgrave.

Mazur, Amy G. (2002) *Theorizing Feminist Policy.* New York: Oxford University Press.

McCormick, John. (2007) *The European Superpower.* London: Palgrave MacMillan.

McDermott, Rose, James H. Fowler and Oleg Smirnov. (2008) "On the Evolutionary Origin of Prospect Theory Preferences." *The Journal of Politics* 70 (April): 335–350.

McGinnis, John O. (2005) "Individualism and World Order," *The National Interest* 28 (Winter): 41–51.

McGirk, Tim. (2010) "Armed Farces." *Time* (June 14): 52–55.

——— (2009) "The Battle over Gaza," *Time* (January 12): 24–28.

McGranahan, Donald. (1995) "Measurement of Development," *International Social Science Journal* 143 (March): 39–59.

McGrew, Anthony. (2005) "The Logics of Globalization," pp. 207–34 in John Ravenhill (ed.), *Global Political Economy.* New York: Oxford University Press.

McGurn, William. (2002) "Pulpit Economics," *First Things* 122 (April): 21–25.

McKibbin, Bill. (2006) "A Special Moment in History," pp. 3–7 in Robert M. Jackson (ed.), *Global Issues 05/06.* Dubuque, Iowa: McGraw-Hill/Dushkin.

——— (1998) "The Future of Population," *Atlantic Monthly* (May): 55–78.

McNamara, Robert S. (2005) "Apocalypse Soon," *Foreign Policy* (May-June): 29–35.

Mead, Margaret. (1968) "Warfare Is Only an Invention—Not a Biological Necessity," pp. 270–74 in Leon Bramson and George W Goethals (eds.), *War.* New York: Basic Books.

Mead, Walter Russell. (2008) *God and Gold: Britain, America, and the Making of the Modern World.* New York: Knopf.

——— (2006) "America's Sticky Power," pp. 8–10 in Robert M. Jackson (ed.), *Global Issues 05/06.* Dubuque, Iowa: McGraw-Hill/Dushkin.

Mearsheimer, John J. (2004) "Anarchy and the Struggle for Power," pp. 54–72 in Karen A. Mingst and Jack L. Snyder (eds.), *Essential Readings in World Politics,* 2nd ed. New York: Norton.

——— (2001) *The Tragedy of Great Power Politics.* New York: Norton.

——— (1990) "Back to the Future: Instability in Europe after the Cold War," *International Security* 15 (Summer): 5–56.

Mearsheimer, John J., and Stephen W. Walt. (2003) "An Unnecessary War," *Foreign Policy* (January-February): 50–58.

Meernik, James David. (2004) *The Political Use of Military Force in US Foreign Policy.* Burlington, Ver.: Ashgate.

Melander, Erik. (2005) "Gender Equality and Intrastate Armed Conflict," *International Studies Quarterly* 49 (December): 695–714.

Melloan, George. (2002) "Bush's Toughest Struggle Is with His Own Bureaucracy," *Wall Street Journal* (June 25): A19.

Mendelsohn, Jack. (2005) "America and Russia: Make-Believe Arms Control," pp. 205–9 in Glenn P. Hastedt (ed.), *America Foreign Policy 04/05,* 10th ed. Guilford, Conn.: Dushkin/McGraw-Hill.

Menkhaus, Ken. (2002) "Somalia: In the Crosshairs of the War on Terrorism," *Current History* (May): 210–18.

Menon, Rajan. (2007) *The End of Alliances.* New York: Oxford University Press.

Mentan, Tatah. (2004) *Dilemmas of Weak States: Africa and Transnational Terrorism in the Twenty-First Century.* Burlington, VT: Ashgate.

Mertus, Julie. (2009) *Human Rights Matters: Local Politics and National Human Rights Institutions.* Stanford, CA: Stanford University Press.

——— (2009) *The United Nations and Human Rights: A guide for a new era.* 2nd ed. New York: Routledge.

de Mesquita, Bruce Bueno. (2009) "Recipe for Failure." *Foreign Policy* (November): 76–81.

Michael, Marie. (2001) "Food or Debt," pp. 78–79 in Robert J. Griffiths (ed.), *Developing World 01/02.* Guilford, Conn.: Dushkin/McGraw-Hill.

Micklethwait, John, and Adrian Wooldridge. (2001) "The Globalization Backlash," *Foreign Policy* (September-October): 16–26.

Midlarsky, Manus I. (2006) *The Killing Trap: Genocide in the Twentieth Century.* New York: Cambridge University Press.

—— (2003) "The Impact of External Threat on States and Domestic Societies," *International Studies Review* 5 (No. 4): 13–18.

—— (ed.). (2000) *Handbook of War Studies II.* Ann Arbor: University of Michigan Press.

—— (1988) *The Onset of World War.* Boston: Unwin Hyman.

Mieville, China. (2006) *Between Equal Rights: A Marxist Theory of International Law.* Chicago: Haymarket Books.

Miller, Mark Crispin. (2006) "What's Wrong With This Picture?" pp. 115–17 in Robert M. Jackson (ed.), *Global Issues 05/06.* Dubuque, Iowa: McGraw-Hill/Dushkin.

Milner, Helen V. and Andrew Moravcsik. (2009) *Power, Interdependence, and Nonstate Actors in World Politics.* Princeton University Press.

Minorities at Risk Project. (2009) "Minorities at Risk Dataset." College Park, MD: Center for International Development and Conflict Management. Available at: http://www.cidcm.umd.edu/mar.

Mintz, Alex. (2007) "Why Behavioral IR?" *International Studies Review* 9 (June): 157–172.

Mitchell, Sara McLaughlin, Kelly M. Kadera, and Mark J.C. Crescenzi (2008) "Practicing Democratic Community Norms: Third Party Conflict Management and Successful Settlements," pp. 243–264 in Jacob Bercovitch and Scott Sigmund Gartner (eds.), *International Conflict Mediation.* New York: Routledge.

Mitchell, Sara McLaughlin, and Brandon C. Prins. (2004) "Rivalry and Diversionary Uses of Force," *Journal of Conflict Resolution* 48 (December): 937–61.

Mitrany, David. (1966) *A Working Peace System.* Chicago: Quadrangle.

Modelski, George. (ed.). (1987a) *Exploring Long Cycles.* Boulder, Colo.: Lynne Rienner.

—— (1987b) "The Study of Long Cycles," pp. 1–15 in George Modelski (ed.), *Exploring Long Cycles.* Boulder, Colo.: Lynne Rienner.

—— (1964) "The International Relations of Internal War," pp. 14–44 in James N. Rosenau (ed.), *International Aspects of Civil Strife.* Princeton, N.J.: Princeton University Press.

—— (1962) *A Theoretical Analysis of the Formulation of Foreign Policy.* London: University of London.

Modelski, George, and William R. Thompson. (1999) "The Long and the Short of Global Politics in the Twenty-First Century," *International Studies Review,* special issue, ed. by Davis B. Bobrow: 109–40.

—— (1996) *Leading Sectors and World Powers.* Columbia: University of South Carolina Press.

Moens, Alexander. (2005) *The Foreign Policy of George W Bush.* Burlington, Ver.: Ashgate.

Moghadam, Reza. (2009) "Transcript of a Conference Call on the New Lending Framework for Low-Income Countries," International Monetary Fund. Available at: http://www.imf.org/external/np/tr/2009/tr072909a.htm.

Moisy, Claude. (1997) "Myths of the Global Information Village," *Foreign Policy* 107 (Summer): 78–87.

Møller, Bjørn. (1992) *Common Security and Nonoffensive Defense: A Neorealist Perspective.* Boulder, Colo.: Lynne Rienner.

Moon, Bruce E. (2008) "Reproducing the North-South Divide: The Role of Trade Deficits and Capital Flows," pp. 39–64 in Rafael Reuveny and William R. Thompson (eds.), *North and South in the World Political Economy.* Malden, MA: Blackwell.

Moorehead, Caroline. (2007) "Women and Children For Sale," *New York Review of Books* (October 11): 15–18.

Moran, Theodore H., Edward M. Graham, and Magnus Blomström (eds.). (2005) *Does Foreign Direct Investment Promote Development?* Washington, D.C.: Institute for International Economics.

Morgan, Patrick. (2005) *International Security: Problems and Solutions.* Washington, D.C.: CQ Press.

Morgenthau, Hans J. (1985) *Politics Among Nations,* 6th ed. Revised by Kenneth W. Thompson. New York: Knopf.

—— (1948) *Politics among Nations.* New York: Knopf.

Morphet, Sally. (2004) "Multilateralism and the Non-Aligned Movement," *Global Governance* 10 (October-December): 517–37.

Morris, Desmond. (1969) *The Human Zoo.* New York: Dell.

Morse, Edward L., and James Richard. (2002) "The Battle for Energy Dominance," *Foreign Affairs* 81 (March-April): 16–31.

Morton, David. (2006) "Gunning for the World," *Foreign Policy* (January-February): 58–67.

Mosley, Layna. (2008) "Workers' Rights in Open Economies: Global Production and Domestic Institutions in the Developing World," *Comparative Political Studies* 41 (4/5): 674–714.

Mowlana, Hamid. (1995) "The Communications Paradox," *Bulletin of the Atomic Scientists* 51 (July): 40–46.

Mueller, John. (2007) *Overblown.* New York: Free Press.

—— (2005) "Simplicity and Spook: Terrorism and the Dynamics of Threat Exaggeration," *International Studies Perspectives* 6 (May): 208–34.

—— (2004) *The Remnants of War.* Ithaca: Cornell University Press.

Mullenbach, Mark J. (2005) "Deciding to Keep Peace," *International Studies Quarterly* 49 (September): 529–55.

Muller, Jerry Z. (2008) "Us and Them: The Enduring Power of Ethnic Nationalism," *Foreign Affairs* 87 (March/April): 18–35.

Murdoch, James C, and Todd Sandler. (2004) "Civil Wars and Economic Growth," *American Journal of Political Science* 48 (January): 138–51.

Murithi, Timothy. (2004) "The Myth of Violent Human Nature," *Peace & Policy* 8: 28–32.

Murray, Williamson, and Allan R. Millett. (2000) *A War to Be Won.* Cambridge, Mass.: Harvard University Press.

Naím, Moisés. (2007) "The Free-Trade Paradox," *Foreign Policy* (September/October): 96–97.

—— (2006a) "The Five Wars of Globalization," pp. 61–66 in Robert M. Jackson (ed.), *Global Issues 05/06.* Dubuque, Iowa: McGraw-Hill/Dushkin.

—— (2006b) "The Most Dangerous Deficit," *Foreign Policy* (January-February): 94–95.

Nardin, Terry. (2005) "Humanitarian Imperialism," *Ethics and International Affairs* 19 (No. 2, Special Issue): 21–26.

Narlikar, Amrita and Rorden Wilkinson. (2004) "Collapse at the WTO: A Cancún Post-Mortem," *Third World Quarterly* 25 (3): 447–460.

National Intelligence Council (NIC). (2004) *Mapping the Global Future.* Washington, D.C.: National Intelligence Council.

NCTC. (National Counter-Terrorism Center). (2009) *2008 NCTC Report on Terrorism.* Washington, D.C.: National Counter-Terrorism Center.

—— (2007) *NCTC Report on Terrorist Incidents.* Washington, D.C.: National Counter-Terrorism Center.

Neack, Laura. (2004) "Peacekeeping, Bloody Peacekeeping," *Bulletin of the Atomic Scientists* 57 (July-August): 40–47.

Nelson, Stephan D. (1974) "Nature/Nurture Revisited: A Review of the Biological Bases of Conflict," *Journal of Conflict Resolution* 18 (June): 285–335.

Nelson, Vaughn. (2009) "SOLUTIONS: Curbing U.S. dependence on foreign oil," *The Washington Times.* Available at: http://washingtontimes.com/news/2009/sep/20/solutions-curbing-us-dependence-foreign-oil//print/.

Neuman, Johanna. (1995–96) "The Media's Impact on International Affairs, Then and Now," *National Interest* 16 (Winter): 109–23.

Neumann, Iver B. (2007) "'A Speech That the Entire Ministry May Stand For,' or: Why Diplomats Never Produce Anything New," *International Political Sociology* 1 (June): 183–200.

Neumayer, Eric and Indra de Soysa. (2005) "Trade Openness, Foreign Direct Investment, and Child Labor," *World Development* 33(1): 43–63.

Newhouse, John. (2003) *Imperial America: The Bush Assault on World Order*. New York: Knopf.

Newell, Richard G. (2005) "The Hydrogen Economy," *Resources for the Future* 156 (Winter): 20–23.

Newsweek. (2008) "The United States Doesn't Have Any Oil," *Newsweek* (July 7/14): 44–45.

Nexon, Daniel H. (2009) "The Balance of Power in the Balance," *World Politics* 61: 330–359.

Nichols, John. (2002) "Enron's Global Crusade," *The Nation* (March 4) http://www.thenation.com/doc/20020304/nichols.

Niebuhr, Reinhold. (1947) *Moral Man and Immoral Society*. New York: Scribner's.

9/11 Commission. (2004) *Final Report of the National Commission on Terrorist Attacks upon the United States: The 9/11 Commission Report*. New York: Norton.

Norberg, Johan. (2006) "Three Cheers for Global Capitalism," pp. 52–60 in Robert M. Jackson (ed.), *Global Issues 05/06*. Dubuque, Iowa: McGraw-Hill/Dushkin.

Nossel, Suzanne. (2004) "Smart Power," *Foreign Affairs* 83 (March-April): 31–142.

Nye, Joseph S., Jr. (2008) "Soft Power and American Foreign Policy," pp. 29–43 in Eugene R. Wittkopf and James M. McCormick, eds., *The Domestic Sources of American Foreign Policy*. Lanham, Md.: Rowman and Littlefield.

——— (2007) *Understanding International Conflicts*, 6th ed. New York: Pearson Longman.

——— (2005) *Power in the Global Information Age*. New York: Routledge.

——— (2004a) "America's Soft Learning Curve," pp. 31–34 in *The World in 2004*, London: Economist Newspapers.

——— (2004b) *Soft Power*. New York: Public Affairs.

——— (1990) *Bound to Lead: The Changing Nature of American Power*. New York: Basic Books.

Oatley, Thomas. (2009) *International Political Economy*, 5th edition. New York: Norton.

——— (2008) *International Political Economy*, 3rd ed. New York: Pearson Longman.

——— (2004) *International Political Economy*. New York: Pearson Longman.

Oberdorfer, Don. (1991) *The Turn*. New York: Poseidon.

O'Brien, Conor Cruise. (1977) "Liberty and Terrorism," *International Security* 2 (Fall): 56–67.

Obuah, Emmanuel. (2006) "Combating Global Trafficking in Persons," *International Politics* 43 (April): 241–265.

OECD. (2007a) *Trends and Recent Developments in Foreign Direct Investment*. Paris: Organisation for Economic Co-operation and Development.

——— (2007b) *World Investment Report*. Paris: Organisation for Economic Co-operation and Development.

——— (2005) *Distribution of Aid by Development Assistance Committee (DAC) Members*. Paris: Organization for Economic Cooperation and Development.

Oneal, John R., and Bruce Russett. (1999) "Assessing the Liberal Peace with Alternative Specifications: Trade Still Reduces Conflict," *Journal of Peace Research* 36 (July): 423–42.

Oneal, John R., and Jaroslav Tir. (2006). *International Studies Quarterly* 50 (December): 755–779.

Onuf, Nicholas. (2002) "Worlds of Our Making: The Strange Career of Constructivism in International Relations," pp. 119–41 in Donald J. Puchala (ed.), *Visions of International Relations*. Columbia: University of South Carolina Press.

——— (1989) *World of Our Making: Rules and Rule in Social Theory and International Relations*. Columbia: University of South Carolina Press.

——— (1982) "Global Law-Making and Legal Thought," pp. 1–82 in Nicholas Greenwood Onuf (ed.), *Law-Making in the Global Community*. Durham, N.C.: Carolina Academic Press.

Opello, Walter C., Jr., and Stephen J. Rosow. (2004) *The Nation-State and Global Order*, 2nd ed. Boulder, Colo.: Lynne Rienner.

O'Reilly, Kelly. (2005) "U.S. Arms Sales and Purchaser's Governments," Occasional Paper, Walker Institute of International Studies. Columbia: University of South Carolina.

O'Reilly, Marc J., and Wesley B. Renfro. (2007) "Evolving Empire," *International Studies Perspectives* 8 (May): 137–151.

Organski, A. F K., and Jacek Kugler. (1980) *The War Ledger*. Chicago: University of Chicago Press.

O'Rourke, Lindsey. (2009) "V-22 Osprey Tilt-Rotor Aircraft: Background and Issues for Congress," Washington, D.C.: Congressional Research Service. (July 14).

——— (2008) "The Woman Behind the Bomb," *International Herald Tribune* (August 5): Op-Ed.

Ostler, Nicholas. (2003) "A Loss for Words," *Foreign Policy* (November-December): 30–31.

Ostry, Sylvia. (2001) Review of *The Challenge of Global Capitalism* by Robert Gilpin, *American Political Science Review* 95 (March): 257–58.

O'Sullivan, John. (2005) "In Defense of Nationalism," *The National Interest* 78 (Winter): 33–40.

Ottaway, Marina (2001) "Reluctant Missionaries," *Foreign Policy* (July/August) 44–55. Owen, John M., IV. (2005) "When Do Ideologies Produce Alliances?" *International Studies Quarterly* 49 (March): 73–99.

Owen, David. (2009) "Comment: Economy vs. Environment," *The New Yorker* (March 30): 21–22.

Pacala, Stephen, and Robert Socolow. (2004) "Stabilization Wedges: Solving the Climate Problem for the Next 50 Years with Current Technologies," *Science* 305 (August): 968–972.

Packenham, Robert. (1992) *The Dependency Movement*. Cambridge, Mass.: Harvard University Press.

Palmer, Glenn, and T. Clifton Morgan. (2007) "Power Transition, the Two-Good Theory, and Neorealism: A Comparison with Comments on Recent U.S. Foreign Policy," *International Interactions* 33 (July/September): 329–346.

Panagariya, Arvind. (2003) "Think Again: International Trade," *Foreign Policy* (November-December): 20–28.

Panitch, Leo. (2009) "Thoroughly Modern Marx," *Foreign Policy* (May-June): 140–143.

Pape, Robert A. (2005a) *Dying to Win: The Strategic Logic of Suicide Terror*. New York: Random House.

——— (2005b) "Soft Balancing Against the United States," *International Security* 30 (Summer): 7–45.

Parker, Georg, Guy Dinmore and Alan Beattie. (2009) "Leaders Seek Trade Deal by 2010," *Financial Times* (July 9, 2009). Available at: http://www.ft.com/cms/s/0/f42cf9e2-6c7e-11de-a6e6-00144feabdc0.html?nclick_check=1.

Parker, Owen, and James Brassett. (2005) "Contingent Borders, Ambiguous Ethics: Migrants in (International) Political Theory," *International Studies Quarterly* 49 (June): 233–53.

Parry, Clive. (1968) "The Function of Law in the International Community," pp. 1–54 in Max Søørensen (ed.), *Manual of Public International Law*. New York: St. Martin's.

Patterson, Eric. (2005) "Just War in the 21st Century: Reconceptualizing Just War Theory after September 11," *International Politics* 42 (March): 116–34.

Paul, T. V., G. John Ikenberry, and John A. Hall (eds.). (2003) *The Nation-State in Question*. Princeton, N.J.: Princeton University Press.

Pauly, Louis W. (2005) "The Political Economy of International Financial Crises," pp. 176–203 in John Ravenhill (ed.), *Global Political Economy.* New York: Oxford University Press.

Paust, Jordan J. (2008) *Beyond the Law.* New York: Cambridge University Press.

—— (2007) *Beyond the Law: The Bush Administration's Unlawful Responses in the War on Terror.* New York: Cambridge University Press.

Payne, Richard J. (2007) *Global Issues.* New York: Pearson Longman.

Peirce, Neal R. (2000) "Keep an Eye on 'Citistates' Where Economic Action Is," *International Herald Tribune* (January 11): 8.

—— (1997) "Does the Nation-State Have a Future?" *International Herald Tribune* (April 4): 9.

Pells, Richard. (2002) "Mass Culture Is Now Exported from All Over to All Over," *International Herald Tribune* (July 12): 9.

Peterson, Erik. (1998) "Looming Collision of Capitalisms?" pp. 296–307 in Charles W Kegley, Jr., and Eugene R. Wittkopf (eds.), *The Global Agenda,* 5th ed. New York: McGrawHill.

Peterson, V. Spike. (2003) *A Critical Rewriting of Global Political Economy: Retrospective, Productive and Virtual Economies.* London: Routledge.

Peterson, V. Spike, and Anne Sisson Runyan. (2009) *Global Gender Issues in the New Millennium.* 3rd edition. Westview Press.—(1993) *Global Gender Issues.* Boulder, Colo.: Westview Press. Petras, James. (2004) *The New Development Politics.* Williston, Vt.: Ashgate.

Petras, James, and Henry Veltmeyer. (2004) *A System in Crisis: The Dynamics of Free Market Capitalism.* London: Palgrave.

Pfaff, William. (2001a) "Anti-Davos Forum is Another Sign of a Sea Change," *International Herald Tribune* (July 25): 6.

—— (2001b) "The Question of Hegemony," *Foreign Affairs* 80 (January-February): 50–64.

Pfetsch, Frank L. (1999) "Globalization: A Threat and a Challenge for the State," paper presented at the European Standing Conference on International Studies, Vienna, September 11–13.

Pham, J. Peter. (2005) "Killing to Make a Killing," *The National Interest* 81 (Fall): 132–37.

Phillips, Nicola (ed.). (2005) *Globalizing Political Economy.* London: Palgrave.

Piasecki, Bruce. (2007) "A Social Responsibility Revolution in the Global Marketplace," *Christian Science Monitor* (August 9): 9.

Pickering, Jeffrey, and Mark Peceny. (2006) "Forging Democracy At Gunpoint," *International Studies Quarterly* 50 (September): 539–559.

Pickering, Jeffrey. (2009). "The International Military Intervention Dataset: An Updated Resource for Conflict Scholars" *Journal of Peace Research* 46(4): 589–599.

Pipes, Richard. (1977) "Why the Soviet Union Thinks It Could Fight and Win a Nuclear War," *Commentary* 26 (July): 21–34.

Pogge, Thomas. (2005) "World Poverty and Human Rights," *Ethics & International Affairs* 19 (No. 1): 1–7.

Polsky, Andrew. (2010) "Staying the Course: Presidential Leadership, Military Stalemate, and Strategic Inertia." *Perspectives on Politics.* 8(1): 127–139.

Porter, Gareth. (1995). "Environmental Security as a National Security Issue," pp. 215–22 in Gearoid O Tauthail, Simon Dalby and Paul Routledge (eds.), *The Geopolitics Reader,* New York, NY: Routledge.

Posen, Barry R. (2004) "The Security Dilemma and Ethnic Conflict," pp. 357–66 in Karen A. Mingst and Jack L. Snyder (eds.), *Essential Readings in World Politics,* 2nd ed. New York: Norton.

Potts, Malcom and Martha Campbell. (2009) "Sex Matters," *Foreign Policy* (July/August): 30–31.

Pouliot, Vincent. (2007) "'Sobjectivism': Toward a Constructivist Methodology," *International Studies Quarterly* 51: 359–84.

Pound, Edward T. and Danielle Knight. (2006) "Cleaning Up the World Bank," *US News & World Report* 140(12): 40–51.

Powell, Colin L. (1995) *My American Journey.* New York: Random House.

Powell, Emilia Justyna and Staton, Jeffrey K. (2009). " Domestic Judicial Institutions and Human Rights Treaty Violation," *International Studies Quarterly.* 53: 149–174.

Power, Jonathan. (2004) "United Nations—Much Maligned, But Much Needed," *International Herald Tribune* (February 26): 6.

Power, Samantha. (2008) *Chasing the Flame: Sergio Vieira de Mello and the Fight to Save the World.* Penguin Press.

Powers, Thomas. (1994) "Downwinders: Some Casualties of the Nuclear Age," *Atlantic Monthly* (March): 119–24.

Prakash, Aseem, and Matthew Potoski. (2007) "Investing Up," *International Studies Quarterly* 51 (September): 723–744.

Prempeh, E. Osei Kwadwo, Joseph Mensah, and Senyo B. S. K. Adjibolosoo. (eds.). (2005) *Globalization and the Human Factor.* Burlington, Ver.: Ashgate.

Prestowitz, Clyde. (2005) *Three Billion New Capitalists.* New York: Basic Books.

—— (2003). *Rogue Nation: American Unilateralism and the Failure of Good Intentions.* New York: Basic Books/Perseus.

Price, Richard. (2003) "Transnational Civil Society and Advocacy in World Politics," *World Politics* 55 (July): 519–606.

Price, Richard, and Christian Reus-Smit. (1998) "Dangerous Liaisons? Critical International Theory and Constructivism," *European Journal of International Relations* 4 (3): 259–294.

Puchala, Donald J. (2003) *Theory and History in International Relations.* New York: Routledge.

Puchala, Donald, Katie Verlin Laatikainen, and Roger A. Coate. (2007) *United Nations Politics.* Upper Saddle River, NJ: Prentice Hall.

Puddington, Arch. (2010) "Freedom in the World 2010: Erosion of Freedom Intensifies." Washington, D.C. Freedom House. Available at http://www.freedomhouse.org/template.cfm?page=130&year=2010.

Putnam, Robert D. (1988) "Diplomacy and Domestic Politics: The Logic of Two-Level Games," *International Organization* 42 (Summer): 427–60.

Quester, George H. (1992) "Conventional Deterrence," pp. 31–51 in Gary L. Guertner, Robert Haffa, Jr., and George Quester (eds.), *Conventional Forces and the Future of Deterrence.* Carlisle Barracks, Pa.: U.S. Army War College.

Quinn, David, Jonathan Wilkenfeld, Kathleen Smarick, and Victor Asal. (2006) "Power Play: Mediation in Symmetric and Asymmetric International Crises," *International Interactions* 32 (December): 441–470.

Quinn, Jane Bryant. (2002) "Iraq: It's the Oil, Stupid," *Newsweek* (September 30): 43.

Quinn, J. Michael, T. David Mason and Mehmet Gurses. (2007) "Sustaining the Peace: Determinants of Civil War Recurrence," *International Interactions* 33 (April/June): 167–193.

Quirk, Matthew. (2007) "The Mexican Connection," *The Atlantic* (April) 26–27.

Raasch, Chuck. (2009) "Obama is America's first global president, historian says," *USA Today News: Opinions* (April 7). Available at: http://www.usatoday.com/news/opinion/columnist/raasch/2009-04-07-newpolitics_N.htm.

Rabin, Matthew. (1993) "Incorporating Fairness Into Game Theory and Economics," *The American Economic Review* 83 (May): 1281–1302.

Rabkin, Jeremy A. (2005) *Law Without Nations? Why Constitutional Government Requires Sovereign States.* Princeton, N.J.: Princeton University Press.

Raloff, Janet. (2006) "The Ultimate Crop Insurance," pp. 166–68 in Robert J. Griffiths (ed.), *Global Issues 05/06.* Dubuque, Iowa: McGraw-Hill/Dushkin.

Ramcharan, Bertrand. (2010) *Preventive Human Rights Strategies.* New York: Routledge.

Rapkin, David, and William R. Thompson, with Jon A. Christopherson. (1989) "Bipolarity and Bipolarization in the Cold War Era," *Journal of Conflict Resolution* 23 (June): 261–95.

Rasler, Karen A., and William R. Thompson. (2006) "Contested Territory, Strategic Rivalries, and Conflict Escalation," *International Studies Quarterly* 50 (March): 145–167.

—— (2005) *Puzzles of the Democratic Peace: Theory, Geopolitics, and the Transformation of World Politics.* London: Palgrave Macmillan.

Ravallion, Martin. (2004) "Pessimistic on Poverty?" *Economist* (April 10): 65.

Ravenhill, John. (2008) *Global Political Economy.* New York: Oxford University Press.

—— (2004) *Global Political Economy.* New York: Oxford University Press.

Ray, James Lee. (1995) *Democracy and International Conflict: An Evaluation of the Democratic Peace Proposition.* Columbia: University of South Carolina Press.

Raymond, Gregory A. (2003) "The Evolving Strategies of Political Terrorism," pp. 71–105 in Charles W. Kegley, Jr. (ed.), *The New Global Terrorism.* Upper Saddle River, N.J.: Prentice Hall.

—— (1999) "Necessity in Foreign Policy," *Political Science Quarterly* 113 (Winter): 673–88.

Redfield, Robert. (1962) *Human Nature and the Study of Society,* vol. 1. Chicago: University of Illinois Press.

Regan, Patrick M., and Aida Paskevicute. (2003) "Women's Access to Politics and Peaceful States," *Journal of Peace Research* 40 (March): 287–302.

Reich, Robert B. (2007a) "How Capitalism is Killing Democracy," *Foreign Policy* (September/October) 39–42.

Reich, Robert B. (2007b) *Supercapitalism.* New York: Knopf.

Reid, T. R. (2004) *The United States of Europe: The New Superpower and the End of American Supremacy.* New York: Penguin.

Reimann, Kim D. (2006) "A View from the Top: International Politics, Norms and the Worldwide Growth of NGOs," *International Studies Quarterly* 50: 45–67.

Reinares, Fernando. (2002) "The Empire Rarely Strikes Back," *Foreign Policy* (January/February): 92–94.

Reiter, Dan. (2003) "Exploring the Bargaining Model of War," *Perspectives on Politics* 1 (March): 27–43.

Renshon, Jonathan and Stanley A. Renshon. (2008) "The Theory and Practice of Foreign Policy Decision Making," *Political Psychology* 29: 509–536.

Reuveny, Rafael, and William R. Thompson. (2008) " Observations on the North-South Divide," pp. 1–16 in Rafael Reuveny and William R. Thompson (eds.), *North and South in the World Political Economy.* Malden, MA: Blackwell.

—— (2004) "World Economic Growth, Systemic Leadership and Southern Debt Crises," *Journal of Peace Research* 41 (January): 5–24.

Reuveny, Rafael and William R. Thompson, eds. (2008) *North and South in the World Political Economy.* Malden, Mass.: Blackwell.

Revel, Jean-Francois. (2004) *Anti-Americanism.* San Francisco: Encounter.

Rich, Frank. (2004) "The Corporate-Military Whiz Kids," *International Herald Tribune* (January 24–25): 8.

Ridley, Matt. (2003) *Nature vs. Nurture: Genes, Experiences and What Makes Us Human.* New York: HarperCollins.

Riedel, Bruce. (2007) "Al Qaeda Strikes Back," *Foreign Affairs* 86 (May/June) 24–40.

Rieff, David. (2005) *At the Point of a Gun: Democratic Dreams and Armed Intervention.* New York: Simon & Schuster.

—— (1999) "The Precarious Triumph of Human Rights," *New York Times Magazine* (August 8): 36–41.

Rifkin, Jeromy. (2004) *The European Dream: How Europe's Vision of the Future is Quietly Eclipsing the American Dream.* New York: Tarcher.

Riggs, Robert E., and Jack C. Plano. (1994) *The United Nations,* 2nd ed. Belmont, Calif.: Wadsworth.

Riker, William H. (1962) *The Theory of Political Coalitions.* New Haven, Conn.: Yale University Press.

Riley-Smith, Jonathan. (1995) "Religious warriors," *Economist* (December 23/January 1): 63–67.

Ripsman, Norrin M. (2005) "Two Stages of Transition from a Region of War to a Region of Peace," *International Studies Quarterly* 49 (December): 669–93.

Ripsman, Norrin M., and T. V. Paul. (2005) "Globalization and the National Security State," *International Studies Review* (June): 199–227.

Roche, Douglas. (2007) "Our Greatest Threat," pp. 137–140 in Robert M. Jackson, ed., *Global Issues 06/07.* Dubuque, Iowa: McGraw-Hill Contemporary Learning Series.

Rochester, J. Martin. (2006) *Between Peril and Promise: The Politics of International Law.* Washington, D.C.: CQ Press.

Rodrik, Dani. (2008) *One Economics, Many Recipes: Globalization, Institutions, and Economic Growth.* Princeton, NJ: Princeton University Press.

—— (1999) *The New Global Economy and Developing Countries.* Washington, D.C.: Overseas Development Council.

Rogoff, Kenneth. (2003) "The IMF Strikes Back," *Foreign Policy* 134 (Jan/Feb): 38–46.

Rosato, Sebastian. (2003) "The Flawed Logic of Democratic Peace Theory." *The American Political Science Review* 97(4): 585–602.

Rose, Gideon. (2005) "The Bush Administration Gets Real," *International Herald Tribune* (August 19): 7.

Rosecrance, Richard. (2005) "Merger and Acquisition," *The National Interest* 80 (Summer): 65–73.

—— (1997) "Economics and National Security," pp. 209–38 in Richard Shultz, Roy Godson, and George Quester (eds.), *Security Studies for the Twenty-First Century.* New York: Brassey's.

—— (1992) "A New Concert of Powers," *Foreign Affairs* 71 (Spring): 64–82.

Rosenau, James N. (1995) "Security in a Turbulent World," *Current History* 94 (May): 193–200.

—— (1980) *The Scientific Study of Foreign Policy.* New York: Nichols.

Rosenberg, Justin. (2005) "Globalization Theory: A Post Mortem," *International Politics* 42 (March): 2–74.

Rosenberg, Shawn W. (1988) *Reason, Ideology and Politics.* Princeton, N.J.: Princeton University Press.

Rosenthal, Elisabeth. (2005) "Global Warming: Adapting to a New Reality," *International Herald Tribune* (September 12): 1, 5.

Rosenthal, Joel H. (1991) *Righteous Realists.* Baton Rouge: Louisiana State University Press.

Ross, Dennis. (2007) *Statecraft and How to Restore America's Standing in the World.* New York: Farrar, Straus and Giroux.

Ross, Michael L. (2004) "What Do We Know about Natural Resources and Civil War?" *Journal of Peace Research* 41 (May): 337–56.

Ross, Philip E. (1997) "The End of Infantry?" *Forbes* (July 7): 182–85.

Rosset, Peter. (1999) "Biotechnology Won't Feed the World," *International Herald Tribune* (September 2): 8.

Rostow, W. W. (1960) *The Stages of Economic Growth.* Cambridge: Cambridge University Press.

Rothkopf, David J. (2005) *Running the World.* New York: Public Affairs.

Rousseau, David L. (2006) *Identifying Threats and Threatening Identities: The Social Construction of Realism and Liberalism*. Stanford, Calif.: Stanford University Press.

Rousseau, Jean Jaques. (1976). *Social Contract*. London: Penguin Books.

Rubenstein, Richard E. (2003) "The Psycho-Political Sources of Terrorism," pp. 139–50 in Charles W. Kegley, Jr. (ed.), *The New Global Terrorism*. Upper Saddle River, N.J.: Prentice Hall.

Rubin, Nancy. (1999) "It's Official: All of the World Is Entitled to Democracy," *International Herald Tribune* (May 18): 8.

Rudolph, Christopher. (2005) "Sovereignty and Territorial Borders in a Global Age," *International Studies Review* 7 (March): 1–20.

Ruggie, John Gerald. (1998) "What Makes the World Hang Together? Neo-Utilitarianism and the Social Constructivist Challenge," *International Organization* 52 (Autumn): 855–885.

—— (1983) "Continuity and Transformation in the World Polity: Toward a Neorealist Synthesis," *World Politics* 35 (January): 261–85.

Rummel, Rudolph J. (1994) *Death by Government*. New Brunswick, N.J.: Transaction.

Runge, Carlisle Ford, and Carlisle Piehl Runge. (2010) "Against the Grain: Why Failing to Complete the Green Revolution Could Bring the Next Famine." *Foreign Affairs* 89(1) (January/February): 8–14.

Russett, Bruce. (2005) "Bushwhacking the Democratic Peace," *International Studies Perspectives* 6 (November): 395–408.

—— (2001) "How Democracy, Interdependence, and International Organizations Create a System for Peace," pp. 232–42 in Charles W. Kegley, Jr., and Eugene Wittkopf (eds.), *The Global Agenda*, 6th ed. Boston: McGraw-Hill.

(2001) *Triangulating Peace: Democracy, Trade, and International Organizations*. New York: Norton.

Russett, Bruce and John Oneal. (1997) "The Classic Liberals Were Right: Democracy, Interdependence, and Conflict, 1950–1985," *International Studies Quarterly* 41 (2): 267–294.

Rynning, Sten, and Jens Ringsmose. (2008) "Why are Revisionist States Revisionist? Reviving Classical Realism as an Approach to Understanding International Change," *International Politics* 45 (January): 19–39.

Sabastenski, Anna (ed.). (2005) *Patterns of Global Terrorism* 1985–2004. Great Barrington, Mass.: Berkshire.

Sachs, Jeffrey. (2005) *The End of Poverty*. New York: Penguin Press.

Sadowaski. Yahya. (1998) "Ethnic Conflict," *Foreign Policy* 112 (Summer): 12–23.

Sagan, Carl. (1989) "Understanding Growth Rates: The Secret of the Persian Chessboard," *Parade* (February 14): 14.

—— (1988) "The Common Enemy," *Parade* (February 7): 4–7.

Sagan, Carl, and Richard Turco. (1993) "Nuclear Winter in the Post-Cold War Era," *Journal of Peace Research* 30 (November): 369–73.

Sageman, Marc. (2008) *Leaderless Jihad: Terror Networks in the Twenty-First Century*. Philadelphia: University of Pennsylvania Press.

—— (2004) *Understanding Terror Networks*. Philadelphia: University of Pennsylvania Press.

Salam, Reihan. (2009) "The Death of Macho," *Foreign Policy* (July/August): 65–71.

Sambanis, Nicholas. (2004) "What Is Civil War?" *Journal of Conflict Resolution* 48 (December): 814–58.

Samin, Amir. (1976) *Unequal Development*. New York: Monthly Review Press.

Samuelson, Robert J. (2009) "A Global Free-for-All?" *Newsweek* (April 13): 25.

—— (2008) "Learning From the Oil Shock." *Newsweek* (June 23): 39.

—— (2007) "The Expanding Power of Capital," Columbia, S.C. *The State* (August 8): A7.

—— (2006) "This Year Could Mark the End of Pax Americana," Columbia, S.C, *The State* (December 19): A9.

—— (2005a) "A Future We Can't Afford," Columbia, S.C, *The State* (April 8): A13.

—— (2005b) "The Dawn of a New Oil Era?" *Newsweek* (April 4): 37.

—— (2002a) "'Digital Divide' Facing Poor Looks Like Fiction," Columbia, S.C, *The State* (April 3): A13.

—— (2002b) "The New Coin of the Realm," *Newsweek* (January 7): 38.

Sandler, Todd. (2010) "Terrorism and Policy: Introduction." *Journal of Conflict Resolution*. 54(2): 203–213.

Sandler, Todd and Walter Enders. (2007) "Applying Analytical Methods to Study Terrorism," *International Studies Perspectives* 8 (August): 287–302.

Sands, Phillippe. (2005) Lawless World: America and the Making and Breaking of Global Rules. New York: Viking Penguin.

Sang-Hun, Choe. (2008) "Hundreds Injured in South Korean Beef Protest," *International Herald Tribune* (June 29).

Sanger, David E. (2009) "Pakistan's Arsenal Raises U.S. Alarms," *International Herald Tribune* (January 10–11): 1, 5.

—— (2009b) "Obama's Worst Pakistan Nightmare," *New York Times Magazine* (January 11).

—— (2005) "The New Global Dance Card," *New York Times* (September 18): Section 4, 3.

—— (1998) "Contagion Effect: A Guide to Modern Domino Theory," *New York Times* (August 2): Section 1, 4–5.

Saul, John Ralstom. (2004) "The Collapse of Globalism and the Rebirth of Nationalism," *Harper's* 308 (March): 33–43.

Saurin, Julian. (2000) "Globalization, Poverty, and the Promises of Modernity," pp. 204–29 in Sarah Owen Vandersluis and Paris Yeros (eds.), *Poverty in World Politics*. New York: St. Martin's.

Saxton, Gregory D. (2005) "Repression, Grievances, Mobilization, and Rebellion," *International Interactions* 31 (No. 1): 87–116.

Schelling, Thomas C. (2006) *Strategies of Commitment and Other Essays*. Cambridge, Mass.: Harvard University Press.

—— (1978) *Micromotives and Macrobehavior*. New York: Norton.

—— (1966) *Arms and Influence*. New Haven, Conn.: Yale University Press.

Schlesinger, Arthur, Jr. (1997) "Has Democracy a Future?" *Foreign Affairs* 76 (September-October): 2–12.

—— (1986) *The Cycles of American History*. Boston: Houghton Mifflin.

Schmidt, Blake and Elisabeth Malkin. (2009) "Leftist wins Salvadoran Election for President" *International Herald Tribune* (March 19): 5.

Schneider, Gerald, Katherine Barbieri, and Nils Petter Gleditsch (eds.). (2003) *Globalization and Armed Conflict*. Lanham, Md.: Rowman & Littlefield.

Schott, Jeffrey. (1983) "The GATT Ministerial: A Post-Mortem," *Challenge* 26 (2): 40–45.

Schraeder, Peter J. (ed.). (2002) *Exporting Democracy*. Boulder, Colo.: Lynne Rienner.

Schroeder, Paul W. (1989) "The Nineteenth-Century System," *Review of International Studies* 15 (April): 135–53.

Schuler, Corinna. (1999) "Helping Children Warriors Regain Their Humanity," *Christian Science Monitor* (October 20): 1, 12–13.

Schulz, William F. (2001*) In Our Own Best Interest: How Defending Human Rights Benefits Us All*. Boston: Beacon Press.

Schwarz, Benjamin. (2005) "Managing China's Rise," *Atlantic Monthly* 295 (June): 27–28.

Schweller, Randall L. (2004) "Unanswered Threats: A Neoclassical Realist Theory of Underbalancing," *International Security* 29 (Fall): 159–201.

—— (1999) Review of *From Wealth to Power* by Fareed Zakaria, *American Political Science Review* 93 (June 1999): 497–99.

Scowcroft, Brent, and Samuel R. Berger. (2005) "In the Wake of War: Getting Serious About Nation-Building," *The National Interest* 81 (Fall): 49–60.

Seck, Manadon Manosour. (1999) "Shrinking Forests," *Christian Science Monitor* (May 3): 9.

Secor, Laura. (2005) *Sands of Empire*. New York: Simon and Schuster.

Selck, Torsten J. (2004) "On the Dimensionality of European Union Legislative Decision-Making," *Journal of Theoretical Politics* 16 (April): 203–22.

Sen, Amartya. (2006) *Identity and Violence: The Illusion of Destiny*. New York: Norton.

Sending, Ole Jacob, and Iver B. Neumann. (2006) "Governance to Governmentality: Analyzing NGOs, States, and Power," *International Studies Quarterly* 50: 651–672.

Sengupta, Somini. (2005) "Hunger for Energy Transforms How India Operates," *New York Times International* (June 5): Section 4, 3.

Senese, Paul D., and John A. Vasquez. (2008) *The Steps to War*. Princeton, N.J.: Princeton University Press.

Serfaty, Simon. (2003) "Europe Enlarged, America Detached?" *Current History* (March): 99–102.

Sezgin, Yüksel. (2005) "Taking a New Look at State-Directed Industrialization," *International Studies Review* 7 (June): 323–325.

Shaffer, Gregory. (2009) "The Future of the WTO," University of Chicago Law School Faculty Blog, Feb 23, 2009. Available at: http://uchicago-law.typepad.com/faculty/2009/02/future-of-the-wtorelevance.html.

Shah, Timothy Samuel. (2004) "The Bible and the Ballot Box: Evangelicals and Democracy in the 'Global South,'" *SAIS Review of International Affairs* 24 (Fall): 117–32.

Shane, Scott. (2005) "The Beast That Feeds on Boxes: Bureaucracy," *New York Times* (April 10): Section 4, 3.

Shannon, Megan. (2009) "Preventing War and Providing the Peace? International Organizations and the Management of Territorial Disputes," *Conflict Management and Peace Science* 26 (2): 144–163.

Shannon, Thomas Richard. (1989) *An Introduction to the World-System Perspective*. Boulder, Colo.: Westview.

Shanker, Thom and Steven Erlanger. (2009) "Afghanistan Presents NATO a Choice of Fusion or Fracture," *International Herald Tribune* (April 3): 1.

Shapin, Steven. (2007) "What Else is New," *The New Yorker* (May 14): 144–148.

Shapiro, Ian. (2008) *Futurecast: How Superpowers, Populations, and Globalization Will Change the Way You Live and Work*. St. Martin's Press.

—— (2007) *Containment: Rebuilding a Strategy Against Global Terrorism*. Princeton, N.J.: Princeton University Press.

Sharp, Travis. (2009) "Fiscal Year 2010 Pentagon Defense Spending Request: February "Topline"," Center For Arms Control and Non-Proliferation. (February 26). Available at: http://www.armscontrolcenter.org/policy/securityspending/articles/022609_fy10_topline_growth_decade/.

Sheehan, Michael. (1996) "A Regional Perspective on the Globalization Process," *Korean Journal of Defense Analysis* 8 (Winter): 53–74.

Sheffer, Gabriel. (2003) *Diaspora Politics: At Home Abroad*. Cambridge: Cambridge University Press.

Shiffman, Gary M. (2006) *Economic Instruments of Security Policy*. Basingstoke, U.K.: Palgrave MacMillan.

Shlapentorkh, Vladmir, Eric Shirae, and Josh Woods (eds.). (2005) *America: Sovereign Defender or Cowboy Nation?* Burlington, Ver.: Ashgate.

Shreeve, Jamie. (2005) "The Stem-Cell Debate," *New York Times Magazine* (April 10): 42–47.

Shultz, Richard H., Jr., Roy Godson, and George H. Quester (eds.). (1997) *Security Studies for the Twenty-First Century*. New York: Brassey's.

Shultz, Richard H., Jr., and William J. Olson. (1994) *Ethnic and Religious Conflict*. Washington, D.C.: National Strategy Information Center.

Siegel, Martin J. (1983) "Survival," *USA Today* 112 (August): 1–2.

Siegle, Joseph T, Michael M. Weinstein, and Morton H. Halperin. (2004) "Why Democracies Excel," *Foreign Affairs* 83 (September-October): 57–71.

Sikkink, Kathryn. (2008). "Transnational Politics, International relations Theory and Human Rights," pp. 172–179 in Karen A. Mingst and Jack L. Snyder (eds.), *Essential Readings in World Politics*, 3rd ed. New York: Norton.

Simmons, Beth A., and Zachary Elkins. (2004) "The Globalization of Liberalization: Policy Diffusion in the International Political Economy," *American Political Science Review* 98 (February): 171–89.

Simmons, Beth A. and Richard H. Steinberg. (2007) *International Law and International Relations*. New York: Cambridge University Press.

Simon, Herbert A. (1997) *Models of Bounded Rationality*. Cambridge, Mass.: MIT Press.

—— (1957) *Models of Man*. New York: Wiley.

Singer, Hans W, and Javed A. Ansari. (1988) *Rich and Poor Countries*, 4th ed. London: Unwin Hyman.

Singer, David. (2010) "Migrant Remittances and Exchange Rate Regimes in the Developing World." *American Political Science Review* 104(2) (May): 307–323.

Singer, J. David. (2000) "The Etiology of Interstate War," pp. 3–21 in John A. Vasquez (ed.), *What Do We Know About War?* Lanham, Md.: Rowman & Littlefield.

—— (1991) "Peace in the Global System," pp. 56–84 in Charles W. Kegley, Jr. (ed.), *The Long Postwar Peace*. New York: HarperCollins.

—— (ed.). (1968) *Quantitative International Politics*. New York: Free Press.

Singer, Max. (1999) "The Population Surprise," *Atlantic Monthly* (August): 22–25.

Singer, Max, and Aaron Wildavsky. (1993) *The Real World Order: Zones of Peace/Zones of Turmoil*. Chatham, N.J.: Chatham House.

Singer, P.W. (2010) "We, Robot: Is it dangerous to let drones fight our wars for us?" *Slate (May)*. Available at: http://www.slate.com/id/2253692.

—— (2009a) "Robots at War: The New Battlefield," *The Wilson Quarterly* (Winter).

—— (2009b) Wired for War: The Robotics Revolution and Conflict in the 21st Century. The Penguin Press.

Singer, Peter. (2004) *One World: The Ethics of Globalization*, 2nd ed. New Haven, Conn.: Yale University Press.

SIPRI (Stockholm International Peace Research Institute). (2009) *SIPRI Yearbook*. New York: Oxford University Press.

—— (2008) *SIPRI Yearbook*. New York: Oxford University Press.

—— (2007) *SIPRI Yearbook*. New York: Oxford University Press.

—— (2006) *SIPRI Yearbook*. New York: Oxford University Press.

Sivard, Ruth Leger. (1996) *World Military and Social Expenditures* 1996. Washington, D.C.: World Priorities.

—— (1991) *World Military and Social Expenditures* 1991. Washington, D.C.: World Priorities.

Siverson, Randolph M., and Julian Emmons. (1991) "Democratic Political Systems and Alliance Choices," *Journal of Conflict Resolution* 35 (June): 285–306.

Skeldon, Ronald. (2010) "Managing Migration for Development Is Circular Migration the Answer?" *The Whitehead Journal of Diplomacy and International Relations* 11(1) (Winter/Spring): 21–33.

Skinner, E. Benjamin. (2010) "The New Slave Trade." *Time* (January 18): 54–57.

—— (2008) "A World Enslaved," *Foreign Policy* (March/April): 62–67.

Sklair, Leslie. (1991) *Sociology of the Global System*. Baltimore: Johns Hopkins University Press.

Slackman, Michael. (2008) "Dreams Stifled, Egypt's Young Turn to Islamic Fervor," *The New York Times* (February 17): 1.

Slater, David. (2005) *Geopolitics and the Post-Colonial: Rethinking North-South Relations*. Malden, Mass: Blackwell.

Slaughter, Anne-Marie. (2004a) *A New World Order*. Princeton, N.J.: Princeton University Press.

—— (2004b) "The Clear, Cruel Lessons of Iraq," *Financial Times* (April 8): 15.

—— (1997) "The Real New World Order," *Foreign Affairs* 76 (September-October): 183–97.

Small, Melvin, and J. David Singer. (1982) *Resort to Arms: International and Civil Wars, 1816–1980*. Beverly Hills, Calif.: Sage.

Smith, Adam. *An Inquiry into the Nature and Causes of the Wealth of Nations*. Edwin Cannan, ed. 1904. Library of Economics and Liberty. Available at: http://www.econlib.org/library/Smith/smWN.html.

Smith, Alastair, and Allan C. Stam. (2004) "Bargaining and the Nature of War," *Journal of Conflict Resolution* 48 (December): 783–813.

Smith, Jackie, and Timothy Patrick Moran. (2001) "WTO 101: Myths about the World Trade Organization," pp. 68–71 in Robert J. Griffiths (ed.), *Developing World 01/02*, Guilford, Conn.: Dushkin/McGraw-Hill.

Smith, Michael J. (2000) "Humanitarian Intervention Revisited," *Harvard International Review* 22 (April): 72–75.

Smith, Steve, and Patricia Owens. (2005) "Alternative Approaches to International Theory," pp. 271–93 in John Baylis and Steve Smith (eds.), *The Globalization of World Politics*, 3rd ed. New York: Oxford University Press.

Smith, Tony. (2007) *Pact With the Devil: Washington's Bid for World Supremacy and the Betrayal of the American Promise*. New York: Routledge.

Snidal, Duncan. (1993) "Relative Gains and the Pattern of International Cooperation," pp. 181–207 in David A. Baldwin (ed.), *Neorealism and Neoliberalism: The Contemporary Debate*. New York: Columbia University Press.

Snyder, David Pearce. (2006) "Five Meta-Trends Changing the World," pp. 13–17 in Robert M. Jackson (ed.), *Global Issues 05/06*. Dubuque, Iowa: McGraw-Hill/Dushkin.

Snyder, Glenn H. (1991) "Alliance Threats: A Neorealist First Cut," pp. 83–103 in Robert L. Rothstein (ed.), *The Evolution of Theory in International Relations*. Columbia: University of South Carolina Press.

—— (1984) "The Security Dilemma in Alliance Politics," *World Politics* 36 (July): 461–495.

Snyder, Glenn H., and Paul Diesing. (1977) *Conflict Among Nations*. Princeton, N.J.: Princeton University Press.

Snyder, Jack. (2005) "A Perfect Peace," *The Washington Post National Review Weekly Edition* (January 10): 33.

—— (2004) "One World, Rival Theories," *Foreign Policy* (November-December): 53–62.

Sobek, David. (2005) "Machiavelli's Legacy: Domestic Politics and International Conflict," *International Studies Quarterly* 49 (June): 179–204.

Sofaer, Abraham. (2010) "The Best Defense?: Preventive Force and International Security." *Foreign Affairs* 89(1) (January/February): 109–118.

Somavia, Juan. (2004) "For Too Many, Globalization Isn't Working," *International Herald Tribune* (February 27): 6.

Somit, Albert. (1990) "Humans, Chimps, and Bonobos: The Biological Bases of Aggression, War, and Peacemaking," *Journal of Conflict Resolution* 34 (September): 553–82.

Sørensen, Georg. (1995) "Four Futures," *Bulletin of the Atomic Scientists* 51 (July-August): 69–72.

Sorensen, Theodore C. (1963) *Decision Making in the White House*. New York: Columbia University Press.

Sorokin, Pitirim A. (1937) *Social and Cultural Dynamics*. New York: American Book.

Soros, George. (2003) *The Bubble of American Supremacy: Correcting the Misuse of American Power*. New York: Public Affairs.

Souva, Mark. (2004) "Institutional Similarity and Interstate Conflict," *International Interactions* 30 (July-September): 263–80.

Spar, Debora. (1999) "Foreign Investment and Human Rights." *Challenge* 42(1): 55–80.

Sperandei, Maria. (2006) "Bridging Deterrents and Compellence," *International Studies Review* 8 (June): 253–280.

Sprout, Harold and Margaret Sprout. (1965) *The Ecological Perspective on Human Affairs*. Princeton, N. J.: Princeton University Press.

Spykman, Nicholas. (1944) *The Geography of Peace*. New York: Harcourt Brace.

Stark, Sam. (2007) "Flaming Bitumen: Romancing the Algerian war," *Harper's* (February): 92–98.

Starr, Harvey. (2006) "International Borders," *SAIS Review* 26 (Winter/Spring): 3–10.

Steele, Brent J. (2007) "Liberal-Idealism: A Constructivist Critique," *International Studies Review* 9 (Spring): 23–52.

Steil, Benn and Manuel Hinds. (2009) *Money, Markets, and Sovereignty*. New Haven: Yale University Press.

Steinberg, Richard. (2009) "The Future of the WTO," University of Chicago Law School Faculty Blog, Feb 23, 2009. Available at: http://uchicago-law.typepad.com/faculty/2009/02/future-of-the-wtorelevance.html.

Stephenson, Carolyn M. (2000) "NGOs and the Principal Organs of the United Nations," pp. 270–94 in Paul Taylor and R. J. Groom (eds.), *The United Nations at the Millennium*. London: Continuum.

Stiglitz, Joseph. (2006) *Making Globalization Work*. New York: Norton.

—— (2003) *Globalization and Its Discontents*. New York: Norton.

Stiglitz, Joseph and Andrew Charlton. (2006) *Fair Trade for All: How Trade Can Promote Development*. New York: Oxford University Press.

Stiles, Kendall. (2005) "The ambivalent hegemon: Explaining the 'lost decade' in multilateral trade talks, 1948–1958," *Review of International Political Economy* 2 (1): 1–26.

Stohl, Rachel. (2005) "Fighting the Illicit Trafficking of Small Arms," *SAIS Review* 25 (Winter-Spring): 59–68.

Stopford, John. (2001) "Multinational Corporations," pp. 72–77 in Robert J. Griffiths (ed.), *Developing World 01/02*. Guilford, Conn.: Dushkin/McGraw-Hill.

Strang, David. (1991) "Global Patterns of Decolonization, 1500–1987," *International Studies Quarterly* 35 (December): 429–545.

—— (1990) "From Dependence to Sovereignty: An Event History Analysis of Decolonization 1870–1987," *American Sociological Review* 55 (December): 846–60.

Strange, Susan. (1997) *Casino Capitalism*. Manchester: Manchester University Press.

Streeten, Paul. (2001) "Human Development Index," pp. 367–68 in Joel Krieger (ed.), *The Oxford Companion to Politics of the World*, 2nd ed. New York: Oxford University Press.

Stross, Randall E. (2002) "The McPeace Dividend," *U.S. News & World Report* (April 1): 36.

Suganami, Hidemi. (1983) "A Normative Enquiry in International Relations," *Review of International Studies* 9: 35–54.

Summers, Lawrence H. (2006) "America Overdrawn," pp. 25–27 in Helen E. Purkitt (ed.), *World Politics 05/06*. Dubuque, Iowa: McGraw-Hill/Dushkin.

Surowiecki, James. (2007) "The Myth of Inevitable Progress," *Foreign Affairs* 86 (July/August): 132–139.

Sutherland, Peter. (2008) "Transforming Nations: How the WTO Boosts Economies and Opens Societies," *Foreign Affairs* 87 (March): 125–136.

Sylvester, Christine. (2002) *Feminist International Relations*. New York: Cambridge University Press.

Talbott, Strobe, and Nayan Chanda (eds.). (2002) *The Age of Terror*. New York: Basic Books.

Talmadge, Eric. (2010) "US-Japan security pact turns 50, faces new strains." *Associated Press* (June 22).

Tan, Sor-hoon (ed.). (2005) *Challenging Citizenship: Group Membership and Cultural Identity in a Global Age*. Burlington, Ver.: Ashgate.

Tarar, Ahmar. (2006) "Diversionary Incentives and the Bargaining Approach to War," *International Studies Quarterly* 50 (March): 169–188.

Tarrow, Sidney. (2006) *The New Transnational Activism*. New York: Cambridge University Press.

Tayler, Jeffrey. (2009) "'What Crisis?' Why Europe's Poorest Country is a Paragon of Financial Stability," *The Atlantic* 304 (1): 28–30.

Tellis, Ashley J. (2005) "A Grand Chessboard," *Foreign Policy* (January-February): 51–54.

Terlinden, Claire and Louise Hilditch. (2003) *Towards Effective Partnership: Untie Aid*. Brussels: Action Aid Alliance.

Teslik, Lee Hudson. (2008) "Council for Foreign Relations Backgrounder: Food Prices," Available at: http://www.cfr.org/publication/16662/price_of_food.html?breadcrumb=%2Findex.

Tessman, Brock, and Steve Chan. (2004) "Power Cycles, Risk Propensity and Great Power Deterrence," *Journal of Conflict Resolution* 48 (April): 131–53.

Tetlock, Philip. (2006) *Expert Political Judgment*. Princeton, N.J.: Princeton University Press.

Thachuk, Kimberley. (2005) "Corruption and International Security," *SAIS Review* 25 (Winter-Spring): 143–52.

Thakur, Ramesh. (1998) "Teaming Up to Make Human Rights a Universal Fact," *International Herald Tribune* (December 10): 10.

Thakur, Ramesh, and Steve Lee. (2000) "Defining New Goals for Diplomacy in the Twenty-First Century," *International Herald Tribune* (January 19): 8.

Thakur, Ramesh and Thomas G. Weiss. (2009) "United Nations 'Policy': An Argument with Three Illustrations," *International Studies Perspectives* 10: 18–35.

Thakur, Ramesh and Thomas G. Weiss, eds. (2009) *The United Nations and Global Governance: An Unfinished Journey*. Bloomington: Indiana University Press.

The Hunger Project. (2009) "Bolivia." Available at: http://www.thp.org/where_we_work/latin_america/bolivia?gclid=CP2K7cvIxpwCFVhJ2godk22zKg.

Thomas, Ward. (2005) "The New Age of Assassination," *SAIS Review* 25 (Winter-Spring): 27–39.

Thompson, Kenneth W. (1960) *Political Realism and the Crisis of World Politics*. Princeton, N.J.: Princeton University Press.

Thompson, Mark. (2007) "Flying Shame," *Time* (October 8): 34–41.

Thompson, William R. (ed.). (1999a) *Great Power Rivalries*. Columbia: University of South Carolina Press.

——— (1999b) "Why Rivalries Matter and What Great Power Rivalries Can Tell Us about World Politics," pp. 3–28 in William R. Thompson (ed.), *Great Power Rivalries*. Columbia: University of South Carolina Press.

——— (1988) *On Global War: Historical-Structural Approaches to World Politics*. Columbia: University of South Carolina Press.

Thrall, Trevor, and Jane Cramer, eds. (2009) *American Foreign Policy and the Politics of Fear: Threat Inflation since 9/11*. New York: Routledge.

Thurow, Lester C. (1999) *Building Wealth*. New York: HarperCollins.

——— (1998) "The American Economy in the Next Century," *Harvard International Review* 20 (Winter): 54–59.

Tickner, J. Ann. (2010) "Searching for the Princess?" pp. 36–41 in Russell Bova (ed.), *Readings on How the World Works*. New York: Pearson.

——— (2005) "What Is Your Research Program? Some Feminist Answers to International Relations Methodological Questions," *International Studies Quarterl y* 49 (March): 1–21.

——— (2002) *Gendering World Politics*. New York: Columbia University Press.

Tiessen, Rebecca. (2010) "Global Actors in Transnational and Virtual Spaces." *International Studies Review* 12: 301–304.

Tilford, Earl H., Jr. (1995) *The Revolution in Military Affairs*. Carlisle Barracks, Pa.: U.S. Army War College.

Tillema, Herbert K. (2008) *Overt Military Intervention in the Cold War Era*. Columbia: University of South Carolina Press.

——— (1994) "Cold War Alliance and Overt Military Intervention, 1945–1991," *International Interactions* 20 (No. 3): 249–78.

Tilly, Charles. (2003) *The Politics of Collective Violence*. Cambridge: Cambridge University Press.

Timmerman, Kenneth. (1991) *The Death Lobby: How the West Armed Iraq*. Boston: Houghton Mifflin.

Tocqueville, Alexis de. (1969 [1835]) *Democracy in America*. New York: Doubleday.

Todaro, Michael P. (2002) *Economic Development*, 8th ed. Reading, Mass.: Addison-Wesley.

——— (2000) *Economic Development*, 7th ed. Reading, Mass.: Addison-Wesley.

——— (1994) *Economic Development in the Third World*, 5th ed. New York: Longman.

Todd, Emmanuel. (2003) *After the Empire: The Breakdown of the American Order*. Translated by C. Jon Delogu. New York: Columbia University Press.

Toft, Monica Duffy. (2007) "Population Shifts and Civil War: A Test of Power Transition Theory," *International Interactions* 33 (July/September): 243–269.

Toner, Robin. (2002) "FBI Agent Gives Her Blunt Assessment," Columbia, S.C., *The State* (June 7): A5.

Toynbee, Arnold J. (1954) *A Study of History*. London: Oxford University Press.

Transparency International. (2009) "Corruption Perceptions Index," Available at: http://www.transparency.org/policy_research/surveys_indices/cpi.

Traub, James. (2005) "The New Hard-Soft Power," *New York Times Magazine* (January 30): 28–29.

Trumbull, Mark and Andrew Downie. (2007) "Great Global Shift to Service Jobs," *The Christian Science Monitor* (September): 1, 10.

Tuchman, Barbara W. (1984) *The March of Folly*. New York: Ballantine.

——— (1962) *The Guns of August*. New York: Dell.

Tures, John A. (2005) "Operation Exporting Freedom," *The Whitehead Journal of Diplomacy and International Relations* 6 (Winter-Spring): 97–111.

Tyler, Patrik E. (2001) "Seeing Profits, Russia Prepared to Become World's Nuclear Waste Dump," *International Herald Tribune* (May 28): 5.

UIA (Union of International Associations). (2006) *Yearbook of International Organizations*. 2005/2006, Edition 42. München: K.G. Saur.

——— (2005) *Yearbook of International Associations 2004/2005*, Vols. 1–5. Munich: K.G. Sauer.

Underhill, Geoffrey R. D., and Xiakoe *Zhang* (eds.). (2003) *International Financial Governance under Stress: Global Structures versus National Imperatives.* Cambridge: Cambridge University Press.

UNDP. (2010) *Human Development Report 2010.* New York: United Nations.

———— (2009) *Human Development Report 2009.* New York: United Nations.

———— (2008) *Human Development Report 2007/2008.* New York: United Nations Development Programme.

UNHCR. 2008. 2007 *Global Trends: Refugees, Asylum-seekers, Returnees, Internally Displaced and Stateless Persons.* Geneva: UN High Commissioner for Refugees.

———— (2007). *2006 Global Trends.* Geneva: UN High Commissioner for Refugees.

United Nations Conference on Trade and Development (UNCTAD). (2010) *World Investment Report 2010: Investing in a Low-Carbon Economy.* New York: United Nations.

———— (2009) *World Investment Prospects Survey 2009–2011.* New York and Geneva: United Nations.

———— (2008) *World Investment Report 2008: Transnational Corporations and the Infrastructure Challenge.* New York: United Nations.

———— (2004) "Global FDI Decline Bottoms Out in 2003," press release.

United Nations Department of Economic and Social Affairs. (2009) "World Population Age 80 or Older." Appeared in *Time Health* (February 22, 2010).

United Nations Department of Peacekeeping Operations. (2010) *Fact Sheet: United Nations Peacekeeping* (March). New York: United Nations.

United Nations Environment Programme (UNEP). (2004) *State of the Environment and Policy Perspective.* New York: United Nations.

———— (2002) *Global Environment Outlook.* New York: Oxford University Press.

UNHCR. (2008) *2007 Global Trends: Refuguess, Asylum-Seekers, Returnees, Internally Displaced and Stateless Persons.* Geneva: UN High Commissioner for Refugeees.

United Nations Peace Operations. (2010) "United Nations Peacekeeping Operations." *Year in Review 2009.* New York: United Nations.

United Nations Population Division (UNPD). (2004) *World Population Prospects.* New York: United Nations.

UNICEF. (2008). *Child Info: Monitoring the Situation of Women and Children.* http://www.childinfo.org/mortality.html. (August 24, 2009).

———— (1996). *Impact of Armed Conflict on Young Children.* Available at: http://www.unicef.org/graca/a51–306_en.pdf.

UNIFEM. (2010) "Democratic Governance." Available at http://www.unifem.org/gender_issues/democratic_governance/.

———— (2009). *Who Answers to Women? Gender and Accountability.* Available at: http://www.unifem.org/progress/2008/media/POWW08_Report_Full_Text.pdf.

Urdal, Henrik. (2006) "A Clash of Generations? Youth Bulges and Political Violence," *International Studies Quarterly* 50 (September): 607–629.

Urquhart, Brian. (2010) "Finding the Hidden UN." *The New York Review* (May 27): 26–28.

———— (2002) "Shameful Neglect," *International Herald Tribune* (April 25): 12–14.

———— (2001) "Mrs. Roosevelt's Revolution," *New York Review of Books* 49 (April 26): 32–34.

———— (1994) "Who Can Police the World?" *New York Review of Books* 41 (May 12): 29–33.

U.S. Agency for International Development. (2004). *Trafficking in Persons: USAIDs reponse* [On-line]. Available at: http://www.usaid.gov/our_work/cross-cutting_programs/wid/pubs/trafficking_in_person_usaids_response_march2004.pdf. (accessed August 24, 2009).

U.S. Arms Control and Disarmament Agency (ACDA). (2002) *World Military Expenditures and Arms Transfers.* Washington, D.C.: U.S. Government Printing Office.

———— (1997) *World Military Expenditures and Arms Transfers 1995.* Washington, D.C.: U.S. Government Printing Office.

U.S. Department of Treasury. (2010) "Gross External Dept Position." Available at http://www.ustreas.gov/tic/debta310.html.

———— (2009) "Major Holders of Treasury Securities," Available at: http://www.treas.gov/tic/mfh.txt.

Valentino, Benjamin. (2004) *Final Solutions: Mass Killing and Genocide in the Twentieth Century.* Ithaca, N.Y.: Cornell University Press.

Vandersluis, Sarah Owen, and Paris Yeros. (2000a) "Ethics and Poverty in a Global Era," pp. 1–31 in Sarah Owen Vandersluis and Paris Yeros (eds.), *Poverty in World Politics.* New York: St. Martin's.

———— (eds.). (2000b) *Poverty in World Politics.* New York: St. Martin's.

Van Evera, Stephen. (1999) *Causes of War.* Ithaca, N.Y.: Cornell University Press.

———— (1994) "Hypotheses on Nationalism and War," *International Security* 18 (Spring): 5–39.

———— (1990–91) "Primed for Peace," *International Security* 15 (Winter): 6–56.

Van Oudenaren, John. (2005) "Containing Europe," *The National Interest* 80 (Summer): 57–64.

Van Riper, Tom. (2009) "The World's Largest Malls," *Forbes* (January 15).

Vasquez, John A. (2005) "Ethics, Foreign Policy, and Liberal Wars," *International Studies Perspectives* 6 (August): 307–315.

———— (2000) *What Do We Know About War?* Lanham, Md.: Rowman & Littlefield.

———— (1998) *The Power of Power Politics: From Classical Realism to Neotraditionalism.* Cambridge: Cambridge University Press.

———— (1997) "The Realist Paradigm and Degenerative versus Progressive Research Programs," *American Political Science Review* 91 (December): 899–912.

———— (1993) *The War Puzzle.* Cambridge: Cambridge University Press.

———— (1991) "The Deterrence Myth," pp. 205–23 in Charles W. Kegley, Jr. (ed.), *The Long Postwar Peace.* New York: HarperCollins.

Vasquez, John A., and Colin Elman (eds.). (2003) *Realism and the Balancing of Power: A New Debate.* Upper Saddle River, N.J.: Prentice Hall.

Verba, Sidney. (1969) "Assumptions of Rationality and Nonrationality in Models of the International System," pp. 217–31 in James N. Rosenau (ed.), *International Politics and Foreign Policy.* New York: Free Press.

Verwimp, Philip, Patricia Justino, and Tilman Bruck. (2009) "The Analysis of Conflict: A Micro-Level Perspective," *Journal of Peace Research* 46 (3): 307–314.

Victor, David G., M. Granger Morgan, Fay Apt, John Steinbruner, and Katharine Ricke. (2009). "The Geoengineering Option: A Last Resort Against Global Warming," *Foreign Affairs* 88 (March/April): 64–76.

Vidal, Gore. (2004). *Imperial America.* New York: Nation Books.

Vital Signs 2007–2008. New York: Norton, for the Worldwatch Institute.

Vital Signs 2006–2007. New York: Norton, for the Worldwatch Institute.

Vital Signs 2005. New York: Norton, for the Worldwatch Institute.

Vital Signs 2004. New York: Norton, for the Worldwatch Institute.

Vital Signs 2003. New York: Norton, for the Worldwatch Institute.

Vital Signs 2002. New York: Norton, for the Worldwatch Institute.

Vital Signs 2000. New York: Norton, for the Worldwatch Institute.

Voeten, Erik. (2004) "Resisting the Lonely Superpower: Responses of States in the United Nations to U.S. Dominance," *Journal of Politics* 66 (August): 729–54.

von Glahn, Gerhard. (1996) *Law Among Nations,* 7th ed. Boston: Allyn & Bacon.

Vreeland, James Raymond. (2003) *The IMF and Economic Development.* Cambridge: Cambridge University Press.

Wagner, R. Harrison. (2007) *War And The State.* Ann Arbor: Pluto Books, University of Michigan Press.

Wallace, Brian. (1978) "True Grit South of the Border," *Osceola* (January 13): 15–16.

Wallerstein, Immanuel. (2005) *World-Systems Analysis.* Durham, N.C.: Duke University Press.

—— (2002) "The Eagle Has Crash Landed," *Foreign Policy* (July/August): 60–68.

—— (1988) *The Modern World-System III.* San Diego: Academic Press.

Walsh, Bryan. (2010) "The Spreading Stain." *Time* (June 21): 51–59.

—— (2009) "The New Age of Exctinction," *Time* (April 1):

—— (2006) "The Impact of Asia's Giants," *Time* (April 3): 61–62.

Walt, Stephen M. (2009) "Alliances in a Unipolar World," World Politics 61: 86–120.

—— (2005) *Taming American Power.* New York: Norton.

Walter, Barbara F. (2004) "Does Conflict Beget Conflict?" *Journal of Peace Research* 41 (May): 371–88.

—— (1997) "The Critical Barrier to Civil War Settlement," *International Organization* 51 (Summer): 335–64.

Walters, Robert S., and David H. Blake. (1992) *The Politics of Global Economic Relations,* 4th ed. Englewood Cliffs, N.J.: Prentice Hall.

Waltz, Kenneth N. (2000) "Structural Realism after the Cold War," *International Security* 25 (Summer): 5–41.

—— (1995) "Realist Thought and Neorealist Theory," pp. 67–83 in Charles W Kegley, Jr. (ed.), *Controversies in International Relations Theory.* New York: St. Martin's.

—— (1993) "The Emerging Structure of International Politics," *International Security* 18 (Fall): 44–79.

—— (1979) *Theory of International Politics.* Reading, Mass.: Addison-Wesley.

—— (1964) "The Stability of a Bipolar World," *Daedalus* 93 (Summer): 881–909.

Walzer, Michael. (2004) *Arguing About War.* New Haven, Conn.: Yale University Press.

WANGO. (2009) "Worldwide NGO Directory." World Association of Non-Governmental Organization: New York. http://www.wango.org/resources.aspx?section=ngodir. Accessed 8 June 2009.

Ward, Michael D., David R. Davis, and Corey L. Lofdahl. (1995) "A Century of Tradeoffs," *International Studies Quarterly* 39 (March): 27–50.

Warner, Bernard. (2008) "A muddy victory for downloaders," *Times Online* (January 30).

Watson, Douglas. (1997) "Indigenous Peoples and the Global Economy," *Current History* 96 (November): 389–91.

Wattenberg, Ben J. (2005) *Fewer: How the Demography of Depopulation Will Shape Our Future.* Chicago: Ivan R. Dee.

WDI. (2007) *World Development Indicators 2007.* Washington, D.C.: World Bank.

—— (2006) *World Development Indicators 2006.* Washington, D.C.: World Bank.

—— (2005) *World Development Indicators 2005.* Washington, D.C.: World Bank.

WDR. (2009) *World Development Report 2008.* Washington, D.C.: World Bank.

—— (2008) *World Development Report 2008.* Washington, D.C.: World Bank.

—— (2007) *World Development Report 2007.* Washington, D.C.: World Bank.

—— (2005) *World Development Report 2006.* Washington, D.C.: World Bank.

Weart, Spencer R. (1994) "Peace among Democratic and Oligarchic Republics," *Journal of Peace Research* 31 (August): 299–316.

Weber, Cynthia. (2005) *International Relations Theory,* 2nd ed. New York: Routledge.

Weidenbaum, Murray. (2009) "Who will Guard the Guardians? The Social Responsibility of NGOs," *Journal of Business Ethics* 87: 147–155.

—— (2004) "Surveying the Global Marketplace," *USA Today* (January): 26–27.

Weiner, Tim. (2005) "Robot Warriors Becoming Reality," Columbia, S.C., *The State* (February 18): A17.

Weir, Kimberly A. (2007) "The State Sovereignty Battle in Seattle," *International Politics* 44 (September): 596–622.

Weisbrot, Mark. (2005) "The IMF Has Lost Its Influence," *International Herald Tribune* (September 23): 7.

Weitsman, Patricia A. (2004) *Dangerous Alliances: Proponents of Peace, Weapons of War.* Stanford, Calif.: Stanford University Press.

Welch, David A. (2005) *Painful Choices: A Theory of Foreign Policy Change.* Princeton, N. J.: Princeton University Press.

Wendt, Alexander. (2000) *Social Theory of International Politics.* Cambridge: Cambridge University Press.

—— (1995) "Constructing International Politics," *International Security* 20 (Summer): 71–81.

—— (1994) "Collective Identity Formation and the International State," *American Political Science Review* 88 (June): 384–396.

Wendzel, Robert L. (1980) *International Relations: A Policymaker Focus.* New York: Wiley.

Wesley, Michael. (2005) "Toward a Realist Ethics of Intervention," *Ethics & International Affairs* 19 (No. 2, Special Issue): 55–72.

Weston, Drew, (2007) *The Political Brain: The Role of Emotion in Deciding the Fate of the Nation.* New York: PublicAffairs.

Western, Jon. (2006) "Doctrinal Divisions: The Politics of U.S. Military Interventions," pp. 87–90 in Glenn P. Hastedt (ed.), *American Foreign Policy,* 12th ed. Dubuque, Iowa: McGraw-Hill/Dushkin.

Wheaton, Henry. (1846) *Elements of International Law.* Philadelphia: Lea and Blanchard.

Wheelan, Charles. (2003) *Naked Economics: Undressing the Dismal Science.* New York: Norton.

White, Ralph K. (1990) "Why Aggressors Lose," *Political Psychology* 11 (June): 227–242.

Wight, Martin. (2002) *Power Politics.* Continuum International Publishing Group.

Wilkenfeld, Jonathan, Kathleen J. Young, David M. Quinn and Victor Asal. (2005) *Mediating International Crises.* London: Routledge.

Will, George F. (2005) "Aspects of Europe's Mind," *Newsweek* (May 9): 72.

Williams, Glyn, Paula Meth and Katie Willis (2009) *New Geographies of the Global South: Developing Areas in a Changing World.* Taylor & Francis.

Wills, Garry. (2004) "What Is a Just War?" *New York Review of Books* (November 18): 32–32.

Wilmer, Franke. (2000) "Women, the State and War: Feminist Incursions into World Politics," pp. 385–395 in Richard W Mansbach and

Edward Rhodes (eds.), *Global Politics in a Changing World*. Boston: Houghton Mifflin.

Wilson, James Q. (1993) *The Moral Sense*. New York: Free Press.

Widmaier, Wesley W. (2007) "Constructing Foreign Policy Crises: Interpretive Leadership in the Cold War and War on Terrorism," *International Studies Quarterly* 51: 779–794.

WIR. (2004) *World Investment Report 2004*. New York: United Nations Conference on Trade and Development.

Wise, Michael Z. (1993) "Reparations," *Atlantic Monthly* 272 (October): 32–35.

Wittkopf, Eugene R., Christopher M. Jones and Charles W Kegley, Jr. (2008) *American Foreign Policy*, 7th edition. Belmont, Calif.: Thomson Wadsworth.

Wittkopf, Eugene R., Charles W Kegley, Jr., and James M. Scott. (2003) *American Foreign Policy*, 6th ed. Belmont, Calif.: Wadsworth.

Wohlforth, William C. (1999) "The Stability of a Unipolar World," *International Security* 24 (Summer): 5–41.

Wohlforth, William C, et. al. (2007) "Testing Balance-of-Power Theory in World History," *European Journal of International Relations* 13: 155–185.

Wolf, Martin. (2005) *Why Globalization Works*. New Haven, CT: Yale University Press.

Wolfe, Tom. (2005) "The Doctrine That Never Died," *New York Times* (January 30): Section 4, 17.

Wolfensohn, James. (2004) "The Growing Threat of Global Poverty," *International Herald Tribune* (April 24–25): 6.

Wolfers, Arnold. (1962) *Discord and Collaboration*. Baltimore: Johns Hopkins University Press.

Wolfers, Arnold, and Laurence Martin (eds.). (1956) *The Anglo-American Tradition in Foreign Affairs*. New Haven, Conn.: Yale University Press.

Wolfsthal, Jon B. (2005) "The Next Nuclear Wave," *Foreign Affairs* 84 (January-February): 156–61.

Wong, Edward. (2005) "Iraq Dances with Iran, While America Seethes," *New York Times* (July 31): Section 4, 3.

Woodard, Colin. (2007) "Who Resolves Arctic Disputes?," *Christian Science Monitor* (August 20): 1, 6.

Woods, Ngaire. (2008) "Whose Aid? Whose Influence? China, Emerging Donors and the Silent Revolution in Development Assistance," *International Affairs* 84: 1205–1221.Woodward, Bob. (2006) *State of Denial*. New York: Simon &Schuster.

——— (2004). *Plan of Attack*. New York: Simon & Schuster.

——— (2002). *Bush at War*. New York: Simon & Schuster.

Woodward, Susan L. (2009) "Shifts in Global Security Policies: Why They Matter for the South," *IDS Bulletin* 40:121–128.

Woodwell, Douglas. (2008) *Nationalism in International Relations*. London: Palgrave Macmillan.

World Bank. (2010) *World Development Report 2010: Development and Climate Change*. Washington, D.C.: The International Bank for Reconstruction and Development/The World Bank.

——— (2009) *Atlas of Global Development*, 2nd edition. Washington, D.C.: World Bank.

——— (2009b) *World Development Indicators 2009*. Washington, D.C.: World Bank.

——— (2008) "World Bank President to G8: 'World Entering a Danger Zone'." Available at: http://go.worldbank.org/FXVBH85XS0.

——— (2007) *Atlas of Global Development*. Washington, D.C.: World Bank.

——— (2005) *World Bank Atlas*. Washington, D.C.: World Bank.

——— (1996) *World Debt Tables 1996*, Vol. 1. Washington, D.C.: World Bank.

World Health Organization. (2009). "Health of Indigenous Peoples." Fact Sheet 326. October 2007. http://www.who.int/mediacentre/factsheets/fs326/en/index.html.

World Resources Institute (WRI). (2009) "What is the state of ecosystems today?" Available at: http://archive.wri.org/newsroom/wrifeatures_text.cfm?ContentID=288.

——— (2004) *SDI: Sustainable Development Index*. Washington, D.C.: World Resources Institute.

World Trade. (2002) *World Trade* 14 (June): 13–15.

World Trade Organization (WTO). (2010) "Understanding the WTO: Settling Disputes." Available at http://www.wto.org/english/thewto_e/whatis_e/tif_e/disp1_e.htm.

——— (2010) *World Trade Report 2010: Trade in Natural Resources*. Geneva: World Trade Organization.

——— (2009a) *World Trade Report 2009*. Available at: http://www.wto.org/english/res_e/booksp_e/anrep_e/world_trade_report09_e.pdf.

——— (2009b) "WTO Secretariat reports increase in new anti-dumping investigations," WTO Press Release (May 7). Available at: http://www.wto.org/english/news_e/pres09_e/pr556_e.htm.

——— (2009c) "Regional Trade Agreements Gateway." Available at: http://www.wto.org/english/tratop_e/region_e/region_e.htm.

——— (2009d) *International Trade Statistics 2008*. Geneva: World Trade Organization.

——— (2003) *World Trade Report 2003*. Geneva: World Trade Organization.

Worldwatch Institute. (2009) *State of the World 2009*. New York: W. W. Norton.

——— (2000) *The World in 2000*. New York: Norton.

Wright, Quincy. (1953) "The Outlawry of War and the Law of War," *American Journal of International Law* 47 (July): 365–76.

——— (1942) *A Study of War*. Chicago: University of Chicago Press.

Yang, David W. (2005) "In Search of an Effective Democratic Realism," *SAIS Review* 15 (Winter-Spring): 199–205.

Yergin, Daniel. (2009) "It's Still the One" *Foreign Policy* September/October, pp. 88–95.

——— (2006) "Thirty Years of Petro-Politics," pp. 106–7 in Robert M. Jackson (ed.), *Global Issues 05/06*. Dubuque, Iowa: McGraw-Hill/Dushkin.

——— (2005) "An Oil Shortage?" Columbia, S.C., *The State* (August 2): A9.

Youde, Jeremy. (2005) "Enter the Fourth Horseman: Health Security and International Relations Theory," *The Whitehead Journal of Diplomacy and International Affairs* 6 (Winter-Spring): 193–208.

Zacher, Mark W. (1987) "Trade Gaps, Analytical Gaps: Regime Analysis and International Commodity Regulation," *International Organization* 41 (Spring): 173–202.

Zacher, Mark W, and Richard A. Matthew. (1995) "Liberal International Theory: Common Threads, Divergent Strands," pp. 107–49 in Charles W Kegley, Jr. (ed.), *Controversies in International Relations Theory: Realism and the Neoliberal Challenge*. New York: St. Martin's.

Zagare, Frank C. (2007) "Toward a Unified Theory of Interstate Conflict," *International Interactions* 33 (July/September): 305–327.

——— (2004) "Reconciling Rationality with Deterrence," *Journal of Theoretical Politics* 16 (April): 107–41.

——— (1990) "Rationality and Deterrence," *World Politics* 42 (January): 238–60.

Zakaria, Fareed. (2009) *The Post-American World*. New York: W.W.Norton.

——— (2008) "The Future of American Power: How America Can Survive the Rise of the Rest," *Foreign Affairs* 87 (3): 18–26.

——— (2007) "Preview of a Post-U.S. World," *Newsweek* (February 5): 47.

———— (2005a) "Does the Future Belong to China?" *Newsweek* (May 9): 26–47.

———— (2005b) "The Wealth of More Nations," *New York Times Book Review* (May 1): 10–11.

———— (2004) "The One-Note Superpower," *Newsweek* (February 2): 41.

———— (2002a) "Europe: Make Peace with War," *Newsweek* (June 3): 35.

———— (2002b) "Stop the Babel over Babylon," *Newsweek* (October 16): 34.

———— (2002c) "The Trouble with Being the World's Only Superpower," *New Yorker* (October 14 and 21): 72–81.

———— (1999) "The Empire Strikes Out: The Unholy Emergence of the Nation-State," *New York Times Magazine* (April 18): 99.

———— (1998a) *From Wealth to Power: The Unusual Origins of America's World Role.* Princeton, N.J.: Princeton University Press.

———— (1998b) "The Future of Statecraft," p. 42 in *The World in 1999.* London: Economist.

Zakaria, Fareed. (1992–93) "Is Realism Finished?" *National Interest* 30 (Winter): 21–32.

Zelikow, Philip. (2006) "The Transformation of National Security," pp. 121–27 in Robert M. Jackson (ed.), *Global Issues 05/06.* Dubuque, Iowa: McGraw-Hill/Dushkin.

Ziegler, David. (1995) Review of World Politics and the Evolution of War by John Weltman, *American Political Science Review* 89 (September): 813–14.

Zimmerman, Tim. (1996) "CIA Study: Why Do Countries Fall Apart?" *U.S. News & World Report* (February 12): 46.

name index

A

Abramowitz, Morton, 205
Adams, John Quincy, 192
Ahmadinejad, Mahmoud, 264–265
Ahtisaari, Martti, 608
Allende, Salvador, 177
Allison, Graham, 203, 292
Altman, Roger, 439
Andropov, Yuri, 86
Angell, Norman, 38
Annan, Kofi, 4, 146, 149, 409, 447, 597
Arbatov, Georgi, 87
Archduke Ferdinand, 67, 69
Ariely, Dan, 202
Aristotle, 605
Atkinson, Brooks, 598
Augustine, Saint, 34, 360

B

Babbar Khalsa, 245
Ball, George W., 193, 195
Balladur, Edouard, 602
Beitz, Charles, 529–530
Benner, Thorsten, 395
Benson, Michelle, 267
Bhagwati, Jagdish, 478, 513–514
Bhutto, Benazir, 247
Bishop, William, 352
Blair, Tony, 45, 516
Boutros-Ghali, Boutros, 146, 232, 597
Brahimi, Lakhdar, 483
Braudel, Fernand, 517
Bremer, Stuart, 601
Brezhnev, Leonid, 87
Brinkley, Douglas, 332
Bronfenbrenner, Urie, 13
Bronowski, Jacob, 613
Brown, Lester R., 556
Brzenski, Zbigniew, 205
Buakamsri, Karuna, 62
Bunche, Ralph, 254
Bunn, Matthew, 296
Bush, George H. W., 345
Bush, George W., 21, 197, 281, 306, 332,

C

Caarlsson, Ingvar, 408
Califano, Joseph A., 191
Campbell, Ian, 471
Carr, E. H., 34
Carré, John Le, 90
Carter, Jimmy, 13, 46, 86, 266, 551
Carter, John, 571
Castro, Raul, 109, 439–440
Chamberlain, Neville, 74

Chan, Steve, 270
Chernenko, Konstantin, 86
Churchill, Winston, 20, 64, 65, 79, 303, 323
Claude, Inis L., 111, 325
Clemenceau, Georges, 73
Clinton, Hillary, 101, 537, 596
Clinton, William, 44, 45, 133, 210, 611
Cobden, Richard, 39, 402
Cole, Juan, 21
Collier, Paul, 112
Comte, Auguste, 163
Cooper, Richard N., 365
Coplin, William, 359
Corleone, Don Vito, 43
Costa, Antonio Maria, 540
Coyle, Philip, 304

D

Darwin, Charles, 253
da Silva, Luiz Inacio, 314
de Cuéllar, Javier Perez, 146, 392–393
de Gaulle, Charles, 294
de Hoop Scheffer, Jaap, 399
de Montesquieu, Charles, 376
de Secondat Montesquieu, Charles, 38
Destler, I. M., 475
de Tocqueville, Alexis, 79, 224
Dobson, William, 21
Doha Round, GATT, 472–473, 480
Doomsday Clock, 300
Dos Santos, Theotonio, 52
Drezner, Daniel, 481
Drucker, Peter, 62
Dubois, W. E. B., 516
Dubos, Rene, 594
Dulles, John Foster, 242, 302
Dworkin, Ronald, 518
Dyson, Freeman, 604

E

Eban, Abba, 353
Einstein, Albert, 6, 58, 138, 293, 376, 613
Eiseley, Loren, 572
Eisenhower, Dwight, 93, 285, 286, 312, 372
Elkind, Sarah, 574
Emerson, Ralph Waldo, 208
Engels, Friedrich, 52
Enlai, Zhou, 348
Enloe, Cynthia, 54
Evans, Gareth, 372

F

Ferguson, Niall, 415, 420
Finkelstein, Robert, 299
Fogel, Robert, 97

Foley, Conor, 370
Franco, Francisco, 75
Frank, André Gunder, 52
Franklin, Benjamin, 14, 459
Freud, Sigmund, 253
Friedman, Thomas, 24, 417–418, 510, 582–583
Frost, Robert, 59–60
Fukuyama, Francis, 253, 609

G

Gandhi, Indira, 608
Gandhi, Mohandas, 576
Garrett, Laurie, 501
Gates, Robert, 93, 232, 285
Gelb, Leslie, 95–96
Gerson, Michael, 37
Ghraib, Abu, 358
Goering, Hermann, 242
Gondomar, Count Diego Sarmiento, 317
Gorbachev, Mikhail, 48, 86, 212
Gottlieb, Gidon, 354
Greenspan, Alan, 437
Grey, Sir Edward, 311–312
Grotius, Hugo, 360, 361
Guterres, António, 497

H

Haass, Richard, 93
Habermas, Jurgen, 50
Hagel, Chuck, 197
Hamilton, Alexander, 460
Hammarskjöld, Dag, 146, 348, 392
Hardin, Garrett, 576–577
Harman, Willis, 613
Hedges, Chris, 233
Hermann, Margaret G., 210
Hitler, Adolf, 74–80, 209, 223, 257
Hobbes, Thomas, 31, 33, 34, 275, 517, 545
Hobson, J. A., 108–109
Hobson, John, 52
Hoffman, Bruce, 174
Hoffman, Stanley, 22
Hoge, James, 339
Holbrooke, Richard, 364
Horkheimer, Max, 50
Hoschschild, Adam, 529
Houdard, Philippe, 240
Hudson, Kimberly, 344
Hughes, Emmet John, 210
Hume, David, 38, 39
Huntington, Samuel, 94, 162, 167
Hussein, Saddam, 197, 219, 292, 363–364
Husseini, Fatima, 516
Huxley, Aldous, 257

J

Jefferson, Thomas, 223, 263
Jeffries, Richard, 51
Jenkinson, Brett, 251
Jervis, Robert, 50, 90, 326
Jintao, Hu, 99, 124, 314
Johnson, Gordon, 299
Jolie, Angelina, 499

K

Kagame, Paul, 126
Kahneman, Daniel, 197, 201
Kant, Immanuel, 37, 38, 39, 221, 223, 263, 400, 404
Kaplan, Morton, 322
Kapstein, Ethan, 540
Kegley, Charles W., 198
Kelsen, Hans, 357
Kennan, George, 46, 83, 223
Kennedy, John F., 85, 213, 230, 346, 614
Kennedy, Paul, 94
Keynes, John Maynard, 428
Khan, A. Q., 295
Khrushchev, Nikita, 85, 303
Kim, Samuel S., 357
Ki-Moon, Ban, 146, 244, 560
Kindlberger, Charles, 420
King, Martin Luther, Jr., 607
Kinnis, J. N., 408
Kissinger, Henry A., 86, 92, 190–191, 200, 210, 234, 390
Klare, Michael, 574
Kluger, Jeffrey, 485
Korb, Lawrence, 289
Krasner, Stephen, 416
Kratochwil, Friedrich, 46
Krauthammer, Charles, 331
Kroenig, Matthew, 295
Krugman, Paul, 467
Kurlantzick, Joshua, 98
Kutcher, Ashton, 506

L

Lama, Dalai, 164
Lamy, Pascal, 429
Laqueur, Walter, 174
Lebow, Richard Ned, 8, 49
Lee, Robert E., 299
Leffler, Melvyn, 81
Lektzian, David, 222
Lenin, Vladimir Ilyich, 52, 71, 82, 107–108, 116
Leo, Stephen, 481
Leontief, Wassily, 604
Levy, Jack, 257
Lie, Trygve, 146, 232
Lieberman, Joe, 174
Lincoln, Abraham, 211
Lindh, Anna, 409
List, Friedrich, 460
Lloyd, William Foster, 576–577
Locke, John, 37
Loder, Bernard C. J., 40

Lomé Convention, 463
Lorenz, Konrad, 253
Lupovici, Amir, 51
Lutz, Ellen, 550
Lynd, Helen Merrel, 599

M

Machiavelli, Niccoló, 31, 32, 34, 242, 599
Mackinder, Sir Halford, 218
Madison, James, 263, 403
Maginot line, 76
Mahan, Alfred Thayer, 218
Malthus, Thomas, 485
Marx, Karl, 51, 52, 107–108, 112
Mathews, Jessica T., 136
Maurice, Sir John Frederick, 376
Mazarr, Michael, 448
Mbeki, Thabo, 101
McCarthy, Joseph, 82
McKibbin, Bill, 566
Mead, Margaret, 190
Mearsheimer, John, 64
Medvedev, Dmitry, 94, 305, 314
Mergenthaler, Stephan, 395
Midlarski, Manus, 531
Milosevic, Slobodan, 45
Mishra, Brajesh, 294
Mitterand, Francois, 608
More, St. Thomas, 254, 360
Morgenthau, Hans J., 34, 65, 600
Mousavi, Mir Hosein, 264–265
Mugabe, Robert, 499
Mussolini, Benito, 77

N

Nicolson, Sir Harold, 347
Niebuhr, Reinhold, 34, 364
Nixon, Richard, 85, 87, 193, 213, 274, 340, 348, 433
Nunn, Nathan, 105
Nye, Joseph, 60, 323

O

Obama, Barack, 33, 307, 335, 358, 381, 387, 584, 696
Onuf, Nicholas, 46
Orwell, George, 523
Osler, Sir William, 599
Overton, Ed, 553

P

Palmerston, Lord, 317
Pape, Richard A., 323
Patten, Chris, 97
Petersen, Spike, 54
Petraeus, David H., 198
Pinochet, Augusto, 240
Pipe, Richard, 86
Plato, 102
Pope John Paul, 171
Pope Nicholas I, 360
Puchala, Donald, 59

Puddington, Arch, 222
Putin, Vladimir, 94, 237, 347
Putnam, Robert, 199

Q

Qaddafi, Muammar, 209, 219
Quindlen, Anna, 250

R

Reagan, Ronald, 86, 304
Redfield, Robert, 518
Renshon, Jonathan, 197
Ricardo, David, 458
Rice, Condolezza, 277
Rieff, David, 551
Rischard, Jean-Francois, 137
Robinson, Mary, 517
Rockefeller, John D. Jr., 551
Rodrik, Dani, 454
Rogoff, Kenneth, 436
Roosevelt, Eleanor, 551
Roosevelt, Franklin, 38, 64, 76, 79, 271
Roosevelt, Theodore, 372, 553
Rosecrance, Richard, 283
Rosenau, James N., 162
Rostow, Walt W., 115
Rotmann, Philipp, 395
Rousseau, Jean-Jacques, 39, 311, 519
Rowley, Coleen, 206
Rubin, Robert, 433
Rumsfeld, Donald, 251
Rusk, Dean, 65

S

Safford, Victoria, 484
Sagan, Carl, 485–486, 608
Saint Augustine, 34, 360
Salas, Rafael M., 484
Samin, Amir, 52
Samuelson, Robert J., 449
Sanchez, Oscar Arias, 290
Santayana, George, 20, 598
Sapir, Edward, 165
Sarkozy, Nicolas, 480
Sazonov, Sergei, 70
Sheeran, Josette, 558
Shultz, George, 304
Schulz, Williams, 551
Schwarzenegger, Arnold, 589
Scowcroft, Brent, 364
Sendero Luminoso, 175
Seneca, Lucius Annaeus, 271
Shalah, Ramadan, 248
Sheeran, Josette, 558
Shelley, Percy B., 271
Simon, Herbert, 200
Sing, Manmohan, 314
Singer, Peter, 513
Smith, Adam, 37, 38, 106, 458
Snyder, David Pearce, 610, 614
Snyder, Jack, 50
Solana, Javier, 45
Somavia, Juan, 422
Sorenson, Theodore, 197

Souva, Mark, 222
Spencer, Herbert, 539
Spinoza, Baruch, 34
Spykman, Nicholas, 218
St. John, Henry, 269
Stalin, Joseph, 64, 76, 79, 81, 223
Steinberg, Richard, 472
Stiglitz, Joseph, 133
Strange, Susan, 441
Summer, William Graham, 107
Surowiecki, James, 603
Sutherland, Peter, 473
Sylvester, Christine, 55

T

Talbott, Strobe, 374
Tessman, Brock, 270
Thant, U, 146
Thurber, James, 599
Tickner, J. Ann, 56
Tolstoy, Leo, 254
Toynbee, Arnold J., 65
Trotsky, Leon, 591
Truman, Harry, 79, 80, 81
Tutu, Desmund, 545

Tversky, Amos, 201
Tzu, Sun, 343, 614

U

ul Haq, Mahbud, 523
Urquhart, Brian, 148, 393

V

van Loon, Hendrik Willem, 598
Van Rompuy, Herman, 159
Vedrine, Hubart, 92
von Clausewitz, Karl, 231

W

Waldheim, Kurt, 146
Wallace, Brian, 520
Walt, Stephen M., 29, 90
Waltz, Kenneth, 35, 603
Weakland, Rombert, 526
Weber, Cynthia, 48
Weber, Max, 203
Weidenbaum, Murray, 414
Weimar Republic, 75

Welch, Jack, 446
Wendt, Alexander, 46, 48
West Berlin, 84
Wheaton, Henry, 352
Whitman, Walt, 6
Whorf, Benjamin Lee, 165
Wilhelm II, Kaiser, 69, 211
Williams, Jody, 384
Wilmer, Franke, 55
Wilson, Woodrow, 38, 40, 72–73, 109, 223, 263, 390–391, 401
Wittkopf, Eugene, 198
Wolfenshohn, James, 412, 522–523
Wolfers, Arnold, 188
Wolfowitz, Paul, 364, 447

Y

Youde, Jeremy, 503

Z

Zakaria, Fareed, 94, 342, 464
Zedong, Mao, 163, 223
Zoellick, Robert, 478, 557

subject index

A

absolute advantage, 458
absolute gains, 459
Abu Ghraib prison, 358, 372
Abyssinia, 75
acid rain, 580
acquired immune deficiency syndrome
  (AIDS), 500–503
activism, 162
actor, defined, 16
actors, nonstate. *See also* multinational
  corporations (MNCs); nongovernmental
  organizations (NGOs); power rivalries;
  terrorism; United Nations
  future trends, 184–186
  issue-advocacy groups, 181–184
  nonstate nations, 164–168
  overview, 137–141
  regional intergovernmental organizations,
    17, 42, 44, 153–162, 217, 396–399
  terrorist groups, 173–176
  transnational, decision making and, 190
  transnational religious movements, 23,
    168–173
  United Nations, overview, 141–149
adjudication, 40, 351
AfDF (African Development Fund), 130, 133
Afghanistan, 86, 87, 93, 292, 516, 538, 542
Africa, 52, 76, 161, 488–190
African Development Fund (AfDF),
  130, 133
African Growth and Opportunities Act,
  463, 470
agency, defined, 518
agenda setting, 508
agent-oriented constructivism, 48–49
AIDS, 500–503
air-launched cruise missiles (ACMs), 297
Albania, 75
Algeria, 110
Alien Tort Claims Act (1789), 371
alignments, 321
ALIR (Army for the Liberation of Rwanda),
  175
alliances
  balance of power, 216, 320–327
  balance of power, models of, 327–333
  future trends, 334–340
  overview, 315–317
  realist theory, 317–319
Allied powers, World War II, 73–80
Al Qaeda, 167, 171–172, 175, 246–248,
  251, 281, 335, 363
alternatives, decision making, 196
Amazon, 165, 569–570
Amnesty International, 140, 541
AMU (Arab Maghreb Union), 161
analysis, levels of, 18–20

anarchy
  armed aggression and, 266
  constructivist theory, 46
  defined, 23
  liberal theory, 41
  neorealism and, 35
  realist view, 33
Angola, 86
Antarctic Treaty, 382
Antiballistic Missile Treaty, 387
antidumping duties, 469
antipersonnel landmines (APL), 384
Antipersonnel Landmines Treaty, 383
antisatellite (ASAT) weapons, 297
anti-Semitic racism, 77
ANZUS (Australia, New Zealand, United
  States), 396–399
APEC (Asia Pacific Economic Cooperation),
  124, 159–160
appeasement, 75
Arab Maghreb Union (AMU), 161
arbitrage market, 420, 423
arbitration, 351
Argentina, 118–119, 123
armed aggression. *See also* conflict
  resolution
  changes in, 232–235
  future of, 270–271, 605–606
  global system, as cause, 265–270
  global trade and, 463
  human nature as cause, 252–255
  judicial framework, 367–372
  Just War Doctrine, 359–366
  long cycle theory, 66, 268–270
  new rules for, 365–366
  overview, 231–232
  state characteristics and, 255–265
  within states, 235–243, 260
  terrorism, 243–252
arms control, 85–86, 87, 376–389
arms race, 33, 86, 287–292, 311–312
Army for the Liberation of Rwanda (ALIR),
  175
Arthashastra, 33–34
ASEAN (Association of Southeast Nations),
  124, 160, 477
ASEAN Nuclear Free Zone Treaty, 383
Asia, 52, 120–121. *See also* Global East;
  specific country names
"Asian Century", 98
Asian Tigers, 120
Asia-Pacific Economic Cooperation (APEC),
  124, 159–160
Association of Southeast Asian Nations
  (ASEAN), 124, 160, 477
asylum, 498
asymmetric war, 243–252, 279. *See also*
  terrorism
atmosphere, earth (ecopolitics), 560–567

atomic bomb, 78–79, 83, 293–299,
  380–383, 582
atrocities, 497. *See also* human rights
Aum Supreme Truth (AUM), 175
Australia, 396–399
Austria, 109
Austrian-Hungarian Empire, 67, 69,
  71–72, 109
authoritarian governments, 224
autocratic rule, 220
avian flu, 502
Axis powers, 73–80

B

balance of payments, 424
balance of power
  changing character of, 283, 286
  financial crisis 2008 and, 444
  future trends, 334–340, 605–606
  hierarchy of, 23, 65
  measures of, 277–279
  models of, 327–333
  overview, 33, 216, 275–276
  realist view, 32, 33, 36, 320–327
  World War I, 69–70
  World War II, 64, 73–80, 328
balance of trade, 424
balancer, 323, 335
Balkans, 76
ballistic missile defense, 304–305
Banco del Sur, 123
bandwagoning, 324
bargaining model of war, 267
Basques, 17, 175
behavioral science, 58–59
Belgium, 69, 76
Berlin, 85, 88
Bhopal, India, 586
bilateral agreements, 378–379
BINGOs (business international NGOs). *See*
  nongovernmental organizations (NGOs)
biodiversity, 567–571
Biodiversity Treaty, 583–584
biogenetic engineering, 568
Biological and Toxic Weapons
  Convention, 382
biological weapons, 299–301
Biological Weapons Convention, 387
bipolarity, 80, 216, 328–330, 337–338
bird flu, 502
blogs, 505
blowback, 291–292
Bolivia, 123
Bolshevik Revolution, 80–81
Bolsheviks, 71
Bono, 184
bounded rationality, 198
bourgeoisie, 52

Brazil, 104, 118–119, 123, 165, 314, 569–570
Brest-Litovsk, Treaty of (1918), 79
Bretton Woods system, 428–433, 455–457
BRIC (Brazil, Russia, India, China), 314
brinkmanship, 302
Britain, 69, 73–80, 217, 281. *See also* Global North
Brundtland Commission, 559
Brunei, 124
Buddhism, 169
bureaucracy, foreign policy, 202–208
bureaucratic politics model, 203
Burundi, 104
Bush Doctrine, 208, 248, 332, 365

C

CAEU (Council of Arab Economic Unity), 160
CAFTA-DR, 123
capital controls, 425
capital flows, 419–420. *See also* global finance
capitalism, 51, 52, 81–88, 107–108, 261–262. *See also* multinational corporations (MNCs); trade
capitalist imperialism, 80–81
Caribbean Community (CARICOM), 160
carrying capacity, 556
cartel, 508–509
cartography, 9–12. *See also* maps
caucuses, 203
Central American-Dominican Republic Free Trade Agreement (CAFTA-DR), 123
Central Bank, 424
Central Intelligence Agency (CIA), 352
change, overview, 20–24
chemical weapons, 299–301
Chemical Weapons Convention, 300, 382
Chernobyl, 585
children
    child labor, 452–455, 541–544
    human rights and, 541–544
    as soldiers, 543
    war and, 240
Chile, 118–119, 123, 177, 240
Chiletelco, 177
China. *See also* Global East
    balance of power, 338
    BRIC, 314
    Cold War, 85
    currency, 427
    development of, 120
    future trends, 96–99
    Taiwan, peace and prosperity, 405–406
    Tibet and, 164
    World War II, 75
choice, decision making, 196
Christian Identity Movement, 245
Christians, 168–173
citizens, coalitions of, 17
civil society, 182, 518
civil wars, 234–243, 260
clash of civilizations, 167
class divide, international, 113–114

classical liberal economic theory. *See also* liberal economic theory
    commercial liberalism, 401–403, 421, 456–461
    defined, 106
    economic freedom map, 465
    free trade, 469–471
    global commerce, 453–454, 457–461
    underdevelopment, 115
classical realism, 35. *See also* realist theory
class struggle, 52
climate change, 560–567. *See also* environment
coalitions, private citizens, 17
Coca Cola, 446
coercive diplomacy, 275, 281, 308–310, 345, 573
coercive power, 367
cognitive dissonance, 12, 198
Cold War
    arms control and disarmament, 379–380
    balance of power, 328–330
    constructivist theory, 48
    détente, 85–87
    nonalignment, 111
    overview, 80–88
    perception and, 13
    realist view, 34–35
    Third World and, 103–104
    weapons trade, 287, 288
collective action dilemma, 462
collective good, 461–462
collective security, 40, 99, 143
colonialism, 75, 103–111
Columbia, 123
COMESA (Common Market for Eastern and Southern Africa), 161
commercial liberalism, 262, 401–403, 421, 456–461
9/11 Commission (2004), 206
Common Market for Eastern and Southern Africa (COMESA), 161
communications, 92, 503–510
communism, 68, 71, 81–88, 107–108, 261–262. *See also* Cold War
Communist Manifesto, 52
communist theory of imperialism, 261–262
community, global. *See* nonstate actors
comparative advantage, 458
compellence, 302–303
complex interdependence, 41
Comprehensive Test Ban Treaty, 383
compromise, 93
concert, defined, 99, 326
conciliation, 351
Confidence- and Security-Building Measures Agreement, 382
conflict, 231. *See also* armed aggression
conflict resolution
    armed aggression, legal control, 359–366
    constructivist theory, 344–345
    disputes, settlement of, 345–351
    international law, 351–359
    judicial framework, international law, 367–372
    liberal theory, 38, 344–345
    perception and, 13–14

Congo, 110
consensus, 37, 93
consequentialism, 45, 196
constitutional democracy, 220
constructivist theory
    bureaucratic politics, 206
    Cold War, 81, 89–91
    common culture, 400–408
    European Union, 154
    game theory, 200
    international law, 358, 367
    international organizations, 390
    leader characteristics, importance of, 193–194, 214
    nonstate actors, 185
    overview, 46–51
    peace, routes to, 344–345, 377
    power, 275–276
    women and negotiation, 350
consumption patterns, 521–523
containment, 84
continuities, overview, 20–24
controversy
    alliances, advantages, 319–320
    arms race and prisoner's dilemma, 385–386
    balance of power, 337–338
    behavioral science and international relations, 58–59
    Cold War, end of, 8–91
    democracy and foreign affairs, 223–224
    development, theories of, 118–119
    global food crisis, 557–558
    global IGOs, 163
    globalization, helpful or harmful, 513–514
    humanitarian interventions, 547–548
    ideology, East-West conflict and, 82–83
    IMF and World Bank policies, 435–436
    international relations theory addressing zombie outbreak, 43–44
    Iraq war, just or not, 363–364
    leaders, impact of, 213–214
    military spending and security, 284–286
    multinational corporations in Global South, 131–132
    perception, 9–12
    religious movements, 171–172
    security, defining, 533–534
    Taiwan, peace and prosperity, 405–406
    war on terror, 251–252
    women and negotiation, 349–350
    World Trade Organization, 474–475
Conventional Forces in Europe, 382
Convention on Cluster Munitions, 383
Convention on the Rights of the Child (CRC), 543–544
cornucopians, 554–555
corporate social responsibility, 179–180
cosmopolitan perspective, 504
cost, United Nations, 146–148
Costa Rica, 104, 124
Council of Arab Economic Unity (CAEU), 160
Council of Europe, 154
Council of Ministers (EU), 157–158
Council on Foreign Relations, 93
counterforce targeting strategy, 302

counterterrorism, 243–252
countervailing duties, 469
countervalue targeting strategy, 302
coup d'etat, 240–241
covert operations, 308
creativity, 206
crime, 174
crimes against humanity, 354
crisis
    Cuban Missile Crisis, 85, 203, 303, 346
    decision making, 212
    financial crisis 2008, 94, 436–441,
        478–481
    food crisis, 557–558
    oil crisis (1973), 41
Crusades, 168
Cuba, 87, 107, 117, 464
Cuban Missile Crisis, 85, 203, 303, 346
cultural conditioning, defined, 258
culture, 256–258, 503–510. *See also*
    globalization
currency, 421, 424, 426, 428–433, 439,
    441–444, 455–457. *See also* global
    finance
cyberspace, 505–510
cyberterrorism, 246
cycles, overview, 20–24
cyclical theory of history, 65, 268–270
Czechoslovakia, 71–72, 76, 84, 109
Czech Republic, 159

D

Darfur, 239
death penalty, 519
debt, 130, 133, 434
decision making
    bureaucratic politics of, 202–208
    domestic influences, 218–225
    influences on, 189–195
    international influences on, 214–218
    leaders, impact of, 208–214
    as rational choice, 196–202
decolonization, 104
deconstructivism, 56–57, 58–59
defensive realism, 35
deforestation, 567–571
democracy
    armed aggression and, 262–265
    foreign affairs and, 223–224
    human development and, 525–528
    liberal theory, 38
    spread of, 112
democratic peace, 221–222, 263, 403–405
demographic stress
    armed aggression, 260–261
    disease, impact of, 499–503
    globalization, 485–493, 494
    migration trends, 493–499
    world growth rates, 485–493, 494
Denmark, 76
dependency theory, 52, 116–117, 523
Depression (1929–1931), 77
deprivation, 258–259
desertification, 570
détente, 85–86, 87
deterrence, 298, 303–306, 330
devaluation, 424

developed countries, defined, 113
developing countries, defined, 112–113
development, 115, 118–119, 556, 559–560
developmental assistance, 151
diaspora, 172, 493–499
digital divide, 507
diplomacy. *See also* conflict resolution
    coercive diplomacy, 308–310, 573
    diplomatic summits, 342
    liberal theory and, 38
    preventive diplomacy, 392–393
diplomatic immunity, 354
disarmament, 378–379
disease, impact of, 499–503
dissent, 206
dissidents, terrorism and, 245
diversionary theory of war, 221, 241–243
doctrines, 330
dollar overhang, 432
domestic politics, 37, 70, 218–225. *See also*
    civil wars
Dominican Republic, 123
domino theory, 82
dualism, 117
Dubai, 121
Dunkirk, 76
Dutch imperialism, 105–111

E

Earth Summit (1992), 583–584
ecological fallacy, 254–255
Economic and Social Council, UN, 145
Economic Community of the Great Lakes
    Countries, 161
Economic Community of West African States
    (ECOWAS), 160
Economic Community of Western African
    States (ECOWAS), 161
economic freedom, 466
economic interdependence, 37
economics. *See also* global finance
    armed aggression and, 261–262
    class struggles, 52
    common culture, 400
    decision making and, 215, 219–220
    emerging powers, map, 95
    European Union, 154
    future trends, 97–98
    Global South, 111–117
    hierarchy of, 23
    international political economy, 416–417
    liberal theory, 44
    multinational corporations, overview,
        176–181
    regional IGOs, 159–162
    Taiwan, 405–406
    underdevelopment, theories of, 115–117
    United States, 91–93
economic sanctions, 463–464
ecopolitics. *See* environment
ECOWAS (Economic Community of West
    African States), 160, 161
ECSC (European Coal and Steel
    Community), 154
Ecuador, 123
education, liberal theory and, 38
EEC (European Economic Community), 154

Egypt, 125
EIR (enduring internal rivalry), 238
electoral process, 220
electromagnetic pulse bombs, 298
El Salvador, 123
embedded liberalism, 429
enclosure movement, 568
end of history, 609–610
enduring internal rivalry (EIR), 238
energy supply and demand, 572–575,
    580–583
English imperialism, 105–111
ENGOs (environmental NGOs). *See*
    nongovernmental organizations (NGOs)
environment
    atmosphere, politics of, 560–567
    biodiversity, deforestation and water,
        567–571
    debate, framing of, 555–556
    energy supply and demand, 572–575
    global solutions, 580–588
    national and local solutions, 588–591
    overview, 554–555
    sustainability, 575–580
    treaties, 583–584
Environmental Modifications
    Convention, 382
Environmental Performance Index, 589
environmental security, 533–534, 555–556
epistemic community, 555–556
epistemology, 57
Estonia, 71–72
ethics, 400–408, 518. *See also* human
    rights
ethnic cleansing, 495–499, 531
ethnic groups, 17, 164–168
ethnicity, defined, 164
ethnic nationalism, 164–168
ethnic prejudice, 70, 77
ethnocentrism, 531
Euro, 442
Europe, 261, 488–491. *See also* European
    Union (EU); Global North; individual
    country names
European Atomic Energy Community
    (Euroatom), 154
European Coal and Steel Community
    (ECSC), 154
European Commission, 157–158
European Court of Justice, 158
European Economic Community (EEC), 154
European imperialism, 105–111
European Parliament, 157–158
European Union (EU). *See also* Global
    North; individual country names
    foreign policy decisions, 217
    liberal theory, 42, 44
    overview, 154–159
    rise of, 17
exchange rate, 423, 433–434. *See also*
    global finance
executions, 519
export-led industrialization, 116–117
export quotas, 468
extended deterrence, 330
externalities, 128–129, 200
extinction, rate of, 568, 579
extraterritoriality, 354

F

facilitation, 349
failed states, 235–237, 493–495, 496
FARC (Revolutionary Armed Forces of Columbia), 175
fascism, 76, 77
Federal Republic of Yugoslavia, 45
feminist theory
  armed aggression and, 258
  financial crisis 2008, 444
  gender inequality, 534–539
  leaders, impact of, 211
  negotiation, women and, 349–350
  overview, 53–56
  peace, routes to, 377
fertility rate, 488
finance
  Bretton Woods system, 428–433
  financial crisis 2008, 94, 436–441, 478–481
  floating exchange rates, 433–434
  globalization of, 417–419
  international political economy, 416–417
  monetary policy, 423–428
  multinational corporations, 451–452
  overview, 419–422
  reforming, 441–444
  Structural Adjustment Policies, 435–436
Finland, 71–72
firebreak, 297
First World, defined, 104
fiscal policy, 424
fixed-but-adjustable exchange rate system, 424
fixed exchange rate, 424, 431
floating exchange rate, 424, 433–434
fog of war, 254
food crisis, 557–558
foreign aid, 124–127, 470
foreign direct investment, 127–130, 419, 451–452
foreign policy
  bureaucratic politics of, 202–208
  domestic influences, 218–225
  influences on, 189–195
  international influences on, 214–218
  leaders, impact of, 208–214
  United States, 13
forests, 567–571
Formosa, 107
formulation, 349
Fourteen Points, 73, 390, 401
France, 69, 73–80
Frankfurt School, 46
free riders, 322, 462
free trade. *See* trade
French imperialism, 105–111
funnel vision, 192

G

game theory, 199
GATT (General Agreement on Tariffs and Trade), 150, 430
Gaza, 259
GDP. *See* gross domestic product (GDP)

gender
  armed aggression, 258
  feminist theory, overview, 53–56
  financial crisis 2008, 444
  inequality and its consequences, 534–539
  leaders, influence of, 211
  negotiations, 349–350
  peace, routes to, 377
Gender Empowerment Measure (GEM), 534–539
General Agreement on Tariffs and Trade (GATT), 150, 430, 455–457, 471
General Assembly, UN, 144
genetic engineering, 558
Geneva Disarmament Conference (1932), 41
Geneva Protocol (1925), 300
genocide, 365, 370, 495–499, 531, 607
geopolitics, 218, 259–260
geostrategic location, 215, 216–218
Germany, 14, 69, 73–80, 109, 217, 257. *See also* Global North
Ghana, 104
global commons, 556, 576–580
global conditions, influence of, 191–193
Global East, 117, 120–121, 449, 469, 564
global finance
  Bretton Woods system, 428–433
  collapse, 1930s, 77
  financial crisis, 2008, 94, 436–441
  floating exchange rate and crisis, 433–434
  globalization of finance, 417–419
  international political economy, 416–417
  monetary policy, 423–428
  multinational corporations, 451–452
  overview, 419–422
  reforming, 441–444
  Structural Adjustment Policies, 435–436
global institutions, 17, 37. *See also* nonstate actors; specific institution names
globalization. *See also* nonstate actors
  balance of power, models of, 327–333
  common culture, 400–408
  cure or curse, 601–603
  defined, 416–419
  disease, impact of, 499–503
  future trends, 510–514
  helpful or harmful, 513–514
  human development and, 525–528
  information age and, 503–510
  institutions, norms and world order, 408–409
  international organizations and security, 389–399
  of labor, 452–455
  population changes, 485–493, 494
  power and, 277
  of production, 450–451
global level of analysis, 19–20, 68–69
globally integrated enterprises, 181
global migration trends, 493–499
global norms, 37
Global North. *See also* Global South; nonstate actors
  climate change, 564
  defined, 102, 104

digital divide, 507
  foreign aid and remittances, 124–127
  free trade, 466–471
  population growth, 487–493
  trade integration, 449
Global South. *See also* nonstate actors
  Asia, 120–121
  climate change, 564
  debt management, 130, 133
  defined, 102, 104
  deforestation, 569–570
  digital divide, 507
  economic development, 111–117
  economic order, reform of, 122–123
  foreign aid and remittance, 124–127
  foreign direct investment, 451–452
  free trade, 466–471
  future of, 133–134
  gender inequality, 536
  imperialism and, 103–111
  military security, 121–122, 261
  modernization, 118–119
  oil and technology, 119–120
  population growth, 487–493
  regional trade regimes, 123–124
  standard of living, 520–523
  theories of underdevelopment, 115–117
  trade and foreign direct investment, 127–130
  trade integration, 449
  war and, 235
global structure, 327
global supply chains, 479
global system
  armed aggression, causes of, 265–270
  defined, 23
global terrorism, persistent threat of, 244
global trade. *See also* multinational corporations (MNCs)
  arms trade, 261
  effects of, 23
  financial crisis, 2008, 478–481
  free trade, 466–471
  future trends, 97–98
  liberal and mercantilist views, 457–461
  multinational corporations, overview, 176–181
  overview, 447–455
  politics and, 461–466
  protectionism, 19–20
  regional trade regimes, 123–124
  security and, 400–403
  strategies for, 455–461
  sustainable development, 584–588
  World Trade Organization (WTO), 471–476
global trends and forecasts
  how people think, 598–600
  key questions, 600–610
  new world order or disorder, 610–614
  overview, 597–598
global village, defined, 485
global warming, 182, 560–567
"global war", 269
GNI (gross national income), 112–113
goals, decision making and, 196
Godfather, The, 43
good offices, 351

government systems, 215, 220–225, 235–237, 262–265, 525–528
Great Britain, 69, 73–80, 217, 281. *See also* Global North
Great Depression (1929–1931), 77, 455–457
Great Patriotic War, 12. *See also* World War II
great powers, defined, 25
Greece, 220, 495
greed, 578
Greenham Common Airbase, 56
greenhouse effect, 561–567
greenhouse gases, 589–590
Greenpeace, 49
gross domestic product (GDP), 420, 434, 448–449
gross national income (GNI), 112–113
Group of 77, 122
groupthink, 206, 255
G-20 Summit, 414
Guantanamo detainees, 358
Guatemala, 123
gunboat diplomacy, 308
guns *vs.* butter, 284–286

H

Haiti, 104
Halliburton, 177
Hamas, 175
hard power, 283, 286
heavily indebted poor countries (HIPCs), 130, 133
hegemonic stability theory, 66, 461
hegemony, 66, 92, 331–332. *See also* balance of power
Hellenic Migration Policy Initiative, 495
Heraclitus, 614
Hezbollah, 175
Hindu religion, 169
HIPC (heavily indebted poor countries), 130, 133
Hiroshima, 78–79, 293
history, cyclical theory of, 65
history-making individuals model, 208–210
HIV, 500–503
H1N1 influenza, 502
Honduras, 123
Hong Kong, 120
horizontal nuclear proliferation, 293
human development
    globalization and, 525–528
    overview, 517–519
    present conditions, 519–523
    security and, 523–525
Human Development Index, 523–525
human immunodeficiency virus (HIV), 500–503
humanitarian intervention, 547–548
human nature, armed aggression and, 252–255
human needs, defined, 523
human rights
    abuses, response to, 544–551
    children and, 541–544
    future trend, 606–608
    gender inequality, 534–539
    humanitarian intervention, 547–548

indigenous peoples, 530–533
internationally recognized rights, 529–530
migration, 497
military interventions, 45, 365
overview, 517–519, 528–529
slavery and human trafficking, 539–541
Human Rights Council (HRC), 549
Human Rights Watch, 49
human security, 517
human trafficking, 539–541
Hungary, 109
hypotheses, 59

I

IDB (Inter-American Development Bank), 130, 133
idealists, 40
ideas, power of, 38
ideology
    defined, 77
    East-West conflict and, 82–83
IGOs. *See* intergovernmental organizations (IGOs)
images, 7–14
IMF (International Monetary Fund), 130, 133, 149–150
imperialism, 52, 75, 105–111, 261–262
imperial overstretch, 92
import quotas, 468
import-substitution industrialization, 116–117
improvised explosive devices (IEDs), 361
income inequality, 521–523
independence, armed aggression and, 256
independent thinking, 206
India, 96–99, 104, 110, 120, 293, 314, 586
indigenous peoples, 103, 164–168, 530–533
individualistic fallacy, 255
individual level of analysis, 18
individuals, importance of, 37
Indonesia, 104, 124, 240
infant industry, 468
inflation, 425, 426
influenza, 502
information, organizing, 8
information age, 174, 503–510
information technology, 505–510
information warfare, 246
infowar tactics, 298
INGOs (international NGOs). *See* nongovernmental organizations (NGOs)
Inhumane Weapons Convention, 382
institutional mind-set, 206
institutions. *See also* nonstate actors; specific institution names
    international, 66
instrumental rationality, 209
Inter-American Convention on Transparency in Conventional Weapons Acquisition, 383
Inter-American Development Bank (IDB), 130, 133
interdependence, 41, 402
interest groups, 181–184, 220, 224
interest rates, 428

intergovernmental organizations (IGOs)
    future trends, 184–186
    international law, 353
    overview, 138–140
    rise of, 17
    security and, 396–399
Intergovernmental Panel on Climate Change (IPCC), 561, 562, 566, 568
Intermediate-Range Nuclear Forces (INF), 379
internal characteristics, influence of, 191, 193
International Bank for Reconstruction and Development, 430, 431
International Court of Justice, UN, 145, 352, 355, 368–372
International Criminal Court (ICC), 369–370, 550
international criminal tribunals, 369–370
International Development Association (IDA), 130, 133
international institutions, 66, 98. *See also* nonstate actors; specific institution names
International Labour Organization, 422
international law
    armed aggression, control of, 359–366
    disputes, settlement of, 345–351
    human rights, 545–551
    International Court of Justice, UN, 145, 352, 355, 368–372
    International Criminal Court, 369–370, 550
    judicial framework, 367–372
    liberal and constructivist routes to peace, 344–345
    overview, 40, 351–359
    World Court, 352, 355, 368–372
international liquidity, 432
International Monetary Fund (IMF)
    currency exchange, 425
    exchange rates, 431
    heavily indebted poor countries, 130, 133
    overview, 149, 152–153, 430
    policies of, 435–436
international monetary system, 419. *See also* global finance
international organizations, 17, 44–45, 389–399. *See also* nonstate actors; specific organization names
international organized crime (IOC) syndicates, 174
international political economy (IPE), 416–417
international regime, defined, 42
international relations theories, 43
international rule-making, 66, 98. *See also* international law
International Telephone and Telegraph (ITT), 177
international terrorism, 172. *See also* terrorism
international trade. *See* global trade
International Trade Organization (ITO), 149
International Union for Conservation of Nature (IUCN), 579
Internet, 505–510
interspecific aggression, 253
intra-firm trade, 451

intraspecific aggression, 253
intrastate conflict, 237–239
investment, foreign direct, 127–130, 419
IOC (international organized crime)
    syndicates, 174
IPE (international political economy),
    416–417
Iran, 264–265, 279, 293, 300
Iraq
    democracy and, 405
    invasion of, 362–364
    military power, 219
    perception and policy, 14
    terrorism, 244
    US war in, 93, 197, 230
Ireland, Republic of, 71–72
irredentism, 77, 172
Islam, 168–173
Islamic Jihad, 175, 245. *See also* terrorism
isolationism, 76, 92
Israel, 13, 125, 273, 294–295
issue-advocacy groups, 181–184
Italian Black Order, 245
Italy, 73–80

J

Japan. *See also* Global East
    development of, 120
    future trends, 96–99
    imperialism, 107–111
    World War II, 73–80
Japanese Red Army, 245
jus ad bellum, 360
jus in bello, 360
just war doctrine, 359–365
just war theory, 307

K

Kach, 245
Kashmir, 110
Kellog-Briand Pact, 34
Korea, 79, 107
Korean War, 84
Kosovo, 45
Kurds, 17, 167, 300
Kurile Islands, 79
Kuwait, 104, 119
Kyoto Protocol (1997), 584

L

labor, globalization of, 452–455
LAIA (Latin American Integration
    Association), 160
laissez-faire economics, 106, 262, 419
landmines, 383, 384
language, 166
laser weapons, 297
Latin America, 52, 118–119. *See also*
    specific country names
Latin American Integration Association
    (LAIA), 160
Latvia, 71–72
law, international
    armed aggression, control of, 359–366
    disputes, settlement of, 345–351

human rights, 545–551
International Court of Justice, UN, 145,
    352, 355, 368–372
International Criminal Court, 369–370,
    550
judicial framework, 367–372
liberal and constructivist routes to peace,
    344–345
overview, 40, 351–359
World Court, 352, 355, 368–372
leadership
    leader characteristics, 191, 193–195
    leaders, impact of, 208–214
    quest for, 66–67
League of Nations, 40, 73, 109–110, 143,
    390–391
least developed of the less developed
    countries (LLDCs), 114
legal procedures. *See* law, international
liberal democratic peace theory, 222
liberal economic theory
    commercial liberalism, 401–403, 421,
        456–461
    defined, 106
    economic freedom map, 465
    free trade, 469–471
    global commerce, 453–454, 457–461
    underdevelopment, 115
liberal-hawk, 364
liberal institutionalism, 43–44
Liberal International Economic Order
    (LIEO), 430
liberalism, defined, 37. *See also* liberal
    theory
liberal theory. *See also* liberal economic
    theory
    alliances, 315–316
    armed aggression, 262–265, 359
    arms race, 385–386
    Cold War, 88, 89–91
    common culture, 400–408
    comparison of theories, 47
    disarmament *vs.* arms control, 378–379
    disputes, settlement of, 346–351
    embedded liberalism, 429
    foreign policy decisions, 223
    global information age, 503–510
    human rights, 544–545
    IGOs, 153, 163
    imperialism, 109
    individual power, 519
    international law, 355, 367
    international organizations, 390
    negotiations, 342
    nonstate actors, 185
    overview, 37–46
    peace, routes to, 344–345, 376–377
    security, 533–534
    state power, 277
    World War I and, 72–73
Liberation Tigers of Tamil Eelam, 175
Libya, 219
LIEO (Liberal International Economic Order),
    430
life expectancy, 490–491
linguistics, 166
linkage strategy, 87
Lisbon Treaty, 159

Lithuania, 71–72
LLDCs (least developed of the less
    developed countries), 114
location, geostrategic, 215, 216–218
long-cycle theory, 66, 268–270
long peace, 235
Long Range Acoustic Device (LRAD), 297
Luxembourg, 76

M

malaria, 502
Malaysia, 104, 120, 124
Manchester School, 38
Manchuria, invasion of, 75
manipulation, 349
Mano River Union, 161
maps
    Africa, colonialism, 105
    biodiversity, 569
    civil war, likelihood of, 260
    class of civilizations, 167
    deforestation, 572
    digital divide, 508
    economic freedom, 465
    emerging power regions, 95
    ethnolinguistic division, 166
    European Union, 156
    gender politics, 538
    geographic influence on foreign
        policy, 217
    global imperialism, 108
    globalization, index of, 418
    Global North and South, 102
    global supply chain, 450
    H1N1 pandemic, 503
    human development, 527
    Mercator projections, 10
    orthographic projection, 11
    perception of, 9–12
    Peter's projection, 10
    population, urbanization, 493
    population growth, 489
    poverty, global, 522
    power potential, 280
    refugees, origin of, 496–497
    regional trade flows, 477
    remittances, 126–127
    United Nations network, 144
    upside down projection, 11
    world religions, 169
    World Trade Organization members, 472
    World War I, changes of, 72
    World War II, 75
Marshall Plan, 431–432
Marxism, 81
massive retaliation, 302–303
matchpolitik, 77
MDRI (Multilateral Debt Relief Initiative),
    130, 133
media, influence of, 220, 508–509
mediation, 349
Mein Kampf (1924), 74
mercantilism
    Bretton Woods System, 428–429
    defined, 106
    economic freedom map, 465

mercantilism *(continued)*
environmental issues, 555
imperialism and, 401
vs. liberalism, 457–461, 469–471
Mercator projection map, 10
Mercosur, 123, 477
MFN (most-favored nation), 456
Middle East, 110, 125, 287–292
migration trends, 493–499
militant religious movements, 170, 245. *See also* terrorism
militarization, 261
military-industrial complex, 290
military intervention
changes in, 232–235
future of, 270–271, 605–606
global system, as cause, 265–270
global trade and, 463
human nature as cause, 252–255
judicial framework, 367–372
Just War Doctrine, 359–366
long cycle theory, 66, 268–270
new rules for, 365–366
overview, 231–232
state characteristics and, 255–265
within states, 235–243, 260
terrorism, 243–252
military necessity, 365
military power. *See also* balance of power
arms race, 86
atomic bomb, 78–79
changing character of, 283, 286
coercive diplomacy, 308–310
distribution of, 69–70
foreign policy decisions and, 215, 218–219
future trends, 98, 605–606
Global South, 121–122
military strategies, 301–307
overstretch, 92
power, overview, 275–276
power transition theory, 267–268
realist approaches, 274–275, 311–312
spending on, 277, 281–283, 284–286
state power, elements of, 276–281
weapons technology trends, 293–301
weapons trade, 287–292
world spending, 147
military spending, 122
Millennium Challenge Account (MCA), 125
Millennium Round, WTO, 474–475
Minorities at Risk Project, 532
mirror images, 13, 81
MIRVs (multiple independently targetable reentry vehicles), 296–299
missile technology, 296–299
Missile Technology Control Regime (MTCR), 382
MNCs. *See* multinational corporations (MNCs)
modernization, defined, 115
modernization, theory of, 118–119
monetary policy, 423–428. *See also* global finance
monetary system, 422. *See also* global finance
money supply, 426. *See also* global finance
morality, 45, 360, 400–408, 518
mores, 400–408

Moscow Olympics, 86
most-favored nation (MFN), 456
MPLA (Popular Movement for the Liberation of Angola), 245
Multi-Fiber Arrangement (MFA), 438
multilateral agreements, defined, 378–379
multilateral arms control, 378–379
Multilateral Debt Relief Initiative (MDRI), 130, 133
multilateralism, 99
multinational corporations (MNCs)
environmental issues and, 584–588
Global South and, 117, 119, 131–132
mass media, 508–509
outsourcing, 120, 452–455
overview, 176–181
rise of, 17
trade globalization, 449–452
multiple advocacy, 203
multiple independently targetable reentry vehicles (MIRVs), 297, 384
multipolarity, 76, 80, 216, 334–340, 337–338
murky protectionism, 479–480
Muslims, 168–173, 175, 245
mutual assured destruction (MAD), 303–304
Myanmar, 104, 117

N

NAFTA, 477–478
Nagasaki, 78–79
NAM (Nonaligned Movement), 111
Napoleonic Wars (1815), 327–328
narcotic trade, 174
nation, defined, 17
national character, 254
National Counter Terrorism Center (NCTC), 243
national interest, 32, 36
nationalism, 70, 77, 256–258
national security
changing character of, 283, 286
coercive diplomacy, 308–310
liberal view, 533–534
military spending, 281–286
military strategies, 301–307
power, overview, 275–276
realist view, 32, 274–275, 311–312
state power, elements of, 276–281
weapons technology trends, 293–301
weapons trade, 287–292
National Security Act (1947), 306
National Security Strategy, U. S., 306
National System of Political Economy, 460
nation-state system, 16
Native Americans, 17
NATO (North Atlantic Treaty Organization), 45, 138, 160, 329, 330, 335, 396–399
nature *vs.* nurture, 254
Nauru, 110
Nazi Germany, 14, 74–80, 257
negotiations
armed aggression, legal control, 359–366
defined, 347
dispute, settlement of, 345–351

international law, 351–359
judicial framework, international law, 367–372
liberal and constructivist routes to peace, 38, 344–345
perception and, 13–14
neoclassical realism, 35. *See also* realist theory
neoidealism, 42
neoliberalism, 42, 185. *See also* liberal theory
neo-Malthusians, 554–555
neorealism. *See also* realist theory
armed aggression, 256, 265–270
balance of power, 337–338
defined, 35
leaders, impact of, 213
World War I, 68
neo-Wilsonian idealism, 42
Netherlands, 76
neutrality, 354
New International Economic Order (NIEO), 123
New People's Army (NPA), 175
newly industrialized countries (NICs), 117, 120–121
New Zealand, 396–399
NGOs. *See* nongovernmental organizations (NGOs)
Nicaragua, 86, 123, 352
NICs (newly industrialized countries), 117
NIEO (New International Economic Order), 123
Nigeria, 104
Non-Aligned Kuala Lumpur Summit Declaration (2003), 111
Nonaligned Movement (NAM), 111
nonalignment, 111, 322
noncombatant immunity, 367
nondiscrimination, trade, 456
nongovernmental organizations (NGOs)
future trends, 184–186
international law, 353
overview, 49, 138, 140–141, 162
religious movements, 171
rise of, 17
nonintervention norm, 309, 354
nonlethal weapons, 297
nonprofit organizations, 140–141. *See also* nongovernmental organizations (NGOs)
nonproliferation regime, 294
nonstate actors. *See also* International Monetary Fund (IMF); nongovernmental organizations (NGOs); United Nations; World Bank; World Trade Organization (WTO)
European Union, overview, 154–159
future trends, 184–186
indigenous peoples, 530–533
issue-advocacy groups, 181–184
multinational corporations, overview, 176–181
nonstate nations, 164–168
oil crisis, 1973, 41
overview, 137–141
regional intergovernmental organizations, overview, 153–154, 159–162
rise of, 17

terrorist groups, 173–176
transnational religious movements, 168–173
nonstate nations, 162, 164–168
nontariff barriers (NTBs), 468
norms, 49
North American Fight Zombies Agreement (NAFZA), 44
North Atlantic Treaty Organization (NATO), 45, 138, 160, 329, 330, 335, 396–399
North Korea, 117, 279, 293
nuclear deterrence, 303–306, 582
nuclear energy programs, 295, 580–582
Nuclear Nonproliferation Treaty (NPT), 294, 296, 380–383, 382, 383
nuclear weapons, 78–79, 85, 293–299, 380–383, 582
nuclear winter, 301

O

OAS (Organization of American States), 138
objectivity, 54
offensive realism, 35
official development assistance (ODA), 124
oil crisis (1973), 41
oil, development and, 119–120
oil spill, 553, 574
oil, supply and demand, 572–575
Olympic Games, 86, 412
OPEC (Organization of Petroleum Exporting Countries), 119, 416, 573
Open Skies Treaty, 382
opportunity costs, 283, 458
orderly market arrangements (OMAs), 468
Organization for Security and Cooperation in Europe (OSCE), 154, 396–399
Organization of American States (OAS), 138
Organization of Petroleum Exporting Countries (OPEC), 119, 416, 573
orthographic projection map, 11
OSCE (Organization for Security and Cooperation in Europe), 154, 396–399
Ottoman empire, 71–72, 109
Our Common Future (1987), 559
Outer Space Treaty, 382
outsourcing, 120, 452–455
ozone layer, 566–567

P

pacifism, 253
Pakistan, 104, 110, 293
Palestine, 110
Palestinian Jihad, 248
Panama Canal, 107
pandemics, 499–503
paradigm, defined, 30
paradigms, security, 275
Paraguay, 123
Partial Test Ban Treaty, 382
peace
    building, 393
    coexistence, 85
    enforcement of, 393
    international law and, 370–372

international organizations and, 390–396
    routes to, 344–345, 376–377
peacekeeping, defined, 392
peacemaking, defined, 392–393
Peace of Westphalia (1648), 16, 184, 325
peace operations, 393
Peloponnesian War, 31
perceptions, 7–14
perceptual psychology, 9–12
Permanent Court of International Justice (PCIJ), 40
Perpetual Peace (1795), 39
Persian Gulf, 86
Persian Gulf War, 219, 292
Peru, 123, 165
Peter's projection map, 10
Philippines, 107, 124
piracy, 42, 365
podcasts, 505
Poland, 71–72, 76, 109
polarity
    balance of power, models of, 327–333
    defined, 216
    future trends, 334–340
polarization, 98, 216, 329
policy agenda, 200
policy networks, 203
political economy, 77
political efficacy, 211
political integration, 154
political system, 220–225, 235–237, 262–265, 525–528
politics of scarcity, 556
pooled sovereignty, 158–159
popular culture, 92
Popular Movement for the Liberation of Angola (MPLA), 245
population
    changes in, 485–493, 494
    density, 492–493
    disease and, 499–503
    growth rates, 485–493, 494
    implosion, 498–499
    migration trends, 493–499
Portugal, 110
Portuguese imperialism, 105–111
positivist legal theory, 357
post-American world, 96
postmodern deconstructivism, 58–59
postmodern terrorism, 174. *See also* terrorism
Potsdam (1945), 79
poverty, 52, 111–117, 152, 258–259, 520–523
Poverty Reduction Strategy (PRS), 152
power. *See also* alliances; military power
    balance of, 33, 216, 327–333
    changing character of, 283, 286
    defined, 16
    financial crisis 2008 and, 444
    future trends, 334–340, 605–606
    hierarchy of, 23, 65
    measures of, 277–279
    overview of, 275–276
    realist view, 32, 33, 36, 320–327
    state power, elements of, 276–281
    women and negotiation, 349–350

World War I, 69–70
World War II, 64, 73–80, 328
power politics, 77
power potential, 95, 277
power rivalries
    Cold War, 80–88
    overview, 64–67
    post-Cold War era, 88, 91–99
    World War I, 67–73
    World War II, 73–80
power transition, 80, 267–268, 331
preemption, 306–307
preemptive war, 306–307
prejudice, 70, 199
preventive diplomacy, 392–393
prisoners dilemma, 385–386
privacy, 506–507
private citizens, coalitions of, 17
private international law, 353
problem recognition, 196
proletariat, 52
proliferation, weapons, 293
propaganda, 357
prospect theory, 201, 325
protectionist trade, 19–20, 467–471, 479
Protection of Nuclear Material Convention, 382
Protestants, 168–173
Protocol to the Inhumane Weapons Convention, 382
PRS (Poverty Reduction Strategy), 152
psychology, 12, 58–59, 198
    perceptual, 9–12
public international law, 353
publicity, 174
public opinion, 220
Puerto Rico, 107
purchasing power parity (PPP), 120, 528

Q

Qatar, 104, 119
QUANGOs (quasi-nongovernmental organizations). *See* nongovernmental organizations (NGOs)

R

racism, 532
radical theory, 353
rapprochement, 86–88
rational choice, 70–71, 196–202, 255, 577
realism, defined, 31. *See also* realist theory
realist theory
    alliances, 316, 317–319
    armed aggression, 261, 262–265
    armed aggression, global system and, 265–270
    arms race, 385–387
    balance of power, 320–327, 337–338
    Cold War, 87–88, 89–91
    comparison of theories, 47
    democratic peace, 405
    disarmament *vs.* arms control, 378–379
    foreign policy decision making, 218–219
    geopolitics, 218
    global finance, 421–422
    global IGOs, 163

realist theory *(continued)*
  global trade, 469
  human rights, 544
  IGOs, 153
  individual power, 518
  international organizations, 389
  leaders, impact of, 209
  mercantilism, 106, 459–461
  military power, 274–275
  negotiations, 348
  nonstate actors, 185
  overview, 31–37
  peace, 376
  power and, 65, 275–276
  security, 311–312, 533–544
  war and, 231
  World War I, 68
realpolitik, 109, 142, 275–276, 312,
  316–317
reasoning, schematic, 8, 12
reciprocity, 347, 455–457
Red Shirts, 62
refugees, 495–499
regional currency union, 442
regional organizations
  overview, 153–154
  rise of, 17
  security and, 396–399
regional trade agreements (RTAs), 123–124,
  476–478
relative burden of military spending, 284–286
relative deprivation, 258–259
relative gains, 32, 459, 461
religion, 23, 168–173, 247–248
remittances, 124–127
renewable energy, 580–583
rent-seeking, 471
replacement-level fertility, 488
repressive terror, 244–245
reprisals, 367
Republic of Ireland, 71–72
resources, 23, 567–571. *See also*
  environment
responsible sovereignty, 137
retorsion, 367
Revolutionary Armed Forces of Columbia
  (FARC), 175
Revolutionary United Front (RUF), 175
revolution in military technology (RMT), 297,
  361
RINGOs (religious international NGOs). *See*
  nongovernmental organizations (NGOs)
robotic military technology, 298–299
roles, defined, 208
Romania, 109
Rome Statute, 369–370
RTAs (regional trade agreements), 476–478
RUF (Revolutionary United Front), 175
Ruhr district, 74
ruling class, 52
Russia. *See also* Soviet Union
  bipolarity, 328–330
  BRIC, 314
  future trends, 97
  post-Cold War era, 94
  World War I, 69, 71–72
  World War II, 12
Rwanda, 239, 531

S

SAARC (South Asian Association for
  Regional Cooperation), 160
SADC (Southern African Development
  Community), 124, 160
sanctuary, 498, 532
Sandinista government, 352
SAPs (Structural Adjustment Policies),
  435–436
satisficing, 200
scapegoat, 221
scarcity, 556
schematic reasoning, 8, 12
scientific study, world politics, 54
Seabed Treaty, 382
secession, 172
second-strike capability, 303
Second World, defined, 104
Secretariat, UN, 145
security. *See also* North Atlantic Treaty
  Organization (NATO)
  changing character of, 283, 286
  coercive diplomacy, 308–310
  collective security, 143
  common culture, 400–408
  Controversy, defining, 533–534
disarmament *vs.* arms control, 378–379
  energy supply and demand, 574–575
  environmental concerns and, 555–556
  future trends, 597–598, 608–609
  Global South, 121–122
  human development and, 523–525
  human security, 517
  institutions, norms and world order,
    408–409
  international organizations and, 389–399
  liberal theory, 44
  military spending, 281–286
  military strategies, 301–307
  overstretch, 92
  peace, routes to, 376–377
  power, overview, 275–276
  realist theory, 36, 274–275, 311–312
  refugees and, 498
  state power, elements of, 276–281
  trade policies and, 470
  weapons technology trends, 293–301
  weapons trade, 287–292
security community, 154
Security Council, UN, 144, 145, 393
security dilemma, 33, 311
security regimes, 322, 359
selective engagement, 92
self-determination, 109
self-help, defined, 32
self-image, leaders, 211
semiperiphery, 120
separative revolts, 172
September 11 attacks (2001)
  anthrax attacks, 299
  bureaucracy and decision making,
    205–206
  decision making after, 197
  globalization and, 167
  transformation and, 21
  war on terror, 93, 246, 251
Serbia, 69

Shanghai, 429
Shining Path, 175
Sicarii Zealots, 173
Sikhs, 17
Singapore, 120, 124
slave trade, 105, 539–541
smart bombs, 298
social construction
  consensus, 206
  constructivist theory, 46–51
  feminist theory, 54
  ideology and, 82
  leaders, impact of, 211
  women and negotiation, 350
social constructivism, 44
Social Darwinism, 253
socialization, 254
social responsibility revolution, 179–180
soft power, 91, 277, 283, 286, 357
Somalia, 142
South Asian Association for Regional
  Cooperation (SAARC), 160
Southern African Development Community
  (SADC), 124, 160
South Korea, 120
South Pacific Nuclear Free Zone (Roratonga)
  Treaty, 382
sovereign equality, 354
sovereignty
  defined, 16
  humans rights and, 546–551
  international law and, 354
  liberal theory, 45
  pooled sovereignty, 158–159
  World Trade Organization, 474–475
Soviet Union. *See also* Russia
  Cold War, 34–35, 80–88, 216, 379–380
  Cuban Missile Crisis, 85, 203, 303, 346
  perception and, 13
  power potential, 281
  World War II, 73–80
Spanish-American War, 107
Spanish civil war, 75
Spanish imperialism, 105–111
speculative attacks, 430
sphere of influence, 80
spiral model, arms race, 311–312
Stages of Economic Growth (1960), 115
standard of living, 520–525
standard operating procedures, 204
START (Strategic Arms Reduction Treaty), 87
state
  defined, 16–17
  power, elements of, 276–281
statelessness, 306
state level of analysis, 19
  armed aggression and, 255–265
  World War I, 70
  World War II, 77
states attributes, defined, 215
state sovereignty
  defined, 16
  human rights, 546–551
  international law, 354
  liberal theory, 45
  pooled sovereignty, 158–159
  World Trade Organization and, 474–475
state-sponsored terrorism, 239, 248, 370

Statute of International Court of Justice, 355
Strategic Arms Limitation Talks (SALT), 85, 379, 383–384
Strategic Arms Reduction Treaty (START), 87, 379
Strategic Defense Initiative (SDI), 304
Strategic Offensive Reductions Treaty (SORT), 379
strategic trade policy, 468
strategic weapons, 297
Structural Adjustment Policies (SAPs), 435–436
structuralism, 68–69
structural realism, 35, 43
structural violence, 356–357
subordinate class, 52
Sudan, 239, 607
superpowers, 53
supply chains, 479
survival of the fittest, 253–254
sustainability
    human security and, 575–580
    ranking, 589
    renewable energy, 580–583
    trade and, 584–588
sustainable development, 556, 559–560
swine flu, 502
Switzerland, 217, 281

T

tactical air-to-surface missiles (TASMs), 297
Taiwan, 84, 107, 120, 405–406
Taliban, 247, 292
tariffs, 466–471
technology, 23, 119–120, 503–510, 604–605
terrorism
    failed states and, 236
    global communications, 509–510
    globalization and, 167
    imperial overstretch, 92
    international law and, 366
    just war doctrine, 361
    overview, 243–252
    persistent threat of, 244
    religious movements, 171–172
    state-sponsored, 370
    transformation and, 21
    transnational terrorist groups, 173–176
    war on, 93, 246, 251, 306–307
    weapons trade, 288
Thailand, 120, 124
theocracy, 170
theories, world politics. *See also*
    constructivist theory; feminist theory;
    liberal theory; realist theory
    Cold War, 89–91
    international theory and future, 57–60
    overview, 30–31
    radical critique, 51–53
    theorizing about theory, 56–57
theory, defined, 30
The Prince, 32
Third Way, 154
Third World, 103–104
Thirty Years' War (1618–1648), 16, 168, 360

Thousand-Year Reich, 78
Thucydides, 31, 32, 221, 315
Tibet, 84, 164
tit-for-tat strategy, 347
Tokyo Round, WTO, 475
torture, 550
trade. *See also* multinational corporations (MNCs)
    arms trade, 261
    Asia Pacific Economic Cooperation (APEC), 159
    balance of, 424, 427
    developing countries, 127–130
    European Union, 154
    financial crisis, 2008, 478–481
    free trade, fate of, 466–471
    future trends, 97–98
    global finance, 420
    globalization, overview, 22–23, 447–455
    global trade and politics, 461–466
    integration of, 448–449
    liberal and mercantilist views, 457–461
    liberal theory and, 38
    protectionism, 19–20, 466–471
    regional trade regimes, 123–124, 476–478
    security and, 400–403
    strategies for, 455–461
    sustainable development, 584–588
    Taiwan, peace and prosperity, 405–406
    World Trade Organization (WTO), 149–150, 430, 456, 463, 471–476
tragedy of the global commons, 576–580
transformation, defined, 21
transgenetic crops, 558
transitional activists, 162
transnational nongovernmental organizations, 49, 140, 190. *See also* nongovernmental organizations (NGOs); nonstate actors; terrorism
transnational norms, 355
transnational relations, 41
transnational religious movements, 23, 168–173
transparency, trade, 456
Treaty of Bangkok, 382
Treaty of Brest-Litovsk (1918), 79
Treaty of Pelindaba, 383
Treaty of Versailles, 72, 73, 109
Treaty on Nuclear Free Zone in Central Asia, 383
trickle-down hypothesis, 528
Tripartite Pact, 76
Truman Doctrine, 83
Trusteeship Council, UN, 145
Turkey, 71–72, 155
two-level games, 199

U

U. S. National Counter Terrorism Center (NCTC), 243
U. S. National Security Strategy (NSS), 306
UFOs (Unidentified Flying Objects), 43
Ukraine, 585
unilateralism, 92
uni-multipolar, defined, 94
Union Carbide, 586

Union of International Associations, 140
unipolarity, 91–93, 216, 328, 337–338
unitary actor, 196
United Arab Emirates, 119
United Nations
    Conference on Trade and Development (UNCTAD), 122
    creation of, 79
    Development Programme (UNDP), 523
    Emergency Force (UNEF), 392
    Human Rights Council (HRC), 549
    Intergovernmental Panel on Climate Change (IPCC), 561, 562, 566, 568
    Monetary and Financial Conference, 150
    overview, 138, 141–149
    peacekeeping, 392–396
    Population Fund (UNFPA), 493
    Register of Conventional Arms, 382
    rise of, 17
United States. *See also* Global North
    bipolarity, 328–330
    Cold War, 34–35, 80–88, 216, 379–380
    Cuban Missile Crisis, 346
    foreign policy, 13
    future trends, 96–99
    imperialism, 107–111
    international law, 352
    invasion of Iraq, 362–364, 405
    post-Cold War era, 88, 91–93
    regional security, 396–399
    trade agreements, 123–124
    unipolarity, 328
    war on terror, 93, 246, 251, 306–307
    World Court and, 370
    World War II, 73–80
Universal Declaration of Human Rights (1948), 354, 528, 529–530
upside down projection map, 11
urbanization, 492–493
Uruguay, 104, 123
Uruguay Round, GATT, 456, 471–473

V

values, 400–408
Venezuela, 123
Versailles, Treaty of (1919), 72, 73, 109
vertical nuclear proliferation, 293
Vietnam, 110, 124
Vietnam War, 14, 279, 281
violence, armed aggression and, 266–267
violence, structural, 356–357
virtual corporations, 451
virtuality, 506
virtual nuclear arsenals, 298
voluntary export restrictions (VERs), 468

W

Wal-Mart, 179–180, 586–588
war
    changes in, 232–235
    future trends, 270–271, 605–606, 608–609
    global system as cause, 265–270
    global trade and, 463
    human nature, as cause, 252–255
    judicial framework, 367–372

war *(continued)*
    just war doctrine, 359–365
    long-cycle theory, 66, 268–270
    new rules for, 365–366
    overview, 231–232
    state characteristics, 255–265
    within states, 235–243, 260
    terrorism, 243–252
war crimes, 358
war weariness hypothesis, 270
Washington, George, 319, 321
Washington Naval Conference, 41
Wassenaar Export-Control Treaty, 382
water shortages, 567–571
Wealth of Nations, The, 106, 458
weapons
    arms race, 33, 85
    Global South, 122
    of mass destruction, 293–301, 301–302,
        380, 582
    nuclear weapons, 78–79, 85, 293–299,
        380–383, 582
    peace, routes to, 377
    proliferation of, 23
    trends, 293–301
    weapons trade, trends, 287–292

women, negotiation and, 349–350. *See also*
    feminist theory; gender
World Bank
    creation of, 430, 431
    debt, Global South, 130, 133
    foreign aid, 124
    NGO, definition of, 141
    overview, 149, 150–152
    policies of, 435–436
World Court, 352, 355, 368–372
World Health Organization (WHO), 502
world law, 353
world maps. *See* maps
world politics. *See also* constructivist theory;
    feminist theory; liberal theory; realist theory
    analysis, levels of, 18–20
    challenges of, 6–7
    international theory and future, 57–60
    keys to understanding, 14–24
    perceptions and images, 7–14
    radical critique, 51–53
    theories of, overview, 30–31
    theorizing about theory, 56–57
world-system theory, 53, 108
World Trade Organization (WTO), 149–150,
    430, 456, 463, 471–476

World War I, overview, 67–73
World War II, 12, 14, 64, 73–80, 328
World Zombie Organization
    (WZO), 43–44
WTO. *See* World Trade Organization (WTO)

X

xenophobia, 498

Y

Yalta, 64, 79
youth bulge, 490
Yugoslavia, 45, 71–72, 109, 496

Z

zeitgeist, 213, 214
zero-sum, defined, 38
zero-sum competition, 461
Zimbabwe, 499
zombies, 43–44